Mitchell Schoen

Mitchell was born in the lowlands of Manhattan, raised on the dunes of Los Angeles and educated in the wilds of Berkeley, California. His initial interest in Latin America was sparked by an exiled Chilean friend. At the University of California at Berkeley he studied political and economic development, particularly in Latin America, where he has travelled extensively. After a short stint as a graduate student in American labour history, Mitchell found honest employment and played parent to Jonathan, who will be 25 in the year 2000. Jonathan travelled with Mitchell in Brazil.

Mitchell graduated from the Columbia Journalism School in New York and has written for newspapers and magazines. He also wrote and produced an award winning documentary on the military presence in New York City's public schools.

William Herzberg

William was conceived – or so he claims – a couple of months before Carnival on a freighter in Guanabara Bay. He led a relatively uneventful life on Long Island until winning the Jericho Jewish Center award for the Best Queen Esther Costume.

William studied bio-chemistry at Harvard and spent his college summers writing for the *Let's Go* travel guide series in Europe, North Africa and the US. He is now a physician in San Francisco who enjoys frequent flier status on many airlines. His next trip is to Gdansk.

Lonely Planet Credits

Editors	Katie Cody
	Mark Balla
Mapping	Todd Pierce
Cover design	Vicki Beale
Design	Trudi Canavan
Illustrations	Trudi Canavan
	Greg Herriman
	Ann Jeffree
Typesetting	Ann Jeffree
	Gaylene Miller

Thanks also to Mabel Botelli and John Maier in Brazil, who did a last minute price update; Maureen Wheeler for proofreading; Graham Imeson and Chris Lee Ack for additional mapping; and Sharon Wertheim for indexing.

Acknowledgements

This book wouldn't have been possible without the help and kindness of many Brazilian friends. Vania Maria Lima

Parente took us in and showed us the Brazilian way. Her 101 kindnesses and big heart kept us going. Marcos Parente put up with an invasion of Lonely Planet creatures who landed with their space-age, paper-less writing machines in the middle of his living room. John Maeir shared his generous spirit, fluency in Monty Python and excellent photographs; Eymard Porto his friendship, good humour and reluctance to speak English; Fausto Nilo his unlimited knowledge of Brazilian music; and Fausto and Sylvia their warmth and generosity. Vivian Stirling showed us around Rio.

Thanks to Dora and Oscar in Bahia for the good times. A warm abraço to the many Parentes we came to know, love and admire. A special nod to Nelson in São Paulo for his wonderfully New Yorkerish love of city. Thanks also to Nil, Dianna and Nelson Cerqueira of Bahiatursa for all their help, and the many Brazilians who met us on the road with open arms offering their homes, affection and cachaça.

Closer to home Jonathan Zachary and Judy Marantz were bloody good spirits on some tough roads. Jonathan, with his stoic countenance and unflagging devotion to the cause, has reminded many of Colonel Fawcett, the great British adventurer who was lost in the wilds of Mato Grosso in the 1920s. Judy showed us how to practice the difficult art of vegetarianism in Brazil and provided us with many photographs. Prof Van Den Dool supplied background material and Dr C Beal his expertise on tropical medicine, and Eric Long, Doug Trent and Marsa Morris wrote about their special knowledge of Brazil.

Thanks also to: the Familia Giesen for a lovely week south of the border; Peter Herzberg for supporting many foolish endeavours; John Freedman for photographs and repeatedly demonstrating the blood/lipid coefficient of cachaça; Scott Plous and Kim Bartholomew for a month of peak experiences, many slides and hours of computer time; John and Anne Neher, Jessica Ult, Michael and Andrew Rosenbach for computer services; UCLA, the California Literature Project and K Garrison for lodging; and Marty Paddock for her friendship and making her home a nurturing work environment.

And finally we would like to thank Tony Wheeler, Jim Hart and the Lonely Planet crew for their patience with our delays and many hours of work on the manuscript.

A Warning & a Request
Things change – prices go up, schedules change, good places go bad and bad places go bankrupt – nothing stays the same. So if you find things better or worse, recently opened or long since closed, please write and tell us and help make the next edition better!

Your letters will be used to help update future editions and, where possible, important changes will also be included as a Stop Press section in reprints.

All information is greatly appreciated and the best letters will receive a free copy of the next edition, or any other Lonely Planet book of your choice.

Contents

INTRODUCTION 7

FACTS ABOUT THE COUNTRY History – Geography – Climate – Government – Economy – 9
Education – Population & People – Culture – Religion – Holidays & Festivals – Language

FACTS FOR THE VISITOR Visas – Money – Costs – Tipping – Tourist Information – 42
General Information – Media – Health – Dangers & Annoyances – Drugs –
Film & Photography – Accommodation – Food – Drinks – Books – Things to Buy –
What to Bring – Sports – Hiking & Climbing

GETTING THERE Air – Overland 72

GETTING AROUND Air – Bus – Car – Hitching – Local Transport 77

THE SOUTHEAST 85

RIO DE JANEIRO 86

RIO DE JANEIRO STATE West of Rio de Janeiro – Ilha Grande – Angra dos Reis – Parati – 129
Around Parati – The Mountains – Petrópolis   Vassouras – Teresópolis –
Nova Friburgo – Itatiaia – Resende – Penedo – Visconde de Mauá – Itatiaia –
East of Rio de Janeiro – Saquarema – Araruama – Arraial do Cabo – Cabo Frio –
Búzios – Barra de São João – Rio das Ostras – Macaé – Biological Reserve Poço
das Antas – Macaé to Campos – Barra de Itabapoana

ESPIRITO SANTO Vitória – Guarapari – Anchieta – Piuma – Marataízes – 156
South of Marataízes – Domingos Martins – Santa Teresa

MINAS GERAIS Belo Horizonte – Sabará – Congonhas – Ouro Prêto – Mariana – São João 160
del Rei – Tiradentes – Prados – Around Minas Gerais – São Tomé das Letras –
Caxambu – São Lourenço – Diamantina

SÃO PAULO São Paulo – São Paulo – Ubatuba – Caraguatatuba – São Sebastião – Ilhabela 186

THE NORTHEAST 201

BAHIA Salvador – Around Salvador – Itaparica – Other Baía de Todos os Santos Islands – 202
The Recôncavo Region – Cachoeira – Candeias – Santa Amaro – Maragojipe –
Nazaré – North of Salvador – Arembepe – North to Praia do Forte – Praia do Forte –
North of Praia do Forte – South of Salvador – Valença – Valença to Ilhéus – Ilhéus –
Around Ilhéus – Porto Seguro – North of Porto Seguro – Santa Cruz Cabrália –
South of Porto Seguro – Arraial d'Ajuda – Trancoso – Caraiva – Parque Nacional de
Monte Pascoal – Prado & Alcobaça – Caravelas – Parque Nacional Marinho dos
Abrolhos – West of Salvador – Feira de Santana – Salvador to Lençóis – Lençóis –
Around Lençóis – Rio São Francisco

SERGIPE & ALAGOAS Sergipe – Estância – São Cristóvão – Laranjeiras – Aracaju – 260
Propriá – Alagoas – Maceió – Penedo – South of Maceió – North of Maceió

PERNAMBUCO Recife – Beaches South of Recife – Olinda – Beaches North of Olinda – 276
Igaraçu – Caruaru

PARAÍBA, RIO GRANDE DO NORTE & FERNANDO DE NORONHA Paraíba – Pitimbu –   291
Jacumã & Praia do Sol – João Pessoa – Baía da Traição – Rio Grande do Norte –
Baía Formosa – Barra do Cunhaú – Tibau do Sul – Búzios to Senador Georgino Alvino –
Pirangi do Sul & Pirangi do Norte – Barreira do Inferno – Ponta Negra – Natal –
North of Natal – Areia Branca – Tibaú – Fernando de Noronha

CEARÁ, PIAUÍ & MARANHÃO Ceará – Fortaleza – South of Fortaleza – South to   301
Rio Grande do Norte – North of Fortaleza – Canindé – Ubajara – Bico do Ipu –
Maranguape – Pacatuba – Serra de Baturité – Piauí – Teresina – Sete Cidades
National Park – The Sertão – Maranhão – São Luís – São Luís Island –
Around São Luís

THE NORTH   325

THE AMAZON Para – Belém – Ilha do Mosqueiro – Praia Algodoal – Salinópolis –   326
Ilha do Marajó – Around Ilha do Marajó – Santarém – Around Santarém – Amapá –
Macapá – Around Macapá – Roraima – Boa Vista – Around Boa Vista – Amazonas –
Manaus – Jungle Tours – Manacapuru – Acre – Rio Branco – Rondônia – Porto Velho –
Around Porto Velho – Around Rondônia – Guajará-Mirim

THE CENTRAL-WEST   375

CENTRAL-WEST Distrito Federal – Brasília – Around Brasília – Goiás – Goiânia –   376
Goiás Velho – Pirenópolis – Caldas Novas – Emas National Park – Tocantins –
Rio Araguaia – Ilha do Bananal – Mato Grosso – Cuiabá – Around Cuiabá –
Around Mato Grosso – Caçeres – Poconé – Pantanal – Mato Grosso do Sul –
Campo Grande – Corumba – Coxim

THE SOUTH   407

PARANÁ Curitiba – Curitiba to Paranaguá – Paranaguá – Paraná Beaches – Ilha do Mel –   408
Baía de Paranaguá – Iguaçu Falls

SANTA CATARINA & RIO GRANDE DO SUL Santa Catarina – Joinville – Joinville to   427
Florianópolis – Blumenau – Florianópolis – Ilha de Santa Catarina – South of
Florianópolis – São Joaquim – Rio Grande do Sul – Porto Alegre – Litoral Gaúcho –
Serra Gaúcho – Jesuit Missions

GLOSSARY   446

INDEX Map Index   451

Facts about the Country

HISTORY

Indians

Anthropologists believe that relatively recently, say 10,000 to 20,000 years ago, the American Indians migrated across the Bering Strait from north-eastern Asia. They were hunter-gatherers who followed the animals across the land bridge connecting Asia and North America. The tribes were highly mobile and once they crossed into Alaska they moved south to warmer climates. Eventually, they reached the Amazon basin in Brazil and spread out from there. It's also likely that a separate, later migration took place across the oceans, jumping from island to island.

The Brazilian Indians never developed an advanced, centralised civilisation like the Incas or Mayas. They left little for archaeologists to discover: only some pottery, shell mounds and skeletons. The shell mounds (*sambaquis*) are curious. They are found on the island of Marajó, the home of Brazil's most advanced pre-Columbian civilisation, and along the coast in the south. They are typically as tall as a human and about 50 metres long, the mounds are naturally formed by the sea and were used as burial sites and sometimes dwellings.

The Indian population was quite diverse. At the time of the Portuguese conquest the Tupi were most prevalent on the coast and best known to the white man. Today, most of the animals in Brazil, nearly all the rivers and mountains and many of the towns have Tupi names.

There were an estimated two to five million Indians living in the territory that is now Brazil when the Portuguese first arrived. Today there are somewhat less than 200,000. Most of them live in the hidden jungles of the Brazilian interior. The Indians of Brazil, as the Portuguese

were to learn, were divided into many groups and were primarily hunter-gatherers. The women did most of the work while the men, who were magnificent archers and fishermen, went to war. They lived in long communal huts. Music, dance and games played a very important role in their culture. Little surplus was produced and they had very few possessions. Every couple of years the village packed-up and moved on to richer hunting grounds.

This natural life, which became the ideal of the noble savage in the minds of the European and inspired many social thinkers such as Rousseau and Defoe, was punctuated by frequent tribal warfare and ritual cannibalism. After battles, captured enemies were ceremonially killed and eaten.

Early Colonisation

In 1500, Pedro Cabral sailed from Lisbon with 13 ships and 1200 men and headed down the coast of Africa, bound for India. Nobody knows how he could have wandered so far off course; some say it was bad winds, others say it was his secret destination all along, but Cabral sailed west and discovered Brazil, landing at present-day Porto Seguro on 22 April.

Cabral and his crew were immediately greeted by some of the many Indians living along the Brazilian shore. Staying only nine days, the Portuguese built a cross and held the first service in the land they dubbed *Terra de Vera Cruz* (land of the true cross). The Indians watched with apparent amazement and then, complying with the exhortations of their guests, knelt before the cross. But it wasn't Catholicism that grabbed their attention. It was the building of the cross. The Indians, living in a stone-age culture, had never seen iron tools.

Cabral sailed on, leaving behind two

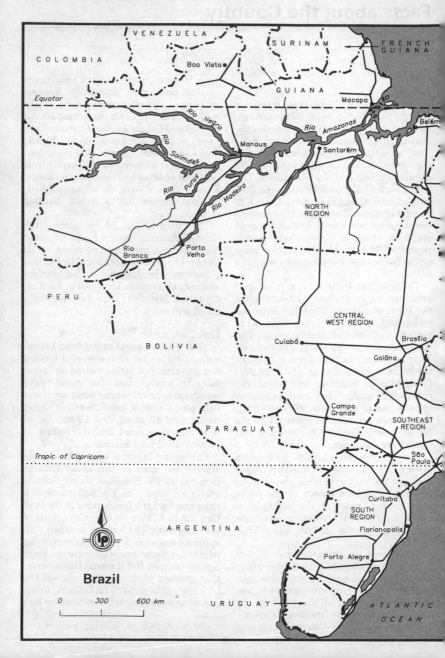

convicts to learn the Indian's ways and taking some logs of the *pau do brasil* – brazil wood tree, which produced a red dye. Subsequent Portuguese expeditions were disappointed by what they found in Brazil. They had little interest in colonisation. Instead they sought the riches of India and Africa where they established trading stations to obtain spices and ivory. Brazil offered the merchants little: the natives' primitive, stone-age culture produced nothing for the European market, and the land was heavily forested, barely passable and very wild.

The red dye provoked the interest of a few Portuguese merchants and the king granted them the rights to the brazil wood trade. They soon began sending a few ships a year to harvest the trees, depending entirely on Indian labour which they procured in exchange for metal axes and knives, objects that are used to this day by Brazilians contacting unknown Indians.

Brazil wood remained the only exportable commodity for the first half of the 16th century – long enough for the colony to change its name from Terra de Vera Cruz to Brazil; an act that was later interpreted, as reports of Brazilian godlessness reached superstition-ridden Portugal, as the work of the devil. But the brazil wood trade was already in jeopardy. It was never terribly profitable and the most accessible trees were rapidly depleted. French competition for the trees intensified and fighting broke out. The Indians stopped volunteering their labour.

In 1531, King João III of Portugal sent the first settlers to Brazil. Martin Afonso de Sousa was placed at the head of five ships and a crew of 400 and after exploring the littoral he chose São Vicente, near the modern port of Santos in São Paulo to set up shop. In 1534, fearing the ambitions of other European countries, the king divided the coast into 12 parallel captaincies. These hereditary estates were given to friends of the crown (*donatário*) who became lords of their land.

European colonisation of the tropics had never before been attempted. The king's scheme was designed to minimise the cost to the crown while securing the vast coastline through settlement. The king wanted to give the captaincies to Portuguese nobility, but the wealthy nobles were interested in the riches of Asia. Instead the captaincies were given to common *fidalgos* (gentry), who lacked the means to overcome the obstacles of settlement in Brazil. Four captaincies were never settled and four were destroyed by Indians. Only Pernambuco and São Vicente were profitable.

In 1549 the king sent Tomé de Sousa to be the first governor of Brazil, to centralise authority and to save the few remaining captaincies. Despite the fact that the Indians had recently driven the Portuguese out, the king chose Bahia for Sousa to rule from; the Baía de Todos os Santos (Bay of All Saints) was one of Brazil's best, as was the land surrounding it.

Ten ships and 1000 settlers arrived safely. On board were Portuguese officials, soldiers, exiled prisoners, New Christians (converted Jews) and the first six Jesuit

Physikalische Karte von SÜD-AMERICA.

priests. The great Caramuru, a Portuguese living among the Indians and married to a chief's daughter, selected a spot on high ground for Salvador da Bahia, the new capital of Portuguese Brazil, a position it held until the colonial capital was transferred to Rio in 1763.

The colonists soon discovered that the land and climate were ideal for growing sugar cane. Sugar was coveted by a hungry European market that used it initially for medicinal purposes and as a condiment for almost all foods and even wine. To produce the sugar cane, all the colonists needed were workers. Growing and processing the cane was hard work. The Portuguese didn't want to do the work themselves so they attempted to enslave the Indians.

Up and down the coast, the Indians' response to the Portuguese was similar.

First, they welcomed and offered the strangers food, labour and women in exchange for iron tools and liquor. They then became wary of the whites who abused their customs and beliefs, and took the best lands. Finally, when voluntary labour became slavery and land abuse became wholesale displacement, the Indians fought back and won many victories.

The capture and sale of Indian slaves became Brazil's second commerce. *Bandeirantes*, men from São Paulo who were often the offspring of a Portuguese father and an Indian mother, hunted the Indians into the Brazilian interior, exploring and claiming vast lands for the Portuguese and making fortunes supplying the sugar estates with Indian slaves. Their bravery was eclipsed only by their brutality.

Spanish dogs attacking Indians

The Jesuit priests went to great lengths to save the Indians from the slaughter. They inveighed against the evils of Indian slavery in their sermons, though they said little about Black slaves. They pleaded with the king of Portugal. They set up *aldeas* or missions to settle, protect and Christianise the Indians.

Fear of God failed to deter the colonists. The monarchy was too weak and ambivalent. Most of the Indians not killed by the guns of the Bandeirantes or the work on the sugar plantations died from imported European diseases and the alien life in the missions. The Jesuits may have delayed the destruction of the Brazilian Indians, but they certainly didn't prevent it. Nonetheless, the Jesuits battled heroically to save the Indians. One Brazilian statesman wrote: 'Without the Jesuits, our colonial history would be little more than a chain of nameless atrocities.'

By the end of the 16th century about 30,000 Portuguese settlers and 20,000 Black slaves lived in isolated coastal towns surrounded by often hostile Indians. There were about 200 prosperous sugar mills; most were in Pernambuco and Bahia. In an often quoted passage, a historian lamented in 1620 that the Brazilian settlers were satisfied with 'sidling like crabs along the coastline from one sugar plantation to another'. But there were good reasons for this. The export economy looked only to Europe, not inland where the forests were dense, the rivers were wild and hostile Indians prevailed. Sugar was extremely lucrative, whereas the gold of El Dorado was elusive. The sugar trade needed the rich coastal soil and access to European markets. Thus the Portuguese settled almost exclusively at the mouths of rivers on navigable bays. Where sugar grew – mainly Bahia, Pernambuco and Rio – so did the fledgeling colony.

The captaincy system failed, but sugar succeeded. The sparsely settled land – that would eventually encompass half a continent – already had the elements that were to define it even into the 19th century: sugar and slavery.

Sugar & Slaves

The sugar plantations were self-sufficient economic enclaves. They were geared to large-scale production that required vast tracts of land and specialised equipment to process the sugar cane. In Brazil this meant the sugar baron needed land, a fair amount of capital and many workers, typically 100 to 150 slaves, both skilled and unskilled.

By the 1550s the wealthier sugar barons began to buy African slaves instead of Indians. The Africans were better workers and more immune to the European diseases that were slaughtering the Indians faster than the Portuguese guns. Soon tremendous profits were being made by merchants in the slave trade. The infamous triangular trade brought slaves and elephant tusks from Africa; sugar, sugar cane liquor and tobacco from Brazil; guns and luxury goods from Europe.

Throughout the 17th century Blacks replaced Indians on the plantations. In the early 1600s about 1500 slaves were arriving each year. From 1550 to 1850, when the slave trade was abolished, about 3 1/2 million African slaves were shipped to Brazil – 38% of the total that came to the New World.

Those Africans who didn't die on the slave ships generally had short and brutal lives. The work on the plantations was hard and tedious. During the busy season slaves worked 15 to 17 hours a day. But working and living conditions, not the amount of work itself, were largely responsible for the high mortality rate of Brazil's slaves. Disease was rampant in Brazil: many succumbed to dysentery, typhus, yellow fever, malaria, syphilis, tuberculosis and scurvy.

The plantation owner ruled colonial Brazil. His control over free whites who worked as share-croppers was almost total, over slaves it was absolute. A slave was dependent on the master. Some were kind, most were cruel and often sadistic.

Slave families were routinely broken up. Masters mixed slaves from different tribes to prevent collective rebellion. The slaves from Islamic Africa, culturally superior to most Portuguese, were particularly feared by the white masters.

Resistance to slavery took many forms. Some slaves responded to their misery with *banzo*, the longing for Africa, which culminated in a slow suicide. Many documents of the period refer to slaves who would stop eating and just fade away. Many slaves fled. Mothers killed their babies. Sabotage and theft were frequent as were work slowdowns, stoppages and revolts.

Those that survived life on the plantations found solace in their African religion and culture, in their dance and song. The slaves were given perfunctory indoctrination into Catholicism. Except for the Islamic element, a syncretic religion rapidly emerged. Spiritual elements from many of the African tribes such as the Yoruba, Bantu, and Fon were preserved and made palatable to the slavemasters with a facade of Catholic saints and ritual objects. These are the roots of modern *macumba* and *candomblé*, prohibited by law until very recently.

Portugal was not an over-populated country. There was no capitalist revolution and no enclosures, as in England, forcing the peasantry off the land. Consequently, the typical Brazilian settler emigrated by choice with the hope of untold riches. These settlers were notoriously indisposed to work. They came to Brazil to make others work for them, not to toil in the dangerous tropics. Even poor whites had a slave or two. There was a popular saying, 'the slaves are the hands and the feet of the whites'.

The sugar barons lived on the plantation part-time and escaped to their second houses in the cities, where they often kept *mulatto* (mixed race) mistresses. The white women led barren, cloistered lives inside the walls of the casa grande. Secluded from all but their husbands and servants, the women married young – usually at 14 to 15 years of age – and often died early.

Sexual relations between masters and slaves were so common that a large mulatto population soon emerged. Off the plantation, with the shortage of White women, many poorer settlers lived with Black and Indian women. Prostitution was prevalent. Many of the free mixed-race women could only survive by working as concubines or prostitutes. Brazil was famous for its sexual permissiveness. By the beginning of the 18th century Brazil was known as the land of syphilis. The disease had reportedly wrought devastation even in the monasteries.

The Church was tolerant of any coupling that helped populate the colony. Many priests had mistresses and illegitimate children. As Gilberto Freyre, Brazil's most famous social scientist, said of the priests, 'a good part if not the majority of them assisted in the work of procreation, and their cooperation was so gratefully accepted that the courts did not arrest or issue warrants for any cleric or friar on the charge of keeping a concubine'.

In the poorer regions of Pará, Maranhão, Ceará and São Paulo, the settlers couldn't afford Black slaves. Indian slaves were more common. Here, miscegenation was more prevalent between Whites and Indians and just as tolerated (this is evident in the racial mix of the people's faces in those states today). As in the rest of the colony, sexual relations were rather licentious. As the Bishop of Pará summed it up:

the wretched state of manners in this country puts me in mind of the end that befell the five cities, and makes me think that I am living in the suburbs of Gomorrah, very close indeed, and in the vicinity of Sodom.

17th Century

Sugar plantations were the first attempt at large scale agricultural production in the New World, not just extraction. Thanks to a virtual monopoly and increasing European demand they were highly profitable. The sugar trade made the Portuguese colonisation of Brazil possible. In later years, as Portugal's Asian empire declined, the tax revenues from the sugar trade kept the Portuguese ship of state afloat.

Although Spain and Portugal had divided the New World exclusively between themselves with the Treaty of Tordesilhas, competing European powers, principally France and Holland, were not deterred from South America. France had successfully operated trading stations in Brazil for many years and had friendly relations with many Indians who saw them as a lesser evil than the hated Portuguese.

In 1555 three boatloads of French settlers led by Nicholas de Villegagnon landed on a small island in Baía de Guanabara. They intended to capture Rio, but were expelled by the Portuguese in 1560. In a second attempt in 1612 the French took São Luis but were driven out by the Portuguese a few years later.

The Dutch posed a more serious threat to Portuguese Brazil. Dutch merchants had profited from the Brazilian sugar trade for many years, but when Portugal was unified with Spain, the traditional enemies of the Dutch, peaceful trade quickly collapsed. The Dutch set up the Dutch West India Company to gain control of part of Brazil. A large expedition took Bahia in 1624. A year later, after bloody and confused fighting, the Portuguese retook the city then repulsed two more attacks in 1627.

The Dutch next conquered Pernambuco in 1630 and from there took control of a major chunk of the Northeast from Sergipe to Maranhão, all of which they held for 20 years. With their superior sea power the Dutch sailed to Africa and captured part of Portuguese-held Angola to supply slaves for their new colony. But the Dutch were undermined by a lack of support from the homeland. Pernambucan merchants, resenting the Protestant invaders, funded Black and Indian soldiers who fought the Dutch on land. The Portuguese Governor of Rio de Janeiro and Angola, Salvador de Sá sailed from Rio and expelled the Dutch from Angola. Finally, when provisions failed to arrive, the Dutch troops mutinied and returned to Europe. A peace treaty was signed in 1654.

Bandeirantes

Throughout the 17th and 18th centuries Bandeirantes from São Paulo continued to march off into the interior to capture Indians. Most Bandeirantes, born of Indian mother and Portuguese father, spoke both Tupi-Guaraní and Portuguese. They also learned the survival skills of the Indians, the use of European weaponry and wore heavily padded cotton jackets that deflected Indian arrows. Travelling light in bands of a dozen to a couple of hundred they would go off for months and years at a time, living off the land and plundering Indian villages. By the mid 1600s they had traversed the interior as far as the peaks of the Peruvian Andes and the lowlands of the Amazon forest. These super-human exploits, more than any treaty, secured the huge interior of South America for Portuguese Brazil.

The Bandeirantes were ruthlessly effective Indian hunters. The Jesuits, who sought desperately to protect their flock of Indians – who had come to the missions to escape Bandeirante attacks – built missions in the remote interior, near the present day borders with Paraguay and Argentina. Far from São Paulo, the Jesuits hoped that they were beyond the grasp of the Bandeirantes. They were wrong, and this was to be their last stand. The Jesuits armed the Indians and desperate battles took place. The Bandeirantes were slowed but they were never stopped. Finally, with the collusion of the Portuguese and Spanish crowns, the missions fell and the Jesuits were expelled from Brazil in 1759.

Gold

El Dorado and other South American legends of vast deposits of gold and precious stones clouded European minds and spurred roving bandeirantes to excess. Despite incessant searching, riches failed to materialise until the 1690s when bandeirantes discovered a magical lustre in the rivers of the Serra do Espinhaço, Brazil's oldest geological formation, an inaccessible and unsettled region inland from Rio de Janeiro.

Soon, the gold rush was on. People dropped everything to go to what is now the south central part of Minas Gerais. Unaware of the hazardous journey, many died on the way. In the orgy to pan no one bothered to plant and in the early years terrible famines swept through the gold towns. The price of basic provisions was always outrageous and the majority suffered. But the gold was there – more than seemed possible.

When gold was first discovered, there were no white settlers in the territory of Minas Gerais. By 1710 the population was 30,000 and by the end of the 18th century it was half a million.

For 50 years, until the mines began to decline, Brazilian gold caused major demographic shifts in three continents. Paulistas came from São Paulo, followed by other Brazilians, who had failed to strike it rich in commercial agriculture. Some 400,000 Portuguese arrived in Brazil in the 18th century, many headed for gold. Countless slaves were stolen away from Africa, to dig and die in Minas.

Fuelled by competition over scarce mining rights, a Brazilian species of nativism arose. Old-time Brazilians, particularly the combative Paulistas, resented the flood of recent Portuguese immigrants who were cashing in on their gold discoveries. The recent arrivals, numerically superior, loathed the favourable treatment they saw the Paulistas receiving. Gold stakes were more often than not settled by guns, not judges, and armed confrontations broke out in 1708. The colonial government was faced with a virtual civil war which lasted over a year, with miners carrying pans in one hand and guns in the other, before government intervention slowed the hostilities.

Most of the gold mining was done by Black slaves. An estimated third of the two million slaves who reached Brazil in the 18th century went to the gold fields where their lives were worse than in the sugar fields. Most slave owners put their slaves on an incentive system allowing the slaves to keep a small percentage of the gold they found. A few slaves who found great quantities of gold were able to buy their own freedom, but for the majority disease and death came quickly.

Wild boom towns arose in the mountain valleys: Sabara, Mariana, São João del Rei and the greatest, Vila Rica de Ouro Prêto (Rich Town of Black Gold). Rich merchants built opulent mansions and grand baroque churches. Crime, gambling, drinking and prostitution ruled the streets. A class of educated artisans and officials provided a sense of European civilisation. The absence of white women led to a large number of mulatto offspring.

Most of Brazil's gold wealth was squandered. A few merchants and miners became incredibly rich and lived on imported European luxury goods. But the gold did little to develop Brazil's economy, create a middle class or better the common worker. Most of the wealth went to Portuguese merchants and the king, where it paused before being traded for English goods.

By 1750, after a half century boom, the mining regions were in decline, the migration to the interior was over and coastal Brazil was returning to centre stage. Aside from some public works and many beautiful churches, the only important legacy of Brazil's gold rush was the shift in population from the Northeast to the Southeast. Some stayed in Minas Gerais and raised cattle on its rich lands. Many ended up in Rio whose population and economy grew rapidly as gold and supplies passed through its ports.

19th Century

In 1807 Napoleon's army marched on Lisbon. Two days before the invasion, 40 ships carrying the Portuguese prince regent (later known as Dom João VI) and his entire court of 15,000 had set sail for Brazil under the protection of British warships. When the prince regent arrived in Rio his Brazilian subjects celebrated wildly, dancing in the streets. He immediately took over rule of Brazil from his viceroy, making Rio the capital of the United Kingdom of Portugal, Brazil and the Algarves. Brazil became the only New World colony to ever have a European monarch ruling on its soil.

As foreigners have been doing ever since, Dom João fell in love with Brazil. Expected to return to Portugal after Napoleon's Waterloo in 1815, he stayed in Brazil. The following year his mother, mad queen Dona Maria I, died and Dom João VI became king. Five years later he finally relented to political pressures and returned to Portugal to rule. He left his son Dom Pedro I in Brazil as prince regent.

According to legend, in 1822, Dom Pedro I pulled out his sword and yelled 'Independendência ou morte!' (independence or death). Portugal was too weak to fight its favourite son, not to mention the British who had the most to gain from Brazilian independence and would have come to the aid of the Brazilians. The Brazilian Empire was born. Without spilling blood, Brazil had attained its independence and Dom Pedro I became the first Emperor of Brazil.

Dom Pedro I only ruled for nine years. From all accounts he was a bumbling incompetent who scandalized even the permissive Brazilians by siring several soccer teams of illegitimate children. He was forced to abdicate, paving the way for his five-year-old son to become emperor.

Until Dom Pedro II reached adolescence Brazil suffered through a period of civil war under the rule of a weak triple regency. In 1840, the nation rallied behind the emperor. During his 50 year reign he nurtured an increasingly powerful parliamentary system, went to war with Paraguay, meddled in Argentine, Paraguayan and Uruguayan affairs, encouraged mass immigration, abolished slavery, and ultimately forged a nation that would do away with the monarchy for ever.

A New Empire

At the beginning of the 19th century Brazil was a country of masters and slaves. There were about three million people, not including the Indians, and roughly one million of them were African slaves.

In the poorer areas there were fewer Black slaves, more poor Whites and more Indians. The Central-West region – Minas, Goiás, the Mato Grosso – was well explored but was settled only in isolated pockets where precious metals had been found. The Northeastern interior, the *sertão*, was the most settled inland section of the country. The arid sertão was unable to sustain much agriculture but cattle could graze and survive. It was a poor business, constantly threatened by drought, but the hardy *sertanejo* (inhabitant of the sertão) – often of mixed Portuguese and Indian extraction – was able to eke out a living.

The South was another story. Settled by farmers from the Portuguese Azores who brought their wives, the area was economically backward. Few could afford slaves. The Indians had been clustered in the Jesuit missions far to the west to save them from the Bandeirantes. The south was, and remains, Brazil's whitest and most European region.

Slavery

Slavery in Brazil was not abolished until 1888, 25 years after abolition in the USA and 80 years behind Britain. Resistance to slavery grew throughout the 19th century and the spectre of Haiti – the site of the first successful slave revolt – haunted the Brazilian planters who, as a result, became more brutal towards their slaves.

In Bahia there were several urban insurrections between 1807 and 1835. Most were led by Muslim Blacks, free and slave. The uprising of 1807 in Bahia was carefully planned so that slaves from the sugar *engenhos* would meet the city slaves at the entrance to the city and together attack the whites, seize ships and flee to Africa. However, the plot was betrayed and the leaders killed. The following year, a similar plan was carried out and the Blacks were defeated in battle. In Minas Gerais, 15,000 slaves congregated in Ouro Prêto and 6000 in São João do Morro, demanding a constitution and freedom. The last big slave revolt in Bahia was in 1835, and was almost successful.

Slaves fought their oppressors in many ways, and many managed to escape from their masters. *Quilombos*, communities of runaway slaves, scattered throughout the countryside, were common throughout the colonial period. The quilombos ranged from small groups hidden in the forests, called *mocambos*, to the most famous, the great republic of Palmares, which survived much of the 17th century.

Palmares covered a broad tract along the *zona da mata* (the lush tropical forest near the coast) of northern Alagoas and southern Pernambuco states. At its height, 20,000 people lived under its protection. Most were Black, but there were also Indians, mulattos, mestiços and bandits. They lived off the land. Agriculture was collective; they grew mostly corn and productivity was higher than on the slave plantations.

Palmares was really a collection of semi-independent quilombos united under the rule of one king to fight off the Portuguese forces. Led by the African king, Zumbí, the citizens of Palmares became pioneers of guerrilla warfare and defeated many Portuguese attacks. Fearing Palmares' example, the government desperately tried to crush it. Between 1670 and 1695 Palmares was attacked an average of every 15 months, until it finally fell to a force led by Paulista Bandeirantes.

Palmares is now the stuff of movies and myths, but there were many quilombos in every state. As abolitionist sentiment grew in the 19th century, the quilombos received more support and ever greater numbers of slaves fled. Only abolition itself in 1888 stopped the quilombos.

Insurrections

With populated settlements separated by enormous distances, few transportation or communication links, and an economy oriented toward European markets rather than local ones, the Brazilian nation together was weak and there was little sense of national identity. Throughout the 19th century the Brazilian empire was plagued by the revolts of local ruling elites demanding greater autonomy from the central government, or even fighting to secede. Rio Grande do Sul was torn by a civil war, called the Farrapos rebellion. There were insurrections in São Paulo and Minas Gerais. And insurrections swept through the North and Northeast in the 1830s and '40s.

The bloodiest and most radical was the Cabanagem in the state of Pará. The rebels laid siege to the capital of Belém, appropriating and distributing supplies. They held the city for a year before their defeat at the hands of a large government force. The peasants fled to the jungle with the army in pursuit and eventually 40,000 of the state's 100,000 people were killed.

The most serious revolts, like the Cabanagem, were the ones that spread to the oppressed peasants and urban poor. But the empire always struck back and the revolts all failed, in part because the upper and middle classes, who led the revolts, feared the mobilised poor as much as they feared the government.

In 1889 a military coup supported by the coffee aristocracy toppled the antiquated Brazilian empire. The emperor went into exile and died a couple of years later. A military clique ruled for four years until elections were held, but because of land and literacy requirements, ignorance and threats, only about 2% of the adult population voted. Little changed, except power to the military and the coffee growers increased, and the sugar barons lost power.

The 19th century was a period of messianic popular movements amongst Brazil's poor. Most of the movements took place in the economically depressed backlands of the Northeast. Canudos is the most famous of these movements. From 1877 to 1887, Antônio Conselheiro, wandered through the backlands preaching and prophesising the appearance of the Antichrist and the coming end of the world. He railed against the new republican government. Eventually he gathered his followers (who called him the Counsellor) in Canudos, a settlement in the interior of Bahia.

In Canudos, the government sensed dissenting plots to return Brazil to the Portuguese monarchy. They set out to subdue the rebels, but miraculously, a force of state police and then two attacks by the federal army were defeated.

Hysterical demonstrations in the cities demanded that the republic be saved from the revolutionary-monarchist followers of the Counsellor. Canudos was again besieged. A federal force of 4000 well-supplied soldiers and cannons took the settlement after ferocious house-to-house

and hand-to-hand fighting. The military was disgraced and suffered heavy casualties and the federal government was embarrassed but Canudos was wiped out. The military killed every man, woman and child, and then they burned the town to the ground to erase it from the nation's memory.

The epic struggle has been memorialised in what is considered the masterpiece of Brazilian literature *Os Sertãos* (Rebellion in the Backlands) by Euclides de Cunha (more recently Mario Vargas Llosa's wrote of Canudos in a lesser work *The War of the End of the World*).

Coffee

The international sugar market began a rapid decline in the 1820s. The sugar planters had depleted much of their best soil. They had failed to modernise and were unable to compete with newly mechanised sugar mills in the West Indies. As rapidly as sugar exports fell, coffee production rose to become Brazil's new monoculture.

The coffee tree flourished on the low mountain slopes of the Paraíba Valley from north-east of São Paulo city up to Rio de Janeiro state and along the border with Minas Gerais. As these lands were snatched up, the coffee plantations moved westward into Minas Gerais and western São Paulo.

Coffee production was labour intensive. Because of the large investment needed to employ so many workers, coffee production excluded the small farmer and favoured large enterprises using slave labour. The master-slave sugar plantation system, complete with the big house and slave quarters was reproduced on the coffee *fazendas* (estates) of São Paulo and Minas Gerais.

Coffee exports increased rapidly throughout the 19th century and profits soared with the introduction of machinery and Brazil's first railroads. In 1889 coffee exports totalled two thirds of the country's exports. The modernisation of coffee production also eased the coffee plantations transition to a free labour force with the end of slavery in 1888. During the next decade 800,000 European immigrants, mostly Italians, came to work on the coffee fazendas. Many more immigrants – Japanese, German, Spanish and Portuguese – flooded into the cities from 1890 to 1916.

These developments in the second half of the 19th century threatened to modernise Brazil's backward, pre-capitalist economy: slavery was abolished, railroads were built, the first industry appeared and millions of Europeans arrived. Brazil was still a rural society – only 10% of the population lived in cities in 1890 – but cities were growing rapidly. São Paulo and Rio in particular were the main beneficiaries of the coffee boom. Nevertheless, the country's place in the world economy remained unchanged: exporter of agricultural commodities and importer of manufactured goods. Some seeds of modernisation were being planted, but there was no economic take-off, no qualitative leap forward.

Vargas Era

Coffee was king until the global economic crisis of 1929 put a big hole in the bottom of the coffee market and badly damaged the Brazilian economy. The coffee planters of São Paulo who controlled the government were badly weakened. In opposition to the pro-coffee policies of the government, a Liberal Alliance formed around the elites of Minas Gerais and Rio Grande do Sul and nationalist military officers. When their presidential candidate, Getúlio Vargas, lost the 1930 elections the military took power by force, handing over the reins to Vargas.

Vargas proved to be a gifted political manoeuverer and was to dominate the political scene for the next 20 years. He skilfully played off one sector of the ruling elite against another but he was careful not to alienate the military. His popular support came from the odd bit of social reform combined with large slabs of demagoguery and nationalism.

In 1937, on the eve of a new election, Vargas sent in the military to shut down congress and took complete control of the country. His regime was inspired by Mussolini's and Salazar's fascist states. Vargas banned political parties, imprisoned political opponents and censored the press. When WW II struck, Vargas sided with the Allies and when the war ended, the contradiction between fighting for democracy in Europe while operating a quasi-fascist state at home was too glaring. Vargas was forced to step down by the military authorities but he remained popular. He was the first Brazilian politician to enact any reforms for the masses.

Under Vargas, with the economic opportunities afforded by the war in Europe, Brazil began its fitful march toward industrialisation and urbanisation. A large network of state corporations including national petroleum and steel companies was established, the first minimum wage was set and peasants flocked to the cities for a better life. In the cities Vargas established state organisations to secure government control and prevent the establishment of independent equivalents. The most important was the Mussolini-inspired Labour Code which established compulsory unions for the small but growing urban working class. This bound them to the Labour Ministry which controlled the union finances, thereby allowing the government to control the labour leaders; it also limited the right to strike to the approval of Labour Courts. These laws worked well to strait-jacket the labour movement until the massive strike wave of 1980 which bypassed the official union leadership and won more democratic and independent unions.

Late 20th Century

Juscelino Kubitschek was elected president in 1956. His motto was '50 years' progress in five'. The critics responded '40 years' inflation in four'. The critics were closer to the mark. Industrial production increased by 80% during Kubitschek's five years.

Kubitschek was the first of Brazil's big spenders. Deficit spending and large loans funded roads and hydroelectric projects. Foreign capital was encouraged to invest and Brazil's auto industry was started. Kubitschek built Brasília, a new capital which was supposed to be the catalyst to developing Brazil's vast interior.

By 1964 the economy was battered by inflation, popular protest was on the rise in the cities and the countryside, and fears of communism were provoked by Castro's victory in Cuba. The military again rose and put the sword to Brazil's limited and fragile democracy by overthrowing Kubitschek. Brazil's military regime was not as brutal as those of Chile or Argentina, the repression tended to come and go in cycles. But at its worst, around 1968 and 1969, the use of torture and murder of political opponents was widespread. For almost 20 years political parties were outlawed and freedom of speech was curtailed.

Kubitschek had made populist and nationalist proclamations, such as defying the IMF so it was impossible to label him a Communist, though some tried. But by 1964 there was a growing threat of increased participation in and even radicalisation of the political process. Much of the middle class welcomed the military, the 'Revolution of 1964', as it was called at first.

Within hours of the coup, President Johnson cabled his warmest good wishes. The USA immediately extended diplomatic relations to the military regime and suspicions ran deep that the USA had masterminded the coup.

Borrowing heavily from the international banks, the generals benefited from the Brazilian economic miracle; year after year in the late '60s and early '70s Brazil's economy grew by over 10%. The trans-

formation to an urban and semi-industrialised country accelerated. Millions came to the cities and *favelas* (shanty towns) filled the open spaces. The middle class grew as did the bureaucracy and military. More mega-projects were undertaken to exploit Brazil's natural resources, to provide quick fixes to underdevelopment and to draw attention from much needed social reforms. The greatest of these was the opening of the Amazon which has brought great wealth to the few and little to most Brazilians, while helping to draw attention away from the issue of land reform.

The military's honeymoon didn't last. Opposition grew in 1968 as the students, and then many in the church – which had been generally supportive of the coup – began to protest against the regime. Inspired by liberation theology the church had begun to examine Brazilian misery. Church leaders established base communities among the poor to fight for social justice. They were appalled by the military's flagrant abuse of human rights which broke all religious and moral tenets.

In 1980 a militant working class movement, centred around the São Paulo auto industry, exploded onto the scene with a series of strikes under the charismatic leadership of Lula.

With the economic miracle petering out and popular opposition picking up steam, the military announced the *abertura* (opening) and began a slow and cautious process of returning the government to civilian rule. Local elections were scheduled then cancelled but congressional elections were held in 1982. Indirect elections for a civilian president were scheduled for 1985. The election process was designed to guarantee the victory of the military's chosen candidate but millions of Brazilians took to the streets in a spontaneous outburst of protest against the dictatorship and joy at the end of military rule. The opposition candidate, Tancredo Neves, won the election, but died the day before

Advertisement for *Mad* magazine
lampooning President Sarney

assuming the presidency. He was succeeded by the vice-president, José Sarney, a relative unknown who had supported the military until 1984.

By 1087, with Sarney at the helm, the politicians were working on a new constitution (Brazil has had several). The military remained behind the curtains of power, having lost little except the responsibility for governing. Little has changed in the day to day life of most Brazilians. There have been no reforms. There has been no redistribution of wealth. There have only been old promises.

GEOGRAPHY

Brazil is the world's fifth largest country – after the Soviet Union, Canada, China and the USA. It borders every country in South America, except Chile and Ecuador, and its 8½ million square kms occupies almost half the continent. Gigantic Brazil is larger than the continental USA, 2½ times the size of India, and larger than Europe excluding the Soviet Union. It spans three time zones and is closer to Africa than it is to Europe or the USA.

As amazing as the size of this enormous expanse, is its inaccessibility and inhospitality to humans. Much of Brazil is scarcely populated: 36% of the nation's territory is in the Amazon basin which,

along with the enormous Mato Grosso to its south, has large regions with population densities of less than one person per square km. Most of this land was not thoroughly explored by Europeans until this century. New mountains, now rivers and new Indian tribes are still being discovered. The Amazon is being rapidly settled, lumbered and depleted.

Brazil's geography can be reduced to four primary regions. The long, narrow Atlantic coastal band that stretches from the Uruguayan border to the state of Maranhaõ; the large highlands – called the Planalto Brasileiro or central plateau – which extend over most of Brazil's interior south of the Amazon basin; and two great depressions – the Amazon basin and the Paraguay basin in the south-east.

The coastal band, stretching for 7408 km, is bordered by the Atlantic and the coastal mountain ranges that lie between it and the central plateau. From Rio Grande do Sul all the way up to Bahia the mountains are right on the coast. Sheer mountainsides, called the Great Escarpment, make rivers impossible to navigate. Especially in Rio and Espírito Santo, the littoral is rocky and irregular, with many islands, bays and sudden granite peaks like Sugar Loaf in Rio.

North of Bahia, the coastal lands are flatter and the transition to highland is

The States of Brazil

Regions

North
North east
Centre West
Southeast
South

1 Rio Grande do Norte
2 Paraíba
3 Pernambuco
4 Alagoas
5 Sergipe

more gradual. Rounded hills signal the beginning of the central plateau. There are navigable rivers and the coast is smooth and calm, well-protected by offshore reefs.

The Planalto Brasileiro is an enormous plateau that covers a part of almost every Brazilian state. The Planalto is punctuated by several small mountain ranges that reach no more than 3000 metres – the highest of these are centred in Minas Gerais – and is sliced by several large rivers. The average elevation of the Planalto is only 500 metres.

From Minas Gerais the Planalto descends slowly to the north. The great Rio São Francisco, called the river of national unity or more informally *velho chico*, which begins in the mountains of Minas, follows this northerly descent. There are several other rivers slicing through the Planalto. The large tablelands or plains between these river basins are called *chapadões*.

From the Brazilian Planalto to the south, the Andes to the west and the Guyana shield to the north, the waters descend to the great depression of the

Amazon basin. In the far west the basin is 1300 km wide, to the east, between the Guyana massif and the Brazilian Planalto, it narrows to less than 100 km.

There are an estimated 1100 tributaries flowing into the Amazon River, 10 of which carry more water than the Mississippi River. The 6275 km long Amazon River is the world's largest. With its tributaries it carries an estimated 20% of the world's fresh water. The Amazon forest contains 30% of the remaining forest in the world.

In the South, there's the Paraná-Paranagua basin. This depression, not as low as the Amazon, includes the Pantanal and runs into Paraguay and Argentina. It is characterised by open forest, low woods and scrubland. Its two principal rivers, the Paraguay and the Paraná, run south through Paraguay and Argentina.

For political and administrative purposes, Brazil is generally divided into five regions: the North, the Northeast, the Central-West, the Southeast and the South.

The North is the Amazon forest. It encompasses 42% of Brazil's land and includes the states of Amazonas, Pará, Rondônia, Acre and the territories of Amapá and Roraima. This is Brazil's least populated region and contains most of the country's Indian population. The two major cities are Manaus and Belém, both on the Amazon river.

The Northeast, Brazil's poorest region, has retained much of Brazil's colonial past. It's also the region where the African influence is most evident. It contains 18% of Brazil's area and includes, moving up the coast, the states of Bahia, Sergipe, Alagoas, Pernambuco, Paraíba, Rio Grande do Norte, Ceará, Piauí and Maranhão. These states are divided into a littoral, the zona da mata and the sertão (the dry interior).

In the old days the Central-West was called the mato grosso (thick forest). It includes the states of Goiás, Mato Grosso, Mato Grosso do Sul and the federal district of Brasília: 22% of the national territory. Only recently opened to road transport, this is Brazil's fastest growing region.

The Southeast is developed, urban Brazil. The states of Rio de Janeiro, São Paulo, Minas Gerais and Espírito Santo make up 10% of the national territory but have 43% of the population and 63% of industrial production.

In the South, Brazil is more European. The prosperous states of Paraná (with the obvious exception of Foz do Iguaçu and its surrounds), Santa Catarina and Rio Grande do Sul are the least interesting for the traveller.

CLIMATE

Many a travel guide suggests a certain sameness to the weather in Brazil. This is misleading. It's true that only the South has extreme seasonal changes like Europe and the USA, but most of the country does have noticeable seasonal variations in rain, temperature and humidity. In general, as you go from north to south, the seasonal changes are more defined.

The Brazilian winter is from June to August. It doesn't get cold in Brazil – except in the southern states of Porto Alegre, Santa Catarina, Paraná and São Paulo where the average temperature during the winter months of June, July and August is between 13°C and 18°C. There are even a few towns that can get snow, which is very strange to most Brazilians who have never touched the white flakes. The rest of the country boasts moderate temperatures all year long.

The summer season is from December to February. With many Brazilians on vacation, travel is difficult and expensive while from Rio south the humidity can be oppressive. It's also the most festive time of year as Brazilians escape their small, hot apartments and take to the beaches and streets. School vacation, corresponding with the hot season, begins sometime in

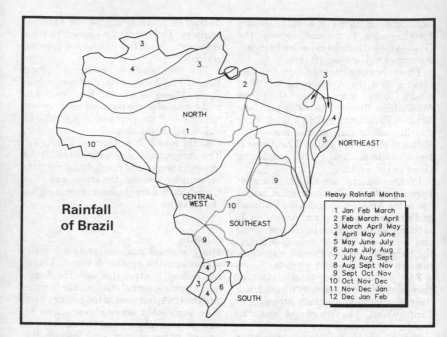

Rainfall of Brazil

Heavy Rainfall Months	
1	Jan Feb March
2	Feb March April
3	March April May
4	April May June
5	May June July
6	June July Aug
7	July Aug Sept
8	Aug Sept Nov
9	Sept Oct Nov
10	Oct Nov Dec
11	Nov Dec Jan
12	Dec Jan Feb

mid-December and goes through Carnival, usually in late February.

In summer, Rio is hot and humid, temperatures in the high 30°Cs are common and sometimes reach the low 40s. Frequent, short rains cool things off a bit, but the summer humidity makes things uncomfortable for people from cooler climes. The rest of the year Rio is cooler with temperatures generally in the mid 20°Cs, sometimes reaching the low 30s. If you are in Rio in the winter and the weather's lousy (the rain can continue for days nonstop), or you want more heat, head to the Northeast.

The Northeast coast gets about as hot as Rio during the summer, but due to a wonderful tropical breeze and less humidity, it's rarely stifling. Generally, from Bahia to Maranhão, temperatures are a bit warmer year-round than in Rio,

rarely far from 28°C. All in all, it's hard to imagine a better climate.

In general the highlands or planalto, such as Minas Gerais and Brasília, are a few degrees cooler than the coast and not as humid. Here, summer rains are frequent, while along the coast the rains tend to come intermittently.

Although there are variations in rainfall (see map), throughout Brazil rain is a year-round affair. The general pattern is for short, tropical rains that come at all times. These rains rarely alter or interfere with travel plans. The sertão is a notable exception – here the rains fall heavily within a few months and periodic droughts devastate the region.

The Amazon basin receives the most rain in Brazil and Belém is one of the most rained on cities in the world, but the refreshing showers are usually seen as a god send. Actually, the Amazon is not nearly as hot as most people presume – the average temperature is 27°C – but it is humid. The hottest part of the basin is between the Solimões and Negro rivers. From June to August the heat tends to decrease a bit.

Whenever you decide to travel in Brazil, there are few regions that can't be comfortably visited all year around.

GOVERNMENT

Brazil's return to democracy in the '80s has been gradual and plagued by the fear that the military can at any moment close the abertura. Every time the opposition party has appeared to be gaining on the military party, the generals have interfered. Nevertheless, in 1982 congressional and state elections were held. In 1985, indirect presidential elections were held and the military's hand-picked successor was defeated.

José Sarney now governs, barely. He has no base, no real party. Without the military's approval he can do nothing. Meanwhile congress is at work on yet another new constitution and democracy flounders.

Amidst work on the constitution, a left-wing congressmen found, to his surprise, that the new constitution had a clause that was in the old constitution. The clause allows for a military takeover in the case of disorder; to be determined by the military (who else). Of course the military doesn't need, and hasn't needed, this legal justification, but they like it and used it in 1964, the last time they took power.

ECONOMY

The only certainty in the economy is its uncertainty. Wild boom and bust cycles have decimated the economy in recent years. Record breaking industrial growth fuelled by foreign capital was followed by negative growth and explosive hyper-inflation. Inflation rates of up to 26% per month, extrapolating to over 1500% per annum is the latest record. Neither tourist

dollars or Brazilian workers' salaries are always able to keep pace with the inflation, however, the dollar does sometimes make gains, whereas Brazilian workers always lose out. In the first half of 1987 real wages for the average Brazilian declined 32%.

Since WW II Brazil has seen tremendous growth and modernisation, albeit in fits and starts. Today, Brazil's economy is the world's eighth largest. It's called a developing country. The military dictators even had visions of Brazil joining the ranks of the advanced, industrialised nations by the year 2000. No one believes that is possible now, but no one denies that tremendous development has occurred.

Brazil is a land of fantastic economic contrasts. Travelling through Brazil you will witness incredibly uneven development. Production techniques barely changed from the colonial epoch dominate many parts of the Northeast and Amazonia, while São Paulo's massive, high-tech auto, steel, arms and chemical industries successfully compete on the world market.

Brazil's rulers, at least since President Kubitschek invented Brasília, have had a penchant for building things big and they have, of course, been encouraged by the IMF and the World Bank. The government borrowed heavily to finance Brasília's construction. The country's external debt began to take off exponentially and a couple of years later inflation followed – neither shows any sign of stopping.

Economic development is slow, but there always seem to be some highly visible mega-projects under way. While many of these are economically ill-advised, they are always good political medicine for whomever is in charge. Some of these mega-projects may produce wealth, but they don't create many jobs, at least once they are built. Utilising the latest technology, much of Brazil's new development is capital intensive. Few jobs are created; not nearly enough to employ the millions of urban poor who have fled the countryside.

Brazil now has an estimated 57 million working people: one third are women; 17% work in agriculture, most as small or landless peasants; 12% work in industry. A majority of the rest cannot find decent work and are forced to sell their labour dirt cheap in jobs that are economically unproductive for society and a dead-end for the individual.

Cheap labour and underemployment abound in Brazil. Middle class families commonly hire two or more live-in maids. This contrasts with five-year-old kids, who will never go to school, selling chewing gum or shining shoes. People are hired just to walk dogs, to watch cars, to deliver groceries. Large crews of street cleaners work with home made brooms. Hawkers on the beaches sell everything and earn almost nothing. Restaurants seem to have more waiters than customers.

Unlike Mexico or Turkey, the poor in Brazil have no rich neighbours where they can go for jobs. With the exception of some minor agrarian reforms, there is no relief in sight. The *fazenderos* (estate owners), with their massive land holdings, are very influential with the government. Apart from the occasional token gesture they are unlikely to be interested in parting with their land.

Instead of land reform, the government built roads into the Amazon: the Belém to Brasília road in 1960 and the Trans-Amazónia and the Cuiabá to Porto Velho roads in the '70s. The idea was to open up the Amazon to mineral and agricultural development, and also encourage settlement by the rural poor.

The mineral-poor Amazonian soil proved hard for the peasants to farm. After cutting the forest and opening the land the peasants were forced off by the hired guns of big cattle ranchers. The settlement of the Amazon continues today, particularly along the Cuiabá-Porto Velho-Rio Branco strip, where violent boom-towns, deforestation and malaria follow in the wake of the settlers.

Brazil is a capitalist country constrained by state intervention and state ownership. Most prices are controlled, off and on, by government decree. Wages and salaries are intermittently controlled as well. There are restrictions on foreign capital and the government has set-up protectionist barriers to help local industry. Car manufacturers must use 95% Brazilian-made parts. Foreign computers are not allowed into the country, although there are no qualms about foreign software – Brazil, which doesn't abide by the international software copyright convention is one of the world's leading software pirates.

All this government tampering politicises economic decision making. Investments are made in a climate of inflation and interest rate uncertainty and government favours, like special subsidies, special licenses, special exemptions from regulations. This leads to many unhappy capitalists and incredible waste. The car industry, for example, which accounts for 10% of the country's output, and was the linchpin of the country's economic miracle of the 1970s has recently fallen on hard times. Ford and Volkswagen have both lost money for several years. They blame government policies like the price freeze that made new cars so cheap in 1986 that anyone who bought one from the manufacturer could resell it the next day with a 60% mark-up.

Petrobras, the national oil company, is about 17 times larger than any other company in the country and the world's 23rd largest corporation. Petrobras handles 40% of Brazil's imports and 20% of its exports. They are now sitting on one of the world's largest untapped oil deposits off the coast of Rio.

Petrobras is one of 600 state-owned companies in Brazil, but with Petrobras the question is who owns who. General Geisel was the head of Petrobras before he became President of Brazil in 1974. Called a government within a government, Petrobras seems to resist pressure – mostly from the IMF – to streamline its operations. Like many government jobs, working for Petrobras is considered a plum. Salaries are among Brazil's best. Housing for most of its white-collar workers is provided at a Rio building called the hanging gardens of Petrobras.

Over 50% of Brazil's industry is clustered in and around São Paulo city. Most important is the car industry. Labour relations with the workers who build cars for Volkswagen, General Motors and Ford were managed by a system modelled on fascist Italy: government-approved unions backed by the power of the military state. From 1968 to 1978 the workers were silent and passive until the day 100 workers at a bus factory went to work and sat down in front of their machines. Within two weeks

78,000 metalworkers were on strike in the São Paulo industrial belt.

Rapidly, the strikes spread to other industries. The government-sponsored unions were replaced; decisions were made by mass assemblies of workers in soccer stadiums. At the invitation of the Catholic church, union offices were moved to the Cathedral of São Bernado. Caught by surprise the corporations and military gave in to substantial wage increases. Both sides prepared for the next time.

In 1980 there was a new wave of strikes. They were better organised, with greater rank and file control. Demands were made to democratise the workplace with shop floor union representation and factory and safety committees. Many improvements were won, many have since been lost, but the industrial working class had flexed its muscles and no one has forgotten.

Brazilian flag

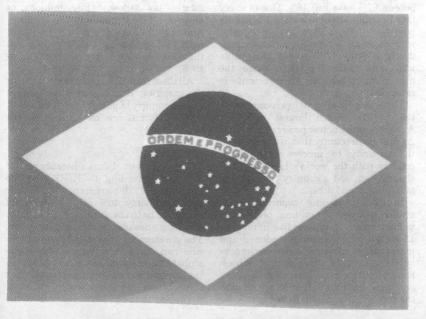

Skyrocketing inflation has battered the Brazilian economy since 1983. The government tried to respond with wage and price freezes, the *plano cruzado* in 1986. It worked for a year, but the freeze was lifted after considerable pressure from the international banks and hyperinflation returned worse than ever. Then, after many people's real income was cut by as much as a half, another freeze was announced in mid 1987. Somehow, while prices were supposedly frozen, the city buses of Rio got judicial permission to double their fares. It was just too much for people who lived on the city's outskirts and spent as much as 25 to 50% of their earnings on buses. Rioting broke out and buses were fire-bombed. Police shot tear gas, the public threw rocks and the next day the price rise was rolled back.

Social Conditions

The richest 4% of Brazilians control a whopping 43% of the nation's wealth; the poorest 67% have just 18%. One of every four Brazilians lives in a state of absolute poverty. Sixty million live in squalor without proper sanitation, clean water or decent housing. Over 60% of the people who work make less than twice the minimum wage. Unemployment is rampant.

These inequities occur in a country with the world's eighth largest economy. A country with nuclear power plants (that don't work), a country that just announced the capacity to process uranium, a country with the world's largest hydroelectric dam and a country that exports automobiles and arms.

In this developing country of 130 million people, 40 million people are malnourished; 25 million live in favelas; 12 million children are abandoned and more than seven million between the ages of seven and 14 don't attend school. Brazil, with its military dreams of greatness, has misery that compares with the poorest countries in Africa and Asia.

As always, these ills hit some groups much harder than others. If you are a woman, a Black, an Indian or from the North or Northeast the odds against escaping poverty are great. One third of the women employed in Brazil work as maids and nannies, most earn less than the minimum wage. Of Brazil's 21 million illiterates, 13 million are Black. Life expectancy in the Northeast is 51 years, compared to 61 for the whole country. The Indians are fighting for survival, less than 200,000 remain from an estimated five million when the Portuguese arrived.

Health in Brazil is wretched. While destitute Nicaragua invests 19% of its budget in health care, Brazil invests 4% and the percentage has been decreasing. The infant mortality rate is 125 for each 1000 births. The number of new cases of malaria reached 160,000 in 1986. Every hour a worker dies at work. In 1986 Brazil led the world in workplace injuries.

The vast majority of the populace supports agrarian reform. Yet, vast estates lay fallow, while millions of desperately poor peasants are landless. And only military might prevents them from taking that land: 261 people lost their lives in vain in the war for land in 1986.

All these facts illustrate the obvious: for the majority, Brazil is as it has always been, a country of poverty and inequality, where reforms are as elusive as the wind.

EDUCATION

The government claims a literacy rate of 80% but according to EDUCAR, the government department for adult education, only 40% of Brazilians old enough to be in the workforce are capable of reading a newspaper with comprehension. The government considers literate those who can write their names, know the alphabet and sound out a few words. In the workplace it has become obvious that these people are functionally illiterate. According to the government, half of the nation's pupils do not pass the first school year and many do not attempt to repeat it. Only two out of every 10 students make it through elementary school. The remainder drop out to support themselves and their family.

Education in Brazil is based on class. Public schools are so bad that anyone with the means, sends their children to private school. Almost all university students are from the private schools, so very few poor children reach university and the poverty cycle is renewed. Many poor children must work to eat and never attend school. Even for those who are able to go, there aren't enough schools, teachers or desks to go around.

The Brizzola government of Rio de Janeiro was one of the first to understand and act upon the connections between poverty, hunger and illiteracy and has set up food programmes in schools. The kids come to school for the food and stay for the lessons. Some schools have classes at night for those children who work during the day. There are televised adult education programmes in mathematics and literacy skills. While these measures are not enough – thousands of Rio's primary school students still have only three hours of class per day – they show that some programmes are successful.

POPULATION & PEOPLE

Brazil's population is around 130 to 135 million, making it the world's sixth most populous nation. With one of the world's highest growth rates – 2½% a year – the population has been rising rapidly over the last 45 years. There were only 14 million Brazilians in 1890, 33 million in 1930, 46 million in 1945, and 71 million in 1960. The population has almost doubled in the last 25 years.

Still, Brazil is one of the least densely populated nations in the world, averaging only 15 people per square km. The USA, by comparison, averages 25 people per square km. This population is concentrated along the coastal strip and in the cities.

There are less than eight million in the enormous expanses of the North and less than 10 million in the Central-West while there are over 60 million in the Southeast and over 40 million in the Northeast. Brazil is also young, half its people are less than 20 years old, 27% under 10. There are 12 million *abandonados*, children without parents or home.

Brazil is now an urban country whereas 40 years ago it was still a predominantly rural society. Due to internal migration, three out of every four Brazilians now live in urban areas. Greater São Paulo has over 15 million residents, greater Rio over 10 million. More than one in every six Brazilians lives in these two urban centres. Greater Belo Horizonte, Porto Alegre, Recife and Salvador all have between two and three million people.

Some 500 years ago Cabral discovered Brazil. When he departed, only nine days later, he left behind two convicts who subsequently married natives. Thus, colonisation though miscegenation was how the Portuguese managed to control Brazil. This strategy was pursued, often consciously and semi-officially for hundreds of years. First with native Indians, then with the Black slaves and finally between Indians and Blacks, miscegenation thoroughly mixed the three races. Brazilians use literally dozens of terms to describe peoples' various racial compositions and shades of skin tones. Most Brazilians are some combination of European, African, Amerindian, Asian and Middle Eastern ancestry.

Accurate statistics on racial composition are difficult to obtain in Brazil. Many are no doubt counted as White who have some Black or Indian blood but the 1980 census showed about 55% technically White, 6% Black and 38% mulatto. Anyone who has travelled Brazil knows these figures are ridiculous. They reflect what people want to think rather than reality. Whiteness in Brazil, they often say, is as much a reflection of one's social standing as the colour of one's skin.

The latest estimates on the number of Indians in Brazil when Cabral arrived puts the number at around five million. Today they live in the Brazilian interior, Amazonas and Mato Grosso. Decimated by disease, war and slavery, this population is, and always was, quite heterogeneous. FUNAI, the government Indian agency, has documented 174 different Indian languages and dialects. Customs and belief systems vary equally widely.

Brazil has had several waves of voluntary immigration. After the end of slavery in 1887, millions of Europeans were recruited to work in the coffee fields. The largest contingent were from Italy, but there were also many Portuguese and Spaniards, with smaller groups of Germans and Russians. Japanese immigration began in 1908 and today São Paulo has the largest Japanese community outside of Japan.

Some 50,000 Portuguese came from 1974 to 1975 with the liberation of Portugal's African colonies. During the '70s many Latin Americans fleeing military dictatorships in Argentina, Chile, Uruguay and Paraguay settled in Brazil.

Indians

Visiting a Reservation If you are a physician, anthropologist or sociologist with an authentic scholarly interest, you can apply to FUNAI for authorisation to visit a reservation.

FUNAI is a large under-funded system with the ambitious and controversial task of protecting the Indians while gently introducing them to the modern world.

If you are not a Brazilian citizen you must first submit a research proposal together with your curriculum vitae, a letter of introduction from your research institute, a letter from the Brazilian researcher or research institute taking responsibility for you and your work and who agrees to accompany you into the field, a declaration that you speak

jornal da
FUNAI

ANO I – Número 02 – Brasília. Setembro de 1986

Portuguese and know Brazilian law, vaccination certificates for yellow fever, typhoid and tetanus and an X-ray to show that you are free from tuberculosis.

All documentation must be in Portuguese and must first be presented to the embassy or consulate of your home country. They must send it to the Ministry of Foreign Relations in Brasília, who will in turn forward it to CNPQ (National Centre for Research). CNPQ will take a minimum of 90 days to consider your proposal. If they agree to authorise your project, the file is passed to the FUNAI office in Rio at the Indian Museum where Professor Neyland further processes it and Dra Cláudia scribbles the final signature.

The procedure is intentionally difficult. It is intended to protect the Indians from the inadvertent spread of diseases to which they have no natural immunity as well as over exposure to alien cultural

ideals. Nevertheless, many make it through all the obstacles and as many as 60 projects have been approved in one three month period.

FUNAI has been criticised for its patronising attitude toward Indians and of manipulating against Indian interest in favour of other claims to Indian lands. It's difficult to pass judgement on the department which is caught between the will of the Indians and the interests of the government, which has been expropriating Indian lands for industry and settlement.

It is beginning to use a computer network and satellite photographs to secure the borders of large and remote tracts of land from invading lumber workers and prospectors. The system is composed of many reservations and posts plus five major parks: Xingu Park in Mato Grosso, Aripuaná Park in Mato Grosso, Araguaia Park on Bananal Island in Goiás, Tumucumaque Park on the Guyanese border of Pará and the Yanomani Park in Roraima.

The ambiguous role of FUNAI in relation to the Indians may be a legacy of the military regime. According to FUNAI magazine, new Indian territories proposed by the Sarney administration would double the current area of Indian lands. Previously 250,000 square km were set aside in 162 areas for an estimated nomadic Indian population of 30,300, located mostly in Mato Grosso, Pará, Amazonas and the territories. An exact Indian count is impossible as tribes are still being 'discovered'. In 1986 for example the Tremembé tribe was discovered on Ceará's coast. But it is questionable whether these proposals will survive the constitution as the Indians have no representation in the national congress since Mário Juruna failed re-election.

Despite their lack of representation, the Indians of Xingu Park are satisfied with the current administration. Raoni, chief of the Metuktire Indians, says, 'things have changed. Now we only have to call by radio and medicines arrive quickly and no more of the tribe's children die'. Speaking of FUNAI's president Jucá, 'the man speaks seriously and wants us to resolve problems with him as they arise'.

CULTURE
Music

Brazilian's are the most musical people on the planet. Wherever you go, you'll find people playing, singing and dancing. Perhaps because of its African roots, Brazilian music is a collective act, a celebration, a festa.

Brazilian popular music has always been characterised by great diversity. Shaped by the mixing of a variety of musical influences from three different continents, the music of the people is still creating new and original forms.

Thus the *Samba Canção*, for example, is a mixture of Spanish bolero with the cadences and rhythms of African music. Bossa nova was influenced by North American music, particularly jazz, and samba. And the music called *jovem guarda* is a mix of musical influences that arrived in Brazil in the '60s including Italian ballads and bossa nova.

Bossa nova was more than a musical style or movement. It initiated a new style of playing instruments and singing. The more operatic, florid style of singing was replaced by a quieter more relaxed sound; remember the soft sound of the *Girl from Ipanema*. João Gilberto is the founding father of bossa nova and many leading figures, like Antônio Carlos Jobim, Baden Powell and Nara Leão, are still playing in Rio. Another bossa nova voice, who became Brazil's most beloved singer, was Elis Regina.

Bossa nova was associated with the rising middle class of urban, university-educated Brazil. It was a musical response to other movements of the '50s and '60s for modernisation. The Cinema Novo, the Brazilian Modern Architecture of Oscar Neiymeyer et al, and other aspects of the cultural life of the nation are reflected in the music and reached a crescendo under the optimistic presidency of Juscelino Kubitschek from 1956 to 1960.

For many years, until the beginning of this century, the samba was considered the music of the poor. It was prohibited not only because of its African origins, but because it was a way for Blacks to meet and congregate. The samba was a festival, intimately linked with the African religious cults, African food and African dance.

Prohibited and persecuted, the samba was revived by the upper class in their search for national cultural roots. The best example was Vila-Lobos, Brazil's great classical composer, who travelled throughout Brazil studying the local folk music and incorporating it into his own work. With the advent of radio, samba – outlawed a few decades earlier – became a national symbol. Born in Rio the samba rapidly became known and played throughout the country.

In the period before bossa nova, there were many styles of samba, like Samba and Samba Canção , which were heard throughout Brazil. But with bossa nova the democratic nature of Brazilian music was altered. Bossa nova was new, modern and intellectual. The middle class stopped listening to the old interpretations of samba and other regional music like the *forró* of the Northeast.

At the end of the '60s the movement known as *tropicalismo* burst onto the scene. Tropicalismo provoked a kind of general amnesty for all the forgotten musical traditions of the past. The leading figures – Gilberto Gil, Caetano Veloso, Rita Lee, Macalé, Maria Betânia, Gal Costa – said that all musical styles were important and relevant. All the styles and traditions in Brazilian music could be freely mixed. This kind of open thinking led to innovations like the introduction of the electric guitar and the sound of electric samba.

Paralleling these musical movements are several incredibly popular musicians

Samba woman

who are hard to categorise and are beyond the normal currents in Brazilian music. They include Chico Buarque de Holanda who mixes traditional samba with a modern, universal flavour. Jorge Bem comes from a particular Black musical tradition of the Rio suburbs but plays an original pop samba without losing its characteristic Black rhythms. Another example is Luis Melodia who combines the samba rhythms of the Rio hills with more modern forms of the '70s and '80s, always with beautiful melody. Then there are people like Egberto Gismonti from Minas who is a wizard with experimental, instrumental music.

These various styles demonstrate the musicality of Brazil. The strengths of Brazilian music are rhythm and melody. Only now, with the rise of Brazilian rock has Brazilian music lost its emphasis on melody. Brazilian rock, derived more from English than American rock, is the least Brazilian of all the Brazilian music. Sadly, it's all the rage with the youngsters.

Samba, Tropicalismo, bossa nova are all national musical forms. But wherever you go in Brazil you'll hear regional specialties. The Northeast has perhaps the most regional musical styles and accompanying dances. The most important is the *forró*, a mix of Northeastern music with Mexican music – maybe brought via Paraguay – with nuances of the music of the Brazilian frontier region. The forró acquired the harmonica from the traditional Northeast via the aldeias of Portugal, and also incorporated the European accordion and the *zabumba* (an African drum).

Frevo is a music specific to Recife. The *trio elétrico*, also called *frevo baiano*, began much more recently and is more of a change in technology than music. It began as a family joke when, during Carnival in Salvador, Dodô and Osmar got up on top of a truck and played frevo with electric guitars. The trio elétrico, is not necessarily a trio, but it is still the backbone of Salvador's Carnival when trucks piled high with speakers, with musicians perched on top, drive through the city surrounded by dancing mobs. But it wasn't popularised until Caetano Veloso, during the period of Tropicalismo, began writing songs about the trio elétrico.

Afochê is another important Black music of Brazil. Religious in origin, it is closely tied to Candomblé, and primarily found in Bahia. Afochê is the most African sounding music in Brazil. It has been rejuvenated by the strong influence of reggae and the growth of a Black consciousness movement in Bahia.

The influence of the music of the Indians was absorbed and diluted as was so much of the Indian cultures in Brazil. In musical terms several whites have idealised what they thought those influences were. The *Carimbó* – the music of the Amazon region – where the majority of Indians live today, is a music influenced primarily by the Blacks of the littoral. Maybe the forró is the Brazilian music that was most influenced by the Indians, via *nordestinos* who have occupied a good part of the Amazon region since the end of the past century.

The musical rage today is *pagode*, a type of samba that existed for some time but was recently picked-up and promoted by the record producers. For some of the best of pagode listen to Bezerra da Silva, who was popular in the favelas before ever recording. Pagode, samba, frevo and forró all have corresponding dances, with their particular choreography, perhaps a reflection of the African influence on Brazilian music and the Brazilian use of music as a celebration of communication.

RELIGION

It's usual to say that Brazil is mainly a Catholic country, that it has the largest Catholic population of any country in the world. Actually, religion in Brazil – contrary to the textbook wisdom – is notable for its diversity and syncretism. There are dozens of sects and religions; though the frontier between them is often tenuous and the relation of some people to a cult is often circumstantial. For example, without much difficulty you can find people from Catholic backgrounds who frequent the church and have no conflict appealing for help at a *terreiro de umbanda*, the house of one of the Afro-Brazilian cults.

The mythical universe of these Brazilians is very rich. Their principal influences are Catholicism and African cults brought by the Blacks during the period of slavery.

The slaves were prohibited from practising their religions by the colonists in the same way that they were kept from other elements of their culture, such as music and dance, for fear that it would serve to reinforce their group identity. Religious persecution led to religious syncretism. To avoid persecution the slaves gave Catholic names and figures to all their African gods. This was generally done by finding the similarities between the Catholic images and the *orixás* (gods) of Candomblé. Thus, the slaves worshipped their own gods behind the representations of the Catholic saints.

Influenced by the rise of liberalism in the 19th century, Brazilians wrote into their constitution the freedom to worship all religions. But the African cults continued for many years to suffer persecution. Candomblé was seen by the white elites as charlatanism that showed the ignorance of the poorest classes.

Today the Afro-Brazilian religions are the fastest growing religions in Brazil (it will be interesting to monitor the onslaught of the American television evangelists; in 1987 Jimmy Swaggert gave his first performance in Maracanã, the world's largest football stadium). There are many cases of scholars who went to study Candomblé and ended up converting.

Gradually, new elements were added to the Afro-Catholic syncretism. The Indian religions and the spiritualism of Kardecism, contributed to the Brazilian religions. Today, you can find all gradations and subdivisions of sects, from the purist cults to those groups that worship Catholic saints, African deities and the Cabóclos of the Indian cults simultaneously.

The popular belief is that all people have orixás that protect them and their spirit. The orixá for each person is identified after a *pai* or *mãe de santo* (literally father or mother of saint; the Candomblé priest or priestess) makes successive throws with a handful of *búzios* (shells). The position of the shells interpret your luck, your future, and your past relation with the gods.

Unlike Catholicism, these religions have an aspect that is quite materialistic. One of the things that is most shocking to Europeans in their first contact with the African images and rituals was the cult of Exú. This entity was generally represented by images mixed from humans and animals with a horn and an erect penis. European Catholics and Puritans looked for an parallel in their own beliefs in whatever they found in the African

religions and identified Exú as the devil. But Exú represents the transition between the material and the spiritual worlds to the Africans. Exú's function in the ritual of Candomblé is to establish the meeting point between the gods and man. Everything related to money, love and protection against thieves, etc comes under the watchful eye of Exú. Ultimately Exú's responsibility is the temporal world.

Each person has their own orixá and Exú in Candomblé. To keep them strong each person should always give them food. In the ritual, the Exú is the first to be given food because he is the point of contact between the individual and their orixá, without him the individual won't reach the god. Exú likes cachaça and other alcoholic drinks, cigarettes and cigars, strong perfumes and meats. The offering to the orixás depends on the preferences of the orixá. For example, to please Iemanjá, the goddess/queen of the sea, one should give perfumes, white and blue flowers, rice and fried fish. Oxalá, the greatest god, the god and owner of the sun, eats cooked white corn. Oxúm, god of fresh waters and waterfalls, is famous for his vanity. He should be honoured with earrings, necklaces, mirrors, perfumes, champagne and honey.

Each orixá is worshipped at a particular time and place. Oxósse, who is god of the forests, should be revered in a forest or park. Xangô, god of stone and justice, receives his offering in rocky places.

In Bahia and Rio the greatest number of people worship the Afro-Brazilian religions during the festivals at the year's end. There are many festivals, such as the night of 31 December and New Year's Day. Millions of Brazilians go to the beach to pay homage to Iemanjá, the queen of the sea. Flowers, perfumes, fruits and even jewellery are tossed into the sea for the mother of the waters, to please or gain protection, and for good luck in the new year.

Like Greek mythology, each of the

orixás has a personality and peculiar history. Struggles for power and conflicts of rule are part of the history of the Candomblé saints.

The orixás are divided into male and female, but there are cases when an orixá can switch from one to the other sex. There is the case of Logunedé, for example, son of two male gods, Ogun and Oxoss, or the example of Oxumaré who is male during six months of the year and female during the other six months. Oxumaré is represented by the river that runs from the mainland to the sea or by the rainbow.

These bisexual saints are generally, but not necessarily, the saints of homosexuals. Candomblé is very accepting of homosexuality and that may explain the foundation of these practices and why they are legitimised by the cult mythology.

The Afro-Brazilian rituals are practised in centros or terreiros directed by a pai de santo or mãe de santo. This is where the initiation of novices takes place as well as consultations and rituals. For more on the practice and how to see Candomblé see the Bahia chapter.

Kardecism
A 19th century spiritism associated with parlour seances, multiple reincarnations and speaking to the dead. This cult incorporates some Eastern religious ideas into a European framework. Frenchman Allan Kardec texts: *The Book of Spirits* and *The Book of Mediums* introduced spiritualism to Brazilian whites in a palatable form.

Candomblé
Candomblé is the most orthodox of the cults. Its origins are in present-day Nigeria and Benin with the Yoruba people. The ceremony is conducted in the Yoruba tongue. The religious hierarchy and structure is clearly established and consistent from one terreiro to the next. In Salvador, Casa Branca on Avenida Vasco

da Gama 436, in the Engenho Velho neighbourhood is the centre for Candomblé. Not all ceremonies are open to the public.

Umbanda
Umbanda, or white magic, is a mixture of Candomblé and spiritism. The ceremony, conducted in Portuguese, incorporates figures from all of the Brazilian races: *preto velho*, the old black slave, *o caboclo* and other Amerindian deities, *o guerreiro* the white warrior, etc. In comparison to Candomblé, Umbanda is less organised, more black magic is involved, and each pai or mãe de santo modifies the religion. The African influence is more Angolan/Bantu. It traces its origins from various sources, but in its present form it is a religion native to Brazil. Quimbanda, is the evil counterpart to Umbanda. It involves lots of blood, animal sacrifice and nasty deeds. The practice of Quimbanda is illegal.

Other Cults Brasília is a capital of the new cults. In the Planaltina neighbourhood, visit Tia Neiva and the Vale de Amanhecer, Eclética de Mestro Yocanan and the Ordem Espiritual Cristo. A few of the Indian religions have been popularised among Brazilians without becoming *macumba*. Union de Vegetal in São Paulo and the South and Santo Daime in Rondônia and Acre are two such cults. A hallucinogenic drink called *auscae*, made from the root and vine of two plants is central to the practice. The use of this drink is tolerated by the government and the religion is otherwise very straight.

HOLIDAYS & FESTIVALS
National Holidays
1 January
New Year's Day
four days before Ash Wednesday
Carnival
March or April
Easter & Good Friday
21 April
Tiradentes Day

1 May
  May Day
June
  Corpus Christi
7 September
  Independence Day
12 October
  All Soul's Day
15 November
  Proclamation Day
25 December
  Christmas Day

Most states have several additional local holidays when everyone goes fishing.

Festivals

Major festivals include:

1 January
  New Year & Festa de Iemanjá (Rio)
  Festa da Boa Viagem (Salvador, Bahia)
1-20 January
  Folia de Reis (Parati, Rio de Janeiro)
3-6 January
  Festa do Reis (Carpina, Pernambuco)
2nd Sunday in January
  Bom Jesus dos Navegantes (Penedo, Algoas)
Sometime in January
  Torneio de Repentistas (Olinda, Pernambuco)
  Festa do Bonfim (Salvador, Bahia)
2 February
  Festa de Iemanjá (Salvador, Bahia)
Sometime in February
  Grande Vaquejada do Nordeste (Natal, Rio Grande do Norte)
  Festa de Itapoã (Itapoã, Bahia)
1st Saturday in February
  Buscada de Itamaracá (Itamaracá, Pernambuco)
February or March
  Shrove Tuesday and the preceding three days to two weeks, depending on the place
February or March
  Carnival (best known places are Rio, Bahia, Recife-Olinda, Manaus, São Luis, Belém, Santarém, Florianópolis, Maceió, Porto Seguro, Angra dos Reis, and Cabo Frio)
After Easter Week (Usually April)
  Feiras dos Caxixis (Nazaré, Bahia)

Mid-April
  Drama da Paixão de Cristo (Brejo da Madre de Deus, Pernambuco)
15 days after Easter (April/May)
  Cavalhadas (Pirenópolis, Goiás)
45 days after Easter (between 6 May and 9 June)
  Micareta (Feira de Santana, Bahia)
Late May/early June
  Festa do Divino Espírito Santo (Parati, Rio de Janeiro)
  Festas Juninas & Bumba-meu-boi (celebrated throughout June in much of the country, particularly São Luis, Belém and throughout Pernambuco and Rio states)
June
  Festival Folclórico do Amazonas (Manaus, Amazonas)
22-24 June
  São João (Cachoeira, Bahia & Campina Grande, Paraíba)
July
  Festa do Divino (Diamantina, Minas Gerais)
  Regata de Jangadas Dragão do Mar (Fortaleza, Ceara
17-19 July
  Missa do Vaqueiro (Serrita, Pernambuco)
August
  Festa da Boa Morte (Cachoeira, Bahia)
15 August
  Festa de Iemanjá (Fortaleza, Ceará)
September
  Festival de Cirandas (Itamaracá, Pernambuco)
  Cavalhada (Caeté, Minas Gerais)
12-13 September
  Vaquejada de Surubim (Surubim, Pernambuco)
12 October
  Festa de Nossa Senhora Aparecida (Aparecida, São Paulo)
Starting 2nd Sunday in October
  Círio de Nazaré (Belém, Pará)
1-2 November
  Festa do Padre Cícero (Juazeiro do Norte, Ceará)
4-6 December
  Festa de Santa Barbara (Salvador, Bahia)
8 December
  Festa de Nossa Senhora da Conceição (Salvador, Bahia)
  Festa de Iemanjá (Belém, Pará & João Pessoa, Paraíba)

31 December
Celebração de Fim de Ano & Festa do Iemanjá (Rio de Janeiro)

LANGUAGE

Quem tem boca vai á Roma
If you can speak you can get to Rome.

Portuguese is similar to Spanish. You will do quite well if you speak Spanish in Brazil. In general, Brazilians will understand what you say, but you won't get much of what they say. So don't think studying Portuguese is a waste of time. Listen to language tapes. Develop an ear for Portuguese. I'll never forget what happened when I asked a Brazilian friend, 'do I speak Portuguese with a Spanish accent?' 'No, not at all,' she responded, 'you simply speak Spanish'.

Brazilians are easy to befriend, but unfortunately the vast majority speak little or no English. This is changing as practically all Brazilians in school are learning English. All the same, don't count on finding an English speaker, especially out of the cities. The more Portuguese you speak, the more you will derive from your trip. Take the time and learn some of the language.

The Portuguese of Brazil has a different pronunciation and vocabulary than the classical language spoken in Portugal. Brazilian Portuguese is softer and more lyrical. Many words and place names are adopted from Tupi-Guaraní and other Indian languages and from African tongues as well as English and French. Within Brazil, accents, dialects and slang (*gíria*) vary regionally. The Carioca inserts the 'sh' sound in place of 's'. The Gaúcho speaks a Spanish-sounding Portuguese, the Bahiano speaks slowly and the accents of the Cearense are often incomprehensible.

Most phrasebooks are not very helpful, their vocabulary is often dated and contains the Portuguese spoken in Portugal, not Brazil. Notable exceptions are Lonely Planet's forthcoming *Brazilian Phrasebook*, and a Berlitz Phrasebook for travel in Brazil. Another option is a pair of pocket paperback Brazilian-Portuguese/English dictionaries. Hygina Aliandro at Ao Livro Técnico S/A, Rua Sá Freiro, 40-CEP 20930, Caixa Postal 3655, Rio de Janeiro publishes the best set. You can purchase them at most university book shops. Make sure any English-Portuguese dictionary is a Brazilian Portuguese one.

If you're more intent on learning the language, we recommend the FSI tape series. Combine this with a few Brazilian samba tapes and you're ready to begin the next level of instruction on the streets of Brazil. If that doesn't suffice, it's easy to arrange tutorial instruction through any of the Brazilian-American institutes where Brazilians go to learn English or at the IBEU (Instituto Brazil Estados Unidos) in Rio.

Useful Words & Phrases

yes	*sim*
no	*não*
perhaps	*talvez*
please, thank you	*por favor*
thank you	*obrigado* (males); *obrigada* (females)
that's alright	*nada*
good morning	*bom dia*
good afternoon	*boa tarde*
good evening	*boa noite*
goodbye	*até logo* or *ciao*
how are you?	*como vai?* or *tudo bem?*
good	*tudo bem*
a pleasure (meeting you)	*muito prazer*
speak more slowly	*fale mais devagar*
I don't speak Portuguese	*não falo português*
do you speak English?	*você fala ingles?*
excuse me	*com licença*
pardon me	*desculpe*
sorry	*perdão*
the bill please	*a conta por favor*
how much	*quanto*

how much time does it take?	*quanto tempo demora?*	70	*setenta*
where	*onde*	80	*oitenta*
where is .... located?	*onde fica .... ?*	90	*noventa*
		100	*cem*
left	*esquerda*		
right	*direita*	**Days of the Week**	
when	*quando*	Sunday	*domingo*
how	*como*	Monday	*segunda-feira*
who	*quem*	Tuesday	*terça-feira*
what	*que*	Wednesday	*quarta-feira*
why	*porque*	Thursday	*quinta-feira*
I want to buy	*eu quero comprar*	Friday	*sexta-feira*
expensive	*caro*	Saturday	*sábado*
cheap	*barato*		
more	*mais*	**Slang**	
less	*menos*		

Brazilians pepper their language with strange oaths and odd expressions (literal translation in parentheses):

yesterday	*ontem*
today	*hoje*
tomorrow	*amanhã*
morning	*a manhã*
afternoon	*a tarde*
what time is it?	*que horas são?*

curse word	*palavrão*
shooting the breeze	*babendo o papa*
too much, no shit! (sperm!)	*porra!*
gosh! (Our Lady!)	*nossa!*
great/cool/OK	*'ta lógico, 'ta ótimo, 'ta legal*

Numbers

0	*zero*
1	*um, uma*
2	*dois, duas*
3	*três*
4	*quatro*
5	*cinco*
6	*seis*
7	*sete*
8	*oito*
9	*nove*
10	*dez*
11	*onze*
12	*doze*
13	*treze*
14	*catorze*
15	*quinze*
16	*dezesseis*
17	*dezessete*
18	*dezoito*
19	*dezenove*
20	*vinte*
30	*trinta*
40	*quarenta*
50	*cinqüenta*
60	*sessenta*

I'm mad at	*eu fiquei chatiado com ....*
money	*grana*
pain in the ass	*pantelho*
fed up with (enlarged scrotum)	*saco cheio*
whoops!	*opa!*
wow!	*oba!*
hello	*oi*
you said it!	*falou!*
bum/ass	*bum-bum/bunda*
bald	*careca*
a mess	*cambalacho*
the famous Brazilian bikini (dental floss)	*fio dental*
I don't like you (son of a whore)	*filho da puta*
marijuana (smoke)	*fumo*
guy	*cara*
beautiful woman	*gatinha*
girl	*garota*

my God	*meu deus*
it's crazy, you're crazy	*'ta loco*
I'm sexually excited or I'm hard up for money (I'm hard)	*estou duro*
everything OK?	tudo bem?
everything's OK	tudo bom
that's great, cool	*chocante*
that's bad, shit (shit)	*merda*
a fix, a troublesome problem	*abacaxí*

* *está* is often shortened to *'ta*

Body Language

Brazilians accompany their oral communication with a rich body language, a sort of parallel dialogue. The thumbs up of *tudo bem* is used as greeting, OK and thank you. The authoritative *não, não* finger wagging is most intimidating when done right under a victim's nose but it's not a threat. The sign of the *figa*, a thumb inserted between the first and second fingers of a clenched fist is a symbol of good luck derived from an African sexual charm. It's more commonly used as jewellery than in body language.

To indicate *rápido!*, speed and haste, thumb and middle finger touch loosely while rapidly shaking the wrist. To threaten someone (*ameaçar*) hold flat hand palm up and slowly rotate it back and forth. If you don't want something (*não quero*), slap the back of your hands as if ridding yourself of the entire affair.

An open hand slapped on top of a clenched fist means screw you and the sign of the *chifra* (goat) or *cornudo* (horned) is made by wagging the hand with index and pinky raised, middle fingers held down by thumb. It indicates a cuckold. Touching a finger to the lateral corner of the eye means, 'I'm wise to you'.

Facts for the Visitor

VISAS

Tourist visas are issued by Brazilian diplomatic offices and are valid for arrival in Brazil within 90 days of issue and then for a 90-day stay in Brazil. They are renewable in Brazil for an additional 90 days.

It should only take about three hours to issue a visa but you need a passport valid for at least six months, a single passport photograph (either black and white or colour) and either a round trip ticket or a statement from a travel agent, addressed to the Brazilian diplomatic office, stating that you have the required ticketing. If you only have a one-way ticket they may accept a document from a bank or similar organisation, proving that you have sufficient funds to stay and buy a return ticket but it's probably easier to get a letter from a travel agent stating that you have a round trip ticket.

For children between the ages of three months and six years, a certificate of vaccination against polio is required, stating kind and dosage of vaccine. There are no vaccination requirements for adults. Visitors under 18 years of age must submit a notarised letter of authorisation from their parents or legal guardian.

Renewing Visas

The Polícia Federal handle visa extensions and they have offices in major Brazilian cities. You must go to them before your visa lapses or suffer the consequences. The tourist office can tell you where they are. In most cases a visa extension seems to be pretty automatic but the police may require a ticket out of the country and proof of sufficient funds.

When I applied in Recife, after waiting a while, they handed me an instruction sheet that indicated three tasks before the golden fleece would be awarded. I had to produce my passport, proof of sufficient funds and go to a Caixa Económica or Banerj and have them fill out a DARF form. Sufficient funds can be travellers' cheques, credit cards or even a ticket out of the country. The granting of a visa extension is completely at the discretion of the police officer. You then pay a tax of about US$7 and in my case the extension was then routinely issued.

While the maximum extension is 90 days, they did ask if I wanted the full 90 days because if you take the full 90 days and then leave the country before the end of that period, you can not return until the full 90 days has elapsed. So if you plan to leave and re-enter Brazil you must plan your dates carefully.

Visas for Adjoining Countries

Visas may be obtained at the following consulates in Brazil:

Argentina
: Visas are required by all travellers except citizens of most West European countries, Canada, Japan and a number of Latin American countries. US, British, Australians and New Zealand citizens do require visas. There is an American consulate in Porto Alegro. From Argentina, most travellers to Brazil pass through Foz do Iguaçu.

Bolivia
: From Bolivia the crossing points are at Quijarro (see the Corumbá section) and near Riberalta at Guayaramerin/Guajará-Mirim (see the Porto Velho section).

Colombia
: From Colombia the border is further down river at Leitícia (see the Manaus section).

Guyana
: Travellers from Guyana fly to Lethem then cross into Brazil at Bom Fim (see the Boa Vista section).

Paraguay
: Travellers from Paraguay can cross the border into Brazil either at Puerto Stroessner to Foz do Iguaçu or at Concepción Pedro Juan Caballero to Ponta Porã (see the Campo Grande section).

Peru
  From Peru the route is via the Amazon at
  Iquitos (see the Manaus section). Rumour
  has it that it is also possible to cross in to
  Peru from São Francisco de Assis in Acre to
  Iñapari in Peru. You have to cross the Rio
  Acre, which is apparently shallow enough to
  wade across. From Iñapari you'll probably
  have to walk the first 70 km or so before
  reaching Iberia. Puerto Maldonado is only
  200 km further, and there may be some kind
  of transport (pillion passenger on a
  motorcycle). Who knows? Best of luck
  anyway, and please let us know if you take
  this route.
Uruguay
  From Uruguay travellers pass either from
  Chuy to Pelotas or from Treinta y Tres or
  Mel to Rio Branco/Jaguarão and then on to
  Pelotas and Porto Alegre.
Venezuela
  Travellers coming from Venezuela must
  pass from Ciudad Bolivar to Santa Elena
  (see the Boa Vista section).

Documents
The only papers you really need are your
passport and visa, an airline ticket, a
yellow WHO health certificate and
money. A credit card is quite handy. Most
other documents are of limited value. To
rent a car you must be at least 25 years old,
and have a credit card and a valid drivers'
licence (or something that can pass for
one). You don't need an International
Drivers' Permit or Inter-Americas license
but it can't hurt.

The International Student Identity
Card is practically useless, as is the
International Youth Hostel card. It's
convenient to have several extra passport
photographs for any documents or visas
you might need to get while in Brazil.

By law you must carry a passport with
you at all times. Sometimes I did this, but
because it's so bulky and rip-offs are
always a threat, I often used a photocopy
of my passport with a driver's licence.
This is probably bad advice to follow
because Brazilian police are not known for
their flexibility and understanding. The

only times I was questioned by police I had my passport and was very glad I did.

If you are particularly worried about carrying your passport with you, you can buy a tourist passport from the accommodation desk at the international airport in Rio. They guarantee that if this document is filled out correctly it is as good as a real passport, and is valid throughout the country. I don't know of anyone who has had the opportunity (or the need) to test that guarantee.

MONEY

February 1986	US$1	cr$13,870 (cruzeiros)
March 1986	US$1	cz$13.87 (cruzados)
March 1987	US$1	cz$24
November 1987	US$1	cz$47
May 1988	US$1	cz$95
October 1988	US$1	cz$297
January 1989	US$1	cz$812
March 1989	US$1	cz$1

Because of the high rate of inflation in Brazil all prices in this book are quoted in US dollars. The unit of currency is the cruzado (cz$), divided into 100 centavos. There are notes of cz$500, cz$100, cz$50, cz$10, cz$5, cz$1, cz$0.500, cz$0.200, cz$0.100 and coins of cz$1, cz$0.500, cz$0.200, cz$0.100. The previous unit of currency, the cruzeiro, was replaced by the cruzado at a conversion rate of 1:1000 in February 1986. In early February 1989, the Brazilian government once again removed three zeros from the currency making the official rate cz$1 to US$1. On 7/3/89 the black market exchange rate was cz$1.56 to US$1

In recent years Brazil has had a parallel exchange system where money can be converted at market, as opposed to official, rates of exchange. Every six months or so the government clamps down on the parallel system but then allows it to operate again after two or three weeks. The black market moves to the street, resulting in lower exchange rates.

Outside of Manaus, São Paulo and Rio, cheques, which have to go back to the US via courier, are difficult to change at parallel market rates.

Cash & Travellers' Cheques

US cash dollars are easier to trade and are worth more on the parallel market, but travellers' cheques are an insurance against loss. It's good to carry a couple of brands of travellers' cheques as well as some emergency US cash for when the banks are closed.

American Express is the most recognised brand, but they charge 1% of the face value of the cheque (on top of the interest that your money makes while sitting in their banks), and sometimes with all the non-accidental losses of cheques they're a little squirrely about giving your money back on the spot. They have offices in Rio de Janeiro, Salvador, Recife, Brasília, Belo Horizonte and São Paulo. Thomas Cook, Barclays and First National City Bank are also good.

Get travellers' cheques in US dollars and carry some small denominations for convenience. If you can't trade on the parallel market, you can always change (trocar) at Banco do Brasil and Banco Económico at the official exchange rate. Keep a close, accurate and current record of your travellers' cheque expenditures. This speeds up the refund process. Guard your travellers' cheques; they are valuable to thieves even without your counter signature. Don't change money on the streets, follow exchangers into unfamiliar areas, or give money or unsigned cheques up-front. Learn in advance how to get refunds from your travellers' cheque company.

COSTS

In 1986 the Brazilian economy seemed to be strong. The government had frozen prices at levels that were great for the Brazilian consumer and the foreign traveller, inflation was stopped, the economy was growing and Brazilians from every class were consuming more than they had in a long while.

Bowing to pressure from the international financial community, the price freeze was lifted a few months later and hyper-inflation soared to more than 20% a month. People stopped buying, unemployment increased and another recession began.

For unknown reasons, the dollar failed to heed the common wisdom by keeping pace with the rate of inflation. This defiance, much to the dismay of anyone in Brazil with dollars, resulted in the buying power of the dollar being cut in half in a matter of months. A Rio/Manaus/Rio flight ticket which was about US$200 suddenly cost US$450. Beer went from 25c to 60c a litre. The bus went from 5c to 13c.

This continuing high inflation means that prices researched earlier in this book may be out of step with prices researched later.

TIPPING
Most services get tipped 10% and as the people in these services make the minimum wage – which is not enough to live on – you can be sure they need the money. In restaurants the service charge will often be included in the bill and is mandatory. If a waiter is friendly and helpful you can give more. When the tip is not included, it's still customary to leave a 10% tip and, unless the service is atrocious, the waiter shouldn't be punished for giving you the option. There are many places where tipping is not customary but is a welcome gesture. The local juice stands, bars, coffee corners, street and beach vendors are all tipped on occasion.

Because of the massive amount of unemployment in Brazil there are some services that you don't need, but are customarily tipped anyway. Parking assistants are the most notable, as they receive no wages, and are dependant on tips, usually the equivalent of 25c to 50c. Gas station attendants, shoe shiners and barbers are also frequently tipped.

Taxis are not usually tipped. Most people round the price up, but tipping is not expected.

TOURIST INFORMATION
The Brazilian tourism authority is called EMBRATUR. It is represented outside Brazil exclusively through the Brazilian Tourism Foundation. To date, the BTF has only four offices world-wide in:

USA
    551 5th Avenue, Room 421, New York, NY 10176 USA (tel (212) 286-9600, telex (23) 452-102)
UK
    32 Green St, London W1Y4AT, UK (tel (01) 499-0877, telex 51-261157)
Germany
    Am Hauptbahnhof 10, 6000 Frankfurt am Main 1, West Germany (tel (069) 251-1966)
Italy
    20122 Via Donizetti, 53 Milan, Italy (tel (392) 796-586)

Brazilian consulates and embassies are able to provide more limited tourist information.

GENERAL INFORMATION
Post
Postal services are pretty good in Brazil. Most mail seems to get through and airmail letters to the USA and Europe usually arrive within a week. The cost, however, is ridiculously high for mail leaving Brazil, almost US$1 for a letter to the USA.

There are mail boxes on the street but it's a better idea to go to a post office. Most post offices (correios) are open all day Monday to Friday and Saturday morning. The poste restante system seems to function reasonably well, although having letters sent to American Express (so long as you are a customer) is more reliable. Post offices send and receive telegrams.

Telephone

International Calls Phoning abroad from Brazil is costly. To the USA and Europe figure approximately US$2 a minute and about US$1 dialling direct if you can use someone's private phone. Prices are 25% lower from 8 pm to 5 am daily and all day Sundays.

Every town has a phone company office for long distance calls, which require a large deposit. If you're calling direct from a private phone dial 00, then the country code number, then the area code, then the phone number. So to call New York you dial 001-212-(phone number). For information on international calls dial 000333. Some of the country code numbers are: UK 44, USA 1, Australia 61, Canada 1, Argentina 54, Chile 56, Peru 51, Paraguay 595.

International collect calls (*cobrar*) can be made from any phone. To get the international operator dial 000111 or 107 and ask for the *telefonista internacional*. If they don't speak English you could experiment with some of the following phrases:

I would like to make an international call to ....
  quero fazer uma ligação internacional para ....
I would like to reverse the charges.
  quero cobrar la

I am calling from a public (private) telephone in Rio de Janeiro.
estou falando dum telefone público (particular) no rio de janeiro
My name is ....
meu nôme é ....
The area code is ....
o código é ....
The number is ....
o número é ....

If you're having trouble, reception desks at the larger hotels can be helpful. Also, the phone books explain all this, but in Portuguese.

National Calls National long-distance calls can also be made at the local phone company office, unless you're calling collect. These are cheap. All you need is the area code and phone number and a few dollars. For calling collect within Brazil dial 107.

Local Calls Brazilian phones use *fichas*, coin-like tokens, which can be bought at many newsstands, pharmacies, etc. They cost less than 5c, but it's a good idea to buy a few extra fichas as phones often consume them liberally.

On almost all phones in Brazil you wait for a dial tone and then deposit the ficha and dial your number. Each ficha is generally good for a couple of minutes but the time can vary considerably. When your time is up, you will be disconnected without warning, so it's a good idea to deposit an extra ficha. To call the operator dial 100, for information 102.

Time
The eastern part of Brazil is one time zone, three hours behind GMT. So when it is midday in Brazil it is 3 pm in London, 10 am in New York, 7 am in San Francisco, 1 am the next day in Sydney or Melbourne.

The cities in the interior, like Manaus, Campo Grande, Cuiabá and Corumbá are one hour later, four hours behind GMT. In the far west, Rio Branco and Benjamin Constant are five hours behind GMT.

Business Hours
Most shops and government services (post office) are open Monday to Friday from 9 am to 6 pm and Saturday from 9 am to 1 pm. Because many Brazilians have little free-time during the week, Saturday mornings are usually spent shopping. Some shops stay open later than 6 pm in the cities and the huge shopping malls often stay open until 10 pm. Banks, always in their own little world, are generally open 10 am to 4.30 pm. Business hours vary by region and are taken less seriously in remote locations.

Weights & Measures
Although the metric system is generally used for all weights and measures, there are a few odd hangers on from the old system. Occasionally petrol (or álcool) is bought in *galões* (gallons), but litres are more usual. It is still quite common to buy cheeses in *libras* (pounds), and lengths of material are still sold in *pés* (feet) as frequently as they are sold in *metros* (metres). There is a metric conversion table in the back of the book.

Laundry
If you own the kind of clothes I do it's cheaper to buy new ones than to have them cleaned at many city laundromats. While all other services are cheap in Brazil, for some reason washing clothes isn't, at least if you send out. Most Brazilian's wash their own clothes or they have domestics do it. If you don't wash your own, see if anyone in your hotel will do it. Often the housekeepers will wash clothes at home to make a few extra cruzados.

MEDIA
Brazil's media industry is concentrated in the hands of a few organisations. The companies that own the two major television stations, *O Globo* and

Manchete, also control several of the nation's leading newspapers and magazines.

Newspapers & Magazines

English In major Brazilian cities you will find three daily newspapers in English. The best by far is the Latin American edition of the *Miami Herald*. The paper isn't cheap, but it's current and fairly comprehensive. The paper's strong points are Latin America and the American sports scene.

The *Latin American Daily Post* is published Tuesday to Saturday in Brazil. It has advertisements in English for both São Paulo and Rio, including apartment rentals, and when the exchange houses close it will have the latest juice on why. The *International Herald Tribune* has articles from the *New York Times* and *Washington Post* but it's a pretty thin paper, and more expensive than the other two newspapers.

Time and *Newsweek* magazines are available throughout Brazil. What can one say about these icons? Their coverage is weakest where the *Miami Herald* is strongest: Latin America and sports. The *Economist* is sold in Rio and São Paulo, but it costs about US$4. In the big cities you can find all sorts of imported newspapers and magazines at some newsstands but they are very expensive.

Portuguese The *Folha de São Paulo* is Brazil's finest newspaper. It has excellent coverage of national and international events and is a good source for entertainment in São Paulo. It's available in Rio and other major cities. The *Jornal do Brasil* and *O Globo* are Rio's main daily papers. Both have entertainment listings. *Balcão* is a Rio weekly with only classified advertisements, a good source for buying anything. *O Nacional* is a weekly paper that has some excellent critical columnists.

Among weekly magazines *Veja*, the Brazilian *Time* clone, is the country's best

selling magazine. It's easy reading if you want to practice your Portuguese. *O Senhor* has the best political and economic analysis and reproduces international articles from the British *Economist*, but it's not light reading. *Isto É* also provides good coverage of current events.

The monthly *Ciência Hoje* is excellent travel reading. Always intelligent and socially conscious, it tackles a wide variety of topics from the ecology of coral reefs, to droughts in the Northeast and the causes of violence in society.

Jornal da FUNAI is a Portuguese-language tabloid about Indian issues put out by FUNAI, the government bureau of Indian affairs. Subscriptions are available for about US$4 in Brazil or US$40 overseas. Write to Jornal do Funai, Setor SDS Venâncio III, sala 310, Caixa Postal 11-1159, CEP 70084 Brasília.

Television

English If you are having second thoughts about visiting Brazil because you don't want to miss the Superbowl or, perhaps, The Miss Teen America Pageant, relax and go ahead and make those reservations. Thanks to the parabolic antenna and the hospitality of the *Sheraton*, the *Inter Continental* or any of several other big hotels, all the major American television events are shown in Rio and São Paulo.

Portuguese Many of the worst American movies and television shows are dubbed into Portuguese and shown on Brazilian television. Brazil's most famous television hosts, who have to be seen to be believed, are Xuxa, the queen of kiddy titillation, and Chacrinha, the Ed Sullivan of Brazil. Both are strong statements on the evil of television. Both are on the tube for countless hours, Xuxa on weekdays, Chacrinha on Saturdays.

Xuxa has coquettishly danced and sang her way into the hearts of tiny Brazilians everywhere. She is living proof that Freud had it right about children's sexuality.

Chacrinha and his dancing girls host Brazil's longest running bump and grind variety show.

What is worth watching? Saturday, around midnight, they show an un-dubbed, quality foreign movie, often in English. Sunday nights, starting at 9 or 10 pm, a soccer game is televised along with the highlights of other matches played that day. And there's a good comedy show that starts around 10 pm Friday.

The most popular programmes on Brazilian television are the novelas (soap operas), which are followed religiously by many Brazilians. These are actually quite good and easy to understand if you speak some Portuguese. They often feature some of Brazil's best actors and pioneer new techniques in the genre; several have had successful runs on European television. The novellas go on the air at various times from 7 to 9 pm.

The news is on several times a night, varying by locale. O Globo and Manchete, the two principal national networks, both have rather pedestrian national news shows. The first channel in Rio is the educational network, which has many wildlife programmes.

Movies

English Most movies in the cinemas are in their original language with Portuguese subtitles, consequently there are plenty of films in English. Brazil gets most of the hits from the USA including many of the violent Rambo type films. Brazilians also adore comedians like Woody Allen and the Marx Brothers. I must admit I don't completely understand why. When I saw *Hannah & her Sisters* in Rio I was the only person in the theatre laughing, and when Woody becomes a Catholic and tries to explain to his father, a New York Jew, his existential crisis I realised that the Brazilians didn't have a clue as to why it was so funny.

The Marx Brothers films are dubbed, which raises the pun problem. When

Groucho tells Chico the lot is out near the viaduct and Chico responds, in his thick accent, 'Vi-a-duck, Vi not a chicken' there is no way this exchange can be duplicated in Portuguese.

Portuguese From the romanticism of *Black Orpheus* to the realism of *Cinema Novo* and Glauber Rocha, Brazil has produced a number of excellent films. Since the end of the dictatorship there has been a film renaissance. Many recent Brazilian films are historical, providing special insight into the country.

Rio has many film aficionados and special events. The Cineclub Botafogo is always a good venue. There are special events like the annual film festival in September and cinema on the beach at Copacabana in the summer.

HEALTH

Before heading abroad travellers should get up-to-date information. In the US you can contact the Overseas Citizens Emergency Center and request a health and safety information bulletin on Brazil by writing to the Bureau of Consular Affairs Office, State Department, Washington, DC 20520. This office also has a special telephone number for emergencies while abroad, (202) 632-5525.

Read the Center for Disease Control's *Health Information for International Travel* supplement of *Morbidity & Mortality Weekly Report* or the World Health Organisation's *Vaccination Certificate Requirements for International Travel & Health Advice to Travellers*. Both of these sources (CDC and WHO) are superior to the Travel Information Manual published by the International Air Transport Association.

The International Association for Medical Assistance to Travelers (IAMAT) at 350 Fifth Avenue, Suite 5620, New York, NY 10001 can provide you with a list of English-speaking physicians in Brazil. In Australia you could contact the

Traveller's Medical and Vaccination Centre in Sydney (02-221 7133) for general health information pertaining to Brazil.

In Brazil, the Rio Health Collective (tel 325-9300 ext 44) can put you in touch with an English speaking doctor. They have a 24-hour answering service.

Yellow Fever
Get your yellow fever shots and keep the yellow WHO certificate to avoid problems when passing into Acre, Amapá, Amazonas, Maranhão, Mato Grosso and Mato Grosso do Sul, Pará, Rondônia and Roraima.

Other Immunisations
Keep the routine immunisations such as polio, tetanus, diphtheria and measles up to date. Most physicians recommend that tetanus booster shots, usually given in combination with diphtheria and whooping cough, be given after major injuries or every 10 years.

Polio is endemic in Brazil, recent outbreaks have been reported in the southern states of Paraná, Santa Catarina and Rio Grande do Sul. A complete immunisation series should be boosted if more than 10 years have elapsed since the last course.

Consider the non-routine shots if your travel exposure and physician so indicates. Protection against typhoid, which is transmitted by lice, is recommended for those interested in rural travel. Protection is not perfect so be cautious with food and water.

Vaccines for hepatitis B are now available. They are not recommended unless you are at risk of contact with blood or secretions. Brazil is a risk area for rabies, but painful pre-exposure rabies vaccinations are not suggested unless you intend to engage in hand to claw combat with the wildlife. A BCG vaccine exists for tuberculosis. It's of questionable value for those planning on a prolonged stay. Consider also a tuberculin skin test and chest X-ray. Cholera shots are probably unnecessary, and not very effective even if taken.

Hepatitis-A is acquired from contaminated water and food, shellfish especially. Avoid urban beaches after rainy days, when there's a higher probability of contracting infectious Hepatitis from sewage-contaminated run-off. Like the daily smog report in Los Angeles, newspapers in Rio do daily beach reports on the E coli counts.

First Aid Kit
Self medication is not a good idea, but when you're on the road, there often are no alternatives. Discuss a drug kit with your physician and find out in what situations self-medication is called for as well as dosages, contra-indications and possible side effects.

On the Road
While you are in Brazil, where you go, how you live and travel, and what you eat will determine your chance of contracting disease. Obviously the least risk accrues to those short term visitors who stay at the better hotels in the urban areas of the developed South and flit around by jet. Those long term budget travellers who tramp through rural areas, travel overland and by boat and suffer local conditions are more susceptible to illness. We empathise with the latter group

There are simple precautions that will keep you healthy while travelling. Assuming that you have seen a physician, had your shots and are taking your anti-malarials, it's most important to eat and sleep well. Budget travellers would be strongly advised not to scrimp on food! It's a bad idea. There comes a time when rice, beans, manioc and multivitamin supplements need to be replaced by a grand meal.

Open up any parasitology or internal medicine textbook, and Brazilian beasties and diseases figure prominently. While there's no worry of any strange tropical diseases in Rio and points further south,

Amazonas, Pará, Mato Grosso, Amapá, Rondônia, Goiás, Espírito Santo and the Northeast have some combination of the following: malaria, yellow fever, dengue fever, leprosy, and leishmaniasis. Health officials periodically announce high rates of tuberculosis, polio, sexually-transmitted diseases, hepatitis and other endemic diseases.

The most common infections in travellers is gastroenteritis, enterotoxigenic E coli, Giardia lamblia and dysentery – both amoebic and bacterial. But if you stay long and travel rough you can become home for a tribe of cattle and pig tapeworms, Ascaris, hookworm or trichura. Schistosomiasis is endemic to eastern Brazil and thus freshwater bathing (rivers, streams, ponds, irrigations ditches, etc) can be dangerous.

Insect borne viruses abound and malaria is a real threat in most rural areas north and west of Rio de Janeiro state. Outside of the Amazon malaria is unlikely in large cities. Incurable Chagas' disease is found throughout Brazil particularly along the north-east coast. It is seen in dwellers of mud and straw huts where the Reduvid bugs live and transmit the disease. Dermal leishmaniasis occurs in jungle areas and a horrible visceral leishmaniasis is seen in the Northeast. This list is by no means exhaustive.

Health Precautions

Mosquitoes Brazilian mosquitoes are not like their North American brethren; they are smaller, quicker, and they land lighter. Their bites are vicious, their appetites insatiable and they're harder to smack. Cover yourself well with clothing and use insect repellent on exposed skin. Burning incense and sleeping under mosquito nets in air conditioned rooms or under fans also lowers the risk of being bitten. Protect yourself especially from dusk to dawn when mosquitoes, including the malaria transmitting Anopheles like to feed. Also nasty are the bites of the pium flies.

Bichos de pé These small parasites live on Bahian beaches and sandy soil. They burrow into the thick skin of the foot at the heel, toes and under the toe-nails and appear as dark boils. They must be incised and removed completely. Do it yourself with a sterilised needle and blade. To avoid *bichos de pé* wear footwear on beaches and dirt trails especially where animals run underfoot.

Worms The majority of people living in rural Brazil have worms. If you adopt the diet and lifestyle of the interior, you are also likely to acquire a worm load. Prevent exposure to parasitic worms (and other fecal-oral diseases) by drinking and brushing teeth with boiled, bottled or filtered water only. Wash produce in the same clean water and make sure all foods, particularly meat, fish, molluscs and pork are well cooked – they harbour flukes and tapeworms. Don't walk around barefoot, Wash hands before preparing meals and after using the toilet, and keep nails short and clean.

Travellers' Diarrhoea If you stay in Brazil long enough, you will get diarrhoea, regardless of how cautious you are, but preventive measures are still important. Avoid tap water, fruit and vegetables that you don't peel yourself (lettuce and fruit salads are notorious), ice cubes and fresh milk. Eat only thoroughly cooked food which is still hot, drink bottled refreshments made from boiled water.

If you are out in the sticks, boiling water for the necessary 10 minutes may be an impossibility. It's easier to treat your drinking water with iodine, which kills most bacteria, giardia and amoebic cysts. Another simple water purification treatment is three drops of Betadine solution per glass of water; it's preferable to allow the solution to mix for a half hour. This kills most bacteria; unfortunately, giardia and amoebic cysts are unaffected.

Drugs like Lomotil or Imodium are handy to have when you've got the shits on interminable toilet-less bus rides; they provide the fastest relief of symptoms, but they do not prevent or cure the diarrhoea. In fact long term use exacerbates diarrhoea and is particularly dangerous with bacterial dysentery. These drugs are good for temporary, symptomatic relief of cramping diarrhoea in adults without high fever, mucous or bloody stools.

Diarrhoea can be dangerous if you lose too many salts and fluids. More Third World children die from the fluid loss and electrolyte imbalance of diarrhoea than anything else. That is why oral rehydration therapy is essential in the management of diarrhoea. With especially watery diarrhoea the following concoction is recommended: one cup of fruit juice mixed with half a teaspoon of honey and a dash of salt (and hold the cachaça). Additional supportive measures include drinking caffeine-free soft drinks, eating salted crackers, rice and bananas. Avoid alcohol and solid foods especially the spicy and greasy foods. Remember to keep up the fluid intake. The more that goes out the more that should go in.

In summary, when you are far from medical help and diarrhoea strikes, bismuth salicylate plus salt and fluid replacement is a good approach to take. If diarrhoea continues, or stools have blood or mucous, you may have bacterial dysentery in which case see a physician immediately or when far from medical help take tetracycline. Severe diarrhoea in children is particularly dangerous and should be brought to the attention of a physician.

Malaria There are four types of malaria: Plasmodium falciparum, the deadliest, P malarie which is still universally sensitive to chloroquine, and finally P vivax and P ovale which are harboured outside of the blood and can relapse. The drug-resistant status of different malarial strains in different parts of the world is constantly in flux. There are two approaches to avoiding malaria: take preventative medications (following your physician's instructions to the letter) and reduce exposure to the Anopheles mosquito which transmits the disease.

Despite preventative measures, it is still possible to contract malaria. Pay attention to symptoms of fever with chills and headache appearing as early as a week or several months after visiting a malarial area. These flu-like symptoms demand medical attention as soon as possible. Delays in treatment of malaria falciparum can be fatal.

Sexually-Transmitted Disease Brazil has the third highest reported incidence of AIDS after the United States and France. Of these, the greatest percentage were in the São Paulo area, but Rio will soon be catching up. Bisexual prostitution will certainly spread the disease among the heterosexual population. Carnival, a time of carefree and careless sexuality, is when health officials believe AIDS is introduced to the nation. Public health measures are directed at educating the public through television and print media advertisements of the dangers of unsafe sex. This conflicts with the 'Brazil, sex vacation capital' image promoted by tourist organisations. Caution is warranted: be abstinent or use condoms (*preservativos*). There is no shortage of other STD's.

Public Health in Brazil
Life expectancy like infant mortality is a gross index of health care and development. In the southern states of Santa Catarina and Rio Grande do Sul the figures approach those of the US and Western Europe; cancer and circulatory diseases are the biggest threat. In the North and Northeast, where infectious and parasitic diseases exact a very high toll, the life expectancy is less than fifty years. Pockets of poverty in the Northeast, like the border region between Pernambuco and Paraíba, have life expectancies as low as 39 – rivalling the worst of war-torn Third World nations in Africa and Asia.

The infant mortality rate is about 90 per 1000 in north-eastern Brazil, but poor health is not confined to the North and the Northeast. The urban slums of the large southern cities are just as miserable. In Nova Iguaçu, a poor and dangerous suburb of Rio de Janeiro 150 out of every 1000 babies dies before the end of their first year. These figures are shocking in comparison to wealthier Brazilian community rates of 10 per 1000.

These statistics are attributable to diarrhoea and other infectious diseases due to lack of sanitation, inadequate access to medical care and poor nutrition. Forty million, or nearly one-third of Brazil's 130 million people, are under nourished according to government statistics. The huge discrepancy in longevity and the quality of health is an indicator of the vast difference between the wealthy and poor in Brazil.

According to transmissible disease reports, there are 160,000 new cases of malaria per year. In 1976 there were 86,000 cases of malaria and 430,000 by 1986. In 1986 there were said to be some six million sufferers of Chagas disease, between six and eight million people with schistosomiasis, 220,000 with leprosy (there are even some cases in the South), 72,000 with measles, 56,000 with tuberculosis, 4200 with typhoid fever, 300 with bubonic plague (there was an outbreak in Paraíba) and there were 156 victims of polio.

Hospitals & Pharmacies Pharmacies stock all kinds of drugs and sell them much more cheaply than in the US. There are few restricted medications. Practically everything is sold over the counter. In the past the German pharmaceutical industry sold European drugs which had exceeded their shelf life to South American firms, but expiration is not as serious a problem nowadays. Nearly all drugs are manufactured by firms in São Paulo under foreign license.

Some pharmacists will give injections (with or without prescriptions). This is true of the Drogaleve pharmacy chain. Sometimes hygiene is questionable, always purchase fresh needles, and make sure other health professionals take similar precautions.

Some private medical facilities in Rio de Janeiro and São Paulo are on a par with American hospitals, but be wary of public hospitals in the interior. They are notorious for re-using syringes after quick dips in alcohol baths, lack of soap and other unsanitary practices. University hospitals are likely to have English speaking physicians. British and American consulates have lists of English speaking physicians.

Brazilian blood banks don't screen carefully. Hepatitis B is rampant. Should you ever require a blood transfusion in Brazil, do as the Brazilians do; have your friends blood-typed and choose your blood donor in advance.

Back Home

Be aware of illness after you return; take note of odd or persistent symptoms of any kind, get a check-up and remember to give your physician a complete travel history. Most doctors in temperate climes will not suspect unusual tropical diseases. If you have been travelling in malarial areas have yourself tested for it.

DANGERS & ANNOYANCES

According to a Gallup survey, Brazil is the world's second most violent nation, topped only by Colombia. Robberies on buses, city beaches and heavily touristed areas are extremely common. Thieves tend to work in gangs, they are armed with knives and guns and are capable of killing those who resist them.

Much of the petty street crime in Rio and Salvador is directed against tourists, known in the jargon of Rio's thieves as *filet mignon*. Foreign tourists have got lots of money. They are easy to pick out in a crowd and they are unfamiliar with the turf and language, and very vulnerable.

The two simplest ways of avoiding these crimes are: don't walk around in high risk areas with anything that's too precious to lose or else avoid high risk areas completely; look and act like a street-smart local. Fair-haired, blue-eyed and light skinned people are at a distinct disadvantage on the streets of Rio. In my more paranoid moments I've considered dyeing my hair. I'm not the only paranoid in Brazil. Citizens have taken to the streets with bodyguards and handguns. Everybody who has been here for a while knows a few horror stories.

On the Beach

Don't bring anything to city beaches apart from just enough money for lunch and drinks. No camera, no bag and no jewellery. Wear your bathing suit and bring a towel. That's it. If you want to photograph the beach go with a friend, then return the camera to your room before staying on the beach. Don't hang out on city beaches at night.

I didn't look like a tourist; I wasn't carrying a camera or wearing flashy jewellery, just a cheap digital watch. I had 50 dollars worth of cruzados plus another 100 in travellers' cheques. I knew better than to go to Copacabana beach with a lot of money, but then I thought nothing bad could happen to me.

Lulled by the beauty of Copacabana and the sound of the surf, I felt safe. I stripped down to my bathing suit, held my jeans, T-shirt and sandals in my hands like weights and started running along the shoreline. There were no bathers or people lying on the sand, but there were plenty of joggers running in pairs and lots of soccer games going on. A man jogging alone on the hard packed sand called for the time, a minute later he turned back, pointed to his bare wrist and shouted hoarsely. He said something about the watch which I couldn't understand, but I shouted back the time anyway, 'It's 4.30.' The sun wouldn't set for an hour and a half.

Ducking my head under the lines of some surfcasters, I slowed down to wade in the water and cool off, holding my things above the water. I turned around in the foot deep surf and a crazed man with an eight inch blade raised over his head was yelling at me in Portuguese, 'Give

me everything you have. Give me your money.' I pulled the wallet out of my jeans handing it to him.

'And the clothes!', he said. His head and neck were cocked to the side, trembling. Two surfcasters were only twenty feet away and they didn't do a damn thing. I could see people in the distance, but the incline of beach at the water's edge seemed like a wall of sand. I didn't shout so as not to alarm the thief.

'The watch too!'

I fumbled with the watch band.

'Come on hurry up! The watch.'

He came towards me. I circled backwards in the water, afraid to trip, afraid he would lose his patience and kill me for the watch. I gave it to him.

The thief sprinted 100 yards down the beach and dropped to the ground with the bundle. He left my clothes and my travellers' cheques on the sand.

A soccer player left his game and approached me.

'It's a good thing you gave him the money because that guy was working with a group. They were standing right there, five men, two men had pistols. The bandits, they don't bother us. We have an understanding with them.'

Maybe he was telling the truth or just covering up for not helping me. But I felt a lot better about just handing over my money. You hear stories about how dangerous Copacabana is, yet it's so beautiful, so wide-open that it puts you off guard. The beach doesn't fit your conception of what a dangerous place should look like. And yet it may well be the most likely place to get robbed in Brazil.

Streets & Buses

Thieves watch for people leaving hotels, car rental agencies, American Express offices – places with lots of foreigners. Then they follow their targets. Don't advertise the fact that you're a foreigner by flashing big bills or wearing jewellery. Keep your watch out of sight in your pocket. Don't carry much money in the streets and even less on the municipal buses. Carry just enough money on your person for the evening's entertainment and transport and keep it discreetly stashed away in a money belt, money sock, secret pockets or shoe. And always have enough money on hand to appease a mugger (about US$2 to US$5).

If you have valuables take taxis, not buses. If you ride the buses, have your change ready. You're less of a target once you have passed the turnstile. Avoid the super-crowded buses. Don't talk out loud.

In Hotels
Place valuables in the hotel safe and get a receipt. Don't leave them in your room.

Precautions
Be prepared for the worst – make copies of your important records: a photostat of passport (page with passport number, name, photograph, location where issued and expiration date), travellers' cheque numbers, credit card numbers, etc. Keep one copy on your person, one copy with your belongings and exchange one with a travelling companion.

A US passport is worth several thousand dollars to some people so keep a close eye on it. If you do lose it, photostats can smooth the issuing of a new passport at embassies and consulates.

Credit cards are useful in emergencies but not for regular purchases. Be quick about cancelling credit cards if lost or stolen. Travel insurance is nice to have if you've lost your airline ticket.

Cabling money is difficult, time-consuming and expensive. You must know the name and address of both the bank sending (record this and keep this with your documents) and the bank receiving your money. Casa Piano on Avenida Rio Branco is the most experienced with overseas transactions.

The Police
If something is stolen from you, you can report it to the police. No big investigation is going to occur but you will get a police form to give to your insurance company. The police aren't to be trusted, however. Brazilian police are known to plant drugs and sting gringos for bribes. The bribes are

like pyramids, the more people are involved, the bigger the bribe becomes.

DRUGS
Marijuana and cocaine are plentiful in Brazil, and very illegal. The military regime had a rather pathological aversion to drugs and enacted stiff penalties. Nevertheless, marijuana and cocaine are widely used, and like many things in Brazil there's a rather tolerant attitude toward them – by everyone except the military and the police. Bahia seems to have the most open climate. But because of the laws against possession, you won't bump into much unless you know someone or go to an 'in' vacation spot with the young and hip like Arraial da Ajuda, Morro de São Paulo, Canoa Quebrada, etc.

Drugs provide a perfect excuse for the police to get a fair amount of money from you, and Brazilian prisons are brutal places. Police checkpoints along the highways stop cars and buses at random. Police along the coastal drive from Rio to São Paulo are notorious for hassling young people and foreigners. Border areas are also very dangerous. A large amount of cocaine is smuggled out of Bolivia and Peru through Brazil. Be very careful with drugs. Don't buy from strangers and don't carry anything around with you.

There are some wild hallucinogenic substances in the Amazon. The best known is Banisteriopsis caapi, better known as *yagé* or *ayahuasca*, which has ritual uses amongst certain tribes. The book *Wizard of the Upper Amazon* centres around this drug's use and the shared consciousness which it is said to provide.

FILM & PHOTOGRAPHY
Cameras are expensive and cumbersome. They will certainly be abused on the road and they may get broken, lost or stolen. But there are so many good shots out there that you'll kick yourself if you don't bring one along. If you are travelling with a fancy camera, cover up the brand on the

prism and case with black electric tape and keep a close eye on your equipment.

It's hard finding a set-up that's right for you. Some people are happy with the automatic 35 mm rangefinders. They take great pictures, are portable and reasonably priced. I brought along a Minolta SLR, a Vivitar 35 to 200 mm zoom and a fast standard lens and I was happy. Had I brought along a small flash, a soft shutter trigger, a few more filters, a lens cleaning kit (fluid, tissue, aerosol) and beanbag (or clamp or monopod), I would have been happier still. Photographic equipment and accessories are expensive and hard to find.

It's foolish to bring a camera to a beach unless it will be closely guarded. If you're shooting on beaches, the glare from water or sand can fool your light meter. This can be avoided by easily forgotten rules of thumb or a photogray card. Some Candomblé temples do not permit photography. Respect the wishes of the locals and ask first if they mind being photographed.

You can not get Ektachrome or Kodachrome slide film developed in Brazil. Print film is expensive, but sold and processed almost everywhere. Bring more film than you think you need and have it processed back home. Use a lead film bag to protect film from airport X-ray machines. This is especially important for the sensitive high ASA films.

If you must get your film processed in Brazil, have it done either at a large lab in São Paulo or in Rio at Kronokroma Foto (tel 285-1993) at Rua Russel 344, Loja E near Praia do Flamengo's Hotel Glória. Bring exposed film in the morning when the chemical baths are fresh. In Rio the Fomar Photo Store (tel 221-2332) at Rua São Jose 90 off Avenida Rio Branco sells some camera accessories. Their friendly staff does quick camera cleaning. If your Nikon is on the blink, speak to Louis (tel 220-1127) at Franklin Roosevelt 39 on the 6th floor near the US consulate.

ACCOMMODATION

A note on prices: while we were writing the first half of this book, Brazil was in the midst of a general price freeze and everything in the country was very cheap. Hotels were no exception. Then suddenly the government lifted all price controls and everything went wild. All hotels raised prices to keep up with inflation, many of them raised their prices well beyond that reasonable ceiling. This wrought hell with our research on hotel prices. Then, equally without warning, the price freeze was reintroduced.

We have managed to tackle the problem of inflation reasonably well by quoting all prices in US dollars, but it is impossible to counteract the weird price changes caused when the government freezes prices, unfreezes them, then freezes them again. Most of the prices listed will be reasonably accurate, but once in a while there is bound to be a shocker.

Lodging

There are plenty of places to stay throughout Brazil. Lodging goes by various names, which doesn't signify all that much.

A *dormitório* is dorm-style sleeping with several beds to a room. These are usually the cheapest places in town, often as little as US$1 or US$2 per night.

A *hospedaria* is similar. Most budget travellers stay at a cheaper *pensão* (small hotel) or *hotel* where a room without a bathroom can go for as little as US$2 or US$3. These rooms with communal bathrooms down the hall are called *quartos*. With a private bathroom, similar rooms are called *apartamentos*.

If you want to travel in style, Brazil has modern luxury hotels all over the place. The best hotels can cost as little as US$30 per night and, at the other end of the scale, as much as US$100 to US$150 per night in Rio and São Paulo. Often a 10% tax is added to the bill.

Aparthotels, available in the larger

cities, provide the comforts of a good hotel without some of the glitter. They are also considerably cheaper. A good, medium priced Aparthotel should cost somewhere from US$10 to US$25 per night.

The better hotels pull one of the best scams around. If you book from abroad, they will try to get you to pay in advance in dollars. Here is the catch, which I call 'catch 22%'. When they charge you in dollars, they calculate it at the official rate which always undervalues the dollar by around 22%. The way around this is to reserve from abroad but not to pay until after your arrival in Brazil, and then only pay in local currency exchanged at the parallel rate.

'Catch 22%' leads some hotels to behave quite strangely. Several better hotels denied me a reservation for Carnival a couple of years ago because they were booked up. A few weeks before Carnival the same hotels had many vacancies and were begging for my business. What had happened? It appears that they had been counting on reservations from abroad on which they could collect an extra 22%. They had obviously been a little over-confident.

Most hotels in Brazil are regulated by EMBRATUR, the state tourism authority. They also rate the quality of hotels from one to five stars. Regulated hotels must have a price list with an EMBRATUR label which is usually posted on the wall in every room.

It's a good idea to look at a room before deciding to take it. Check the shower for hot water, check the bed, check the lock on the door. Two big sleep killers in Brazil are mosquitoes and heat. Fans do wonders at stopping both.

Many medium priced and expensive hotels have safes which are 'safe' to use so long as you get a receipt.

In the off-season many hotels have promotional rates. Ask about them, even bargain if you know the place is empty. Sometimes good hotels have a few quartos or cheaper rooms which are not advertised.

It pays to enquire about these, as they allow you to use all the facilities of the hotel while paying considerably less than the other guests.

There are a few games played by hotel clerks to get you into a more expensive room. If you want a single room there are only doubles; if you want a quarto, there are only apartamentos. Don't say yes too quickly – if you feign a desire to look for alternative lodging, they will often remember that there is a cheaper room after all. In reality, some hotels don't have singles. It is generally much cheaper to travel with someone, as rooms for two are nowhere near twice as expensive as rooms for one.

If you're staying in middle to high class hotels, reservations are a good idea in touristed centres (especially in Rio) during vacations – July, and December to February – and in any vacation-mecca (eg Búzios) during weekends. We try to list hotel phone numbers for this purpose, but you can also get them from travel agents and tourist information offices. Be wary of taxi drivers, particularly in Rio, who know just the hotel for you. They'll often take you to an expensive hotel which pays the cabby for his services.

To avoid summer crowds, it is not a bad idea to travel during the week and stay put, usually in a city, during the weekends when the locals are making their pilgrimages away from the cities. This minimises crowded buses and hotels and gets you into the city for the weekend music and festivities.

If you're travelling where there are no hotels – the Amazon or the Northeast – a hammock and a cover are essential. With these basics, and friendly locals, you can get a good night's rest anywhere. Most fishing villages along the littoral have seen an outsider or two and will put you up for the night. If they've seen a few more outsiders, they'll probably charge you a couple of dollars.

Motels

Motels are a Brazilian institution and should never be confused with hotels. Rented by the hour, for short stays only, the motel is the Brazilian solution to the lack of privacy caused by overcrowded living conditions. Used by adults who still live with their parents, kids who want to get away from their parents, and couples who want to get away from their kids, they are an integral part of the nation's social fabric, a bedrock of Brazilian morality and are treated by Brazilians with what most outsiders consider to be incredible nonchalance.

The quality of motels runs a gamut, reflecting their popularity with all social classes. Most are out of the city centre, with walled-in garages for anonymity. I've heard of a suite in a fancy motel (no really, I only heard this) that had a hot-tub in one room with opening skylights. In the next room was a sauna. The suite had circular vibra-beds with mirrors overhead, a video recorder with adult movies piped over loudspeakers, and room service with a menu full of foods and sex toys (with instructions).

Most travellers don't spend much time in motels, but they can be quite useful. If you're having trouble finding accommodation, they're not too expensive. I for one wouldn't hesitate to head straight for a motel in that situation.

FOOD

Vou matar quem 'tá me matando
I'm going to kill the person who's killing me
   a popular saying when sitting down to eat

The hub of the Brazilian diet revolves around *arroz* (white rice), *feijão* (black beans) and *farofel* (manioc flour). It's possible to eat these every day in Brazil and in some regions it's hard not to. The tasty black beans are typically cooked in bacon. The white rice is often very starchy. Farofel, the staple of the Indians, slaves and Portuguese for hundreds of years, is a hardy root that grows everywhere. It seems to be an acquired taste for foreign palates.

Lunch is the big meal in Brazil, except in the modern cities. From the rice-bean-farofel group meals go in one of three directions: *carne* (steak), *galinha* (chicken) and *peixe* (fish). This makes up the typical Brazilian meal and is called *prato feito* (made plate) or *prato do dia* (plate of day) in luncheonettes from Xique Xique to Bananal. They are typically enormous meals and incredibly cheap but after a while they can become a trifle monotonous. If quantity is your thing, you can live like a king.

What is done with the meat, chicken or fish? It's cooked, and that's about it. Don't get me wrong, it's generally very good meat, but Brazilians don't do much with it. Steak is the national passion. They like it big and rare. The best cuts are *filet* and *churrasco*. Chicken is usually grilled, sometimes fried. Fish is generally fried.

But that's not the end of the story. In the cities you can get many of the dishes that you like back home. There's also fine dining. For US$5 to US$10 you can have a superb Italian, Japanese or Indian dinner in Rio or São Paulo. *Churrascarias* and *rodízios* bring you all the meat you can eat and a variety of other goodies for a fixed price (around US$5 in Rio). They must be tried – vegetarians have no problem filling-up if they don't mind seeing all that meat. Rodízios are especially good in the South.

Lanchonetes are stand-up fast-food bars where you can order sandwiches and *pasteis* (crumbed hors d'oeuvres). *Restaurantes* have more proper sit down meals. Never order *um almoço* unless you have a big appetite or care to share with a friend. Portions are immense.

Despite much sameness there are regional differences. The cooking in the North has a heavy Indian influence, the Northeast has African, and in the South, more Italian, German and Japanese influences. From Africa came peppers, spices and the delicious oil of the dendê palm tree. The slaves introduced greater variety in the preparation of meat and fish and dishes like *vatapá* and *caruru*. Afro-Brazilian cuisine is the country's most distinct and flavourful. Nature has also provided variations in regional cuisines. The fruits of the Amazon, the barbecue meats of the Southern gaucho, the fish of the Pantanal, the crustaceans of Fortaleza may not be available in other parts of the country.

Breakfast

Breakfast is called *café* or *café da manhã*, café is also coffee. Served at most hotels (with the possible exception of the very cheapest places), for no extra charge café includes coffee, steamed milk, fruit, biscuits or bread, maybe cheese and meat, and rarely eggs. If you tire of this, or don't like it in the first place, I'd recommend the following: go into any *paderia* (bakery) or market and buy a good *iogurte* (yoghurt), then get some fruit, always abundant and delicious. This meal got me away from café da manhã and off coffee.

Lunch

Lanchonetes, as mentioned earlier, are everywhere. Portions are almost always big enough for two. Most cities now have vegetarian restaurants with salads, casseroles, brown rice, etc. With any luck the food might be healthy, but it's rarely tasty. A better choice may be a *suco* (juice) bar for a natural fruit juice and sandwich.

Dinner

Dinner doesn't vary much from lunch, unless you go to a better restaurant. Most dishes can be easily divided between two people (if you can't eat it all ask for a doggie bag (*embalagem*) and give it to someone on the street).

In the cities, Brazilians dine late. Restaurants don't get busy in Rio and São Paulo until 10 pm on weekends. A 10% tip is generally included in the bill. If not it's

customary to leave at least 10%. Most places in Rio will bring you a *couvert*, whether you ask or not. This is optional so you are perfectly within your rights to send it back. The typical couvert is a ridiculously overpriced and tedious basket of bread, crackers, pheasant eggs and a couple of carrot and celery sticks. Most restaurants will still bring bread with your soup at no extra charge.

Standard operating procedure in most Rio restaurants is to overcharge the customer. Some places don't even itemise their bills. Don't hesitate to look at the bill and question the waiter. It's all part of the game. They good-naturedly overcharge and you can good-naturedly hassle them until the bill is fixed. They are used to it.

Local Specialities

We have run across some exceptional dishes in the course of our travels. In Fortaleza, *peixe a delícia*, fish with a banana and cheese sauce, and *caldo de peixe*, fish broth, were excellent. The *moqueca de sururu* of Maceió, the *ensopado de peixe* in Lençois and the spicy shrimp of Arraial da Ajuda were all memorable. And the taste of succulent ham and pineapple sandwiches from Copacabana's *Restaurante Cervantes* will haunt me for years to come.

Brazilian Dishes

Acarajé – this is what the Bahianas, Bahian women in flowing white dresses, traditionally sell on street corners throughout Bahia. The Bahianas are an unforgettable sight but you're likely to smell their cooking before you see it. It's the wonderful-smelling dendê oil. The Acarajé is made from peeled brown beans, mashed in salt and onions, and then fried in dendê oil. Inside these delicious fried balls is *vatapá* (see near the end of this list), dried shrimp, pepper and tomato sauce. The dendê oil is strong stuff. Many stomachs can't handle it.

Angú – a cake made with very thin corn flour, called *fubá*, and mixed with water and salt.

Bobó de Camarão – manioc paste cooked and flavoured with dry shrimp, coconut milk and cashew-nut.

Camarão á Paulista – unshelled fresh shrimp fried in olive oil with lots of garlic and salt.

Canja – a big soup with chicken broth. More often than not a meal in itself.

Carne de Sol – a tasty, salted meat, grilled and served with beans, rice and vegetables.

Caruru – the Caruru, one of the most popular Brazilian dishes brought from Africa, is made with okra or other vegetables cooked in water. The water is then drained, and onions, salt, shrimps and malagueta peppers are added, mixed and grated together with the okra paste and dendê oil. The fish, traditionally a sea-fish called garoupa, is than added.

Carangueijada – a kind of crab cooked whole and seasoned with water.

Casquinha de Carangueijo or *Siri* – stuffed crab. The meat is prepared with manioc flour.

Cozido – any kind of stew, usually with more vegetables than other stew-like Brazilian dishes (eg potatoes, sweet potatoes, carrots and manioc)

Dourado – found in fresh waters throughout Brazil, a scrumptious, clean fish.

Feijoada – the national dish of Brazil, feijoada is a meat stew served with rice and a bowl of beans. Feijoada is served throughout the country and there are many different variations, depending on what animal happens to be walking through the kitchen while the chefs are at work. All kinds of meats go into feijoada. Orange peels, peppers and farinha accompany the stew.

Frango ao Molho Pardo chicken pieces stewed with vegetables and then covered with a seasoned sauce made from the blood of the bird.

Moqueca – a kind of sauce or stew and a style of cooking from Bahia. There are many kinds of moqueca: fish, shrimp, oyster, crab or a combination. The moqueca sauce is defined by it's heavy use of dendê oil and coconut milk, often with peppers and onions. A moqueca must be cooked in a covered clay-pot.

Moqueca Capixaba – a moqueca from Espírito Santo uses lighter *urucum* oil from the Indians instead of dendê oil.

Pato ao Tucupi – roast duck flavoured with garlic and cooked in the *tucupi* sauce made from the juice of the manioc plant and *jambu*, a local vegetable. A popular Pará dish.

Peixada – fish cooked in broth with vegetables and eggs.

Peixe a Delícia – broiled or grilled fish usually made with bananas and coconut milk. Delicious in Fortaleza.

Prato de Verão – literally summer plate, served at many suco stands in Rio. Basically, it's a fruit salad.

Pirarucu ao Forno – pirarucu is the most famous fish from the rivers of Amazonia. It's oven-cooked with lemon and other seasonings.

Tacacá – an Indian dish, it's dried shrimp cooked with pepper, jambu, manioc and much more.

Tutu á Mineira – a bean paste with toasted bacon and manioc flour, often served with cooked cabbage. Typical of Minas Gerais.

Vatapá – a seafood dish with a thick sauce made from manioc paste, coconut and dendê oil. Maybe the most famous Brazilian dish with African roots.

Xinxim de Galinha – pieces of chicken flavoured with garlic, salt and lemon. Shrimp and dendê oil are often added.

Fruit

This is a partial list of Brazilian fruits, particularly those found in Rio. Many of the fruits of the Nordeste and Amazon have no English equivalent, so there's no sense translating, you'll just have to try them. They include *ingá, abiu, marimari, bacuri, murici, pitanga, taberebá, sorva, pitamba* and *jambo* as well as the more common *jenipapo* and plantains. Although much of it is grown in Bahia, cocoa is native to the Amazon. The spiked *graviola* used in juices and ice creams is also a transplant to the Northeast.

abacate – avocado
abacaxí – pineapple
açaí – fruit of açaí palm tree used in wines and syrups
ameixa – plum, prune
bacaba – Amazonian fruit used in wines and syrups
betarraba – beetroot
biribá – Amazonian fruit eaten plain
buriti – a palm tree fruit used in ice cream and in making wine
cacau – cacao fruit, the seeds are used to make chocolate
cajú – fruit of cashew
cenoura – carrot
cupuaçú – Amazonian fruit used to make a conserve
fruto-do-conde green, sugar-apple fruit, very popular
goiaba – guava
graviola – yellow, stringy fruit with a green, bumpy skin
jaca – large fruit of the jackfruit tree
laranja – orange
limão – lemon
mamão – papaya
maracujá – yellow fruit
melancia – watermelon
melão – honeydew melon
morango – strawberry
pera – pear
pêssego – peach
pupunha – a fatty, vitamin-rich Amazonian fruit taken with coffee
tangerina – mandarin orange, tangerine
uva – grape

DRINKS
Fruit Juice
Sucos in Brazil are divine. They vary by region and season (the Amazon has fruits you won't believe). Request *sem açúcar e gelo* or *natural* if you don't want sugar and ice. Often you'll get some water mixed into a suco, if you're worried about getting sick ask for a *suco com leite* (with milk) or a *vitamina*, which is the same thing. Banana and avocado are great with milk.

Another way to avoid water is orange juice, rarely adulterated, it mixes well with papaya, carrot, and several other fruits. An orange juice, beet and carrot combo is popular in Rio. There is an incredible variety of fruits and good combinations. Spend some time experimenting.

Coffee
Brazilians take their coffee as strong as the devil, as hot as hell, and as sweet as love. They call it *cafezinho* and drink it as an espresso-sized coffee without milk and cut with plenty of sugar. The cafezinho is taken often and at all times. It's sold in stand up bars and dispensed in offices to keep the workers perky. I've known Brazilians to take one to bed with them to go to sleep.

Chá or tea is not nearly as important a drink as coffee.

Soft Drinks
Soft drinks (*refrigerantes*) are found everywhere and are cheaper than bottled water. Coke is number one, guaraná is number two. Made from the berry of an Amazonian plant, guaraná has a delicious, distinct taste.

Alcoholic Drinks
para que nossas mulheres não fiquem viúva
May our wives never be widows
  (a drinking toast)

Beer When the price of beer was doubled in 1986 words of revolt rang through the streets. When rumours of an impending producer boycott followed, the revolution was being plotted in many a bar.

seu
forte
é o
sabor

A *cerveja* is a 600 ml bottled beer. Of the common brands Cerma is the best followed by Antártica, Brahma and Malt 90. Brazilians gesture for a tall one by horizontally placing the Boy Scout sign (two fingers together) a foot above their drinking tables. A *cervejinha* is 300 ml of bottled or canned beer. *Chopp* (pronounced 'shoppee') is a pale blond pilsner draft, lighter and far superior to canned or bottled beer. Usage: *Moço, mais um chopp!* (waiter, one more 'shoppee'!).

Wine Jorge Amado wrote a satire about nationalist generals running Brazil who drink Brazilian wine in public and avoid the stuff like the plague in private. Well, Brazilian wine is improving but it's not great. Forrestier is at the top of a very low heap of vintages. The whites are better than the reds and the Argentine wines are much better than both.

Cachaça *Cachaça, pinga* or *aguardente* is a high-proof, dirt cheap, sugar-cane alcohol produced and drunk throughout the country. Cachaça literally means booze. Pinga (drop) is considered more polite but by any name it's cheaper than spit and far more toxic. The production of cachaça is as old as slavery in Brazil. The distilleries grew-up with the sugar plantations, first to supply local con-

sumption and then to export to Africa to exchange for slaves.

There are well over 100 brands of cachaça with differences in taste and quality. A cheap cachaça can cut a hole in the strongest stomach lining. Velho Barreiro, Ypioca, Pitú, Carangueijo, and São Francisco are some of the better labels. Many distilleries will allow you to take a tour and watch the process from raw sugar to rot gut and then sample some of the goodies.

Cachaça is found everywhere – even in the most miserable frontier shantytowns. Bottled beer usually follows the introduction of electricity to a region. At the pinnacle of Brazilian civilisation is *chopp* (a draft beer), which is only found in large and prosperous economic centres with paved roads and electricity.

Caipirinha is the Brazilian national drink. The ingredients are simple: cachaça, lime, sugar and crushed ice, but a well made caipirinha is a work of art. *Caipirosca* is a caipirinha with vodka replacing cachaça. *Caipirissima* is still another variation with Bacardi rum instead of cachaça. *Batidas* are wonderful mixes of cachaça, sugar and fruit juice.

BOOKS
Fiction

There are a few dozen excellent Brazilian works of fiction translated into English but, sadly, many of today's best writers have not been translated.

Machado de Assis is simply world class. The son of a freed slave, Assis worked as a typesetter and journalist in late 19th century Rio. A tremendous stylist, with a great sense of humour Assis had an understanding of human relations which was both subtle and deeply cynical, as the terse titles of books like *Epitaph of a Small Winner* (Avon Bard 1977) or *Philosopher or Dog* (Avon Bard 1982) might suggest. He wrote five major novels, my favourite is *Dom Casmurro* (Avon Bard 1980).

The most famous writer in Brazil is the

regionalist Jorge Amado. Born near Ilhéus, Bahia in 1912, and a long time resident of Salvador, Amado has written colourful romances of Bahia's people and places. Strongly influenced by Communism during his early work, Amado's later books are better, although the subjects are lighter. The best are *Gabriela, Clove & Cinnamon* (Avon Bard 1974) which is set in Ilhéus and *Dona Flor & Her Two Husbands* (Avon Bard 1977) whose antics occur in Bahia. Amado's *Tent of Miracles* (Avon Bard 1978) explores racial relations in Brazil and *Pen, Sword and Camisole* (Avon Bard 1986) laughs its way through the petty worlds of military and academic politics. *The Violent Land* (Avon Bard 1979) is another of Amado's classics.

Without a word to waste, Graciliano Ramos tells of peasant life in the sertão in his best book *Barren Lives* (University of Texas Press 1965). The stories are powerful portraits. Strong stuff. Autran Dourado's *The Voices of the Dead* (Taplinger 1981) goes into the inner-world of a small town in Minas Gerais. He has a couple of other books about Minas Gerais, his home state. Read anything you can find by Mário de Andrade, one of Brazil's pre-eminent authors. His *Macunaíma* is comic and could only take place in Brazil.

Clarice Lispector has several collections of short stories, all are excellent. Lídia Fagundes Telles' books contain psychologically rich portraits of women in today's Brazil. Dinah Silveira de Queiroz's *The Women of Brazil* is about a Portuguese girl who goes to 17th century Brazil to meet her betrothed.

Márcio Souza is a modern satirist based in Manaus. His biting humour captures the horror of the Amazon and his imaginative parodies of Brazilian history reveal the stupidity of personal and governmental endeavours to conquer the rainforest. Both the *Emperor of the Amazon* (Avon Bard 1980), his first book, and *Mad Maria* (Avon Bard 1985) shouldn't be missed if you're going to the Amazon but I found his latest farce, *The Order of the Day* (Avon Bard 1986), disappointing.

The bizarre and brutal *Zero* (Avon Bard 1983), by Ignácio de Loyola Brandão, had the honour of being banned by the military government until a national protest helped lift the ban. *The Tower of Glass* (Avon Bard 1982), by Ivan Ângelo, is all São Paulo; an absurdist look at big-city life where nothing that matters, matters. It's a revealing and important view of modern Brazil 'where all that's solid melts into air'. João Ubaldo Ribeiro's *Sergeant Getúlio* (Avon Bard 1980) is a story of a military man in Brazil's Northeast. No book tells better of the sadism, brutality and patriarchy which run through Brazil's history.

The Amazon & Indians
The first and last word on the history of the Portuguese colonisation, the warring and the enslavement of the Indian is *Red Gold* (Harvard University Press 1978) by John Hemming (see the History section). Other interesting titles are *The Last Indians, South America's Cultural Heritage* by Fritz Tupp, *Aromeri Brazilian Indian Feather Art* by Norberto Nicola and Sónia Ferraro and *Aborigines of the Amazon Rain Forest: The Yanomani* by Robin Henbury-Tenison.

Alex Shoumatoff has written two excellent Amazon books, both of them entertaining combinations of history, myth and travelogue. Anthropologist Darcy Ribeiro's interesting novel *Maíra* (Random House 1983) is about the clash between Indian animism and Catholicism.

Armchair adventurers will enjoy Spix and Martius' *Travels Brazil*, a three volume chronology of the pair's 3½ year's journey from 1817 to 1820. Illustrated with wonderful etchings, it is a biologist's record of customs, social life, ethnology and a description of flora and fauna.

Those interested in *yagé*, the hallucinogenic drug used by certain tribes of the upper Amazon, will find *Wizard of the Upper Amazon – the Story of Manuel Códrova-Rios* (Houghton Mifflin 1975) by F Bruce Lamb interesting reading .

Travel

Peter Fleming's *Brazilian Adventure* (Penguin 1978) is about the young journalist's expedition into Mato Grosso in search of a famed explorer who had disappeared. At the time this area was the world's last, vast unexplored region. What Fleming found is less important than the telling; written with the humour of the disenchanted Briton, travel adventures don't get any funnier than this. Highly recommended.

In the 19th century practically every westerner who visited Brazil seems to have written a travelogue and some, with their keen powers of observation, are quite good. Maria Graham's *Journal of a Voyage to Brazil & Residence there During Part of the Years 1821, 1822, 1823* is as precise as the title suggests. Henry Koster wrote *Travels in Brazil* in 1816; Herbert H Smith wrote *Brazil, the Amazon & the Coast* in 1880.

History

Brazil has a fascinating and fantastic history but for some reason, none of the good surveys of Brazilian history have been translated into English. So the best way to go, if you want to understand the flow of Brazilian history in English, is via several excellent narratives.

John Hemming's *Red Gold: The Conquest of the Brazilian Indians* (see The Amazon & the Indians), follows the colonists and Indians from 1500 to 1760, when the great majority of Indians were effectively either eliminated or pacified. Hemming, a founder of Survival International, doesn't water-down the extent of Portuguese atrocities.

Caio Prado Junior, Brazil's leading economic historian, presents a descriptive analysis of the legacy of Brazil's colonial past in *The Colonial Background of Modern Brazil*. Probably the single best interpretation of the colonial period in English, Prado presents a sweeping view of Brazil's lack of development, which he blames on the export-based economy and the social relations of slavery.

Celso Furtado, a leading economist and the current Minister of Culture in Brazil, has written a good introductory economic history of the country titled *The Economic Growth of Brazil* (Greenwood 1984).

Charles R Boxer is from the good old school of British economic history, which took writing seriously. All his books are fine reading and illuminating history. The *Golden Age of Brazil, 1695-1750* (University of California Press 1962) has an excellent introductory chapter summarising life in 17th century Brazil and then focuses on the gold rush in Minas Gerais and its consequences in the rest of the colony. Boxer has also written *Salvador de Sá & the Struggle for Brazil & Angola, 1602-1686* and *The Dutch in Brazil, 1624-1654*.

The most famous book on Brazil's colonial period is Gilberto Freyre's *The Masters & the Slaves: A Study in the Development of Brazilian Civilization* (University of California Press 1986). There's a new paperback edition from the University of California Press which also is publishing Freyre's other works *The Mansions & the Shanties: The Making of Modern Brazil* (University of California Press 1986) and *Order & Progress: Brazil from Monarchy to Republic* (University of California Press 1986).

Freyre's argument that Brazilian slavery was less harsh than in the USA and that through miscegenation Brazil has avoided the racial problems of the USA is deeply flawed. It contributed to the myth of racial democracy in Brazil and has been severely rebuked by academics over the last 20 years. Still, Freyre's books can be read on many levels, including social history, and there are fascinating comments (read the footnotes) on folklore, myths and superstition, religion, sexuality, etc.

Emília Viotti da Costa has a collection

Top: Hang-gliding in Rio (SP)
Bottom: Hang-gliding at the beach, Rio (JM)

of well-written essays in English which is one of the best treatments of 19th century Brazil. *The Brazilian Empire: Myths & Histories* (University of Chicago Press 1986) interweaves the ideological and economic components of Brazilian history and the results are illuminating and suggestive. Her essays, particularly on slavery and the landless poor, explode many of the harmony myths that hide the realities of oppression and poverty.

The English narratives on 20th century Brazilian history are less satisfying. Peter Flynn's *Brazil: A Political Analysis* presents a political history from 1889 to 1977. Thomas Skidmore's *Politics in Brazil, 1930-1964* is good. And Irving L Horowitz covers the Goulart era in *Revolution in Brazil.*

Alfred Stepan has edited a collection of essays on *Authoritarian Brazil: Origins, Policies & Future* (Yale University Press 1973). These are often theoretically heavy, but quite interesting, particularly the essays by Fishlow, Cardoso and Schmitter.

Other Subjects

The African Religions of Brazil (John Hopkins 1978) by Roger Bastide is fascinating. Ruth Landes' *The City of Women* is about Candomblé in Bahia. Florestan Fernandes' *The Negro in Brazilian Society* was one of the first to challenge the myth of racial democracy. Thomas Skidmore's *Black into White: Race & Nationality in Brazilian Thought* is an intellectual history of the racial issue.

Carolina Maria de Jesus lived and wrote in the slums of São Paulo. Her book *Child of the Dark* (NAL 1965) is strong and compelling. In *The Myth of Marginality: Urban Politics & Poverty in Rio de Janeiro* (University of California Press 1976) Janice Perlman debunks some of the myths of life in the favelas.

Finally, the not-to-be-believed rebellion in Canudos by the followers of the mystic Antônio Conselheiro has been immortalised in *Rebellion in the Backlands* (University of Chicago Press (1985), by Euclides da Cunha. Mixing history, geography and philosophy *Os Sertões* (in Portuguese) is considered the masterpiece of Brazilian literature. It's an incredible story about the outcasts of the Northeast and a sort of meditation on Brazilian civilisation. The story of the author and the rebellion is told by Mário Vargas Llosa in his novel *The War of the End of the World* (Avon Bard 1985); entertaining, light reading for the traveller.

THINGS TO BUY

A smart souvenir hunter can do well in Brazil provided they know a little about Brazilian culture. Most people find music, native crafts and artwork to be the best souvenirs.

Brazilian music (discussed in the Facts for the Visitor chapter) is sure to evoke your most precious travel memories. Unfortunately Brazilian recordings haven't yet switched to CD format, so you have to make do with cassettes or LPs. Take note that cassette recordings are generally of poor quality. The best record stores in the country are in the big shopping malls of São Paulo.

Although nearly everything can be found in Rio and São Paulo, there is a premium for moving craft and art pieces from the hinterland to the fancy stores of the big cities. The inexpensive exceptions include the weekly hippie fair of Ipanema (see Rio chapter), the ubiquitous FUNAI stores and museum gift shops.

Most of the Indian crafts sold in FUNAI stores are inexpensive, but the quality generally matches the price. Museum gift shops, on the other hand, stock some very worthwhile souvenirs. They are particularly good for prints of local art. The Carmen Miranda museum sells great t-shirts of the great lady herself complete with her fruit headdress.

Outside the big cities your best bet for craftwork are artisan fairs, cooperative stores and government-run shops. The Northeast has a rich assortment of artistic items from which to choose. Salvador and nearby cachoeira are notable for their rough-hewn wood sculpture. Artisans in Fortaleza and the southern coast of Ceará specialise in fine lace cloths. The interior of Pernambuco, in particular Caruaru, are famous for the wildly imaginative ceramic figurines and the traditional leather hats worn by the sertanejos. Functional and decorative hammocks are available in cities throughout the Amazon. These string, mesh or cloth slings are fixtures in most Brazilian homes. They are indispensable for travellers and make fine, portable gifts.

The state of Minas Gerais is most famous for its gemstones. However, if you're in the market for fine jewellery and precious stones wait until you return to the big cities to make your purchases. Buy from a large and reputable dealer like Amsterdam-Sauer, Roditi or H Stern. Stern is an international dealer based in Ipanema whose reputation for quality and honesty is beyond reproach. It isn't a discount store, but their jewellery in Brazil is less expensive than in their outlets in other parts of the world.

Brazilian leather goods are moderately priced, but the leather isn't particularly supple. The better Brazilian shoes, belts, wallets, purses and luggage are sold in the upmarket shops of Ipanema and Copacabana. Brazilian shoes are extremely good value, but much of the best is reserved for export and larger sizes are difficult to find. High quality, cheap, durable, leather soccer balls with hand-stitched panels are sold all over Brazil in sporting goods stores. Inflated soccer balls should not be put in the cargo hold of a plane.

In an effort to draw industry to the Amazon, the Brazilian government lifted many tax and tariff restrictions in Manaus. The advantage to tourists in this free trade zone is minimal unless you are particularly interested in picking up electrical equipment which has been assembled in Brazil.

Finally, here are a few more ideas for the avid souvenir hunter. Coffee table picture books on Brazil, videotapes of carnival and highlights of the Brazilian national team and Pelé in various world cup matches are hawked in the streets of Copacabana. Guaraná powder, a stimulant (said to be an aphrodisiac), is sold in health food stores and chemists. Mounted reprints of old Rio lithographs are sold in Rio's Cinelândia district on the steps of the opera house. The smallest of Brazil's bikinis (fio dental – dental floss) are sold at Bum-Bum or Kanga shops. Candomblé stores are a good source of curios, ranging from magical incense guaranteed to bring good fortune, increase sexual allure, wisdom and health to amulets and ceramic figurines of Afro-Brazilian gods. If you're in Brazil for Carnival make sure you pick up a copy of the Carnival edition of Manchete magazine.

WHAT TO BRING

The happiest travellers are those who can slip all of their luggage under their plane seats. Pack light. We found that a bookpack/Daypack that can be attached or nested inside a larger backback to be a versatile combination. Travel packs are backpacks which can be converted into more civilised looking suitcases. They are cleverly compartmentalised, and have internal frames and special padding.

Use small padlocks to secure your pack, particularly if you have to leave it unattended in one of the more down-market hotels that you are bound to encounter. What you bring will be determined by what you do. If you're planning a river or jungle trip read the Amazon chapter in advance. If you're travelling cheap, a cotton sheet sleeping-sack will come in handy.

In terms of clothing you don't need more than a pair of shorts, trousers, a couple of T-shirts, a long sleeved shirt, bathing suit, towel, underwear, walking

Clubs

For anyone interested in climbing and hiking, Rio's clubs are the single best source of information as well as the best meeting place for like-minded people (Believe it or not, Brazil does have ecologically minded people.) The clubs meet regularly and welcome visitors. All of the following clubs are well organised and have bulletin boards listing excursions on the weekends.

Centro Excursionista Brasileiro
  Avenida Almirante Barroso 2-8 Andar, Centro, Rio de Janeiro, RJ CEP 20031. CEB has a membership of 900, meets on Wednesday and Friday evenings and is geared toward trekking and day hikes. CEB also runs a small restaurant which is open from 6 pm, Monday to Friday, where people meet informally to plan excursions.
Centro Excursionista Rio de Janeiro
  Avenida Rio Branco 277/805, Centro, Rio de Janeiro, RJ CEP 20040. CERJ, with an active membership of 50, meets on Tuesday and Thursday evenings. CERJ offers the greatest diversity of activities ranging from hikes to technical climbing.
Clube Excursionista Carioca
  Rua Hilário de Gouveia 71/206, Copacabana, Rio de Janeiro, RJ CEP 22040. Meeting on Thursday and Friday evenings, this club specialises in difficult technical climbing only.

Climbing Guides

As a testament to the growing interest in climbing and hiking in Rio, 1987 witnessed the first publication of a climbing magazine, *Revista Montanha*, and the establishment of a guiding association, Associação de Guias Independentes. They are both located at Rua Mexico 148/204, Rio de Janeiro, RJ CEP 20030. Phone 262-9703 and ask for Bruno Menescal for information on arranging a guided climb or trek.

Doing it Yourself

Rock climbing is still a novelty in Brazil and practised by only a few dedicated fanatics. Climbing gear is barely existent

so bring your own. It is very easy to sell good quality gear at premium prices to local climbers. In all of Brazil there is only one rock climbing store, Alta Montanha, which carries a few used hardware items. Its owner, Francisco, is also a very good source of information. The store is at Rua Senador Dantas 117, Sobreloja 202, in the centre of Rio.

As yet Brazil does not have hiking or climbing guides published in Portuguese or any other language for that matter. However, old editions of *Revista Montanha* feature documented routes with designs and topographical maps.

Popular Hikes & Climbs

Tijuca The National Park of Tijuca is a 120-square km park with an excellent trail system. It is also home to different species of birds and animals including iguanas and monkeys. The Alto da Boa Vista section of Tijuca forest, which is part of the national park, has several good day hikes. Maps of the forest are obtained at the small artisan shop just inside the park entrance, which is open from 7 am to 9 pm daily. To get there take bus 221 from Praça 15 in the centre to Praça Afonso Viseu in Alto da Boa Vista.

Pão de Açúcar On Pão de Açúcar (396 metres), Rio's Sugar Loaf, there are 32 established climbing routes. Climbers are often seen scaling the western face below the cable cars. *Revista Montanha* has detailed information about routes for anyone wanting to climb without a Brazilian guide.

One of the best hikes is up the back side of Pão de Açúcar. Besides the breathtaking view of the ocean below, one is also compensated by not having to pay for the cable car ride. The hike takes 1½ hours and doesn't require equipment or a lot of climbing experience, but does have two 10 to 15 metre exposed parts that require agility and common sense.

The hike begins on the left-hand side of Praça General Tibúrcio (the same praça where the cable cars are boarded) where a paved jogging track runs for 1200 metres along the base of Morro de Tijuca and Pão de Açúcar. At the end of the track pick up the trail on the other side of the cement tank in the tall grass. Follow this trail (always taking the up-hill forks) for 100 metres. At the old foundations, some 30 metres above the water, the trail ascends steeply for 60 metres until levelling off on the narrow ridge. From the ridge, the broad eastern flank of Pão de Açúcar is seen. The trail to follow is up the far left-hand side ridge.

At the base of the rock the trail deviates slightly to the right for the next 40 metres until coming to two iron bolts on the smooth exposed rock. This is the first exposed area, which while crossed easily without ropes, requires agility and alertness. There is nothing below to break a fall except the rocks in the ocean 120 metres below.

From the second bolt stay next to the rock slab for the following six metres. In the gap between the first rock slab and the next slab it is safer to step up on to the second rock slab rather than continuing along the exposed face. Twenty metres higher up there is a third iron bolt, which is a good place to take in the view before tackling the crux of the climb – above the clearly defined path. At the fourth bolt, the hike becomes a climb for the next 10 metres. This section is best climbed by finding the holds behind the rock slabs and pulling yourself up. After the sixth and final bolt, the climbing is over. Follow the well defined path up 200 metres to the small children's park at the top.

Corcovado Corcovado (710 metres) offers technically difficult climbs with fantastic views of Pão de Açúcar and Lagoa Rodrigo. Private guides and the clubs are the best means for unravelling its many diverse routes. Well-equipped and ex-perienced climbers can easily climb its eastern face on the route K-2 (rated 5.9).

The climb begins 200 metres below the summit. To get to the base of the climb, take the train to the top and instead of ascending the stairs to the left, follow the road out of the parking lot for 15 minutes. After the first rocky outcrop, on the northern side, descend two more turns in the road. At the second turn there is a cement railing, behind which is a poorly maintained trail.

Follow this trail as it hugs the base of the rock for 200 metres around to the eastern face of the mountain. Don't get discouraged by the tall grass which obstructs the trail, just keep to the base of the rock. On the eastern face the start of the climb is at the 20 metre crack in the whitened rock. From there the climb is clearly marked with well placed bolts to the top, just underneath the statue of Christ.

Dedo de Deus A third popular climb is Dedo de Deus (God's Finger) (elevation 1675 metres), a 200 metre needle-like pinnacle in the National Park of the Serra dos Órgãos, where rock climbing began in Brazil back in 1912. On the Rio to Teresópolis highway, five km from Teresópolis, Dedo de Deus is a frequent goal of the climbing clubs. The climb, rated 5.4, consists mostly of chimney routes, but is spectacular for abseiling. The top offers views of the rest of the park as well as Rio de Janeiro in the distance.

The trail to the base of the climb is found 200 metres below the small dam on the side of the highway. From the highway, it is a good two hour hike straight up in the steamy jungle. Dedo de Deus is best climbed with someone who knows the trail and the hidden chimney routes.

National Park of Itatiaia Three hours from Rio, off the Rio to São Paulo highway, the National Park of Itatiaia hosts the state of Rio's highest rock climb – Pico das Agulhas Negras (peak of the black needles) (2787 metres). The climb takes two days.

In addition to the great climbing, the

park is a wonderful place to get away from the oppressive summer heat. In the summer, the average temperature is a cool 13°C. The park's terrain is expansive, with small bushes, cactus and rocks on the lower elevations and forests with hidden waterfalls at higher altitudes (see State of Rio de Janeiro – Itatiaia).

Climbing Vocabulary

Although most Brazilians in the clubs know a little English, not everyone does. It helps to know a little Portuguese to smooth the way.

equipment	*equipamento*
bolt	*grampo*
rope	*corda*
carabiner	*mosquetão*
harness	*baudrie*
backpack	*mochila*
webbing	*fita*
chalk powder	*pó de magnésio*
rock	*rocha*
summit	*topo/cume*
crack	*fenda*
route	*via/rota*
a fall	*queda*
to be secured	*esta preso*
a hold	*uma agarra*
to belay	*dar segurança*
to make a stupid mistake and fall	*tomar uma vaca*

Getting There

AIR

Cheap deals on air travel are volatile. With some leg-work you can usually save a couple of hundred dollars. Check newspapers and discount or Latin American specialist travel agents for good deals.

Varig is Brazil's international airline and they fly to many major cities in the world. From the USA the basic carriers are Varig, Pan Am and Japan Air (from the West coast); from England British Airways and Varig; from Australia QANTAS, Aerolineas Argentinas and Lan Chile.

Discount tickets have restrictions. The most pernicious is the limit on the amount of time you can spend in Brazil. Charter flights are often as little as one to three weeks. Most other tickets have a 90-day limit. There's usually a premium for tickets valid over 180 days. The Brazil Air Pass must be purchased outside of Brazil. (See Getting Around for more information).

In 1986 the Brazilian government slapped a 25% tax on all international airlines tickets, to off-set the good deals because of the parallel market. The only way you can still purchase international tickets without the tax is with a foreign credit card, but then you lose the parallel market rate.

The cheapest flights to the USA are charters from Manaus to Miami (the Disneyworld express). Manaus is halfway between Rio and Miami. Flights to Miami are cheap, and domestic Brazilian flights can be cheap with the 14 or 21-day Airpass (see Getting Around chapter), so the missing link is a cheap Miami/Manaus flight. Only Varig and Pan Am are licensed to operate unlimited flights to the big US market, and their international flights go out of Rio and São Paulo. The lesser Brazilian airlines VASP and Transbrasil are authorised to fly a limited number of flights. For a while Transbrasil flew three times a week Manaus/Orlando/Manaus for US$399 (In Rio call Concorde Turismo 258-0344, in São Paulo call Intravel 220-2371). Transbrasil has been knocked out of this service (temporarily?), but VASP has filled in the gap with a US$550 roundtrip Rio/Miami flight via Manaus and Kingston, Jamaica. (Between Jamaica and Miami they've circumvented the US flight quota by using a Jamaican carrier.) LAB (Lloyd Aero Boliviano) sometimes flies Manaus/ Miami. If you can swing it, start your Brazilian travels in Manaus.

Keep in mind that there's a US$7 airport tax when you leave Brazil.

From the US

When flying from the US consider charter flights, especially for brief visits of one to three weeks. Look into Tower Air and CIEE (offices in New York, San Francisco, Boston). They often have the best deals, but they have crazy restrictions and generally suffer from acute disorganisation. At one stage Tower had a New York / Rio de Janeiro / New York fare for US$600.

LAP (Lineas Aereas Paraguayas) has been the budget traveller's choice with a cheap Miami / Asunción / Rio de Janeiro flight. Contrary to what you may think, they are punctual, although we have heard of a few cases of the lost luggage blues. Canadian Pacific also has a cheap flight, from Toronto to Rio.

Aside from charters, Brazilian or Latin American travel agencies are the best places to go for discounted tickets. These agencies usually buy tickets in bulk from the airlines, which they then discount to their customers, or they sell what are called fill-up fares for the airlines which are an even better deal (but there are some additional restrictions). These discounts range from 10 to 25 percent less than normal economy fares. Look for ads in the newspaper. Gleiser Travel in New York is recommended. We've had reports of hassles with Brazil Tours in Los Angeles.

From the USA the major carrier gateway cities are New York, Los Angeles and Miami. All have basically the same fare structure. Economy fares often have to be purchased two weeks in advance and you must stay from at least two weeks and no more than three months. The three month time limit is a real drag but we were unable to find a way around it, even the charters have it.

Long Stays If you are planning to stay in Brazil for more than 90 days, cheap airline tickets are a big problem. You are required to buy a return ticket before you will be issued with a visa in the USA, but it's not hard to get around this (see visa section). Unfortunately, the cost of a one-way ticket is more than twice the price of a return economy fare. For example: from Los Angeles to Rio return costs about US$900 if you buy from the airlines, but from discounted travel agents it gets as low as US$700. The fare for a one way ticket is US$850, for a round trip of over three months the fare is double that. Absurd! This means it may be cheaper to buy a discounted return ticket with a 90 day limit and bury the return portion ticket and then buy a ticket in Brazil when you are ready to go home.

If you plan to stay more than six months in Brazil you also have to plan around leaving the country to get a new visa. Ask about package deals. We were able to get a round-trip Aerolineas Argentinas ticket from New York to Buenos Aires with an unlimited stopover in Rio. This gave us a free ride to Buenos Aires to get new visas after several months in Brazil – but check if this is still available.

From Australia/New Zealand
Aerolineas Argentinas (in Rio 224-9242) flies over the south pole once a week via Rio de Janeiro / Buenos Aires / Auckland / Sydney. Lan Chile (in Rio 221-2882) flies Rio de Janeiro / Santiago / Papeete / Sydney for US$2387. QANTAS (Rio 511-0045) flies Sydney/Rio de Janeiro via Los Angeles for US$2350. The LA-Rio leg is on Varig; a maximum of two stopovers is allowed in the Pacific (US$50 each) in places like Honolulu and Tahiti.

From Europe
Varig and British Airways fly from London. TAP is now flying from Portugal. Air France flies Paris/Cayenne (French Guyana) and Paris/Rio de Janeiro, but they have discontinued their Cayenne/Belém flight. On Mondays, Varig flies Belém/Cayenne (US$140); the same flight continues to Paramaribo, Surinam (US$185). There are lots of charters flying between Europe and Rio de Janeiro. Schwabb is the only one which operates out of Brazil. Maximum stay is the major restriction. Lan Chile has charter flights (60 day maximum stay) between Rio de Janeiro and several European capitals (eg, Madrid US$799 roundtrip versus normal fare of US$1023).

From Asia
From the Orient, the hot tickets are JAL, Singapore Airlines and Pan Am. Japan Airlines flies Tokyo / Los Angeles / Rio de Janeiro / São Paulo and they often have the best fares to Rio from the West coast of the US.

OVERLAND
To/From Argentina
Coming from or going to Argentina most travellers pass through Foz do Iguaçu (see Foz do Iguaçu for more information).

To/From Bolivia
Corumbá The main crossing point between Bolivia and Brazil is at the Rio Paraguai between Corumbá and Quijarro. Corumbá is serviced by two daily trains: the 11 hour slow train departs from Campo Grande at

8.15 or 9 am and the ten hour express leaves at 8.10 or 9 pm.

There is a Bolivian consulate in Corumbá for those who need visas. The red tape involved in crossing this border can involve a fair amount of running around.

Those who need visas must go to the Bolivian Consulate at Rua Antônio Mário Coelho, 852 (231-5605); it's open Monday to Friday from 8 am to midday and 3 pm to 6 pm, and on Saturdays from 8 am to midday. There's also a Bolivian consulate in Campo Grande at Rua Pernambuco, 1772 (624-5038). If you don't need a visa for Bolivia then don't come here or they'll try to persuade you that you do need one. The procedure for crossing the border changes from time to time but at present it involves a lot of running around. First you have to get your Brazilian exit stamp from the police at Corumbá railway station (open only in the mornings and evenings when the trains come in). After that take a bus to the border and get your passport stamped by Bolivian Immigration (there are three buses in the morning and one in the afternoon from the town centre). After that it's back to town where you get your passport stamped again by the Bolivian Consul.

From Corumbá you must take either a bus or taxi to the Bolivian border town of Quijarro, 4 km from Puerto Suarez. From here the *ferrobus* to Santa Crúz de la Sierra, known as the train of death, leaves daily at 9 pm. Tickets for the twelve hour journey go on sale at 3 pm the same day. Ordinary trains are also available, but not recommended – they take about 24 hours.

Guajará-Mirim There is a border crossing into Bolivia at Guajará-Mirim. Although the Madeira to Mamore railroad has long since been abandoned, there are bus connections twice a day (during the dry season) from Porto Velho to Guajará-Mirim at 7 am and 9 pm; twelve hour bus ride. If you need a Bolivian visa have two photographs ready. Regardless of your

visa status there are four things you must do: get your passport stamped at the Bolivian consulate at Avenida Leopoldo dos Matos, 239 (541-2862); get a Brazilian exit stamp from the Polícia Federal at Avenida Benjamin Constant; take the ferry from Guajará-Mirim across the Rio Mamore to the Bolivian sister city of Guayaramerín; get a Bolivian entrance stamp on your passport.

There is a corresponding Brazilian consulate in Guayaramerín for travellers going in the opposite direction; open weekdays from 11 am to 2 pm. There are two daily buses from Guayaramerín to Riberalta at 9.30 am and 4 pm; it's a 2½ hour ride. Riberalta is linked to Cochambamba by air.

Cáceres From Cáceres north of Cuiabá you can cross to San Matías in Bolivia, but if you want to go further into Bolivia from there, you will have to fly to Roboré or Santa Crúz in order to connect with terrestrial transport.

To/From Colombia
The Colombian border is at Leitícia (see Manaus for further information).

To/From French Guyana
Rumour has it that non-Brazilians can enter French Guyana from Oiapoque by motorised dugout. It is, on the other hand not possible to enter Brazil by the reverse route unless you happen to hold a Brazilian passport, so don't try going to St George (the town on the French Guyanese side) unless you intend to fly out of Cayenne or to re-enter Brazil near Boa Vista.

To/From Guyana
You may want to save yourself the trouble of a difficult overland passage by flying directly to Georgetown. There are two Guyana Airways flights a week from Boa Vista.

There's a daily 8 am bus from Boa Vista to Bom Fim (three hours, 125km, US$5) returning from Bom Fim at 2 pm. Get an exit stamp then hike five miles to the border where you can hire a canoe across the Rio Tacutu to Lethem, Guyana and get an entrance stamp. Lethem is linked to the rest of Guyana by air, not road.

To/From Paraguay

Foz do Iguaçu See the Foz do Iguaçu section in the Paraná chapter.

Ponta Porã There is a Paraguayan Consulate in Corumbá at Avenida Antônio João, 226 (231-4803). In Campo Grande the Paraguayan Consulate is at Rua 14 de Julho, 1845, 3rd floor (624-9916). You can also arrange visas 340 km from Campo Grande at Ponta Porã. It is a border town of 25,000 people divided from the Paraguayan town of Pedro Juan Caballero by Avenida Internacional.

Ponta Porã, Guaraní for pretty square, was a centre for the yerba-mate trade in the late 1800s, long before it started attracting Brazilians who like to play in the Paraguayan casinos, shop (duty free purchases of up to US$150 permitted) and hang out in ritzy hotels like *Pousada do Bosque* (Avenida Presidente Vargas, 1151 (431-1181].

There are five daily buses between Campo Grande and Ponta Porã and two daily trains. The slow eight hour train leaves Campo Grande at 9 am; the six hour express train leaves at 4.45 pm. The express returns to Campo Grande from Ponta Porã at 6.40 am and the slow train at 8.45 am. The Paraguayan consulate in Ponta Porã is on Avenida Internacional and a corresponding Brazilian consulate in Pedro Juan Caballero. The daily buses to Concepción and Asunción, normally five and ten hours away, may be interrupted in the rainy season.

To/From Peru

To or from Peru the route is via the Amazon at Iquitos (see Manaus for further information).

To/From Surinam

It is not possible to enter Surinam overland from Brazil without passing through one of the other two Guyanas first.

To/From Uruguay

Coming from Uruguay, travellers pass either from Chuy to Pelotas or from Treinta y Tres or Mel to Rio Branco/Jaguarão.

To/From Venezuela

A gravel road runs through the Venezuelan towns of Ciudad Bolívar, Tumeremo and El Dorado to Santa Elena (on the border) then onto Boa Vista Brazil. You can get as far as El Dorado on buses, from there to Santa Elena you'll have to hitch or hire a jeep (it's actually much easier to fly between Santa Elena and Ciudad Bolívar on daily Aeropostal flights). Before and after Santa Elena you can count on numerous encounters with unpleasant police and border patrols. They have a well deserved reputation for stealing travellers belongings.

Most people arrive in Santa Elena in the evening, but it's best to time your arrival earlier in the afternoon in order to get a hotel room. Consider taking a jeep instead of the bus. If it's convenient, try to get an exit stamp at DIEX, the day before crossing the border rather than suffering through the following morning border turmoil.

When departing for Brazil, board the bus for Boa Vista in front of the Hotel Frontera at 7 am even though the bus will only pull out by 8 am or later. The first stop is DIEX for exit stamps. Be wary of fellow passengers and officials who board the bus. Theft is common, particularly during the periodic clumsy searches which punctuate the ride to the border.

At the border after the final Venezuelan baggage search, there is a 100 yard walk to the Brazilian post for an entry stamp on your visa. Although the Venezuelans are lax, the Brazilians are strict about border control. They absolutely will not permit entry of people with irregularities, particularly those who have overstayed their visas in the past. Weather permitting it's a dull eight hour ride (not including two hours at the border). The bus fare from

Santa Elena to Boa Vista is US$8 payable in bolivars or cruzados. In Boa Vista, the Venezuelan consulate (224-2182) is at Rua Benjamim Constant 525 near the Hotel Lua Nova.

Getting Around

AIR

Flying in Brazil is not cheap. But with the seemingly endless expanses of sertão, amazon and pantanal between many destinations, the occasional flight can be an absolute necessity. And even if you don't use it, having extra money to fly can add flexibility to your travel plans. Brazil has three major national carriers and several smaller regional airlines. The biggies are Varig/Cruzeiro, Vasp, and Transbrasil. Together, they cover an extensive network of cities; they don't all go to the same places, but at least one of them goes to every major city. There is very little price competition between them. Prices on most flights, no matter which airline, are based on distance, and because flying is expensive, it's rarely difficult getting on a flight, with the exception of the vacation periods from December up to Carnival and July. Make reservations as early as possible for Carnival time!

Air Pass

There are two different Brazil Air Passes: the first, costs US$330 for 21 days. This allows for unlimited flights within that time. The second costs US$250 for 14 days and is limited to four destinations (eg, from Rio you can fly to Salvador, and on to Belém, then to Manaus, and Porto Alegre, and finally back to Rio – the city you start from is not counted among the destinations, so if you are returning to that same city you have five flights).

The air pass must be purchased outside of Brazil, where you'll get an MCO in your name with Brazil Air Pass stamped on it, which you exchange for an air pass from one of the three airlines in Brazil. All three airlines offer the same deal, all three fly to most major cities, but Varig/Cruzeiro flies to more cities than the other two. If you are buying an airpass and plan to go to a specific smaller city, you may want to check with a travel agent to see which airline goes there (for example, only VASP flies to Corumbá the port entry to the southern Pantanal).

The air pass cannot be used to fly on the Rio to São Paulo shuttle, which lands at the downtown airports of both cities, but it can be used to fly between the international airports of both cities. The MCO is refundable if you don't use it in Brazil.

Before buying an airpass, you should sit down and work out whether it is really a good investment for your purposes. There are often delays flying in Brazil and it's rare that you don't waste a day in transit. Unless you're intent on a whistle stop tour of the country, there are only so many flights that you will want to take in two or three weeks. The other question is the cost of airfares in Brazil. There has been drastic variation in prices over the past few years (when travel agents quote airfares from abroad in dollars, they are probably using the official exchange rate which boosts the price considerably).

Within Brazil, there are a few discounted flights and you should check to see if there are any new ones when you arrive. Night flights after 10 pm on certain routes are discounted by 30 percent. Children under 12 fly for half price.

The smaller domestic airlines include Nordeste, Rio Sul, Taba, Votec and Tam. They mostly use the Bandeirante a small Brazilian-built prop-plane (which some claim is not too safe) and fly to smaller cities where the major carriers don't go. We used Nordeste to fly to Ilhéus once when we couldn't get a seat on a plane directly to Salvador.

There are also many air-taxi companies, which mostly fly in the Amazon. These flights are expensive, although usually

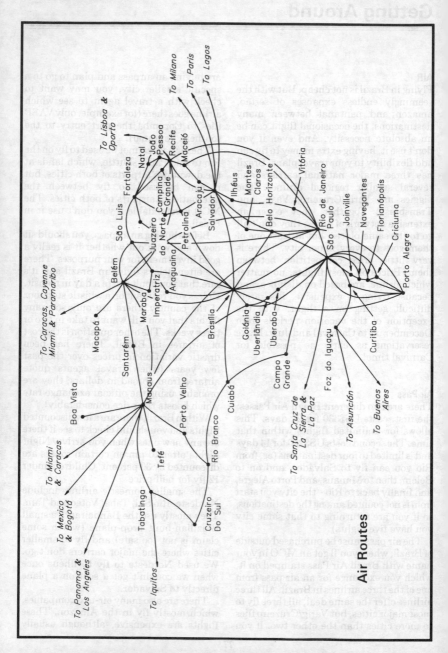

Air Routes

always a danger on domestic flights. Planes flying along the coast often stop at every city, so if you're going from Rio to Fortaleza it's possible that the plane will stop at Salvador, Maceió, Recife and João Pessoa, on the way. Sometimes these outrageously indirect flights are unavoidable, but not always.

FAB (Força Aerea Brasileira) has been known to give free flights when they have extra space. Go to the desk marked CAN in the airport and ask about the next military flight, then show up again two days before scheduled departure time and sign up. It helps to have a letter of introduction from a consulate. Some air bases restrict flights to Brazilian nationals (eg, Santarém), but it's not as rigid as it often appears. The whole process is hit and miss but it's particularly worth a try in the North in cities like Boa Vista, Macapá, Brasília, Cuiabá, Porto Velho, Manaus, Santarém, Rio Branco, Belém, São Luís.

BUS
Onde fica essa cidade? Lá onde o vento faz a volta
Where is that city? There where the wind turns around
(popular saying about distances in Brazil).

the price comes down with more people flying and sometimes you can bargain.

Air reservations can appear and disappear mysteriously. If you have a reservation it's often necessary to confirm it and reconfirm it, even if you've already bought the ticket. If you have been told a flight is full, keep trying to make the reservation every so often and go directly to the airlines central ticket office or the airport. Several times travel agents were unable to get us reservations, assuring us that there wasn't a ticket to Salvador within two months of Carnival, and we got the reservation by going to the airline counter at the airport. Another option if you are looking for a cheap flight is to go stand-by.

Strange routes, bizarre connections, long lay-overs and frequent stops are

Except in the Amazon basin, buses are the primary form of long-distance transportation for the vast majority of Brazilians. Bus service is generally excellent. The buses are clean, comfortable, and well serviced Mercedes, Volvos and Scanias. The drivers are generally good, and a governor limits their wilder urges to 80 km per hour.

Bus travel throughout Brazil is very cheap (fares work out to less than a dollar per hour): for example, the six hour trip from Rio to São Paulo costs US$4; the 18 hour trip from São Paulo to Foz do Iguaçu is only US$11.

All major cities are linked by frequent buses – one leaves every 15 minutes from Rio to São Paulo during peak hours – and there is a surprising number of scheduled long-distance buses. It's rare that you will have to change buses between two major cities, no matter what the distance. There are also inter-country buses. From several major cities you can get a direct bus to Argentina, Paraguay, Bolivia or Chile.

'Progress is roads' goes the saying in Brazil. And wherever there is a road in Brazil, no matter how bad a road, or so it seems, there is a bus that travels it. We will never forget the bus that rescued us on an almost deserted peninsula out near Ponta do Mutá – a place where no one goes, and no one ever seems to have heard of. How we got there is hard to explain, how the bus got there is impossible to explain. It was a road, more like a wide trail, that was impassable by normal car and apparently unknown to Brazilian cartographers. But the bus came and eventually delivered us to a humble fishing village of no more than a hundred people.

In every big city, and most small ones, there is a central bus terminal (*rodoviária*). The rodoviárias are most frequently on the outskirts of the city. Some are modern, comfortable stations. All have restaurants, news-stands, toilets, etc. Most importantly, all the long-distance bus companies operate out of the same place making it easy to find your bus.

Inside the rodoviária you'll find ticket offices for the various bus companies. They usually post bus destinations and schedules in their windows; occasionally they are printed on leaflets; sometimes you just have to get in line and ask the teller for information. This can be difficult if you don't speak much Portuguese and the teller is in a highly agitated state after his 23rd cafezinho or speaks with an accent from the interior of Ceará. The best strategy is probably to have a pen and paper handy and ask him to write down what you need to know.

When you find a bus company that goes to your destination, don't assume it's the only one, there are often two or more and the quality rarely varies markedly between them (although our favourite is Itapemirim whose buses have super air-suspension).

Usually you can go down to the rodoviária and buy a ticket for the next bus out. Where this is difficult, for example in Ouro Prêto, we try to let you know. In general though it's a good idea to buy a ticket a few hours in advance and if it's convenient, the day before. On weekends, holidays and from December to February this is always a good idea.

Aside from getting you on the bus, buying a ticket early has a few other advantages. First, it gets you an assigned seat. Many common buses fill-up the aisles with standing passengers. Second, you can ask for a front row seat, with extra leg space, or a window seat, with a view (ask for a *janela* or an odd numbered seat).

You don't always have to go to the rodoviária to buy your bus ticket. Selected travel agents in major cities sell long-distance bus tickets. This is a great service which can save you a long trip out to an often chaotic rodoviária. The price is the same and the travel agents are more likely to speak some English and be less rushed.

There are two types, or classes, of long-distance buses. The ordinary or *comum* is the most common. It's quite comfortable, usually with air-conditioning and a toilet. The *leito* or *executivo* is Brazil's version of the couchette. Although they usually take as long to reach their destination as a comum and cost twice as much, leitos, which often depart late at night, are exceptionally comfortable. They have spacious, fully reclining seats, blankets and pillows, and more often than not a steward serving coffee, soda and água mineral. If you don't mind missing the scenery, a leito bus can get you there in comfort and save you the cost of a hotel room.

With or without bathrooms, buses generally make pit stops every three or four hours. These stops are great places to meet other bus passengers, buy bizarre memorabilia and wish you were back home eating a healthy vegetarian quiche.

Like everything in Brazil, bus service varies by region. The South has the most and the best roads. The coastal highways are usually good, at least until São Luis. The Amazon and the sertão are another story. It's no surprise that roads in the sertão are bad. It's the way in which they are bad that's so strange. In several areas the road alternates every few hundred yards between dirt (which is better) and pot-hole infested paved road (which is much worse). This pattern is without logic, it conforms to no obvious geographical or human design, and it forces a constant speeding-up or slowing-down.

Highlighted by the transamazônia highway, there has been a tremendous growth of roads into unsettled regions in Brazil, particularly the Amazon; they have been a corner-stone of the military governments economic development strategy. But many of these roads are precarious at best. Most are unpaved and are constantly being washed out during the rainy season when buses get stuck and are always being delayed. In the dry season buses are usually scorching hot, dusty and stuffed with people. As countless books have documented, bus transportation in the Amazon is always an adventure, teaching a healthy respect for the power and the size of the forest.

CAR

The number of fatalities caused by motor vehicles in Brazil is quite high. The roads

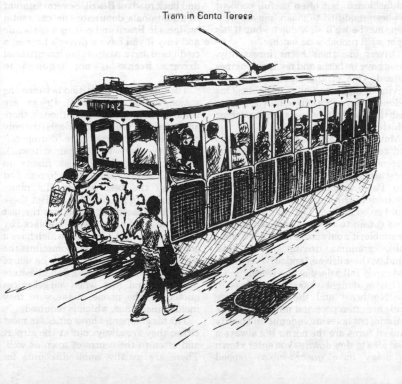

Tram in Santa Teresa

can be very dangerous, especially busy highways like the Rio to São Paulo corridor. Most of the problems stem from the Brazilian driver. If you thought the Italians were wild drivers, just wait. This isn't true everywhere, but in general the car owner is king of the road and shows it. Other motorists are treated as unwelcome guests at a private party. Pedestrians are shown no mercy, and certainly no courtesy.

Especially in Rio, the anarchic side of the Brazilian personality emerges from behind the drivers' wheel as lane dividers, one-way streets and even side walks are disregarded and violated. Driving is un-policed, traffic violations unheard of. Despite all appearances to the contrary, Brazil does hold to the convention that a red light means 'stop'. In practice, this old-fashioned, but often useful, concept has been modified to mean 'maybe we'll stop, maybe we'll slow down –but if it's night we'll probably do neither.'

Drivers use their horns incessantly, buses have no horns and rev their engines instead. One of the craziest habits is driving at night without headlights. This is done, as far as we can tell, to be able to flash the headlights on to warn approaching vehicles.

Many drivers are Formula I racing fans and tend to drive under the influence, pretending they are Nelson Piquet. The worst are the Rio bus drivers, or maybe the São Paulo commuter, or maybe the Amazonian truck driver, or maybe . . . I could go on and on. This cult of speed, a close cousin to the cult of machismo, is insatiable; it's only positive aspect is that, unlike grandma driving on an Iowa Sunday, these drivers tend to be very alert and rarely fall asleep at the wheel.

Driving at night is hazardous, at least in the Northeast and the interior where roads are often poor and unreliable. Like malaria, pot holes are endemic and poorly banked turns are the norm. It's always a good idea to slow down as you enter a town as many have *quebra-molas* (speed bumps) which you never see until it's too late. Another big danger are the farm trucks with inexperienced drivers carrying workers and cargo to town.

On the bright side, many trucks and buses in the Northeast help you pass at night with their indicators. A flashing right indicator means it's clear to go, a flashing left means that a vehicle is approaching from the opposite direction. Everything happens more slowly in the Northeast, and this holds true for driving too.

Car Rental

Renting a car is expensive, with prices similar to those in the US and Europe. But if you can share the expense with friends it's a great way to explore some of the many remote beaches, fishing villages and back roads of Brazil. Several familiar multinationals dominate the car rental business in Brazil and getting a car is safe and easy if you have a driver's license, a credit card and a passport (an international driver's license is not required in Brazil).

There is little competition between the major rental companies. Prices are usually about the same, although there are occasional promotional deals (the only ones we encountered were during off-season weekends in non-tourist towns). Volkswagen beetles (called *fuscas* in Brazil) are the cheapest cars to rent and are also the best on Brazil's many alternatives to the paved road. But these are being phased-out (1986 was the last year Brazil produced fuscas); replaced by Volkswagen Gol, Chevettes (which have a good reputation) and Fiat. Sometimes the rental companies will claim to be out of these cheaper models, if so, don't hesitate to shop around. Also, when you get prices quoted on the phone, make sure they include insurance, which is required.

The big companies have offices in most cities; they are always out at the airport and often in the centre of town as well. There are usually small discounts for weekly and monthly rentals, and no drop-off charges.

Motorcycles

Mar e Moto (274-4398) in Rio rents motorcycles, but it's quite expensive. If you want to buy a bike, Brazil manufactures its own, but they are also expensive.

Motorcycles are popular in Brazil, especially in and around the cities. Theft is a big problem; you can't even insure a bike because theft is so common. Most people who ride keep their bike in a guarded place, at least overnight. For the traveller this can be difficult to organise, but if you can manoeuvre around the practical problems, Brazil is a great place to have a motorcycle.

HITCHING

Hitching in Brazil, with the possible exception of the Amazon and Pantanal, is difficult. The word for hitching in Portuguese is *carona*, so *pode dar carona* is 'can you give (me/us) a lift'. The best way to hitch – practically the only way if you want a ride – is to wait at a petrol station or a truck stop and talk to the drivers. But even this can be difficult. A few years back there were several assaults by hitchhikers and the government began to discourage giving rides in public service announcements.

LOCAL TRANSPORT
Local Bus

Local bus service tends to be pretty good in Brazil. Since most Brazilians take the bus to work everyday, municipal buses are usually frequent and their network of routes is comprehensive. They are always cheap and crowded.

In most city buses, you get on in the back and exit from the front. Usually there's a money collector sitting at a turnstile at the rear of the bus, with the bus price displayed nearby. If you're unsure if it's the right bus, it's easy to hop on the back and ask the money collector if the bus is going to your destination – *você vai para .... ?* If it's the wrong bus no one will mind if you hop off, even if the bus has gone a stop or two.

Crime can be a problem on buses. Rather than remain at the rear of the bus, it's safer to pay the fare and go through the turnstile. Try to avoid carrying valuables on the buses if you can. If you must take valuables with you then keep them well hidden.

Jumping on a local bus is one of the best ways to get to know a city. With a map and a few dollars you can tour the town and maybe meet some of the locals.

Taxis Taxis are fine. Prices are reasonable, if not cheap, and most drivers are honest, at least outside of Rio. The big city taxis tend to have meters, which are inevitably updated by a *tabela* that converts the price on the meter to a new price. This is OK as long as the meter works and the tabela is legal and current (don't accept photocopies). If the meter doesn't work

then negotiate a fare before getting on board or find another cab.

The same goes for taxis without meters. Agree on the price beforehand, and make sure there is no doubt about it. You don't want to have an argument at the end of the ride; it's not worth it, even if you win.

The worst place to get a cab is wherever the tourists are. Don't get a cab near one of the expensive hotels. Walk a block away

from the beach at Copacabana to flag down a cab. Many airports have special airport taxis which are about 50 percent more expensive than the regular taxi which is probably waiting just around the corner. If, however, you are carrying valuables, the special airport taxi, or a radio-taxi, can be a worthwhile investment. These are probably the safest taxis on the road.

THE SOUTHEAST
REGIÃO SUDESTE

Rio de Janeiro

Rio is *a cidade maravilhosa* (the marvellous city). Jammed into the world's most beautiful city setting – between ocean and escarpment – are nine million *cariocas*, as the inhabitants are called. This makes Rio the world's biggest tropical city and one of the most densely populated places on earth. This thick brew of cariocas pursue pleasure like no other people: beaches and the body beautiful; samba and cerveja; football and cachaça.

Rio has its problems, and they are enormous. A third of the people live in favelas that blanket many of the hillsides. The poor have no schools, no doctors, no jobs. Drug abuse and violence are endemic. Police corruption and brutality are commonplace. There is no law or order.

Nevertheless in Rio, everything ends with samba – football games, weddings, work, political demonstrations and, of course, a day at the beach. There's a lust for life, a love of romance, music, dance and talk that seems to distinguish the carioca from everyone else. For anyone coming from the efficiency and rationality of the developed capitalist world this is potent stuff. The sensuality of Carnival is the best-known expression of this Dionysian spirit, but there are plenty more.

Rio has its glitzy side, its international tourism crowd, its lives of the rich and famous. But happily it's also a good city for the budget traveller. There are plenty of cheap restaurants and hotels. The beaches are free and democratic. There's lots to explore in the city centre and in several other neighbourhoods with their parks and museums . Mass transportation is fast and easy. And if you can meet some locals - not nearly so hard as in New York, London or Sydney – well, then you're on easy street.

Expect some rain in Rio. In the summer, from December to March it gets hot and humid. Temperatures in the high 30°Cs are common. There's more rain but it rarely lasts for too long. In the winter temperatures range from the 20°Cs to low 30°Cs with plenty of good days for the beach.

History

Gaspar de Lemos set sail from Portugal for Brazil in May 1501 and entered a huge bay in January 1502. Mistaking the bay for a river he named it Rio de Janeiro. It was the French, however, who first settled along the great bay. Like the Portuguese, the French had been harvesting brazil wood along the Brazilian coast, but unlike the Portuguese they hadn't attempted any permanent settlements until Rio de Janeiro.

As the Portuguese colonisation of Brazil began to take hold, the French became concerned that they'd be pushed out of the colony. Three ships of settlers reached the Guanabara Bay in 1555. They settled on a small island in the bay and gave it the name of Antarctic France. Almost from the start the French town seemed doomed to failure. It was torn by religious divisions, isolated by harsh treatment of the Indians and demoralised by the puritanical rule of the leader, Nicolas de Villegagnon, who prevented his men from having sexual relations with the Indians unless they married! Antarctic France was weak and disheartened when the Portuguese attacked and drove the French from their fortress in 1560.

A greater threat to the Portuguese were the powerful Tamoio Indians who had allied with the French. A series of battles occurred, but the Portuguese were better armed and better supplied by the motherland than the French. The Portuguese finally expelled the French and drove the Tamoio from the region in a series of bloody battles.

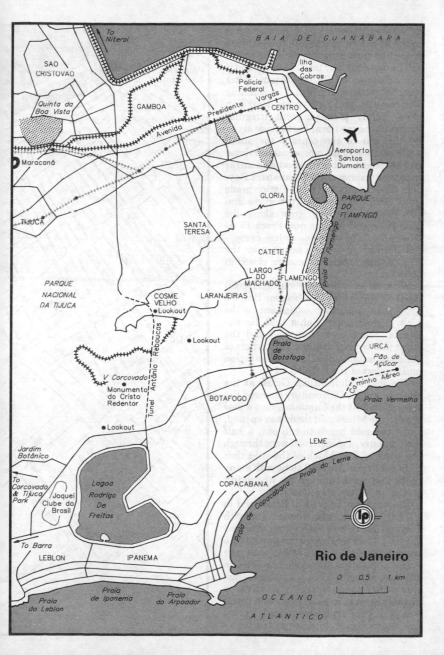

The Portuguese set up a fortified town on the Morro Castelo in 1567 to maximise protection from European invasion by sea and Indian attack by land. They named it São Sebastião do Rio de Janeiro, after King Sebastião of Portugal. The founding 500 cariocas built a typical Brazilian town; poorly planned, with irregular streets in the medieval Portuguese style. By the end of the century the small settlement was, if not prosperous, surviving on the export of brazil wood and sugar cane, and fishing in the Guanabara Bay.

In 1660 the city had a population made up of 3000 Indians, 750 Portuguese and 100 Blacks. The city grew along the waterfront and what is now Praça 15 de Novembro. The religious orders came – the Jesuits, the Franciscans and the Benedictines – and built austere, closed-in churches.

With its excellent harbour and good lands for sugar cane, Rio became Brazil's third most important settlement in the 17th century after Bahia and Recife-Olinda. Slaves were imported and the sugar plantations thrived. The owners of the sugar estates lived in the protection and comfort of the fortified city.

The gold rush in Minas Gerais at the beginning of the 18th century changed Rio forever. In 1704 the *Caminho Novo* a new road to the Minas gold fields was opened. Until the gold began to run out, a half century later, a golden road went through the ports of Rio. Much of the gold that didn't end up in England along with many of the Portuguese immigrants who didn't end up in Minas, stayed in Rio.

Rio was now the prize of Brazil and in 1710 the French, who were at war with Portugal and raiding her colonies, attacked the city. The French were defeated, but a second expedition succeeded and the entire population abandoned the city in the dark of night. The occupying French threatened to level the city unless a sizeable ransom in gold, sugar and cattle was paid. The Portuguese obliged. During the return voyage to an expected hero's

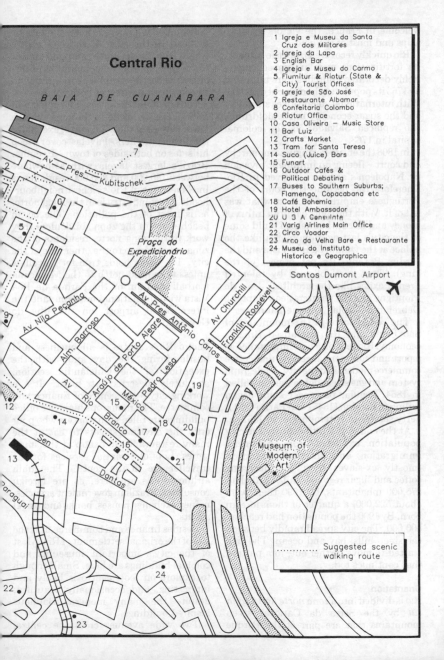

Central Rio

BAIA DE GUANABARA

1 Igreja e Museu da Santa
   Cruz dos Militares
2 Igreja da Lapa
3 English Bar
4 Igreja e Museu do Carmo
5 Flumitur & Riotur (State &
   City) Tourist Offices
6 Igreja de São José
7 Restaurante Albamar
8 Confeitaria Colombo
9 Riotur Office
10 Casa Oliveira – Music Store
11 Bar Luiz
12 Crafts Market
13 Tram for Santa Teresa
14 Suco (Juice) Bars
15 Funart
16 Outdoor Cafés &
   Political Debating
17 Buses to Southern Suburbs;
   Flamengo, Copacabana etc
18 Café Bohemia
19 Hotel Ambassador
20 U S A Consulate
21 Varig Airlines Main Office
22 Circo Voador
23 Arco da Velha Bare e Restaurante
24 Museu do Instituto
   Historico e Geographica

Praça do
Expedicionário

Av Pres Kubitschek

Av Nilo Peçanha

Av Pres Antônio Carlos

Alm. Barroso

Av Rio Araújo de Porto Alegre

México

Pedro Lessa

Av Rio Branco

Sen Dantas

Paraguai

Av Churchill

Franklin Roosevelt

Santos Dumont Airport

Museum of
Modern
Art

Suggested scenic
walking route

welcome in France, the victors lost two ships and most of the gold.

Rio quickly recovered from the setback. Its fortifications were improved, many richly decorated churches were built and by 1763 its population had reached 50,000. With international sugar prices slumping and the sugar economy in the doldrums, Rio replaced Salvador as the colonial capital in 1763.

In 1808 the entire Portuguese monarchy and court – fleeing an imminent invasion by Napoleon's armies – arrived in Rio. Therefore Rio became the court of the Portuguese empire or at least what was left of it. With the court came an influx of money and talent that helped build some of the city's lasting monuments like the palace at the Quinta da Boa Vista and the Jardim Botânico (a pet project of the king). They were followed by talented French exiles like the architect Jean de Montigny and the painters Jean Baptiste Debret and Nicolas Antoine Taunay.

The coffee boom in the mountains of São Paulo and Rio revitalised Brazil's economy. Rio took on a new importance as a port and commercial centre, and coffee commerce modernised the city. A telegraph system and gas street lights were installed in 1854. Regular passenger ships began sailing to London (1845) and Paris (1851). Ferry service to Niterói began in 1862.

At the end of the 19th century the city population exploded from European immigration and internal migration (mostly ex-slaves from the declining coffee and sugar regions). In 1872 Rio had 275,000 inhabitants, by 1890 there were about 522,000, a quarter of them foreign born. By 1900 the population had reached 800,000. The city spread rapidly between the steep hills, bay and ocean. The rich started to move further out, in a pattern that continues today.

Orientation

Rio is divided into a *zona norte* and a *zona sul* by the Serra da Carioca, steep mountains that are part of the Parque Nacional da Tijuca. These mountains descend to the edge of the city centre where the zona norte and sul meet. Corcovado, one of these mountain peaks, offers the best geographical orientation to the city with its view of both zones.

Rio is a tale of two cities. The upper and middle classes reside in the zona sul, the lower classes in the zona norte, except for the favela dwellers. Favelas cover steep hillsides on both sides of town – Rocinha, Brazil's largest favela with somewhere between 150,000 and 300,000 residents, is in Gávea, one of Rio's richest neighbourhoods. Most industry is in the zona norte, as is most of the pollution. The ocean beaches are in the zona sul. Unless they work in the zona norte, residents of the zona sul rarely go to the other side of the city. The same holds true for travellers unless they head north to the Maracanã football stadium or the Parque da Boa Vista with the national museum, and the international airport, on the Ilha do Governador.

Centro Rio's centre is all business and bustle during the day and, with the exception of the Cinelândia section, absolutely deserted at night. It's a working city – the centre of finance and commerce. The numerous high-rise office buildings are filled with workers who pour onto the daytime streets to eat at the many restaurants and shop at the small stores. Lots of essential services for the traveller are in the centre. The main airline offices are here, as are foreign consulates, Brazilian government agencies, money exchange houses, banks and travel agents.

Besides finance and commerce, it is the site of the original settlement of Rio. Most of the city's important museums and colonial buildings are here. Small enough to explore on foot, centro is lively and interesting, and occasionally beautiful; despite the many modern, Bauhaus inspired buildings.

Two wide avenues cross the centre.

Typical favela

Avenida Rio Branco, where buses leave for the zona sul, and Avenida Presidente Vargas, which heads out to the sambódromo and the zona norte. Rio's modern subway follows these two avenues as it burrows under the city. Most banks and airline offices have their headquarters on Avenida Rio Branco.

Cinelândia At the southern edge of the business district, Cinelândia's shops, bars, restaurants and movie theatres are popular day and night. There are also several decent hotels there that are reasonably priced. The bars and restaurants get crowded at lunch and after work, when there's often samba in the streets. There's a greater mix of cariocas here than in any other section of the city. Several gay and mixed bars stay open late.

Lapa By the old aqueduct that connects the Santa Teresa trolley and the city centre, Lapa is the scene of many a Brazilian novel. This is where the boys became men and the men became infected. Prostitution still exists here but there are also several music clubs, like the Circo Voador and Asa Branca, and some very cheap hotels. Lapa goes to sleep very late on Fridays and Saturdays.

Santa Teresa This is one of Rio's most unusual and charming neighbourhoods. Along the ridge of the hill that rises from the city centre, Santa Teresa has many of Rio's finest colonial homes. In the 1800's Rio's upper-crust lived here and rode the *bonde* (cable car) to work in the city. The bonde is still there but the rich moved on and out long ago.

During the '60s and '70s many artists and hippies moved into Santa Teresa's mansions. Just a few metres below them the favelas grew on the hillsides. Santa Teresa was considered very dangerous for many years and is now heavily policed. It's still necessary to be cautious here, especially at night.

Flamengo & Catete Moving south along the bay, these areas have the bulk of inexpensive hotels in Rio. Flamengo was once Rio's finest residential district and the Catete Palace housed Brazil's president until 1954, but with the new tunnel to Copacabana the upper classes began moving out in the 1940s. Flamengo is still mostly residential, the apartments are often big and graceful, although a few high-rise office buildings have recently been built amongst them. With the exception of the classy waterfront buildings Flamengo is mostly a middle class area.

There is less nightlife and fewer restaurants here than in nearby Botafogo or Cinelândia, which are five minutes away by subway.

Parque do Flamengo & Praia do Flamengo Stretching along the bay from Flamengo all the way to the city centre, the Parque do Flamengo was created in the 1950s by an enormous landfill project. Under utilised during the week, with the exception of the round-the-clock football games (joining a few hundred spectators at a 3 am game is one of Rio's stranger experiences), the park comes to life on weekends.

The museum of modern art is at the northern end of the park; at the south end is Rio's, a big outdoor restaurant that's ideal for people and bay watching. The park is not considered safe at night.

Botafogo Botafogo's early development was spurred by the construction of a tram that ran up to the botanical garden linking the bay and the lake. This artery still plays a vital role in Rio's traffic flow and Botafogo's streets are extremely congested. There are several palatial mansions here that housed foreign consulates when Rio was the capital of Brazil. Also this area of town has fewer high rise buildings than in much of the rest of Rio.

There are not many hotels in Botafogo but there are lots of good bars and restaurants where the locals go to avoid the tourist glitz and high cost of Copacabana.

Copacabana The famous curved beach you know about. What's surprising about Copacabana is all the people who live there. Fronted by beach and backed by steep hills, Copacabana is for the greater part no more than four blocks wide. Crammed into this narrow strip of land are 25,000 people per square km, one of the highest population densities in the world. Any understanding of the Rio way of life and leisure has to start with the fact that so many people live so close together and so near to the beach.

Only three parallel streets traverse the length of Copacabana. Avenida Atlântica goes along the ocean. Avenida NS de Copacabana, two blocks inland, is one-

way, in the direction of the business district. One block further inland, Rua Barata Ribeiro is a one-way street in the direction of Ipanema and Leblon. These streets change their names when they reach Ipanema.

Copacabana is the capital of Brazilian tourism. It's possible to spend an entire Brazilian vacation without leaving it and some people do just that. The majority of Rio's medium and expensive hotels are here and they are accompanied by plenty of restaurants, shops and bars. For pure city excitement, Copacabana is Rio's liveliest theatre. It is also the heart of Rio's recreational sex industry. There are many *boîtes* (bars with strip shows) and prostitutes; anything and everyone is for sale.

From Christmas to Carnival there are so many foreign tourists, that Brazilians who can't afford to travel abroad, have been known to go down to Avenida Atlântica along the Copacabana beach and pretend they are in Paris, Buenos Aires or New York.

As always when there are lots of tourists there are problems. Prices are exorbitant, hotels are filled and restaurants get over-crowded. The streets are noisy and hot, and Copacabana is the place where you are most likely to get robbed in Brazil.

Ipanema & Leblon These are Rio's two most desirable districts. They face the same stretch of beach and are separated by the Jardim de Alah, a canal and adjacent park. They are residential, mostly upper class and becoming more so as rents continue to rise. Most of Rio's better restaurants, bars and nightclubs are in Ipanema and Leblon; there are only a few hotels, although there are a couple of good aparthotels.

Barra da Tijuca Barra is the Ipanema of tomorrow. Despite the long drive from the centre and the appallingly unplanned urban development, the city is quickly expanding into Barra. The beach is

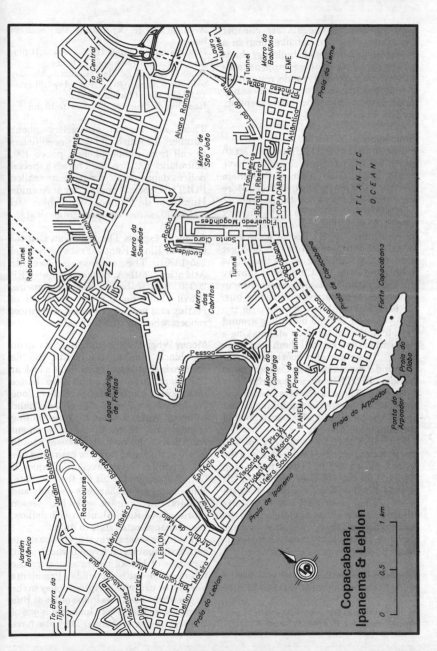

Copacabana, Ipanema & Leblon

beautiful and apartments are cheaper than those closer in, but like fungi in a rainforest hundreds of buildings have sprung-up wherever there happens to be an open space. Whether condo, restaurant, shopping centre or discotheque, these big, modern structures are, without exception, monstrosities.

Information

Tourist Office Both RIOTUR (tel 242-8000) and FLUMITUR (tel 252-4512) have tourist information hotlines. Call them from 9 am to 5 pm for any questions. More often than not they know the answer.

RIOTUR (tel 297-7177) is the Rio city tourism agency. They have offices at Rua da Assembléia 10, 8th floor, Centro with maps and brochures. You can also get these at their information booths at the main rodoviária, the Cinelândia subway station, Sugar Loaf and sometimes in your hotel. When arriving in Rio by bus, the RIOTUR booth at the rodoviária can save you a lot of time by calling around town to find a vacant hotel and making a reservation (you just tell them your price range). There are also booths at Sugar Loaf and downstairs in the Carioca metro station. RIOTUR is a powerful city agency, in charge of Carnival and many city events. It is often incredibly inefficient and is the target of many accusations of corruption and the like.

FLUMITUR (tel 252-4512) is the Rio state tourism agency. Their office is in the same building as RIOTUR's (metro stop Carioca) on the 7th floor. EMBRATUR (tel 274-2212) is Brazil's national tourism agency. Their main office is at Rua Mariz e Barros 13 near Praça da Bandeira on the north side of town. For the average traveller, neither of these agencies is worth a special trip.

Telephone International phone calls can be made from the following locations in Rio:

Aeroporto Santos Dumont, 5.30 am to 11 pm
Praça Tiradentes 41, open 24 hours

Avenida NS de Copacabana 462, open 24 hours
Rua Visconde de Pirajá 111, 6.30 am to 11 pm
Rodoviária Novo Rio, open 24 hours
Rua São José, 35 Ed Menezes Cortes, Monday to Friday 6.30am to 10 pm, Saturday 6.30 am to 12.30 pm, closed Sundays
Rua Dias da Cruz 182, 12.30 am to 10 pm

There are certain emergency phone numbers for which you don't need fichas to call from public phones: police 190, ambulance 192, fire 193. There is a special police department for tourists called POLTUR, open 24 hours a day at Avenida Humberto de Campos 315, Leblon (tel 259-7048), across the street from Scala.

American Express The American Express agent in Rio is Kontik-Franstur SA (tel 235-1396). The address is Avenida Atlântica 2316-A, Copacabana CEP 20040, Copacabana, Rio de Janeiro, Brazil. They do a pretty good job of getting and holding onto mail. Beware of robbers when leaving their office.

Money When the government eases up on the black market, trading in Rio de Janeiro is simple and open. Take a look at the *dólar paralelo (comprar)* exchange rates posted on the front page of *O Globo* or *Jornal do Brasil* (lower left hand column). At least when they are trading openly and there is no government crackdown, the exchange houses should give you the listed rate (for cash) and one or two points less for travellers' cheques. If not, shop around a bit for the best rate. Since currency exchange is a supply and demand ruled market, when high season tourists flood Rio de Janeiro with dollars, the exchange rate tends to drop.

There are several travel agents/casas de câmbio in the city on Avenida Rio Branco, a couple of blocks before and after the intersection with Avenida Presidente Vargas (be cautious carrying money in the city centre). The Casa Piano office at Rua Visconde de Pirajá 365, Ipanema is one of the best places to change. They also have an office in the centre at Avenida Rio Branco 88.

Cambitur has several offices: Rua Visconde de Pirajá 414, Ipanema; Avenida NS de Copacabana 1085, Copacabana and Avenida Rio Branco 31, Centro. Another is Exprinter at Avenida NS de Copacabana 371, Copacabana and Avenida Rio Branco 128 and 57, Centro.

If there is a crackdown and the government shuts down the exchange houses you may have to get a bit more creative. Hotels, travel agents and jewellers are good places to make enquiries. Perseverance is the key.

Consulates The following countries have consulates in Rio:

Argentina
    Praia de Botafogo 228, 2nd floor, Botafogo (tel 551-5198); open Monday to Friday midday to 5 pm.
Australia
    Rua Voluntários da Pátria 45, 5th floor, Botafogo (tel 286-7922); this is only an office; for the Australian embassy call Brasília (tel 061) 248-5569.
Bolivia
    Avenida Rui Barbosa, 664, No.101, Botafogo (tel 551-1796).
Canada
    Praia do Botafogo 228, 10th floor, Botafogo (tel 551-9542)
Chile
    Praia do Flamengo 382, No.401, Flamengo (tel 552-5349); open Monday to Friday 8.30 am to 1.30 pm.
Columbia
    Praia do Flamengo 82, No.202, Flamengo (tel 225-7582); open Monday to Friday 9 am to 1 pm.
Ecuador
    Praia do Flamengo 382, No.402, Flamengo (tel 552-4949); open Monday to Friday 8.30 am to 1 pm.
Great Britain
    Praia do Flamengo 284, 2nd floor, Flamengo (tel 552-1422); open Monday to Friday 9 am to midday and 1.30 to 4 pm.
Paraguay
    Rua do Carmo 20, No.1208, Centro (tel 242-9671); open Monday to Friday 9 am to 1 pm.

Peru
    Avenida Rui Barbosa 314, 2nd floor, Botafogo (tel 551-6296); open 9 am to 2 pm.
Uruguay
    Rua Arthur Bernardes 30, Catete (tel 225-0089); open 9 am to 1 pm.
United States
    Avenida Presidente Wilson 147, Centro (tel 292-7117); open Monday to Friday 8 am to 4 pm.

Visa Extension If you need to renew your visa for another three months go to the Polícia Marítima building (tel 203-2142, ramal (extension) 34) at Avenida Venezuela 2, Centro (near the far end of Avenida Rio Branco). They are open from 11 am to 5 pm for visa extensions. Bring a passport and money (the fee is around US$10).

Airlines All three major Brazilian airlines have their main offices in the centre (metro stop Cinelândia). You can also walk over to Aeroporto Santos Dumont where they have ticket counters and make reservations from there.

Varig/Cruzeiro (tel 292-6600 or 297-4400) has its main office in Centro at Avenida Rio Branco 277. There are also offices at Ipanema (tel 541-6343) Rua Rodolfo Dantas 16, and Rua Visconde de Pirajá 351, Ipanema (tel 287-9040). The city office is much more reliable and knowledgeable than the other Varig offices.

VASP (tel 292-2080) has a city office at Rua Santa Luzia 735. They also have offices at Copacabana (tel 235-3260) Avenida NS de Copacabana 291, and Ipanema (tel 292-2112) Rua Visconde de Pirajá 444.

Transbrasil (tel 297-4422 or 297-4477) is in the centre at Avenida Calógeras 30. The other offices are at Copacabana (tel 236-7475) Avenida Atlântica 1998, and Ipanema (tel 521-0300) Rua Maria Queteria 77.

Nordeste Linhas Aéreas (tel 220-4366) is at Aeroporto Santos Dumont. They go to Porto Seguro, Ilhéus and other smaller cities in the Northeast. Rio Sul (tel 262-6911) does the same for the South and is also at Aeroporto Santos Dumont. Cruzeiro do Sul (tel 297-4400) has an office at Avenida Rio Branco 128, and in Copacabana (tel 257-1257) at Avenida NS de Copacabana 291.

International airlines include:

Aer Lingus
    Avenida Rio Branco 25, 2nd floor, Centro (tel 233-5633);
    Rua Visconde de Pirajá 595, No 503, Ipanema (tel 259-5198)
Aerolineas Argentinas
    Rua São José 40, Centro (tel 224-9242);
    Avenida NS de Copacabana, Copacabana 312 (tel 255-7144)
Aero Peru
    Praça Mahatma Gandhi 2, Centro (tel 240-1622 or 240-0722)
Air France
    Avenida Rio Branco 257, Centro (tel 220-3666)
Alitalia
    Presidente Antônio Carlos 40, Centro (tel 210-2192)
Avianca
    Rua México 11-C (tel 240-4413)
British Airways
    Avenida Rio Branco 108, 21st floor (tel 221-0922 or 242-6020)
Equatoriana
    Avenida Almirante Barroso 63, No.1908 (tel 240-1075)
Iberia
    Avenida Presidente Antônio Carlos 51, 8th floor, Centro (tel 210-2415)
Japan Air Lines
    Avenida Rio Branco 108, 19th floor (tel 221-9663)
KLM
    Avenida Rio Branco 311 (tel 210-1342)
Lan Chile
    Rua São José 70, 8th floor (tel 242-1423)
LAP-Lineas Aereas Paraguayas
    Avenida Rio Branco 245, 7th floor (tel 220-4148)
Lloyd Aero Boliviano
    Avenida Calógeras 30 (tel 220-9548)
Lufthansa
    Avenida Rio Branco 156 (tel 398-3855 or 262-0223)

Pan Am
    Avenida Presidente Wilson 165 (tel 240-2322)
SAS
    Avenida Presidente Wilson 231, 21st floor (tel 210-1222)
Viasa
    Rua do Carmo 7, 4th floor (tel 224-5345)

Travel Agents Rio has no shortage of tourist agents eager to give advice, book bus and plane tickets and organise tours. They can also save you unnecessary trips to the rodoviária by selling bus tickets in advance. Many agents are brusque and unhelpful but some are quite the opposite so it's usually worth walking out on type one to find type two.

Quest Tours (tel 224-7843) is in the centre at Rua do Carmo 11, apt 701 and is run by Argentines who speak some English, Spanish and French. They do tours, hotel reservations – and they can be helpful with discount airline tickets if you're flying out of the country, something most travel agents know little about. Le Monde Passagems, Viagems e Turismo (tel 287-4042) on Rua Visconde de Pirajá 260, Ipanema is useful (speak to Mark or Carlos) as is Paxtur Passagems e Turismo (tel 205-1144) on Largo do Machado 29.

Guidebooks There are several guidebooks to Rio. *Guia Rio* by Quatro Rodas has the most comprehensive list of restaurants, hotels, bars and activities. It's well-worth buying if you're going to be in Rio a long time and is sold at newsstands. It's in Portuguese, with a small English section, and only covers the upper end of the price spectrum. The *Insider's Guide to Rio* by Christopher Pickard covers a lot of ground, has excellent descriptions of Rio's fine restaurants and is in English, but it's also not oriented to the budget traveller (you can find it in hotel souvenir shops).

A few years ago EMBRATUR put out a great book called *Rio Antigo: Roteiro Turístico-Cultural do Centro da Cidade*. Filled with detailed maps and descriptions of the city's historic buildings, it's a great book if you're a student of colonial architecture and plan on seeing the remains of old Rio. The book is hard to find, but some bookstores and museums still have back copies.

Bookstores Finding good English books is difficult outside of Rio and São Paulo, so stock up before heading into the interior. Nova Livraria Leonardo da Vinci is Rio's best: Avenida Rio Branco, 185 (it's one floor down on the sobreloja level). Edifício Marques do Herval (tel 224-1329) is a serious bookstore, with Rio's largest collection of foreign books and a knowledgeable staff which, for a tidy sum, will order just about any book you want. They're open 9 am to 7 pm Monday to Friday and 9 am until midday on Saturday.

Livraria Dazibão at Rua Visconde de Pirajá 571-B in Ipanema stocks many Penguin paperbacks. Livraria Kosmos, next to the Copacabana Palace Hotel, has many foreign language books. Each of the Livraria Siciliana chain has a collection of paperbacks in English. They are at Visconde de Pirajá 511, Ipanema and Avenida NS de Copacabana 830, Copacabana.

Stúdio Livros at Rua Visconde de Pirajá 462 has current magazines and paperbacks in English. At the Leblon end of Ipanema, Rua Visconde de Pirajá 640, there's a small used-book store that has old, funky and cheap books in English.

Libraries IBEU (Instituto Brasil-Estados Unidos) has an English library with a large fiction collection, many books about Brazil in English and a good selection of current magazines from the US. To check out books you have to take classes there or buy a membership, but it's cheap. The library is at Avenida NS de Copacabana 690, 3rd floor.

With an American passport you can get into the American consulate which has a fantastic periodical room. It's on the corner of Avenida Presidente Wilson and Rua México; open 8 am to 4 pm, Monday to Friday.

Language Classes IBEU (tel 255-8939) has a variety of Portuguese language classes that start every month or two. The cost for a six week course that meets three times a week is only about US$50. For information stop by Avenida NS de Copacabana 690, 5th floor. There are several companies that offer group and private lessons but they are expensive; for information check the English language newspaper the *Latin America Daily Post*.

Next door there is a Casa Matos store which sells the language books for the IBEU courses. It's a good place to pick up a book or dictionaries to study Portuguese on your own.

Health The Rio Health Collective offers a free telephone referral service. They speak English and can hook you up with an English-speaking doctor or specialist, and in any part of the city. If you can speak some Portuguese, Jaime Rabacov (tel 286-5394 or 286-9345) is an excellent general practitioner.

24 Hour Pharmacies Drogaria Cruzeiro (tel 287-3636), Avenida NS de Copacabana 1212, Copacabana; Farmácia Piauí (tel 274-8448) Avenida Ataulfo de Paiva 1283, Leblon and Rua Barata Ribeiro 646, Copacabana (tel 255-7445).

Hair A haircut can be a real treat in Brazil. For men at least we can recommend a couple of master barbers in Copacabana who eschew high-tech electric cutters and rely on sharp scissors, a precise eye and skilled hands. Omar (tel 287-2991) is at Avenida NS de Copacabana 1344 at the corner Rainha Elizabeth; and José (tel 227-7894) is at the Salão Juvenil Rua Raul Pompeia 168-C.

Art Supplies Casa Matos is the big chain. They have a store in Ipanema at Avenida Atlântica 690. The small Arte Técnica is in Flamengo at Rua do Catete 228, loja 119. They have better quality supplies and also have poster tubes which can carry home some of Rio's best gifts – art prints, giant photos, posters, etc.

Walking Tour

There's more to Rio than beaches. Don't miss exploring some of the city's museums, colonial buildings, churches (of course) and traditional meeting places – restaurants, bars, shops and street corners. Here's our suggested walking tour. Many of the places mentioned are described in more detail in the appropriate sections. The centre of Rio, now a pot-pourri of the new and old, still has character and life.

Take a bus or the metro to Cinelândia and find the main square along Avenida Rio Branco, called Praça Floriano, today the heart of Rio. Toward the bay is the Praça Mahatma Gandhi. The monument was a gift from India in 1964. Behind the praça and across the road, the large aeroplane hanger is the Museum of Modern Art.

Praça Floriano comes to life at lunch time and after work when the outdoor cafes are filled with beer drinkers, samba musicians and political debate. The square is Rio's political marketplace. There's daily speechmaking, literature sales and street theatre. Most city marches and rallies culminate here on the steps of the old Câmara Municipal.

Across Avenida Rio Branco is the Biblioteca Nacional. Built in 1910 in the neoclassic style, it's open to visitors and usually has an exhibition. The most impressive building on the square is the Teatro Municipal, home of Rio's opera, orchestra and gargoyles. The theatre was built in 1905 and revised in 1934 under the influence of the Paris Opera. The front doors are rarely open, but you can visit the ostentatious Assyrian Room restaurant and bar downstairs (entrance on Avenida Rio Branco). Built in the '30s it's completely covered in tiles, with beautiful mosaics.

In Avenida Rio Branco you'll find the Museu Nacional de Belas Artes, housing some of Brazil's best paintings, and Funart which exhibits excellent popular art.

Now do an about-face and head back to the other side of the Teatro Municipal and walk down the pedestrian-only Avenida 13 de Maio (on your left are some of Rio's best suco bars). Cross a street and you're in the Largo da Carioca. Up on the hill is the recently restored Convento de Santo Antônio. The original church here was started in 1608, making it Rio's oldest. The church's Saint Antônio is an object of great devotion to many cariocas in search of husbands. The church's sacristy, from 1745, has some beautiful jacaranda-wood carving and Portuguese blue tiles.

Gazing at the skyline from the convent notice the Rubix-cube-like Petrobras building. Behind it is the ultra-modern ultra-ugly Metropolitan Cathedral (if you want to take a look, the inside is cavernous and cold with huge stained glass windows). If you have time for a side-trip, consider heading over to the nearby bonde that goes up to Santa Teresa.

Next find the shops along 19th century Rua da Carioca. The old wine and cheese shop has some of Brazil's best cheese from the Canastra mountains in Minas Gerais. They also have bargains in Portuguese and Spanish wines. Two shops sell fine Brazilian-made instruments, including all the Carnival rhythm-makers, which make great gifts. There are several good jewellery stores off Rua da Carioca, on Rua Ramalho Ortigão.

Whenever I'm near Rua da Carioca 39 I stop at the *Bar Luis* for a draft beer and lunch or snack. Rio's longest running restaurant, it was opened in 1887 and named Bar Adolf until WW II. For decades, many of Rio's intellectuals have chewed the fat while eating Rio's best German food here.

At the end of the block you'll pass the Cinema Iris, which used to be Rio's most elegant theatre, and emerge into the hustle of Praça Tiradentes. It's easy to see that this was once a fabulous part of the city. On opposite sides of the square are the Teatro João Caetano and the Teatro Carlos Gomez, which show plays and dance. The narrow streets in this part of town house many old, mostly dilapidated, small buildings. It's worth exploring along Rua Buenos Aires as far as Campo de Santana and then returning along Rua da Alfândega. Campo de Santana is a pleasant park, once the scene – re-enacted in every Brazilian classroom – of Emperor Dom Pedro I, King of Portugal, proclaiming Brazil's independence from Portugal.

Back near Avenida Rio Branco, at Rua Gonçalves Dias 30, hit the *Confeitaria Colombo* for coffee and turn-of-the-century Vienna. Offering succour to shopping-weary matrons since 1894, the Colombo is best for coffee (very strong) and desserts.

From here, cross Avenida Rio Branco, go down Rua da Assembléia, stop at Riotur and Flumitur if you want tourist information, then continue on to Praça 15 de Novembro. In the square is the Pyramid Fountain, built in 1789, and a crafts market. Facing the bay, on your right is the Palácio Imperial which was the royal palace of the king and seat of the government. With independence it was ingloriously relegated to the Department of Telegraphs. The building was recently restored and a couple of museums are being installed.

On the opposite side of the square there is the historic arch, the Arco de Teles, running between two buildings. Walking through the arch you'll see, immediately on your left, the elegant and very British *English Bar*. A good place for a quiet, expensive lunch or drink. The stores along the stone streets here have a waterfront character. There are several seafood restaurants, fishing supply stores and a couple of simple colonial churches. It's a colourful area.

Back at Praça 15 de Novembro take the overpass to the waterfront, where ferries leave to Niterói and Ilha da Paquetá. The ferry to Niterói takes only 15 minutes and you never have to wait long. Consider crossing the bay and walking around central Niterói if you have some time (the feel is different from Rio, much more like the rest of Brazil). Even if you return immediately the trip is worth it just for the view.

Facing the bay, the *Albamar Restaurant* is a few hundred metres to your right. It's in a green gazebo overlooking the bay. The food is good and the atmosphere just right. On Saturdays the building is surrounded by the tents of the Feira de Antiguidades, a strange and fun hodgepodge of antiques, clothes, foods and other odds-and-ends.

Maracanã

The stadium, Brazil's temple of soccer, and a colossus among coliseums easily accommodates over 100,000 fans and on occasion – the World Cup Game of 1950 or Pelé's last game – has squeezed in close to 200,000 crazed fans (although it's difficult to see how). If you like sports, if you want to understand Brazil, or if you just want an intense, quasi-psychedelic experience, then by all means go see a game of *futebol*, preferably a championship game or one between rivals Flamengo (Fla) and Fluminense (Flu).

Brazilian soccer, if not the best in the world, is certainly the most imaginative and exciting. Complementing the action on the field, the stands are filled with fanatical fans who cheer their team on in all sorts of ways: chanting, singing and shouting; waving banners and streamers with team colours; pounding huge samba drums; exploding firecrackers, Roman candles and smoke bombs (in the team colours); launching incendiary balloons; throwing toilet paper, beer and even dead chickens – possibly Macumba inspired. The scene, in short, is sheer lunacy.

Obviously, you have to be very careful if you go to Maracanã. Don't wear a watch or jewellery. Don't bring more money than you need for tickets, transport and refreshments. The big question is how to get to and from the game safely.

The big games are held Sundays at 5 pm year-round. Tourist buses leave from major hotels at 2.30 pm (they often run a bit late) for 5 pm Sunday games. They cost about US$15, which is a rip-off, but it's the safest and easiest way to get to the game. They drop you off and pick you up right in front of the gate and escort you to lower-level seats. Unfortunately this is not the best perspective for watching the game, but it is the safest because of the overhead covering which protects you from descending objects.

However you get to the stadium, it's a good idea to buy these lower-level seats, called *cadeira*, instead of the upper-level bleachers, called *arquibancada*. The price is US$3, unless it's a championship game when it's more.

The metro is closed on Sundays, and taking a bus or cab can be a hassle. Getting to the stadium isn't too difficult, catch a bus marked Maracanã (from Zona Sul 433, 432, 464, 455; from Centro 260) and leave a couple of hours before game-time. Returning to your hotel by bus is often a drag. The buses are flooded with passengers and thieves set to work on the trapped passengers. Taking a cab is a possible alternative, but they can be hard to flag down, the best strategy is to walk away from the stadium a bit.

Surprisingly, driving a car to the stadium is pretty easy. You should leave a couple of hours before kick-off and, for easy departure, park away from the stadium. The traffic isn't all that bad and if you arrive early you can watch the preliminary games.

Pão de Açúcar (Sugar Loaf)

Sugar Loaf, God's gift to the picture postcard industry, is dazzling. Two cable cars lift you 1300 metres above Rio and the Guanabara Bay. From here, Rio is undoubtedly the most beautiful city in the world. There are many good times to make the ascent, but sunset on a clear day is the most spectacular. As day becomes

night and the city lights start to sparkle down below, the sensation is delightful.

Everyone must go to Sugar Loaf, but if you can, avoid going from about 10 to 11 am and 2 to 3 pm when most tourist buses are arriving.

The two-stage cable cars leave about every 30 minutes from Praça General Tibúrcio (tel 541-3737) at Praia Vermelha in Urca. They operate Tuesday to Sunday from 8 am to 10 pm and Monday from 8 am to 7 pm. Occasionally they close an hour or so early for special shows so you might want to call ahead if you're going late at night. The price is US$1.

On top of the lower hill there's a restaurant/theatre. The Beija Flor samba school puts on a show Monday 9 pm to 1 am. Less touristy shows are the Friday and Saturday Carioca Nights. They have some excellent musicians, check the local papers for listings.

To get to Sugar Loaf take a bus marked Urca/Praia Vermelha from Centro and Flamengo (No 107 or No 442) and from Zona Sul No 511 or No 512. The open-air bus that runs along the Ipanema and Copacabana beaches also goes to Sugar Loaf.

Corcovado & Cristo Redentor

Corcovado is the mountain (hunchback) and Cristo Redentor is the statue (Christ the Redeemer). The mountain rises straight up from the city to 709 metres. The statue, with it's welcoming out-stretched arms, stands another 30 metres high and weighs over 1000 tons (a popular song talks about how the Cristo should have it's arms closed to it's chest because for most who come to Rio the city is harsh and unwelcoming).

The statue was originally conceived as a national monument to celebrate Brazil's 100 years of independence from Portugal. The 100 years came and went in 1922 without the money to start construction but in 1931 the statue was completed by French sculptor Paul Landowski, thanks to some financial assistance from the Vatican.

Corcovado lies within Tijuca National Park. You can get there by car or by taxi, but the best way is to go up the cog train – sit on the right hand side going up for the view. The round trip costs US$1.50 and leaves from Rua Cosme Velho 513 (Cosme Velho). You can get a taxi there or a bus marked Rua Cosme Velho – a 422, 498 or 108 bus from Centro, a 583 from Largo Machado, Copacabana and Ipanema or a 584 from Leblon.

During the high season, the trains, which only leave every 30 minutes, can be slow going. Corcovado, and the train, are open from 8 am to 8 pm, although the train sometimes closes at 6 pm in the slow season. Needless to say, the view from up top is spectacular.

Santa Teresa Bondinho

The 'little tram' goes over the old aqueduct to Santa Teresa from Avenida República do Chile and Senador Dantas in Centro. Santa Teresa is a beautiful neighbourhood of cobblestone streets, hills and old homes. Favelas down the hillsides have made this a high-crime area. Go, but don't take valuables. Public transportation stops at midnight, so you'll need a car if you are going anywhere after that time. There's a small Museu do Bonde at the central tram station with a history of Rio's tramways since 1865 for bonde buffs.

The Museu Chácara do Céu Rua Murtinho Nobre, 345 Santa Teresa (tel 224-8981) is up in Santa Teresa. It has a good collection of art and antiques.

Hang-Gliding

If you weigh less than 80 kg (about 180 lb) and have US$45 you can do the fantastic – hang-glide off Pedra Bonita on to Pepino Beach in São Conrado. This is one of the giant granite slabs that towers above Rio. No experience is necessary. To arrange a double flight (voo duplo) go out to Pepino and the pilots will be waiting on the beach.

We're told that the winds are very safe here and the pilots know what they are doing. Guest riders get their bodies put in a kind of pouch that is secured to the kite.

Our pilot, Assad, picked us up in his beat-up Volkswagen with the asa delta (hang-glider) rack. The climb up to the take-off point was awesome. Pedra Bonita looms over São Conrado's Pepino beach like Fantasia's Bald Mountain. The road winds up through the lush green Tijuca forest. Assad's driving was not soothing, in fact if his driving was any indication of how he was going to pilot the hang-glider, I didn't want to have anything to do with him. We were waved on through the private entrance to the hang-gliding area and the engine whined as we climbed the extremely steep hill.

When we reached the top Assad assembled the glider, untangled the cables, tightened the wing nuts and slipped elastic bands over the wing struts. Up close the glider looked flimsy. We put on our flight suits and practised a few take-off sprints near the platform, literally a five-metre-long runway of wooden boards inclined 15° downhill. We were 550 metres above sea level and a few km inland from the beach. If I were a rock and Rio were a vacuum, it would take me over 10 seconds to kiss the dirt.

I wore old sneakers for traction and two good luck charms to amuse the ambulance crew I anticipated would be piecing through the tangled ball of crumpled metal, torn nylon and mangled flesh down below.

With the glider resting at the top of the runway we clipped ourselves onto it and checked the balance of the craft as we hung side by side. Assad adjusted his weight belt, all the straps, the velcro leg cuffs and helmet and gave me very brief instructions: hold on to the cuff of his shorts, keep my hands to myself, resist the temptation to hold the control bar or cables (this can throw the glider so don't touch), and when he gave the count 'um, dois, tres, ja!', go very fast.

Assad checked the windsocks on either side of the platform, the surface of the sea and the rippling of the leaves to ascertain the direction, speed and flow of the wind. He wanted a smooth wind coming inland from a flat sea.

'Um, dois, tres, ja!'. Four bounding steps and we were flying. It's not the free fall sinking feeling you get from elevators, but a perfect calm. I closed my eyes and felt as if I was still –

the only movement, a soft wind caressing my face. Miraculously, it seemed I was suspended between earth and sky. To our left was Rocinha, the most famous of Zona Sul's favelas, to the right Pedra Bonita, and below us the fabulous homes of Rio's rich and famous. We floated over skyscrapers and Pepino beach, made a few lazy circles over the water and before I knew it, it was time for the descent. Upon landing we stood upright, Assad pointed the nose up, the glider stalled and we touched down on the sand gentle as a feather.

It wasn't until after the flight that Assad told me that he is not without recourse. In an emergency, like a sudden change in weather, a hang-glider pilot can fly down to the beach in less than 90 seconds. Assad also carries a never-used parachute which is designed to support the weight of two passengers and the glider itself which is supposed to fall first and cushion the blow.

Flight Information Assad can mount a camera with flash, wide-angle lens, motor drive and a long cable release on a wing tip to take pictures of you in flight. Other flyers provide this service, too. If you want to take pictures yourself you must realise that take-off and landing pictures are impossible since you can't be encumbered with equipment. Your camera must fit into the velcro pouch in the front of your flight suit. It's a good idea to have the camera strap around your neck and a lens cover strapped to the lens or you will risk beaning a carioca on the head and losing equipment. Flights are usually extremely smooth so it's possible to take stable shots. Hang-gliders themselves are dramatic shots especially when taken from above.

Know your exact weight in kg in advance. Ideally your pilot should be heavier than you. If you're heavier than the pilot, he will have to use a weight belt and switch to a larger glider. If you're over 80 kg, you're out of luck. You don't need any experience or special training, anyone from seven to seventy years can do it.

Cautious flights depend on atmospheric conditions. Assad reckons he can fly all but three or four days per month and conditions during winter are even better.

For the experience of a lifetime, it's not that expensive, US$45 for anywhere from 10 to 25 minutes of extreme pleasure. For US$60 Assad will supply film and camera gear, for US$70 he will drive you to and from your hotel. Arrive early and allow for plenty of time to get things assembled, move things around, etc. If you fly early in the day, you have more flexibility with delays.

The best way to arrange a flight is to go right to the far end of Pepino beach on Avenida Prefeito Mendes de Morais where the fly-boys hang out (and Niemeyer is building the headquarters of the Voo Livre club). Assad can be reached on 237-5117. Other tandem glider pilots are Casimiro (tel 511-1500), Maurício (tel 208-1625) and Ruy (tel 226-5207). For more information call the Associação Brasileiro de Voo Livre (tel 220-4740 & 208-1625). They also offer classes.

Bateau Mouche
This private company has modern boats that cruise Guanabara Bay and go out into the Atlantic. They usually have a morning and afternoon cruise that costs from US$20 to US$30. The scene is too slick-touristy for my taste but the voyage out into the ocean is undeniably beautiful. Don't take their bay cruise because for a fiftieth of the price you can take a ferry or hydrofoil to Paquetá Island and cover much of the same ground while travelling with the locals.

City Sunset
Sunset is a nice time to be around the central plaza in the city. The sky can be beautiful and floodlights illuminate the big buildings like the municipal theatre and national library.

Ilha de Paquetá
This island in the Baía de Guanabara was once a very popular tourist spot and is now frequented mostly by families from zona norte. There are no cars on the island. Transport is by foot, bicycle (there are

literally hundreds for rent) and horse-drawn carts. There's a certain dirty decadent charm to the colonial buildings, unassuming beaches and businesses catering to local tourism. Sadly the bay is too polluted to safely swim in and the place gets very crowded.

Go to Paquetá for the boat ride through the bay and to see cariocas at play – especially during the Festa of São Roque which is celebrated over five days in August. Boats leave from near the Praça 15 de November in Centro. The regular ferry takes one hour and costs 5c. The hydrofoil is worth taking, at least one way. It gets to the island in 25 minutes and costs US$1. The ferry service (tel 231-0396) goes from 5 am to 11 pm, leaving about every hour. From January to April and in July the hydrofoil leaves every hour on the hour from Rio (7 am to 5 pm) and returns every hour on the half hour from Paquetá (7.30 am to 5.30 pm). The rest of the year, there are only four hydrofoils a day, each way.

Ferry to Niterói from Praça 15

This is the poor man's Bateau Mouche. It costs about 3c and the views are great, particularly returning to Rio around sunset. Over at Niterói you can walk around a bit to see Rio's poor relation or catch a local bus to Niterói's beaches. Leaving from Praça Quinze (in the centre) the ferry goes every couple of minutes and is always full of commuters. Buses to Praça Quinze include from Flamengo the 119; from Copacabana 119, 413, 415, 154, 455 and 474; from Ipanema 474 and 154.

Jóquei Clube

There's lots to see at the race track. The stadium, which seats 35,000, is on the Gávea side of the Lagoa at Praça Santos Dumont 31 (take any of the buses that go to Jardim Botânico). It's a beautiful horse racing track with a great view of the mountains and Corcovado; it costs only a few cents to enter. It's rarely crowded and the fans are great to watch – it's a different slice of Rio life. Racing is usually every Saturday and Sunday afternoon, and Monday and Thursday night.

Parks & Gardens

Tijuca Forest Tijuca is all that's left of the tropical jungle that once surrounded Rio de Janeiro. In 15 minutes you can go from the concrete jungle of Copacabana to the 120 square km tropical jungle of Tijuca Forest. A more rapid and drastic contrast is hard to imagine. The forest is exuberant green, with beautiful trees, creeks and waterfalls, mountainous terrain and high peaks. Candomblistas leave offerings by the roadside, families have picnics, and serious hikers climb the summit of Pico da Tijuca (1012 metres).

The heart of the forest is the Alto da Boa Vista with several waterfalls (including the 35 metre Cascatinha Taunay), peaks and restaurants. It's a beautiful spot. You can get maps at the entrance.

The entire park closes at sunset and is rather heavily policed. Kids have been known to wander off and get lost in the forest, it's that big. It's best to go by car, but if you can't catch a No 221, No 233 or No 234 bus marked Vista Chinesa, which will get you to the entrance of Alto da Boa Vista.

The best route by car is to take Rua Jardim Botânico two blocks past the Botanical Garden (heading away from Gávea). Turn left on Rua Lopes Quintas and then follow the Tijuca or Corcovado signs for two quick left turns until you reach the back of the Botanical Garden where you go right. Then follow the signs for a quick ascent into the forest and past the Vista Chinesa (get out for a view) and the Mesa do Imperador. Go right when you seem to come out of the forest on the main road and you'll see the stone columns to the entrance of Alto da Boa Vista on your left in a couple of km.

You can also drive up to Alto da Boa Vista by driving out to São Conrado and turning right up the hill at the Tijuca Forest signs.

Jardim Botânico Open daily from 7 am to 5 pm, the garden was first planted by order of the prince-regent Dom João in 1808. There are over 5000 varieties of plants on 141 hectares. Quiet and serene on weekdays, the botanical garden blossoms with families and music on weekends. The row of palms, planted when the garden first opened, and the Amazonas section with the lago Vitória Regia are some of the highlights.

The garden is on Rua Jardim Botânico 920. To get there take a Jardim Botânico bus: from Centro any one of the bus Nos 172, 409, 438; from zona sul, Nos 558, 571; from Leblon No 574. Note that these buses don't coincide with Rio tourist booklet info. It's not a bad idea to take insect repellent.

After the garden walk go a few blocks down Rua Jardim Botânico, away from the beach, to *Alfaces* at Rua Visconde da Graça 51 for an excellent light lunch with an assortment of salads, good desserts and outdoor tables.

Parque Lage Just a few blocks down from the Jardim Botânico at Rua Jardim Botânico 414 this is a beautiful park at the base of Tijuca Forest. There are gardens, little lakes and a mansion which now houses the Instituto de Belas Artes – there are often art shows and sometimes performances there. It's a tranquil place, with no sports allowed and a favourite of families with small children. It's open from 8 am to 5.30 pm. Take a Jardim Botânico bus.

Parque do Flamengo Flamengo is a park with loads of fields and a bay for activities and sports. There are three museums – Museu Carmen Miranda, Museu dos Mortos da Segunda Guerra Mundial, and Museu de Arte Moderna. Inside the park, along the bay, the *Barracuda Rio* restaurant (tel 265-3997) is a great spot for bay and people watching. There's a deck and tables outside where you can drink or eat, and inside you can get a more substantial meal; they are also open for dinner.

To get there take the bus marked Aterro do Flamengo; from Centro No 125 or No 132 and from zona sul No 511 or No 512.

Parque da Catacumba With high-rise buildings on both sides, Catacumba is on the Morro dos Cabritos, which rises from the Lagoa. It was the site of a favela which was destroyed to make the park. A shaded park for walkers only, it's a good place to escape the heat and see some excellent outdoor sculptures. At the top of the hill there is a great view. Catacumba also has free Sunday afternoon concerts, during the summer in its outdoor amphitheatre, featuring some of Rio's best musicians. Check the Sunday newspaper for details.

Parque da Cidade Up in the hills of Gávea, this park is also calm and cool, and popular with families. Open daily from 7 am to 5 pm, the Museu da Cidade is on the park grounds.

Parque do Catete The grounds of the old presidential palace are now the Parque do Catete, a quiet refuge from the city, which has monkeys hanging from the giant trees.

Quinta da Boa Vista Rio's main park and museum of natural history makes a great Sunday outing and if you want to make a day out of it the nordeste fair (see Things to Buy) and Maracanã soccer stadium are both nearby.

Museums
National Museum The Museu do Primeiro Reino and its grand imperial entrance are still stately and imposing, and the view from the balcony to the royal palms is majestic. However the graffitied buildings and unkempt grounds have suffered since the fall of the monarchy. The park is large and busy, and because it's on the north side of the city you'll see a good cross-section of cariocas.

Open Tuesday to Sunday 10 am to 5 pm, museum admission is 40c (free on Thursdays). The old palace museum has many interesting exhibits: dinosaur fossils, sabre tooth tiger skeletons, beautiful pieces of pre-Columbian ceramics from the littoral and planalto of Peru, a huge meteorite, hundreds of stuffed birds, mammals and fish, gory displays of tropical diseases and exhibits on the peoples of Brazil.

The latter are most interesting. Rubber gatherers and Indians of the Amazon, lace workers and *jangadeiro* fishermen of the Northeast, candomblistas of Bahia, gaúchos of Rio Grande do Sul and *vaqueiros* of the sertão are all given their due. What's neat about these exhibits is that with a little bit of effort and a lot of travelling you can see all of these peoples in the flesh. The Indian exhibit is particularly good – better than that of the FUNAI Museu do Índio. Take buses marked Quinta; from Centro take the metro or bus No 284; from zona sul bus Nos 474 or 475.

Museu Nacional de Belas Artes At Avenida Rio Branco 199 (tel 240-0160) this is Rio's premier fine art museum. There are over 800 original paintings and sculptures in the collection. The most important gallery is the Galeria de Arte Brasileira with 20th century classics such as Cândido Portinari's Café. There are also galleries with foreign art (not terribly good) and contemporary exhibits.

The museum is open Tuesday and Thursday from 10 am to 6.30 pm; Wednesday and Friday from midday to 6.30 pm; and Saturday, Sunday and holidays from 3 to 6 pm. Photography is prohibited. Take any of the city-bound buses and get off near Avenida Rio Branco, or take the metro to Carioca station.

Museu Histórico Nacional Recently restored, this colonial structure is filled with historic relics, but the displays are not particularly interesting, more a hodge podge of whatever the curator found in the closet. This may change, the museum is supposedly being completely reorganised. The building is near the bay at Praça Marechal Âncora (tel 240-7978).

Fundação Nacional de Arte (FUNART) FUNART, at Rua Araújo Porto Alegre 80 (right next to Museu de Belas Artes on Rio Branco), is actually the Ministry of Culture. It also has excellent exhibitions of contemporary and popular art in forms such as photos and cartoons. They are often quite topical and political.

Walk past the guards and there are three small galleries right in front of you. On the 2nd floor there are exhibits in the broad hallways and Rio's finest public bathrooms. The men's bathroom has one of Brazil's best collections of 19th century English plumbing technology. Of particular interest are the rare, giant urinals, which, like imperial England herself, humble all who stand before them. The galleries are open during working hours and sometimes later into the night. To get there, take a bus headed for the centre and get off at Avenida Rio Branco, or take the subway and get off at Carioca station.

Museu do Folclore Edson Carneiro The small Edson Carneiro museum should not be missed – especially if you're staying nearby in the Catete/Flamengo area. It has excellent displays of folk art – probably Brazil's richest artistic tradition – a folklore library and a small crafts store with some wonderful crafts and books at very cheap prices.

The museum is part of FUNART, the government art agency. It's now in two buildings; one next to the grounds of the Catete Presidential Palace, the other inside the grounds. The address is Rua do Catete 181, Catete and it's open Monday to Friday from 11 am to 6 pm and Saturday, Sunday and holidays from 3 to 6 pm.

Museu da República & Catete Palace The Museu da República and the Catete

Palace have been closed for restoration. Built between 1858 and 1866, the palace was occupied by the president of Brazil from 1896 until 1954, when Getúlio Vargas killed himself. The museum, which occupies the palace, has a good collection of art and artefacts from the republican period.

Museu do Índio At Rua das Palmeiras 55, Botafogo the Museu do Índio (tel 286-8799) has a good library with over 25,000 titles, a map and photo collection and a quiet garden. The Indian exhibits in the National Museum at the Quinta da Boa Vista are better.

Museu H Stern At Rua Visconde de Pirajá 490 you may find the 12 minute guided jewellery tour interesting if you're in the neighbourhood. With a coupon you can get a free cab ride to and from the store and anywhere in Rio Sul.

Carmen Miranda Museum The small Carmen Miranda Museum in Parque do Flamengo is across the street from Avenida Rui Barbosa 560 (near the Hotel Glória) and is open Tuesday to Friday from 11 am to 5 pm and Saturday and Sunday 1 to 5 pm. Carmen, of course, was the Brazilian bombshell although she was actually born in Portugal. She made it to Hollywood in the 1940s and has become a cult figure in Rio. During Carnival hundreds of men dress up as Carmen Miranda look-a-likes. The museum is filled with Carmen memorabilia and paraphernalia including costumes, posters, postcards, T-shirts (US$8) records (US$3) and a small exhibit.

Museu de Arte Moderna At the northern end of Parque do Flamengo, looking a bit like an airport hanger, is the modern art museum. Construction began in 1954, but for much of the past few years all that one has been able to see of the museum are its grounds, done by Brazil's most famous landscape architect Burle Marx (who landscaped Brasília).

The museum was devastated by a fire in 1978 which consumed much of its collection. It is still being renovated and therefore is often closed so tel 210-2188 before going.

Naval Museum In Bauru, behind the Modern Art Museum, the Naval Museum is open Tuesday to Friday 11.30 am to 5.30 pm, Saturday and Sunday from 9 am to 5.30 pm. It documents the Brazilian Navy's role in WW II and has ship models.

The Beaches
The beach, a ritual and way of life for the carioca, is the common denominator. People of all walks of life, in all shapes and sizes congregate on the sand. To the casual observer one stretch of sand is the same as any other. Not so. The beach is complex. Different times bring different people. Different places attract different crowds. Before and after work exercise is the name of the game. Tanning is heaviest before 2 pm. On prime beach days, the fashionable pass the morning out at Pepino or Barra beaches and the afternoon back at their spot in Ipanema.

Every 20 metres of coastline is populated by a different group of regulars. For example, Arpoador beach has more surfers and people from the zona norte. In front of the luxury hotels you'll always find tourists and a security force watching over them. Wherever you do go, don't take valuables.

Praia Flamengo This popular beach is a thin strip of sand on the Guanabara Bay with a great view – the park and beach were a landfill project. Within an easy walk of most of the budget hotels in Catete/Flamengo, there's a different class of carioca here than on the luxurious beaches to the south, and it's fun to watch them play. Swimming isn't recommended in any of the bay beaches because of the sewage and industrial waste that pollutes the water.

Praia Botafogo This small beach is on a calm bay inlet looking out at Sugar Loaf. The Rio Yacht Club and Bateau Mouche are next door.

Praia Copacabana/Leme The world's most famous beach runs 4.5 km in front of one of the world's most densely populated residential areas. From the scalloped beach you can see the granite slabs that surround the entrance to the Guanabara Bay – a magnificent meeting of land and sea. The last km to the east, from Avenida Princesa Isabel to the Leme hill, is called Leme beach. When you go to Copacabana, which you must, do as the locals do, bring only the essentials. This is the best place in Brazil to get robbed. It's also not a good idea to walk down by the water at night.

There's always something happening on the beach during the day and on the sidewalks at night: drinking, singing, eating and all kinds of people checking out the scene; tourists watching Brazilians, Brazilians watching tourists; the poor, from nearby favelas, eyeing the rich, the rich avoiding the poor; prostitutes looking for tricks, johns looking for treats.

Praia Arpoador This small beach is wedged between Copacabana and Ipanema. There's good surfing here and a giant rock that juts out into the ocean with a great view.

Praia Ipanema/Leblon These two are really one, although the beach narrows on the Leblon side, separated by the canal at Jardim de Alah. Ipanema, like the suburb, is Rio's richest and most chic beach. There isn't quite the frenzy of Copacabana, and the beach at Ipanema is a bit safer and cleaner. There are only two sidewalk cafes facing the ocean in Ipanema – *Barril 1800* and *Albericos* – and one in Leblon – *Canecão*.

Ipanema is an Indian word for dangerous, bad waters. The waves can get big and the undertow is often strong. Be careful and swim only where the locals are swimming.

Different parts of the beach attract different crowds. Posto nine is Garota de Ipanema beach, right off Rua Vinícius de Morais. Today it's also known as the Cemetério dos Elefantes for the old leftists, hippies and artists who hang-out

there. The Farme de Armoedo at Rua de Armoedo, also called Land of Marlboro, is the gay beach. In front of the Caesar Park Hotel there's a very young crowd.

Praia Vidigal Under the Sheraton Hotel and the Morro Dois Irmãos, the beach is a mix of the hotel and favela dwellers who were pushed further up the hill to make way for the Sheraton.

Praia Pepino/São Conrado After the Sheraton there is no beach along the coast for a few km until Pepino beach in São Conrado. You can also take Avenida Niemeyer to the tunnel leading to Barra da Tijuca.

Pepino is a beautiful beach, less crowded than Ipanema. Currently Rio's most 'in' beach, it's popular with the surfing set and many in their 20s. Along the beach are two big, resort hotels, the Hotel Inter-Continental and Hotel Nacional. Behind them, nestled into the hillside, is Brazil's biggest favela, Rocinha.

Bus Nos 546 and 553 go to Pepino. Don't take valuables as these buses are frequent targets of robbers. There is also an executive bus (No 2016 São Conrado) that goes along Copacabana and Ipanema beaches to Pepino.

Praia Barra da Tijuca The next beach out is Barra. It's 12 km long, with clean, green water. The first few km are filled with bars and seafood restaurants (*Peixe Frito* is recommended). Further out there are only barracas on the beach. It's calm on weekdays, and crazy on hot summer weekends.

Ten years ago Barra was semi-deserted, today its skyline is rapidly being filled in with high-rise condominiums. It's a shame to see this kind of uncontrolled, unplanned growth in such a beautiful place.

Further Out The beaches further south – Prainha, Grumari, Marambaia – are very beautiful and worth exploring but not easily accessible by public transport.

They only get busy on weekends, when bus lines swell. All have barracas. Prainha, the next beach past Barra, is one of the best surfing beaches in Rio. Grumari, is arguably the prettiest beach near the city. There is a restaurant on the beach where the crabs are good.

To reach these beaches by car you can either turn off the Rio to Santos road, BR101, at Barra and follow the beach road. If it's a busy weekend, wait a few km and turn left at Estrada Bemvindo Novais at Recreio dos Bandeirantes or Estrada Vereador.

Carnival

A pagan holiday originating perhaps in the Roman Bacchanalia celebration of Saturn or in the ancient Egyptian festival of Isis. Carnival was a wild party during the middle ages until tamed in Europe by Christianity, but the sober church of the Inquisition could not squelch Carnival in the Portuguese colony, where it came to acquire African rhythms and Indian costumes.

People speculate the word Carnival derives from *caro-vale* meaning 'goodbye meat'. The reasoning goes something like this: for the 40 days of Lent, nominally Catholic Brazilians give up liver or flank steaks. To compensate for the big sacrifices ahead they rack up sins in a delirious carnal blow-out in honour of King Momo.

Carnival is celebrated everywhere in Brazil and each region has a particular way of celebrating. In Bahia, Carnival is celebrated in the streets under the blasting loudspeakers of the trio elétrico trucks; in Recife and Olinda merry-makers dance the frevo. These are more authentic Carnivals than Rio's glitzy celebration which has become the big draw for the tourism industry. More than anywhere else in Brazil, it is a spectator event, but it's a fantastic spectacle nonetheless. Every year wealthy and spaced-out foreigners descend on Rio en masse, get drunk, get high, bag some sunrays and exchange exotic diseases. Everyone gets a bit unglued this time of year and there are lots of car accidents. Some of the leaner and meaner cariocas can get a little ugly with all the sex, booze and flash of money. Apartment rates and taxi fares triple and quadruple and some thieves keep to the spirit of the season by robbing in costume.

The excitement of Carnival builds all year and the pre-Lenten revelry begins well before the official dates of Carnival. A month before Carnival starts, rehearsals at the *escolas de samba* (samba clubs) are open to visitors on Saturdays. The rehearsals are usually in the favelas. They're fun to watch, but for your safety go with a carioca. Tourist Carnival shows are held all year round at Scala, Plataforma 1 and up top at Pão de Açúcar.

The escolas de samba are actually predated by *bandas* (non-professional equivalents of the escolas de samba) which are now returning to the Carnival scene as part of the movement to return Rio's Carnival to the streets. In 1986 there was a Banda da Ipanema, a Banda do Leblon, a Banda dos Mendigos (beggars), and a Banda da Carmen Miranda, among others. The bandas are great fun, a good place to loosen up your hip-joints for samba and excellent photo opportunities; transvestites always keep the festivities entertaining. Try RIOTUR for information on the scheduled bandas or just show up in Ipanema (most of them are in Ipanema) at Praça General Osório or Praça Paz around 5 pm or so, a couple of weekends before official Carnival.

Other street festivities are held in Centro on Avenida Rio Branco. RIOTUR has all the information.

Carnival Balls Carnival balls are surreal and erotic events. In one ball at *Scala* I saw a woman (transsexual?) bare her breasts and offer passers-by a suck while rickety old ladies were bopping away in skimpy lingerie. A young and geeky rich guy was dancing on tables with whores past their prime, young models and lithe young nymphets, all in various stages of undress. Breasts were painted, stickered with adhesive tattoos, covered with fish-net brassieres or left bare. Bottoms were spandexed, G-stringed and mini-skirted.

In Monte Líbano, all the action took place on the stages. One stage had a samba band, the other was crushed with young women. They didn't dance but ground their hips and licked their lips to the incessant, hypnotic music and the epileptic flashing of the floor lights. Throngs of sweaty photographers and video crews mashed up to the stage. Everyone played up for the camera, vying for space and the attention of the photographers. The Vegas headdresses, the pasty-faced bouncers and the rich men in private boxes overlooking the dance floor lent a Mafiosi feel to the place.

Carnival is the holiday of the poor. Not that you could tell from the price of the tickets to the balls. Some of them cost more than the monthly minimum wage. There are snooty affairs like the Pão de Açúcar ball (tel 541-3737, tickets about US$75) and the Hawaiian ball at the yacht club and raunchier parties in Leblon at *Scala* (tel 239-4448, US$40) and *Monte Líbano* (tel 239-0032, US$16). Tickets go on sale about two weeks before Carnival starts and the balls are held nightly for the week preceding Carnival and through Carnival.

In 1986 *Scala* held the Flamengo soccer club's Baile Vermelho e Preto (red and black ball) and the inimitable Gala Gay Ball. *Monte Líbano* the wildest place safe enough for tourists, hosted many hot events: Bum-Bum Night, Baile das Panteras, Baile das Gatas, Baile Fio Dental and the grand Baghdad Night. There are three rules of thumb: beautiful, flirtatious and apparently unescorted women are either escorted by huge, jealous cachaça crazed men wielding machetes or they are men with make-up and tits; everything costs several times more within the club, than outside; don't bring more money than you're willing to lose – the club bouncers are big, but not that effective.

The Sambódromo Parades In the sambódromo, a tiered street designed for samba parades, the Brazilians harness sweat, noise and confusion and turn it into art. The 16 top-level samba schools prepare all year for an hour of glory in the Sambódromo. The best escola is chosen by a hand picked set of judges on the basis of many components including percussion, the *samba-enredo* theme song, harmony between percussion, song and dance, choreography, costume, story-line, floats and decorations and others. The championship is hotly contested; the winner becomes the pride of Rio and Brazil.

The parades begin with moderate mayhem then work themselves up to a higher plane of frenzy. The announcers introduce the escola, the group's colours and the number of wings. Far away the lone voice of the *puxador*, starts the samba. Thousands more voices join him, then the drummers kick in, 600 to 800 per school. The booming drums drive the parade.

The samba tapes flood the air waves for weeks prior to the beginning of Carnival. From afar the parade looks alive. It's a throbbing beast and slowly it comes closer, a pulsing Liberace-glittered, Japanese-movie-monster slime-mould threatening to engulf all of Rio in samba and vibrant, vibrating mulatas.

The parades begin with a special opening wing or *abre-alas* which always displays the name of the school and the theme of the escola. The whole shebang has some unifying message, some social commentary, economic criticism or political message but it's usually lost in the glitter. The abre-alas is then followed by the *commissão de frente* who greet the crowds. The escola thus honours its

elderly men for work done over the years.

Next follow the main wings of the escola, the big allegorical floats, the children's wing, the drummers, the celebrities and the bell-shaped Baianas twirling in their elegant hoop skirts. The Baianas honour the history of the parade itself which was brought to Rio from Salvador in 1877. The *mestre-sala* (dance master) and *porta-bandeira* (standard bearer) waltz and whirl. Celebrities, dancers and tambourine players strut their stuff. The costumes are fabulously lavish: 1½-metre-tall feathered headdresses, flowing sequin capes, rhinestonestudded G-strings.

The floats gush neo-baroque silver foil and gold tinsel. Sparkling models sway to the samba, dancing in their private Carnivals. A nubile young lady falls into my neighbour's lap. He adjusts her sequins and sets her back on her path. All the while the puxador leads in song, repeating the samba-enredo for the duration of the parade. Over an hour after it began, the escola makes it past the arch and the judges' stand. There is a few minutes pause. Globo and Manchete TV cranes stop bobbing up and down over the Pepsi caps and bibs of the foreign press corps. Now garbage trucks parade down the runway clearing the way for the next escola. Sanitation workers in orange jump-suits shimmy, dance and sweep, gracefully catch trash thrown from the stands and take their bows. It's their Carnival, too. The parade continues on through the night and into the morning, eight more samba schools parade the following day, and next week the top eight schools will parade once more in the parade of champions.

Getting tickets at the legitimate prices can be tough. Many tickets are sold 10 days in advance of the event. People queue up for hours and travel agents and scalpers snap up the best seats. Seats in private boxes have been sold for US$200. But don't fret. It's possible to see the show without paying an arm and a leg. The parades last eight to 10 hours each and no-one can or wants to sit through them that long. Unless you're an aficionado of an escola that starts early, don't show up at the sambódromo until midnight, three or four hours into the show. Then you can get tickets at the grandstand for about US$16. And if you can't make it during Carnival, there's always the cheaper (but less exciting) parade of champions the following week. If you can avoid it, don't take the bus to or from the Sambódromo.

Carnival Dates Starting dates for Carnival in coming years are:

1990	25 February	1994	14 February
1991	10 February	1995	26 February
1992	1 March	1996	17 February
1993	21 February	1997	9 February

Places to Stay

Rio has a star system. Hotels are ranked from one star for the cheapest to five for the most luxurious. Rio has 11 five-star hotels to choose from, 14 four-star hotels, 27 three-star hotels, 29 two-star hotels, three one-star hotels and 47 hotels unclassified by EMBRATUR (our specialty), but still regulated. Hotels which are not regulated by Embratur sometimes slip in additional charges and other assorted petty crimes against the tourist. Threaten to call SUNAB price regulation if this happens, discuss a price before accepting a room, and also ask if a 10% service charge is included. Unless otherwise indicated breakfast is included in the following hotels.

At Carnival time hotel prices go up and everyone gives dire warnings of no place to stay. For the past couple of years, etc however, there have been enough rooms as many people go to other cities for Carnival.

Also, when there is a big discrepancy between the official and parallel exchange rates, the big hotels will try to hold their rooms for overseas bookings which are paid at the official rate. This means that sometimes these hotels claim to be booked-up far in advance and then will have rooms available at the 11th hour.

Places to Stay – bottom end

The best area for budget hotels is Glória/Catete/Flamengo. This used to be a desirable part of the city and is still quite nice. Many of the places used to be better hotels so you can get some nice rooms at very reasonable prices. These hotels are often full from December to February so reservations are not a bad idea.

From Glória to Lapa, near the aqueduct, on the edge of the business district there are several more budget hotels. Generally, these are hardly any cheaper than the hotels further from the city in Catete, yet they are run-down and the area is less safe at night. If, however, everything else is booked-up you'll see several hotels if you walk along Rua Joaquim Silva (near the Passeio Público), then over to Avenida Mem de Sá, turn up Avenida Gomes Freire and then turn right to Praça Tiradentes. The *Hotel Marajó* at Avenida Joaquim Silva 99 is recommended.

Glória The *Hotel Turístico* (tel 225-9388), Ladeira da Glória 30, is one of Rio's best budget hotels. It's across from the Glória metro station, 30 metres up the street that emerges between two sidewalk restaurants. The rooms are clean and safe, with small balconies. Senhor Antônio, the owner, is from Spain and very friendly. The hotel is often full but they do take reservations. Singles/doubles start at US$5.50/9.

The *Monte Castelo* (tel 222-1733), Rua Cândido Mendes 201, is another very popular hotel. It's on the other side of the Glória Metro station one block away back towards the centre of town. Singles/doubles start at US$4/5.50. Nearby, the *Hotel Cândido Mendes* is at Rua Cândido Mendes 117. It's just a bit more expensive and they have modern rooms with air-con.

Right near the Glória metro station, the *Hotel Benjamin Constant*, Rua Benjamin Constant 10 is one of the cheapest places around. The rooms are small and dingy, but the cost is only US$1.50 per person.

Flamengo The *Hotel Flórida* (tel 245-8160), one of Rio's best budget hotels, is at Rua Ferreira Viana 69, near the Catete metro station. The *Flórida* has only two faults: it's not in Ipanema and it always seems to be booked up. Rooms have private baths with good, hot showers and polished parquet wood floors. Singles/doubles cost US$9.50/11 (air-con is available). There's a cheap little restaurant and a safe deposit for valuables. Make your reservations well in advance for stays during high season.

Across the street is the *Hotel Ferreira Viana* (tel 205-7396) at Rua Ferreira Viana 58 with cramped, but cheap rooms at US$3.50/5 for singles/doubles (US$6.50 with air-con) and an electric shower down the hall.

A few doors down the block at Rua Ferreira Viana 29 the *Regina Hotel* (tel 225-7280) is a respectable middle range hotel with a snazzy lobby, clean rooms and hot showers; singles/doubles start at US$16/20.

Close by on busy Rua do Catete are three budget hotels worthy of note. The *Hotel Monte Blanco* (tel 225-0121) at Rua do Catete 160 a few steps from the Catete metro stop is very clean, has air-con, and singles/doubles for US$6/10. Ask for a quiet room in the back. The *Hotel Imperial* (tel 205-0212) at Rua do Catete 186 is a tacky hotel with parking. The quality and prices of the rooms vary from US$12/15 for doubles without/with bathrooms. Some of the rooms have air-con. The *Hotel Rio Claro* (tel 225-5180), a few blocks down at Rua do Catete 233 has musty singles for US$6.50 and doubles with air-con, TVs and hot showers for US$11.50.

Turn down the quiet Rua Arturo Bernardes for a couple more budget hotels: the *Monterrey* and *Rio Lisboa* (tel 265-9599) are at 39 and 29 respectively. The first is a little more expensive but friendlier. Singles start at US$2.00 and doubles at US$3/4.50.

Further into Flamengo, near the Largo do Machado metro station, the elegant palm-tree lined Rua Paissandú has two excellent low to middle range hotels. The *Hotel Venezuela* (tel 205-2098) at Rua Paissandú 34 is clean and cosy. All the rooms have double beds, air-con, TV and hot water; it costs US$5.50/$11 for singles/doubles. The *Hotel Paissandú* (tel 225-7270) at Rua Paissandú 23 is a two-star Embratur hotel with singles ranging from US$7 to US$12.50 and doubles from US$13.50 on up to US$17. It's hard to get a room and for some unknown reason, the doors shut at midnight.

Other hotels in Flamengo include the *Hotel Barão do Flamengo* (tel 245-7965) at Rua Barão do Flamengo 36 which charges US$7/10 for singles/doubles. All rooms have air-con. The *Hotel Hispánico Brasileiro* (tel 225-7537) at Rua Silveira Martins 135 is near Flamengo beach. It has big, clean rooms, but none of them has showers. Singles are US$8 and doubles US$8 to US$15.

Places to Stay – middle

If you want to be near the beach, there are several reasonably priced hotels in Copacabana, a couple in Ipanema and even some in Leblon. They all get busy in the high season, so it might pay to book ahead. For the same price you can get a cheerier room in Flamengo or in the centre near Cinelândia (the Cinelândia hotels are also convenient if you're heading to the airport or rodoviária soon). But if you want to stay where the sun always shines and the lights never go out, you can probably find a Copacabana hotel room for US$10 to US$15.

Another relatively inexpensive option in Copacabana, Ipanema and Leblon is to rent an apartment by the week or the month. There are loads of agencies. You could try Brasleme Imóveis (tel 542-1347), Rua Barata Ribeiro 92-A, Copacabana and Apartur Imóveis (tel 287-5757), Rua

Visconde de Pirajá 371 S/204, Ipanema. If you are interested in renting an apartment, you could look under *temporada* in any daily newspaper. Renting an apartment really makes sense if you're staying a while or if there are several people in your group, but remember it's inevitably a bit of work finding and securing a place. There are also residential hotels or aparthotels that are often more spacious and less expensive.

Cinelândia The *Nelba Hotel* (tel 210-3235) at Rua Senador Dantas 46 is in a good central location in the heart of Cinelândia. A two-room, three-bed suite with a high pressure hot shower, air-con, phone and Tv is US$7.50/10.50 for singles/doubles. The *Itajuba Hotel* (tel 210-3163) at Rua Álvaro Alvim 23 has better rooms (with refrigerators) than the Nelba Hotel and is quieter. Singles/doubles are US$11.50/19.50 and suites US$23.

Rodoviária The *Hotel Turismo Ltd* (tel 263-4148) is near the Rodoviária Novo Rio bus station at Rua Sara 85. They have US$17 doubles with very hot air-con, TV and revolting but clean decor. Call them from the rodoviária and they will send a cab to pick you up free of charge. For something cheaper, the *Hotel Conceição* is close by at Rua Garibaldi 165.

Santa Teresa The *Hotel Santa Teresa* (tel 222-4355) is attractive and has a small pool, car parking and rates that include three meals. Singles/doubles with a bath are US$8/10.50. Santa Teresa is a beautiful neighbourhood, but somewhat dangerous and after midnight there is no public transport. The hotel is at Rua Almirante Alexandrino 660. To get there take the bondinho to Vista Alegre then follow the tracks down hill to the old mission-style building on the hill.

Leme *Hotel Praia Leme* (tel 275-3322) at Avenida Atlântica 866 is a two-star Embratur hotel costing US$17 for doubles with bath. It's right across the street from the beach and the employees are friendly and speak English. They also have apartments for rent at weekly and monthly rates on Avenida Princesa Isabel 7 (tel 275-5449). The rooms all have TVs and hot showers. The minimum stay is five days.

Copacabana The *Copa Linda* (tel 255-0938) is one of Copacabana's cheapest hotels. They have small and very basic singles/doubles for US$11 with a bath. It's at Avenida NS de Copacabana 116 on the 2nd floor. A couple of blocks away, the *Hotel Angrense* (tel 255-3875) is almost as cheap. The clean but dreary rooms cost US$8 a single and US$14 a double. It's at Travessa Angrense 25. The road isn't on most maps but it intersects Avenida NS de Copacabana just past Rua Santa Clara.

There are several hotels that offer more for the money than the two just mentioned. Right nearby, the *Grande Hotel Canada* (tel 257-1864), Avenida NS de Copacabana 687, has singles from US$22 to US$28 and doubles from US$25 to US$31 (there is no elevator for the cheapest rooms). The rooms are modern with air-con and TV.

The *Hotel Martinique* (tel 521-4552) combines a perfect location with good rooms at a moderate cost. It's on the quiet Rua Sá Ferreira at number 30, one block from the beach at the far end of Copacabana. Clean, comfortable rooms with air-con start as low as US$17/24 for singles/doubles.

In the same class, the *Hotel Toledo* (tel 257-1990) is at Rua Domingos Ferreira 71. The rooms are as fine as many higher priced hotels. Singles/doubles start at US$22/24.50. The *Hotel Biarritz* (tel 255-6552) is a small place at Rua Aires Saldanha 54. Singles/doubles start at US$12/25 and all rooms have air-con and TV. Also try the *Apa Hotel* (tel 255-8112) at Rua República do Peru 305. Singles/doubles are US$20/29.

For more money the *Hotel Trocadero* (tel 257-1834), Avenida Atlântica 2064 is a good deal with singles/doubles at US$48/53. Along with the old *Excelsior* (tel 257-1950), Avenida Atlântica 1800, the *Riviera* is the least expensive hotel on the beachfront with singles/doubles at $US35/37.

Ipanema There are two inexpensive hotels in Ipanema. The *Hotel San Marco* (tel 239-5032) is a couple of blocks from the beach at Rua Visconde de Pirajá 524. Rooms are small but with air-con, TV, and fridge. Singles/doubles start at US$23/32. The *Hotel Vermont* (tel 521-0057), Rua Visconde de Pirajá 254 also has very simple rooms at $US15/16.50. Call for reservations at both these hotels.

There are a few other hotels that are relatively inexpensive for the area, with rooms starting at around US$30. The *Ipanema Inn* (tel 287-6092) Rua Maria Quitéria 27 is on a quiet street half a block from the beach. Singles cost from US$26/30 and doubles are US$29/35. You can get an ocean side apartment at the *Arpoador Inn* (tel 247-6090), Rua Francisco Otaviano. This six-floor hotel is the only hotel in Ipanema or Copacabana that doesn't have a busy street between your room and the beach. The beachfront rooms are more expensive than those facing the street but the view and the roar of the surf makes it all worthwhile. Singles cost between US$20/44 and doubles are between US$26/49. This must be one of the best deals in Rio.

The *Hotel Carlton* (tel 259-1932), Rua João Lire 68, is on a very quiet street in Leblon. It's a small, friendly hotel, away from the tourist scene (children are free). There is an excellent hotel bar. Singles/doubles are US$33/35.50.

Places to Stay – top end
The *Rio Flat Service* (tel 274-7222) has three residential hotels that are more like apartments. All rooms have a living room and a kitchen. Without the frills of fancy hotels, they still have a swimming pool, breakfast and maid service. Apartments start at US$33. The *Apart Hotel* (tel 256-2633), Rua Barata Ribeiro, 370, Copacabana and the *Copacabana Hotel Residência* (tel 256-2610), Rua Barata Riveiro 222, are both very similar.

Of the many top hotels in Rio, the *Ouro Verde* (tel 542-1887), Avenida Atlântica 1456, is recommended for its comfort and service. The *Everest Rio* (tel 287-8282), Rua Prudente de Morais 1117 is one of the few hotels in Ipanema and not too expensive with US$72/85 singles/doubles. Avoid the *Rio Sheraton*, (tel 274-11222) which is removed from the city and somewhat isolated, and has offended the gods by displacing a favela. Singles/doubles cost US$103/114.

Places to Eat
As in most of Brazil, restaurants in Rio are abundant and cheap. The plates at the many lanchonetes are big enough to feed two and the price is only US$1 to US$2. For something lighter, and probably healthier, you can eat at a suco bar. Most have sandwiches and fruit salads. Make a habit of asking for an *embalagem* (doggie bag) when you don't finish your food. Wrap it and hand it to a street person.

Centro *Bar Luis*, Rua da Carioca 39 is a Rio institution, that opened in 1887. Bar Luis, the city's oldest cervejaria, on Rio's oldest street, is a bar-less old dining room serving good German food and dark draft beer at moderate prices. It's open Monday to Saturday for lunch and dinner, until midnight.

Hotel Ambassador at Rua Santa Luzia 651 off Avenida Graça Aranha has a businessman's lunch buffet which is a good way to fill your belly. For US$3 it's all you can eat, with plenty of fruits and desserts included.

Café do Teatro (tel 262-6164) at Avenida Epitácio Pessoa 1244 under the Teatro Municipal is a place to recall the good old days. Entering the dark, dramatic Assyrian room, with it's elaborate tile work and ornate columns, is like walking into a Cecil B De Mille film. The 70-year-old restaurant is where Rio's upper-crust used to dine and drink after the theatre; it must be seen to be believed. They serve lunch only and close on Saturdays and Sundays. It's somewhat expensive and semi-formal but don't be deterred, you can have a drink and light snack by the bar, listen to piano music, and breathe in the Assyrian atmosphere.

Confeiteria Colombo is at Rua Gonçalves Dias 34, one block from and parallel to Rio Branco. It's a big Viennese coffee house/restaurant where you can sit or stand and eat with a dessert or cake. The Colombo is best for coffee and cake or a snack.

Haku-San (tel 263-2719) at Rua Buenos Aires 45 is open from 11.30 am to 3 pm and then from 6 to 10 pm. It has all your favourite Japanese dishes and the plate of the day costs US$2. Other dishes are a little more expensive.

The *English Bar* (tel 224-2539) at Travessa do Comércio 11, Arco do Teles is open 11.30 am to 4 pm Monday to Friday. It's a quiet and classy English pub that serves a good lunch. Steaks go for US$3 to US$4, fish a bit less. It's off the Praça 15 de Novembro, right through the Arco do Teles.

The green gazebo structure near the Niterói ferry is *Alba Mar* (tel 240-8378) at Praça Marechal Âncora 184. It looks out on the Baia de Guanabara and Niterói. Go for the view and the seafood. It stays open from 11.30 am to 10 pm Monday to Saturday. Dishes start at US$3 and the peixe brasileira is recommended.

Cinelândia *Macrobiótica* (tel 220-7585) is one floor up at Rua Embaixador Regis de Oliveira 7. Macrobiotics is pretty popular in Brazil's cities and the food here is inexpensive and simple. Try the soup and rice dishes. They are open Monday to Friday from 11 am to 5.45 pm.

Lanchonete Bariloche is at Rua Alcindo Guanabara 24-D, across from Rua Senador Dantas. This cheap little counter joint has wood-grilled steaks for US$2 and is open until 2 am. *Churrascolândia Restaurante* (tel 220-9534) at Rua Senador Dantas 31 is a steakhouse which also has tasty steaks cooked on a wood grill for US$2.

Santa Teresa/Glória/Lapa *Arco da Velha Bar e Restaurante* at Praça Cardeal Câmara 132, Lapa is literally under the arch of the viaduct that the trolley crosses to head up to Santa Teresa. The Arco da Velha has great Bahian food and there is live music upstairs. It's a good place to eat if you're going to a show in the city.

Catete/Largo do Machado Area *Salé & Douce Ice Cream & Delicatessen* (tel 285-7347) is at Rua do Catete 311 next to the São Luis cinema and across from the Largo do Machado subway entrance. In addition to the *Babushka* ice-cream they have healthy sandwiches for about 75c.

Restaurant Amazónia (tel 225-4622) at Rua do Catete 234 has good steak and a tasty broiled chicken with creamed corn sauce, both for about US$3.

Adega Real do Flamengo (tel 265-7549) at Largo do Machado 30-A is an Iberian-style bar and restaurant, with garlic and meat hanging from the ceiling and wine bulging off the shelves. It serves various fish and meat dishes that vary from the usual Rio fare. Try the bolinhos de bacalhau (cod fish balls) for 80c with a Portuguese wine. For a feast try the roast cabrito (kid – the four-legged kind with little horns growing out of its head) US$3.

Flamengo/Botafogo/Catete David, the owner of *Rajmahal* (tel 541-6999) at General Polidoro 29, Botafogo, is British, but the food is all Indian and quite good. Meals cost about US$4 and the place is a bit off the beaten path. The restaurant is spacious and refreshingly calm for Rio. It's open in the evenings from Tuesday to Sunday.

Sol e Mar (tel 295-1896), Avenida

Repórter Nestor Moreira 11 is somewhat pricey and stuffy, complete with serenading violinists. It's one of the few places in the city that's right on the bay and the outdoor tables provide a spectacular view. Seafood dominates the menu. The restaurant is next to the Bateau Mouche at Botafogo beach and is open daily from 11 am to 3 am.

The popular *Churrascaria Majórica* (tel 245-8947), Rua Senador Vergueiro 11/15, Flamengo has good meat, reasonable prices and an interior done in gaúcho kitsch. It's open for lunch and dinner.

Cafe Lamas (tel 205-0198) at Rua Marques de Abrantes 18-A, Flamengo has been operating since 1874 and is one of Rio's most renowned eateries. It has a lively and loyal clientele and is open for lunch and dinner with a typical meaty menu and standard prices; try the grilled linguiça or filet mignon.

Leg Leg Lanches, Rua da Catete 228, loja 111, Flamengo is behind a shopping plaza. This little lunch and pastry place has some excellent, light and healthy lunches for less than US$1.

Leme *Mário's* (tel 542-2393) at Avenida Atlântica 290, Leme has an all you can eat for US$6 deal. Many people think this is Rio's best churrascaria and they may be right. Be prepared to wait during prime time as they get a big tourist crowd. It's open from 11.30 am to 1.30 pm.

Restaurante Shirley at Rua Gustavo Sampaio 610-A has delicious Italian seafood plates from US$3 to US$8. Try the mussel vinaigrette appetiser or the octopus and squid in ink for US$5.

Copacabana *Lope's Confeiteria* at Avenida NS de Copacabana 1334 off Júlio de Castilhos is an excellent lanchonete with big portions and little prices for typical Brazilian food.

The *Americana Restaurant* on Avenida Rainha Elizabeth off Avenida NS de Copacabana has lunches and dinners which are hearty and reasonably priced.

The steak with potatoes or vegies is excellent for US$2.50.

Restaurante Lucas at Avenida Atlântica 3744 is across from Rua Lima 247-1606 and has reasonably priced German dishes starting at US$2.

Confeitaria Colombo at Avenida NS de Copacabana and Barão de Ipanema is a smaller version of the Colombo in the centre, but with the same colonial charm. For coffee, desserts and snacks stay downstairs, but take a look upstairs at the elegant dining room. Their cafe Viennese is excellent.

O Rei Do Caranguejo (tel 235-1249) at Rua Barata Ribeiro 771 is king of the seafood in Copacabana. They have enormous portions of fish and seafood. The crab is excellent and the price can't be beaten (US$2 to US$3) especially if you split dishes. This is one of our Rio favourites.

Arataca at Rua Domingues Ferreira 41 (near the American Express office) is one of several Arataca restaurants in Rio which feature the exotic cuisine of the Amazon. This place is actually a counter lunch stand and deli, around the corner from one of their regular restaurants, with the same food as the restaurants but for only half the price. In addition to the regional dishes such as vatapá US$2 and pato (duck) US$2.50 they serve real guaraná juice (try it) and delicious sorbets made from Amazonas fruits.

Mab's at Avenida Atlântica (the Copacabana side of Princesa Isabel, across from the Meridien) has excellent seafood soup in a crock, chock full of piping hot creepy-crawlies for US$2.50.

Cervantes at Avenida Prado Junior is Rio's best sandwich joint and is also a late night hangout for a strange and colourful crew. It's on the infamous Avenida Prado Junior, where everyone and everything goes at night. Meat sandwiches come with pineapple (US$1). The steaks and fries are excellent too.

The *Bahian Restaurant* at Rua Miguel Lemos 56 is not really called that but it's the style of food that Toninho and his wife Jacira serve. Toninho was a Brazilian soccer great and played for the world cup team in 1978. The food's good and the place is decorated with soccer memorabilia.

Macro Nature is across the road and down the Travessa Cristiano Lacorte from the Bahian Restaurant. It's the best vegetarian restaurant/health food store in Copacabana. The menu is brief and very natural; the soups excellent. They have sucos, sandwiches, yoghurt and health foods to go and everything is cheap. The *ponto de encontro de pessoas saudáveis* (the meeting point for healthy people) as they call themselves is open Monday to Friday from 9 am to 10.30 pm, Saturday and Sunday from 9 am to 6 pm.

Ipanema *Via Farme* (tel 227-0743) at Rua Farme de Amoedo 47 offers a good plate of pasta at a reasonable price, something which is usually hard to find. The four cheese pasta and the seafood pasta dishes are excellent and portions are large enough for two to share. Most dishes are less than US$3. They are open from midday to 2 am.

Barril at 1800 Avenida Vieira Souto and Avenida Rainha Elizabeth at the beach is open late into the night. This trendy beach cafe, below Jazzmania (see Entertainment), is for people meeting and watching.

After a day at Ipanema beach, you can stroll over to the *Shell Station* across the street from Barril 1800 for Babushkas terrific ice cream.

La Guillotine is at Teixeira de Melo 19, right off the beach. For a good typical lunch at the beach this small restaurant serves chicken, beef or fish with a choice of three salads all for about US$1. They have chopp beer (remember – it's pronounced 'shop-ee') and outdoor tables.

Next door to La Guillotine, the *Mustang Pancake & Steakhouse* is a great place to eat before or after the beach.

They have a couple of outdoor tables and serve inexpensive hamburgers, steaks and pancakes (these are not American-style pancakes, but more like crepes). The pancakes are big and tasty, but sometimes too salty.

Boni's, Rua Visconde de Pirajá 595 is a favourite for fast food. Excellent pastries and fresh coffee with enough force to turn Bambi into Godzilla.

Chaika, Rua Visconde de Pirajá 321 is open from 8 am to 2 pm; this is where the girl from Ipanema really eats. There's a stand-up fast food bar, and a restaurant in the back with delicious hamburgers, the sweetest pastries and good cappuccino (a rarity in Rio). Chaika's stays busy late into the night.

La Veronese Rua Visconde de Pirajá 29A is off Gomes Carneiro. For an inexpensive meal, Veronese has take-away Italian pastas, pizzas and pastries.

Porção de Ipanema (tel 521-0999), Rua Barão da Torre 218 has steadily been moving up in the churrasco ratings game. Again, it's all you can eat for about US$6 a person and they open at 11 am and close at 2 am.

Bar Lagoa on the lake, is Rio's oldest bar/restaurant. It doesn't open till 7 pm but only closes at 3 am. There's always a good crowd and you can just drink beer, or you can eat a full meal for US$3 to US$4. The food is excellent, the menu typical, and the atmosphere great.

Restaurante Natural (tel 267-7799) at Rua Barão da Torre 171 is a very natural health food restaurant which has an inexpensive lunch special with soup, rice, vegies and beans, for less than US$1. Other good dishes are pancakes with chicken or vegetables for US$1.50.

Delikats at Avenida Henrique Dumont near Rua Visconde de Pirajá is Rio's only deli and has lots of homemade food. They make the best potato knish south of New York. They also have pastrami, herring, rye bread and other treasures from the old country, but sadly no bagels.

Le Bon Jus at the corner of Teixeira de

Meio and Visconde de Pirajá is one of the best juice and sandwich stands in the city.

Leblon *Sabor Saúde*, Avenida Ataulfo de Paiva 630, Leblon is Rio's best health food emporium and is open daily from 8 am to 11 pm. They have two natural food restaurants; downstairs has good meals for US$1, while upstairs is more expensive (on Sundays upstairs they have great buffet feasts for US$2.50). There's also a small grocery store and take away food counter.

Cantinho de Gôa at Rua Almirante Guimarães 65-D near Ataulfo de Paiva (tel 259-0945) is a small friendly Indian restaurant and Charlie speaks English. It's best for lunch and at Saturday lunch you can sample all the dishes. For dinner they sometimes close early, so it is best to call ahead and let Charlie know you're coming. It's a bit on the expensive side with vegetarian curry for US$2 and meat curry at US$2.75.

Don't let the silly name put you off at *Restaurante Bozó* (tel 274-0147), Rua Dias Ferreira 50, Leblon, these people are very serious about their food. Try the scrumptious and filling post-cruzado-plan medallions of filet mignon wrapped in bacon and smothered in pepper sauce.

Most cariocas have a favourite churrascaria. The serious carnivores have a current favourite because last months favourite has slipped a bit. *Plataforma* (tel 274-4052) at Rua Adalberto Ferreira 32, Leblon is one of the best. It's always busy late at night and is a big hangout for actors and musicians. Prices don't vary much between churrascarias, it's all you can eat for about US$6. The restaurant is open from 11 am to 2 am daily.

Gávea *Guimas* (tel 259-7996), Jose Roberto Macedo Soares 5, Gávea is my favourite restaurant and the food is terrific although the prices are just a bit more than a typical filet at any one of a

hundred Rio restaurants. That's because the portions are not enormous.

Guimas offers what most restaurants in Rio lack: creative cooking. This is a US$20 a plate restaurant in the USA. Try the pernil de carneiro (lamb with onions) for US$3 or the oriental shrimp curry (US$4) and a Rio salad. The small, but comfortable open-air restaurant opens at 8 pm and gets crowded later in the evening.

Tijuca Forest *Os Erquilos* is a beautiful colonial restaurant in Alto da Boa Vista, Tijuca Forest. It has a typical menu which is not expensive. It is open Tuesday to Sunday from midday to 7 pm.

Breakfast If you're hungry for an American-style breakfast, head to one of the big hotels like the *Meridien*. They offer all you can eat, buffet-style breakfast with eggs, pancakes – the works – for US$3 a person. It's often possible to split a portion.

Ice Cream *Babushka's* and *Alex* are the two best ice cream chains in town.

Fine Dining Rio is loaded with fancy restaurants which are not that expensive for the visitor. In most you can go and spend less than US$10 – especially if you decline the couvert which is always a rip-off – and the most expensive are often less than US$20. Here's a list of some of the best:

Chinese
    Mr Zee (tel 294-0591), Rua General San Martin 1219, Leblon
French
    Laurent (tel 266-3131), Rua D Mariana 209, Botafogo
    Clube Gourmet (tel 295-1097), Rua General Polidoro 186, Botafogo
    Ouro Verde (tel 542-1887), Avenida Atlântica 1456
Italian
    Quadrifoglio (tel 226-1799), Rua Maria Angélica 43, Jardim Botânico

Polish
  A Polonese (tel 237-7378), Rua Hilário de Gouveia 116, Copacabana
Portuguese
  Antiquarius (tel 294-1049), Rua Aristides Espinola 19, Leblon
Swiss
  Casa da Suiça (tel 252-2406), Rua Cândido Mendes 157, Glória

Entertainment

To find out what's going on at night, pick up the *Jornal do Brasil* at any newsstand and turn to the entertainment section. On Sundays they insert an entertainment magazine called *Domingo* which lists the week's events. If you can't deal with another word of Portuguese, the big shows and fancier clubs will have announcements in the *Latin America Daily Post*.

Nightlife varies widely by the neighbourhood. Leblon and Ipanema have up-

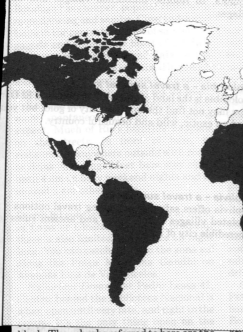

poorer areas on the outskirts of the city. The bar is frequented by many gays, blacks and zona norte people. It's a good change from the zona sul club scene but don't bring too much money to this part of town late at night. There's no cover charge.

Cafe Bohémia is a vegetarian restaurant by day and has wild transvestite shows on Friday, Saturday and Sunday nights. Cafe Bohémia is also unique, for a couple of dollars you get dancing and a very funny show if you can get by in Portuguese. It's in the centre on Avenida Santa Luzia, right off Avenida Rio Branco. The show starts about 1 or 2 am.

Bar Brasil in Lapa is an old bohemian hangout and is always alive. Lapa is generally an interesting area to explore at night.

Flamengo/Botafogo *O Viro da Ipiranga* (tel 25-4762) at Rua Ipiranga 54 in ...go is a warm bar with a relaxed ... great local musicians and it costs ... couple of dollars to get in. The ... varies but they have a couple of ... a week of Chorrinho, a bittersweet ... mental music from Rio.

...nga Rosa (tel 266-4996) at Rua ...ove de Fevereiro 94, Botafogo is off ...Voluntários da Pátria. There are ... inside and out, in a pleasant ...ard, and they have samba and ...e music from Thursday to Sunday ... minimal cover charge.

...a Branca, Rua do Catete 112, has ...ggae every Sunday night until 4 am ... good dance floor and low prices.

...o Da Pimenta, Rua Real Grandeza ...Botafogo is a great little joint for ...a, pagode and traditional Rio music ...t's very cheap. There's a lively, ...l crowd that knows how to dance and

...chrane, off Rua Voluntários da ...a, is one of Rio's more popular gay ... *Vaticano*, Rua da Matriz 62, ...fogo is a hip bar, popular with the

block. The suburbs referred to here are the ... artsy Rio set. Others to check out in

Botafogo are *Razão Social* on Rua Conde de Irajá, *Barbas* on Rua Álvaro Ramos and *Tamino* on Rua Arnaldo Quintela.

Copacabana *Galeria Alaska* on Avenida NS de Copacabana has a transvestite show and dancing and is a centre of gay Rio.

If you are homesick for punk culture try *Crepúsculo Sobre Cubatão* at Barata Ribeiro 543. It's frequented by 'darks' – Brazilian punks who wear black clothing and listen to Brazilian rock – they've come a long way from the Girl from Ipanema days. The club is owned by famous British train robber Ronald Biggs and suitable attire is required to enter.

Botanic (tel 294-7448) is a bar frequented almost exclusively by women. It is in Jardim Botânico at Rua Pacheco Leão 70.

Ipanema & Leblon *Jazzmania* (tel 287-0085), Rua Rainha Elizabeth at the sea, is Rio's most serious jazz venue. They have more international stars than any other club, but also the best of Brazilian jazz. The club is expensive at around US$8 cover on weekends and a little less on weekdays. The music starts about 11 pm and goes late.

People's (tel 294-0547), at Avenida Bartolomeu Mitre 370 in Leblon, is a posh club with some of the best names in jazz. To hear the great music you have to endure a US$8 cover charge and incessant smoking and talking from a snobby crowd. When it gets crowded the Ralph St Laurent crowd seems to get in and seated while the Lonely Planet crowd gets left at the door.

There are several other expensive restaurants/clubs in Ipanema and Leblon which have good jazz but look like a scene right out of Los Angeles or New York. *Chiko's Bar*, Avenida Epitácio Pessoa 560 on the Lake goes late and has no cover charge so you don't need to stay long. *Double Dose* (tel 294-9791), Rua Paul Redfern 44 has top names as does *Mistura Up* at Rua Garcia D'Avila 15, *Un Deux Trois* (tel 239-0198) at Rua Bartolomeu

Mitre 123 and *Equinox* (tel 247-0580) at Rua Prudente de Morais 729.

If you want to speak English, *Lord Jim's* British pub is the place. It's at Rua Paul Redfern 63 in Ipanema. The *Garota de Ipanema* is at Rua Vinícius de Morais 49 and has open-air dining. There are always a few foreigners checking out the place where Tom Jobim was sitting when he wrote 'The Girl from Ipanema'.

My favourite bar is also Rio's oldest. In a town that's losing it's tradition rapidly to modern western schlock, *Bar Lagoa* is a comforting breeze. They are trying to close it down to build a high-rise, high-tech, condo complex, but I don't think they'll succeed. Popular opposition is strong and militant. It's open from about 9 pm to 3 or 4 am with food, drink and a loud carioca crowd.

For something completely different in Ipanema the tiny *Salada Salada* restaurant has samba on its sidewalk on Fridays and Saturdays, after work until late. The crowd is mostly maids, porters, chauffeurs and clerks who work in Ipanema and stop by for some music and beer before heading to the far off suburbs where they live. It's a great scene and it's free. It's at the corner of Rua Garcia D'Avila and Barão da Torre.

Brazilian Dancing The following clubs have popular Brazilian music like samba and forró and Rio's popular dance classes. You're unlikely to find any tourists, or middle class Brazilians there. If you want to learn about Brazil and dance, or just watch Brazilians dancing, these are the places.

Pagode da Passarela has samba and pagode on Friday and Saturday nights. It's very crowded because it's affordable to almost everyone: 50 cents for women and US$1 for men. It's in the centre near Praça 11. *Bola Preta* (tel 240-8049) is a big dance house with different types of popular music each night. They have serestas, roda de samba and pagode. The club's right in the centre, on Avenida 13 de Maio.

Another good place to samba, but out in the suburbs, is *Pagode Domingo Maior* (tel 288-7297) at Rua Gonzaga Bastos 268, Vila Isabel. It's probably a good idea to go with a Brazilian if you don't speak Portuguese.

If you'd rather not go into town, *Clube do Samba* (tel 399-0892) is out in Barra at Estrada da Barra 65. They have samba and pagode Friday and Saturday nights. On Sunday you can get a feijoada there. This is a middle class club, with admission costing about US$3.

Forró is the popular dance music of Brazil's Northeast and there are plenty of Northeasterners in Rio going out dancing every weekend. I actually like the accordion-laced forró more than most of the current samba, and the dancing is a blast. *Forró Forrado* (tel 248-0524) is close to the budget hotels in Catete at Rua do Catete 235. From Thursday to Sunday nights they do the forró, starting up at 10 pm and going late. Admission is US$2.50 for men and US$1 for women. Another club for forró is *Estdantina* (tel 232-1149) at Praça Tiradentes 79, downtown. They go Friday and Saturday nights until about 4 am.

Big Shows *Circo Voador* under the Arcos da Lapa is a big tent with reggae, samba and trio elétrico music. The crowd is mostly from the north side. It's one of my favourites and is very reasonably priced. They get many of the best bands from Bahia and São Paulo.

Down the block is *Asa Branca* (tel 252-0966). They have samba and pagode shows that aren't for tours, though they are staged shows. *Scala*, *Plataforma I* and *Oba Oba* have expensive Vegas-style shows with naked samba. *Scala II* has many top musicians like Gilberto Gil playing there these days. It's a show house, flashy and artificial, but I'd go anywhere to see a Gil show.

Pão de Açúcar has a regular performance of the samba school *Beija Flor* Mondays from 9 pm to 1 am. It's expensive and touristy, but it's samba. Carioca Nights are held Fridays and Saturdays from 10 pm to 4 am. Mostly rock, but not always, the shows are not terribly expensive and are under the small pavilion on Morro da Urca – the first stop to Sugar Loaf. It's a spectacular view.

Canecão also gets the big stars of music. It's right next to the giant Rio Sul shopping mall at the entrance to the Copacabana tunnel.

Maracanãzinho is the smaller stadium next to Maracanã in São Cristóvão. The biggest shows, like Milton Nascimento play there.

Parque Catacumba, along the Lago, often has free outdoor concerts on Sundays at 5 pm. Check the newspaper.

Discos There are many discos with bright lights and loud music in the big city, but I can't help you much here if you're interested – pick up a tourist brochure. Interestingly, many of the discos have stiff dress codes and admission charges designed, in part, to deter the many prostitutes who come to meet tourists. Some are even called private clubs and require that you go through a concierge at your five-star hotel to pay US$20 to enter.

Help calls itself the biggest disco in Latin America and no one seems to doubt it. It's at Avenida Atlântica 3432 in Copacabana. *Apocalypse* is at the Hotel Nacional in São Conrado. *Circus* in Leblon is smaller. *Calígula* in Ipanema is where you might meet Sylvester Stallone, Brigitte Nielson or Ed Koch.

Samba Schools As early as October or November the samba schools begin holding rehearsals and dances, typically on Saturday nights. These are generally open to the public for watching and joining in the samba. Almost all the escolas da samba are on the north side of town and, of course, things get going late so you need a car or a taxi. Check with Riotur or the newspaper to get the schedules and locations. Each school has a club/arena but they also hold rehearsals around town. The school addresses are:

Portela, Rua Clara Nunes 81, Madureira
Mocidade Independente de Padre Miguel, Rua Coronel Tamarindo 38
São Clemente, Rua Assunção 63, Botafogo
Império Serrano, Avenida Ministro Edgard Romero 114, Largo de Madureira
Mangueira, Rua Visconde de Niterói 1072, Mangueira
Beija Flor, Rua Praçinha Wallace Paes Leme 1562, Nilópolis
Império da Tijuca, Rua Conde de Bonfim 1226, Usina da Tijuca

Things to Buy

Most stores are open Monday to Friday from 9 am to 7 pm (some stay open even later). Saturday is a half day of shopping, from 9 am to 1 pm. The malls usually open from 10 am to 10 pm, Monday to Friday, and 10 am to 8 pm on Saturdays. It's illegal for stores to open on Sundays.

Pé de Boi This store sells the traditional artisan handicrafts of Brazil's Northeast and Minas Gerais, and it's all fine work. There's lots of wood, lace, pottery and prints. It's not an inexpensive store; you have to buy closer to the source to get a better price, but if you have some extra dollars – ten to twenty at a minimum – these pieces are the best gifts to bring home from Brazil: imaginative and very Brazilian.

The small store is worth a visit just to look around. Ana Maria Chindler, the owner, knows what she's selling and is happy to tell you about it. Pé de Boi (foot of bull) (tel 285-4395) is in Botafogo on Rua Ipiranga 53. It is open Monday to Friday until 7 pm and on Saturdays from 10 am to 1 pm.

FUNAI Brazil's Indian agency, has a tiny craft shop at Avenida Presidente Wilson 16-A (it's actually around the corner from the main entrance). Open Monday to Friday from 9 am to midday and 1 to 6 pm, the store has woven papoose slings for

US$5, jewellery from 50c to US$5 and musical instruments.

Casa Oliveira (tel 222-3539) is at Rua da Carioca 70, Centro, Rio's oldest street. This beautiful music store sells a wide variety of instruments. They have all the noise makers that fuel the Carnival *baterias* (rhythm sections), a variety of small mandolin-like string instruments, accordions and electric guitars. These make great presents and it's a fun place to play even if you don't buy.

Rio Sul Brazilians', like Americans, seem to measure progress by shopping malls. They love to shop at these monsters. Rio Sul was the first mall to maul Rio. There are all kinds of stores. The C&F Department Store has a good range of clothes and is inexpensive. Rio Sul is right before you enter the Copacabana tunnel in Botafogo. There are free buses from Copacabana.

Hippie Fair This is an arts and crafts fair, with many booths selling jewellery, leather goods, paintings, samba instruments, clothes, etc. There is some awful stuff here and some OK stuff. Prices go way up during the peak tourist season and the air rings with the sounds of New Yorkers hunting down good buys.

The fair is every Sunday at the Praça General Osório in Ipanema. But you can find the same items at Praça 15 in the centre or at the end of Copacabana beach. If you're just beginning to travel in Brazil skip it.

Nordeste or São Cristóvão Fair

The nordeste fair is at the Pavilhão de São Cristóvão on the north side of town every Sunday, starting early and going until about 3 pm. The fair is very Northeastern in character. There are lots of *barracas* (stalls) selling meat, beer and cachaça; bands of accordions, guitars and tambourines playing the forró; comedy, capoeira battles and men selling magic potions. It's a great scene.

Of course there's plenty to buy. Besides food, they have lots of cheap clothes, some good deals on hammocks and a few good nordeste gifts like leather vaqueiro (cowboy) hats. If you're ready for adventure and have a car, it's best to arrive the night before the market. This is set-up time and also party time. At about 9 or 10 pm the barracas open for dinner and beer. Some vendors are busy setting up, others are already finished. Music and dance starts and doesn't stop until sunrise. It's great fun so long as you're careful.

Bum Bum Since your bathing suit has too much fabric attached to the seams, resign yourself to buying a new one. Bum Bum is the trend setter of the bikini world, and it knows it. It's not cheap, but you're paying for style not fabric. It's in Ipanema at Rua Visconde de Pirajá 437. If you're on a budget, there are plenty of other boutiques that sell bikinis for less money but with just as little fabric. Ki-Tanga is a good example.

Getting There & Away

Air Flights go to all of Brazil and Latin America. Shuttle flights to São Paulo leave from the convenient Aeroporto Santos Dumont, in the city centre along the bay. Almost all other flights – domestic and national – leave from Aeroporto Galeão.

Bus Buses go everywhere. All leave from the loud Novo Rio Rodoviária in São Cristóvão on the north side of town. Excellent buses leave every 15 minutes or so for São Paulo (six hours). Most major destinations have *leito* (executive) buses leaving late at night. These are very comfortable. Many travel agents in the city

sell bus tickets. It's a good idea to buy a ticket a couple days in advance if you can.

national bus times

Angra dos Reis	4 hours
Belém	70 hours
Belo Horizonte	7½ hours
Brasília	20 hours
Cabo Frio	3 hours
Curitiba	12 hours
Florianópolis	20 hours
Foz do Iguaçu	25 hours
Ouro Preto	9 hours
Parati	6 hours
Petrópolis	1½ hours
Recife	38 hours
Salvador	28 hours
São João del Rei	6½ hours
Vitória	8 hours

international bus times

Asunción, Paraguay	32 hours
Buenos Aires, Argentina	50 hours
Montevideo, Uruguay	39 hours
Santiago, Chile	75 hours

Getting Around

Airport Transport All international and nearly all domestic flights use Galeão International Airport, 15 km north of the city centre on Ihla do Governador.

There are two air-con airport bus routes operating from 5.20 am to 12.10 am, every 40 minutes to one hour (about US$1). One route goes to the centre and to the smaller Santos Dumont Airport (flights to São Paulo) and points in the centre, the other route goes to the city centre and along the beaches of Copacabana, Ipanema, Leblon, Vidigal, and São Conrado. The driver will stop wherever you ask along the route. Both stop at the rodoviária if you want to catch a bus out of Rio immediately.

You can catch the bus on the 2nd floor (arrivals) of the airport, at the Galeão sign. The tourist desk inside the airport has schedule and price information. If you're heading to the airport you can get the bus in front of the major hotels along the beach, but you have to look alive and flag them down. The bus company is Empresa Real. Galeão should be written on the direction sign.

Many taxis from the airport will try to rip you off. The safe course is to take a radio taxi where you pay a set fare at the airport. This is also the most expensive way to go. A common yellow and blue taxi is less expensive if the meter is working and if you pay what is on the fare schedule. A sample fare from the airport to Ipanema is US$6 in a common yellow and blue taxi versus US$12 in a radio-dispatched taxi. If you're entering Brazil for the first time, on a budget, a good compromise is to take a bus to somewhere near your destination and then take a short taxi-ride to your hotel.

Sharing a taxi from the airport is a good idea. Taxis will take up to four people. To ensure a little bit of security, before entering the taxi at the airport you can usually get a receipt with the licence plate of your taxi and a phone number to register losses or complaints. If you're headed to Leblon or Ipanema the Tunnel Rebouças is more direct than the beach route.

Aeroporto Santos Dumont is in the heart of the city on the bay. It's used for the São Paulo shuttle and some flights to a variety of other destinations like Porto Seguro or Belo Horizonte. You can take the same bus as for Galeão airport or get to the city and take a taxi, or simply walk to the airport from Centro.

Bus All buses going out of metropolitan Rio leave from the Novo Rio Rodoviário, Avenida Francisco Bicalho in São Cristóvão, about 20 minutes north of the centre (call 291-5151 for information). At the rodoviária you can get information on transportation and lodging at the Riotur desk on the 1st floor.

Special air-con buses go directly to the southern suburbs – Copacabana, Ipanema and Leblon. These buses or the taxis are safer than public buses if you have many valuables. They leave from in front of the main terminal exit. On the far corner, to your right as you leave from the same door, there is a small terminal for city buses on Rua Ecuador. There are bus numbers and routes posted, so it's pretty easy to get oriented.

For Copacabana, the best are bus Nos 126, 127 or 128. The best bus to Ipanema and Leblon is No 128, but you can also take No 126 or No 127 to Copacabana and then catch another bus to Ipanema and Leblon. For the budget hotels in Catete and Glória, take bus No 170 which goes down Rua do Catete or any bus that goes to the centre on Avenida Rio Branco. Get off near the end of Avenida Rio Branco and hop on the metro. Get off the metro at Catete station, which is in the heart of the budget hotel area.

Municipal Buses These are a real mixture of the good, the bad and the ugly. The good: Rio's buses are fast, frequent, cheap and, because Rio is long and narrow, it's easy to get the right bus and usually no big deal if you're on the wrong one. The bad: Rio's buses are often crowded, slowed down by traffic and driven by raving maniacs who drive the buses as if they were motorbikes. The ugly: Rio's buses are the scene of many of the city's robberies.

Don't carry any valuables on the buses. Don't advertise being a foreigner and have your money ready when you enter the bus. Be particularly cautious if you're boarding a bus in a tourist area. If you feel paranoid about something on the bus, get off and catch another.

In addition to their number, buses have their destinations, including the areas they go through, written on the side. Nine out of 10 buses going south from the centre will go to Copacabana and vice versa. All buses have the price displayed above the head of the money collector. The buses you need to catch for specific destinations are listed in the Things to See section.

There are also special air-con, executive buses called *ônibus frescão* or *Castelo*. Almost all of them go along Copacabana,

Ipanema and Leblon to the Castelo or Terminal Menezes Cortes (224-7577) on Avenida Erasmo Braga in Centro. They all have Castelo and one other destination (eg Leblon, Jardim de Alah, Copacabana) displayed on the front. The price is about double that of the regular buses, which is still pretty cheap. They are very comfortable and pretty safe. The Castelo – Hotel Nacional and Castelo – São Conrado buses are good to take for Pepino Beach. From the Castelo station there are buses to Petrópolis and Terosópolis, which saves a trip out to the rodoviária.

There is an open-air tourist bus that goes along the beaches and then over to Sugar Loaf.

If you're staying in the Catete/Flamengo area and want to get to the beaches by bus you can either walk to the main roadway along Parque Flamengo and take any bus marked Copacabana or you can walk to Largo do Machado and take the No 570 bus.

Metro Rio's excellent subway system is limited to points north of Botafogo and is open 6 am to 11 pm daily, except Sundays. The two air-conditioned lines are cleaner, faster and cheaper than buses (discounts are offered with multiple tickets). The main line from Botafogo to Saens Pena has 15 stops: Botafogo, Flamengo, Largo do Machado, Catete, Glória, Cinelândia, Carioca, Uruguiana, Presidente Vargas, Central, Cidade Nova and Estácio which is in common with both lines. At Estácio the lines split, the main line continues west towards the neighbourhood of Andarai making stops at Afonso Pena, Engenho Velho and Tijuca and the secondary line goes north towards Maracanã stadium and beyond. The main stops for Centro are Cinelândia and Carioca.

Taxi A Rio taxi is quite reasonable, if you're dividing the fare with a friend or two. Taxis are particularly useful late at

Rio Metro

Linha II

Irajá

Inhaúma

Linha I

Del Castilho

Tijuca

Mo da Graça

Engenho Velho

Maracanã

Afonso Pena

Estácio

São Cristavão

Cidade Nova

Central

Pres Vargas

Uruguaiana

Carioca

Cinelândia

Glória

Catete

Largo do Machado

Flamengo

Botafogo

usually posted on the passenger window, which is used to determine the fare.

Now, what to watch out for: most important make sure the meter works. If it doesn't, ask to be let out of the cab. The meters have a flag that switches the meter rate; this should be in the number one position (20% less expensive) except on Sundays, holidays, evenings from 10 pm to 6 am and when driving outside of Rio Sul (some taxi's will switch to the high rate near the airport which is legal). Make sure meters are cleared before you start (find out the current starting number). Make sure the tabela is original, not a photocopy. The taxi drivers that hang out near the hotels are sharks. It's worth walking a block to avoid them. Most people don't tip taxi drivers, although it's common to round off the fare to the higher number.

The meters are weighted towards distance not time, this gives the drivers incentive to drive quickly (for a head rush tell your driver that you are in a bit of a hurry) and travel by roundabout routes. Taxis don't always run during thunderstorms because alcohol powered cars stall easily, but buses usually plough on ahead. It's illegal for cabs to take more than four passengers. This is, of course, irrelevant except for the fact that most cabs won't do it because of conventions of the trade.

The white radio-taxi's (tel 260-2022) are 30% more expensive than the common taxi, but they will come to you and they are safer.

night and when carrying valuables, but they are not a completely safe and hassle-free ride. First, there are a few rare cases of people being assaulted and robbed by taxi drivers. Second, and much more common, the drivers have a marked tendency to exaggerate fares.

Here's how the taxi is supposed to operate: there should be a meter and it should work; there should be a current tabela to determine the fare; upon reaching your destination, check the meter and look that up on the tabela,

Car Rental These agencies can be found at the airport or clustered together on Avenida Princesa Isabel in Copacabana. There doesn't seem to be much price competition between the companies. Prices are not cheap, at about US$40 a day, but they go down a bit in the off-season. When they give prices on the phone the agencies usually leave out the cost of insurance, which is mandatory. Most agencies will let you drop off their cars in another city without an extra charge.

Motorcycle Rental Mar e Moto (tel 274-4398) rents motorcycles but it is cheaper to rent a car. They are in Leblon at Avenida Bartolomeu Mitre 1008.

Train The train station, Estação Dom Pedro II, is at Praça Cristiano Ottoni on Avenida Presidente Vargas. To get there take the metro to Central station.

Walking For God's sake be careful! Drivers run red lights, run up on sidewalks and stop for no one and nothing.

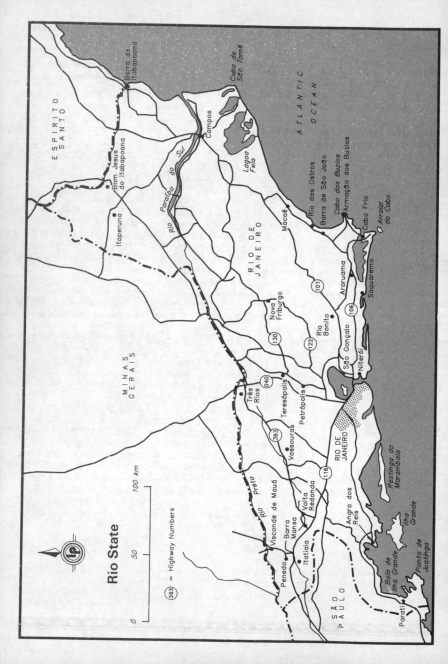

Top: Ipanema, Rio (SP)
Bottom: Offering to the Sea God, New Year in Rio (JM)

Top: Buzios, Rio State (WH)
Left: Cristo Redentor, Rio (WH)
Right: Sunset, Buzios, Rio State (WH)

Rio de Janeiro State

The small state of Rio de Janeiro offers the traveller much more than just the cidade maravilhosa. Within four hours of any point in the state, and often much less, there are beaches, mountains and forests that equal any in Brazil. Many of these places offer more intimate settings to meet cariocas who have known about the natural wonders surrounding the city for years. You won't find virgin sites, undeveloped for tourism, like you'll find in the Northeast. Tourism here is fairly developed and prices are higher than in most of Brazil. But if you only have a couple of weeks in Brazil and think that you'll be returning some day, an all Rio de Janeiro itinerary would be one of the best possible. And if you have all the time in the world, it's easy to pass a month or two in Rio de Janeiro.

The state, lying on the Tropic of Capricorn, has an area of 44,268 square km – about the size of Switzerland – and a population of about 13 million. The littoral is backed by steep mountains which descend into the sea around the border with São Paulo and gradually move slightly further inland in the north. This forms a thin strip of land nestled between the lush green mountains and the emerald sea, with beaches that are the most visually spectacular in Brazil.

Divided by the city of Rio and the giant Baía de Guanabara, with 131 km of coast and 113 islands, there are two coastal regions, with somewhat different natural characteristics: the Costa Verde to the west and the Costa do Sol to the east. Along the Costa Verde, where the mountains kiss the sea, there are hundreds of islands, including Ilha Grande and the Restinga de Marambaia, which soften the seas for easy swimming and boating. The calm waters, coupled with the natural ports and coves, allowed safe passage for Portuguese ships that came to Parati to transport sugar cane, and later gold, to Europe. It also protected pirates who found a safe haven on Ilha Grande.

There are beaches waiting to be explored, particularly further away from Rio city, where the coastal road stays close to the ocean and the views are spectacular. The most famous spots are Angra dos Reis, Parati and Ilha Grande.

To the north, the mountains begin to rise further inland. The littoral is filled with lagoons and swamp land. Stretching ever further from the coast are *campos* (plains) which extend about 30 km to the mountains. Búzios and Cabo Frio, famous for their beauty and luxury, are only two hours from Rio by car. Saquarema, one of Brazil's best surfing beaches, is even closer.

Driving due north from Rio city, after passing through the city's industrial and motel sections, you soon reach a wall of jungled mountains. After the climb, you're in the cool Serra dos Órgãos. The resort cities of Petrópolis and Teresópolis are nearby, as well as many smaller villages where cariocas go to escape the tropical summer heat. Hiking and climbing among the fantastic peaks of the Parque Nacional da Serra dos Órgãos, outside Teresópolis, is superb.

The other mountain region where cariocas play is in the corner of the state that borders São Paulo and Minas Gerais. Getting there is a longer trip, although it still only takes four hours. The route passes near the steel city of Volt Redonda.

Indian Names
Many places in Rio State include words in their names. These in

Araruama – place where the m
Baré – in the middle of many
Cunhambebe – women who

Grataú – ghost's den
Grumari – a kind of tree
Guanabara – arm of the sea
Guaratiba – place with much sun or place with many holes
Ipanema – place that gives bad luck or place of dangerous sea
Itacuruçá – stone's cross
Itaipu – stone that the sea hits
Itaipuaçu – little Itaipu
Jabaquará – crack in the earth
Jeribá – a kind of coconut palm
Mangaratiba – banana orchard
Maricá – belly
Parati – a kind of fish
Paratininga – dry fish
Sapeca – burned
Saquarema – lagoon without shells
Tijuca – putrid smelling swamp

West of Rio de Janeiro

ILHA GRANDE

Ilha Grande is what Hawaii must have been before the arrival of the British. It's all tropical beach and jungle, and because of a maximum security prison and a limitation on new hotels it is likely to remain this way. There are only three towns on the island. Freguesia de Santana is a small hamlet with no regular accommodation. Parnaioca has a few homes by a lovely strip of beach near the prison. Abraão has a hotel, an inexpensive pension and ferry connections to Mangaratiba and Angra dos Reis.

If you really want to get away from it all, Ilha Grande may well be the place to go. The options are pretty attractive. You can ~~r~~ent a boat for US$6 per hour, and buzz ~~a~~round to Freguesia or Parnaioca. There ~~are t~~rails through the lush steamy jungle ~~to var~~ious beaches around the island. For ~~exampl~~e, it is a 2-½ hour trek to Praia ~~Lopes Me~~ndes, claimed by some to be the ~~most beaut~~iful beach in all Brazil. Praia ~~__ __ __ __ __ __~~ also ranks up there. And ~~__ __ __ onl__~~y two of the island's 102

Abraão

Abraão could be a movie set for Papillon. It has a gorgeous palm tree studded beachfront of light faded homes and a tidy white church. Guards and military police compete for beer and curb space. It's OK to rouse the dogs sleeping on the dirt and cobblestone streets. They're friendly and seem to enjoy tramping around the island to the abandoned old prison, to the beaches, to the forest, to the hills and the waterfalls.

Information & Orientation In Abraão, to the left of the dock (when you're facing the ocean), are the ferry ticket office, a guest house for military police, the road to the commandant's house and the trail to the ruined old prison. To the right of the dock is the cobblestoned Rua da Igreja, and at the far end of the beach a clockwise trail leads around the island to Praia Lopes Mendes and the other beaches of Ilha Grande.

Places to Stay & Eat Lodging on Ilha Grande can be difficult to find. There are two expensive hotels on the island, a small

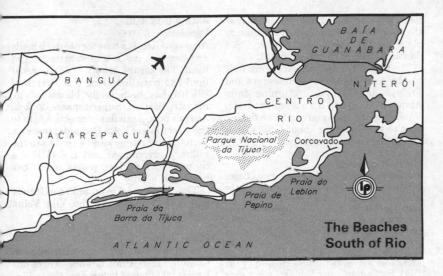

The Beaches
South of Rio

pension and a few campgrounds in Abraão including *Gilson Camping*, a small fenced in dirt plot. It may be possible to arrange a stay in a private home in Freguesia. Off-site camping is forbidden and not advised.

Perpendicular to the beachfront, Rua da Igreja is the second most important street on the island featuring a white church, a few bars and the *Hotel Mar da Tranquilidade* (tel 789-1614 or for reservations from Rio (021)392-8475). The hotel has charming doubles with hot showers and includes breakfast and lunch for US$13. The hotel restaurant is open to everyone – just give the cook several hours advance notice.

Right around the corner is *Restaurante Janethe's*, serving prato feitos with abundant portions of fresh fish (US$1.50). Rua da Igreja becomes a dirt road and continues over a little footbridge to the house of *Dona Pena*. Look for the yellow gate on the right hand side. Dona Pena has two rooms to let and is building a few more. One room for US$6 has pebble floors, foam mattresses on stone slabs, hot showers and mosquito screens. The other

room which costs US$7.50 has a kitchen and refrigerator.

Ilha Grande's other hotel, *Paraiso do Sol*, is minutes away by boat or two hours away on foot from Abraão at Praia das Palmas on the trail to Praia Lopes Mendes. The hotel is open from October through the high season. Doubles with full board are US$28. For information and reservations call (021) 263-6089.

Getting There & Away Going from Rio, catch a Conerj ferry either from Mangaratiba or Angra dos Reis. If you take the 5.30 am bus to Mangaratiba on EVAL bus lines, you can catch the daily 8.30 am ferry from Mangaratiba to Abraão. There are five buses a day from Rio to Mangaratiba at 6 am, 9 am, 12.30 pm, 3 and 7pm. Outgoing bus schedules are similarly staggered, beginning half an hour earlier.

The boat returns from Abraão Mangaratiba on Mondays, Wednes and Fridays at 5 pm, on Saturday Sundays at 4 pm and on Tuesda Thursdays at 11 am. Mangar nothing more than a poor litt town. If you're stuck there, you can stay at the *Hotel Rio Branco*, a small and dumpy place on the main square with US$4 doubles (US$9 with private bath).

The ferry schedule from Angra dos Reis to Abraão is Mondays, Wednesdays and Fridays at 3.30 pm, returning from Abraão at 10.15 am. It's a 90-minute ride. If you miss the ferry you can hire a fishing boat to the island for about US$24 from either Mangaratiba or Angra.

Life on Ilha Grande

We were on our way out the door to Praia Lopes Mendes when Dona Pena suggested we go to the police station and enquire about the fugitive situation. The convicts – some of Brazil's most dangerous and hardened criminals – make regular breaks from the prison and hide on the island until they can find a boat and take off. We didn't think much of Dona Pena's cautionary advice, but still we stopped by the DPO. Half a dozen armed military police were milling about the chief's desk.

'Have any fugitives escaped?' we asked.

'Yes, seven,' replied an MP.

'Is it dangerous?' we queried.

'Where do you want to go?'

'Praia Lopes Mendes.'

'On foot?'

Without waiting for our answer, the chief raised an eyebrow and continued, 'are you going to camp there?'

'No. Is it dangerous?'

There was no answer, or comforting looks from the other men. We persisted, 'would you go?'

'You can go. I am not going to stop you. But they are desperate men. They have nothing to lose.'

We joined up with three fishermen and two prison guards who were drinking chopp and snacking on olives.

Their conversation turned toward the prison break. 'The fugitives? They escaped 10 days ago and they're certainly off the island by now. You have nothing to worry about'.

We walked a km so down the beach where a ioca sporting speedos, a tan and a martini us to the trailhead to Praia Lopes es.

ANGRA DOS REIS

Population: 60,000

Angra dos Reis is a base for nearby islands and beaches, not a tourist attraction in itself. The savage beauty of the tropical fjord-like coastline along this stretch of BR-101 has been badly blemished by industrialisation. Super-tankers dock in Angra's port, a rail line connects Angra to the steel town of Volta Redonda, there's a Petrobras oil refinery and – thanks to the military government and the IMF – a controversial nuclear power plant has been built nearby.

The closest beaches are at Praia Grande and Vila Velha. Take the Vila Velha municipal bus.

Places to Stay

The *Hotel Sol da Praia*, Estrada do Contorno 1890, Praia Grande, Angra dos Reis is 200 metres before the Angra Inn. Take the Vila Velha bus from the rodoviária. The hotel has a beautiful courtyard and classy doubles for US$12.50.

The *Palace Hotel* (65-0032) at Rua Coronel Carvalho 275 is a clean 2-star Embratur hotel with TV, air-con, telephone, hot water and US$30 doubles. The *Cherry Hotel* at Rua Peroia Peixoto 64 is in the heart of Angra off Rua Coronel Carvalho and they charge US$4.50 per person. There's also the *Grande Hotel Acrópolis* (tel 65-0566) at Rua da Conceição 231 with doubles for US$20.

Getting There & Away

Angra dos Reis is three hours (150 km) from Rio de Janeiro's Novo Rio bus station.

PARATI

Population: 9000

Oh! Deus, se na terra houvesse um paraíso, não seria muito longe daqui!
(Oh! God if there were a paradise on earth it wouldn't be very far from here!)

Américo Vespúcio

Américo was referring to steep, jungled mountains that seem to leap into the sea, a scrambled shoreline with hundreds of islands and jutting peninsulas, and the clear, warm waters of the Baia da Ilha Grande, as calm as an empty aquarium. All this still exists, if in a less pristine state, as well as one of Brazil's most enchanting towns – the colonial village of Parati – which Américo did not get to enjoy.

Parati is both a great colonial relic, well-preserved and architecturally unique, and a launching pad for a dazzling section of the Brazilian littoral. The buildings are marked by simple lines that draw the eye to the general rather than the specific and earthy colours and textures that magnify, through contrast, the natural beauty that envelopes the town. So while the individual buildings in Parati may well be beautiful, the town when viewed as a whole is truly a work of art.

Dozens of secluded beaches are within a couple of hours boat or bus ride from Parati. There are good swimming beaches close to town, but the best are along the coast toward São Paulo and out on the bay islands.

One of the most popular spots between Rio and São Paulo, Parati is crowded and lively during the summer holidays, brimming with Brazilian and Argentine holiday-makers, and good music. That the town is all tourism there is no doubt; there are too many boutiques and too few cheap places to eat and sleep for it to be anything else. If you get around these obstacles Parati is a delight and there are plenty of beaches to accommodate all visitors.

History

Parati was inhabited by the Guianas Indians, when Portuguese from the capitania of São Vicente settled here in the early part of the 16th century. With the discovery of gold in Minas Gerais at the end of the 17th century, Parati became an obligatory stopover point for those coming from Rio de Janeiro, the only point where the escarpment of the Serra do Mar could be scaled. The precarious road was an old Guianas Indian trail that cut past the Serra do Facão (nowadays Cunha, São Paulo) to the Valley of Paraíba and from there to Pindamonhangaba, Guaratinguetá and then the mines.

Parati became a busy, important port as miners and supplies disembarked for the gold mines and gold was shipped to Europe. The small town prospered and, as always, the wealthy built churches to prove it. There was so much wealth in Parati that in 1711 Captain Francisco do Amaral Gurgel sailed from Parati to save Rio de Janeiro from a threatened French siege by handing over a ransom of 1000 crates of sugar, 200 head of cattle and 610,000 cruzados of gold.

The town's glory days didn't last long. After the 1720s a new road from Rio to Minas Gerais via the Serra dos Órgãos cut 15 days off the route from Parati and it started to decline. In the 19th century the local economy revived with the coffee boom and now, with the recent construction of the road from Rio, the town's coffers are once again being refilled.

Information & Orientation

Parati is a couple of km off the Rio to Santos highway, at the south-west corner of Rio de Janeiro state. Until 1954 the only access to Parati was by sea. In that year a road was built through the steep Serra do Mar passing the town of Cunha, 47 km inland. In 1960 the coastal road from Rio, 253 km away, was extended to Parati and beyond to São Paulo 330 km away.

Like Rio, Parati gets hot and muggy in the Brazilian summer. The rains are most frequent in November, January, and May. Be ready for plenty of nasty mosquitoes.

Tourist Office The Centro de Informações Turísticas (tel 71-1186) on Avenida Roberto Silveira is open daily from 8 am to

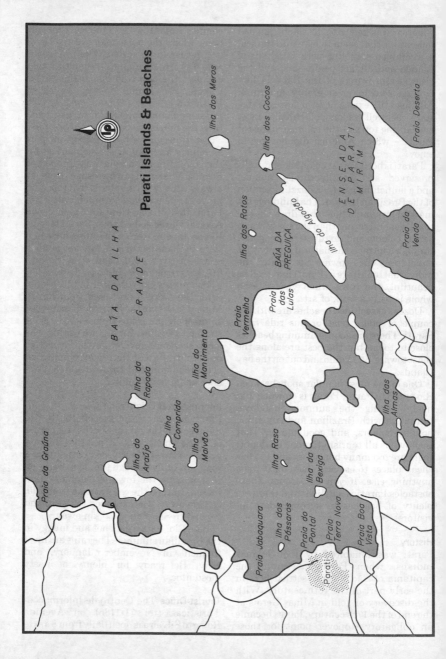

Parati Islands & Beaches

10 pm. The Secretaria de Turismo e Cultura (tel 71-1256), in the Antigo Quartel do Forte near the port, is open daily from 9 am to 6 pm.

Telephone The telephone office stations are in front of the Centro de Informações Turísticas and at Rua Dr Samuel Costa 29. Hotel Pousada Pardeiro and the Restaurante Mare Alta, among others, have fale facil (easy speaking) phones.

Churches

Parati is easy to look around; just walk on the *pes-de-moleque*, the local name for the irregular cobblestone streets washed clean by the rains and high tides. Parati's 18th century prosperity is reflected in its beautiful old homes and churches. Three main churches were used to separate the races – NS do Rosário (1725) for slaves, Santa Rita for freed mulattos and NS das Dores for the White elite.

The Igreja NS do Rosário e São Benedito dos Homens Pretos (1725), Rua Samuel Costa, was built by and for slaves. Reformed in 1857, the church has gilded wood altars dedicated to Our Lady of the rosary, St Benedict and St John. The pineapple crystals are for prosperity and good luck.

Igreja Santa Rita dos Pardos Libertos (1722), Praça Santa Rita, has a tiny museum of sacred art and some fine woodwork on the doorways and altars. Igreja de NS das Dores (1800), Rua Dr Pereira, was reformed in 1901. The cemetery is fashioned after the catacombs.

Matriz NS dos Remédios (1787), Praça Mons Hélio Pires, was built on the site of two earlier 17th century churches. Inside there is art from past and contemporary local artists. The construction of the church, according to legend, was financed by a pirate-treasure hidden on Praia da Trindade.

Forte Defensor Perpétuo

The Forte Defensor Perpétuo was built in 1703 to defend the gold being exported from Minas Gerais from pirate attacks. The fort was rebuilt in 1822, the year of Brazilian independence, and was named after Emperor Dom Pedro I. It's on the Morro da Vila Velha, the hill just past Praia do Pontal, a 20-minute walk north from town. The fort houses the Casa de Artista e Centro de Artes e Tradições Populares de Parati.

Beaches & Islands

Many tourists take the big schooner that leaves from the docks at midday and returns at 5 pm. It costs US$7 per person. Lunch is served on board for an additional US$4. The boat makes three beach stops for about 45 minutes each. Because it's the least expensive cruise in the bay, the schooner is usually crowded and stifling.

A much better alternative is to rent one of the many small motorboats at the port. For US$6 per hour (somewhat more in the summer) the skipper will take you where you want to go. Bargaining is difficult but you can lower the cost by finding travelling companions and renting bigger boats – they hold from six to 12 passengers.

The closest fine beaches on the coast – Vermelha, Lula and Saco – are about an hour away by boat (camping is allowed on the beaches). The best island beaches nearby are probably Araújo and Sapeca but many of the islands have rocky shores and are private. The mainland beaches tend to be better. These beaches are all small and idyllic, most having a barraca serving beer and fish and, at most, a handful of beachgoers.

So at a minimum, if you figure on an hour boat ride and an hour at the beach, you need to rent a boat for three hours. Of course, there are even more beautiful beaches further away.

The strategy of the boat drivers, since they usually can't return to port for another boatload, is to keep you out as long as possible. So don't be surprised the first beach you go to is out of beer, the next beach would be much pleasa because of its cleaner water. These can be very compelling reasons not to return as scheduled, but paradise has a price.

Parati reputedly has access to 65 islands and 300 beaches. Whatever the count, there are enough. Following is a list of the most accessible beaches, just north of town, and the best beaches, to the south. Don't limit yourself to this list, as there are plenty more to be found. If you do come across any really special beaches, and you can bare to share your secret, we'd love to know about them.

Praia do Pontal On the other side of the canal, 10 minutes on foot, this is Parati's city beach. There are several barracas and a lively crowd but the beach itself is not attractive and the water gets dirty.

Praia do Forte On the side of the hill, hidden by the rocks, Praia do Forte is the cleanest beach within a quick walk of the city, relatively secluded and frequented by a youngish crowd.

Praia do Jabaquara Continue on the dirt road north past Praia do Pontal, over the hill, for two km to Praia do Jabaquara, a big, spacious beach with great views in all directions. There is a small restaurant and a campground that's better than those in town. The sea is very shallow and it's possible to wade way out into the bay.

Festivals

Parati is known for its colourful and distinctive festivals. The two most important are the Festa Do Divino Espírito Santo, which begins nine days before Pentecostal Sunday and the NS dos Remédios on 8 September. The former is planned throughout the year and features all sorts of merrymaking revolving around the *fólios*, musical groups that go from door to door singing and joking.

The Festas Juninas during the month of June are filled with dances including the *xiba*, a circle clog dance, and the *ciranda*, a xiba with guitar accompaniment. The festivals culminate on 29 June with a maritime procession to Ilha do Araújo. Parati is a good option for Carnival if you want to get out of Rio for a couple of days.

The Parati region produces excellent Pinga (cachaça), and in 1984 the town fathers, in their wisdom, inaugurated an annual Festival da Pinga. The pinga party is held over an August weekend.

Places to Stay

Parati has two very different tourist seasons. From about October to February hotels get booked up and room prices double so reservations are a good idea. Many places require the full amount to be paid in advance, usually placed in their bank account in Rio or São Paulo. This is often non-refundable. The rest of the year, finding accommodation is easy and not expensive, the town is quiet and some of the boutiques and restaurants close for the winter. The prices quoted are off-season rates.

Places to Stay – bottom end

Cheap accommodation can be hard to find in Parati, but if Naoemi Maciel is renting rooms in her house you're in luck. It's a beautiful, big 300-year-old house at Rua da Praia 41. Naoemi is friendly and relaxed about sharing her place. She charges US$3 a person for a bed in a room with anywhere from two to seven beds.

The showers are incredibly good and you can use her living room and kitchen. It's a terrific place.

The *Pousada Fortaleza* (tel 71-1338), Rua Abel de Oliveira 31 has doubles starting as low as US$11. The *Hotel Estalagem* (tel 71-1626), Rua Mal Santos Dias 9, charges US$6 a person. There are several campgrounds on the edge of town.

Places to Stay – middle
If you can get one of the less expensive rooms at the *Hotel Coxixo* (tel 71-1400, see top end) then try there first as they have doubles from US$20. The *Hotel Solar dos Gerânios* (tel 71-1550) on Praça da Matriz (also known as Praça Monsenhor Hélio Pires) is a beautiful old hotel with wood and ceramic sculptures, flat brick and stone, rustic heavy furniture and *azulejos* (Portuguese tiles). Rooms have hot showers. Doubles start as low as US$14.

The *Bela Vista* (tel 71-1429), Rua do Comércio 46, is a good choice with doubles from US$22 to US$28. Another possibility is the *Pousada Aconchego* (tel 71-1598) at Beco do Propósito s/n (without a number). They have doubles from US$10 to US$20. The *Pousada da Matriz* (tel 71-1610), Rua Mal Deodoro 334, is a bit less expensive with doubles as low as US$6.

Places to Stay – top end
There are three splendid 4-star colonial pousadas in Parati. Owned by a famous Brazilian actor, the *Pousada Pardeiro* (tel 71-1370), Rua Tenente Francisco Antônio 74 has a tranquil garden setting, refined service and impeccable decor. If I had the money I'd blow it here. This is one of Brazil's best hotels, with doubles starting at US$40/46.

The *Hotel Coxixo* (tel 71-1460), Rua Tenente Francisco Antônio 362, is just a notch below the Pousada Pardeiro, but they have some standard rooms that are a fantastic deal at US$20. The pousada is cosy and colonial, with beautiful gardens and a pool, the rooms are simple but comfortable and pretty. To get the US$20 doubles make reservations early. Most doubles go for US$35 to US$40.

Pousada do Ouro (tel 71-1311), Rua da Praia 145, is the kind of place where you can imagine bumping into Mick Jagger, Sonia Braga or Marcello Mastriani, especially when you enter the hotel lobby and see photos of them posing in front of the pousada. The hotel has everything – bar, pool and a good restaurant. Doubles cost US$35 to US$40.

The *Hotel Pescador* (tel 71-1466), Avenida Beira Rio, is outside of the colonial part of town and is more of a family scene. It's not a bad hotel, but the competition is so much better. Doubles start at US$25. The *Hotel Mercado de Pouso* (tel 71-1114), Rua Dona Geralda 43, is a better choice at US$92.

Places to Eat
Parati has many pretty restaurants that all seem to charge too much. To beat the inflated prices in the old part of town try the sandwiches at the lanchonete on Praça Matriz.

Chicken costs US$2 for a big portion with rice and a mixed salad at *Restaurante e Churrascaria do Gaspar*, Rua Marechal Deodoro, or at the lanchonetes in the new part of town.

The best restaurants in the old town include the *Galeria do Engenho*, Rua do Comércio 40 which serves large and juicy steaks for US$4 and *Vagalume*, Rua Comendador José Luis 5. *Hiltinho*, Rua Marechal Deodoro 233, at the edge of the Praça Matriz, is more expensive and the food is oversalted, but there's a good menu and ample portions. Another recommended restaurant is *Mare Alta*, Praça da Bandeira.

Entertainment
Listen to Nando and Jimmy sing and strum guitar at the Art Café. Or just wander the streets and you'll hear some music outside at the restaurants by the canal or inside one of the bars.

Getting There & Away
The rodoviária (tel 71-1186) is on the main road into town, Rua Roberto Silveira, a half km up from the old town.

There are five daily buses from Parati to Rio; it's a five hour trip with buses leaving Rio for Parati at 6.30 and 9 am, 12.30, 3.00, 6.20 and 8 pm. Atlântico has a couple of daily buses from Rio that continue to Ubatuba.

Five daily Coltur buses go from Parati to Angra dos Reis, taking two hours. The first leaves at 8 am, the last at 8.30 pm, There are four daily Maringa buses for São Paulo which take six hours. Three daily São José buses go to Ubatuba and three more go to Cunha.

AROUND PARATI
Praia Barra Grande
About 20 km up the Rio to Santos highway, Barra Grande is an easy-to-reach alternative to the beaches in Baia de Parati. There are four municipal buses a day leaving from Parati.

Praia de Parati Mirim
For accessibility, cost and beauty this beach is hard to beat. Parati Mirim is a small town, 27 km from Parati. The beach has barracas and houses to rent. From Parati, it's a couple of hours by boat, but if you're on a budget catch a municipal bus that makes the 40 minute trip for only 30c. Get the Parati Mirim bus from the rodoviária at 6.50 am or 1 pm.

Praia do Sono
They don't get much prettier than this beach. Past Ponta Negra on the coast going south, about 40 km from Parati, Praia Sono can have rough water and is sometimes difficult to land on. It's a four to five hour boat ride. The much cheaper alternative is to take the Laranjeiras bus from Parati and get directions in Laranjeiras for the 1½ hour walk to Sono. Buses leave Parati at 5.15 am, 12.30 pm and 6.40 pm. There's food but no formal lodging at the beach.

Praia da Trindade
About five km before Sono, this is another beautiful beach and it has a simple pousada so you can stay for a night or two. In addition to boats, the beach is accessible by the same bus as for Praia do Sono. Ask the driver to let you off at the entrance to Trindade.

Inland
The old gold route, now the road to Cunha (6 km), is a magnificent jungle ride up the escarpment. The steep dirt part of the road gets treacherous in the rain. Catch the Cunha bus.

Take the Ponte Branca bus from Parati to the Igrejinha da Penha, a small triple-turreted hillside church. You'll find a ¾ km jungle trail to a beautiful waterfall and water slide. Circular buses cost 10c and leave at 5, 6, 7 and 11.30 am and 4.30 pm.

Fazenda Bananal-Engenho de Murycana is four km off the Parati to Cunha road, 10 km from town. It's a touristy spot with an old sugar mill, a restaurant, a zoo, and free samples of cachaça and batidas.

The Mountains

PETRÓPOLIS
Population: 149,000
Petrópolis is a lovely mountain retreat with a decidedly European flavour, only 60 km from Rio de Janeiro. This is where the imperial court spent their summer when Rio got too muggy. Bucolic appearances aside, Petrópolis is also the home of Father Boff, a liberation theologist actively involved in peasant campaigns for agricultural reform and censured by the Vatican for his politicisation of the church.

Museu Imperial & Other Buildings
Petrópolis' main attraction is the Museu Imperial, the perfectly preserved and impeccably appointed palace of Dom Pedro II. A 20 minute audiovisual

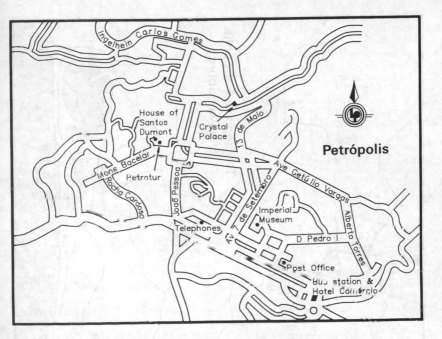

documentary entitled 'Petrópolis: Imperial City' is shown Tuesday to Sunday every half-hour.

After the Museu Imperial you can visit the home of Brazil's first aeronaut, Casa de Santos Dumont and the Palácio Cristal (1884). Then take a horse and carriage ride through the city's squares and parks, past bridges, canals and old fashioned lamps.

Places to Stay

The *Hotel Comércio* (tel 42-3500), at Rua Dr Porciúncula 56, is directly across from the rodoviária. Rooms are clean and cheap at US$3.50/5 for singles/doubles. There is a hot water shower down the hall.

Around Town

If you have use of a car take a ride out on the Estrada Industrial. It's 70 km to the little church of São José de Rio Preto.

You'll pass a few good restaurants on the way; Tarrafa's and Boi na Brasa for steak and in Correias the expensive French restaurant One For the Road.

In Itapaiva visit the Recanto porcelain factory. In Pedra do Rio find the hiking trail to the Rocinha waterfalls in the Secretaria neighbourhood, then visit the farms and ranches of Posse.

VASSOURAS

Population: 13,000

Vassouras, a quiet resort 118 km south of Rio, was home of the 19th century coffee barons. They were literally barons, for 18 of them were given titles of nobility by the Portuguese crown.

Buildings & Fazendas

There are a few old churches in the centre as well as old buildings of the schools of medicine, philosophy and engineering, but the real attractions of Vassouras are

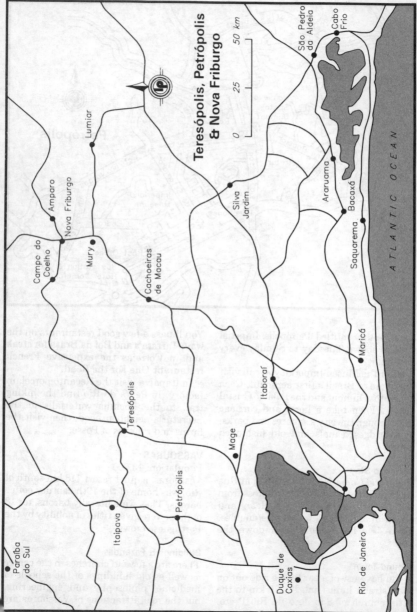

Teresópolis, Petrópolis & Nova Friburgo

the old coffee fazendas. Although protected by the historical preservation institutes, permission must be requested from the owners before touring the grounds.

Museu Chácara da Hera

Vassouras' favourite grande dame is the noble heiress, Eufrásia, a woman who claims devotion to Vassouras despite palaces in London, Brussels and Paris. Her home, the Museu Chácara da Hera, is located on Rua Fernandes Junior and is open from Tuesday to Sunday from 1 to 4 pm. Fazenda Santa Eufrásia (three km) and Fazenda Dom Carlos (five km) are within walking distance.

Places to Stay

There are a few cheap pensions which charge US$10 for room and board but otherwise accommodation is expensive. The *Mara Palace* (tel 71-1003), at Rua Chanceler Dr Raul Fernandes 121, charges US$19/35 for a deluxe double. The *Hotel Parque Santa Amália* (tel 71-1346), at Avenida Rui Barbosa 526, charges US$30 for doubles.

TERESÓPOLIS

Population: 79,000

Do as Empress Teresina did and escape the steamy summer heat of Rio in the cool mountain retreat of Teresópolis (910 metres), a city nestled in the strange organ-pipe mountains of the Serra dos Órgãos. The road to Teresópolis first passes the sinusoidal bumps of a padded green jungle then winds and climbs past bald peaks which have poked through the jungle cover to touch the clouds.

The city itself is modern, prosperous and dull. The principal attraction is the landscape and its natural treasures – in particular the strangely shaped peaks of Pedra do Sino (2263 metres), Pedra do Açu (2230 metres), Agulha do Diabo (2020 metres), Nariz do Frade (1919 metres), Dedo de Deus (1651 metres), Pedra da Ermitage (1485 metres) and Dedo de Nossa Senhora (1320 metres). With so

many peaks, it's no wonder that Teresópolis is the mountain climbing, rock climbing and trekking centre of Brazil.

There are extensive hiking trails and it's possible to trek over the mountains and through the jungle to Petrópolis. Unfortunately the trails are unmarked and off the maps, but it's easy and inexpensive to hire a guide at the Parque Nacional. Guidebooks to Teresópolis with trail maps are sold at the Cupela Banco de Jornais in the square in front of the Igreja Matriz.

Teresópolis is not simply for alpinists, but a centre for sports lovers of all kinds. The city has facilities for motorcross, volleyball and equestrianism – many of Brazil's finest thoroughbreds are raised here – not to mention soccer. Teresópolis bears the distinction of hosting Brazil's world cup soccer team; the national team is selected and trained there.

Information & Orientation

Teresópolis is built up along one main street which changes names every few blocks. Starting from the highway to Rio in the Soberbo part of town and continuing north along the Avenida Rotariana (with access to the National Park) the road is renamed Avenida Oliveira Botelho, Avenida Feliciano Sodré and then Avenida Lúcio Meira. Most of the sites are west of the main drag and up in the hills. The cheap hotels are found in the neighbourhood of the Igreja Matriz de Santa Tereza, Praça Baltazar da Silveira.

Tourist Office There's a tourist stand at the rodoviária (open daily 8 am to 11 pm). It's better staffed than the office on Avenida Lúcio Meira, which is open from Monday to Friday from 1 to 5 pm. The rodoviária also has a Telerj station for long distance calls.

Serra dos Órgãos National Park

The main entrance of the Serra dos Órgãos National Park is open daily from

8 am to 5 pm (admission 25c). There's a 3½ km walking trail, waterfalls, swimming pools, tended lawns and gardens. It's a very pretty park for a picnic. There are some chalets for rent at the park substation, 12 km towards Rio. There are also camping sites. For more information see the climbing section in the Facts for the Visitor chapter.

Museum of Natural History

The Von Mártius Museum of Natural History named after Botanist Carl Phillip Von Mártius is at km 47 of the Rio-Teresópolis highway. It's not a big deal.

Other Attractions

The Mulher de Pedra rock formation, 12 km out towards Nova Friburgo, does indeed look like a reclining woman.

Colina dos Mirantes is a good place to view the Serra dos Órgãos range and the city. On clear days you can see as far as Guanabara Bay. The Quebra Frascos, royal family of the second empire, lived in this neighbourhood. Take Rua Feliciano Sodré. The best spot for viewing the Dedo de Deus peak is from Soberbo.

Places to Stay – bottom end

The *Várzea Palace Hotel* (tel 742-0878) at Rua Prefeito Sebastião Teixeira 41/55 behind the Igreja Matriz is a grand old white building with red trim which has been a Teresópolis institution since 1916. Can this be a budget hotel? Cheap and classy doubles without a bath are US$4. With a bath they cost US$10.

Other budget hotels are nearby, including the *Hotel Center* (tel 742-5890) at Sebastião Teixeira 245 which has singles/doubles for $US15/18. The *Novo Hotel* is in front of the Igreja Matriz on Rua Delfim Moreira.

Places to Stay – top end

The more expensive hotels are out of town. *Hotel Alpina* (tel 742-5252) is three km on the road to Petrópolis and has singles/doubles for $US30/34. *Hotel Rosa dos Ventos* (tel 742-8833) is at Km 23 on the Nova Friburgo highway and has rooms for honeymooners and couples but no one under 16 is permitted to stay there. Rooms here are $US72/82 for singles/doubles with breakfast and lunch included. *São Moritz* (tel 742-4360) is further along at Km 36. The *Hotel Alpina* (tel 742-5252) is also along the road to Petrópolis and has singles/doubles for $US32/35.

Places to Eat

There are several lanchonetes on the main street. *Churrascaria Bife Grande* at Avenida Feliciano Sodré 420 is a charmless aeroplane-hangar-style restaurant with fluorescent lights. They serve a huge steak for US$2.

Restaurante Irene (tel 742-2901) Rua Seada 730 (parallel to Rua Sebastião Teixeira) basks in its reputation for Teresópolis' best *haute cuisine*. Reservations are required.

Bar Gota da Água at Praça Baltazar da Silveira 16 is also known as *Bar do Ivam* and is a comfy little place which serves trout with a choice of sauces for US$5. Try it with alcaparra, a bitter pea-like vegetable, or almond sauce. For dessert have some apple strudel and Viennese coffee a few doors down at *Lanches Mickey*.

Parreirinha do Lamego at Avenida Delfim Moreira 359 serves Angolan and Portuguese food. Their bacalhau (cod) is good. *Tudo em Cima*, Avenida Delfim Moreira 409 serves an admirable soufflé of bacalhau for US$4.

Getting There & Away

The rodoviária is on Rua 1 do Maio off Avenida Tenente Luis and has buses to Rio every 30 minutes from 5 am to 10 pm (50c, 1 hour 15 minutes, 95 km). There are also buses to Petrópolis (every second hour from 9 am to 9 pm) and Nova Friburgo. You must purchase return tickets in the rodoviária.

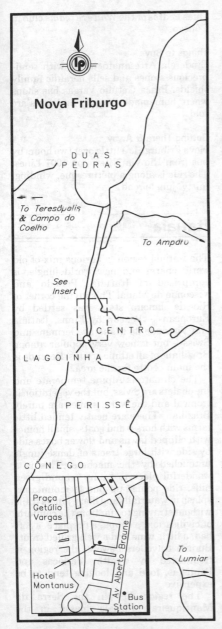

Nova Friburgo

DUAS PEDRAS

To Teresópolis & Campo do Coelho

To Ampato

See Insert

CENTRO

LAGOINHA

PERISSÊ

CÓNEGO

To Lumiar

Praça Getúlio Vargas

Av. Alberto Braune

Hotel Montanus

Bus Station

Getting Around
Hopefully, Viação Dedo de Deus on Avenida Lúcio Meira 594 now operates a tourist bus that covers the sights. Otherwise you will have to take the local buses or taxis or just hoof it.

NOVA FRIBURGO
Population: 90,000
During the Napoleonic wars Dom João II encouraged immigration to Brazil. At the time people were starving in Switzerland, so 300 families in the Swiss canton of Friburg packed up and took off for Brazil in 1818 The passage to Brazil was horrible, many died, but enough families survived to settle in the mountains and establish a small village in the New World.

Like Teresópolis and Petrópolis, Nova Friburgo has good hotels and restaurants plus many lovely natural attractions: waterfall, woods, trails, sunny mountain mornings and cool evenings. (It's chilly and rainy during the winter months from June through August). The Cónego neighbourhood is interesting for its Germanic architecture and its apparently perpetually blooming flowers.

Mountains & Views
Scout out the surrounding area from Morro da Cruz. The cable-car station is in the centre at Praça do Suspiro. Gondolas to Morro da Cruz (1800 metres) run from 9 am to 5.30 pm. Most of the nice sights are a few km out of town. Pico da Caledônia (2310 metres) offers fantastic views and jump-off points for hang-gliders.

You can hike to Pedra do Cão Sentado or explore the Furnas do Catete rock formations, visit the mountain towns of Bom Jardim (23 km north on BR-492), or Lumiar (25 km from Mury and a little bit before the entrance to Friburgo). Hippies, cheap pensions, waterfalls, walking trails and white-water canoe trips abound in Lumiar.

Places to Stay – bottom end

Hotel Fabris (tel 22-2852) at Avenida Alberto Braune 148 asks US$6/6.50 for clean singles/doubles. *Hotel Montanus* (tel 22-1235) at Rua Fernando Bizzotto 26 has simple singles/doubles for $US5/6.

Places to Stay – top end

Rates at the top hotels are all for double occupancy and include full board. *Sans Souci* (tel 22-7752) in town at Rua Itajai charges US$26/45 for doubles/singles. *Hotel Olifas* (tel 22-7840) in Lagoinha at Parque Olifas charges US$42/48 for singles/doubles.

Hotel Garlipp (tel 42-1330) is in Mury, 10 km out on the road to Niterói, and charges US$25/31 for singles and $US31/38 for doubles. *Hotel Bucsky* (tel 22-5052) is five km from town at Ponte de Saudade and charges US$28/38 for singles/doubles with full board.

Places to Eat

For cheap eats try the self-service buffet at *Cantina Ismério* at Praça Getúlio Vargas 122A. One trip to the buffet table is US$1.30 and two trips costs US$2. If you want to eat very well try one of the two Swiss/German delicatessens on Rua Fernando Bizzotto for a hefty cold cut sandwich on black bread with dark mustard. One of the two delis, *Oberland* (tel 22-9838) at number 12, doubles as a restaurant. It's a very cosy wood-panelled room where the menu is short and the food is great. Try the weisswurst (veal sausage) with sauerkraut US$2 and the chocolate cakes for desert.

The *Churrascaria Majórica*, in the centre at Praça Getúlio Vargas 74, serves a decent cut of filet mignon for US$6. *Chez Gigi*, a fancy French restaurant on the Mury to Lumiar road, serves a US$14 feast of smoked trout, pate of truffles, cheeses, salads, caviar and snails every day but Monday.

Entertainment

There's dancing either at *Clube 86* in Duas Pedras or the *White Streams* club in Cónego.

Things to Buy

Cinderela Artesanato works with semi-precious stones and sells heraldic family shields. Praça Getúlio Vargas has shops where homemade liqueurs and jams are sold.

Getting There & Away

Nova Friburgo is a little over two hours by bus from Rio via Niterói on 1001 Lines. The ride is along a picturesque, winding, misty, jungle road.

Itatiaia

The Itatiaia region, a curious mix of old world charm and new world jungle, is comprised of Itatiaia, Penedo and Visconde de Mauá. This idyllic corner of Rio de Janeiro state was settled by Europeans – Penedo by Finns, Itatiaia and Visconde de Mauá by Germans and Swiss – but is now very popular among Brazilians of all ethnic groups. Resende is the main centre for the area.

The climate is Alpine temperate and the chalets are Swiss, but the vegetation is tropical and the warm smiles are purely Brazilian. There are neatly tended little farms with horses and goats, small homes with clipped lawns and flower boxes side by side with large tracts of dense jungle untouched by the machete. This is a wonderful place to tramp around green hills, ride ponies up purple mountains, splash in waterfalls and blaze jungle trails without straying too far from the comforts of civilisation: a sauna, a fireplace, a soft bed, a little wine and a well-grilled trout! Budget travellers beware, the region is frequented by wealthy cariocas and Paulistas, food and lodging tend to be expensive.

The region lies in the Serra da Mantiqueira's Itatiaia massif in the

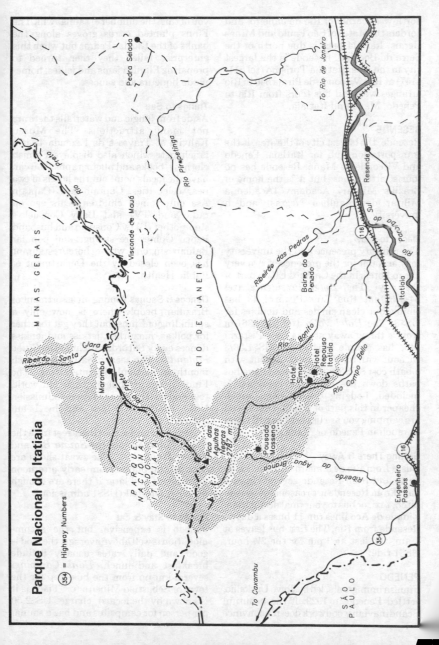

Parque Nacional do Itatiaia

(354) = Highway Numbers

north-west corner of Rio de Janeiro, and borders the states of São Paulo and Minas Gerais. Itatiaia park is due north of the Serra de Bocaina. Resende is the largest city in the area. Itatiaia Turismo (tel 511-1147) at Rua Visconde de Pirajá 540 in Rio arranges weekend bus tours from Rio to Penedo, Mauá and Itatiaia.

RESENDE
Resende, the largest city of the area, is the transportation hub for Itatiaia, Penedo and Visconde de Mauá. Resende has no tourist attractions, but it is the home of Brazil's Military Academy (Academia Militar das Agulhas Negras) and a university.

Places to Stay
The military presence and the university may account for the presence of two very cheap hotels in the Campos Elízio part of the city. The *Hotel Presidente* (tel 54-3052) at Rua Luis Pistarni 43 has simple but clean singles and doubles for US$3. The *Hotel Valin* (tel 54-0836), a stone's throw away at Rua Luis Pistarni 140, has simple singles for US$1.50/3 without/with bath. Doubles without/with a bath cost $US3/5. Both hotels have hot baths down the hall, and breakfast is included. Lodging doesn't come much cheaper in this part of Brazil. Unless you are camping you are likely to pay 10 times as much in Penedo or Mauá.

Getting There & Away
Buses from Rio de Janeiro and São Paulo go to and from Resende several times a day. From Resende it's reasonably easy to hitch, taxi, or bus to your final destination. Cidade de Aço lines run 11 buses a day to Resende from Rio. The first bus leaves at 7 am, the last at 9 pm for the 2½ hour, US$1 ride.

PENEDO
Finnish immigrants, led by Toivo Uuskallio, settled Penedo in 1929. If the beautiful Scandinavian woodwork doesn't convince you of this, the number of saunas will. The Finns planted citrus groves along the banks of the Rio das Pedras but when this enterprise failed they then turned to preparing Finnish jams and jellies, homemade liqueurs and sauces.

Things to See
Aside from jungle and waterfalls there are not many attractions. The Museu Kahvila at Travessa da Fazenda 45 is a lanchonete which also displays Finnish clothing, books and photographs. You can have the locals point out the hotels of two near celebrities: Captain Asa (Captain Asa entertained children years ago on radio and TV) and Baby Consuelo's stepmother (Baby Consuelo and husband Pepeu Gomes are strange and popular Bahian singers) whose hotel/restaurant has been closed by the Department of Public Health.

Dances & Saunas Among an assortment of Brazilian people there is now only a sprinkling of Finns, but they get together for polkas, mazurkas, letkiss and jenkiss dances every Saturday night at the *Clube Finlandês*. The second Saturday of each month is particularly interesting. The Finnish dancers put on their old world togs and do traditional dances (admission US$1, starts at 9 pm and by 1 am it's over).

Next door and across the street from the *Clube Finlandês* are the *Sauna Bar* and *Sauna Finlandesa*. The sweat shops are open to the public from early afternoon until 10 pm and later if there are enough people interested (US$1 admission).

Places to Stay & Eat
Penedo is expensive, but the accommodation is well above average, the food is good and daily rates usually include breakfast and lunch. *Hans Camping*, several km up from the bus-stop for the town of Sebastião Mineiro (or 'Tião' as it is known by the locals), charges US$2.50 per person for campsites and has a sauna,

swimming pool, bar and a waterfall nearby. Hans is closed in August.

The *Pousada Challenge* (tel 51-1389) about a km up from Tião on the Estrada da Fazendinha has very clean pre-fab chalets which sleep three. It costs US$20 for a doubles plus US$12 for each other person, and includes breakfast and lunch (buffet-style dinner is US$3), use of the pool and sauna.

The *Hotel Baianinha* (tel 51-1204), next to Tião on the Cachoeiras, asks for US$11/14 for singles/doubles. The Baianinha kitchen specialises in fish and Bahian dishes which range in price from US$3 to US$9. The food is good and portions are huge. *Bate Papo*, on Avenida Casa das Pedras at the lower end of the city centre, is supposed to have good and cheap food. *Restaurante Mariska*, Rua Esporte Clube near the Telerj station, serves tasty but expensive Hungarian food.

Things to Buy

Paulo of Mato Grosso builds and sculpts wonderful things from hard eucalyptus woods. He's ecologically minded and uses felled wood he finds in the forest. Penedo's small craft shops specialise in jellies, honey, chutneys and preserves, chocolates, cakes and candles.

Getting There & Away

From Resende it's much easier to get to Penedo and Itatiaia than to Mauá. Auto Viação Tupi has 24 Penedo-bound buses daily from 5.50 am to 8.40 pm. The bus services the three km main street (which is considered to be the centre of town) and continues past the end of the paved road to Tião which is the final stop. The Hotel Baianinha is near the bus terminal. Pousada Challenge is a brisk 30-minute walk from Tião and Hans Camping is another 20 minutes further up. Taxis to Penedo charge US$5 to US$10.

Around Town

There are three waterfalls worth visiting.

They are Tres Cachoeiras near Tião, Cachoeira do Roman which is very pretty but on private grounds and 10 minutes uphill from the Pousada Challenge, and Cachoeira do Diabo right near the Pousada Challenge. About 40 minutes of uphill hiking from Hans Camping takes you into very dense jungle, although there are trails inside. Hopefully you will run into the large bands of big monkeys and steer clear of the wildcats. At the point where Penedo's main asphalt road turns to dirt you can rent horses for US$2.50 per hour, and horse and carriage for US$5 per hour.

VISCONDE DE MAUÁ

Mauá is a little more tranquil and pretty than Penedo and harder to reach. It's a lovely place with streams, tinkling goat bells, cosy chalets and country lanes graced with wildflowers. There are horses for hire by the footbridge for US$2.50 per hour, but some of them are small.

The Santa Clara Cachoeira, the nicest waterfall in the area, is a 40-minute walk from Vila Maromba in Maringa. For a mini jungle experience climb up on either side of the falls through the bamboo groves.

The young and the restless can follow the trail from Maromba to the Cachoeira Veu de Noiva in Itatiaia Park. It's a full day's hike each way. It's possible to kayak the rapids of the Rio Preto if you are so inclined. The Rio Preto, which divides Minas Gerais from Rio, also has small river beaches and natural pools to explore.

Places to Stay

Hotel Casa Alpina (tel 54-0530) has US$35 doubles with full board, private sauna and fireplace. For reservations call Rio (021) 221-2022, São Paulo (011) 259-5226.

There are many other hotels of this calibre in this price range (eg *Os Condes*), but the cheapest place to stay aside from the campgrounds is the *Chalezinho*

Eliane. Eliane rents out a duplex chalet with hot water and two double beds for US$7.50. Breakfast is not included.

Places to Eat
Natural/vegetarian food, as served in *Restaurants Colher de Chá* and *Pureza*, is popular in Mauá. People here like brown rice, granola with tropical fruits and yoghurt mixed in and caipirinhas with natural honey. The food is good, but expensive.

Restaurante Maina serves abundant portions of standard fare at low prices. Big meals cost US$3, prato feito costs US$2 (includes a bottomless bowl of soup, tough meat, salad, beans, rice and liberally salted French fries). After thorough and painstaking research we concluded that the *Colher de Chá* is the best place to get drunk.

Things to Buy
The Companhia Visconde de Mauá is a hippie store with embroidered blouses, T-shirts, natural perfumes and soaps.

Getting There & Away
The one daily bus from Resende to Visconde de Mauá (about two hours on a winding dirt road, 40c) leaves Monday to Saturday at 4 pm, so you must catch the 1 pm bus from Rio to make it, or else pay for a taxi which costs US$20. The bus returns to Resende at 8 am every morning except for Sundays when it returns at 5 pm. Visconde de Mauá is not a single town but a group of villages: Vila Mauá, Vila Maromba and Vila Maringa. Take the bus beyond Vila Mauá to the end of the line at Maromba and Maringa.

PARQUE NACIONAL DO ITATIAIA
This is a national park established in 1937 to protect 120 square km of ruggedly beautiful land. It contains over 400 species of native birds, jaguars, monkeys, sloths, lakes, rivers, waterfalls, alpine meadows and primary and secondary Atlantic rainforests. Don't let the tropical

house plants fool you; it gets below freezing point in June! Itatiaia even has a few snowy days some years!

Museum
The park headquarters, museum and Lago Azul (Blue Lake) are 10 km in from the Rodovia (highway) Presidente Dutra. The museum, open Tuesday to Sunday from 8 am to 4 pm, has glass cases full of stuffed and mounted animals, pinned moths and snakes in jars.

Climbing & Walking
Mountain climbing, rock climbing and trekking enthusiasts will want to pit themselves against the local peaks, cliffs and trails.

Every two weeks a group guided by Senhor Hans Bauermeister scales the Agulhas Negras peak, at 2787 metres the highest in the area. For more information call the Grupo Excursionista de Agulhas Negras (tel 54-2587) and refer to the section on hiking & climbing in the Facts for the Visitor chapter.

A walk to the Abroucas refuge at the base of Agulhas Negras is a 26 km, eight hour jungle trek from the park entrance. The mountain refuge can sleep 24 people and is accessible by car from the Engenheiro Passos to São Lourenço road near the Minas Gerais and Rio de Janeiro border. Reservations are required. Call the IBDF in Resende (tel (0243) 52-1461) and get maps and advice from the park IBDF office before setting off.

Simpler hikes include the walk between Hotel Simon and Hotel Repouso (where the painter Guignard lived, worked and left a few of his paintings), and the 20-minute walk from the Sítio Jangada to the Poronga waterfalls.

Places to Stay

There are four hotels and a camping area within the park but the hotels are expensive 3-star Embratur affairs with saunas and swimming pools like the *Hotel Repouso Itatiaia* (tel 52-1110) which charges US$37 for a double and full board in a chalet. There are also four more hotels outside the park.

Getting There & Away

Every 20 minutes on weekdays, every 40 minutes on weekends (from 5.30 am to 11.20 pm) there is a bus from Resende to the town of Itatiaia. From the town take a *circular* bus to the park entrance.

East of Rio de Janeiro

SAQUAREMA

Population: 25,000

After the famous beaches of Rio and Guanabara Bay with their high-rise hotels and bars spilling out onto the sands, the quiet and clean beaches east of Rio are a welcome change.

Saquarema, 100 km from Rio de Janeiro, sits between miles of open beach, lagoons and jungled mountains. The town takes unusual pride in the natural beauty of its setting. Polluting industries are forbidden in the municipality, so it's still possible to find sloths and bands of monkeys in the jungles. Motorboats aren't allowed to muck up the lakes and lagoons which means the water is still pure, and the fish and shrimp are abundant. The long shoreline of fine white sand and clean water attracts surfers, sports fishers and sun worshippers.

Saquarema is a horse breeding and fruit growing centre. You can visit the orchards and pick fruit or hire horses and take to the hills. Adventurers who tramp the jungle trails in search of the elusive mico-leão monkey are sure to discover beautiful waterfalls, if not primates. All in all there are plenty of things to do away from the beach.

Ah, but the beaches . . . Bambui, Ponta Negra and Jaconé, south of town, are long and empty save for a couple of fishing villages. The waves are big, particularly in Ponta Negra and three km north of Saquarema in Praia Itaúna where an annual surfing contest is held during the last two weeks of May.

History

On 17 March 1531, Martim Afonso de Sousa founded a Portuguese settlement and met with the Tamoio Indian chief Sapuguaçu. Nonplussed by Afonso de Sousa's five ships and 400 sailors, Sapuguaçu chose to ally the Tamoios with the French. In 1575 Antônio Salema, then governor of Rio de Janeiro, decided to break the Tamoio-French alliance and with an army of over 1000 men massacred the Indians and their French military advisors.

The next big event in Saquarema's history was the slave revolt of Ipitangas when 400 slaves took over the plantation mansion and kicked out their master. For a few days, the slaves held the town and fought against the cavalry which rode out from Niterói. The town pillory, Bandeque's Post, named after the leader of the slave revolt, was in use as recently as the end of last century.

Festivals

Saquarema hosts the NS de Nazaré mass on 7 and 8 September which attracts 150,000 pilgrims, second only to the Nazaré celebrations of Belém.

Places to Stay

There are five hotels, four pousadas and three camping areas to choose from. Most of the hotels are on Avenida Saquarema or on Avenida Oceânica and most of the hotel rooms will accommodate up to four people. The cheaper hotels are on Avenida Saquarema, *Roda da Água* (tel (021) 781-4151 in Rio) at 3557, *Lagoa Azul* (tel (021) 252-7980 in Rio) at 1580 and *Iate Hotel* (tel 51-2211) at 565.

The fancier hotels are *Pousada Berro da Água* (tel 51-2271) at Avenida Oceânica 165 and *Marinas da Lagoa* (tel 51-2228) at Avenida Saquarema 1503 which has doubles for $US35. Also recommended are *Hotel Saquarema* (tel 51-2254), *Pousada da Mansão* (tel 51-2254) and *Estalagem de Itaúna* (tel 51-2156).

Getting There & Away

Saquarema is serviced by frequent 1001 buses from Rio de Janeiro, Niterói and Cabo Frio.

ARARUAMA

Araruama is 114 km from Rio, with a calm lagoon ideal for windsurfing. The ocean beaches are 18 km from town, the closest is Praia Seca. This is actually part of Maçambaba beach which continues all the way to Arraial do Cabo where it's known as Praia Grande. The saltworks on the lakeshore are interesting to visit.

Places to Stay

The cheapest beds in town are in the *Pousada Luar da Lagoa*.

ARRAIAL DO CABO

Population: 5000

Arraial do Cabo sits on a square corner of land with Cabo Frio due north 10 km and Praia Grande stretching due west 40 km (continuous with Praia Maçambaba). The village of Arraial do Cabo spreads out from the edges of four bays and has beaches that compare with the finest in Búzios, but unlike Búzios, Arraial is a place where people live and work. The saltworks of the Companhia Nacional de Alcalis, north of town, extract table salt and *barrília*, a type of phosphate tied to the salt.

Beaches

Discovered years ago by Américo Vespúcio, Praia dos Anjos has beautiful turquoise water and a little too much boat traffic for comfortable swimming. The favourite beaches in town are Praia do Forno, Praia Brava and Praia Grande. Stretching along a pretty piece of road to Cabo Frio, Praia do Forte has bleached white sand and a backdrop of low scrub, cacti and grasses. The Oceanographic Museum on Praia dos Anjos is open Tuesday to Sunday from 8 am to 5 pm.

Go to the Gruta Azul (blue cavern) on the far side of Ilha de Cabo Frio, ask fisherfolk at Praia dos Anjos for a tour – it should cost about US$12 to US$15 – or enquire at the Pousada Restaurante dos Navegantes. Be alert to the tides, the entrance to the underwater cavern isn't always open.

To see the wild orchids between Cabo Frio and Arraial do Cabo ask the bus driver to let you off at the access road, and then hike inland.

Places to Stay

Hotel A Resurgência at Rua Luis Joaquim Correa 350, Praia dos Anjos is operated by and for the navy and its research scientists. Call ahead on (0246) 22-1615 for permission to stay there. A dorm-style bed costs US$3.50, private rooms US$12.50/14 for singles/doubles.

The *Pousada Restaurante dos Navegantes* (tel 22-1611) on Praia Grande is a very pretty resort hotel with a courtyard pool and singles for US$12.50, doubles for US$17.50. *Camping Praia Grande* is a walled-in grassy area reasonably close to the beach.

The *Mini Hotel Carreitero* on the corner of Rua Dom Pedro I and Rua Martin Afonso on the outskirts of town has small, cheap-o US$2.50 singles and US$4 doubles. *Hotel Churrascaria Gaucha* (tel 22-1533), Praça Lions Clube 35 has large beat-up rooms with hot showers and plenty of mosquitoes for US$4 per person. It's not worth it.

Places to Eat
Garrafa de Nancy Restaurante is a classy seafood place where you can eat very well for about US$6 per person. Cheaper eats are at the *Hotel Churrascaria Gaucha*, where US$2 buys you a prato feito with chicken, beef, sausage, salad, manioc, rice and beans.

Getting There & Away
Take the municipal bus from Cabo Frio (10c) which loops around Arraial and returns to Cabo Frio every 20 minutes.

CABO FRIO
Population: 41,000
The Cabo Frio district was formerly comprised of Cabo Frio, the most populous town, Búzios, the wealthy and sophisticated resort, and Arraial do Cabo which has since become independent politically and economically because of its salt industry.

History
According to local historian Márcio Verneck, Cabo Frio was inhabited at least 5500 years ago. Before the Portuguese arrived, the warring Tamoios and Goitacazes tribes lived here. In 1503 the Portuguese armada, under the command of Américo Vespúcio, landed at Praia dos Anjos in Arraial do Cabo. Twenty-four men were left behind to start a settlement, one of the first prefects in the Americas. Fantastic reports about this community were the model for Thomas Moore's Utopia.

The economy of the Portuguese settlement was based on the coastal brazil wood which was felled and shipped back to Europe. Portuguese vessels were at the mercy of Dutch and French corsairs until 1615 when the Portuguese defeated their European foes and founded Santa Helena de Cabo Frio, and took the French-built fort of São Mateus to protect their trade. In time the Franciscans joined the settlement and built the Nossa Senhora dos Anjos convent. They were followed by the Jesuits at Fazenda Campo Novo. By the 1800s the brazil wood stands were completely destroyed and the economy was geared toward fishing and, more recently, tourism, saltworks and chemical industries.

Information & Orientation
Canal do Itajuru links the Lagoa de Araruma to the ocean. Cabo Frio lies to one side of this canal. The town is a two km hike from the bus station along Avenida Júlia Kubitschek. The cheap hotels are located on Rua José Bonifácio and Rua Jorge Lossio.

Forte São Mateus
The Forte São Mateus, a stone fortress stronghold against pirates, was built in 1616 and is open from 10 am to 4pm Tuesday to Sunday. It's at the end of Praia do Forte.

Dunes
There are three spots in and about Cabo Frio with sand dunes. The dunes of Pero beach, a super beach for surfing and surfcasting, are six km north in the direction of Búzios, near Ogivas, and after Praia Brava and Praia das Conchas. The Dama Branca (white lady) sand dunes are on the road to Arraial do Cabo. The Pontal dunes of Praia do Forte town beach stretch from the fort to Miranda hill. The dunes can be dangerous because of robberies so

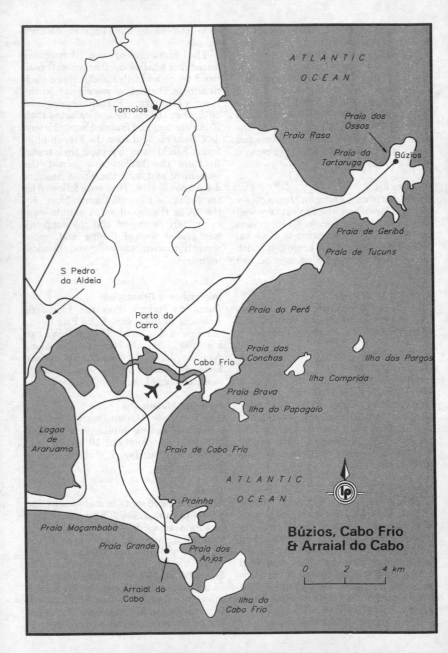

ATLANTIC OCEAN

Tamoios

Praia Rasa

Praia dos Ossos

Praia da Tartaruga

Búzios

S Pedro da Aldeia

Praia de Geribá

Praia de Tucuns

Porto do Carro

Praia do Peró

Cabo Frio

Praia das Conchas

Ilha dos Pargos

Ilha Comprida

Praia Brava

Ilha do Papagaio

Lagoa de Araruama

Praia de Cabo Frio

ATLANTIC OCEAN

Prainha

Praia Maçambaba

Búzios, Cabo Frio & Arraial do Cabo

0   2   4 km

Praia Grande

Praia dos Anjos

Arraial do Cabo

Ilha do Cabo Frio

get the low-down from the locals before heading out to the beaches and dunes.

Getting There & Away
The old coastal road takes longer than BR-101 but it's a beautiful level route winding around foggy green mounds. There are regular 1001 buses from Rio de Janeiro and Niterói (two hours 15 minutes).

BÚZIOS
Population: 20,000
Búzios, a lovely beach resort, is a peninsula (scalloped by 17 beaches) which juts into the Atlantic. Originally it was a simple fishing village until discovered by Brigitte Bardot and her Brazilian boyfriend. The village is now littered with boutiques, fine restaurants, fancy villas, bars and posh pousadas. It's twice the price of the rest of Brazil but affordable for foreigners.

Búzios is not a single town but three settlements on the peninsula – Ossos, Manguinhos, and Armação – and one further north on the mainland called Rasa. Ossos (bones) at the northernmost tip of the peninsula is the oldest and most attractive. It has a pretty harbour with a yacht club, a few hotels, bars and a tourist stand. Manguinhos at the isthmus is the most commercial and even has a 24-hour medical clinic. Armação, in between, has the best restaurants along with city necessities like international phones, a bank, petrol station, post office and pharmacy. North-west along the coast is Rasa and the island of Rasa where Brazil's political dignitaries and rich relax.

Information
Change money in Rio, but if you forget, try one of the French restaurants.

The Ekoda Tourist Agency (tel 23-1490) in Armação at Avenida José Bento Ribeiro Dantas 222 is open seven days a week from 10 am to 8pm. They sell maps of Búzios, organise dune buggy beach tours and have direct buses to Rio.

Boat Rental You can rent a boat for excursions to Ilha Branca from Pablo and Carmen, a Chilean couple who live on a boat off Praia Azeda Ossos.

Beaches
In general the southern beaches are trickier to get to, but they're prettier and have better surf. The northern beaches are more sheltered and closer to the towns.

Working anti-clockwise from south of Maguinhos, the first beaches are Geribá and Ferradurinha (the little horseshoe). These are beautiful beaches with good surf but the Búzios Beach Club is building condos here.

Next on the coast is Ferradura, which is large enough for windsurfing, and Lagoinha, a rocky beach with rough water. Praia da Foca and Praia do Forno have colder water than the other beaches. Praia Olho de Boi (bull's-eye) was named after Brazil's first postage stamp. It's a pocket-sized beach reached from the long clean beach of Praia Brava by a little trail.

João Fernandinho and João Fernandes are both good for snorkelling, as are the topless beaches of Azedinha and Azeda. Praia dos Ossos, Praia da Armação, Praia do Caboclo and Praia dos Amores are pretty to look at, but not for lounging around. Praia da Tartaruga is quiet and pretty. Praia do Gaucho and Manguinhos are town beaches further along.

Places to Stay
Lodging is somewhat on the expensive side, especially in the summer, so consider staying in Saquarema or Cabo Frio or renting a house and staying for a while. In general, rooms to let are cheaper than pousadas. All accommodation listed has showers and includes a light breakfast. Prices range from US$15 to US$40 for doubles in the low season. The high season is January to February and again in July.

In Ossos *Pousada dos Sete Pecados Capitais* (tel 23-1408 or reservations 399-1431) on Praça Eugênio Harold (also known as Praça dos Ossos) charges US$15 off season and US$20 high season for a small double. The place is clean, attractive and among Búzios' cheapest. *Casa Márcia Vanicoru* (tel 23-1542), Rua João Fernandes 60 is a private home with rooms to let. Márcia runs a progressive household and has doubles for US$23 off season, US$28 in the high season. Márcia speaks English, is an excellent cook and will rent you bikes to get to the beaches.

Vila Mediterrânea (tel 23-1322) at Rua João Fernandes 58 is a white-washed and tiled little hotel. Off-season doubles with a lovely inland view are US$20. *Pousada la Chimere* (tel 23-1460), Praça Eugênio Harold 36, is an excellent splurge with a lovely courtyard and large well-appointed rooms with a view over the square. Low season doubles are US$35, high season US$50.

In Armação, try *Pousada do Arco Iris* (tel 23-1256) at Rua Manoel Turibe de Farias 182 with US$15 doubles off season, US$24 high season.

Places to Eat
For good cheap food have grilled fish right on the beaches. Brava, Ferradura and João Fernandes beaches have little thatched-roof fish and beer restaurants. Most of the better restaurants are in or about Armação. *Bar David* in Armação, on Rua Manoel Turibe de Farias, has good cheap food. An ample US$1.50 prato feito usually includes shark fillet with rice, beans and salad.

Búzios is also a good place to indulge in some fancy food. *Le Streghe* (the witch) in Armação, on Rua das Pedras, has great pasta and northern Italian dishes and obsequious service. *Au Cheval Blanc*, a few doors down, has a reputation for fine French food. Both have main courses starting at US$6 and up.

Chez Michou Creperie, also on Rua das Pedras, is a popular hangout because of their incredible crepes. They'll make any kind of crepe you want and the outdoor bar has delicious pinha coladas for US$1. On Avenida Beira Mar, between Ossos and Armação, are *Satíricon* with overpriced Italian seafood and *La Nuance*, a fun outdoor French restaurant and bar.

Things to Buy
If you are capable of lifting one and willing to lug it around Brazil, a whale vertebrae makes an interesting conversation piece for a budding comparative zoologist or chiropractor.

Getting There & Away
The 1001 bus line runs many buses a day to Cabo Frio from the Novo Rio Rodoviária. It's a three hour, 140 km ride. From Cabo Frio to Búzios (Ossos) take the municipal bus for a 50 minute, 20 km bone-crunching cobblestone run. Hitching is possible, but probably not worth it from Niterói along coastal RJ-106 or the inland from near Araruana. Búzios is 16 km away from the turn off of RJ-106.

BARRA DE SÃO JOÃO
Population: 2500
Barra de São João, not to be confused with São João da Barra further north up the coast, is an easy going, friendly place set on a narrow spit of land between a small river and the Atlantic. Old, well-preserved colonial homes with azulejos give it a warm Portuguese feel. The village architecture is protected by law. The picturesque and quiet beach is good for surfcasting.

Places to Stay
The *Pousada Castelinho* at Avenida Marcílio Dias 833 has a ping-pong table and a pool table. Singles cost US$5 to US$7.50 while simple seaside suites cost US$10. The *Hotel Brasil* is cheaper, but not as good, and a third hotel is being built.

Getting There & Away
Thirty-five km from Macaé and 57 km from Cabo Frio, Barra de São João is serviced by 10 daily Macaénse line buses.

RIO DAS OSTRAS

Rio das Ostras is 10 km north of Barra de São João and is full of hotels and restaurants, but not nearly as charming as Barra de São João. For some reason the hotels are more expensive here. The best beaches are Costa Azul and Praia da Joanna, near the yacht club across the wooden bridge.

Places to Stay & Eat

The *Hotel Restaurante Ostrão* (tel 64-1379), Avenida Beira Mar has clean but overpriced doubles with fridge-bar, TV and ocean views. There are several cheaper hotels back on the highway. Try *Sandy's* for light snack food, drinks and breakfast.

MACAÉ

Population: 40,000

Macaé was once a calm fishing village but now its a fast growing petroleum refinery city with Petrobras oil rigs 100 km offshore. Two to three years ago the place was swarming with American technicians, resulting in the gas pipeline which is now being built to Rio. Due to helicopter traffic to and from the oil rigs, Macaé is perhaps the third busiest airport in Brazil after Rio and São Paulo. The best beach in town, Praia Cavalheras, is not polluted. . . yet.

Places to Stay & Eat

The *Pousada Del Rey* (tel 62-2896) at Rua Vereador Manuel Braga 192, only a block from the bus station, is clean and a good deal with US$4.50 singles and US$6 doubles. The owner, Daniel, a Spaniard from Salamanca, recommends the *Cantinho do Bobo* for family style food.

BIOLOGICAL RESERVE POÇO DAS ANTAS

A few km off BR-101 between Casmiro de Abreu and Silva Jardim, the Poço das Antas reserve was created to protect the endangered mico-leão (lion monkey) and its natural habitat, coastal jungle. Fifty mico-leões were sent from a breeding programme in the US. The small monkeys with their golden, lion-like manes are hard to spot. More monkey business is conducted in nearby Cachoeiras de Macaco in the Instituto de Estúdos de Simiologia (Simian Studies Institute).

MACAÉ TO CAMPOS

From Macaé to Campos is rolling ranch land. Here and there are remnants of tropical forest, palms and scraggly undergrowth in uncleared ravines and hill clefts. A dark mountain range runs along the coast 50 km inland. Most of the land between the Atlantic and the mountains is planted with sugar cane.

BARRA DE ITABAPOANA

At the extreme north-east corner of Rio de Janeiro state Barra da Itabapoana borders the Atlantic Ocean and Espírito Santo on the far side of the Rio Itabapoana. There's not much to the town: a beat-up church, a few riverboats, two or three street lights, a TELERJ station, a fish market and a menagerie of pigs, chickens, horses and dogs. The beach is two km from the church out of town (turn left at the cemetery).

Places to Stay & Eat

Dona Sede runs a pension near the church and charges US$3 per person. She can fix you meals, but your best bet is *Restaurante São Remo* by the fish market. It is possible to get good food in the middle of nowhere; their pasteis de camarão are superb and US$1.50 buys a plate of fried fish with shrimp sauce plus rice, beans and salad.

Getting There & Away

There is one daily bus at 6 am that crosses into Cachoeiro do Itapemirim, Espírito Santo. From here the choice is either to head directly to Vitória or take the slower, more picturesque coastal route. Two Grajaú line buses go the three hours and 76 km of dirt road back to Campos in Rio de Janeiro state. One bus leaves at 3 pm, the other at 6 pm.

Espírito Santo

If Brazil were to have a contest for the least appealing state, Piauí would be a contender, but Espírito Santo would win the booby prize. Perhaps Espírito Santo suffers most due to the glory of its neighbouring states, Minas Gerais, Rio de Janeiro and Bahia. In any case it's a small state with little to interest the tourist.

Colonised in the 16th century, Espírito Santo grew as an armed region to prevent gold from being smuggled out of Minas. In the 1800s, Germans and Italians came to the state and settled in the hills of the interior. Until the 1960s, coffee plantations were the prime source of income but that has since been superseded by heavy industry.

The coastline away from Vitória is clean but not particularly pretty. The turbulent surf kicks up sand which gives the water a muddy brown hue rather than the aquamarine found in Bahia or Rio.

In all fairness Espírito Santo does have some attractions, humble as they may be. Some of the fishing villages and beaches on the southern coast are attractive, but they have no provisions for tourists. Excellent seafood is available in Espírito Santo; especially noteworthy is the moqueca capixaba which is made without dendê oil.

VITÓRIA
Population: 144,000
Although founded in 1551, Vitória, capital of Espírito Santo, has remarkably little to show for it. Other than the historic suburb of Vila Velha, 12 km away with some beach and barracas, a little nightlife and some pleasant old buildings, there's not much to see.

Praia de Camburi is the hotel and staurant strip off Avenida Dante chelini. Praia da Costa, the 16th ury pink Anchieta palace (Cidade at Praça João Climaco) and Parque Moscoso (off Avenida da República) are worth a look.

Places to Stay
Hotel Mineira Praia at Rua Joaquim Lírio 363, Praia do Canto, has mostly dorm-style lodging, but there are some single rooms for the same low price of US$2.50 including breakfast.

Hotel Senac (tel 325-0111) at Rua VII 417, Ilha do Boi, could be the cheapest five-star hotel in Brazil; the most expensive suites are only US$54.

Places to Eat
Restaurante Piratas at Avenida Dante Michelini 747, Praia de Camburi has a good squid vinaigrette for US$4. Ask for the couvert. Churrascaria Minuano at Avenida Dante Michelini 337 has a US$4 rodízio. The Natura Restaurante for vegetarians is near the Carlos Gomes theatre at Praça Costa Pereira in the Cidade Alta.

Getting There & Away
It's all too easy to get here, the trick is to get away. The bus station on Ilha do Príncipe has connections to all major cities. Vitória is 500 km from both Rio de Janeiro and Belo Horizonte.

GUARAPARI
Guarapari is the most prominent resort town of Espírito Santo. It's too big a city to be a proper beach town but there are 23 beaches in the municipality, each with a lovely mountain backdrop. The best beach is Praia do Morro; unlike the others it doesn't have too many stones, but it does have the healing monazitic radioactive sands touted in Espírito's brochures.

Places to Stay
There are two budget pousadas on Rua Dr Silvo Melo, Pousada Maryland (tel 261-

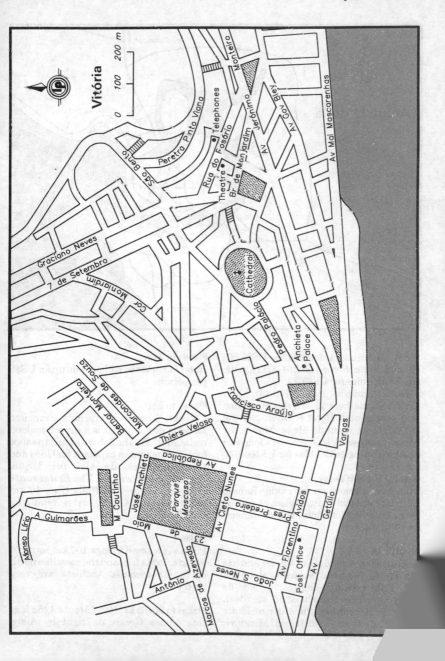

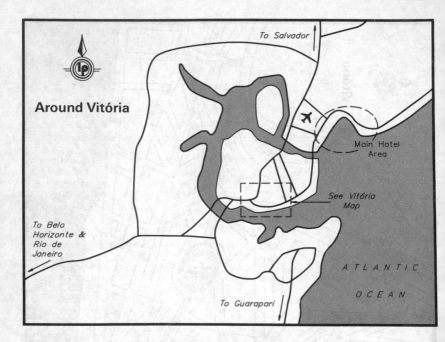

Around Vitória

To Salvador

Main Hotel Area

See Vitória Map

To Belo Horizonte & Rio de Janeiro

ATLANTIC OCEAN

To Guarapari

0553), with singles/doubles for US$8.50/13, and *Areia Preta* (tel 261-2717), with singles/doubles for US$9/12.

Hotel Rádium (tel 261-1014), Rua Ciriaco Ramalhete 52, is a recommended mid-range hotel. *Hotel Porto do Sol* (tel 261-0011) at Avenida Beira Mar 1, by Muquiçaba beach, is Guarapari's four-star hotel with singles/doubles for US$60/67.

Getting There & Away

The bus station on Avenida Ramon Calmon has local coastal buses as well as buses to Belo Horizonte, Rio de Janeiro and Vitória.

ANCHIETA

Anchieta is 88 km south of Vitória and has the Padre Anchieta museum alongside the 16th century church of NS de nção. The church is no big deal, ough it contains the chair of Padre eta and some relics (closed Monday).

Places to Stay

Hotel Porto Velho will put you up for US$5 per person.

Places to Eat

Cabana Senzala at Avenida Francisco Lacerda de Aguiar 81 is a superb seafood restaurant. Try the fish with shrimp sauce for US$6, moqueca capixaba for US$4 and the frigideira de siri for US$6. Portions are enormous. The *Restaurante Peixada do Garia* on Praia Ubu, 10 km north towards Guarapari is reputedly excellent.

PIUMA

Piuma is a small village 100 km south of Vitória. Praia Iriri and the coastline north of Piuma towards Anchieta are very pretty.

Places to Stay & Eat *Hotel Monte Agha* is at Rua Minas Gerais 20, right by Aiaca beach. The small and cheap *Pousada Vela Branca* is also on the beachfront at Rio Novo do Sul 1137.

Restaurante Belabatok on Avenida Beira Mar has fine seafood.

MARATAÍZES

The town of Marataízes caters to the Mineiro holiday crowd during high summer season, but lives off its small fishing industry the rest of the year. Every morning the town beach throbs with fishermen who pull lines in teams, haul in and sort the catch, fix nets and push tiny boats into the foamy sea. It is possible to hire a boat from Marataízes or Itapaiva beach to the islands of Francês, Ovos or Itaputera.

Places to Stay

The *Praia Hotel* (tel 532-2144), at Avenida Atlântica 99, on the beachfront with singles/doubles for US$22, is nicer than its rivals the *Hotel Balneário* (tel 532-1436) at Avenida Lacerda de Aguiar 353, with singles/doubles for US$11.50, or the *Hotel Saveiros Palace* (tel 532-1413) at Avenida Miramar 119, with singles/doubles for US$17.50.

Getting There & Away

There are bus connections to Vitória, Belo Horizonte, and the smaller towns of Anchieta, Guarapari and Cachoeiro de Itapemirim. Two daily buses service the coast all the way to Vitória while other buses go to Vitória via an inland route through Cachoeiro de Itapemirim.

SOUTH OF MARATAÍZES

Praia Marape is a lovely beach adjacent to a poor little fishing village about 30 km south of Marataízes. There is no formal accommodation here, but hardy travellers can make do. Praia das Neves, Praia Moroba and Praia Lagoa Boa Vista are reasonable beaches further to the north.

DOMINGOS MARTINS

Domingos Martins, also known as Campinho, is a small village settled by Germans in 1847. The pride of the town is the musical water clock decorated with figures of the 12 apostles in the Restaurante Vista Linda, seven km before the town proper.

Recanto dos Colibris in town at the far end of Avenida Presidente Vargas is a pretty gathering spot. The town is a good base for exploring the streams and forests of the mountains. Fifty km further into the mountains at Aracê are some fancier resort hotels with horses for hire.

Places to Stay

Hotel e Restaurante Imperador (tel 268-1115) at Rua Duque de Caxias 275 has a sauna and charges US$6.50 for doubles.

Getting There & Away

Five buses a day make the 41 km, hour long trip from Vitória.

SANTA TERESA

Santa Teresa is a small town settled by Italian immigrants. The town has a pretty, flowered plaza and a cool, mountain climate suitable for vineyards. The Biology Museum of Professor Melo Leitão and the orchid gardens have been closed for restoration ever since director Augusto Ruschi died. Nearby trips include the valley of Canaa and the Nova Lombárdia forest reserve.

Places to Stay & Eat

Hotel Pierazzo (tel 259-1233) at Avenida Getúlio Vargas 115 has very nice singles/doubles for US$4.50/9. A few doors down from the hotel is the *Restaurante Zitus* which does good pasta.

Getting There & Away

Santa Teresa is two hours and 76 km from Vitória on the Nossa Senhora das Graças bus line.

Minas Gerais

The state of Minas Gerais, as large as France, is part of a vast plateau that crosses Brazil's interior. Rising along the state's southern border with Rio and São Paulo is the Serra da Mantiqueira with some of Brazil's highest peaks. These mountains stalled the development of Minas Gerais until the gold boom at the beginning of the 18th Century. Running south to north, from São João del Rei through Ouro Prêto and past Diamantina is the Serra Do Espinhaço, Brazil's oldest geological formation. This range separates Minas' two principal river systems: the great São Francisco to the west and the Rio Doce to the east.

Minas has good roads, but travel is usually a sinuous affair. Much of the terrain is characterised by hills, deep valleys, and plateaus running off the larger mountains. With plentiful rains the south, east and much of the centre were once thickly forested, but the land has been cleared for mining and agriculture and today there is little forest left. In the rainy season the land is still green, but forests are pretty much limited to Minas' several large parks and reserves. The northern extension of the state is sertão and less populated than the rest of the state. It's an arid land with shrub-like trees that look dead during the dry season but quickly regain their foliage when it rains. The most common tree is the pepper tree (*aroeira*).

For the traveller Minas presents a welcome contrast to the rest of Brazil. Nestled in the Serra Do Espinhaço are the historic colonial cities which grew-up with the great gold boom. The foothills and streams of these mountains were scoured for gold throughout the 18th century. Minas' exquisite colonial towns are seemingly frozen in another epoch. Their baroque churches and sacred art – most of these are sculptures from one of the world's great artists, Aleijadinho – represent over half of Brazil's national monuments.

Minas also has several hydro-mineral spas in the mountainous south-west corner and a number of prehistoric caves close to the capital, Belo Horizonte. Founded as recently as 1897, Belo Horizonte is Brazil's third largest city. While residents often speak well of this sprawling city, there is little of natural or man-made beauty to stimulate the visitor.

The major historical cities are clustered in three main spots along the Serra do Espinhaço range. São João del Rei, with Tiradentes and Prados nearby is 200 km south of Belo Horizonte. Ouro Prêto and Mariana are 100 km south-east of Belo Horizonte. Diamantina, with Serro further down the road, is 290 km north of Belo Horizonte.

Ouro Prêto, declared a World Cultural Heritage Site by UNESCO, has more of everything than any city in Brazil – more homogeneous baroque architecture, more churches, more Aleijadinho, more museums and more fame. Ouro Prêto also has more tourists, more traffic, more boutiques, more locals hawking things to visitors and more expensive hotels and restaurants. If you go to Ouro Prêto and don't have time to visit the other clusters of historic cities, be sure to visit nearby Mariana which remains less affected by tourism.

It's hard to tell anyone to bypass Ouro Prêto, and if you really like colonial or baroque art and architecture, or the sculpture of Aleijadinho and churches then you should definitely go. But if your time is limited and your visit is during the peak tourist season it's worth considering spending more time at some of the other historic cities and less time at Ouro Prêto.

Diamantina has the fewest tourists and

Top: Ouro Prêto, Minas Gerais (WH)
Left: Fountain in Ouro Prêto, Minas Gerais (WH)
Right: Ouro Prêto, Minas Gerais (WH)

Top: The historic colonial village of Paraty (JM)
Left: Street scene in Tiradentes, Minas Gerais (MS)
Right: Igreja São Francisco, São João del Rei, Minas Gerais (MS)

is the least disturbed of the historic cities. Its many buildings form a beautiful display of colonial architecture. Between them, São João and Tiradentes are a good combination to visit: the former has several churches and works of Aleijadinho in a small lively city with little tourism, and the latter is a tiny colonial town untouched by time and a perfect place to relax and reflect.

The mystery card when shuffling around your itinerary is the town of Congonhas. Congonhas is a couple of hours bus ride from Belo Horizonte, São João or Ouro Prêto. Bus connections are inconvenient going from São João to Ouro Prêto or vice versa and there is one, and only one, attraction: the masterpiece of Aleijadinho. You only need a few hours to view the statues at the Basílica, but it's an inspirational moment and well worth the trouble.

Climate

Minas Gerais has two distinct seasons: wet from October to February and dry from March to September. The rainy season is characterised by almost daily downpours, but they rarely last for long, and although it is warm it is still much cooler than the heat of Rio. The dry season is cool and from July to September it can actually get cold. There is often fog during September and October.

Even during the rainy season travel – with umbrella – is quite practical, with one proviso: From December to February Ouro Prêto, Brazil's most splendid colonial city, is deluged with tourists who can be more of a nuisance than the rain.

History

No one really knows when gold was first discovered in the backwoods of Minas Gerais. But sometime around 1695 *Bandeiras*, groups of explorers from São Paulo, in search of Indian slaves and precious metals saw gold along the riverbanks and in the riverbeds flowing from Brazil's oldest mountains. The gold deposits were called *faisqueiras* (sparkles) because the larger pieces were actually visible and all the miner had to do was pick them up.

Soon the word was out. Brazilians flocked to Minas Gerais and Portuguese immigrated to Brazil. The two groups soon fought over land claims in the War of the Emboadas. Slaves were brought from the sugar fields of Bahia and the savannahs of Angola as few whites did their own mining. Until the last quarter of the 18th century the slaves of Minas Gerais were digging up half the world's gold.

Over 100 years before the more famous California gold rush, Brazil's gold rush was just as crazy, wild and violent. Disease and famine were rampant. The mine towns were known for their licentiousness and prostitutes such as the famous Xica da Silva in Diamantina have been immortalised in the cinema.

Merchants and colonial officials became rich, as did a few gold miners. Gold siphoned off to Portugal ended up in feeding England's industrial revolution, and so the only lasting benefits to come to Brazil were the development of Rio de Janeiro, the main port for the gold, and the creation of the beautiful, church-clad mining cities that dot the hills of Minas Gerais. Ouro Prêto was the most splendid of these. Vila Rica de Ouro Prêto (rich town of black gold), as it was known, grew to 100,000 people and became the richest city in the New World.

Economy

Unlike many appellations, Minas Gerais (general mines) wears its name well. Minas produces more iron, tin, diamonds, zinc, quartz and phosphates than any other state in Brazil. It has one of the world's largest reserves of iron. The industrial growth rate of the state has been well above the national average over the past few years and the state should soon pass Rio de Janeiro as the second most powerful economy behind São

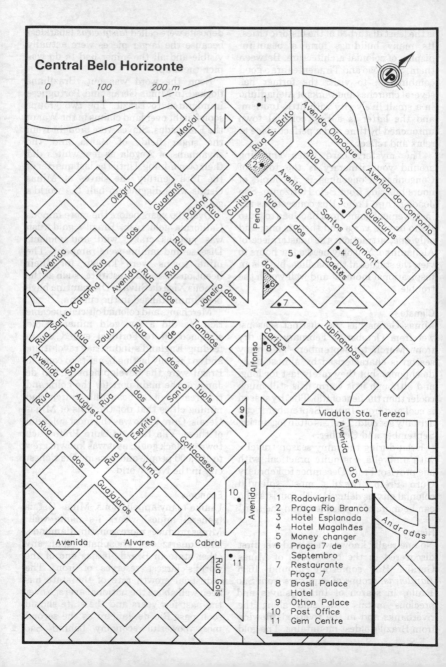

Central Belo Horizonte

0   100   200 m

1   Rodoviaria
2   Praça Rio Branco
3   Hotel Esplanada
4   Hotel Magalhães
5   Money changer
6   Praça 7 de
    Septembro
7   Restaurante
    Praça 7
8   Brasil Palace
    Hotel
9   Othon Palace
10 Post Office
11 Gem Centre

Paulo. Belo Horizonte is the site of a large Fiat automobile plant.

Minas is known for its large milk and cheese production. The agriculture sector is diverse and strong, with fruit and cattle as well.

BELO HORIZONTE

Population: 1,450,000

Belo is the capital of mineral-rich Minas Gerais state. It's a rapidly industrialising city, founded in 1897 and already the third largest city in the country. Belo is a planned city, a giant sprawling affair surrounded by hills which lock in the thick grey-black layers of smog. Belo has nothing of special interest for the tourist; most travellers who stop here are on their way to Ouro Prêto or Diamantina with perhaps the occasional soul heading to Brasília.

Information

Everything is located around the centre so it's easy to get business done. There are no money exchange houses in Belo, but banks abound. Changing dollars at parallel rates isn't difficult, but travellers' cheques are a bit of a hassle. If you are changing money for Ouro Prêto, the jewellery stores there will usually change dollars and travellers' cheques at close to the parallel rate.

Places to Stay

Lots of hotels are central or close to the rodoviária, which is the place to be. Prices are generally inexpensive, and there are many cheap places. From the front of the rodoviária there are several hotels within 10 blocks along the following routes: walk down Avenida Santos Dumont and then turn right and go up Rua Espírito Santo or walk up Avenida Afonso Pena, the major diagonal street.

Places to Stay - bottom end

The *Hotel Esplanada* (tel 222-7411), a 2-star Embratur hotel at Avenida Santos Dumont 304 (cross street Espírito Santo), charges US$5.50/7 for singles/doubles without bath or US$8.50/12.50 with bath.

Hotel Magalhães (tel 222-9233) at Rua Espírito Santo 237 has singles/doubles for US$1.50/2.50 without bath and doubles with bath for US$5. It is clean and comfortable.

Next door is *Hotel São Salvador* (tel 222-7731) at Rua Espírito Santo 237 with singles/doubles for US$1.50/4 without baths and US$4 for doubles with bath. *Continental* (tel 201-7944) at Avenida Paraná 241, in the centre, is a couple of blocks on the other side of Avenida Afonso Pena. It's clean, friendly, not too noisy and some rooms have little balconies. Fifties'-style doubles are a good deal at US$9.50.

If you want to stay out in the Pampulha district the *Mineirão* (tel 441-6133) on Avenida Antonio Abraao Caram is good and cheap with singles for 70c. In the centre, the *Sul America* (tel 201-1722) at Avenida Amazonas 50 is good and mid priced. For a bit less try the *Ambrosio Porto* (tel 224-1626) at Rua Espírito Santo 1502.

Places to Stay - top end

In the centre, across from the park, the *Othon Palace* (tel 273-3844) is Belo Horizonte's 5-star hotel. It's brand new and has singles/ doubles for US$55/61 without bath.

The *Hotel Amazonas* (tel 201-4644) at Avenida Amazonas 120 is a classy 3-star Embratur place. They charge US$18.50 for doubles with TV, air-con and balcony. *Brasil Palace Hotel* (tel 273-3811) at Rua dos Carijos 269 has singles/doubles without bath for US$10/12.

Entertainment

Bampís (tel 201-9312) is a good samba-type dance spot at Avenida Alvares Cabral 967, Lourdes.

Right near the central hotels on Praça Sete de Setembro Praça 7, the *Restaurante Praça 7* has a beer-hall atmosphere with good local music from 10 pm to 3 am. If you can stand the horrible sound system it's fun. The cover charge is only 50c.

Cantina do Adnan is a somewhat sleazy place, but they have some terrific, very unusual, local music. It's a few blocks up from the Hotel Magalhães, on Rua Espirito Santo.

Things to Buy

The Centro de Artessanato Mineiro (tel 222-2765) on Avenida Afonsi Pena 1537, Palacio das Artes (at the edge of the Municipal Park) has a varied assortment of Mineiro crafts: ceramics, jewellery, tapestries, rugs, quilts and soapstone sculptures. It's open daily 9 am to 9 pm and it's a government store.

The hippie fair at the Praça da Liberdade has local crafts and good food on Sundays and Thursday nights.

The Gem Centre is not far from the municipal park, at Avenida Alvares Cabral 45. There are around 20 reputable gem dealers with small shops in the building.

Getting There & Away

Air Belo Horizonte is connected to Rio and São Paulo by frequent one hour VASP/Cruzeiro/Transbrasil *ponte aeria* (air bridge) flights. There are flights to just about anywhere in Brazil.

Bus Buses take seven hours to Rio, 9½ to São Paulo, 12 hours to Brasília, 21 to Salvador. There are 10 daily buses to Ouro Prêto (98 km); the first leaves at 6.45 am, the last at 9 pm. The trip takes 1¾ hours.

There are seven daily buses to Mariana (115 km); six daily to Diamantina (248 km), the first at 5.30 am and the last at midnight; 11 daily to São João del Rei (187 km), the first at 6.15 am and the last at 11 pm. From 4 am to midnight frequent buses go to Sabará, 15 minutes away.

If you're heading to the mineral spring resorts, there are four daily buses to Poços das Caldas and two dailies to Caxambu.

Getting Around

Airport Transport There are two airports. Most planes use the new international Aeroporto Confins which is 40 km from the city. The closer, sleepy Aeroporto da Pampulha has some of the Rio and São Paulo shuttle flights.

The best way to get to the airport is by bus from the rodoviária. Empresa Zeze has a conventional bus that leaves every 30 minutes starting at 4.45 am until 9.15 pm, 50c. Even though it's not advertised, this bus will stop at Aeroporto da Pampulha on the way to Aeroporto Confins but make sure the driver knows your destination.

There is also an executivo bus that costs 75c and is air conditioned. It leaves from the executivo terminal every 45 minutes starting at 5.15 am until 10 pm.

SABARÁ

Sabará stands on the muddy banks of the Rio das Velhas (Old Ladies River). Sabará was one of the world's wealthiest mining centres, but is now a poor town dominated by a Belgian metal works. In the boom years of the early 1700s, when the Rio das Velhas was 15 times wider, slave boats would sail all the way down the Rio São Francisco from Bahia. Sabará produced more gold in one week than the rest of Brazil produced in one year. You can still pan the river bed for gold flakes, but the nuggets are long since gone.

Matriz de NS de Conceição

The Portuguese Jesuits, cultural ambassadors of the far flung Portuguese empire, were among the first westerners to make contact with the Orient. As a result the Matriz de NS de Conceição (1720) is a fascinating blend of Oriental arts and Portuguese baroque; overwhelming with its gold leaf and red Chinese scrolls.

Re-stationed in Brazil, the Jesuits brought the Oriental arts to Sabará, as is evident in the pagodas on some of the church door panels by the sanctuary. There are several other interesting little details in the church. Floorboards cover

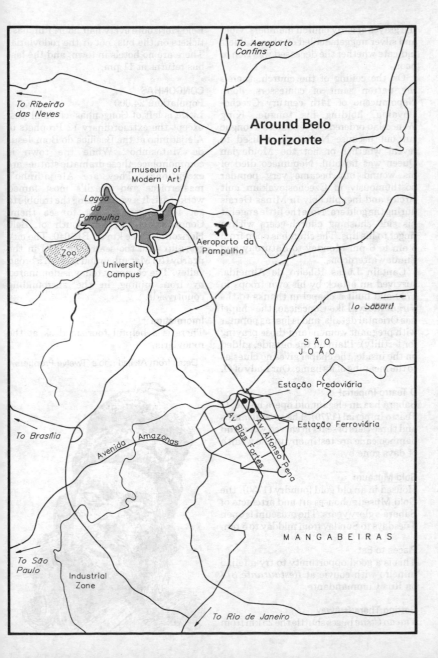

Around Belo Horizonte

To Aeroporto Confins

To Ribeirão das Neves

museum of Modern Art

Lagoa da Pampulha

Zoo

University Campus

Aeroporto da Pampulha

To Sabará

SÃO JOÃO

Estação Predoviária

Estação Ferroviária

Av. Bias Fortes

Av. Afonso Pena

To Brasília

Avenida Amazonas

To São Paulo

Industrial Zone

MANGABEIRAS

To Rio de Janeiro

the graves of early church members. Gold and silver nuggets nailed on these tablets indicate whether the deceased was rich or poor.

On the ceiling of the church, there's the patron saint of confessors, John Nepomuceno of 14th century Czechoslovakia, holding his tongue. King Wenceslau ordered St Nepumeco's tongue cut out because Nepumeco refused to reveal whether or not the Moldavian Queen was faithful. Nepumeco died of his wound but became very popular posthumously in Czechoslovakian cult circles and inexplicably in Minas Gerais during the gold era. Note the little angel at his side shushing church-goers with a finger to his lips. The church is open from 8 am to 6 pm Monday to Saturday and Sunday afternoons.

Captain Lucas Ribeiro de Almeida, survived an attack by his own troops in 1720 and built a chapel in thanks to the Virgin Mary. Like Conceição, the chapel has Oriental details, and is just as popular with pregnant women (and those praying for fertility). Plain on the outside, gilded on the inside, the chapel gives no clues as to the meaning of its name, Our Lady of O.

O Teatro Imperial
Sabará has an elegant old opera house, O Teatro Imperial (1770). The crystal lamps and three tiers of seats in carved wood and bamboo cane are testimony to the wealth of days gone by.

Gold Museum
Housed in an old gold foundry (1730), the Gold Museum houses art and artefacts of Sabará's glory years. The museum is open Tuesdays to Sunday from midday to 5 pm.

Places to Eat
This is a good opportunity to try a feijão mineiro with couvie at *Restaurante 314* on Rua Commandante.

Getting There & Away
Viação Cisne buses shuttle the 25 km from

Belo Horizonte every half hour. Purchase tickets on the bus, not at the rodoviária. There are no hotels in town, and the last bus returns at 11 pm.

CONGONHAS
Population: 24,000
Little is left of Congonhas' colonial past except the extraordinary 12 Prophets of Aleijadinho at the Basílica do Bom Jesus de Matosinhos. While the town is commonplace, these dramatic statues are exceptional. They are Aleijadinho's masterpiece and Brazil's most famed work of art. It's worth taking the trouble to get to Congonhas just to see them. Congonhas is 72 km south of Belo Horizonte, three km off BR-040. The city grew-up with the search for gold in the nearby Rio Maranhão and is set in a broad valley. The economy today is dominated by iron mining in the surrounding countryside.

Information
There is a helpful tourism desk at the rodoviária.

Detail from Aleijadinho's 'Twelve Prophets'

The 12 Prophets

Already an old man, sick and crippled, Aleijadinho sculpted the 12 Prophets from 1800 to 1805. Symmetrically placed in front of the Basílica of Bom Jesus do Matozinho each of the prophets from the Old Testament was carved out of one or two blocks of soapstone. Each prophet carries a message from the scrolls, six of them are good, six bad, and all in Latin.

Much has been written about these sculptures: their dynamic quality, the sense of movement (many talk of the appearance of a Hindu dance or a ballet), how they complement each other and how their arrangement in front of the church prevents them from being seen in isolation. The poet Carlos Drummond de Andrade wrote that the dramatic faces and gestures are 'magnificent, terrible, grave and tender' and commented on 'the way the statues, of human size, appear to be larger than life as they look down upon the viewer with the sky behind them'.

Before working on the prophets, Aleijadinho carved or supervised his assistants in carving 6 wooden statues, which were placed in the six little chapels that represent the Passion of Christ: The Last Supper, Calvary, Imprisonment, Flagellation and Coronation, Carrying of the Cross and The Crucifixion.

Some of the figures, like the Roman soldiers, are very crude and clearly done by assistants, while others are finely chiselled. The statues were restored in 1957 by the painter Edson Mota and the gardens were designed by Burle Marx.

Festivals

From 7 to 14 September the Jubileu do Senhor Bom Jesus de Matosinhos is one of the great religious festivals in Minas Gerais. Each year, approximately 600,000 pilgrims arrive at the church to make promises and penitence, receive blessings and give and receive alms. The Holy Week processions in Congonhas are also famous, especially the dramatisations during Good Friday.

Places to Stay

Hotel Cova do Daniel (tel 731-1834) is old, antique and definitely not restored. This hotel is right across the street from the 12 Prophets. Single rooms cost US$2/4.50 without/with bath, doubles are US$4.50/9 without/with bath. There is a restaurant downstairs.

The only other hotel in town is the cheaper and funkier *Hotel Freitas* (tel 731-1543), downtown at Rua Mal Floriano 69.

Getting There & Away

Getting an early start, you can go from São João del Rei to Congonhas – spending a few hours at the 12 Prophets – and then on to Conselheiro Lafaiete and Ouro Prêto in one day (or vice versa). We've included detailed bus schedules to enable you to make quick connections between the three buses you must take.

There are nine daily buses from Belo Horizonte to Congonhas (one hour and 40 minutes, US$1). The last return bus to Belo Horizonte leaves Congonhas at 8 pm. Buses leave every 30 minutes for Conselheiro Lafaiete where you can get buses to Rio.

From Congonhas to Ouro Prêto you can go to Belo Horizonte or make a connection in Conselheiro Lafaiete. The latter route can be faster if you make a good connection. The drive from Lafaiete to Ouro Prêto is almost all dirt road and very slow and often crowded, but quite scenic with a view of several large mining projects. Try to get to Lafaiete a bit early to make sure you get a bus, although if you miss the last bus there are a couple of hotels across from the rodoviária.

From Lafaiete to Ouro Prêto is US$1.25 and 2½ hours: Monday to Friday 7.15 am, 9.40 am, midday, 3 pm and 6.45 pm; Saturday 7.15 am, midday, 3 pm and 6 pm and Sunday 6 am, midday, 3 pm and 6 pm.

From Ouro Prêto to Lafaiete buses leave Monday to Saturday at 5 am (except Saturday), 9 am, midday, 2.40 pm and 6 pm and Sunday at 6 am, midday, 2.40 pm and 6 pm.

Buses leave Congonhas for São João del Rei at 7.20 am, 9.40 am, 1.20 am, 2.50 pm, 4.20 pm, 6.10 pm, 8.10 pm, 8.20 pm, 9.20 pm and a 10.20 pm bus on Sundays only.

Getting Around

From the Congonhas rodoviária the 'Basílica' bus leaves every 30 minutes and costs 5c. It's a 15-minute ride up the hill to the Basilica and the 12 Prophets. Try to get off the bus just after passing the church, as it begins to go downhill, for the best approach and first view of the statues. The same bus returns you to the rodoviária.

OURO PRÊTO
Population: 30,000

History

According to the Jesuit Antonil, a mulatto servant in the Antonio Rodrigues Arzão expedition went to the Rivulet Tripui to quench his thirst and pocketed a few grains of an odd black metal he found in the stream bed. The little nuggets were reported to the governor of Rio and turned out to be gold. The exact location of the river was forgotten during the long expedition and only the strange shape of the peaks of Italcolomy were remembered.

On 24 June 1698 Antonio Dias de Oliveira rediscovered the area, convinced he had found the promised El Dorado. The mines were the largest deposits of gold in the western hemisphere and the news and gold fever spread fast. Stories tell of men who acquired fabulous wealth from one day to the next, and others who died of hunger with their pockets full of gold.

King Dom João V back in Portugal was quick to tax a royal fifth, and a chain of posts was established to ensure the crown was getting its cut. In theory, all the gold was brought to these *Casas de Intendencias* to be weighed and turned into bars, and the royal fifth taken. Tax shirkers were cast into dungeons or exiled to Africa. One common technique used to avoid the tax was to hide gold powder in hollow images of the saints. Bitter over the tax, the Paulista miners rebelled against the Portuguese in the unsuccessful Guerra dos Emboabas (1709). Two years later Vila Rica, the predecessor to Ouro Prêto, was founded.

The finest goods from India and England were made available to the simple mining town. The gold bought the service of baroque artisans who turned the city into an architectural gem. At the height of the gold boom in the mid 18th century there were 110,000 people in Ouro Prêto (the vast majority slaves) versus 50,000 in New York and about 20,000 in Rio de Janeiro. The royal fifth, estimated as 100 tons of gold in the 18th century, quickly passed through the hands of the Portuguese court, built up Lisbon and then financed the British Industrial Revolution.

The greed of the Portuguese led to the sedition of Vila Rica (1720). As the boom tapered, the miners found it increasingly difficult to pay ever larger gold taxes. In 1789 poets Claudio da Costa and Tomas Gonzaga, the dentist Tiradentes and others whose heads were full of the French revolutionary philosophies hatched the Incofidencia Mineira. The attempt to overthrow the Portuguese was crushed by agents of the crown in the early stages. Gonzaga was exiled to Mozambique, and Costa did time in prison. Tiradentes, the only man not to deny his role in the conspiracy, was abandoned by his friends, jailed for three years without defence, then drawn and quartered.

By decree of Emperor Dom Pedro I, Vila Rica, capital of Minas Gerais since 1721, became the Imperial City of Ouro Prêto. In 1897 the state capital moved from Ouro Prêto to Belo Horizonte. This was the decisive move that preserved Ouro Prêto's colonial flavour. The former capital of Minas Gerais, assumes the symbolic role

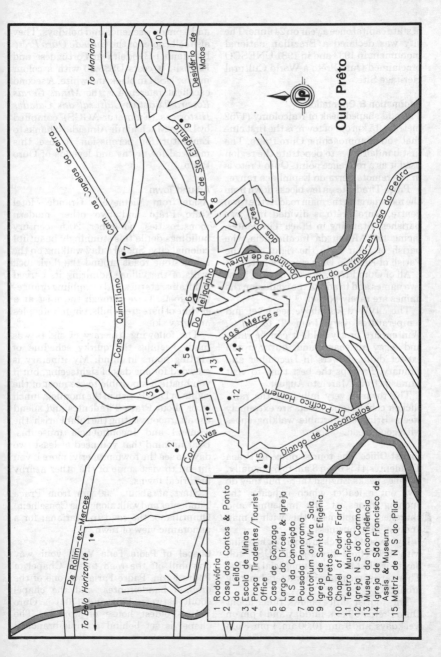

Ouro Prêto

1 Rodoviária
2 Casa dos Contos & Ponto do Leilão
3 Escola de Minas
4 Praça Tiradentes/Tourist Office
5 Casa de Gonzaga
6 Largo do Dirceu & Igreja N S da Conceição
7 Pousada Panorama
8 Oratorium of Vira Saia
9 Igreja de Santa Efigênia dos Pretos
10 Chapel of Padre Faria
11 Teatro Municipal
12 Igreja N S do Carmo
13 Museu da Inconfidência
14 Igreja de São Francisco de Assis & Museum
15 Matriz de N S do Pilar

of state capital once a year on 24 June. The city was declared a Brazilian national monument in 1933 and in 1981 UNESCO proclaimed Ouro Prêto a World Cultural Heritage Site.

Information & Orientation

The odd shaped peak of Italcolomy (1752 metres), 15 km out of town, is the first clue that you're approaching Ouro Prêto. The first bandeirantes to penetrate the region used it as a reference point. Ouro Prêto is in the remote Serra do Espinhaço range.

Praça Tiradentes, a few blocks down from the rodoviária on the main road, is the town centre. Ouro Prêto is divided into two parishes. Standing in Praça Tiradentes, facing the Museu da Incofidência, the parish of Pilar is to the right and the Parish of Antonio Dias is to the left.

All of Ouro Prêto's streets have at least two names and to add to the confusion the names are rarely posted.

The city is a km above sea level and temperatures vary from 2 to 28°C. Winters are pretty cold. It can be rainy and foggy all year round, but you can expect daily showers in December and January. Perhaps the best time to visit Minas is from March to August.

The town is very hilly and the rain-slicked cobblestone streets are extremely steep. Bring comfortable walking shoes with good tread.

Tourist Office The tourist office at Praça Tiradentes 41 is open 8 am to 5 pm daily. No one speaks English there, but they do give out a leaflet which indicates the opening times of the museums and churches. Supplement this with a map and you're in business.

If you want to pack in a lot of sightseeing with little effort hire a guide (US$7 full day tour), but beware of unofficial guides. There are some nasty characters hanging around.

The tourist office shows films about Ouro Prêto at 9 am, midday and 4 pm on weekdays, and 9 am, 10.30 am, 1 pm, 3 pm and 4 pm on weekends and holidays. They also sell copies of the *Guia de Ouro Prêto* by Manuel Bandeira in Portuguese and English. It costs US$3.50 with a colour map or US$1 in black and white. A second excellent reference is the *Minas Gerais Roteiro Turistico-Cultural das Cidades Historicas* (Embratur-AGGS) compiled by Lucia Machado de Almeida. Thanks to Embratur for permission to use this material for myths and legends of Ouro Prêto.

Around Town

Aside from Niemeyer's Grande Hotel Ouro Prêto and two other modern monstrosities no other 20th century buildings defile this stunningly beautiful colonial city. Spend a day walking on the cobblestone roads around the dark rock walls of the village admiring its carved fountains, statues and crumbling orange-tiled roofs. Gaze through the mist at a skyline of bare green hills, church steeples and grey skies.

The following itinerary of sights was made keeping the quirky schedule of visiting hours in mind. My itinerary is crowded for one day of sightseeing, but if you hustle it's possible to see most of the sights in Dias Parish in the morning, lunch in or about Praça Tiradentes and spend the afternoon visiting the Pilar Parish, the Mineral and Inconfidência museums. Bear in mind that you need at least two days to see the town properly, more if you intend to visit some of the other nearby historical towns.

Start at about 7.30 am from Praça Tiradentes and walk along Rua Conselheiro Quintiliano, the road to Mariana, for a panoramic view of town.

Chapel of Padre Faria Work your way downhill off the road to the Chapel of Padre Faria. Padre Faria was one of the original bandeirantes, and the chapel (built between 1701 and 1704) is Ouro Prêto's oldest house of worship. The chapel is set behind a triple-branched papal cross (1756), the three branches representing the temporal, spiritual and material powers of the pope. It's the richest chapel in terms of gold and artwork, but unfortunately due to poor documentation the artists are anonymous. In 1750 the church bell rang for Tiradentes (when his body was brought to Rio), and then the church bell rang once again for the inauguration of Brasília. Note that the angel on the right-hand side of the high altar has butterfly wings. The church is open from 8 am to midday.

Igreja de Santa Efigênia dos Prêtos
Descending the Ladeira do Padre Faria back towards town is the Igreja de Santa Efigênia dos Prêtos. The church was built between 1742 and 1749 by and for the black slave community. Santa Efigênia, patroness of the church was the queen of Nubia, and the featured saints, Santo Antonio do Nolo and São Benedito, are black. The slaves prayed to these images so that they wouldn't be crushed in the mines.

The church is Ouro Prêto's poorest in terms of gold and richest in art work. The altar is by Aleijadinho's master, Francisco Javier do Briton. Many of the interior panels are by Manuel Rabelo de Souza (see if you can find the painting of Robinson Crusoe), and the exterior image of Nossa Senhora do Rosário is by Aleijadinho himself. The church was financed by gold extracted from Chico-Rei's gold mine, Encardadeira. Slaves contributed to the church coffer by washing their gold-flaked hair in baptismal fonts. Others managed to smuggle gold powder under fingernails and inside tooth cavities. The church is open from 8 am until midday.

The first abolitionist in Brazil was Chico-Rei, an African tribal king. Amidst the frenzy of the gold rush an entire tribe, king and all, was captured in Africa, placed in chains, sent to Brazil and sold to a mine owner in Ouro Prêto. Chico-Rei worked as the foreman of the slave-miners. Working Sundays and holidays, Chico-Rei finally bought his freedom from the slave-master, then freed his son Osmar. Together, father and son liberated the entire tribe. The collective bought the fabulously wealthy Encardadeira gold mine and Chico-Rei assumed his royal functions, once again holding court in Vila Rica and celebrating African holidays in traditional costume. News of this reached the Portuguese king, who immediately prohibited slaves from purchasing their own freedom. Chico-Rei is a folk-hero among Brazilian Blacks.

Vira-Saia Oratory
At the beginning of the 18th century there was a rash of ghost incidents in the city. Phantoms would spring from the walls near Santa Efigênia church and wing through town spooking the townspeople. The simple village folk would faint and drop their bags of gold powder which the bandit-like ghosts would snatch. The terrorised people asked the bishop for permission to build oratories and the bishop complied. Designed to keep evil spirits at bay, the oratories (glass-encased niches containing images of saints) were built on many street corners. Not many oratories remain, there's one on Rua dos Paulista (also called Bernardo Vasconcelos) and another on Antonio Dias, but the most famous one of all is the Oratorio Vira-Saia. Nowadays these few remaining oratories are used to scare off evil spirits during Holy Week.

At the bottom of the Ladeira de Santa Efigênia (also known as Vira-Saia), on the corner with Rua Barão do Ouro Branco, is the small oratory of Vira-Saia. The meaning of vira-saia is two-fold, originating either from the Portuguese *virar* (turn) and *sair* (depart) or the direct translation of *vira-saia*, turncoat or traitor.

In the latter part of the 18th century gold caravans destined for the Portuguese crown were robbed on a regular basis, despite measures to cloak shipments by altering dates and routes. It didn't take long to surmise that it was an inside job. Someone working in the Casa de Fundição was leaking information.

Who would suspect that Antonio Francisco Alves, pillar of the community, upstanding citizen, mild-mannered businessman and gentle father, was in reality the head and brains behind the Vira-Saia bandits – the very same outfit which looted the government's gold caravans? After the route of the gold caravan was planned, Alves would steal out to the oratory and turn the image of Nossa Senhora das Almas within the sanctuary (thus pinpointing the direction of the gold traffic).

The plot thickens. A reward was posted for revealing the secret identity of the criminal. Finally a member of Alves' own band, Luis Gibut, turned him in. Gibut was a French Jesuit who fell in love with a beautiful dame, abandoned the order, became a highway bandit and the turncoat's turncoat. Whew. This same Luis Gibut is responsible for teaching misspelled Latin phrases which Aleijadinho incorporated into many of his works.

Alves, his wife and his daughters were dragged off into the jungle to meet their fate. Sra Duruta, a good neighbour, came to the rescue and saved Alves, but it was too late for his wife and kids. Alves was one step ahead of the long arm of the law, but he didn't get off scot-free. Shortly afterwards, he was plugged by another unnamed Vira-Saia. The criminal gang continued to do successful robberies without its first chief. Luis Gibut, ex-Jesuit, traitor and poor speller, is probably still doing time in purgatory.

Largo do Dirceu

Largo do Dirceu is next, right before the Igreja Matriz NS da Conceição de Antônio Dias. This used to be a popular hangout of the poet Tomás António Gonzaga and his girlfriend and muse, Marília. It figures prominently in *Marília de Dirceu*, the most celebrated poem in the Portuguese language.

Matriz NS da Conceição de Antônio Dias

The cathedral of the António Dias parish, Matriz NS da Conceição de Antônio Dias, was designed by Aleijadinho's father, Manuel Francisco Lisboa, and built between the years 1727 and 1770. Note the painting of the eagle, its head points downward and is symbolic of the domination of the Moors by the Christians. Aleijadinho is buried by the altar of Boa Morte.

The Museu do Aleijadinho adjoins the church and opens the same hours of 8 to 11.30 am and 1 to 5 pm. Nearby is Encardideira, the abandoned mine of Chico-Rei. Ask around for directions. It's rumoured to be haunted, dangerous, full of crumbling secret passageways and ripe for a Hardy Boys adventure.

Tomás Antônio Gonzaga's House

Rua do Ouvidor 9 is the address of Tomás Antônio Gonzaga's house and now the seat of the municipal government. Back in 1789, the gold tax and anti-monarchist sentiment in Minas were rising concurrently. This is where Gonzaga, his poet-friend Claudio da Costa (author of *Vila Rica*), Tiradentes the dentist and others conspired unsuccessfully to overthrow the Portuguese monarchy. The sad little event came to be known as the Incofidência Mineira.

Igreja de São Francisco de Assis

Across the street from Gonzaga's house is the Igreja de São Francisco de Assis. After the 12 Prophets in Congonhas do Campo, Aleijadinho's (Antonio Francisco Lisboa) masterwork, it is the single most important piece of Brazilian colonial architecture. The entire exterior, a radical departure from the military baroque style, was carved by Aleijadinho alone, from the soapstone medallion to the cannon waterspouts and the military (two bar) cross. The interior was painted by Aleijadinho's long-term partner Mestre Manuel da Costa Ataíde.

The sacristy is haunted by the spirit of an 18th century woman. In the dead of night her head dissolves into a skull and she screams, 'I'm dying, call Father Carlos!' The church and adjoining Aleijadinho museum is open from 8 to 11.30 am and 1 to 5 pm.

Aleijadinho

The church of São Francisco de Assis, the Carmo church façade, the 12 Prophets of Congonhas do Campos and innumerable relics in Mariana, Sabará, Tiradentes and São João del Rei were all carved by Aleijadinho. Brazil's Michelangelo lost the use of his hands and legs at the age of 30 but with hammer and chisel strapped to his arms, advanced art in Brazil from the excesses of the baroque to a finer, more graceful rococo. The Mineiros have reason to be proud of Aleijadinho – he is a figure of international prominence in the history of art. Aleijadinho angels have his stylistic signature: wavy hair, wide-open eyes and big round cheeks.

Son of a Portuguese architect and Black slave, Aleijadinho lived from 1730 to 1814 and was buried in the Matriz Dias within 50 paces of his birth site. By federal decree he was declared patron of Brazilian arts in 1973. For many years Manuel da Costa Ataíde, from nearby Mariana, successfully collaborated with Aleijadinho in many churches: Aleijadinho would sculpt the exterior and a few interior pieces and Ataíde would paint interior panels. With his secretly concocted vegetable dyes, Costa the colour man fleshed out much of Aleijadinho's work.

Praça Tiradentes Praça Tiradentes is the centre of town and a good place to have lunch, catch your breath by the statue of Tiradentes or take in some museums before the churches of the Pilar parish open in the afternoon.

The Museu da Incofidência, formerly the old municipal building and jail, is an attractive civic building built between 1784 and 1854. Used as a prison from 1907 until 1937, the museum contains the Tiradentes tomb, documents of the Incofidência Mineira, torture instruments and important works by Ataíde and Aleijadinho. The museum is open midday to 5.30 pm.

Igreja NS do Carmo The Igreja NS do Carmo was a group effort by the most important artists of the area. Begun in 1766 and completed in 1772, the church features a façade by Aleijadinho. It's open 1 pm to 5 pm.

Other Buildings

The Escola de Minas in the old governor's palace in Praça Tiradentes has a very fine museum of mineralogy. It's open midday to 5 pm, Monday to Friday. The Casa dos Contos (Counting House) is now a public library and art gallery. Claudio da Costa was imprisoned here after participating in the Inconfidência Mineira. It is open 12.30 to 5 pm. Next door is the old Ponto do Leilão where slaves were taken to be tortured.

Casa de Tiradentes, the home of Joaquim Jose da Silva Xavier (better known as Tiradentes - toothpuller), is nearby. After his failed rebellion against the Portuguese and execution in Rio his head was paraded around town, his house was demolished and the grounds were salted so that nothing would grow there.

Matriz de NS do Pilar

The Matriz de NS do Pilar is the second most opulent church in Brazil (after Salvador's São Francisco) in terms of gold, with 434 kg of gold and silver and one of Brazil's finest showcases of artwork. Note the wild bird chandelier holders, the laminated beaten gold, the scrolled church doors, 15 panels of Old and New Testament scenes by Pedro Gomes Chaes and the hair on Jesus (the real stuff, donated by a penitent worshipper).

Legend has it that both the Pilar and Antonio Dias parishes vied for the image of Nossa Senhora dos Passos. In order to settle the argument, the image was loaded on a horse standing in Praça Tiradentes and rockets were fired to scare the horse. The image would belong to the parish to which the horse bolted, but since the horse only knew one path it galloped straight to the Matriz do Pilar.

Teatro Municipal

Built in 1769 by João de Souza Lisboa, the Teatro Municipal is the oldest theatre in Minas Gerais and perhaps in all of Brazil. The theatre is open to visitors from 1 to 5 pm.

Other Attractions

This is only a partial list of places to see in Ouro Prêto. If you're still enthusiastic for more, the tourist office can sell you some fine guidebooks. If you're after something more strenuous hike to the peak of

Itacolomy; it takes three hours to walk the 18 km from Praça Tiradentes.

Parque Itacomory (easiest approach from Mariana) is a pleasant excursion – the park has good walking trails, waterfalls and orchids, and the colonial town of Mariana is only 12 km away. Buses leave every half hour and on weekends at 9.30 am a steam train leaves from Ouro Prêto's Barrio da Barra.

Minas de Passagem

I got a kick out of Minas de Passagem. It is probably the best gold mine to visit in the Ouro Prêto region. The immense system of tunnels goes way down deep, then spreads horizontally. Only a fraction of the mine is open to the public, but for most terrestrials it's enough. The descent into the mine is made in an antique, steam-powered cable-car that gives you a very good idea of just how dangerous and claustrophobic mining can be.

The mine was opened in 1719. Until the abolition of slavery it was worked by Black slaves, many of whom died (not from the cable-car ride as you might think after taking it), but from the job of dynamiting into the rock. My guide who had been working in the mine as recently as 1985, and was then earning the minimum wage of US$35 a month, told us that the life of the 'free' miner was little better than that of the slave.

The mandatory guided tour, led by former miners, is short and quite informative, especially if someone in the group asks the right questions. The mine is open from 9 am to 6 pm daily and is well worth the US$2 entry fee.

The mine is between Ouro Prêto and Mariana. Take any local bus that runs between the two and ask the driver to let you off at Minas de Passagem.

Festivals

The Semana Santa Holy Week Procession held on the Thursday before Palm Sunday and sporadically until Easter Sunday is a spectacle. The Congado is to Minas what Candomblé is to Bahia and umbanda is to Rio; the local expression of African-Christian syncretism. The major Congado celebrations are for Nossa Senhora do Rosario on 23 to 25 October at the Capela do Padre Faria, the New Year and 13 May, the anniversary of abolition.

The Cavalhada held in Amarantina (near Ouro Prêto) during the Festa de São Gonçalo from 17 to 23 September isn't as grand as the one in Pirenópolis, but impressive nonetheless. The Cavalhada is a re-enactment of the battles between Christians and Moors in Iberia.

Places to Stay

Ouro Prêto is a university town with schools of pharmacy and biochemistry, mineralogy, geology and engineering. No less than 20% of the homes in Ouro Prêto are devoted to student lodging. Although they are the cheapest places to stay in town, most of the repúblicas are closed from Christmas to Carnival. Consult the list in the tourist office for a complete list of student repúblicas. Regular lodging tends to be expensive and hard to find on weekends, holidays and during exam periods.

Places to Stay – bottom end

The *Serigi República* (tel 551-1279) on Rua Nova charges US$3 for a bed.

More expensive places include the *Pousada Panorama* (tel 551-3366), past Hotel Solar de Lajes on Rua Barão do Camargos and about 1½ km from Praça Tiradentes. David, an Arizonian, and his Brazilian wife, Lucia, have a charming place with a super view, fireplace and video player. They also sell crafts. Rates are reasonable for the area with singles/doubles for US$7/9.

Pousada Ciclo do Ouro (tel 551-3201) at Rua Felipe dos Santos 241 is a small friendly, family run place with doubles for US$5/10 without bath or US$11 with.

There are a number of mid-range hotels closer to the centre of town. *Hotel Pilão* (tel 551-3066), Praça Tiradentes 57, has

US$8 to US$12 doubles. *Pouso Ouro Prêto* (tel 551-2778) at Praça Tiradentes 70 has US$10 doubles and *Hotel Colonial* (tel 551-3133) at Avenida Cônego Cabio Veloso 8 has US$10 doubles.

Places to Stay – top end
Pouso Chico Rei (tel 551-1274) Rua Brigideiro Mosqueira 90 has wonderful doubles completely furnished in antiques for US$25. Reserve way in advance.

Hotel da Estrada Real (tel 551-2122) on Rodovia dos Inconfidêntes (BR-356) is seven km out of the way, but it's the next best of the top end hotels; doubles are US$32. *Luxor Pousada Ouro Prêto* (tel 551-2244), Rua Alfredo Baeta 10, has the dubious distinction of being the most expensive hotel with US$42 doubles. *Hotel Quinta dos Barões* (tel 551-1056) at Rua Paudiá Calógeras 474 has fancy US$35 doubles.

Places to Eat
The typical dish of Minas is tutu a mineira, a black bean feijoada with couve, a type of kale. *Restaurante Casa Do Ouvidor* on Rua Conde de Bobadela is the place to try it. The best pizza I've tasted in Brazil is served at *Casa Nova*, Rua Direita 97, right on Praça Tiradentes. The cebola and Portuguesa pizzas (US$2.50 and US$3.50 for medium-sized pies) are excellent. It is only open for dinner.

Entertainment
The kids hangout in Praça Tiradentes before thronging to *Club Ouro Prêto* for some slow and steamy dancing. It's open Saturday and Sunday nights 8 to 11 pm. Admission for women/men is 10c/50c and alcoholic drinks are 10c to 75c.

Things to Buy
A soapstone quarry 28 km away in Santa Rita de Ouro Prêto provides endless supplies for attractive Henry Moore-style carvings, and imitations of Aleijadinho. Unglazed ceramics, woodcarvings and basket work are sold in the souvenir shops

of Praça Tiradentes. Wilson Prolin, a fine local painter, has a studio in town.

Although Imperial Topaz is only found in this area of Brazil, don't buy here unless you are knowledgeable about gemstones. The larger firms in Rio and São Paulo like Stern, Roditi, Amsterdam Sauer are more trustworthy.

Getting There & Away
There are 10 buses a day from Belo Horizonte to Ouro Prêto. The first bus leaves at 6.45 am and the last bus at 9 pm (98 km, one hour 45 minute trip). Buy bus tickets at least a day in advance, or you may find yourself without a ride.

MARIANA
Mariana is a beautiful old mining town with a character unlike its busy neighbour, Ouro Prêto. Only 12 km by paved road from Ouro Prêto, Mariana is touristed but not overrun. Founded in 1696, it retains the high-altitude tranquillity of many of the mining towns and is a great place to unwind. It's also a good place to stay if you want to avoid Ouro Prêto by night.

There are plenty of interesting sights to visit. The 18th century churches of São Pedro dos Clérigos, NS da Assuncão, São Francisco and the museum at Casa Capitular are all worthwhile. While walking through the old part of town you'll come across naive painters and wood sculptors at work in their studios.

Places to Stay & Eat
Hotel Central (tel 557-1630) is a real budget hotel at US$2/3.50 for singles/doubles with bath. *Hotel Faisca* (tel 557-1206) also costs US$2/3.50 for singles/doubles. *Hotel Muller* (tel 557-1188) is US$11 for a room.

Restaurante Tambaú near the town square has good regional cooking at reasonable prices.

Getting There & Away
A bus leaves Ouro Prêto for Mariana every 30 minutes from the far side of the School

of Mineralogy. The trip takes 15 minutes. There are direct buses from Mariana to Belo Horizonte, 113 km away.

An old train leaves Ouro Prêto for Mariana on Saturdays and Sundays at 9.30 am. It is advisable to arrive at the station by 9 am. The train returns at 4 pm, but if you miss it there is always the bus.

SÃO JOÃO DEL REI
Population: 50,000

One of Minas Gerais original gold towns, São João del Rei is a thriving small city with an old central section with several of Brazil's finest churches. With hotels and sights all within walking range in the old city centre there's little cause to see the more modern part of town, nevertheless, it's evident that the city hasn't been frozen in time like most of the other historic cities of Minas Gerais.

The old section is protected by Brazil's Landmarks Commission and police guard the churches at night. The city is cut in half by Rio Lenheiro, which is traversed by two 18th century stone bridges. In addition to the Aleijadinho-inspired churches, there are several fine colonial mansions – one that belonged to the late and still popular president Tancredo Neves – a good museum and a surprising variety of other sites and activities.

The city sits between the Serra de São José and Serra do Lenheiro, near the southern end of the Serra Espinhaço. It's hilly country near the Rio das Mortes (river of death), where many prospectors were killed during the gold rush days. The most famous incident took place in 1708 when a band of *Emboadas*, recent Portuguese immigrants, surrounded about 50 Paulistas or Bandeirantes, natives of São Paulo of mixed Portuguese and Indian blood. The Paulistas were massacred after laying down their arms to surrender. This was the bloodiest atrocity in the near civil war that these two groups fought over control of the mines, and is called the Capão da Traição (copse of treason).

The city is sandwiched between two

1	Ascent to Bonfim
2	Pousada Casarão
3	Igreja de São Francisco de Assis
4	Casa da Intendência
5	Igreja de São Gonçalo e Monumento ao Expedicionário
6	Capela de Santo Antonio
7	Capela de NS das Dores
8	Secretaria de Turismo, Museo Municipal & Biblioteca Municipal
9	Estação Ferroviária
10	Teatro Municipal
11	Prefeitura Municipal
12	Novotel Porto Real
13	Ponte da Cadeia
14	Hotel Colonial
15	Museu de Arte Regional
16	Hotel Lenheiro
17	Hotel Hespanhol
18	Capela de NS da Piedade
19	Largo do Rosário
20	Igreja de NS do Rosário
21	Ponte do Rosário
22	Museu de Arte Sacra
23	Igreja de NS do Carmo
24	Chafariz Colonial
25	Tourist Office
26	Old House
27	Solar do Barão de Itambé
28	Pelourinho
29	Catedral de NS do Pilar
30	Gold Mine
31	Igreja de NS das Mercês

hills, both of which provide excellent views, particularly at sunset. The Cristo Redentor monument, overlooking the city, stands on one hill and the Capelinha do Senhor do Bonfim on the other. Both hilltops are the last stop for the local city bus 'Sr dos Montes' which leaves in front of the train station.

Information

São João is big enough to have most services. There is a Banco do Brasil. The Secretaria de Turismo is across from the Igreja de São Francisco and is open from 8 am to 4.30 pm. They have maps, and if you need more esoteric information there

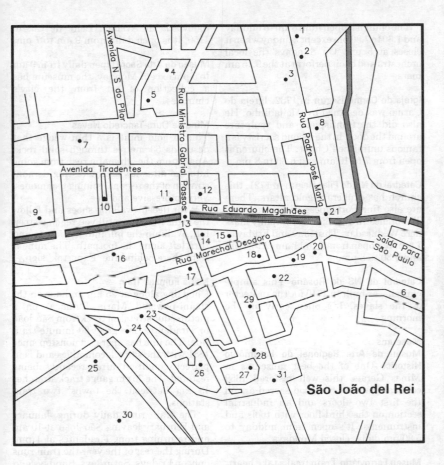

São João del Rei

is a professor working in the building who knows his regional history.

Churches

Floodlights illuminate the churches at night and give them a fantastic appearance. Be sure to take a walk at night.

São Francisco de Assis This exquisite baroque church, full of curves and carvings, looks out on a palm-tree-lined plaza shaped like a lyre. Begun in 1774, this church was Aleijadinho's first complete project, but much of his plan was not realised. Still the exterior, with an Aleijadinho sculpture of the Immaculate Virgin and several angels, is one of the finest in Minas. There is some uncertainty about what Aleijadinho did and did not do on the church interior. He probably did the main altar, but his work was completely altered. In the second altar to the left there is an image of São João Evangelista which is the work of Aleijadinho, as is the Santo Antonio. Notice the fine woodwork, particularly in the rear of the church.

The church is open from 8 am to midday and 1.30 to 7.30 pm except Sunday when it closes at 5 pm. On Sundays the local orchestra and choir perform at the 9.15 am mass.

Igreja do Carmo Begun in 1732, Igreja do Carmo was designed by Aleijadinho. He also did the frontispiece and sculpture around the door. In the second sacristy is a famous unfinished Christ. The church is open from 7 to 10 am and 5.30 to 8 pm.

Catedral de NS do Pilar Begun in 1721, this church has exuberant gold altars. There are also fine Portuguese tiles (*azulejos*). The orchestra and choir accompany mass here Wednesday, Thursday and Friday at 7 pm. It's open from 7 to 11 am, 2 to 4 pm and 5.30 to 8 pm.

Catedral de NS do Rosário This simple church was built in 1719 for the protector of the slaves. It's open early in the morning.

Museums
Museu de Arte Regional do Patrimônio Historico One of the best museums in Minas Gerais, this well restored 1859 colonial mansion has good sacred art on the first two floors and an industrial section on the third floor with tools and instruments. It's open from midday to 5.30 pm daily, closed Mondays.

Museu Ferroviário Train freaks take heart. Recently renovated, the railway museum has a wealth of artefacts and information about the old train days in the late 19th century. It's in the train station, under the large rotunda that looks like a coliseum. The cost is 25c and it's open daily from 9 am to midday and 1.30 to 5.30 pm.

Museu do Estanho John Somers This is a pewter factory with a display and store for visitors. It's owned by an Englishman (there is a small English community in São João). The museum is down the river toward the

rodoviária at Avenida Leite de Castro 1150. It is open daily from 9 am to 7 pm.

Museu de Arte Sacra Open daily from 9 am to 5 pm except Monday, the museum has a collection of art from the city's churches.

Mina de Ouro-Tancredo Neves
This ex-gold mine is a thin wedge that descends 53 metres through solid rock. Apart from the adrenalin rush from going into the mine it's an interesting demonstration of the regional mining techniques. Very impressive and free.

Wear decent walking shoes and follow the signs from town till you reach a steep hill. Walk up the hill into the favela and turn left along the footpath. The mine is right there behind the 'Exportak' sign.

Maria Fumaça Train
Chugging along at 25 km an hour on the steam-powered Maria Fumaça, on a picturesque stretch of track from São João to Tiradentes, is a great 30-minute train ride. The line has operated nonstop since 1881 with the same locomotives and is in perfect condition after recently being restored. The 76 cm gauge track stretches 13 km between the towns' two train stations.

The train runs daily during January and February leaving São João at 10 am and returning from Tiradentes at 1 pm. During the rest of the year the train runs only on Fridays, Saturdays, Sundays and holidays departing São João at 10 am and 2.15 pm and returns from Tiradentes at 1 pm and 5 pm. This schedule often changes so it's best to double-check. The train is often crowded, so get there early. It costs 75c. Going to Tiradentes sit on the left side for a better view. Don't forget that if you're only going to Tiradentes for the day and need more time than the return train allows you can easily take a later bus.

Festivals
São João has a very lively Carnival – the

locals claim it's the best in Minas Gerais. With all the music in town – there's a school of music and several bands and orchestras – it's a credible boast. The Semana da Inconfidência from 15 to 21 April celebrates Brazil's first independence movement and the hometown boys who led it (also in Tiradentes).

The list of festivals is too long to repeat here – 15 religious and 10 profane on one calendar – so stop by the tourist office to get a calendar of events; there's a good chance someone is celebrating something in São João.

Places to Stay - bottom end

There is a good stock of inexpensive hotels in the old section of the city, right where you want to be.

The *Hotel Hespanhol* (tel 371-4677) at Rua Marechal Doodoro 131 is hard to beat. They have singles without bath for US$3 and doubles with bath for US$8. All rooms are clean and relatively spacious. The *Brasil* (tel 371-2804) at Avenida Tancredo Neves 395 facing the river has good singles for US$2.

The historic *Colonial* (tel 371-1792) is clean, if a bit funky, and very colonial. Rooms without bath go for US$2.50 a person and most have a view of the river. The *Aparecida Hotel* (tel 371-1548) has singles for US$3, not bad if the other hotels are full.

Places to Stay - top end

The *Lenheiro Palace* (tel 371-3914) facing the river at Avenida Tancredo Neves 257 has charm and style for US$21 a double.

Up the hill behind the Igreja São Francisco is the *Pousada Casarão* (tel 371-1224), Rua Ribeiro Bastos 94. Like many of Minas' elegant mansions turned pousada this place is exquisite, but the rooms are on the small side and the beds on the short side. There is a small swimming pool and the cost is US$10/12 for singles/doubles.

The *Hotel Porto Real* (tel 371-1201) is São João's modern hotel; it's also the biggest eyesore on the riverfront. They have singles/doubles for US$15/17.

Places to Eat

It's hard to get excited about eating in São João. *Pizzeria Primus* has good pizza – try the primus special. It's open late at Rua Arthur Bernardes 97. The *Cantina do Italo* on Rua Ministro Gabriel Passos has a good reputation for meat, which it doesn't live up to. For regional cooking try the *Restaurant Rex* at Rua Arthur Bernardes 137 or *Quinto Do Ouro* Praça Severiano de Resende 4.

For cheaper food *Top Top* has sandwiches and outdoor dining, usually on Avenida Tiradentes. On the same street, *Zoti* below the Igreja São Francisco, is a lively late night place for beer and light meals.

Entertainment

The music of Minas is extremely good and different to anything else you've ever heard. Try the Teatro Municipal for weekend concerts. The restaurant *A Tasca da Portuguesa* (tel 371-2331) has live music Thursday, Friday and Saturday. It's at Avenida Tiradentes 207. Another central place to try is *Feitic, O Mineiro*.

Getting There & Away

The long and winding road from Rio to São João traverses the Serra da Mantiqueira. The roads and scenery are good on this 5½ hour bus ride. São João is 190 km south of Belo Horizonte, 3½ hours by bus.

Buses leave Rio direct for São João daily at 9 am, 4 pm and 11 pm. The return from São João to Rio leaves at 8 am, 4 pm and 11.30 pm Monday to Saturday and at 4 pm, 10.15 pm and 11.30 pm Sunday. The fare is US$3.50. There are also frequent buses to Juiz de Fora where you can then transfer to a São João or Rio bus.

From São João to Belo Horizonte – via Lagoa Dourada – there are eight buses a day. Monday to Saturday the first bus leaves at 6 am and the last at 6.40 pm. There are extra buses Sunday night until 10 pm. The trip takes 3½ hours and costs

US$2. This is also the bus to Congonhas, two hours and US$1 down the road. If you want a seat buy your ticket a few hours early.

For the quickest route to Ouro Prêto, catch a bus to Lagoa Dourado (they leave every 30 minutes), then take a bus to Lafaiete and from there take the bus to Ouro Prêto (for schedule see Congonhas section).

Getting Around
The 'Villa Cidade' and 'Trevo Cidade' local buses will get you to the rodoviária in 10 minutes. They leave from the small bus stop in front of the train station. You can also take a taxi for US$1.50 or walk.

TIRADENTES
Population: 2500
They don't make 'em any prettier than Tiradentes. Ten km down the valley from São João del Rei, its gold era rival, colonial Tiradentes sits on a hill below a mountain. With few signs of change over the last two centuries, the town has that magic quality of another era – and for some odd reason that's a very good feeling.

Originally Arrail da Ponta do Morro (hamlet on a hilltop), Tiradentes was renamed to honour the martyred hero of the Inconfidência who was born at a nearby farm. The town's colonial buildings run up a hillside where they culminate in the beautiful Igreja de Santo Antonio. If you stand between the church's Aleijadinho-carved frontispiece and famous sundial there is a colourful view of the terracotta-tiled colonial houses, the green valley and the towering wall of stone formed by the Serra São Jose.

Information
São João del Rei has the usual banks, travel agencies, etc. There is a local tourism office at the city hall on Rua Resende Costa.

Igreja Matriz de Santo Antônio
Named after the town's patron saint, construction began on this church in 1733 at the site of a former church. Restored in 1983, this is one of Brazil's most beautiful churches. There are two bell towers and a frontispiece by Aleijadinho (one of the last that he completed), who also made the sundial in front of the church.

The inside is all gold and rich in symbols from the Old Testament. There is a painting by João Batista showing the miracle of Santo Antonio making a donkey kneel before the Pope. There is also a polychrome organ built in Portugal and brought to Tiradentes by burro in 1798. Out of order for some 50 years, the organ was recently repaired by German technicians. Ask about performances.

The church is open from 8 am to 5 pm and usually closes from midday till 1 pm for lunch.

Museu do Padre Toledo
Dedicated to another hero of the Inconfidência, Padre Toledo lived in this 18-room house where the *inconfidêntes* used to meet. The museum features regional antiques and documents from the 18th century.

Igreja da Santissima Trindade
After a two km walk on Rua Santissima Trindade you arrive at this simple pilgrimage church.

Solar da Ponte
This colonial mansion, now an expensive hotel, is impeccably restored and decorated and is well worth walking through. It's the first building on the other side of the little stone bridge and it's marked by a small sign.

Serra de São Jose
Mãe d'Agua is at the base of these mountains. It's lush with moss and plants, and the waters are clear and fresh. A 25-minute, three km walk, Mãe d'Agua can also be reached by car. For guides and

information about walks into the mountains talk to the tourist office.

Places to Stay

Tiradentes has several good but expensive pousadas and a lack of cheap places. If you can't find anything within your budget ask around for homes to stay in or commute from São João del Rei.

Places to Stay – bottom end

Pousada dos Inconfidêntes (tel 355-1218) doesn't offer much, but is relatively inexpensive at US$5/10 a single/double. *Pousada do Laurito* and *Pousada Bebeto* are better. Ask Bebeto at the Loja Bebeto in the centre of town to show you his pousada. *Hotel Wellerson* (tel 355-1226) has singles/doubles for US$7.

Places to Stay – top end

Solar do Ponte (tel 355-1255) is an old colonial mansion. The rooms are simple, small and beautifully decorated. There's a salon and sauna and afternoon tea is included in the US$49 a double price. A good place to splurge.

The *Pousada Maria Barbosa* (tel 355-1227), near the train station, has a pool and is US$22 a double. Across the stone bridge and to the left, *Pousada Tiradentes* (tel 355-1232) has charm and costs US$15 a double and US$10 a single.

Things to Buy

Tiradentes has surprisingly good antiques, woodwork and silver jewellery for sale. There is furniture, clocks, china and even chandeliers in the antique stores.

Getting There & Away

Tiradentes is about 20 minutes from São João del Rei. The best approach is the wonderful railroad trip from São João del Rei (see that city for details). Buses come and go between São João and Tiradentes every 40 minutes (slightly less frequently on weekend afternoons). The first and last buses leave for Tiradentes Monday to Friday at 5.50 am and 6.20 pm, Saturday at 8.15 am and 10.30 pm, Sunday at 7 am and 6.20 pm. There is no other direct bus service from Tiradentes.

PRADOS

Population: 3000

Prados is a small colonial town with virtually no tourism. The town has good colonial buildings and the Igreja da NS da Conceição, built in 1711. It's a quiet place with a certain charm, but few important sights.

Places to Stay

The town hotel, the *São Sebastião*, is simple and cheap.

Getting There & Away

The journey is an hour by bus from São João to Prados for 40c; Monday to Friday at 7.30 am, 10.30 am, 12.15 pm, 3.30 pm, 5.30 pm, 6.30 pm; Saturday at 7.30 am, 12.15 pm, 3.30 pm and 6 pm, and Sunday at 12.15 pm and 10 pm.

Around Minas Gerais

SÃO TOMÉ DAS LETRAS

In southern Minas, 310 km from Belo Horizonte, Letras is a small village of less than a thousand, at 1450 metres. The name refers to the inscriptions on some of the many caverns in the region. If you're into mysticism or superstition, this is the place to go. Fuelled by the inscriptions, the town is filled with strange stories of flying saucers, visits of extraterrestrials, a cave that is the entrance to a subterranean passageway to Machu Picchu, Peru and more.

This is also a beautiful mountain region, with great walks and several waterfalls (*cachoeiras*) like Véu da Noiva, Corredeiras, da Prefeitura and da Eubiose. The town's churches and buildings are old and made of stone. There's a great view from the top.

Places to Stay & Eat

There are two simple pousadas, *Tatá* and *Capote*. It's easy to rent a room in a house and there's camping on the edge of town. The *Bar do Gê* is a surprisingly good restaurant.

Getting There & Away

The town is best reached from Três Corações, 40 km to the west. Buses leave Monday to Saturday at 3.30 pm. The dirt road up the mountains is precarious and buses are cancelled during hard rains. Hitching is possible. São Tomé das Letras can also be reached from Caxambu, 60 km to the south.

CAXAMBU

Population: 70,000

Caxambu is a combination of two African words *cacha* (drum) and *mambu* (music). Cacha-mambu or caxambu is a conically shaped drum from the Congo which the city fathers likened to the knolls of the area. In 1748, with the construction of a chapel dedicated to Our Lady of Cures in the parish of Baependi, the settlement of 'Cachambum', later called Caxambu, was put on the map.

In 1814, according to tradition, the first mineral fountains were discovered by an illustrious European traveller whose name was not recorded, but it wasn't until 1870 that the springs were first tapped. Realising the curative properties of the waters medical men flocked to the town. In 1886 Dr Policarpo Viotti founded the Caxambu water company (nationalised in 1905). The water of Caxambu was celebrated in the international water circuit, winning gold medals long before Perrier hit Manhattan singles bars. Caxambu took the gold medal in Rome's Victor Emmanuel III Exposition of 1903, and another gold medal in the St Louis International Fair of 1904, then the Diploma of Honour in the University of Brussels Exposition of 1910. Water Olympics were discontinued during WW I, and Caxambu's history was uneventful until 1981 when Supergasbras and Superagua, private firms, took over the government concession. Caxambu is sold throughout Brazil and in Miami, Florida where the US Food & Drug Administration has approved it. Caxambu is the only Brazilian mineral water thus honoured.

Caxambu is a tranquil resort for the elderly and middle class – people come here to escape the heat of Rio and the madness of Carnival. The town has not changed for 50 years and some couples have been coming here every summer for 30 years and more.

Parque das Aguas

The Parque das Aguas of Caxambu is like a Disneyland for the rheumatic. Given the proper temperament and surroundings, nursing your ailments can be fun. Like Disneyland, the grounds are swept clean around the clock, but instead of an army of Mickey Mouses, groundspeople cleverly disguised as arthritics are on dust patrol. People come to take the mineral waters, smell the sulphur, compare liver spots, watch the geyser spout every two or 2½ hours, rest in the shade by the canal or walk in the lovely gardens.

The park is not only good, it's good for you. Liver problems? Go to the Dona Leopoldina magnesium fountain. Skin disorders? Take the sulphur baths of Tereza Cristina. Anaemic? The Conde d'Eu e Dona Isabel fountains are rich in iron. VD? The Duque de Saxe fountain helps calm the bacteria causing syphilis. For stomach troubles drink the naturally carbonated waters of Dom Pedro (there's a water bottling plant on the premises). The alkaline waters of the Venancio and Viotti fountains are good for dissolving kidney stones while the Beleza waters soothe the intestines. The multi-purpose water of the Mayrink fountains 1, 2 and 3 is good for gargling, eye irritations and table water (without the bubbles).

The park is open daily from 7 am to 6 pm, and admission to the grounds is 15c. Separate fees are required for paddleboats

(75c per hour), the rifle-range, hydro-therapeutic massages at the bathhouse (US$1), jacuzzi, sauna (50c), clay tennis courts (US$1 per hour), swimming pool (50c), skating rink, etc.

Other Attractions
There are other attractions in town. Morro Cristo hill has an eight metre high image of Jesus. On Rua Princesa Isabela is the St Isabel of Hungary church, built by the princess once she conceived, due to the miraculous waters of Caxambu.

Take a horse and buggy ride into the countryside; a 1½ hour ride from the park entrance will only set you back US$6. The standard tour includes the mini-zoo, the Fabrica de Doce and the Chacarra Rosallan. The mini-zoo at the Hotel Campestre has caged monkeys, a wilting peacock and a sariema bird which looks like an eccentric European aristocrat, disgraced and in exile. The Fabrica de Doce has locally produced honey (US$2), liqueurs (25c) and preserves (50c). The last stop is Chacara Rosallan's; an old farm with a flower orchard and fruit grove. Rosallan is famous for two of her fruit liqueurs; jaboticaba and bottled tangerine. Empty bottles are passed over the tiny tangerines and strapped to the tree; the tangerine grows within the bottle and weeks later is made into a liqueur.

Places to Stay - bottom end
Seedy US$1.75 singles with bath are available at Rua Major Penha 363. The *Hotel Lider* (tel 341-1398) at Rua Major Penha 225 is a broken down 1-star Embratur hotel with humble charm and US$7 singles with full board.

Hotel São Jose (tel 341-1094) at Rua Major Penha 264 is a 2-star Embratur hotel with TVs, big double beds, and hot showers. Singles/doubles are US$8/16 or with full board US$14/24. The *Hotel Marques* (tel 341-1013) at Rua Oliveira Mafra 223 is cheaper with singles/doubles with full board for US$12.50/16.50. Next

door the *Hotel Alex* (tel 341 1331) has US$12 doubles with full board.

Places to Stay - top end
The 4-star *Hotel Gloria* (tel 341-1233) at Avenida Camilo Soares 590 is a very posh resort complex with a range of activities for the leisure set. Doubles with TV, bath, bar, telephone and three meals a day are US$82 for two. Facilities include a big gym with indoor basketball court, tennis (clay courts in the park), physical rehabilitation centre and sauna.

The *Hotel Braganca* (tel 341-1117), directly in front of the Parque das Aguas entrance at Rua Antonio Miguel Arnati 34, is not quite as fancy but more than adequate. Singles/doubles are US$18/24 and the rates include full board.

Getting There & Away
There are seven daily buses between Caxambu and São Lourenço on 49 km of windy wooded road, four to São Paulo, and four to Rio via Cruzeiro and Resende.

SÃO LOURENÇO
Population: 23,000
São Lourenço is another pleasant city of mineral waters –just south of Caxambu – 275 km from Rio de Janeiro, 296 km from São Paulo and 401 km from Belo Horizonte. The principal attraction is the Parque das Aguas, featuring waters with a variety of healing properties, sauna, and a lake with paddle boats. It is open daily from 7 am to 5.30 pm. Other diversions include goat cart rides for children, horse and buggy rides for adults and the courtesy bus to Fazenda Ramos for a day of picnic swimming and leisure. Try their doce de leite.

Circuito das Aguas (Water Circuit)
VW Kombi-van half-day tours of the Circuito das Aguas (water circuit) can be arranged for US$6 per person. The vans will take up to eight people and normally visit Caxambu, Baependi, Cambuquira,

Lambari and Passo Quatro, but you can also talk the driver into taking you to the mysterious stone village of São Tome das Letras (80 km away).

Places to Stay

The *Dormitorio Rodoviária* at Avenida Getúlio Vargas 176 at US$2 per person is the cheapest place to crash in town. The rooms are tiny, dimly lit and not very secure.

Around the corner at Avenida Dom Pedro II 611 is the *Hotel Colombo* (tel 331-1157), which is several notches above the dormitory in quality with clean and attractive carpeted rooms. Quartos (rooms without bath) are US$4, apartamentos (with bath) are US$6.

The *Hotel Metropole* (tel 331-1290) has doubles ranging from US$12 to US$24 with full board.

Places to Stay – top end

The *Hotel Primus* (tel 331-1244) at Rua Justino 681 has singles/doubles for US$55/80 with full board – less 20-30% out of season. *Hotel Brasil* (tel 331-1422) at Rua João Loage 87, across from the park are the top of the line 4-star hotels of São Lourenco. Doubles with full board start at US$99 – less 30% out of season.

Places to Eat

The restaurants in town can't compete with the food served in the hotels. *Kibe-Lave* serves mediocre food while *Restaurant Chalet* has poor and expensive food.

Entertainment

The nightlife is pretty tame. In the evenings teenagers and young adults pretty up and hang out on the fence and entrance of the *Hotel Metropole*. The club there has dances with a large-screen music video and bar. There's no cover charge. Social outcasts and pinball wizards spend the evening in the two 'Flipper' parlours on Avenida Dom Pedro II.

Getting There & Away

There are four buses daily to Rio de Janeiro on Cidade de Aço lines (five hours), four daily buses to São Paulo (six hours) and seven to Caxambu.

Around São Lourenço

Members of the Brazilian Society of Euboise believe that a new civilisation will arise in the seven magic cities of the region – São Tome das Letras, Aiuruoca, Conceição do Rio Verde, Itanhandu, Pouso Alto, Carmo de Minas and Maria da Fe.

Taxis and VW-vans congregate at Avenida Getúlio Vargas.

Visit Poços das Caldas, a city built on the crater of an extinct volcano, another mineral spring town settled by crystal glass blowers of the Island of Murano, near Venice. Full day US$15 tours to Pocos das Caldas leave at 7 am.

DIAMANTINA

Diamantina is a five-hour drive north from Belo Horizonte. One of Brazil's prettiest colonial gems, the city boomed when diamonds were discovered in the 1720s after the gold finds in Minas. The diamonds are gone, but fine colonial mansions and excellent hiking in the surrounding mountains still draw visitors.

While you are here walk a couple of km down the Caminho dos Escravos (built by the slaves) to the Serra da Jacuba. Then walk eight km on the road to São Goncalo to the *furnas* (caverns).

Diamond Museum

The house of Padre Rolim, one of the Inconfidentes, is now a museum with furniture, coins, instruments of torture and others relics of the diamond days. It's open from midday to 5.30 pm except Mondays.

Igreja NS do Carmo

Built in 1758, this church is rich in gold. The bell tower is in the back of the church because Chica da Silva disliked being awakened by early tolls.

Places to Stay

The *Nosson Hotel* (tel 931-1022), opposite the bus terminal, is friendly and cheap. The better hotel in town is the *Tijuco* (tel (031) 222-2268) at Rua Macau do Meio 211. The *Dalia* (tel 931-1477) is at Praça Juscelino Kubitschek 25 and the *Grande Hotel* (tel 931-1520) is at Rua Da Quitanda 70.

Places to Eat

Restaurant Confiança at Rua da Quitanda

39, next to the post office, has good regional food but is a bit expensive. The *Grupiara* at Rua Campos Carvalho 12-A is also recommended.

Getting There & Away

Diamantina is a five-hour bus ride from Belo Horizonte for US$3. Buses leave for Diamantina daily at 5.30 am, 9 am, 11.30 am, 2.30 pm, 6.30 pm and midnight. They return to Belo Horizonte Monday to Friday at 6 am, 10.45 am, midday, 3.15 pm and 6 pm; Saturday at 6 am, 10.45 am, midday, 3.30 pm and 6 pm; Sunday at 6 am, midday, 3.30 pm and 6 pm.

São Paulo

SÃO PAULO

Population: 10 million

São Paulo is another world. It is South America's largest city, with over 10 million inhabitants – one in every 12 Brazilians live there. It's the industrial engine that motors Brazil's economy: 30 of Brazil's largest 50 companies and 50% of the nation's industry is in the São Paulo region.

The city is Brazil's most cosmopolitan and modern. It is a city of immigrants and ethnic neighbourhoods. Millions of Italians came at the end of the 19th century. Millions of Japanese have come in this century. Millions of Brazilians from the countryside and from the Northeast are still pouring in. From this diversity and industrial development has sprung Brazil's largest, most cultured and educated middle class. These Paulistas are lively and make well-informed companions.

The city's population explosion has occurred at an astonishing pace. In the 1870s, when the coffee boom began to awaken the city's commerce, São Paulo was still a lesser Brazilian city. The population reached 580,000 by 1920, 1.2 million by 1940, two million by 1950, 3.1 million by 1960, and 5.2 million by 1970. Behind these numbers are, of course, extraordinary urban problems. One that you'll notice immediately is traffic. Another is urban sprawl; the city doesn't stop.

São Paulo gets cold in the Brazilian winter and smoggy-hot in the summer. But if you know someone there who can show you around or you just like big cities, it's worth a visit. At it's best it offers the excitement and night life of one of the world's great cities.

Information & Orientation

Getting around SP is difficult even if you speak Portuguese, have a car, time and money, and know the streets and traffic patterns. For the rest of us it's simply impossible. Why? First, it's a big, sprawling city. Second, there is no plan or pattern to the arteries. Third, there are few natural or artificial landmarks to orient oneself. There is no ocean or river (of importance) and either few dominating boulevards or so many, depending on how you look at it, that they are of little use to the visitor. Visibility is limited by buildings everywhere.

All of these obstacles are overcome, with time, but it takes much longer to get a feel for the layout of SP than just about any city in the world. Even maps reflect the difficulty of bringing SP down to comprehensible dimensions. At first glance, they are of practically no use.

Parks, museums, art galleries, zoos, and you name it, are spread-out through the metropolitan area. It's best to pick up *Veja* at a newsstand or go to a tourism booth for a good list.

Tourist Office The city's many tourist information booths vary greatly in quality but they do have excellent city and state maps, as well as *São Paulo this Month* – a monthly entertainment guide with an English section. They are also good for bus and metro information.

There are information booths on Praça da República (along Avenida Ipiranga); Praça da Sé (in front of the Sé metro station entrance); Praça da Liberdade (in front of Liberdade metro station entrance); Teatro Municipal; Avenida São Luis (on the corner of Praça Dom José Gaspar); and Aeroporto de Congonhas. They are open Monday to Friday from 9 am to 6 pm and Saturday and Sunday from 9 am to 1 pm.

The shopping centres Ibirapoera, Iguatemi, and Morumbi also have information booths. The phone numbers for the main tourism office are 257-7248 and 229-3011.

Paulistas would not dream of driving in the city without one of several large city street directories. If you are staying in the city for awhile the *Guia São Paulo* by Quatro Rodas has street maps and hotel and restaurant listings. *O Guia* has the clearest presentation of any street guide and it lists tourist points as well. Another street guide to check out is the *Guia Caroplan*.

Post American Express/Kontik-Franstur (tel 259-4211) is at Rua Marconi (2nd and 4th floors). From the Praça da República, on the Avenida Ipiranga side, go down Barão de Itapetininga and turn left after two blocks. They close for mail pick-up from midday to 2 pm.

Money Changing money should be easy in São Paulo and at top dollar. Ask at the usual places – hotels, travel agents, funeral parlours – just about anywhere. There are several travel agents and casas de câmbio across from the airline offices on Avenida São Luis which are a good bet.

Consulates
The following countries have consulates in São Paulo:

Argentina
Rua Araújo 216, 8th floor (tel 256-8555), open 9 am to 1 pm.
Bolivia
Rua Quirino de Andrade 219, 3rd floor (tel 255-3555), open 9 am to 1 pm.
Chile
Avenida Paulista 1009, 10th floor (tel 284-2044), open 8.30 am to 1.30 pm.
Paraguay
Avenida São Luis 112, 10th floor (tel 255-7818), open 9 am to 1 pm.
Peru
Rua Suécia 114 (tel 852-2392), open 8 am to 4 pm.
UK
Avenida Paulista 1938 (tel 287-7722) open 8.30 am to 12.30 pm and 1.30 to 5 pm.

USA
Rua Padre João Manoel 933 (tel 881-6511), open 8.30 am to 3 pm.

Airlines Most of the major airlines have offices on Avenida São Luis, near the Praça da República. Varig-Cruzeiro (tel 258-2233) is at Rua da Consolação 362, Transbrasil (tel 259-7066) is at Avenida São Luis 250 and VASP (tel 257-6370) is at Avenida São Luis 91.

Books There's a good selection of English books at the Book Centre at Rua Gabus Mendes 29, near the Praça da República.

Health For serious health problems, Einstein Hospital is one of the best in Latin America.

The Museu de Arte de São Paulo (MASP)
The Museum of Art is at Avenida Paulista 1578. To get there take the metro to Paraiso station and then walk or catch a bus down Avenida Paulista. You'll probably want to walk since it's only about 20 minutes and you'll pass the latest, largest and most daring skyscrapers in Brazil. To bus to the museum from Praça da República hop on the 805A 'Avenida' and from Liberdade the 'Shopping Continental' bus.

With Latin America's best collection of western art, the museum has many French Impressionists and a few great Brazilian paintings: the Candido Portinaris are worth the trip alone. There are also temporary exhibits in the basement and outside on Sundays, from 10 am to sunset, there is the Feira de Antiquidades do MASP. The fair is full of old odds and ends, big and small – including furniture, books and toys. The museum is open 2 to 5 pm from Tuesday to Sunday. Go early as the light can be very bad late in the day.

For a bit of R&R after the museum, there is a small park – a tropical oasis in the midst of the mountains of concrete – across Avenida Paulista.

São Paulo

0   250   500 m

Rua Martim Francisca
Rua Frederico Abranches
Avenida São João de Caxias
Avenida Rio Branco
Budget Hotel Area
1 Star Hotels
Avenida Duque
Avenida São João
Ipiranga
Avenida
2 & 3 Star Hotels
Avenida Vieira de Carvalho
Rua Rego Freitas
3 Star Hotels
3
Praça da República
4
República M
Avenida Ipiranga
3 Star Hotels
Airlines Tourist & Money Exchange
Anhangabáu M
5
6
Rua da Consolação
7
Via 9 de Julho
Viaduto Jacarei
20
Rua Augusta
2 Star Hotels
Rua Santo Antonio
Rua Major Diogo
Rua da Abolição
8
Avenida Nove de Julho
Silva
Lixado
Brig Luis Antonio
Rua Jaceguai
9
Rua 13 de Maio
Rua Rui Barbosa
11   10
13
12
Rua Cons Carrao

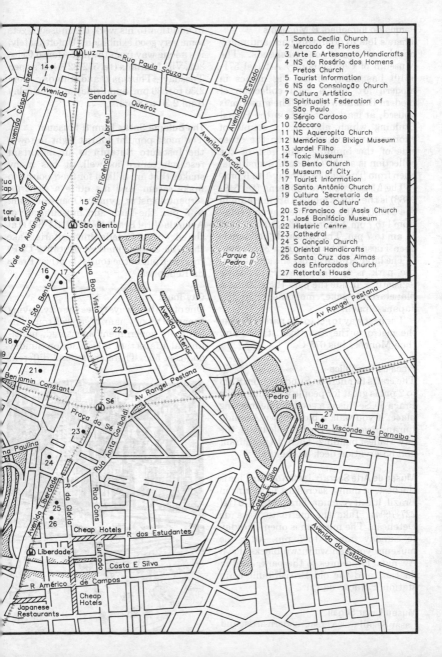

1 Santa Cecília Church
2 Mercado de Flores
3 Arte E Artesanato/Handicrafts
4 NS do Rosário dos Homens Pretos Church
5 Tourist Information
6 NS da Consolação Church
7 Cultura Artística
8 Spiritualist Federation of São Paulo
9 Sérgio Cardoso
10 Záccaro
11 NS Aqueropita Church
12 Memórias do Bixiga Museum
13 Jardel Filho
14 Toxic Museum
15 S Bento Church
16 Museum of City
17 Tourist Information
18 Santo Antônio Church
19 Cultura 'Secretaria de Estado da Cultura'
20 S Francisco de Assis Church
21 José Bonifácio Museum
22 Historic Centre
23 Cathedral
24 S Gonçalo Church
25 Oriental Handicrafts
26 Santa Cruz das Almas dos Enforcados Church
27 Retorta's House

Parque D Pedro II

Parque do Ibirapuera & Museums

There's lots to do in this park and many people doing it on weekends. The Museum of Contemporary Art (tel 571-9610) has many of the big names in modern art and a good collection of modern Brazilian artists. The museum is housed, at least part of it, in the Bienal Building which also has a couple of enormous exhibition halls on the other side of the building. The rest of the collection is at the Cidade Universitaria, open from Tuesday to Sunday 1 to 6 pm.

The Museu de Arte Moderna (tel 549-9688) is the oldest modern art museum in the country. It's open Tuesday to Friday from 1 to 7 pm, Saturday and Sunday from 11 am to 7 pm. The Museu de Folklore is open Tuesday to Sunday from 2 to 5 pm.

The large edifice across the street from the park is the new São Paulo state legislature. Inside the park there is also a planetarium, lake, monuments and a Japanese pavilion.

The best way to get to the park is to take the metro to the Ana Rosa station and then Monções bus 675-C.

Praça da República

The crafts fair here on Sundays from 8 am to 2 pm is great for people watching. Like Praça de Sé this is a good public meeting place. If you walk a block down Avenida Ipiranga, you'll see the Edificio Itália, the city's tallest building. There's a restaurant and observation deck on the top.

Museu de Arte Sacra & Jardim da Luz This is

the best, of many, sacred art museums in Brazil. It's at Avenida Tiradentes 676 (tel 227-7694). Take the metro to Casa de Detencão. The museum is open Tuesday to Sunday from 1 to 5 pm. After the museum you can walk two blocks down Avenida Tiradentes to the park, Jardim da Luz, and the old British-built train station, Estação da Luz.

Museu Lasar Segall

Lasar Segall was a great modern artist and in addition to his work the museum gets some very good exhibitions. Unfortunately, it's a long way from town at Afonso Celso 362, Vila Mariana (tel 572-8211). It's open Tuesday, Thursday and Sunday from 2.30 to 6.30 pm, and Friday and Saturday from 2.30 to 8 pm.

The Butantã Snake Farm & Museum

The most popular tourist sight in town, the Instituto Butantã is an important research centre as well. It has many snakes that are milked for their poison to make serum, and it's quite a sight for serpentologist or layman. Open from 8 am to 5 pm, the farm and museum are at Avenida Vital Brasil 1500 (tel 211-8211) at the edge of the Cidade Universitaria. Take the 702-U bus marked Butantã-USP from in front of the tourist booth at Praça da Rebública.

City Tours

One of the best ways to see the city, saving time and money, is an organised tour. The tours are government sponsored, multi-lingual affairs that take place on Sunday and cost 50c. There are several different

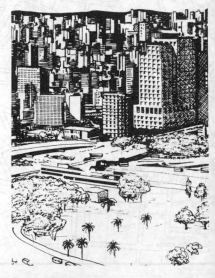

itineraries and two different agencies – one goes by bus, the other metro. For information go to a tourist information booth or call Circuito Cultural (tel 267-2122) and Turismetro (tel 229-3011).

Liberdade

Liberdade, the oriental district, has a big street fair all day Sundays and is only five minutes from the centre by metro. Get off at Liberdade station.

Places to Stay

São Paulo has plenty of hotels and they come in groups, which makes it easy to go to a street and find one that suits your style. Prices tend to be reasonable. Most hotels have a 10% surcharge, but many give weekend discounts of 20%. Rooms are hardest to find midweek and for the middle to high-priced hotels it's a good idea to make reservations a week or so in advance.

Places to Stay – bottom end

Down and out in São Paulo is done in an area between the Estação da Luz and the Praça da República. There are dozens of budget and below budget hotels on Rua dos Andradas and Rua Santa Efigênia and the streets that intersect them from Avenida Ipiranga to Duque de Caxias. The area is pretty safe during the day but seedy at night. There's much prostitution and many of the hotels cater to this high-turnover clientele. These are often the cheapest hotels and the management will usually show you that you're not welcome.

The *Hotel Ofir* (tel 223-8822), Rua dos Andradas 258, has good rooms with baths and hot water with singles/doubles at US$4/6.50. The *Hotel Copacabana* (tel 222-0511) Rua Aurora 264 has single/double quartos for US$5/8 and apartments for about a dollar more. Less expensive is the *Santa Teresinha* down Rua Aurora at 205. Singles/doubles go for US$1.75/3, without bath.

There are several places on Santa

Efigênia. The *Pauliceía* (tel 220-9433), Rua Timbiras 216 (at the corner of Santa Efigênia), is a very good deal. It's clean and safe. A room for two goes for US$4, apartments for US$5.50. The *Hotel Braga* is at Santa Efigênia 493 and has very basic doubles without bath for US$3. At Santa Efigênia 348 the *Hotel Luanda* (tel 222-3666) has singles for US$3/4.50 without/with bath. Doubles cost twice as much. At Santa Efigênia 163 the *Hotel San Remo* (tel 229-6845) is similar in quality and price to the Hotel Luanda.

The *Galeão* (tel 220-8211) at Rua dos Gusmões 394 is excellent. It's really a middle price hotel (apartments start at US$8) with cheap quartos that cost only US$3 per person. They also do laundry.

Places to Stay – middle

There are loads of middle-priced hotels on the streets around Praça da República. They tend to come in clusters, by price, along certain streets. The cheaper ones are on Avenida São João (from Avenida Duque de Caxias all the way to the Vale do Anhangabaú).

Avenida Vieira de Carvalho has some very good deals for a few dollars more. It's a dignified, quiet street with some very expensive hotels as well. On the other side of the Praça da República Avenida Ipiranga (toward Avenida São João), Rua 7 de Abril and Rua Casper Libero all have several hotels for even a bit more.

On the fringe of the budget hotel area, just across Avenida Rio Branco at Rua Vitória 390, the *Las Vegas* (tel 221-8144) has many amenities and nice singles/doubles for US$4/6. Three blocks further, at Praça Júlio Mesquita 90 and 34, are the hotels *America do Sul* (tel 223-6699) and *Lux* (tel 221-9077). The first has singles for US$8/11 without/with bath and doubles for US$13/20 without/with bath. The second is older and classier, with singles/doubles starting at US$13/20.

The *Manchete* and *Plaza* are two of many hotels on Avenida São João which are about the same price. It's a busy street, which is particularly noisy during the day. The *Manchete* (tel 221-9844) at 1124 has singles without/with bath for US$5/6.50. The *Plaza* (tel 222-1355) is at 407. Doubles start at US$11. The *Cineasta* (tel 222-5533) at Avenida São João 613 is a good deal, but the rooms are noisy.

A favourite is the *Itamarati* (tel 222-4133) at Avenida Vieira de Carvalho 150. It's a well-kept old hotel, the rooms are clean and the management helpful. Single/doubles start at US$8.50/11. The *Amazonas* (tel 220-4116) is in a great spot, at the corner where Avenida Vieira de Carvalho meets the Praça da República. Singles/doubles start at US$10/12.

Across from the Estação da Luz, the *Hotel Florida* (tel 220-2811) has singles/doubles for US$20/15. With rooms starting in the same price range, there are three big hotels to choose from on the 700 block of Avenida Ipiranga: *Plaza Maraba Hotel* (tel 220-7811) with singles/doubles with bath for US$16/19.50, *Excelsior* (tel 222-7377) and *Terminus* (tel 222-2266). The *Excelsior* is the best and the most expensive of the three.

An alternative to staying in a hotel in the central district is to head over to Liberdade, the Japanese, Chinese and Korean district. The subway stops very close to the hotels, and it's quieter, safer and more interesting at night. There are several less expensive hotels as you walk downhill from the metro station at Praça da Liberdade (there's an information booth here that can give directions). The *Hotel Ikeda* on Rua dos Estudantes has singles starting at US$6. The *Hotel Isei* (tel 278-6677) at Rua de Gloria 290 has singles/doubles for US$8/11. *Hotel Long Mung* (tel 278-1449) is on the same street at number 470 and has singles/doubles with bath and fan for US$7/8. The *Pensão Araki* is at Rua S Joaquim 139.

More expensive places in Liberdade include the *Banri* (tel 270-8877) at Rua Galvão Bueno 209. They have singles/doubles starting at US$14/15. The *Osaka Palace* (tel 270-1311) is right across the street from the metro. It has all the modern amenities and doubles starting at US$25/30. Reservations are often needed about a week in advance for these two hotels.

Places to Stay - top end

As in Rio, the residential-hotels are an excellent deal. The *Trianon Residence* (tel 283-0066) – near Avenida Paulista at Alameda Casa Branca 363, Cerqueira César – features an excellent location, close to the centre but not in it. It has comfortable doubles for US$30.50. The *Augusta Park Residence* (tel 255-5722), Rua Augusta 922, Consolação, is similar value with singles/doubles for US$30/35.

The *Nikkey Palace* (tel 270-8511) in Liberdade at Rua Galvão Bueno 425 has a sauna and restaurant. Singles/doubles cost US$50/55. In town there is the *Othon Palace* (tel 239-3277) at Rua Libero Badaró 190 with singles/doubles starting at US$45/50.

Over on Avenida Casper Libero, a quiet street for the centre of town, there are three hotels. The *Marian Palace* (tel 228-8433) has singles/doubles starting at US$28/36. Down the block, the *Planalto* (tel 227-7311) has all the amenities too. It's a bargain with singles/doubles starting at US$18/26. The same applies to the *Delphos* (tel 228-6411), next door with singles/doubles for US$20/23. The *São Paulo Centre* (tel 228-6033) at Largo Santa Efigênia 40 is an old, elegant beauty. Singles/doubles cost US$35/38 and up.

São Paulo's luxury hotels include the *Maksoud Plaza* (tel 251-2233) with singles/doubles for US$65/89, the *Grand Hotel Ca'd'Oro* (tel 256-8011), the *São Paulo Hilton* (tel 256-0033) with singles/doubles for US$75/89, and the *Eldorado Boulevard* (tel 256-8833) with singles/doubles for US$65/85.

Places to Eat

The best reason to visit São Paulo is to eat. Because of the city's ethnic diversity you can find every kind of cuisine and, if you can spend a few dollars, it's easy to find great food at reasonable prices. There are also a million cheap lanchonetes, great pizzerias and churrascarias, and some of the best Italian and Japanese food that you'll find outside of those countries.

The Paulistas love to go out to dinner and they go out late. Although they open earlier, most restaurants don't fill up until 9 or 10 pm on weekdays and later on weekends. Many stay open on weekends until 2 or 3 am.

If you are staying in the city for awhile and like to eat out and eat well, ask at a tourist booth about the Secretaria de Esportes e Turismo's *Mapa Gastronomico de São Paulo* or go to the Secretaria at Avenida São Luis 115. On one side there's a detailed city map with 303 of the city's best restaurants (expensive and not) and the other side has the restaurant's addresses, hours and special dishes. A great source, with a surprisingly good choice of restaurants.

Central District If you're staying here, there are a few inexpensive places that are close by and several notches above the rest. *Ponto Chic* is a friendly, informal restaurant, but the best reason to go is the famous Brazilian sandwich, the 'Bauru', which Ponto Chic invented many moons ago. The Bauru is beef, tomato, pickle and a mix of melted cheeses served on French bread. The price is US$1.25. Not only is the Bauru popular in urban and backland Brazil, but it is also served in Paris. Ponto Chic is only a few blocks from the Praça da República at Largo Paissandu 27 and is open until 4 am

Another winner is the *Lanches Aliados* at the corner of Avenida Rio Branco and Rua Vitória. It's a cheap lunch spot with excellent food. The *Casa Ricardo* features 20 different sandwiches and is reasonable. Open until 7.30 pm, it's at Avenida Vieira de Carvalho 48.

For vegetarians *Superbom* is pretty fair. It's open Monday to Friday for lunches only (closes at 3 pm). There are branches at the Praça da República 128 (4th floor), 9 de Julho 180 and Praça da Sé 62. The *Mel* has some excellent natural and vegetarian lunches. It's open from 10 am to 6 pm Monday to Friday at Rua Araujo 75 (Centro).

The *Bar e Restaurante Leão* at Avenida São João 320 has all-you-can-eat Italian meals with salad bar, at reasonable prices. Nearby, in Bela Vista, there are two very good and very Italian restaurants on Rua Avanhandava. *Gigetto* and *Famiglia Mancini* have large selections of pastas and wines, stay crowded very late with the after theatre crowd and are moderately priced – US$4 buys a large plate of pasta. *Gigetto* is supposed to be an actors' hangout.

Cantina e Pizzeria Lazzarella Due (tel 289-3000), Rua Treze de Maio 590, Bixiga is full of Brazil kitsch. The live, if dated, music features a multi-lingual sing-along. It's festive, and the food is good and large plates of pasta are only US$4. The Bixiga district is loaded with Italian restaurants and bars; it's one of the best places in the city at night.

Ca'd'Oro (tel 256-8011) in the hotel of the same name is considered the best. It's very expensive; sports jacket and reservations recommended. *A Camorra* (tel 280-0741) at Rua da Consolação 3589, Cerqueira César is open for dinner only. The waiters here have an uncanny mafia-like appearance. *Giordano* (tel 64-8686) has excellent seafood and is somewhat expensive. Open for lunch and dinner (closed Mondays) it's at Alameda Lorena 1884, Jardim Paulista.

There are several other fine, but more reasonably priced Italian restaurants. *Cantina Balilla* (tel 228-8282) at Rua do Gasômetro 332, Brás stays open until 2 am and serves a delicious grilled capon chicken. *Jardim de Napoli* (tel 66-302?) at Rua Doutor Martinico Prado 4? Higienopolis is open for lunch and din? *L'Osteria do Piero* (tel 853-108? Alameda Franca 1509, Cerqueira features roast kid with broccoli and agnollotti. It is only open for dinner.

There's good pizza all over town. The best pizzerias include *Speranza* (tel 288-8502) at Rua 13 de Maio 1004, Bela Vista (dinner only). *Zi Tereza* at Rua da Consolação 1950, Consolação is open for lunch only. *Babbo Giovanni* (tel 853-2678), Rua Bela Cintra 2305, Cerqueira César is open for dinner only (inexpensive). The various *Micheluccio* restaurants about town are also good.

For a big splurge many think *Massimo* (tel 852-0947) at Alameda Santos 1826, Cerqueira César is the city's best restaurant. Another costly treat is the Indian cuisine at *Govinda* (tel 531-0269), Rua Princesa Isabel 379, Brooklin Paulista; open for dinners only. If it's lean meat you seek, *Baby-Beef Rubaiyat* has three churrascarias: the one in the centre (tel 813-2703) is at Avenida Vieira de Carvalho 116. A bit less expensive, *Morais* (tel 221-8066) at Praça Júlio Mesquita 175 is also central. Open until 3 am, *Morais* specialises in steak with fried garlic and French fries.

For everyone who has travelled extensively in Brazil and been disappointed by one lousy chinese restaurant after another *China Massas Caseiras* (tel 853-7111) is required therapy. It's inexpensive and delicious. Try the pasties. The place is at Rua Mourato Coelho 140, Pinheiros and open for lunch and dinner (closed Wednesdays). The *Schnapshaus* (tel 211-9886) has good German food and is informal and affordable, with meals at about US$4. It's at Rua Diogo Moreira 119, Pinheiros.

Liberdade has several Oriental restaurants and good food at the Sunday street fair. Ask for Yosaku at the *Teisoko*, Rua Gloria 730, and you'll get a fine, full lunch for US$2. There are several good Japanese restaurants to choose from on Rua Tomás Gonzaga. The *Sushi-Yassu* is the most famous and the most expensive at about US$8 a meal.

Entertainment

This city swings at night. Everyone is out playing until the wee hours and you feel it – where else can you get stuck in a traffic snarl at 3 am. São Paulo's nightlife approaches the excitement, diversity and intensity of New York's. To enjoy it, all you need is money and transportation.

The best list of events is probably the weekly *Veja* magazine which has a special São Paulo edition. They also list restaurants, bars, museums, fairs, etc.

Rua 13 de Maio in Bixiga hums at night. There are several clubs, restaurants and even a revival movie theatre. It's a young crowd so the prices are reasonable. You can go there, look around and plan out a full evening in one neighbourhood. The biggest club is the *Café Piu-Piu* (tel 258-8066) at number 134. They have music every night but Monday: jazz, rock and a sequin-shirted, 20-gallon-hatted band that plays American country music.

Bela Vista is another good area for nightlife. There's lots happening and it's central, although the clubs are not as close together as in Bixiga. *Spazio Pirandello* (tel 255-7586) at Rua Augusta 311 is always lively – the crowd both gay and straight. There's art on the walls and a bookstore downstairs. *Estacão Madame Sata* (tel 285-6954) is from another world. It's a new wave and dark club – darks are Brazil's version of punks – but there's no heavy scene. The place is free and easy, the live, avant garde music unusual and often superb. A special experience, it opens at about 10 pm, but go late – very late. The club is at Rua Conselheiro Ramalho 873, Bela Vista.

For the best jazz in town try *Café Teatro Opus 2004* (tel 256-9591), Rua da Consolação 2004. At the *Luar do Sertão* (sertão moonlight) you'll find the music of the sertão and many nordestinos swaying to the *forrós*, the *xotes* and various other wild dances. This music is one of the great cultural treasures of Brazil and with the mass migration from the Northeast to São Paulo there's plenty of authentic talent.

The *Bar Brahma* is the city's oldest drinking establishment. It's at the corner of Rua São João and Avenida Ipiringa, in the heart of the central hotel district. From 7 pm to midnight the antique surroundings are accompanied by equally dated live music. The best tables are upstairs. The bar is friendly and relaxing and a popular after-work hangout for many Paulista professionals.

Another time-capsule bar is the *Riviera Restaurant & Bar* at the corner of Rua Consolacão and Avenida Paulista. This bar takes you back to the seedy '40s. It's inexpensive and unassuming; a good place to go with a friend to talk and unwind. A couple of doors down is a popular late-night bar and croissant shop. The *Paris Cafe* is the famous cafe hangout by the university.

Vou Vivendo (tel 815-7021) is a medium size music club/restaurant. It's informal and prices are reasonable. Upstairs there's excellent samba, jazz, etc. It's at Rua Pedroso de Moraes 1017, Pinheiros. Across the street the *Avenida Club* (tel 814-7383) features orchestra dancing – for couples – Fridays and Saturdays from 10 pm to 4 am. The 18-piece orchestra plays the old tunes and the dance hall is a fantastic recreation of the '30s scene. The cover charge is US$5 for men and US$4 for women. Downstairs is a classy restaurant.

Getting There & Away

Air There are flights to everywhere in Brazil and many of the world's major cities. Before buying your ticket make sure to check which airport the flight departs from and how many stops it makes (flights to coastal cities often make several stops along the way).

The São Paulo to Rio shuttle flies every 30 minutes or less from Congonhas airport into Santos Dumont, central Rio. The flight is less than an hour and you can usually go right to the airport, buy a ticket and be on a plane within the hour.

Bus The terminal Tieté is easy to reach – just get off at the Tieté metro station, which is adjacent and connected. It's an enormous building and not easily navigated. The information desk at the middle of the main concourse on the 1st floor is of limited value. Only Portuguese is spoken.

Bus tickets are sold on the 1st floor, except for the Rio shuttle which has its ticket offices on the ground floor at the rear of the building. Buses leave for all of Brazil and there are also buses to major cities in Argentina, Paraguay, Chile and Uruguay.

All of the following buses leave from the Tiete rodoviária. Frequent buses traverse the 429 km of the Via Dutra highway to Rio in six hours. The cost is US$5 for the regular bus, US$9 for the leito. The bus to Brasília takes 15 hours for US$14, to Belo Horizonte nine hours for US$8.50, to Foz do Iguaçu 20 hours for US$11, to Cuiabá 25 hours for US$22, to Campo Grande 16 hours for US$17, to Salvador 30 hours for US$24, to Curitiba six hours for US$3, to Joinville nine hours for US$4, to Blumenau 10 hours for US$4.50, and to Florianópolis 12 hours for US$5.

Buses to Santos and São Vicente leave every five minutes from a separate bus station at the end of the southern metro line (Jabaquara station). It's a one hour trip.

If you're staying outside the city centre find out if there is a local bus station nearby where the buses make a stop on their way out of town. For example there's Itapemirim Turismo (tel 212-5402) at Avenida Valdemira Feirrara 130, near the University City. Several southbound buses stop here on their way to Florianópolis, Curitiba, etc. If you catch the bus here, it will save an hour's drive into the city and an hour's drive back.

Rail Estação da Luz train station services the long-distance routes: Rio, Brasília and Campo Grande and Corumbá. To get there take the metro to the Luz station.

The nine hour train ride to Rio is

supposedly quite scenic. At least it used to be – unfortunately the train now leaves both Rio and São Paulo at 11 pm so you don't see much. A cabin for two costs about US$16 and the agents recommended buying your tickets a week in advance. The 22 hour trip to Brasília offers daylight and interesting terrain. It leaves Sundays at 10.05 pm with stops at the bigger cities along the way. A double cabin costs US$26, a leito seat US$12 and economy seats as low as US$3.

You can't get a direct train to Campo Grande or Corumbá from São Paulo. What you have to do is take the train or bus from São Paulo to Bauru. At Bauru, there's a 3.45 pm daily train that goes through Campo Grande and Corumbá and all the way into Bolivia. For information telephone Bauru (tel (0142) 22-6826). The trip from São Paulo to Corumbá, which crosses the southern edge of the Pantanal, takes close to 40 hours.

Getting Around

Airport Transport São Paulo has three airports. Congonhas serves Rio and other local flights. It is the closest airport – 14 km south of the city centre. Avoid the radio taxis up front and ask for the regular taxi (comums), There's a small sign marking the place. The ride into town is about US$4.

To catch a bus into the city, walk out of the terminal and to your right where you'll see a busy street with a pedestrian overpass. Head to the overpass, but don't cross: you should see a crowd of people waiting for the buses along the street, or ask for the bus marked 'Banderas'. This bus will get you there in about an hour. The last bus leaves around 1 am.

The Aeroporto Viracopos is 97 km from the city and near Campinas. Avoid this airport if possible. A taxi from here into town will cost about US$45.

Aeroporto Internacional de São Paulo/ Guarulhos is 30 km east of the city. There's a bus that takes you to Praça da

República, or look for a comum instead of a special radio or airport cab.

Metro If you're on a limited budget, São Paulo by metro and foot is the best way to see the city. The metro is new, cheap, safe and fast. It's open from 5 am to midnight. There are currently two lines that intersect at Praça da Sé. Liberdade is one stop away, the budget hotel area is served by the Luz station, and the rodoviária, Terminal Tieté, is three stops down the line. Get off at Tieté.

Bus Buses are slow, crowded during rush hours and not too safe. Unlike Rio, you can wait quite a while for the one you want, and trying to figure out which that is can be difficult.

Taxi Both the regular (comum) and radio taxi service are metered. Radio taxi (tel 251-1733) costs 50% more than the comum and will pick you up anywhere in the city.

UBATUBA

Population: 30,000

The Ubatuba littoral is a stunning stretch of beach along the northern São Paulo coast. It's the pre-eminent beach resort for the well-to-do of São Paulo and there are many elegant beach homes and hotels, especially to the south of the town of Ubatuba. To the north of town, all the way to Parati, the beaches are wilder, cleaner and often deserted. There are few hotels, but plenty of campsites.

Most travellers don't go to Ubatuba, unless they are spending some time in São Paulo and want to escape for the weekend, or are driving the Rio to Santos coastal road. It's not that the beaches aren't top-notch, they are, but they get crowded in the summer, are rather expensive and there is little that remains of the old fishing culture that animates so many coastal towns in Brazil.

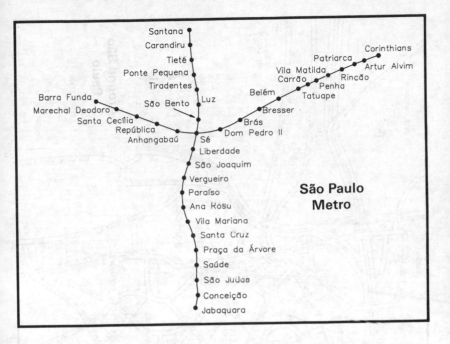

São Paulo
Metro

Information & Orientation

Ubatuba is 72 km south-west of Parati on the paved coastal road; a 1½ hour drive at a reasonable speed. Rio is 310 km away; a six hour drive. Heading south on the coast Caraguatatuba is 54 km, São Sebastião and Ilha Bela are 75 km and Santos is 205 km. After Caraguatatuba the road begins to deteriorate and an unending procession of speed bumps rear their ugly heads.

São Paulo is 240 km from Ubatuba and the fastest route, by a long shot, is to turn off the coastal road at Caraguatatuba on SP-099 and climb the escarpment until you meet the Rio to Santos highway, BR-116, at São José dos Campos. This is a beautiful, rapid ascent, and the road is in good condition.

Ubatuba is large enough to have most services. There is a Banco do Brasil. The post office is on Rua D Maria Alves, and the posto telefônico is at Rua Prof Thomaz Galhardo 81.

Tourist Office There's a tourist office shack in Ubatuba where Rua Prof Thomaz Galhardo hits the bay. Open from 8 am to 6 pm, they are somewhat helpful and have maps of the coast.

Beaches

Beaches, beaches and more beaches. Within the district of Ubatuba there are some 74 beaches and 15 islands. If you're staying in the city and don't have wheels there's a fine beach a couple of km south of town with barracas and some surfing. Other recommended beaches south of Ubatuba include Toninhas and Enseada eight km, Flamengo 12 km, Lazaro and Domingas Dias 14 km.

To the north of town the beaches are hidden away down the steep hillside.

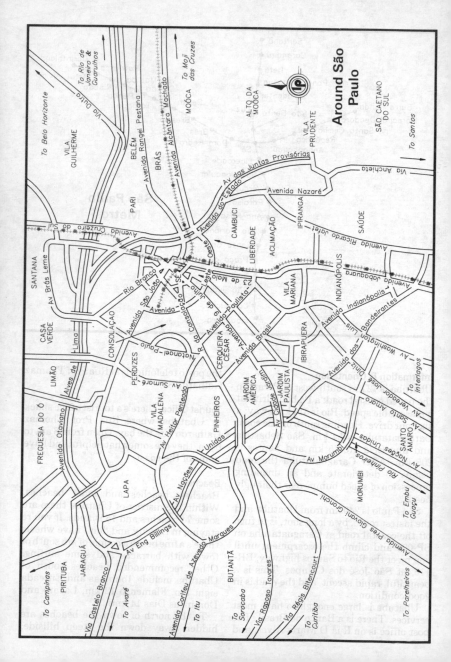

Around São Paulo

They are harder to find, but well worth the effort. The best beaches are Vermelha nine km, Itamambuca 11 km, Promirim 22 km and Ubatumirim 32 km.

Port
The port is at Praia de Saco de Rebeiro, 12 km south of Ubatuba. Mykonos Turismo (tel 42-0388) has offices at the port and offers daily cruises into the Baía da Enseada and out to the Ilha Anchieta. They also have a ship that sails to Ilha Bela Saturdays at 10 am. Prices are high.

Festivals
On 29 June, Ubatuba celebrates the Festa de São Pedro Pescador with a big maritime procession.

Places to Stay
Many hotels dot the shoreline to the south of Ubatuba. Outside the city of Ubatuba, Praia da Enseada probably has the most facilities. There are several lesser priced hotels, including three along the beach. The *Pousada Beija Flor* has rooms for US$39. You will also find a couple of the areas best hotels, the *Hotel Mediterraneo* (tel 42-0112) and *Hotel Cassino Sol e Vida* (tel 42-0188) with singles/doubles for US$52. Hotel rates change dramatically with the seasons.

Staying in Ubatuba is the most convenient and cheapest place if you don't have a car. Good hotel deals within a couple blocks of the bus stations include the *Hotel Xareu* (tel 32-1525) at Rua Jordão Homem da Costa 413, the *Hotel São Nicolau* (tel 32-1267) at Rua Conceição 213 with singles/doubles for US$13/15, and next door the *Parque Atlântico* (tel 32-1336) at Rua Conceição 185 with singles/doubles for US$10/14.

The *São Charbel* (tel 32-1090), Praça Nobrega 280, is a somewhat better hotel with singles/doubles for US$16 and the *Ubatuba Palace* (tel 32-1500) is the city's finest with singles/doubles for US$24.

Getting There & Away
There are two bus stations in Ubatuba, less than two blocks apart. The Atlântico Rodoviária is on Rua Professor T Galhardo between Rua Hans Staden and Rua Cunhambebe. The Maringa Rodoviária is on Rua Conceição across from Praça 13 de Maio.

Buses leave every 45 minutes to São Paulo and Caraguatatuba. There are six daily buses to Parati. Buses to Rio leave at 12.45 pm and 8.15 pm.

CARAGUATATUBA
Population: 35,000
The coastal town of Caraguatatuba is 55 km from Ubatuba and 25 km from São Sebastian. This is not a very attractive town, and the beaches around the city are below the regional standard and not worth visiting.

Places to Stay & Eat
If you do get stuck here there are a few cheap hotels – ask around for *Hotel Central*, *Hotel Atlântico* or *Hotel Binoca* – and plenty of restaurants. There are also several hotels at Praia Massaguaçu, 10 km north of town.

Getting There & Away
The rodoviária (tel 22-1669) is at Praça Díogenes Ribeiro de Lima 227 and buses leave for points north and south along the coast and to São Paulo and Rio.

SÃO SEBASTIÃO
Population: 20,000
The coastal town of São Sebastião faces the Ilha de São Sebastião, popularly known as Ilhabela, only a 15 minute ferry trip acoss the channel. Huge oil tankers anchor in the calm canal formed by the island and mainland, waiting to unload at São Sebastião. The town itself is unassuming. There's not much here, but at least it has avoided the tourist industry blight, thanks to the poor beaches. Most visitors stay in São Sebastião, either because they can't find lodging at Ilhabela

or to enjoy the canal's excellent windsurfing conditions.

Places to Stay

The *Porto Grande* (tel 52-1101), on the coast road just north of town, is the best hotel around and the owner changes dollars at close to parallel market rates. It's on the beach. Basic singles/doubles are US$30/33, while more luxurious singles/doubles are US$33/42. They also have a good dinner and a maritime museum. For something cheaper, and right downtown, try the *Hotel Roma* (tel 52-1016) at the Praça Major João Fernandes 174. Doubles start at US$14.

Places to Eat

Along the waterfront you'll find several good fish restaurants including *Superflipper*. Eat the fish, not the shrimp.

Getting There & Away

The Rio to Santos highway from São Sebastião to Santos is slow going. A much quicker route to São Paulo (200 km) is through Caraguatatuba, despite a zillion speed bumps along the coastal road.

The rodoviária (tel 52-1072) at Praça da Amizade 10, has a regular service to São Paulo, Rio and Caraguatatuba.

ILHABELA

Population: 14,000

With 340 square km, Ilhabela is the biggest island along the Brazilian coast. The island's volcanic origin is evident in the steeply rising peaks, which are covered by dense, tropical jungle. There are 360 waterfalls and the flatlands are filled with sugar cane plantations. The island is known for it's excellent jungle hiking and fine cachaça.

Unfortunately, visiting Ilhabela can be a bit of a drag. During the summer the island is besieged by multitudes of Paulistas. Besides the threat this poses to the environment, the crowds create all sorts of logistical difficulties: many hotels fill-up, waits of two to three hours for the ferry are common and prices soar.

The time to go to Ilhabela is weekdays in the off-season. Once you arrive, the name of the game is to get away from the west coast, which faces the mainland, and where almost all human activity is concentrated. To get to the other side of the island requires either 4WD, catching a boat, or a guide and a strong pair of hiking legs. Of the sheltered beaches on the island's north side, Praia Pedra do Sino and Praia Jabacuara are recommended. On the east side, where the surf is stronger, try Praia dos Castelhano, Praia do Gato or Praia da Figueira.

Places to Stay

On Rua Dr Carvalho try the *Hotel São Paulo* (tel 72-1158) for relatively inexpensive lodging or the *Pousada dos Hibiscos* (tel 72-1375), Avenida Pedro Paula de Morais 714. Consider staying in São Sebastião where the hotels are cheaper. There are no hotels on the far side of the island but it's possible to find a bed in a barraca.

Getting There & Away

The ferry takes 15 minutes and runs frequently. The service starts at 5.30 am and goes until midnight, although during the summer it often goes much later. The price is 25c a person.

THE NORTHEAST

REGIÃO NORDESTE

Bahia

Bahia is Brazil's most historic state, most African state and one of its most beautiful. Its capital, Salvador da Bahia, was the capital of colonial Brazil from 1549 to 1763 and the centre of the sugar civilisation, the country's lifeblood until the 18th century decline in international sugar prices. The city is loaded with colonial relics – including many richly decorated churches, one for every day of the year according to popular belief.

Much of Bahian life revolves around the Afro-Brazilian religion known as Candomblé. To the Christian observer, Candomblé provides a radically different view of the world. Candomblé also provides a context for cultivating African traditions – the music, the dance, and the language – into a system of worshipping life and enjoying it in peace and harmony.

Salvador da Bahia is a fascinating city. A city that gets better as you discover more of it, as you peel away the tourist layers. You should also get out of Salvador into the smaller cities, into the towns and fishing villages where life is unaffected by tourism and even less affected by the 20th century.

If beaches are what you want the only difficulty is choosing. You can stay in Salvador and do fine. You can go to Porto Seguro for deserted beaches with fancy hotels and restaurants or cross the river to Arraial d'Ajuda for a hipper, less developed beach scene. To really escape civilisation you can go to the island beaches of Morro de São Paulo or even better the beaches up north around Conde.

Going inland, Cachoeira and Lençóis are both preserved-like-a-pickle colonial towns. Cachoeira is known for its Candomblé, Lençóis for its legends and superstition. Both cities have good lodging and beautiful surrounding country-side. The sertão is another world, like the moon perhaps. There is no tourism there, in fact there is no there there, but you can explore. The people who live along the Rio São Francisco – which flows over 3000 km – have maintained a rich culture despite the poor environment.

Economy

Despite a terrible drought in Bahia's interior in 1987, the state has the rosiest economic outlook in Northeastern Brazil. Because of Bahia's substantial oil and natural gas the large Camaçari petro-chemical complex has been growing quickly.

Cacao prices have been up on the world market and it's still the state's most valuable export crop. Corn and soybeans are the primary market crops in the interior, where there is mostly subsistence farming. Much of the state's economy revolves around the port of Salvador – castor oil seeds, coconut butter, coffee, sisal ropes, petroleum products and chemicals all pass through here.

Geography

The state of Bahia divides into three distinct regions: the recôncavo, the sertão and the littoral. The recôncavo is a band of hot and humid lands which surround the Baia de Todos os Santos. The principal cities are Cachoeira, Santo Amaro, Maragojipe and Nazaré which were once sugar and tobacco centres and the source of wealth for Salvador, the heart of colonial Brazil. The soil is rich and rivers are abundant.

The sertão (backlands), the land of droughts, immortalised by Euclides da Cunha's book *Rebellion in the Backlands* and the Cinema Novo films of Glauber Rocha, is dominated by a dry and temperate climate. The land is called the *caatingas*. Caatinga is a scrubby shrub plant. There is little diversity, just thorny caatinga that covers the land and stretches to the horizon. The biggest towns stretch along the Rio São Francisco.

The littoral, with beautiful, endless beaches, produces cacao south of Salvador, where there are important cities like Valença, Ilhéus and Itabuna. North of Salvador the coast is only sparsely populated with a few fishing villages. The southern beaches are calm, while the northern beaches are often windy with rough surf. Salvador da Bahia is the heart and soul of Bahia.

Religion

The Afro-Brazilian religious cults in Bahia are called Candomblé. Brought from Africa by the Nago, Bantu and Jeje peoples, Candomblé revolves around the worship of the orixás – spirits or gods. For slaves in Brazil, these African beliefs, as well as African songs and dances, were prohibited. Only the Christian celebrations were tolerated, so to survive the African religions took on the outward appearance of Christianity.

Candomblé was prohibited in Bahia until 1970. Much of Candomblé is secret but the public ceremony, conducted in the original Yoruba tongue, takes place in a *terreiros*. Display figures of Catholic saints are one of the few signs of Christianity.

For more on Candomblé see the religion section in Facts About the Country. It's a subject well-worth reading more about. The strength and cultural richness of Candomblé has attracted and inspired a number of perceptive western authors, several of whom were converted. *Orixás* by Pierre Fatumbi Verger is a photo book comparing the Brazilian and African religions. Edison Carneiro is the most famous student of Candomblé, capoeira and other aspects of Bahian life and folklore. Several of his books are in English. On religion, look for *Candomblés da Bahia. The African Religions of Brazil*, by the well-known French anthro-pologist Roger Bastide, is a scholarly look at social forces which shaped Candomblé. For lighter reading try Jorge Amado's *Dona Flor & Her Two Husbands*.

An Evening of Candomblé

The mãe-de-santo or pai-de-santo run the service. The *mãe-pequena* is entrusted with the training of priestesses: two *filhas-de-santo*, one a girl over seven years of age the other a girl under seven. The initiates are called *abian*.

In the morning of an orixá's day animals are sacrificed to the orixá of the celebration. Only initiates may attend the morning service. Later in the afternoon the *padê* ceremony calls Exú. Then comes the chanting, accompanied by atabaques drummers called *alabés*, to the orixás.

The long evening of Candomblé in Casa Branca, Salvador's oldest terreiro, is quite an experience. The mon drum complex and powerful African rhythms. The women dress in lace and hooped skirts, and dance slowly and chant in the Yoruba language. The terreiro is female dominated. Only the women dance, only they enter a state of trance, the principal goal of the ceremony. The men play supporting roles. The dance is very African, with slow graceful hand motions, swaying hips and light steps. When the trance strikes one dancer she'll shake and writhe while assistants embrace and support her. Other dancers also fall into a trance while dancing. Sometimes, spectators even go into trances, which is discouraged.

The festival I witnessed was for Omolú, the feared and respected orixá of plague and disease. He is worshipped only on Mondays and his Christian syncretic counterpart is either Saint Lazarus or Saint Roque. His costume consists of a straw belt encrusted with sea-shells, a straw mask, a cape and dress to cover his face and body which have been disfigured by smallpox.

When dancers receive the spirit of Omolú in the trance, some leave the floor. They return shortly with one who represents Omolú and is covered from head to toe in long straw-like strands. The dancing resumes.

Although the congregants of Casa Branca are friendly and hospitable, they don't orient their practice to outsiders. Several westerners attend, and many white Brazilians are members. After the ceremony the guests are invited to the far end of the house for sweets and giant cakes – one is decorated like the Brazilian flag.

Culture

Capoeira Capoeira is an African martial art developed by the slaves to fight their oppressors. Prohibited by the slave-masters, capoeira was pushed out of the slave barracks (*senzalas*) and into the jungle. Later, to disguise it from the authorities, Capoeira developed into a kind of acrobatic dance. Clapping of hands and the plucking of the *berimbau*, a fishing-rod-like instrument, originally alerted the fighters to the approach of the boss and subsequently became incorporated into the dance-form to maintain the rhythm.

As recently as the 1920s, capoeira was still prohibited and Salvador's police chief organised a police cavalry squad to ban capoeira from the streets. In the 1930s, Mestre Bimba established his academy and capoeira, no longer a tool of insurrection but a form of artistic expression, became an institution in Bahia.

Today, there are two schools of capoeira: the Capoeira de Angola led by Mestre Pastinha and the more aggressive Capoeira Regional of Mestre Bimba. The former school holds that Capoeira came from Angola, the latter believes that it was born in the plantations of Cachoeira and other cities of the Recôncavo region.

Capoeira is a fight, a game and a dance. The movements are always fluid and circular, the fighters always playful and respectful. It has become very popular in recent years and throughout Bahia and Brazil you will see *roda de capoeiras*,

The martial art Capoeira

semi-circles of spectator-musicians who sing the initial *chula* before the fight and provide the percussion during the fight. In addition to the berimbau, blows are exchanged to the beat of *caxixis*, *pandeiros*, *reco-recos*, *agogós* and *atabaques*.

Jogo dos Búzios

The Jogo dos Búzios (game of shells) can be traced back to numerology and caballism. It is a simple version of the Ifa tray in which the orixá Ifa is invoked to transmit the words of God to the people. The mãe de santo casts 16 seashells on a white towel. She interprets the number and arrangement of face-up and face-down shells to predict the future.

The Jogo is a serious, respected force in Bahia. In 1985 the Jogo dos Búzios was used by many politicians to forecast the election returns. Visitors can consult a mãe-de-santo for Candomblé-style fortune telling any day of the week, except for Fridays and Mondays, but Thursdays are best.

Bahian Folk Art

Bahia has some of Brazil's best artisans, who usually have small shops or sell in the local market. You can buy their folk art in Salvador, but the best place to see or purchase the real stuff is in the town of origin.

Leather, wood, earth, metal and fibre are the materials used, while production is regional and specialised. Feira de Santana is known for its leather work, the best examples are in the city's Casa do Sertão Folklore Museum. Maragogipinho, Rio Real and Cachoeira produce earthenware. Caldas do Jorro, Caldas de Cipo and Itaparica specialise in straw crafts. Rio de Contas and Muritiba have metal work. Ihla de Maré is famous for lace work. Jeuie, Valença, and Feira de Santana are woodworking centres. Santo Antônio de Jesus, Rio de Contas and Monte Santo manufacture leather and silver goods.

Salvador

Population: 1,500,000
Salvador da Bahia, often called Bahia by Brazilians, is like no other city in the New or Old World. A fascinating place, Salvador is Brazil's most festive city.

For rich and poor alike, the beach is a great escape. There are long stretches of sand lapped by calm seas, lined with coconut trees and scented with dendê oil, the backbone of the African cuisine.

The best way to enjoy Bahia is to go slow, but do some exploring, be somewhat adventurous, and get out of the safe hotel districts. Look for music. It's a great way to meet people and see Bahians at play.

History

The first contact with the Portuguese was made on 1 November 1501, All Saints Day, when Américo Vespúcio sailed in to the bay which was accordingly named Baia de Todos os Santos. In 1549 Tomé de Souza came from Portugal bringing city plans, a statue, 400 soldiers and 400 settlers including priests and prostitutes. He founded the city in a location which had good defenses on a clifftop facing the sea. After the first year a city of mud and straw had been built and by 1550 it was surrounded by walls to protect against Indian attacks. It was to be the capital of the new lands and for three centuries Brazil's most important city.

For its first century of existence the city depended upon the export of sugar cane but later tobacco growing developed and cattle were raised in the sertão. With the mining of the Chapada Diamantina, Salvador also exported gold and diamonds. The city's baroque architecture dates from this period.

Bahia remained the seat of government until 1763 when, with the decline of the sugar cane industry, the capital was moved to Rio. Overlooking the mouth of

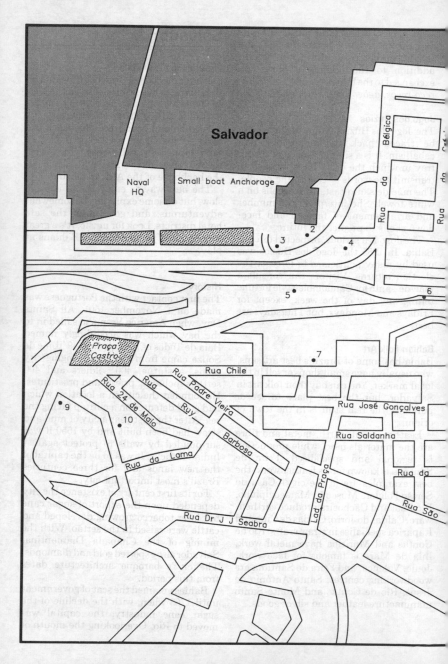

Salvador

Naval HQ

Small boat Anchorage

Praça Castro

Rua Chile

Rua Padre Vieira

Rua 24 de Maio

Rua Ruy

Barbosa

Rua da Lama

Rua Dr J J Seabra

Rua José Gonçalves

Rua Saldanha

Rua da

Rua São

Lad da Praça

Bélgica

Rua da

Rua da Ca

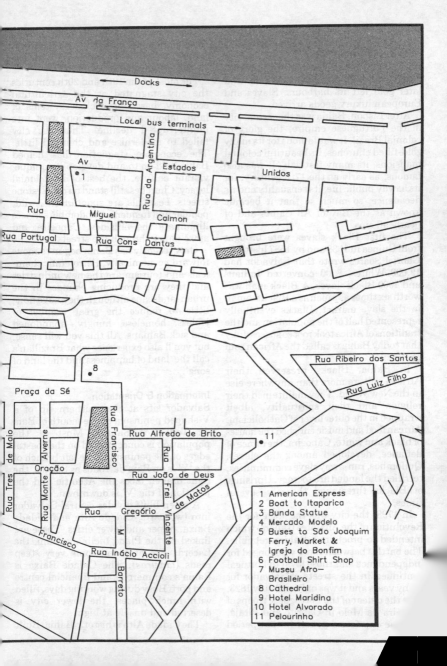

1 American Express
2 Boat to Itaparica
3 Bunda Statue
4 Mercado Modelo
5 Buses to São Joaquim
  Ferry, Market &
  Igreja do Bonfim
6 Football Shirt Shop
7 Museu Afro–
  Brasileiro
8 Cathedral
9 Hotel Maridina
10 Hotel Alvorado
11 Pelourinho

the Baía de Todos os Santos, which is surrounded by the Recôncavo, Brazil's richest sugar and tobacco lands, Bahia was colonial Brazil's economic heartland. Sugar, tobacco, sugar cane brandy and later gold left its harbours. Slaves and European luxury goods arrived.

After Lisbon, Bahia was the second city in the Portuguese empire, the glory of colonial Brazil. It was famous for its many gold-filled churches, its beautiful colonial mansions, its many festivals. It was also famous, as early as the 17th century, for its bawdy public life, its sensuality and its decadence, so much so that it became known as the Bay of All Saints and of nearly all sins.

The first Black slaves were brought from Guinea in 1538 and by 1587 historian Gabriel Soares wrote that Salvador had 12,000 Whites, 8000 converted Indians and 4000 Black slaves. A Black man was worth six times as much as a Black woman in the slave market. Blacks eventually represented half of the population and the traditions of Africa took root so successfully that today Bahia is called the African soul of Brazil.

In Bahia, Blacks preserved their African culture more than anywhere else in the New World. They maintained their religion and their spirituality, albeit wrapped in the outer layer of Catholicism. African food and music enriched the houses of black and white. Capoeira, the dance of defiance, developed among the slaves. Quilombos, run-away slave communities, terrified the landed aristocracy. Uprisings of Blacks threatened the city several times.

In 1798, the city was the stage for the Revolution of the Alfaiates (tailors) which intended to proclaim a Bahian republic. The battles between those who longed for independence and those loyal to Portugal continued in the streets of Salvador for many years and it was only on 2 July 1823, with the defeat of the Portuguese troops of Madeira de Melo in Cabrito and Pirajá, the city found peace. In that period

Salvador had 45,000 inhabitants and was the commercial centre of a vast territory. Its area of influence increased with the spread of railways.

For most of the 19th and 20th centuries the city stagnated as the agricultural economy, based on archaic systems of land, labour and production, went into uninterrupted decline. Thus the city failed to modernise and changed little. The economic stagnation has helped Bahia hold on to and develop its unique, vibrant culture, the best of its colonial legacy. Churches still stand on cobblestone streets. Festivals are spontaneous, wild, popular and frequent. Candomblé services illuminate the hillsides. Capoeira and afoxé dance through the streets.

Only recently has Bahia begun to move forward economically. Petroleum, chemicals and tourism are the new industries and they are producing changes in the urban landscape although they have done little to reduce the great number of jobless, homeless, hungry, abandoned and sick Bahians. All this you will sense, but you'll also experience what Brazilian's call the 'land of happiness and the land of song'.

Information & Orientation

Salvador sits at the southern tip of a V-shaped peninsula at the mouth of Baia de Todos os Santos. Most of the population is concentrated on the coastal edges of the peninsula. The left branch of the 'V' is on Baia de Todos os Santos, the right branch faces the Atlantic and the junction of the 'V' is downtown.

A steep bluff divides central Salvador into two parts, Cidade Alta and Cidade Baixa, upper and lower cities. These are linked by the Plano Inclinado tram, the Lacerda Elevator and some very steep roads (ladeiras). The Cidade Baixa is Bahia's commercial and financial centre and port. Busy during working days, filled with lunch places, the lower city is deserted and unsafe at night.

The Cidade Alta is historic Bahia. Built

Top: Favela dwellers in Salvador, Bahia (JM)
Left: Resident of Salvador, Bahia (JM)
Right: A typical 'Bahiana' in native dress, Salvador, Bahia (JM)

Top: Fishermen hauling nets in Salvador, Bahia (JM)
Bottom: Salvador delicacies, Bahia (JM)

on hilly, uneven ground, the site of the original settlement was chosen to protect the new capital from Indian attacks. The most important buildings went up on the hilltops – the churches, convents, government offices and the houses of the merchants and landowners. Like most Portuguese cities there was almost no rational planning.

Today, the colonial neighbourhoods of Pelourinho, Terreiro de Jesus and Anchieta are filled with 17th century churches and houses. These aren't the safest parts of town – several streets are centres of prostitution – but they are certainly the most interesting. Most of the city's best cheap hotels are here. There is relatively little nightlife.

Walking past the praça with the Lacerda Elevator you'll see a big, creamy pink colonial building which houses Bahiatursa, the excellent state tourism agency. A few blocks further is the Praça Castro Alves, centre for carnival festivities.

The main street here is Avenida 7 de Setembro which parallels the bay until it reaches the Atlantic Ocean and the section called Barra, which has many of the city's upper and middle-end hotels and bars.

The main road along the Atlantic coast, sometimes called Avenida Presidente Vargas (at least on the maps), hugs the shore all the way to Itapoã. Along the way it passes the middle class Atlantic suburbs and a chain of great tropical beaches.

Heading away from the ocean along the bay, starting at the Cidade Baixa, you pass the port, the ferry to the island of Itaparica and the bay beaches of Boa Viagem and Ribeira (very lively on weekends). These are poor suburbs along the bay and the further you go from the centre the greater the poverty. Watch for the incredible architecture of the algados; favelas built on the bay.

CIA, the Centro Industrial de Aratu, is three times the size of Salvador and sprawls around the bay of Aratu, which empties into Baia de Todos os Santos. It's the first rationally planned industrial park of Brazil and over 100 firms operate there.

Finding your way around Salvador can be a bitch. Besides the upper city and lower city, there are too many one-way, no-left-turn streets that wind through Salvador's valleys and lack any coherent pattern or relationship to the rest of the existing paved world. Traffic laws are left to the discretion of drivers. Gridlock is common at rush hour.

Perhaps most difficult for the visitor, street names are not regularly used by the locals and when they are there are often so many different names for each street that the one you have in mind probably doesn't mean anything to the person you're asking to assist you – the road along the Atlantic coast, sometimes known as Presidente Vargas, has at least four aliases.

Some of the street names variations include:

Praça 15 de Novembro, popularly known as Terreiro de Jesus

Rua J J Seabra is popularly known as the Bairro do Sapateiro or the shoemaker's neighborhood. In early colonial days, this street was the site of a moat, the first line of defense against the Indians.

Rua Francisco Muniz Barreto is known as the Rua das Laranjeiras or St of Orange Trees.

Inácio Accioli known as Boca do Lixo which means, believe it or not, garbage mouth!

Rua Leovigildo de Caravalho is known as Beco do Mota.

Rua Padre Nobrega is known as Brega. The street was named after a Bahian priest. The street came to be the main drag of the red light district and with time Nobrega was shortened to Brega which in Brazilian usage is now synonymous with brothel.

Tourist Office Your first stop in Salvador should be Bahiatursa, (tel 254-7000), Praça Tomé de Souza, Palácio Rio Branco. They also have offices at the rodoviária (tel 231-2831) and airport (tel 240-1244). More than just a brochure stand, Brazil's best organised tourist outfit will help you find lodging, dispense maps and events calendars and tell you where and when to see capoeira and candomblé. They have good pamphlets for walking tours and there's a message board for finding friends, renting houses and boats, buying guidebooks and even overseas airline tickets, etc.

Bahiatursa operates an alternative lodging service that locates rooms in private houses and the like during Carnival and summer holidays. This can be an excellent way to find cheap and friendly rooms.

Bahiatursa also provide information on travel throughout the state of Bahia, but they are not nearly as knowledgeable or reliable as when they stick to the city.

Telephone Many hotels have international phone service, which is easier than running off to a phone station. If you are not so lucky the Telebahia posts are:

Telebahia Mercado Modelo
    Praça Visconde de Cayru, s/n (no number), open Monday to Saturday 8 am to 6 pm.
Telebahia Barra
    Avenida Sete de Setembro 533, Porto da Barra, open daily 6.30 am to 10 pm.
Telebahia Rodoviária
    open daily 6.30 am to midnight.
Telebahia Aeroporto
    Aeroporto Internacional Dois de Julho, open daily 6.30 am to midnight.

There are also phone stations in Iguatemi Shopping Centre, Campo da Pólvora and Centro de Convenções da Bahia.

American Express There's an American Express/Kontik-Franstur SA (tel 242-2494) office in the Cidade Baixa at Praça da Inglaterra 2 which holds mail for travellers. It's open Monday to Friday 8 am to 6 pm, but the mail office often closes for lunch.

Money The tourism industry is big in Bahia, so you can always find a place to change money although the rates are slightly below Rio. The difficulty is not wasting too much time doing it and not getting ripped-off. Whatever you do, don't change money with guys on the street, particularly near the Lacerda elevators or the Cantina Luau.

Out of every 100 foreigners who go near the Lacerda elevator, 98 are approached by men posing as money changers and offering exchange rates that are too good to be true. Many of them will lead you to some side alley or empty lobby to conduct the transaction and rip you off. Salvador is a poor city and there is much petty crime. Keep your wits about you and guard your wallet.

The basic strategy, as always, is to ask around. It's always safer to change with someone who has an address, a building, a business, so there's some accountability (eg a hotel or jewellery store).

Airlines Following is a list of the airlines represented in Salvador:

LAP – Paraguay Airlines
    Rua Visconde do Rosário 3 (tel 243-8981)
Nordeste
    Avenida D João VI, Brotas (tel 233-3370 & 244-7533)
Transbrasil
    Rua Carlos Gomes 616, Centro (tel 241-1044) & airport (204- 1100)
Varig/Cruzeiro
    Rua Carlos Gomes 6, Centro (tel 243-1344) & airport (tel 204- 1030)
Vasp
    Rua Chile 27, Centro (tel 243-7044) & airport (tel 249-2495)

Travel Agents The following travel agents sell bus tickets in addition to all the normal services. They can save you a trip out to the rodoviária, but check first as some agents do not sell tickets to all destinations:

Amaralina Viagems (tel 235-1263), Barra
Antares (tel 247-7588), Barra
Itapemirim (tel 247-6633), Avenida Sete de Septembro 1420

Itapoan Turismo (tel 243-4648), Campo da Pólvora 21, Centro
Remundi Turismo (tel 243-3011), Rua Grécia 8, Cidade Baixa
Rumo Turismo (tel 258-1684) Avenida Antônio Carlos Magalhães 1034, Loja 31, Pituba
Transamazonas Turismo (tel 247-7025)
Turbahia (tel 242-3474), Cidade Baixa

Time In Bahia, shopkeepers close for lunch until 3 instead of 2, and then go home at 3.45 pm instead of 5 pm. Café da manhã becomes *café da tarde*. Work has a different flavour: slow, relaxed and seemingly nonchalant. It's as if the capitalist revolution – and the changes in the concept of time that it engenders – has not been completed in Salvador. There are fewer clocks on walls, fewer watches on wrists. The bus drivers even go at reasonably safe speeds.

The slow Bahian pace often frustrates and irritates visitors, but if you can reset your internal clock and not get uptight or unsettled, the Bahians are likely to reward you with many kindnesses and surprises. They will pass time with you in ways unheard of in the modern world. For example, when in a taxi and unable to find an obscure restaurant, the taxi driver stopped, turned off his meter, and started to read my map. After 10 minutes we drove on and he turned the meter back on.

Candomblé
Before doing anything in Bahia, find out the schedule of Candomblé so you don't miss a night in a terreiro. Bahiatursa has many Candomblistas on its staff and is well-informed. They have a complete list of terreiros, houses of Candomblé, and can tell you the schedule for the month. Activities usually start around 8 or 9 pm and can be held any day of the week.

Cultural Events
If you want to plug into the arts, the Fundação Cultural do Estado da Bahia (tel 243-4555), Rua General Labatut 27, Barris organises a listing of museums, libraries, theatres and cultural events (fine arts) including performances at the Teatro Castro Alves (tel 235-7616), Praça Dois de Julho (Campo Grande). Call or stop by at either address for a monthly program.

Churches
Bahia has plenty of churches, many built during the 17th and 18th centuries. The city boasts of having 365 churches, one for every day of the year, but the actual number of churches is somewhat closer to 70. Some churches have been converted into museums, others are perpetually being restored. Some convents have been refurbished as hotels and their chapels are now convention rooms. If you're into seeing them all, Bahiatursa has a complete list and the most interesting churches are described here.

Capoeira School
To visit a Capoeira school it's best to get the up-to-date schedule from Bahiatursa. They have a complete listing of schools and class schedules. The Associação de Capoeira Mestre Bimba is an excellent school. It's at Rua Francisco Muniz Barreto 1, Terreiro de Jesus and operates Monday to Saturday 9 to 11 am and 4 to 7 pm. Speak to Manuel or Ari.

Around Town
Historic Salvador is easy to see on foot and you should plan on spending a couple of days wandering among the splendid 16th and 17th century churches, homes and museums. One good approach is to hit the old city in the morning and head out to the beaches in the afternoon.

The most important part of Bahia's colonial quarter runs from the Praça Castro Alves along Rua Chile and Rua da Misericórdia to Praça da Sé and Praça 15 de Novembro and then down through the Praça Pelourinho and up the hill to the Largo do Carmo.

There's no sense being too precise here, it's easy to stay in the colonial district. If you make a wrong turn you'll jump into another century. Also, you can keep oriented with our map or the Bahia Tours pamphlet that Bahiatursa gives out.

Cathedral of Bahia Starting at the Praça da Sé, walk a block to the Terreiro de Jesus (Praça 15 de Novembro on many maps). The biggest church on the plaza is the Cathedral of Bahia. Currently under renovation, the Cathedral was built of Lioz stone from 1657 to 1672. Many consider this the city's most beautiful church. The inside has many segmented areas and the emphasis is on verticality. It's open daily from 7 to 11 am and 2 to 6 pm.

Afro-Brazilian Museum Next door is the old medical school which now houses my favourite museum in Bahia, the small Afro-Brazilian Museum. The museum collection focuses primarily on displays of the orixás from both Africa and Bahia. There is a surprising amount of African art from pottery to woodwork. A highlight is the artist Caribe's carved wooden panels representing the Oxum. There are also capoeira artefacts. The museum (tel 243-0384) is open Tuesday to Saturday 9 to 11.30 am and 2 to 5.30 pm. There is an adjoining library.

In the middle of the plaza you'll meet drug dealers, honest hammock vendors and rip-off money changers. Be careful, don't change money.

Igreja São Francisco Exiting the museum, walk to the far end of the plaza and continue one block to the Igreja São Francisco. Defying the teachings and vows of poverty of its namesake, this baroque church is crammed with displays of wealth and splendour. Gold-leaf is used like wallpaper. There's an 80 kg silver chandelier and imported Portuguese ceramic tiles.

Forced to build their masters' church and yet prohibited from practising their own religion (Candomblé terreiros were hidden and kept far from town) the

African slave-artisans responded through their work: the faces of the cherubs are distorted, some angels are endowed with huge sex organs, some appear pregnant. Most of these creative acts were chastely covered by 20th century sacristans. Traditionally Blacks were seated in far corners of the church without a view of the altar.

Notice the polychrome of São Pedro da Alcântara by Manoel Inácio da Costa. The artist like his subject was suffering from tuberculosis. He made one side of the figure's face more ashen than the other so that São Pedro appears more ill as you walk past him. The hallway ceiling by José Joaquim da Rocha was painted with the then new perspective technique.

The poor come to Igreja São Francisco on Tuesdays to venerate Santo Antônio and receive bread. The Candomblistas respect this church's saints and come to pray here as well as in the Igreja NS do Bonfim.

Church of the Third order of São Francisco Next door to the Igreja São Francisco is the 17th century Church of the Third order of São Francisco. Notice the frontispiece, in the Spanish Baroque or Plateresco style, which was discovered 30 years ago hidden behind plaster.

Igreja São Pedro dos Clérigos The Igreja São Pedro dos Clérigos is back on the Terreiro de Jesus. This Rococo church, like many others built in the 18th century, was left with one of its towers missing in order to avoid a tax on finished churches. It opens only during mass.

Pelourinho
Along the Cantina La Luau is Rua Alfredo Brito, which goes to the Pelourinho district, with the city's oldest architecture. Pelourinho means whipping post, and this is where the slaves were tortured and sold (whipping of slaves was legal until 1835 in Brazil).

The old slave auction site on Praça José

de Alencar (also known as Largo do Pelourinho) has recently been renovated and converted into the Casa da Cultura Jorge Amado. According to a brass plaque across the street, Amado lived in the Hotel Pelourinho when it was a student house. The exhibition is disappointing but you can watch a free video of *Dona Flor* or one of the other films based on Amado's books.

If you're hungry while in the Pelourinho area there are two good restaurants serving typical Bahian food. Senac is buffet style and has a great selection of typical dishes. You can sample them all and it's open from midday to 2 pm for lunch and 7 to 10 pm for dinner. They also have folklore shows. Over at the Hotel Pelourinho Restaurant the food's good, the bay view's fantastic and the service is slow.

Museu da Cidade Next door is the Museu da Cidade. Among bits of whimsy (fleas in a matchbox dressed up to get married) there are costumes of the orixás of Candomblé and the personal effects of the Romantic poet Castro Alves, author of *Navio Negreiro* and one of the first public figures to protest slavery. The museum is open Monday to Friday 8 am to and 2 to 6 pm, Saturdays 8 am to midday.

Igreja N S do Rosário dos Pretos Across the Largo do Pelourinho, this church was built by and for the slaves. The 18th century church has some lovely coloured tiles.

Igreja dos Passos
From Pelourinho go down the hill and then head up to the Igreja dos Passos which has the same flavour as the Spanish steps of Rome. The first Brazilian film to win an award at the Cannes film festival, *O Pagador do Promessa*, was filmed here.

Convento do Carmo

At the top of the hill, inside the Convento do Carmo, there's the ritzy five-star Luxor Convento do Carmo Hotel and the Igreja and Museu Do Carmo, which is moderately interesting. Among the sacred and religious articles is a treaty declaring the expulsion of the Dutch from Salvador on 30 April 1625. The document was signed at the convent which served at the time as the general's quarters. It's open from Monday to Saturday from 8 to 11.30 am and 2 to 5 pm.

Continue on a few blocks for some unspoilt, old Bahia. The buildings are very old, but run-down and lived-in. There's an odd-looking public oratory called the Cruz do Pascoal in the middle of the street.

Praça Municipal

Starting at Praça da Sé again, walk over to the Praça Municipal. While not officially recognised or protected by the Brazilian historical architecture society SPHAN, the municipal plaza has several beautiful and important sites. The Palácio Rio Branco, was built in 1549 to house the offices of Tomé de Souza, the first general governor of Brazil; the palace has been rebuilt and refurbished over the years. The big pink birthday-cake building is now headquarters for Bahiatursa.

Elevador Lacerda

The Elevador Lacerda was inaugurated in 1868. It was an iron structure with clanking steam elevators until the new Lacerda elevator system was built in 1928. The electric elevators truck up and down a set of 85 metre vertical cement shafts in less than 15 seconds, carrying over 50,000 passengers daily.

Things weren't always so easy. At first, the Portuguese used slaves and mules to transport goods from the port in the Cidade Baixa to the Cidade Alto. By 1610 the Jesuits had installed the first elevator to negotiate the drop. Manually operated, the elevator was powered by a clever system of ropes and pulleys and carried freight and a few brave souls.

Mercado Modelo

Descending into the lower city you'll be confronted by the Mercado Modelo, filled with restaurants and shops, Salvador's worst concession to the tourism business. If you've missed Capoeira, they often have some for the tourists out in back. The horrendous modernist sculpture across the street is referred to as *bunda* (arse) by the locals. There are many cheap lanchonetes in the Cidade Baixa and it's worth exploring.

Mercado São Joaquim

To see a typical market, take the Ribeira or Bon Fim bus in front of the bottom of the elevator for about three km and get off after the Pirelli Pneus store on your left. On the waterfront, the Mercado São Joaquim is a small city of barracas open all day every day except Sunday. Watch out for the meat neighbourhood, it can turn the unprepared into devout vegetarians.

You are bound to come across some great singing and dancing at the barracas serving cachaça.

Igreja NS do Bonfim

Further along the Itapagipe peninsula past the mercado São José, is the Igreja NS do Bonfim, the site of the important procession of the same name held on the third Sunday in January. Built in 1745, the shrine is famous for its miraculous curing power. In the ex-voto room you'll see offerings – replicas of feet, arms, heads, hearts – the body-parts that devotees claim were cured by the Bonfim.

The Bonfim church is the church of Oxalá for Candomblistas and is their most important church. In January the festa do Bonfim, one of Bahia's most important, takes place here and the Candomblé priestesses (mães de santo) lead the festivities together with the Catholic priests.

Approaching the church you'll undoubtedly be offered a ribbon to put around your wrist. With the ribbon you can make three wishes that will come true by the time the ribbon falls off. This usually takes over two months and you must allow it to fall off from natural wear and tear. Cutting it off is said to bring bad luck.

The Bay

From the church there's a very interesting half-hour walk to the bay where you'll find the old Monte Serrat lighthouse and church (good crab at the barracas). Nearby is Praia da Boa Viagem where on New Year's Eve one of Bahia's most popular and magnificent festivals takes place: the maritime procession of Senhor Bom Jesus dos Navegantes.

The beach is lined with barracas and is very animated on weekends. It's a poorer part of town and quite interesting. From Boa Viagem there are frequent buses back to the França bus stop below the Lacerda Lift.

Museu de Arte Sacra da Bahia

The square belongs to the people as the sky belongs to the condor.

the poet Castro Alves

From the Praça Castro Alves, jammed with tens of thousands of people at Carnival time, it's a short walk to the Museu de Arte Sacra da Bahia. It's at the bottom of Ladeira de Santa Teresa at the corner of Rua do Sodré. The sacred art is excellent and the building, a 17th century convent, has been beautifully restored. They have a wide variety of sculptures and images in wood, clay and soapstone, many brought over from Portugal.

Museu de Arte Moderna

On the bay, toward Campo Grande from the centre, is the Solar do Unhão, an old sugar estate that now houses the small Museu de Arte Moderna, a restaurant (see Places to Eat) and a ceramic workshop. It's a lovely spot, the art is often good and I recommend the restaurant for its tranquillity and view.

Beaches

Pituba, Armação, Piatã, Placaford, and Itapoã beaches may not be as famous as Ipanema and Copacabana, but they are more beautiful. These are incredibly pristine beaches, all within 45-minutes by bus from the centre. For information on beaches north of Itapoã see the North of Salvador section.

To get to the beaches find the air-con executive bus marked Praça da Sé/Aeroporto. It leaves from Praça da Sé and travels along the beaches. You can flag it down anywhere on its path. Otherwise take a municipal bus to Campo Grande and then take the bus marked Aeroporto (you can also catch this bus along its route). Both these buses will take you along the Atlantic as far as Itapoã, but if you are going to one of the further beaches it's worth taking the executivo bus.

After driving for 20 minutes it's hard to find an ugly stretch of beach. There's no real secret to choosing, just get off where it suits your fancy and avoid spots with water run-offs emptying into the sea (it's often sewage dirtying the water). If you're looking for a beach which is both beautiful and convenient, and you're not hell-bent on having your own beach, I'd recommend Placaford.

If you don't want to go that far or you want the city beach scene, Barra is the first Atlantic beach and the liveliest. Swimming is calmest at the bay-like Porto da Barra. There are plenty of restaurants, barracas and bars. You can see Bahia's oldest fort, the polygonal Santo Antônio da Barra which was built in 1598 and fell to the Dutch in 1624. The view of Itaparica is splendid.

Festivals

Carnival in Bahia is justly world famo

For four nights and three days, beginning on a Thursday night, the masses go to the streets and stay until they fall. There's nothing to buy, so all you have to do is follow your heart – or the nearest trio elétrico – and play.

But Carnival isn't the only festival worth going out of your way for. There are many others, particularly in January and February, with strong roots among Bahians. Since the 17th century, religious processions have remained an integral part of the city's cultural life. Combining elements of the sacred and profane, Candomblé and Catholicism, many of these festivals are as wild as and possibly more colourful than Carnival.

Carnival Carnival starts on a Thursday night and goes until the following Monday. Everything, but everything goes for these four days. In recent years Carnival has revolved around the trio elétricos. The trios, a distinctly up-beat musical style, play from the tops of trucks that slowly wind their way through the main carnival areas (Praça Castro Alves, Campo Grande and Barra). Surrounding the trios is a sea of dancing, drinking fools.

Carnival brings so many tourists, and so much money, to Bahia that there's been an inevitable pull towards commercialisation though it's still light years behind Rio. Fortunately, residents of the city have been very critical of recent Carnivals and in 1986 the Carnival controls were taken away from the bureaucrats and handed over to Waly Salomão, a local poet and friend of Gilberto Gil.

Waly promoted Carnival's most authentic manifestations. Events were decentralised. Freer and more spontaneous expressions were encouraged. Let's hope the trend continues.

Take a look at the newspaper or go to Bahiatursa for a list of events. Don't miss the Afro blocos, afoxés, like Badauê, Ayê, orun, Ilê, Muzenza and the most famous, O Filhos de Gandhi. The best place to see them is in Liberdade, Salvador's largest Black district.

Also, explore Carnival Caramuru in Rio Vermelho and the smaller happenings in Itapoã, the old fishing and whaling village which has a fascinating ocean procession on Carnival's last day that delivers a whale to the sea.

The traditional gay parade is held on Sunday at Praça Castro Alves. Many of Brazil's best musicians return to Bahia for Carnival and the frequent rumours that so and so will be playing on the street are often true (Gilberto Gil and Baby Consuelo have appeared for example).

Many clubs have balls just before and during Carnival. If you're in the city before the festivities start you can also see the blocos practising. Just ask at Bahiatursa.

Hotels do book up during Carnival, so reservations are a good idea. Stay near the centre or in Barra. Violence can be a problem during Carnival. Some women travellers have reported violent approaches by locals. Since you should only carry money for food and drink, the most common danger at Carnival is probably getting sucked into the pack right behind a trio elétrico. This is mostly a problem at Castro Alves, where you're unable to avoid the flying elbows.

Processão de Senhor Bom Jesus dos Navegantes Actually two maritime processions, this is one of Bahia's most popular festivals. On New Year's Eve, the image of Senhor dos Navegantes goes from the Basílica da Conceição in Largo da Boa Viagem and then during the day of 1 January the image is taken on the bay and returned to the beach at Boa Viagem which is packed with people. A happy celebration, there's typical music, food and drink. The festival began in Portugal in 1750.

Festas de Reis Also originating in Portugal, the festival on 5 and 6 January takes place in the Igreja da Lapinha.

Festa do Bonfim The festival centres around the Candomblistas most important Catholic church, Igreja do Bonfim, and the orixá Oxalá. It takes place sometime between 9 and 18 January. The festivities are jubilant and crowded; they culminate with the Candomblé Mães and Filhas de Santo conducting the washing of the church. The Filhos de Gandhi and trios elétricos sing and flowers are everywhere.

Focta de São Lázaro This is the festival for Omulu for Candomblistas. On the last Sunday in January there's a mass, procession, festival and cleaning of the church.

Festa de Iemanjá A grand maritime procession takes flowers and presents to Iemanjá, the Mãe e Rainha das Águas (mother and queen of the waters). One of Candomblé's most important festivals, it's centred in Rio Vermelho. There are trios elétricos, afoxés and plenty of food and drink.

Lavagem da Igreja de Itapoã Out in Itapoã, 15 days before Carnival, this warm-up for Carnival is all music and dance with blocos and afoxés.

Procissão do Encontro Sometime in mid-March, this big religious procession represents the meeting of NS das Dores with Sr dos Passos.

São João Celebrated in the third week of June, there are many parties on the street where people drink a local liqueur called ginepapo.

Santa Bárbara This is the Candomblé festa of the markets. Probably the best spot to see festivities from 4 to 6 December is in Rio Vermelha at the Mercado do Peixe.

Festa de NS da Conceição The festival begins on 29 December and culminates with a procession and party on 8 December.

Passagem do Ano Novo Down on the beaches, the evening of 31 December is Carnivalesque.

Places to Stay

Salvador has many hotels but they can all fill up during the summer season – reservations are a good idea. Bahiatursa can help you find lodging. Just give them your price range and a general idea of where you want to stay. They also have names of houses that take in tourists and these can be excellent, cheap lodgings when hotels are full, especially during summer holidays and Carnival. But beware, the tourist office makes selective referrals and it helps if you don't look too burnt-out or broke. In addition to Bahiatursa you can call 243-6150, 243-6138 and 243-2247 for accommodation.

Places to Stay – bottom end

Most of the cheap hotels are in the old part of town around Terreiro de Jesus, Praça da Sé, Pelourinho and Praça Anchieta.

For something inexpensive head over to the Praça Anchieta area. The *Hotel Solar São Francisco* (tel 242-6015), Praça Anchieta 16, is clean. They have singles/doubles for US$1.50/5 with bath down the hall. The *Hotel Colon* (tel 321-1531) next door is slightly more expensive with singles/doubles for US$4.50. Also consider the *Hotel Império* with singles at US$2 and doubles US$3. This neighbourhood is not too safe at night.

Another good, clean cheapy is the *Hotel Solar* in the Pelourinho area at Rua José de Alencar 25. It has doubles starting at US$4.50. Over at Praça Castro Alves the *Hotel Alvorado* has doubles for US$2 without bath. It seems pretty secure. The *Hotel Maridina* (tel 242-7176), 7 de Septembro 6 is an excellent deal with singles/doubles starting at US$4/6.50.

The *Hotel Chile* (tel 243-2294) at Rua Chile 7 is 50 metres from Bahiatursa. They have singles in the US$3 to US$8 range (with air-con in the more expensive rooms) and doubles cost from US$5.50 to US$14 (also with air-con in the better rooms). It's a bit grubby, but a good deal. Although it's a little more expensive, the *Hotel Themis* (also known as Uirapuru Inn) (tel 243-1668) is the best value you'll find in a hotel here. It's at Praça da Sé 57, Edifício Themis, 7th floor. A French hangout, with a great view, they have doubles for US$12 (one bed only) and a few singles without baths for US$8. There is a good bar and restaurant with prato feito for US$2.

The *Hotel Anglo-Americano* (tel 247-7681) at Avenida Sete de Setembro 1838, Vitória has singles for US$2.50/5 without/with bath and doubles for US$4. It's similar to the Hotel Chile but in a quieter part of town. The *Pousada Iemanjá* (tel 241-1870), Rua Direita da Piedade 20, Piedade has a good reputation; singles/doubles are US$1.50/3 without bath. The *Casa de Studante* at Avenida 7 de Septembro 3513, Barra, is cheap. Another option if you need a place for only one night is the *Hotel Paraíso* (tel 243-4426) at Rua Demócrata 45, Largo Dois de Julho. This is actually a sex motel, but it has decent rooms, some with incredible views, and you get all this for as little as US$6.50 for two (or however many you can fit on one round bed with mirrors overhead).

If you plan to pass most of your days at the beach and just go into the city on occasion, consider staying in Itapoã, the nicest Atlantic beach suburb. It's a good 45-minute ride to the city, but the beaches are top-notch, there are several hotels and the town itself is an old fishing village with a good feel and few tourists. It's also close to the airport which can make it convenient if you're flying out the next day.

Along the beach, in the heart of Itapoã, the *Hotel Europa* (tel 249-9344) is a personal favourite. They have very clean

doubles for US$9/12 (all have bath). Across the street you have beach, barracas and buses to the centre of Salvador.

Places to Stay – middle

The *Hotel Pelourinho* (tel 243-9144) at Rua Alfredo Brito 20 is right in the heart of the historic Pelourinho area, a great central location during the day. It's an older, converted mansion with character. There's a good restaurant-bar and rooms have views of the bay, hot bath and frigo bar (the upper end rooms also have air-con). Singles are US$10 to US$22 and doubles are US$13 to US$26.

The *Palace Hotel* (tel 243-1155) at Rua Chile 20 is good value and right in the centre of the city. Rooms cost US$10/12 for singles and US$20/24 for doubles.

If you'd rather stay near the beach there are several hotels in Porto da Barra. *Barra Turismo Hotel* (tel 245-7433) is at Avenida Sete de Septembro 3691. Rooms have a good ocean view, TV, balcony and air-con. Singles/doubles cost US$13/14.50. The *Hotel Porto da Barra* (tel 247-4939) at Avenida Sete de Septembro 3783 has singles/doubles for US$12/16, but it's not as nice. Also nearby, the *Hotel Solar da Barra* (tel 247-8689) at Avenida Sete de Setembro 2998 has singles/doubles for US$9/12. On the same street, at number 106, the *Baia de Todos os Santos* (tel 321-6344) is recommended.

A cheaper alternative is the *Hotel Caramaru* (tel 247-9951) at Avenida Sete de Septembro 2125 in Vitória near the Museu do Bahia. Singles/doubles cost from US$8/11. The less expensive rooms have access to a bath down the hall.

Places to Stay – top end

The *Hotel da Bahia* (tel 237-3690) at Praça Dois de Julho in Campo Grande gets rave reviews. It has all the amenities but it's not on the beach and with doubles starting at US$48 it should be.

The *Quatro Rodas* (tel 249-9611) is Bahia's luxury palace, it's way out past Itapoã and it's not on the beach either.

Singles/doubles here are US$85/95. The *Meridien Bahia* (tel 248-8011) with singles/doubles for US$50/55; the *Bahia Othon Palace* (tel 247-1044) with singles/doubles for US$51/5; and the *Salvador Praia* (tel 245-5033) are all top hotels, on the beach and not too far out.

The government-owned *Luxor Convento do Carmo* (tel 242-3111) near Pelourinho is a beautiful converted monastery built in 1580. There is a pool, but the rooms are a bit small. The area is deserted at night (you have to use taxis) and it's overpriced with singles/doubles for US$39/45.

Moving down in price a bit, the best value is the *Hotel do Farol* (tel 247-7611), Avenida Presidente Vargas 68 in Barra. They have comfortable doubles for US$37 and if you can get one with a view you're in business. There's a small pool. Also in Barra, the *Marazul Hotel* (tel 235-2110), Avenida Sete de Septembro 3937 has singles/doubles for US$32/35. It's in an excellent location and has a small pool, but the hotel is not very well kept.

Further up the coast in Pituba, the *Pituba Plaza* (tel 248-1022 with singles/doubles for US$26/29 is also recommended, as is the *Itapoã Praia* (tel 249-9988) at Rua Dias Gomes 4 with singles/doubles for US$21/26. Back toward the centre the *Hotel Vila Velha* (tel 247-8722) is at Avenida Sete de Setembro 1971. It offers good value at US$17.50/19.50 for a single/double.

Places to Eat

Bahian food can be savoury and distinct, but it usually isn't. In general, the restaurants in Salvador are disappointing. All too often the food tastes bland and isn't terribly fresh. There are, of course, important exceptions.

Dendê, the African palm oil used to cook many regional dishes, has a terrific flavour – you'll smell it everywhere – but it has stirred up a lot of trouble in traveller's bellies. Many visitors suffer stomach trouble in Bahia so be careful.

With a big working population, the Cidade Baixa has lots of cheap, lunch-only restaurants. If you're in a hurry, there are several cafes across from the Mercado Modelo offering standard fare but the best lunch around is *Restaurante Juarez*. Going out toward the ferry, find the Mercado D'Ouro on Avenida Frederico Pontes. It's a bit hard to find, the *Juarez* is inside. The food's simple but good, cheap and abundant: for example, filet mignon with rice, beans and salad costs US$2.

Cheap food is easy to find in the Cidade Alto. Probably the best is *Dona Benta Restaurante Lanches* at Rua Carlos Gomes 328, out past Praça Castro Alves. It's open for lunch and you can get meat or vegetable stew with rice and beans for 75c. A step up is the *Apolo* at Rua Miguel Calmon 3. It's open Monday to Friday for lunch only.

A hangout with cheap vittles is *Cantinho da Lua* on Terreiro de Jesus at the edge of the Pelourinho district. *Restaurante Bela Nápoli*, (tel 243-5125), Rua Nova de São Bento 194 has good Italian lunches and dinners (closed Sundays).

Go down Rua Alfredo de Brito to the *Hotel Pelourinho*. There's a restaurant across the courtyard. They have good Bahian food for US$2 to US$3 a plate and a great view of the bay (lunch and dinner). Across the street is *Senac* (tel 242-5503). For US$3 there's a buffet with 30 regional dishes. It's not the best Bahian cooking, but you can discover which local dishes you like and eat till you explode. It's open from midday to 2 pm and 7 to 10 pm every day except Sundays, and they often have folklore shows after the meal. The *Peres Restaurant*, next to the Vila Velha theatre, is another good place with a view.

The *Solar do Unhão* (tel 245-5551) sits on the bay at Avenida do Contorno; there's an old sugar estate that's been turned into the Bahia Modern Art Museum, a ceramic complex and a restaurant. The restaurant is on the lower level in the old senzala (slaves quarters). Legend has it that the place is haunted with the ghosts of tortured slaves. Given the old pelourinho and torture devices on display, it's easy to believe.

Ironically, this is one of the prettiest spots in the city. Open daily, except Sunday, for lunch and dinner, with a folklore show at 10 pm for an extra US$3. It has good Bahian cooking. Lunches cost about US$2 and dinners US$4. Reservations are recommended for dinner.

Continuing along the bay toward Barra is another quiet restaurant with a great view, *Iate Clube da Bahia* at Avenida Sete de Septembro 3252. Open for lunch and dinner, it's pricey, with small portions, but if you want to splurge the seafood is excellent. Afterward, try *La Basque* at Avenida Sete de Septembro 3667 for some great pistachio and tangerine ice cream.

There are several restaurants along Porto da Barra. *Van Gogh* at Avenida Presidente Vargas 3749 stays open until midnight serving meat and fish at moderate prices. Nearby is *Manga Rosa*, Rua César Zama 1, with good health food. *Salad's* is open daily for light lunch and dinner. It's at Avenida Presidente Vargas 68. *Desicatese* is very good.

In Rio Vermelho, *O Marisco* has great seafood. Their *Mariscada Tropical* plate is a sort of Bahian fish stew which can feed three (US$6). The *polvo* (octopus) and *ensopado de camarão* are also excellent. It's at Rua Euricles de Matos 123, open daily (except Wednesdays) for lunch and dinner. If you want a drink after eating try the *Vagão*, a hip bar in a train car right up the hill from Marisco.

Baby Beef (tel 244-0811) in the Hipermercado Pais Mendoça, Pituba has expensive but very fine steaks and ribs. Also in Pituba, *San Mei* (tel 248-2214), Rua Mato Grosso 64 serves up all the greasy Chinese food you can stomach for US$2 per person.

Salvador's finest Bahian cuisine is found at *Restaurante Iemanjá*, Avenida Otávio Mangabeira, s/n Armação and *Casa da Gamboa* (tel 245-9777), Rua da

Gamboa 51, Gamboa which is famous for its moqueca. Both are moderately priced. *Chez Bernard* (tel 245-9402), Rua Gamboa de Cima 11, Aflitos has fancy French food with a nice view. It's closed on Sundays and on Saturdays it's only open for dinner. Try *restaurant Gan* (tel 245-2206) at Praça Alexandre Fernandes 29, Fazenda Garcia for Japanese food (dinner only).

Last, best and hardest to find is *Bargaço*. The seafood is Bahia's finest. The ensopada de camarão is divine and the price is right (US$2 to US$4 a big plate). The atmosphere is quite simple, it has a picnic bench motif. It's on a small residential street near the convention centre.

Entertainment

I'd go to Bahia just to hear the music. It's that good. The backbone of the musical tradition is African, but the music is clearly Bahian. Today's popular styles include trio elétrico (which dominates Carnival), tropicalismo, afoxé, the caribé, reggae, jazz and Gilberto Gil.

Bars and clubs tend to come and go quickly in Salvador, so ask around and check the newspaper to confirm the following suggestions. In general, Barra has the most nightlife in Bahia, many of the city's best non-tourist places are in Rio Vermelho and many of the better hotels, such as the *Salvador Praia* have fancy nightclubs.

Teatro Castro Alves at Campo Grande is the biggest music theatre in Bahia. The big acts play here and they're often Brazil's best. Across the plaza *Cruz Vermelha* is a popular outdoor club. The crowd is young and very Bahian, the music is trio elétrico, reggae and rock. The *Raso da Catarina* is a nearby bar with a lively, left-wing flavour. Their postered wall is a good source for interesting cultural and political happenings in the city. It's downstairs at Avenida Sete de Setembro 1370.

Holmes is a gay men's bar in Gamboa not far from Campo Grande. The *Ladeira*

dos Aflitos in the centre is owned by the famous musician Batatinha. It's a fun scene here, with a different slice of Bahian life. Bahia's strangest bar is the *Boteco do Fariah* in Garcia. It's a somewhat typical outdoor bar with a street running through the middle of it.

The Pelourinho area often has blocos (musical street groups) practising on Sunday nights. African culture is kept alive in Liberdade which is a good place to see afoxé. Go with someone who knows the area.

Barra is full of bars, discos and music. Some places are quite good, but it's more touristy and westernised than other neighbourhoods. If you just want to sit, drink and watch, *Oceânia* at Avenida Presidente Vargas 01 is a good spot, as is *Barravento* on Mar Vista beach along Avenida Presidente Vargas. It's one of the few spots in Brazil where you can see the sun set into the sea.

Rio Vermelha is sort of the art and foreign district and they have Bahia's best music clubs. *Ad Libitum*, João Gomes 88, has great Brazilian jazz and gafeira. It's a big place with inside/outside seating and dancing. It's always hopping on weekends, the crowd is mixed and informal, the cover charge is usually US$1.

The *68 Bar* is just down the block from Ad Libitum at Lago de Santana 3. The number 68 refers to the worst year of repression during the 20-year military dictatorship. Although there is no live music the joint jumps. It's unpretentious and drinks are cheap. Outdoor seating provides refuge from the cigarettes.

There are several bars with music along the Pituba coast. *Travessia* is a good cafe/bar to hang out and watch people. *Chambarril* is a lot of fun with a very local scene. It's not sophisticated and the sound system is shockingly bad, but it's jammed with revellers doing the *merengue*, a dance you shouldn't miss.

Things to Buy

Camping equipment sales and rentals are available at AMP Camping, Rua Conselheiro Pedro Luis 492, Rio Vermelho. Surfing enthusiasts will find equipment at Sailer (tel 237-1120), Rua Afonso Celso 05, Barra.

Getting There & Away

Air The big three domestic airlines all fly to Bahia, as does the Nordeste, which goes to smaller cities in the region like Ilhéus and Porto Seguro. You can fly to anywhere in Brazil from Bahia, but make sure you find out how many stops the plane makes. If you're flying north many (maybe all?) planes stop at every city along the Atlantic seaboard which makes for a long ride.

Bus Ten daily buses depart to Aracajú. The five-hour trip costs US$2, with a leito bus leaving at 12.20 am for US$4. Five daily buses go to Recife, the 12-to-14-hour trip costs US$6.50. The daily common bus goes to Fortaleza and takes 20 hours and costs US$8. There's a leito for US$18 that leaves three times a week. A daily bus goes to Belém, 36 hours away.

Seven daily buses go to Rio (including one leito). The price is US$9.50 and US$22 for a leito. The trip takes 28 hours. Three buses go to São Paulo in 33 hours for US$11, leito for US$26. Belo Horizonte is 24 hours away and Brasília is 22 hours away. Both have daily bus service.

Many buses operate to Lençóis (seven hours), Valença (five hours), Ilhéus (seven hours), Porto Seguro (12 hours) and Paulo Afonso (10 hours).

Boats Boats to points on Baía de Todos os Santos leave from the Terminal Turístico Marítimo (tel 243-0741) on Avenida da França, one block towards the water from the Mercado Modelo. There are tours of the bay featuring Itaparica and Frade islands and boats to Maragogipe. (See Baía de Todos os Santos and Recôncavo sections for schedules.) There may now be regular boat connections to Morro de São Paulo. The other docks in front of the

Mercado Modelo have motorboats to Mar Grande and Itaparica.

Getting Around

Airport Transport Ipitanga Airport is over 30 km from the city centre, inland from Itapoã. There are always airport taxis available for US$8 to US$12 (tickets are available at the airport desk). The best way to go is by an executivo bus marked Praça da Sé/Aeroporto (75c). It starts at Praça da Sé (there's a small signpost) and goes down Avenida 7 de Septembro to Barra where it continues all the way along the coast. You can flag it down along the way.

In light traffic, the ride to the airport takes 45 minutes, with traffic 1½ hours. A municipal bus marked Aeroporto (15c) follows the same route but it gets very crowded and isn't recommended if you're carrying a bag.

Local Transport Venice has its canals and gondolas, Salvador has its bluff, elevators, trams, hills, valleys and one-way streets. The Lacerda elevator runs all the time linking the low and high cities. The Plano Inclinado Gonçalves, behind the cathedral near the Praça da Sé, makes the same link and is more fun, but only operates from Monday to Friday 6 am to 8 pm and Saturdays 6 am to 1 pm.

There are three municipal bus stops downtown worth knowing about: Praça da Sé, Barroquinho and Avenida da França. Buses from Praça da Sé go to Campo Grande, Vitória and Itapoã via Barra. Air-conditioned executive buses marked Praça da Sé/Aeroporto also leave from here and go along the beaches from Barra to Itapoã (75c). This is the most comfortable way to go to the Atlantic coast beaches.

The Avenida da França stop is in the lower city in front of the Lacerda lift. From here take the Ribeira or Bom Fim bus to the Itaparica ferry (get off after a couple of km when you see the Pirelli Pneus store on your left), the São Joaquim market (get off at the stop after Pirelli Pneus), or the Igreja NS do Bonfim.

Rodoviária The bus terminal (tel 231-5711) is five km from downtown, but it's a bit messy taking a bus there – many buses marked rodoviária drive all over the city – and can take up to an hour during rush-hour. It's a good occasion for a taxi. Buses to the rodoviária leave from Barroquinho. Take the bus marked Rodoviária R3, get off at Iguatemi and cross over the highway (for what it's worth there is a pedestrian crossing). Alternatively take a bus to Campo Grande and change there. The best bus for Praça da Sé is marked Rodoviária/Sé.

Around Salvador

ITAPARICA

Many Bahians love the island, the biggest in the bay, but it's really not a must-see destination. Weekends are crowded, transportation is slow without a car, it's fairly expensive and the beaches aren't as pretty as the more accessible beaches to the north of the city.

The largest island of Baía de Todos os Santos, Itaparica is popular with many Brazilians who prefer a swim in the calm waters of the bay to the rough and tumble of the ocean. The island is built-up with many weekend homes, but few budget hotels. Many of the beaches are dirty and the best part of the island is owned by Club Med. Yet there still are a few clean beaches where you can just kick back on the sand, lie beneath wind-swept palms and gaze across the bay at the city (try Barra Grande for example).

Orientation

Itaparica City Starting at the northern tip of the island is the city of Itaparica and its São Lourenço Fort. Built by the Dutch invaders in the XVII century, the fortress figured prominently in Bahia's battle for

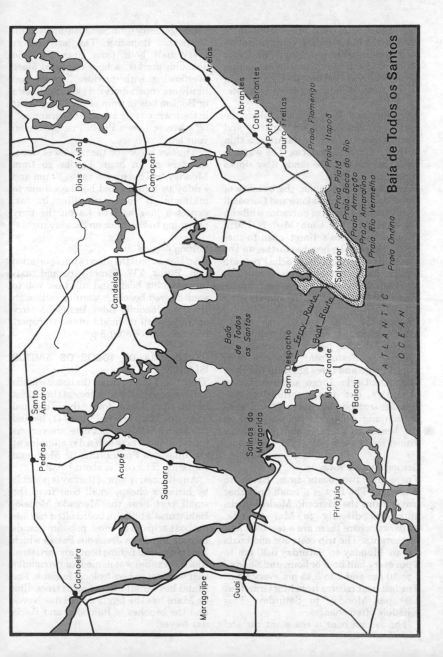

Baía de Todos os Santos

independence in 1823. The mansion of Lieutenant Botas (Solar Tenente Botas) on the square of the same name, the Igreja Matriz do Santissimo Sacramento on Rua Luis Gama and the Fonte da Bica mineral water fountain round out the city sights.

Along the Coast Working south along the coast, between Cidade de Itaparica and Bom Despacho, is Ponte da Areia, a thin strip of sand with barracas. The water is clear and shallow, the sandy floor slopes gently into the bay.

South of Mar Grande, the beaches of Barra do Gil, Barra do Pote and Coroa all have excellent views of Salvador while on the other side of Club Med is Barra Grande, Itaparica's finest open-to-the-public beach. The beaches further to the south up to and including Cacha Prego are dirtier and generally less beautiful, although many Bahians consider Cacha Prego the best beach on the island.

Places to Eat

The best eating on the island is the seafood at the beach barracas. The *Timoneiro Restaurant*, 10 km from Cacho Prego and three km from the Bom Despacho/Cacho Prego junction, serves expensive but tasty shrimp dishes. Another seafood place is the *Restaurante & Camping A Lagosta* (tel 839-1988) on the beach at Barra Grande. A lobster dinner feeds two for US$7.50.

Getting There & Away

There are two boats from Bahia to Itaparica. The first is a small boat that leaves from the Mercado Modelo docks and goes directly to Mar Grande, Itaparica where there are a few bars and restaurants. The trip costs 50c and boats depart Monday to Saturday 6.30 am to 4 pm every half hour or hour, and Sunday 7 to 10 am and 2 to 5.45 pm every hour. The last boat returns from Mar Grande at 4.30 pm Monday to Saturday. This schedule often changes.

The second boat is the giant car and passenger ferry from São Joaquim to Bom Despacho, Itaparica. The ferry leaves every half hour from near the São Joaquim market, a busy colourful place overflowing with produce, spices and hardware (open daily). Take the Ribeira or Bonfim bus in front of the Lacerda lift in the lower city for a couple of km and get-off when you see a Pirelli Pneus store on your left.

The fare is 10c and the ride takes three-quarters of an hour. Ferries go from Monday to Thursday 6 am to 10 pm and Friday to Sunday and holidays 6 am to midnight. If you're travelling by car, expect a long wait to get on the ferry returning to Salvador on Sunday nights.

Getting Around

Bom Despacho is the island's transportation hub. Buses, VW Kombi-vans and taxis meet the big boats and will take you to your desired beach. A warning, although the São Joaquim-Bom Despacho ferry operates until midnight island transport becomes scarce after 8 pm.

OTHER BAÍA DE TODOS OS SANTOS ISLANDS

The easiest way to cruise the lesser islands and the bay itself is to get one of the tourist boats that leave from the Terminal Turístico Marítimo (tel 243-0741) behind the Mercado Modelo. There are various tours but most take half a day stopping at the Ilhas dos Frades, Ilha de Maré and Itaparica. The cost is about US$9.

An alternative tour of the bay is possible by hiring a cheap, small boat from the small port near the Mercado Modelo. Bahiatursa's bulletin board often has ads for boat trips. The most popular islands include Ilha Bom Jesus dos Passos which has traditional fishing boats and artisans. Ilha dos Frades was named for two monks that were eaten here by local Indians. The island has waterfalls and palm trees. Ilha de Maré has the Igreja de NS das Neves and the beaches of Itamoabo and Bacia das Neves.

Top: Pelourinho, Salvador, Bahia (WH)
Left: Salvador, Bahia (JM)
Right: Housing in Salvador, Bahia (JM)

Top: Shanty town on the outskirts of Salvador, Bahia (JM)
Left: Catburger sign, north-east of Ilheus, Bahia (MS)
Right: Beach scene, Bahia (JM)

The Recôncavo Region

The Recôncavo is the region of fertile lands spread around the Baía de Todos os Santos. Some of the earliest Brazilian encounters between Portuguese, Indian and African peoples occurred here and the lands proved to be among Brazil's best for growing sugar and tobacco.

Along with the excellent growing conditions, the region prospered due to its relative proximity to Portuguese sugar markets, the favourable winds to Europe and the excellent harbours afforded by the Baía de Todos os Santos. By 1570 there were already 18 mills, by 1584 there were 40. The sugar plantation system was firmly entrenched by the end of the 16th century and continued to grow from the sweat of African slaves for another 250 years.

Tobacco came a bit later to the Recôncavo. Traded to African slave-hunters and kings it was the key commodity in the triangular slave trade. Tobacco was a more sensitive crop to grow than sugar and the estates were much smaller. Big fortunes were made growing sugar, not tobacco. On the other hand, fewer slaves were needed, about four per tobacco farm, so many poorer Portuguese settlers went into tobacco and a less rigid social hierarchy developed. Many even did some of the work!

A second subsidiary industry in the Recôncavo was cattle ranching which provided food for the plantation hands, and transport for the wood that fuelled the sugar engenhos and for getting the processed cane to market. Cattle breeding started in the Recôncavo and spread inland, radiating west into the sertão and Minas Gerais, then north-west into Piauí.

If you have time for only one side trip from Salvador, visit Cachoeira and perhaps squeeze in Santo Amaro or Maragojipe on the way. A suggested itinerary is to take the weekday afternoon boat to Maragogipe and then the bus along the Paraguaçu to Cachoeira or if you can rent a car drive up through Santo Amaro. If your timing is good, usually Friday or Saturday nights, you can attend a terreiro de Candomblé at Cachoeira, then return to Salvador by bus.

CACHOEIRA

Population: 11,520

Cachoeira – the jewel of the Recôncavo – is a small city in the centre of Brazil's best tobacco growing region. Set below a series of hills, along the Rio Paraguaçu, Cachoeira is full of beautiful colonial architecture, uncompromised by the presence of modern structures. Because of this, the city was pronounced a national monument a few years ago. Today, the state of Bahia is trying to turn Cachoeira into a tourist centre. So far their activities have been mostly beneficial as many old churches and municipal buildings have been, or are being, restored and saved and there are still only a few tourists around. This could change.

Like Ouro Preto, Cachoeira feels like a living museum. It is timeless and tranquil. It is also an important centre of Candomblé – often curious and mysterious and never easily written about – and the home of many traditional craftsmen and artists. Cachoeira can be visited in a day from Salvador, but get an early start, or even better, plan to stay overnight.

History

Diego Álvares, the father of Cachoeira's founder was the sole survivor of a ship bound for the West Indies that wrecked in 1510 on a reef near Salvador. The Portuguese Robinson Crusoe was saved by the Tupinambá Indians of Rio Vermelho who dubbed the strange white sea creature, Caramuru or Fish-man. Diego Álvares lived 20 years with the Indians and married Catarina do Paraguaçu, the daughter of the most powerful Tupinambá chief. Their sons João Gaspar Aderno Álvares and Rodrigues Martins Álvar

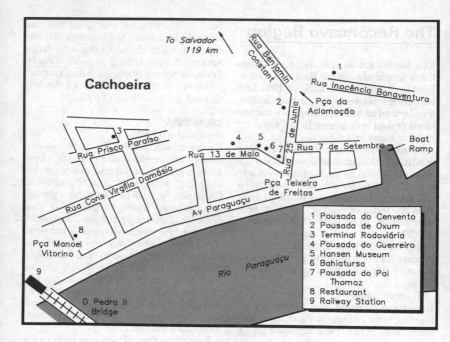

Cachoeira

To Salvador
119 km

Rua Benjamin Constant

Rua Inocência Bonaventura

Pça da Aclamação

Rua 25 de Junio

Rua Prisco Paraíso

Rua 13 de Maio

Rua 7 de Setembro

Boat Ramp

Rua Cons Virgílio Damásio

Pça Teixeira de Freitas

Av Paraguaçu

Pça Manoel Vitorino

Rio Paraguaçu

D Pedro II Bridge

1 Pousada do Cenvento
2 Pousada de Oxum
3 Terminal Rodoviária
4 Pousada do Guerreiro
5 Hansen Museum
6 Bahiatursa
7 Pousada do Pai Thomaz
8 Restaurant
9 Railway Station

killed off the local Indians, set up the first sugar cane fazendas and founded Cachoeira.

By the 18th century, tobacco from Cachoeira was considered the world's finest, sought by rulers in China and Africa, and was more profitable than sugar. Tobacco also became popular in Brazil. The holy herb as it was called, was taken as snuff, smoked in a pipe or chewed.

Cachoeira, 121 km from Salvador and 40 km from Santo Amaro, is separated from São Felix by the Rio Paraguaçu – spanned by an old bridge built by the British in 1885. The river flows into the Baía de Todos os Santos. The main crops in the region are tobacco, cashews and oranges.

Information

There's a tourist office in the Casa da ultura.

Candomblé

Do whatever you can to see Candomblé in Cachoeira. This is one of the strongest and perhaps purest spiritual and religious centres for Candomblé. Terreiros de Candomblé are held in small homes and shacks up in the hills, usually on Friday and Saturday nights at 8 pm. The ceremony is long and mysterious. Go with respect. Visitors are not as common here as in Salvador and the tourist office is sometimes reluctant to give out this sort of information. Do persist.

Around Town

Cachoeira and São Felix are best seen on foot. There's nothing you really have to see, so it's best to just take it easy and explore whatever comes your way. In addition to the main sites, look-out for the old two-storey homes on Rua Ana Neri, Rua Benjamin Constant, Rua Aristedes

Milton, Rua Sete de Setembro and Rua Treze de Maio.

Museum of the Third Order of Carmelites The Museum of the Third Order of Carmelites on Praça da Aclamação alongside the Pousada do Convento features a gallery of suffering polychrome Christs imported from the Portuguese colonies in Macau. Christ's blood is made with bovine blood mixed with Chinese herbs and sparkling rubies. The museum also has a beautiful, unrestored baroque gilded church and a creepy room-full of offerings. There's also massive termite damage throughout the church. Visiting hours are Monday to Friday from 8 to 11.30 am and 2 to 5 pm, weekends from 9 to 11.30 am (cost 5c).

Casa da Câmara e Cadeia Nearby on the same square is the Casa da Camara e Cadeia, the old prefecture and prison. Organised criminals ran the show upstairs and disorganised criminals were kept behind bars downstairs. The structure in yellow with white trim dates back to 1698 and at one time served as seat of the Bahian government. The old marble pillory in the square was destroyed after abolition. Across the square is the humble SPHAN museum with squeaky bats flapping over colonial furnishings.

Hansen Bahia Museum The Hansen Bahia Museum, next door to the tourist office, was set up in the home and birthplace of Brazilian heroine Ana Neri, who organised the nursing corps during the Paraguay War. Now the work of German (naturalised Brazilian) artist Hansen Bahia is displayed here. Among his powerful lithographs of human suffering is a series of illustrations of Castro Alves' poem *Návio Negreiro* (Slave Ship). The museum is open from 10 am to midday and from 2 to 5 pm and is closed Tuesday and Sunday afternoons. Prints are on sale for 25c each.

NS do Rosário do Porto do Cachoeira The blue church with yellow trim, up from the Hansen Bahia Museum at the corner of Rua Ana Neri and Rua Lions Club, is the NS do Rosário do Porto do Cachoeira. The church has beautiful Portuguese tiles and a ceiling painted by Teófilo de Jesus. It's open Tuesday through Saturday from 9 am to midday and 2 to 4 pm, on Sundays 8 am to midday. The museum alongside has remnants from the abandoned 17th century Convento de São Francisco do Paraguaçu.

NS da Ajuda & the Casa da Cultura Next to the Irmandade de Boa Morte meeting hall on Largo da Ajuda is Cachoeira's oldest church, the tiny NS d'Ajuda, built in 1595 when Cachoeira was known as Arraial d'Ajuda. Also on the praça is the newly restored Casa da Cultura.

Built in 1873 to house Dannemann's cigar factory, the brick building now contains excellent woodwork (for sale), old photographs of the twin cities and of cachoeira festivals and Candomblé, as well as a theatre, a tourist office and a snack place.

Santa Casa de Misericórdia Where Praça Aristedes Milton meets Rua da Santa Casa, is the municipality's oldest hospital, Santa Casa de Misericórdia. The complex contains a pretty chapel (1734) with a painted ceiling, gardens and an ossuary. It's open weekdays 2 to 5 pm.

Other Attractions At the far end of town near the bridge and train station is the Igreja NS de Conceição do Monte. From the top of Rua Simões Filho alongside the 18th Century church there is a good view of Cachoeira and São Felix.

Across from the ruined grand facade of the train station, the wide, empty and cobblestoned Praça Manoel Vitorino feels like an Italian movie set. Try your Italian on the ice-cream man or the pigeons, the move on to São Felix.

Crossing the old Ponte Dom Pedro

narrow and dilapidated bridge where trains and cars must wait their turn, watch your step; loose planks claimed the life of one man in 1986. Other than a view towards Cachoeira, São Felix has two attractions, the Casa da Cultura Américo Simas and the Casa da Hansen Bahia.

The Casa da Hansen is a bit of a climb up Ladeira de Santa Barbara so use the Hansen museum as a litmus test for deciding whether you like his work and want to make the climb. There are interesting and beautiful relics of the Hansens' life and art including a full colour version of the 14 stages of the cross set in Nazi Germany.

Festivals
Festa da NS de Boa Morte usually falls around 15 August and lasts three days. This is one of the most fascinating Candomblé festivals going – it's worth a special trip to see it. Organised by the Irmandade da Boa Morte (Sisterhood of the Good Death) – a secret, Black, religious society – descendants of slaves celebrate their liberation with dance and prayer and a mix of themes from Candomblé and Catholicism.

The Festa de São João, from 22 to 24 June, is the big popular festival of Bahia's interior. It's a great tapestry of folklore with music and dancing, plenty of food and drink. Don't miss it if you're in Bahia at the time.

Other festivals include NS do Rosário (second half of October) with games, music and food; NS da Ajuda (first half of November) with a church lavage and street festival; Santa Barbara or Iansã (4 December), a Candomblé celebration in São Felix at the fountain of Santa Bárbara.

Places to Stay – bottom end
Pousada Cabana do Pai Tomás (tel 724-1288), Rua 25 de Junho 12, has spartan athless rooms which cost US$3.50 for two ngle beds. See the carved wooden panels the restaurant downstairs.

Pousada do Guerreiro (tel 724-1203), Rua 13 de Maio 14 has ragged but cheap singles (US$2.50 to US$5) and doubles (US$5 to US$7.50) with and without bath and air-con.

Places to Stay – top end
Managed by Bahiatursa, *Pousada do Convento de Cachoeira* (tel 724-1151) is on Praça da Aclamação (along Rua Inocência Bonaventura) and is a lovely hotel with a courtyard and swimming pool. The dark wood rooms of the old convent now have air-con, fridge and hot showers and are a good deal at US$12.50 a single and US$14 a double. They do a good breakfast too.

Places to Eat
The *Gruta Azul* (tel 724-1295), Praça Manoel Vitorino 2 is Cachoeira's best restaurant, but it's only open for lunch. The place has character – secret recipes, a lush courtyard, a huge tropical bird cage – and good food and drink. Try the shrimp dishes for US$3 or maniçoba, the spicy local version of manioc and meat. If you're adventurous ask for the boa morte (good death) drink. The *Pousada do Convento* and *Pousada Pai Tomás* also serve good meals.

Entertainment
Check out the beer drinking and forró dancing at the riverside bars.

Things to Buy
Cachoeira has a wealth of wood sculptors, some of whom do very fine work. This is some of the best traditional art still available in Brazil. There are working shops at Praça Teixeira de Freitas, Rua 25 de Julho, Praça Dr Aristedes Milton and Rua Ana Neri and you will see plenty of studios as you walk through town. Doidão and Coucou are two of the best. They carve beautiful, heavy wood pieces.

Getting There & Away
Bus Take an Autoviação Camurujipe bus

marked São Felix from Salvador's Rodoviária. The two hour, 80c ride passes through Santo Amaro. Cachoeira's bus station (tel 724-1214) on Rua Prisco Paraíso also has regular buses to Maragogipe and Valença.

Train Salvador and Cachoeira are also connected by rail, but service is poor.

Boat Ever since the Paraguaçu (Big River) was blocked by the Pedra do Cavalo dam, Cachoeira no longer has the waterfalls for which it was named. The river has since silted up making boat passage up from Maragogipe and Salvador difficult and irregular. Enquire about Vapor do Cachoeira boat service at the Companhia de Navegação Bahiano (Mercado Modelo docks, Salvador). Apparently, during the festival of São João there is an attempt at regular boat service to Salvador.

Getting Around
You can rent a sail boat from Escuna of Paraguaçu Turismo Ltda for US$25 for the day, visit the ruins of the Convento de Santo Antônio do Paraguaçu and take as many 20 people along. Contact Sr Joel on 724-1692 or 724-1524.

Near Cachoeira
If you have the use of a car or like long walks, you can visit the Pimantel Cigar Factory, 10 km out of town. Suerdieck is another cigar factory in town on Rua da Feira. Continue on Rua da Feira out of town for a look at Cachoeira's poor neighbourhoods and the surrounding countryside.

There are also two old sugar mills near town, the Vitória and Guaiba engenhos, four and eight km respectively along the road to Santo Amaro.

CANDEIAS
The Museu do Recôncavo includes an old sugar plantation with Engenho de Freguesia, the engenho de açúcar Freguesia (sugar mill), an old church and one of the

original senzalas (slave quarters). To get there from Salvador take the BR-324 to BA-017 near Monte Recôncavo.

SANTA AMARO

Population: 28,000

Santo Amaro is on the road from Salvador to Cachoeira. It's an old run-down sugar town that knows no tourism. I like Santo Amaro a lot. If you're going to Cachoeira think about stopping for a few hours, especially if it's a market Saturday, when the town comes to life. If you decide to stay the night, there's often very good local music. The town's two pousadas are on the Praça da Purificação.

In colonial days, Santo Amaro was a sugar town. Today the major industry is paper production at the paper mill along the road to Cachoeira. The mill has spoiled the Rio Subaé and bamboo has replaced sugar cane on the hillsides. Today's reminders of Santo Amaro's sugar legacy are the decrepit pastel mansions of the sugar barons and the many churches.

The plantation owners lived on Rua General Câmara, the old commercial street. Many of the churches have been closed since a gang of thieves stole most of the holy images and exported them to France. The largest church, Santo Amaro da Purificaço, is still open. The festa of Santo Amaro (6 to 15 January) is celebrated by the ritual *lavagem* (washing) of the church steps. Santo Amaro is the birthplace of the singers Caetano Veloso and his sister Maria Betânia. During Carnival, they've been known to put in an appearance between trios elétricos.

Step out to the square across from the church for an evening's promenade. Despite active flirting, the sexes circle separately.

Getting There & Away

Santo Amaro is 73 km from Salvador and 32 km before Cachoeira/São Felix. There are frequent buses.

MARAGOJIPE

Circled by rich green fields patched with crops and the Baía de Todos os Santos, Maragojipe is a pleasantly decaying tobacco-exporting port. Would-be cowboys tie up their horses and hangout in dockside bars where posters of Jesus and automotive pin-ups vie for wall space. The crumbling plaster facades of the bars look out onto rows of *saveiros* (homemade fishing boats), dugout canoes and mangrove swamps. Old, cross-legged fishermen mend nets while the younger fishermen cast nets, and draw for shrimp.

Maragojipe is 12 km from Nazaré and 32 km from Cachoeira.

Things to See

The Suerdieck & Company Cigar Factory (established 1920) is open for tours from 7 am to 6 pm Monday to Friday and Saturday mornings. On weekend nights head down to the dockside bars for local music. Swimming off the cement pier is popular.

Strolling through town look out for the wrought-iron grill and sculpted facade of the pale-blue building on Rua D Macedo Costa.

Places to Stay

The *Oxumaré Hotel* (tel 726-1104), Rua Heretiano Jorge de Sonza 3 has cramped singles/doubles with bath down the hall for US$2/4.

Places to Eat

Try the suco bar on Largo da Matriz. Make enquiries into jumbo shrimp at the few restaurants in town.

Getting There & Away

Bus Viazul buses from Salvador to Maragojipe go via Santo Amaro and Cachoeira. There are six buses daily, the first at 7.10 am, the last at 6.20 pm. The trip takes three hours and costs 50c. There are no buses via Itaparica. We recommend going by boat.

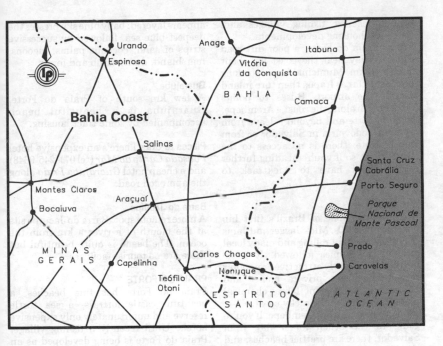

Bahia Coast

Urando
Espinosa
Anage
Itabuna
Vitória da Conquista
BAHIA
Camaca
Salinas
Montes Claros
Araçuaí
Bocaiuva
MINAS GERAIS
Capelinha
Carlos Chagas
Nanuque
Teófilo Otoni
ESPÍRITO SANTO
Santa Cruz Cabrália
Porto Seguro
Parque Nacional de Monte Pascoal
Prado
Caravelas
ATLANTIC OCEAN

Boat The boat from Maragojipe to Salvador leaves at 5 am Monday to Friday. Get there an hour early to buy passage. Boats leave from Salvador to Maragojipe Monday to Friday at 1 pm (40c) from the Terminal Turístico Marítimo (tel 243-0741) at Avenida da França one block towards the water from Mercado Modelo. Stops are made at São Roque, Barra do Paraguaçu and Enseada and the trip takes three hours.

There are no boats to Cachoeira since the Rio Paraguaçu has silted up but there are frequent buses.

NAZARÉ
Population: 18,000

Nazaré is an 18th century city with some colonial buildings and churches and a good market known for its *caxixis* – small ceramic figures. The town is 70 km from Salvador via ferry boat.

The big festivals are the folkloric NS de Nazaré (24 January to 2 February) and Feira dos Caxixis (Holy Week), which features a large market on Thursday and Good Friday of Holy Week, followed by the holiday of Micareta.

Places to Stay
The riverside *Hotel Caxixis* (tel 736-1138) is reasonably priced.

North of Salvador

The coastal road north from Salvador is called the Rodovia do Coco (the Coconut Highway). The excellent, paved road runs a few km from the ocean as far as the entrance to Praia do Forte, 80 km north of Salvador. There are several access roads along the way that get you down to the coconut beaches, fishing villages and, sadly, new housing developments.

After Praia do Forte, a poor dirt road winds its way near the coast for about another 40 km. Municipal buses go along the coast as far as Itapoã then turn inland towards the airport. Buses to points further north along the coast – Arembepe, Praia do Forte and beyond – leave from the main rodoviária in Salvador or from Itapoã. Note: there is no access to the BR101 road, so if you're heading further north, you'll have to backtrack to Itapoã.

AREMBEPE

Arembepe was one of Brazil's first hip beaches in the '60s. Mick Jagger and Janis Joplin got the joint rolling and many local and foreign hippies followed. It is no longer a particularly attractive or popular retreat. Exclusive private homes and pollution from the giant Tibras chemical plant have tainted the rocky coast.

I don't recommend Arembepe. If you're going to the beach for a day from Salvador, there are prettier beaches, and if you're getting out of Salvador there are less spoiled fishing villages along the Bahian littoral.

Places to Stay

If you do end up in Arembepe, there is a cheap pension that the locals use on the south side of town and *Praias de Arambepe Hotel* (tel 824-1115), across from the praça, with doubles for US$11.

Just south of town, along the sea, the *Pousada da Fazenda* (tel 824-1030) looks like one of the few holdovers from the hippie days. They have small cabanas and healthy cooking. Lodging costs US$15 a double.

Getting There & Away

There is a convenient direct bus to Itapoã for 25c.

NORTH TO PRAIA DO FORTE

Driving north from Arembepe the littoral

appears layered: baby blue sky presses the deepest-blue sea, followed by successive strips of sand, coconut palms, lagoons, marshland, dune, scrub and forest.

Guarajuba

A few km south of Praia do Forte, Guarajuba is a beautiful beach accompanied by some tract housing.

Places to Stay There's an expensive hotel *Pousada Canto do Mar* (tel 071-245-0648) and a cheap hotel *Guarajuba Praia* along the approach road.

Barra do Jacuípe

A more remote spot, Barra do Jacuipe sits at the mouth of a river a km from the ocean. The beach is quite beautiful but there are no tourist facilities.

PRAIA DO FORTE

Praia do Forte has fine beaches, a beautiful castle fortress, a sea turtle reserve and unfortunately only expensive hotels. Until recently a fishing village, Praia do Forte is being developed as an ecologically minded, upscale beach resort (European tourists, we are told, are now coming directly from Salvador's airport to Praia do Forte). While it's way too early to know how this attempt will fare – scepticism is the only sane attitude – the main result thus far is the absence of cheap accommodation.

Praia do Forte is the seat of one of the original 12 captaincies established by the Portuguese. The huge estate extended inland all the way to the present day state of Piauí. Desperate to colonise and thereby hold his new land, the King of Portugal set about granting lands to merchants, soldiers and aristocrats. For no apparent reason Garcia d'Avila, a poor, 12-cow farmer, was granted this huge tract of land.

Garcia chose a prime piece of real estate to build his home and castle; an aquamarine ocean-view plot studded with palm trees four km up the road from town on Morro Tatuapaçu. Today, the castle is in ruins, completely overgrown with weeds and grasses, but it still made a fine tropical setting for director Márcio Meyrelle's production of Macbeth a few years back. The castle is worth a visit.

TAMAR Turtle Reserve

The TAMAR turtle reserve is on the beach right next to the light house and the overpriced Pousada Praia Forte. TAMAR (Tartaruga Marinha) is a jointly funded IBDF and Navy project started in 1982 to protect several species of marine turtles that are, or were, threatened: tartaruga xibirro, tartaruga de ponte, tartaruga mestica do cabeada and tortuga de couro.

What you see is actually quite modest, several small feeding pools with anywhere from two to several dozen turtles depending on the season. The TAMAR project gathers 30,000 turtle eggs a year along the coast. The eggs – moist, leathery, ping-pong-size balls – are buried in the sand to incubate. When the turtles hatch, they're placed in the feeding pools until big enough to tackle the Atlantic.

TAMAR also has stations at Comboios, Espírito Santos (north of Vitória near Lineares) to protect the leatherback and loggerhead turtles and on Fernando de Noronha to preserve the green turtle.

Nowadays commerce in endangered turtle species is illegal but shells are still sold in Salvador's Mercado Modelo and in Sergipe turtle eggs are still popular hors d'oeuvres. Of the 60 km of beach under the jurisdiction of the TAMAR project in Bahia, 13 km of coastline are patrolled by the scientists alone, the remainder is protected by a cooperative effort in which fishermen – the very same who used to collect the eggs for food – are contracted to collect eggs for the scientists.

Places to Stay & Eat

The only cheap place to stay is the camping grounds. They are very good and very cheap with cold-water showers, shady, sandy sites, washing basins for clothes and a daily cost of 25c per person. It's a 10-minute walk to the beach.

Pousada-Restaurante Oxun-Mare (tel 226-9411) costs US$20 a double without a bath and US$30 with a bath. Three meals are included. The *Pousada Praia do Forte* (tel 241-5653) has bungalows on the beach for US$50 for two. This price also includes three meals. Everyone in town seems to be money hungry.

Getting There & Away

The 2½ hour bus ride from Salvador's rodoviária costs 60c. Buses leave at 7 and 8 am, and 1 and 4 pm, they return from Praia do Forte at 5 and 9.30 am, midday and 4.30 pm.

NORTH OF PRAIA DO FORTE

To get to the beaches further north of Praia do Forte, head inland to BR-101 at Alagoinhas or Entre Rios. Going north, BR-101 parallels the coast approximately 60 km inland. Before you leave the state of Bahia, there are three roads back to the coast to Subaúma, Conde and Mangue Seco (the first two can be reached by bus from Salvador, Alagoinhas and Entre Rios).

Because there is no road that goes along the coast the beautiful beaches and fishing villages have been left somewhat undisturbed but this may soon change. All through this region there are fenced off tracts of land and small real estate offices selling beachfront property. If the government goes ahead as planned and paves the Rodovia do Coco from Salvador all the way to Maceió, tremendous changes would be set in motion. With good roads, all these beaches would be close enough to major urban areas to become weekend beach resorts.

Subaúma, Suipé & Palame

From Entre Rios there is a 75 km dirt road, curvy and precarious, to the beach town of Subaúma. There is no sign for the turnoff, so you should ask locals for directions. Hitching is possible. From Subaúma,

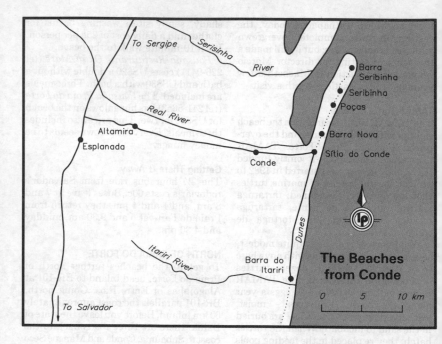

The Beaches from Conde

0   5   10 km

there is access to the tiny beach towns of Porto Suipé and Palame. These are very good, empty beaches but there are no hotels and the surf can be rough and dangerous.

Conde

On the Rio Itapicuru, Conde is about 12 km from the sea. It's the little big-town of the area and the jumping-off point for several beaches, the closest being Sítio do Conde. The food and lodging is a bit better here than in the other towns, but if you want beach there's little reason to stay in Conde for long.

Conde has a good Saturday market where fishermen and artisans come to peddle their goods. There's plenty of river traffic on market days which makes it easy to get a ride down the river to the ocean. From there you can hike or possibly hitch a ride on a tractor.

Places to Stay The *Hotel Santa Bárbara* is clean and comfortable. It's a simple place with rooms on the courtyard and bath down the hall, but nicer than places in Sítio. It's on the outskirts of town on the road to Sítio (US$5 a double, breakfast is an additional US$2.50).

Conde's other hotel is the *Pousada do Conde*, on the main street as you enter town. Doubles go for US$2.50 without cafe. The rooms are clean and face a courtyard.

Getting There & Away The town is serviced by regular buses from the BR-101 turn-off. The road is paved and the drive is beautiful, passing several enormous pine tree plantations. This route offers the easiest access to some of the great beaches of northern Bahia.

Sítio

Whether you walk, hitch or bus, you can't miss the many birds feeding at the lagoons that cover the six km drive to Sítio from Conde. When you arrive in Sítio, the beach is fine, but often windy, with choppy surf. From Sítio you can get to several beaches by walking along the shore or finding a fishing boat going up to the Rio Itapicuru.

Places to Stay & Eat Where the road meets the beach, there are a few restaurants. The *Restaurante Santa Maria* has five rooms to rent at US$2 a double, they are not too clean and the bath is down the hall. A cleaner deal is Dona Negra's house with rooms. At US$2 per person, it's very basic, but at that price you can't complain. She makes a big breakfast, but check the price before tucking in.

If you want a good place to stay, ask around for Iracema, near the *Santa Maria*. She has a beach house for rent just outside of town and it's a notch above anything else around. The price is US$10.

When you're hungry, hit the *Bar Lesco* which serves grand portions of seafood. It's also a friendly hangout and a good place for information.

Getting There & Away The bus schedule is geared to getting the kids to school: Conde to Sítio 6.50 am, Sítio to Conde 2 pm, Sítio to Barra 9 am, Barra to Sítio 1.30 pm.

Barra de Itariri

Barra is a 14 km dirt-drive south from Sítio. There are a few cars that come along so a walk/hitch combination is possible or you can walk along the stunning beach. The road is never more than a few hundred metres from the sea, which is hidden behind a running dune spotted with coconut trees. Away from the ocean there is a larger, more distant bluff.

Barra itself is all magic. The Rio Itariri slowly snakes into the sea, sand dunes cascade seaward, children and burros

explore the waters, coconut trees are ubiquitous. The beach is deserted except on weekends and the seas are choppy.

Places to Stay & Eat The town of Barra is tiny, with one lone restaurant looking out at the river. There are no pousadas, but some of the locals rent rooms (ask for Duda or Dona Nequinha) and there are some longer-term houses for rent.

Getting There & Away The bus leaves Barra for Alagoinhas (on BR-101) at 1.20 pm for 75c and returns from Alagoinhas at 6 am, passing through Conde and Sítio.

Mangue Seco

Mangue Seco is at the northern border of Bahia, at the tip of a peninsula formed by the Rio Real. You won't find it on most maps, but it's as beautiful as it is difficult to get to. Mangue Seco is a tiny town with a big, wide-open beach. The surf can be rough.

Places to Stay & Eat There are a couple of bars and a restaurant, open only on weekends, but there is no accommodation.

Getting There & Away Mangue Seco and Praia da Costa Azul can be reached by land from Jandaira at the BR-101. It's a very poor road, sometimes impassable after heavy rain, that weaves for 65 km until it reaches Mangue Seco. There is no bus service on this road.

You can also get there by sea from Saco in the state of Sergipe. Saco is not on most maps either, but it's at the southern end of the coast of Sergipe. To reach Saco, head to Estância on the BR-101 in Sergipe. From Estância there is a decent 28 km road to the coast and Praia do Abais. Saco is another 23 km further south on a rough dirt road. There are buses from Estância on Sundays and Mondays, but double-check this. From Saco you can catch a small boat to Mangue Seco. Reportedly, you can also reach Mangue Seco by boat from the towns of Pontal and Craxto in Sergipe.

Saco

Saco, actually across the border in the state of Sergipe, gets weekenders from Estância, but is quiet during the week. It's a fine beach with good swimming. There is no accommodation, but bars and restaurant open on weekends.

Abais

This is another weekend spot, but with a pousada. The beach, however, is not as good as the others in the area.

South of Salvador

VALENÇA

Population: 30,000

For most travellers, Valença is simply a stepping-stone to the beaches of Morro de São Paulo but it's also a small, friendly city that's a great place to see the people and work of the region. Everything centres around the busy port and large market, along the Rio Una where there are buses and boats, historic buildings, food and lodging. There are shipbuilders, vaqueiros (cowboys), textile manufacturers, peasants, craftsmen and fisherman. It's a lively scene, well worth exploring.

After routing the local Tupininquin Indians, the Portuguese settled here along the Rio Una in the 1560s, but were in turn expelled by the Aimores tribes. It wasn't until 1799, when the Portuguese returned from their posts in the mangrove archipelago to resettle and found Vila de Nova Valença do Santíssimo Coração de Jesus, that the city became a permanent fixture.

Information

If you're stuck, you can change money at Banco do Brasil and Banco Económico on Rua Governador Gonçalves. There's a Vatur office on Rua Comendador Madureira.

Around Town

In the centre of town wander around the port, the central plaza (under restoration) and the market. At the far end of the port, the timbered ribbing of boat hulls look like dinosaur skeletons. Some of the *saveiros*, wooden sail boats, are built for export to Uruguay and Paraguay. The remaining saveiros are used by the local fishermen who pull out of port early in the morning and return by mid-afternoon with the catch of the day.

The smell of sap and sawdust, old fish and sea-salt mingles with the wonderful smell of nutmeg. Picked from nearby groves of shrubby nutmeg trees, the cloves are set on a cloth and left to dry in the sun. The cattle ranching a bit further upstream and downwind has its own peculiar aroma. Vaqueiros sporting leather caps with braided chin straps straddle their horses and guide the cattle to market. Once in a while a loose bull goes charging through town.

For a good trek follow the left bank of the Rio Una upstream towards the NS de Amparo church up on the hill. At the base of the hill there's a trail straight up to the church and a beautiful view.

Cotton Factory

Back down the hill there's a large, white fortress-like building that houses a textile factory. Personal tours of the factory show the entire hot, noisy, smelly transformation of raw cotton into finished fabrics. This factory is typical of the old Brazilian economy – still prevalent in the Northeast – with its use of antiquated US machinery and cheap Brazilian labour. It's a good tour for those interested in issues of economic development.

The factory is open for visits on Saturdays from 9 am to 5 pm and you may be able to arrange a tour on other days. Authorisation is provided at the colonial building to the front-left of the factory.

Festivals

In addition to the traditional festivals of

Bahia like São João, Terno de Reis, Queima de Judas and Bumba Meu Boi, Valença celebrates holidays peculiar to the area. Sagrado Coração de Jesus is a mass held for the patron of the city sometime in June or July. The mass, novena and festival in honour of the patron saint of workers, NS do Amporo, is celebrated on 8 November.

The Boi Estrela is a folklore festival where men and women dressed as cowhands accompany Catarina the Bahiana while they play tambourines and chant. Zabiapunga, another folklore fest, features musical groups playing weird instruments and running through the city streets at dawn of the new year.

There's a good Carnival, with trios elétricos and the Carnival-like Micareta festival held 15 days after Lent. Other festivals include Festa de Reis (6 January), São João (23 June), NS do Rosário (24 September to 3 October), São Benedito on Cairu Island (26 December to 6 January) and Iemanjá (31 December & 1 January).

Places to Stay

Hotel Guaibim (tel 741-1110), Praça da Independência 74 is one block in from the port. Singles cost US$5.50 to US$9, doubles US$11 to US$12 depending on whether or not the rooms have air-con and a fridge. *Hotel Rio Una* (tel 711-1614) on Rua Maestro Barrinhão on the riverside has more comforts and is accordingly more expensive.

Places to Eat

There are plenty of typical lanchonetes. The *Bar Luis* in Cajaíba is recommended for seafood. *Restaurant Akuários* is in the same building as the Hotel Guaibim and the Hotel Rio Una has its own restaurant, the *Panorama*.

Getting There & Away

Air There is a small airport which is serviced by Nordeste airlines.

Bus Valença is a five-hour bus ride from Salvador (272 km). Valença's rodoviária (tel 741-1280) is by the port on Rua Maçônica. There are five daily buses to Salvador. Some go via Itaparica Island (190 km) and drop you off at Bom Despacho for the 45 km ferry ride to Salvador. Others go all the way around Baía de Todos os Santos (290 km) into Salvador.

Boat Although Salvador is only 110 km by sea, boat service is irregular.

Near Valença

The best mainland beach in the vicinity is 14 km north of town at Guaibim. There are local buses and it's popular on weekends.

The islands of Boipeba and Cairu have colonial buildings and churches, but their beaches don't compare with Morro de São Paulo.

VALENÇA TO ILHÉUS
Morro São Paulo

What Porto Seguro must have been 15 years ago, Morro São Paulo is today: a tranquil, isolated fishing village with incredible beaches, recently discovered by hip Brazilians and international travellers. Unfortunately, the secret is out. Morro is on everyone's lips and has even made it onto several Brazilian magazines' best beach lists.

At the northern tip of Ilha do Tinharé, Morro has grass streets where only mules, beach bums and horses tread – no cars and few facilities for tourists. The waters around the island are very clear, ideal for scuba diving and the underwater hunt for lobster, squid and fish. The settlement is comprised of three hills – Morro de Mangaba, Morro de Galeão and Morro de Farol. Climb up from the harbour through the 17th century fortress gate and up to the lighthouse (1835). From the top you can see over the island and its beaches. The west side of the island, the river or

Gamboa side, is bordered by mangroves, the eastern side is sandy.

There are three beaches in Morro de São Paulo: the rather dirty village beach, followed by the barraca and camping beach and the fazenda beach. These three are merely preludes to the long lovely stretch of sand graced by tall swaying palms which borders the eastern half of the island.

Beware, there are many bichos de pé, little critters that burrow into human feet, so keep something on your feet when walking through town.

Places to Stay & Eat The food and lodging scene is changing quickly and accommodation can be scarce during the summer. There are about 40 pousadas or you may be able to rent a house from one of the local fisherman.

The *Restaurante-Pousada Gaucho* charges US$5 per room which can sleep three people. They also rent two-room houses for US$12 per day.

Ilha da Saúde Pousada-Restaurant (tel 741-1702 in Valença) has attractive singles/doubles for US$20/22. They serve their tasty shrimp prato feito (US$2) excruciatingly slowly. *Restaurante Verdão Tropical* serves a prato feito for US$2.

Getting There & Away Take the Brisa Biônica (Bionic Breeze) and Brisa Triônica between Morro de São Paulo and Valença for a relaxed 2½ hour, 50c boat ride. You'll pass mangroves and coconut-palm-lined beaches that rival the Caribbean and South Pacific in beauty, yachts and double-masted square-rigged Brazilian 'junks'.

During the summer the schedule is as follows: Monday to Saturday two boats per day at 9 am and 2 pm go from Valença to Morro de São Paulo and return at 6 am and 12.20 pm. The Sunday schedule is the same but directions are inverted to afford day-trippers an opportunity to enjoy Morro.

The rest of the year there is only one boat per day in either direction. It leaves Monday to Saturday at 6 am from Morro to Valença and returns to Morro at 12.30 pm. On Sundays there is a 6 am boat to Morro and a 12.30 pm boat returning to Valença. If you're coming from Salvador you can confirm these times at Bahiatursa.

Try bolo e mingau for breakfast when the boat stops at the Gamboa pier. Bolo is cake and mingau is a warm, white, sweet, gummy manioc-brew spiced with nutmeg cloves.

Camamu

Camamu sits on a hill behind a labyrinth of mangrove-filled islets and narrow channels (no beaches). The town is the port of call for the many tiny fishing villages in the region. There's a lively dock-side morning market with fish, fruit and drying nutmeg.

Saveiro fishing boats are built and repaired right outside of the port. The Açaraí waterfalls are five km away by bus or taxi and worth a visit.

Places to Stay Camamu offers the overpriced and under-maintained *Hotel Assunção* (tel 255-2168) at US$7 for two. The *Hotel Rio Açaraí* is soon to open.

Getting There & Away Buses depart for Valença and Ubaitaba every hour or so.

Ponta do Mutá

If you want to get off the beaten path, this is the place. The peninsula that goes out to Ponta do Mutá has one long dirt road, no hotels, infrequent buses and a handful of very small fishing villages (you won't find any of them on a map). It's a completely unspoilt area but the beaches are hard to get to without a car.

Beer is sold in the villages, but little else, so you might have to work at finding food and lodging. Several of the villages have small, early morning boats that take the locals to market across the bay to Camamu. This is a delicious two-hour voyage and it eliminates a heap of time backtracking on the peninsula.

Itacaré

Itacaré is a quiet colonial town at the mouth of the Rio de Contas. They could film *A Hundred Years of Solitude* here, if they could find the town. Distance and bad roads have shielded Itacaré from tourism (it's a two-hotel town), but there are endless empty beaches to the north and south with gentle waves and calm water. The meeting of river and ocean is beautiful. Ribeira beach is recommended for a swim.

Be warned that there is no road along the coast here, so you must return the way you came – unless you hike or hitch a ride on a fishing boat.

There is one blemish on this tropical hideaway, brought to you by Petrobras, the government oil company. There are little coin-sized spots of oil on many parts of the beach (I did not, however, get any oil on me when I went swimming).

To get to the beaches north of Itacaré' cross the river by long dug-out canoe for 50c to US$1. This odd yet tranquil scene – mangrove trees lining the riverbanks and Petrobras choppers thrashing overhead – looks like the opening of *Apocalypse Now*, just before the jungle goes up in napalm flames.

In Itacaré you can also rent a canoe to visit O Pontal, a beautiful promontory just south of the bay. It's best to leave your camera behind as the canoes are precarious.

Places to Stay The *Hotel-Restaurant Iemanjá* with breakfast (US$2.50) is the better of the town's two hotels.

Getting There & Away There is no road along the coast from Itacaré, so you must return to the main highway inland, unless you sail or walk along the coast. Buses depart for Ilhéus at 6 am and 4 pm, Ubaitaba 9 am (for connections north), Itabuna 5.30 am and 2 pm (via Ubaitaba).

On the map it appears possible to walk along the shore to the next town north, thereby eliminating a lot of backtracking. After getting several opinions, all conflicting, on the feasibility of this idea we decided to try it.

It is a long walk, around 20 km in the sand, and you have to cut inland at some point to hit the next road. It's only recommended if you want to camp out and explore some fantastic super-isolated stretches of beach.

Itacaré to Ilhéus

From Itacaré to Ilhéus is 110 km. The trip takes four hours by bus. The route is slow but stunning, one of my favourites in Brazil. The bus stops every few km to pick up another couple of locals. Each face has a unique blend of Black, Indian and White features.

There are occasional cacao plantations where the locals seem to both live and work. Just like in *A Violent Land*, Jorge Amado's novel about the cacao belt, a man with a rifle guards the fazenda gate. As the sun sets, families appear on the front step of their single-room, thatched-roof houses. The entire extended family watches the bus pass. The patriarch always stands with a machete in hand.

The first two hours from Itacaré to Uruçuca are along a bad dirt road, the bus travelling at a snail's pace. Uruçuca is a tiny village – secluded and timeless, with brilliant light and surrounded by lush valleys where the cacao trees grow. If you have some time, it's well worth exploring the town a little. Make sure you check what time the next bus comes through or you could find yourself stuck here with nowhere to stay.

From here the road heads down through lush Atlantic coastal jungle, reaching the coast shortly before Ilhéus. The rolling hills are covered by a wide variety of trees – I recognised groves of cacao, coconut and enormous bamboo.

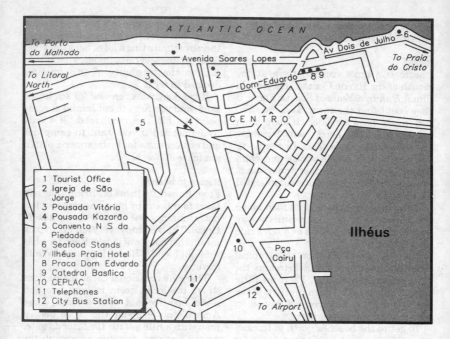

Map legend:

1 Tourist Office
2 Igreja de São Jorge
3 Pousada Vitória
4 Pousada Kazarão
5 Convento N S da Piedade
6 Seafood Stands
7 Ilhéus Praia Hotel
8 Praca Dom Edvardo
9 Catedral Basílica
10 CEPLAC
11 Telephones
12 City Bus Station

Map labels: ATLANTIC OCEAN; To Porto do Malhado; Avenida Soares Lopes; Av Dois de Julho; To Praia do Cristo; To Litoral North; Dom Eduardo; CENTRO; Ilhéus; Pça Cairu; To Airport

ILHÉUS

Population: 75,000

Ilhéus' Catedral Basílica, the city's most important building, is an enormous edifice with a striking facade and a grand entrance. After climbing its many steps and passing through the massive doors, I was even more reverential than usual as I walked into the church's enormous chamber where I saw a sporty, bright-red, Ford Escort parked before the pews. Nothing has ever looked so out of place. The temporary use of the city's most famous House of the Lord to shelter an automobile was, it turned out, prompted by a raffle to fund a badly needed church restoration.

Ilhéus, the town that Jorge Amado, Brazil's best-known novelist, lived in and wrote about in *Gabriela* and *Clove & Cinnamon* retains some of the charm and lunacy that Amado fans know well. There's a half-hearted attempt to portray the city as an up-and-coming tourist mecca, but nobody believes it will happen. Ilhéus remains largely unaffected by tourism, the colonial centre is small and distinctive with its strange layout and odd buildings, the people are warm and friendly, the city beaches are broad and beautiful and 15 minutes away the beaches are even better.

History

Ilhéus was a sleepy town until cacao was introduced into the region from Belém in 1881. At the time, Brazil's many uncompetitive sugar estates, which had not incorporated new production techniques that had drastically increased sugar output in other countries, were reeling from a drop in world sugar prices. Simultaneously, the slave system was finally coming to an end with many slaves escaping and others being freed. With the sugar plantations in the doldrums, impoverished agricultural workers from the Northeast – black and white – flocked to the hills surrounding Ilhéus to farm the new boom crop: cacao, the *ouro branco* (white gold) of Brazil.

Sudden, lawless and violent, the rush for the white fruit of the cacao had all the leading elements of a gold rush. When the dust settled, the land and power belonged to a few ruthless *coroneis* and their hired-guns. The landless were left to work, and usually live, on the fazendas where they were subjected to a harsh and paternalistic labour system. This history is graphically told by Amado, who grew up on a cacao plantation, in his book *The Violent Land*.

Cacao still rules in Ilhéus. The lush tropical hills are covered with the large, pod-shaped fruit that dangles from skinny trees and if you take a drive you will still see the cacao fazendas and rural workers who look like they came right out of Amado's book. You can also visit the small Regional Museu do Cacao, the port and, with effort and luck, a fazenda.

Information & Orientation

The city is sandwiched between hills, beach and a small harbour at the mouth of the Rio Cachoeira. Getting around is baffling. I have never lost my sense of direction so often in such a small place. Fortunately central Ilhéus is small, so it doesn't matter much.

The airport and the road to the Olivença beaches are in the southern part of town, on the other side of the circular harbour.

Tourist Office There is a poor imitation of a tourist office which claims to occasionally have maps ('you should have been here yesterday', they said, day after day). If you want to check it out, it's a five-minute walk up the beach sidewalk, away from the centre.

Money Money exchange at good rates is difficult. For official rates there's the Banco do Brasil at Marques de Paranágua 112.

Around Town

The best thing to do in Ilhéus is just wander. The centre is lively, with several old, gargoyled buildings such as the Prefeitura. If you walk up the hill to the Convento NS da Piedade there's a good view of the city and littoral. Wherever you end up, it won't be more than a stone's throw from the beach. The Praia da Avenida, along the city, is always active, but reportedly polluted from the port.

Churches

The Igreja de São Jorge (1534) is the city's oldest church and houses a small sacred art museum. It's on Praça Rui Barbosa, open Tuesday through Sunday 8 to 11 am and 2 to 5.30 pm. The Catedral de São Sebastião (Basílica) on Praça D Eduardo is being restored.

Museu Regional do Cacao

The Museu Regional do Cacao has local, modern painting and cacao artefacts. It's at Rua A L Lemos 126 and is open Tuesday to Friday from 2 to 6 pm, Saturday and Sunday from 3 to 6 pm.

Festivals

As any knowledgeable Jorge Amado fan would guess, Ilhéus has highly spirited festivals. The best are the Gincana da Pesca in early January; Festa de São Sebastião (much samba and capoeira) from 11 to 20 January; Festa de São Jorge (with Candomblé) on 23 April; Festa das Águas (Candomblé) in December and a trio elétrico filled Carnival.

Places to Stay – bottom end

There are not enough hotels in Ilhéus, consequently they seem to be overpriced and often full up. Most are close by, within a 15-minute walk from the central bus station. Several hotels are worth avoiding, including the *Lukas* (tel 231-4071) with doubles for US$12, the *Central* and *Britânia* (tel 231-1722) for about the same price.

The *Hotel Ilhéus* (tel 231-4242), Praça Firmino Amaral 144 costs US$10 a single/double with breakfast. *Pousada Kazarão* (tel 231-5031) at Praça Coronel Pessoa 38 has the nicest rooms in town for US$9 a double and US$6 a single, without breakfast. *Pousada Vitória* (tel 231-4105) which is down the block has singles/doubles for US$4.50.

Places to Stay – top end
At the top end, the best hotel in town is the three-star *Ilhéus Praia Hotel* (tel 231-2533), right across from the Catedral Basílica and the beach on the Praça D Eduardo.

Places to Eat
Locals boast about the regional flavoured cooking at *Moqueca de Ouro*. For about US$4 you get a plate of seafood for two, with a waterfront view. It's out near the airport. Take the bus marked Pontal. For more good seafood in the same price range try *Os Velhos Marinheiros* at Avenida 2 de Julho and *O Céu é o Límite* two km out on Avenida Itabuna.

Behind the Catedral Basílica, along the beach, there are several reasonably priced seafood stands with outdoor tables. The centre is filled with cheap restaurants with prato feitos for US$1. The tiny, but mighty, *Asa Branca* with a wide array of natural juices and cheap sandwiches is at Rua Pedro II 110.

Getting There & Away
Air There is a small airport which is serviced by Nordeste Varig/Cruzeiro and air-taxis. You can fly to several major cities including Rio, Salvador, Recife and Belém. If you're returning to Rio, the flight stops at Salvador but is still cheaper than flying from Salvador.

Bus Ilhéus is about 460 km south of Salvador and 315 km north of Porto Seguro. From highway BR-101 at Itabuna, Ilhéus is a beautiful 30 km descent through the cacao belt to the sea. Most major destinations have more frequent buses leaving from Itabuna than Ilhéus, so it's usually quicker to go to Itabuna then shuttle down to Ilhéus.

The Ilhéus Rodoviária (tel 231-1015) is a 15-minute bus ride from the centre. Buses to Salvador use two different approach routes. The more common is along the Recôncavo. You can take this if you want to stop at Cachoeira on the way to Salvador. The other route goes through Nazaré and Itaparica Island and lets you off at the ferry for a stunning 35 minute ferry ride into the city.

Ilhéus has several buses daily to Salvador including one at 5.55 pm via the ferry (seven hours, US$2.50), two a day to Valença (four hours, US$1.50), three daily to Porto Seguro (4- 1/2 hours, US$2) and buses to Itacaré at 7 am and 4 pm (four hours, US$1).

Getting Around
Airport Transport The airport (tel 231-3015) is at Praia do Pontal, four km from the centre.

Local Transport The city bus station is at the edge of the centre, away from the ocean. Buses go from there to Olivença, the rodoviária and the airport.

AROUND ILHÉUS
Centro de Pesquisa do Cacao (CEPLAC)
You don't have to be a chocaholic to enjoy CEPLAC's model cacao plantation and research station at Itabuna. CEPLAC is the government cacao agency and they give tours of the facility demonstrating the cultivation and processing of the funny fruit. It is open to the public from Monday to Friday from 9.30 to 11 am and again from 2.30 to 5 pm.

If you're already in Ilhéus you can confirm the times with CEPLAC's office in town before going. It's the big building by the city bus station (in Itabuna you can call 211-2211, ext 132). Buses leave every 20 minutes for Itabuna from the Rodoviária. Ask the bus driver to let you off at Ceplac, eight km before Itabuna.

Olivença Beaches

There are good clean beaches, many with barracas, all the way to Olivença, 20 km to the south. You can even go south of Olivença for more remote beaches, but after a few km the coastal road turns inland. Beaches are busy on weekends and there's supposed to be some good surfing.

Places to Stay On the way you'll pass two simple hotels, *Pousada & Bar Grapiuna* and *Paraíso Mar Azul*. In Olivença proper there is the *Pousada Olivença*.

Getting There & Away To get there take an Olivença marked bus from the central rodoviária; they leave frequently and cost a few cents. The bus travels close to the beaches so you can pick one to your liking and quickly hop-off.

Reserva Biológica Mico Leão de Una

This small (50 square km) biological reserve was designed to protect the *mico leão* (lion monkey) in its natural habitat of

Praia Ilhéus

coastal jungle. It's not a park and it does not cater to visitors but you can visit and it's well worth the trip. The monkeys (leontopithecus rosalia chrysomelas) have the look and proud gaze of miniature lions: a blazing yellow, orange and brown striped coat, a Tina Turner mane and a long, scruffy tail. The mico-leões are hard to spot in the wild, but behind the biologist's quarters there is one monkey in captivity and one monkey-boarder who comes in from the forest every evening for milk, cheese, bananas and some shut-eye. If you're lucky you will also see tapu, paca, capybara and deer which are also native to the area.

Getting There & Away Getting to the beasts is a bit difficult without a car. Take the bus marked Canaveiras from the Ilhéus Rodoviária and go 35 km south of Olivença along the coastal highway until a MA-IBDF sign marks the turn-off to the reserve.

From here you have to hitch, which is difficult, or hike. Follow the turn-off for five km on a pitted dirt track over the Rio Mariu and past a fazenda. Turn right at the marker, the working station is three km further within the park. To arrange a visit and perhaps an MA-IBDF jeep ride from the highway call Dr Saturnino, director of the reserve, at his home in Una (236-2166 from 7 to 8 am or after 5.30 pm).

PORTO SEGURO
Population: 5000

Porto Seguro was a pioneering settlement in this part of Brazil, but today it is neither a naval or colonial outpost but a refuge for swarms of Brazilian and international tourists who come to party and take in some mesmerising beaches. Tourism is the number one industry in Porto Seguro. At last count the small city had nearly 50 hotels and pousadas. Other regional industries are lumber, fishing, beans, sugar cane, manioc and livestock.

1	Igreja NS da Pena
2	Igreja da Misericórdia
3	Passo Municicpal e Museu
4	Igreja NS Rosário
5	Pharmacy
6	Supermarket
7	Tourist Office
8	Delegacia de Polícia (Police Station)
9	Telephones
10	Banco – Baneb
11	Banco do Brasil
12	Igreja NS do Brasil
13	Pousada do Cais
14	Capitania dos Portos
15	Bus Station
16	Restaurante do Japonês

History
After sighting land off Monte Pascoal in April 1500, Cabral and his men sailed three days up the coast to find a safe port. The Portuguese landed not at Porto Seguro (literally safe port), but 16 km further north at Coroa Vermelha. The sailors celebrated their first mass in the New Land, stocked up on wood and fresh water and set sail after only 10 days on shore. Three years later the Gonçalvo Coelho expedition arrived and planted a marker in what is now Porto Seguro's Cidade Alta. Jesuits on the same expedition built a church in Outeiro da Glória, to minister to the early colonists and convert the Tupiniquin Indians. The church is now in ruins. In 1526, a naval outpost was built in the Cidade Alta and once again the men from the Companhia de Jesus built a chapel and convent, the Igreja da Misericórdia.

In 1534, when the colonies were divided into hereditary captaincies, Porto Seguro was given to Pero de Campos Tourinhos. In the following year Tourinhos founded a village at the falls of the Rio Buranhém, Porto Seguro, and seven other villages each with a church. Despite the churches, Tourinhos was denounced to the Holy Inquisition as an atheist, apparently the

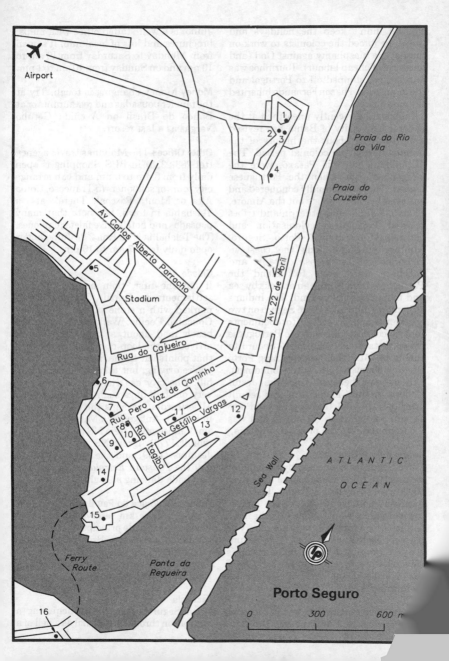

Porto Seguro

captain didn't keep the holidays and worse, he forced the colonists to work on Sundays, a blasphemy against God (and an abuse of cheap labour). Tourinhos was imprisoned, shipped off to Portugal and the Inquisition. His son Fernando inherited the captaincy.

Information recently unearthed at the Federal University of Bahia has revised some thinking about the history of the Indians during the colonial period. The Tupiniquin, not the Pataxó, were the indigenous tribe when the Portuguese landed. They were rapidly conquered and enslaved by the colonists but the Aimoré, Pataxó, Cataxó and other inland tribes resisted Portuguese colonisation and constantly threatened Porto Seguro. Military outposts along the coast in Belmonte, Vila Viçosa, Prado and Alcobaça were built to defend the Portuguese from European attacks by sea and Indian attacks by land. The Indians still managed to take Porto Seguro on two occasions, and according to documents sent by colonial judges to the Portuguese crown, attacks reduced Porto Seguro to rubble in 1612 (thus undermining Porto Seguro's claims to 16th century buildings).

It is now believed that the Jesuit College in the Cidade Alta was rebuilt after 1620. In 1759, the captaincy of Porto Seguro passed on to the crown and was incorporated into the province of Bahia.

Information & Orientation

Porto Seguro is connected by an asphalt road to BR-101 at Eunápolis, a little over 660 km south-west of Salvador. The town itself has no beaches, but is the largest town in the area and the one with the most facilities for tourists – there are plenty of perfect beaches nearby. The Porto Seguro coast is protected by reefs; the ocean is clear, shallow, and as calm as a meeting of the Native Daughters of California. Swimming is safe.

Tourist Office Porturismo, at the corner of Pero Vaz de Caminha and Rua 2 de Julho, is a well-staffed office with maps, brochures and lots of local info. It's open from Monday to Saturday from 10 am to 10 pm and on Sunday from 10 am to 1 pm.

Money Money changing is tough. Try at the fancier pousadas and restaurants or at Banco do Brasil on Avenida Getúlio Vargas as a last resort.

Other Offices The Malvinas travel agency (tel 288-2335) in BPS Shopping is open daily from 8 am to 6 pm and can arrange city tours or schooners to Trancoso, Coroa Alta or Monte Pascoal. There's also a Telebahia in town, but note that many pousadas and hotels have falefacil phones. The Telebahia is on Rua 2 de Julho and is open daily from 7 am to 10 pm.

Cidade Alta

If not the first, then among the first settlements in Brazil, Cidade Alta is marked with a stone placed in 1503 by Gonçalvo Coelho. Walk north along the beach road about a km. Once you've arrived at the loop don't follow the sign that points left to the historic city unless you're driving, but take the dirt road up hill. The city has views of beaches and very old buildings such as Igreja NS da Misericórdia (perhaps the oldest church in Brazil), Antigo Paco Municipal (1772, small museum), Igreja NS da Pena (1535, rebuilt 1773), Igreja NS do Rosário dos Jesuitas (1549) and the old fort (1503). Try the *Pousada Estrela* for drinks and Lambada dancing at night.

Reserva Biológica do Pau Brasil

This 10 square km reserve, 15 km from town, was set aside principally to preserve the brazil wood tree. Brazil's namesake was nearly completely felled from the littoral in the early years of colonisation. Enquire at Porturismo.

Festivals

Porto Seguro's Carnival is acquiring a reputation throughout Brazil as a hell of a party, though not at all traditional. In 1984 the theme was the Adam and Eve story. Costumes were pretty skimpy at first, then everyone stripped off as if on cue. The police were called in the following year.

Many of Brazil's favourite musicians have beach homes nearby and they often perform during carnival. The Sunday before Carnival a beauty pageant is held at the Praia Hotel. Municipal holidays celebrated include:

5-6 January

The Torno de Reis is celebrated in the streets and by the doors of the church, Women and children carrying lanterns and *pandeiros* (tambourines) sing *O Reis* and worship the *Reis Magos* (three wise men).

3 January until February

Bumba-meu-boi is celebrated in the streets of the city with a musical parade (see São Luis de Maranhão).

20 January

The Puxada de Mastro is a group of men who carry a figure to the door of the church. Decorated with flowers, the mastro is hung in front of the church with the flag and image of São Sebastião and the women sing to the Saint.

19-22 April

The discovery of Brazil is commemorated with an outdoor mass and Indian celebrations.

15 August

The Festa de NS d'Ajuda is the culmination of a pilgrimage starting on 9 April. A mass procession, organised in homage to the miraculous saint, is followed by food, drink and live music.

8 September

The Festa de NS da Pena is the same as the Festa de NS d'Ajuda with the added extra of fireworks.

25-27 December

The Festa de São Benedito is on 27 December during the Cucumbi activities at the door of the church of Nossa Senhora do Rosário. Cidade Alta boys and girls in blackface perform African dances like *Congo da Alma*, *Ole* or *Lalá* to the music of drums, *cuica atabaque* and *xeque-xeque*.

31 December

On New Year's everyone rushes around shouting 'Feliz ano novo Bahiana!', strangers kiss and serious partying ensues.

Places to Stay

Accommodation in Porto Seguro is fancier and there is more of it than further south at Arraial. During the low season there must be at least 20 vacant rooms per tourist, so bargain. On the other hand in the high season (December to February) accommodation can be very tight. It's a good job Porto Seguro has nine hotels and 37 pousadas.

Places to Stay – bottom end

For US$2.50 per person the clean rooms of *Pousada Inaia* (tel 288-2866) at Avenida Portugal 526 are a good deal.

Many of the middle range pousadas are charming, homey hotels which reflect the character of their owners. The *Pousada do Cais* (tel 288-2121) at Avenida Portugal 382 has singles/doubles for US$18.50/23.50 or US$23/29 with air-con. All the rooms are different and tastefully decorated.

The *Pousada Aquarius* (tel 288-2738) at Rua P A Cabral 174 offers low season singles for US$7.50 and doubles for US$8, high season doubles are only US$12. *Pousada dos Navegantes* (tel 288-2390) at Avenida 22 de Abril 212 is a little bit out of the way, but all rooms have fans, double hammocks and a good breakfast. In the low season singles/doubles are US$20 or US$22 with air-con. In the high season rooms are 25% more expensive.

The *Pousada Caravelas* (tel 288-2706), Avenida 22 de Abril s/n (no number) has pleasant US$21 doubles near the sea.

Places to Stay – top end

The fanciest hotel in the area, the *Porto Seguro Praia* (tel 288-2321), about four km north of town, is set back off the coastal road on Praia Itacimirim. The *Hotel Phonécia* (tel 288-2411), Avenida 22 de Abril 400 is closer to town and on the beach. Both are big, expensive and impersonal.

Places to Eat

The *Bar-Restaurant Tres Vintens* Avenida Portugal 246 serves a delicious bobo de camarão for US$3.50. With a side dish this is a meal for two. For good sushi, sashimi and hot shrimp dishes (US$2 to US$5), take the ferry across to the Ajuda side and pop into the *Restaurante do Japonês* in the orange building. For dessert have a mango popsicle (picole) which you can buy nearby on the street.

La Tarrafa, Avenida Portugal 360 is a rustic oyster bar. A plate of buttery clams or oysters for US$1 goes best with a cold brew. *Restaurant Prima Dona*, Praça dos Pataxos 247 is run by honest-to-God Italians from Turin, they understand what *al dente* means. Pastas start at US$2, seafood US$3.50 and up. It's open after 7 pm but it's closed on Mondays.

Casa da Esquina on Rua Assis Chateaubriand has been recommended for seafood. *Nativo* on Avenida Getúlio Vargas is the place to go for pastries and juices. Try cacao juice – it's not at all like chocolate, but it is very good. *Tia Seissa*, Avenida Portugal 170 makes home-made liqueurs from tropical fruits and cachaça. Try pitanga (like cherry) and jenipapo at 50c a pop.

Entertainment

For live music and booze go to Porto Seguro's Passarela de Alcool. *Posto 38*, a *lambada* dance hall, starts hopping after 10 pm. There's no cover charge. The lambada is an erotic and entertaining local dance which involves some agitated leg tangling and exaggerated hip wiggling whilst pressing belly buttons.

Boat Trips

Excursions can be arranged with Companhia do Mar Passeios de Escunas (tel 288-2381) on Praça dos Pataxós, which runs five-day schooner trips south along the coast then off to Abrolhos.

Airacata (tel 282-1121) has day-trips which depart from Cabrália at 10 am and return by 4 pm touring Rio João de Tiba, Coroa Alta and Santo Andre. Macunaíma (tel 288-2381) runs tours of the coast south of Porto Seguro. They set sail daily at 9 am from Porto Seguro's ferry port and return at 5 pm after stops at Trancoso, Recife de Fora and Coroa Alta.

You can windsurf in front of the Hotel Phonécia for US$5 per hour. Here the reef protects you from choppy surf.

Things to Buy

Pataxó Indians imported from the interior of Brazil are nominally under the care of FUNAI. A few Pataxó are hanging on south of Caraiva and are trying to maintain some semblance of their traditional way of life. The few Pataxó north of Porto Seguro sell trinkets (overpriced coloured feathers, pieces of coral, fibre wrist bands with beads) to tourists at Coroa Vermelha. This make-believe village is simply a sad little collection of thatched-roof huts and dugout canoes by the beach. Porto Seguro also has souvenir shops that sell Pataxó jewellery, basketware and earthenware ceramics. Please don't buy items made of turtle shell!

Getting There & Away

Air Nordeste has a daily milk run to Porto Seguro, originating in São Paulo with stops in Rio (Santos Dumont airport), Brasília and Ipatinga, Minas Gerais. From Rio the flight leaves daily at 12.50 pm and costs US$40. It returns from Porto Seguro at 8.55 pm. They also have Saturday and Sunday flights to Belo Horizonte and daily flights to Salvador. Nordeste fly Bandeirantes, a small Brazilian-built plane that some say has a bad safety record.

Rio Sul airlines has Sunday flights to Vitória and Rio de Janeiro, TAM flies to São Paulo on Saturdays.

Bus The station is across from the ferry at Praça dos Pataxos. Viação São Geraldo runs a daily bus to São Paulo at 10.45 am and Rio at 5.45 pm (17 hour ride). There are more buses during the high season. Viação São Jorge has two daily buses to Salvador with a leito at 6.20 pm. Vitória is served by one leito and one common bus per day. There are three buses a day to Ilhéus and Itabuna.

There's a bus to Eunápolis, from where there are more frequent bus departures than in Porto Seguro, nearly every hour from 5.20 am to 8 pm. Buses to Santa Cruz de Cabrália run six times daily from 6.20 am to 7 pm.

Getting Around

For bike rentals (50c per hour, US$4 per day) enquire at Porturismo.

The ferry across the Rio Buranhém towards Arraial d'Ajuda, Trancoso and Caraiva charges 10c per person, US$1 per car and operates 6.30 am to 11 pm. The return trip is free and the fare doubles on Sundays. The *Nova Lusitânia* and *Iracema*, both tired barges, make the five minute crossing past the rotting and listing old hulks of beached fishing boats.

NORTH OF PORTO SEGURO

North of Porto Seguro, right by the paved coastal road, lie several attractive beaches such as Mundai and Coroa Vermelha and finally at Km 25 the town of Santa Cruz Cabrália. These beaches are easily accessible by bus and, consequently, not as primitive and pristine as those to the south.

About five km north of town is the nicest of the northern beaches, Mundai, with barracas at the mouth of the Rio Mundai. North of Rio dos Mangues at Ponta Grande the highway cuts inland a bit. The beach is good – uncrowded, tranquil waters – and hard to get to. Six km before Cabrália is Coroa Vermelha with Pataxos craft stands, a monument to the discovery of Brazil and some fair beaches.

SANTA CRUZ CABRÁLIA

There's not much to Cabrália, but its terracotta roofs and palm trees are pleasant enough. Climb up to the bluff over-looking the town for the view and to visit the lonely white church. The Igreja Imaculada Conçeição dates back to 1630 and was built by the Jesuits. The elderly caretaker will tell you the history of the region as well as the inside scoop on Cabral's expedition. Fried shrimp and a batida de coco at the barracas by the church enhance the view of the offshore reef, the boats and the palm trees in and about the bay of Cabrália.

Places to Stay & Eat

Pousada Xica da Silva (tel 282-1104), Rua Frei Henrique de Coimbra (by the bus stop) charges US$7/14 singles/doubles in clean rooms with fans and hot showers. The pousada has a restaurant, bar and swimming pool. Across the street at *Restaurante Vanda* lobster goes for a hefty US$8.

Getting There & Away

Over 10 Sulba buses a day head north to Cabrália. The last bus back to Porto Seguro leaves at 4.30 pm, sometimes 5.10 pm. The 23 km trip takes 25 minutes.

SOUTH OF PORTO SEGURO

After the Rio Buranhém crossing there is a long stretch of dreamlike beaches, with a bluff backdrop. Up on the bluff, a short walk from the beach, are the villages of Arraial d'Ajuda (also known as NS da Ajuda), Trancoso and Caraiva, at 4.5 km, 12 km and 37 km from the ferry crossing, respectively. In general the further south you tread from Porto Seguro, the more 'uncivilised' things get. Porto Seguro has paved roads, electricity, modern hotels as well as pousadas, chopp (and of course bottled beer). Arraial d'Ajuda has dirt roads, electricity, good pousadas (no hotels) and no chopp, just bottled beer. There is only a poor unpaved road south to Trancoso and the road completely peters out beyond there towards Caraiva.

ARRAIAL D'AJUDA

Ten years ago, before electricity or the road from Porto Seguro, Arraial was a poor fishing village removed from the world. Since then, the international tourist set has discovered Arraial and its desolate beaches, and a time-honoured way of life is dying. The village has gone too hip too fast; by day all is beach blanket Babylon, by night Arraial is something out of a Fellini film: marijuana smoke clouds the main street, white horses gallop wildly through the town, wasted minstrels sing songs, and ancient village women wear Nina Hagen T-shirts.

Yet, for some, Arraial is the place to be. Younger, hipper and wilder than Porto Seguro, small and rustic Arraial is a wonderful place to tan and slough off excess brain cells. Newcomers soon fall into the delicious routine: going crazy every evening, recovering (hopefully) the following morning, only to stare blankly at strange, new bed-mates and crawl weakly back onto the beach for more surf, sun and samba.

Information & Orientation

Arraial d'Ajuda is built on a little hilltop by the sea. The main street running from the church to the cemetery is called Broadway. The restaurants and bars plus a cheap pousada are here. This is where the bus and taxis stop. Most of Arraial's pousadas are located on the ocean-side of this hilltop in a maze of nameless dirt streets. Mucugê is the name of the beach below the maze.

Heading south towards Trancoso the beaches are called Pitinga, Taipe, Rio da Barra and finally Trancoso. Descending from Arraial the smooth 4.5 km road to the ferry runs about 100 metres inland of Praia do Arraial and passes several pousadas.

Beaches

Praia Mucugê is good until 3 or 4 pm when the sun hides behind the hill. The nine barracas are home to do-it-yourself samba and guitar music. The far right barraca facing the ocean tends to have the best music and a fantastic batida de abacaxi (vodka and pineapple) for US$1. The far left barraca, Tia Cleuza, has indescribably good fried shrimp. A shrimp experience can be had for US$2.

Notes on nude sun-bathing: it's OK for women to go topless anywhere. Nude sun-bathing is OK for both men and women on Pitinga beach and points further south.

Places to Stay

Pousadas are popping up every day. Old pousadas change their names, management comes and goes and owners trade property deeds like baseball cards. In short, this information may be dated six months from now. Most of the pousadas don't have phones, but you may make reservations by leaving a message at Arraial's phone station. Camping is permitted on Arraial's beaches. The pousadas in Arraial tend to be rustic and often have fierce mosquitoes, so make sure your room has either a well-fitting mosquito net over the bed or preferably a fan.

The luxurious *Aldeia do Sol* below town on the way to the ferry, has beach chalets and cabanas with all the facilities you can imagine. *Pousada os Coqueiros* (follow the signs) is a very pretty, very hip and very noisy hangout for wandering musicians, the chic, the young and the wanna-be-young crowd. Rooms are US$8 to US$14 and you should bargain.

The *Pousada e Restaurante Erva Doce* in the maze is quiet, with attractive split-level units. For reservations (high season US$20, low season US$12.50) call São Paulo (011) 652-866 or leave your name and message at Arraial's phone station. *Hotel Pousada Tororão* accepts reservations (tel Rio (021) 247-0864) for its single/double/triple chalets which cost US$19/24/30. Cosy, very clean rooms, friendly staff, restaurant and bar make this a good deal. Across the street is *Pousada Cajueiros* with good breakfasts, mosquito nets, private bath and hammocks at negotiable prices.

Pousada Iemanjá, a dumpy little place on Broadway, has rooms with mosquito nets and private bath for as little as US$2.50 per person. For other cheap deals check out the pousadas by the ferry crossing.

Places to Eat

Restaurants on Broadway serve the unavoidable prato feito. Also on Broadway, *Restaurante Mama Mia* features people watching, drugs and respectable pizza (US$2.50). The barracas down at the beach have excellent fried shrimp and other seafood.

Entertainment

Arraial is pretty lively in the evenings. Cruise Broadway for drinking and lambada or forró dancing. Arraial's pousadas host open fiestas with musicians every evening. Pousada os Coqueiros is a favourite party spot. Once a month people gather on Mucugê to sing, dance and howl at the moon.

A Warning

At less than one-third the cost in the US, many people are tempted by cocaine, but be very cautious. Police in Porto Seguro are aware of Arraial's drug traffic and there have been a couple of drug-related murders.

Getting There & Away

See Porto Seguro above for ferry details. From the ferry landing there are four approaches to Arraial d'Ajuda: a lovely four km hike along the beach, a taxi to town, a VW Kombi-van to Mucugê beach or bus to town.

TRANCOSO

The village lies on a grassy bluff overlooking the ocean and Trancoso's fantastic beaches. Pousadas and restaurants are simple, campgrounds OK, but your best bet is to rent a house on the beach.

Trancoso does have electricity and overpriced bottled beer.

Places to Stay & Eat

Pousadas *Miramar, Sembura, Fonte das Canoas* and *Tudo Azul no Verde* offer simple rooms: bargain for low season rates and count on US$8 to US$12.50 in the high season.

Take your pick from Restaurants *Santa Rita, Evani, Malu, Quadrado* and others for the dreaded prato feito.

Getting There & Away

The bus to Trancoso from Arraial leaves three times a day at 7 am, 10 am and 2 pm from the ferry landing and Broadway (50c). There are more buses during the high season. Trancoso is 22 km from Arraial on a poor and winding road versus 13 km by foot along the beach. Passengers must leave the bus while it crosses the rickety bridge spanning the Rio Taipe (to lighten the load and allow the *cobrador* (conductor) to fix the planks) and pray fervently while the bus attempts the 35° incline killer-hill just before town.

The walk back from Trancoso to Arraial along the beach is beautiful. Hikers must ford two rivers ankle or arm-pit deep according to the tides and season. The road down to the beach is hidden near the right side of the square facing the ocean. One beach holds the coveted position between ocean surf and a fresh water lagoon. Praia Pitinga, the river beach closest to Arraial, has red and green striped sandstone cliffs, sparkling water and large grained sand.

CARAIVA

Without running water, electricity or throngs of tourists, the hamlet of Caraiva is primitive and beautiful. The beaches are lined with coconut palms and cashew trees and dashed by a churning white surf. Boats to Caraiva (40 km south of Trancoso) leave from Trancoso's pier daily during high season as soon as the boat fills (US$4 per person) and irregularly

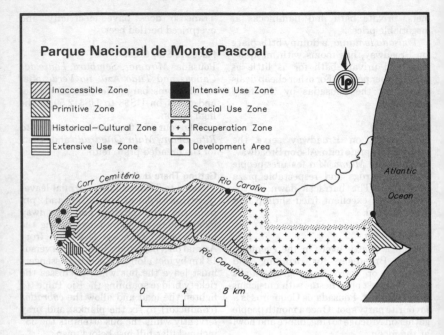

Parque Nacional de Monte Pascoal

Inaccessible Zone
Primitive Zone
Historical–Cultural Zone
Extensive Use Zone
Intensive Use Zone
Special Use Zone
Recuperation Zone
Development Area

Atlantic Ocean

Corr Cemitério
Rio Caraíva
Rio Corumbau

0   4   8 km

the rest of the year. Purportedly the municipality also operates a daily (high-season) boat to Caraiva for 75c, leaving from the pier at 3 pm.

PARQUE NACIONAL DE MONTE PASCOAL

On 22 April 1500 the Portuguese, sailing under the command of Pedro Álvares Cabral, sighted the broad 536 metre hump of Monte Pascoal, their first glimpse of the new world. Pero Vaz de Caminha, who was with Cabral, wrote about the event nearly 500 years ago:

And thus we continue our course on this sea, at length, until Tuesday of the Oitavas of Easter, which made twenty-one days of April, being from that island a work of 660 or 670 leagues according to what the pilots said, we encountered some signs of land which were long grasses which the sailors call *botelho* just like others which are given the name asses' tail. And

Wednesday the following morning we saw the birds they call *furabuchos*.

On this day, at vespers, we sighted land! First a great hill, very high and round, and other lower peaks to the south of it, and on the land great groves of tea: to the tall hill the captain gave the name of Monte Pascoal (Mount Easter) and the land, Terra de Vera Cruz (Land of the True Cross).

The park, 690 km from Salvador and 479 km from Vitória, contains a variety of ecosystems: Atlantic rainforest, secondary forests, swamplands and shallows, mangroves, beaches and reefs. The variety of the landscape is matched by the diversity in flora and fauna. There are several monkey species including the endangered spider monkey (brachyteles arachnoides), two types of sloths, anteaters, rare porcupines, cavies, capybaras (the world's largest rodent), deer, jaguar, cougar and an endless number of birds.

There are plans for a visitor's centre, marked trails, picnic tables, etc. Visitors can climb Monte Pascoal and roam through the forests at the western/BR-101 end of the park. The coastal side is accessible by boat or on foot but the north-eastern corner of the park below Caraveiras is home to a small number of Pataxó Indians and is closed to tourism.

PRADO & ALCOBAÇA

South of Monte Pascoal is Prado (Portuguese for meadow) which has fine beaches with very clean water and several hotels.

Twelve km north of town on a dirt track are the semi-deserted beaches of Paixão and Tororão. Twenty-two km further on a bad stretch of road is the lovely and lonely Praia Areia Preta and the village of Cumuruxatiba. North of Cumuruxatiba past the ocean border of Monte Pascoal Park, the village of Caraiva and all the way to Trancoso is a 50 km stretch of undeveloped coastline. There are no tourist facilities; just virgin beach for the savage tan. The road peters out beyond Caraiva and there is only a miserable unpaved road from Trancoso to Porto Seguro.

South from Prado is Alcobaça, the beach town immediately north of Caravelas.

Places to Stay

Prado has a number of hotels including the low priced *Praia do Mar Azul* (tel 298-1264) on Avenida 2 de Julho with singles/doubles for US$4/6.50. Out of town towards Barra do Farol there's also a *Camping Club do Brasil* with shady sites near the beach.

The middle range *Costa Sul* (tel 298-1069) is on Avenida José Fontes Almeida with singles for US$6.50. At the top end of the Prado price scale *Júlio César* (tel 298-1168) is Rua Dom Pedro II on the beach. Further north at the village of Cumuruxatiba there's a modest pousada and a restaurant. Camping is permitted.

South towards Caravelas, Alcobaça has hotels, restaurants and good beaches.

CARAVELAS

Caravelas, 54 km from Teixeira de Freitas on BR-101, is not only a gateway to Abrolhos but also a respectable beach town. In addition to Praia Grauça (10 km north of town on a dirt track) and Pontal do Sul across the river, Caravelas has the island beaches of Coroa da Barra (30 minutes by boat) and Coroa Vermelha (1½ hours by boat).

Places to Stay

There are two hotels in and about town. *Shangri-La* (tel 297- 1059) at Rua Sete de Setembro 219 has singles/doubles for US$3.50. *Pousada das Sereias* is on Praia Grauça, a beach 10 km from town in Barra de Caravelas. Pousada das Sereias rents out scuba gear.

PARQUE NACIONAL MARINHO DOS ABROLHOS

Abrolhos, Brazil's first and only marine park, is a pristine archipelago 80 km off-shore from Caravelas. Santa Bárbara, the only inhabited island of the archipelagos' five, has a lighthouse built in 1861, and a handful of buildings. Abrolhos is being preserved because of its coral reefs and crystal clear waters, which are supposed to be great for scuba diving. But the only approach is by boat, and staying on the islands is prohibited. The Brazilian navy considers the area strategic, therefore only underwater photography is permitted.

You can reach Abrolhos from Caravelas, by fishing boats which leave early each morning (four hour ride each way, US$75 per boat load). For more information call Antônio Carlos, Secretaria de Turismo de Caravelas (073) 297-1149. From Porto Seguro, the Companhia do Mar Passeios de Escunas (tel (073) 288- 2381) on Praça dos Pataxós organises five-day schooner trips which cruise south along the Bahian coast then on to Abrolhos. The fare of US$150 per person includes food, lodging (bunks on the boat), transport and visitor's licence from the Capitania of Porto Seguro. A minimum of 10 passengers is needed.

West of Salvador

FEIRA DE SANTANA
Population: 230,000

At the crossroads of BR-101, BR-116 and BR-124, this is the main city of Bahia's interior and a great cattle centre. There's not much to see here except the Feira de Gado, the big Monday cattle market (lot's of tough leather), which is great fun but don't expect to buy much, and the Mercado de Arte Popular (open daily except Sundays). The Casa do Sertão Folklore Museum might also be worth a look.

Two months after carnival, Feira de Santana is the scene of the Micareta – a 60-year-old local version of Carnival which brings together the best trios elétricos of Salvador, with local blocos, samba schools and folklore groups.

The heart of the Micareta is on Avenida Getúlio Vargas, the city's main street, where 20 trios sing-along for five days. The festivities begin on Thursday with the gay dance and the opening ceremony. The Tennis and Cajueiro clubs hold big dances like the traditional *Uma Noite no Havaí* (a night in Hawaii). For those who missed out on Carnival in Salvador, the Micareta could be the next best thing.

Places to Stay
There are many cheap hotels near the rodoviária like the *Hotel Samburá* (tel 221-8511) or the *Hotel Solar Santana* on Avenida Senhor dos Passos, near the festivities. The *Feira Palace* (tel 221-5011) at Avenida Maria Quitéria 1572 is a four-star affair with singles starting at US$24 and doubles US$28.

Getting There & Away
Frequent buses make the two-hour journey from Salvador for US$1. The bus station mural by Lénio Braga was painted in 1967.

SALVADOR TO LENÇÓIS
The seven hour bus odyssey from Salvador to Lençóis first goes through Feira de Santana and then continues through some sertão, the journey punctuated by circling hawks, patches of low scrub and cactus, thin cows and a long narrow road pointing toward low buttes on the gently curving horizon.

The bus stops for lunch at Itaberaba's rodoviária restaurant. The menu includes two typical sertão dishes: *carne de sol com pirão de leite* (dried salted beef with manioc and milk sauce to take the edge off the salt) for US$2 and *sopa de feijão* (bean soup with floating UPO's – unidentified pig's organs) for 25c.

If you go by car, there are fuel station on BR-242 east in Tanquilo, some 22 km out of town. The nearest station to the west is around 30 km away.

LENÇÓIS
Population: 2228

Lençóis lies in a gorgeous, wooded, mountain region – the Chapada Diamantina – an oasis of green in the dusty sertão, where you'll find solitude, small towns steeped in the history and superstition of the garimpeiros (prospectors), and great hiking to peaks, waterfalls and rivers. If you want to see something completely different, and have time for only one excursion into the Northeastern interior, this is the one.

The natural beauty of the region and the tranquillity of the small, colonial towns has attracted a steady trickle of travellers for several years; some have never left. These new residents have spearheaded an active environmental movement that successfully lobbied the government to declare the region a national park.

History

The history of Lençóis epitomises the story of the diamond boom and bust. After earlier expeditions by bandeirantes proved fruitless, the first diamonds were found in the Chapada Velha in 1822. After the large strikes in the Rio Mucujê in 1844, prospectors, roughnecks and adventurers arrived from all over Brazil to seek their fortunes.

The garimpeiros began to work the mines searching for diamonds near kimberlite, an indicator stone, and in alluvial deposits. They settled in makeshift tents which, from the hills above, looked like sheets of laundry drying in the wind, hence the name of Lençóis (Portuguese for sheets). The tents of the diamond prospectors grew into cities: Vila Velha de Palmeiras, Andaraí, Piatã, Xique-Xique and the most attractive of them all, the stone city of Lençóis. Exaggerated stories of endless riches in the Diamantina mines precipitated mass migrations, but the area was rich in dirty industrial stones, not display-quality gems.

At the height of the diamond boom the French, who purchased diamonds for drilling the Panama Canal (1881-1889), built a vice- consulate in Lençóis. French fashions and *bon mots* made their way into town but with the depletion of diamonds, the fall-off in French demand (and subsequently the fall in diamond prices on the international market) and the newly discovered South African mines, the boom went bust at the beginning of the 20th century.

Nowadays, the town economy has turned to coffee, manioc and tourism but the locals still dream of diamonds. The last few garimpeiros are using powerful and destructive water pumps to wrench diamonds from the riverbeds.

A Little Geology

According to geologists, the diamonds in the Chapada Diamantina were formed in ancient volcanoes millions of years ago in an area near present day Namibia.

Ironically, Bahia was contiguous to Africa before the continental drift. As the volcanoes were eroded the diamonds were mixed with pebbles, swept into the depths of the sea – which covered what today is inland Brazil – and imprisoned as the conglomeration turned to stone. With the formation of the Chapada Diamantina this layer of conglomerate stone was elevated, and the forces of erosion released the trapped diamonds and brought them to rest in the riverbeds.

Information & Orientation

The Prefeitura Municipal at Praça Otaviano Alves 8 is a pretty building with black and white photos of old Lençóis and some scanty tourist information which can be supplemented by local experts. Biologist Roy Funch, ex-American from Arizona and now a naturalised citizen, came to Brazil 10 years ago with the Peace Corps. He pushed for the creation of a National Park and is now director of the Parque Nacional da Chapada Diamantina.

Luis Krug from São Paulo is a friendly, bearded guide who knows the history, geography and biology of the area as well as the trails. Eliane, who works at Pousalegre, knows the local history of garimpeiros; African princes; and men of letters.

Things to See

The city is pretty and easily seen on foot, although unfortunately most of the buildings are closed to the public. See the French vice-consulate, a blue 19th century building where diamond commerce was negotiated. Other buildings include the Casa do Artesão, the first lapidary of Lençóis, the House and Museum of Afrânio Peixoto with the personal effects and works of the writer, the Quartel of Colonel Horácio Matos, and the Urbano Duarte Library.

Parque Nacional da Chapada Diamantina

Many of the foreigners who came only to visit have settled permanently in Lençóis.

They have been the backbone of a strong ecological movement which is in direct opposition to the extractive mentality of the garimpeiros and many of the locals. Riverbeds have been dug up, waters poisoned and game hunted for food and sport. Much of the land has been ravaged by forest fires. The hunting and depletion of habitat has thinned the animal population severely.

After six years of bureaucratic battles, Roy Funch helped convince the government to create the Parque Nacional da Chapada Diamantina to protect the natural beauty of the area. Signed into law in 1985, the park roughly spans the quadrangle formed by the cities of Lençóis and Mucujê, Palmeiras and Andaraí. The park, 1520 square km of the Sincora range of the Diamantina plateau, has several species of monkeys, beautiful views, clean waterfalls, rivers and streams, and an endless network of trails. Although bromelias, velosiaceas, philodendrons and strawflowers are protected by law, these plants have been uprooted nearly to extinction for the ornamental plant market.

The park is particularly interesting for rock hounds who will appreciate the curious geomorphology of the region. There is no park infrastructure, and there are no maps of the park so it's best to arrange for a guide at the Pousada de Lençóis.

Near Lençóis The Salão de Areias Coloridas (room of coloured sand) is where artisans gather their matéria prima for bottled sand paintings. It's only one km from town. The Rio Ribeirão, tributary of Rio São José, has swimming holes and a natural water-slide (bring old clothes or borrow a burlap sack). It's 45 minutes from town, ask local children to guide you. From Capitação (water company) above Pousada do Lençóis follow the trail to the Rio Lençóis and walk upstream a few minutes to a pretty little waterfall. Some trails continue further along the river and up into the hills. These trails are poorly marked, the terrain is confusing and it's easy to get lost.

Festivals
According to legend, a horrible serpent covered with feathers lives under the Ponte dos Arcos Romanos. Every year the parade for Nosso Senhor dos Passos, the patron saint of prospectors and the city of Lençóis, passes back and forth over the bridge to appease the monster and keep him from devouring the city. The celebration starts on 24 January and culminates on 2 February with the *Noite dos Garimpeiros* (prospectors night).

The author's week, Semana de Afrânio Peixoto, is 11-18 December and coincides with the municipality's emancipation from slavery.

Jarê is the regional variation on Candomblé. The principal holidays take place in January and September. Lamentação das Almas is a mystic festival held during Lent.

Places to Stay
The choices for lodging are simple. *Pousalegre* (tel 334-1124) on Praça Aureliano Sé is the traveller's hangout and the clear favourite at US$3 per person, including hot showers down the hall. The price includes a superb breakfast featuring the standard fare plus cous-cous, eggs and *baje* (a warm, buttered manioc pancake with the consistency of a very chewy styrofoam polymer). It's booked solid on weekends.

Pousada Bugrinhos is not quite as cheap or as good. *Camping Lumiar* on Praçca Afrânio Peixote is in town, but it is quiet. There are shady sites, dirty bathrooms, a bar and a restaurant but watch out for Pablito and his marauding chickens. *Camping da Granja* is 11 km out of town towards BR-242.

The middle range candidate is *Hotel Colonial* (tel 344-1114) on Praça Otaviano Alves. They have brand new

Top: Camamen, Bahia (MS)
Left: 'Jangada' boat, Bahia (JM)
Right: Valença, Bahia (MS)

Top: Fishermen and houses, Maceio, Alagoas (KM)
Left: Fishermen in Alagoas (JM)

singles for US$9 and doubles for US$12 with private bath.

At the top end the *Pousada de Lençóis* (tel 334-1102) on Praça Otaviano Alves is an attractive Bahiatursa operation with a swimming pool, frigobar, air-con, restaurant and bar. Singles/doubles are from US$13/15.

Places to Eat

Without a doubt the best meals and deals are at the *Pousalegre*, with a huge ensopado de peixe (fish stew) for US$2. *Frutaria-Lanchonete Flor da Terra*, next door, is good for light lunches of natural food: yoghurt, juices, omelettes and pancakes. The *Pousada de Lençóis* also has a restaurant.

Skip the *Dom Ratão* which is reputed to serve game illegally caught in the park. The *Lagedo Bar & Restaurant* (across the bridge on the other side of town) is the evening hangout.

Things to Buy

Funkart at Praça do Matos 854 (Antiga Praça do Mercado) and other artisan/trinket shops sell crochet, lace-work, and bottles of coloured sand.

Getting There & Away

It's a hot seven hour bus ride inland from Salvador to Lençóis, which is 12 km off BR-242 (Salvador-Seabra highway) at an altitude of 400 metres.

The Paraíso Bus Company at Rua Almirante Barroso 16 (Antiga Rua das Pedras) is a few doors down from the Praça Aureliano Sé (Antiga Praça dos Nagôs) bus stop. Buses to Salvador leave at 9 am and 9 pm. Buses from Salvador leave at 9.15 am and 8.15 pm. The fare is US$3. Buses to Palmeiras and Seabra leave at 3 am and 4 pm.

AROUND LENÇÓIS

There are many natural wonders, known only by a handful of locals, throughout the Chapada Diamantina as well as many inaccessible, but fascinating, ghost towns like Xique Xique de Igatu. A car and a guide are often recommended for these excursions, so ask around. There are many surprises in the region.

The Rio Mucujezinho, 30 km from town, is a super day trip. Rita and Marco are cave dwellers with a snack bar there. Ask local children to help you pick your way about two km along the river to a 30 metre waterfall and swimming hole. Take the 7.30 to 8 am Palmeiras/Seabra bus, ask the driver to stop at Mucujezinho and to pick you up on his return trip. Morro do Pai Inácio, the tallest peak in the immediate area (1200 metres) is 27 km away by road. An easy trail takes you to the summit (200 metres above the highway) for a beautiful view. The Cachoeira Glass, named after missionary George Glass, plummets 450 metres. It may be the highest waterfall in Brazil. It's easy to get to the top (68 km by road and two hours on foot), but to get to the bottom of the falls is a very long day trip or a better overnight hike. Speak to Luis Krug.

Other trips from Lençóis include Praia do Rio São José (Zaida), Cachoeira de Primavera (1½ hours on foot), Estrela de Céu in the Garimpo region (two hours on foot), Gruta da Pratinha (70 km by car), Gruta da Lapa Dolce (70 km car then 45 minutes on foot, bring a light), Capão (18 km, one day on foot, bring overnight gear), Palmeiras to see the house of João Macedo (56 km), Andaraí (100 km), Mucujê (150 km), Lagoa Encantada (121 km) and Xique Xique de Igatu (highly recommended).

RIO SÃO FRANCISCO

For the Brazilian, particularly the Nordestino, it's impossible to speak about the Rio São Francisco without a dose of pride and emotion. The third most important river in Brazil, after the Amazon and Paraguay, there is no river that is anthropomorphised like the São Francisco. Everyone who knows the São Francisco, especially those who live along its banks, speak of it as a friend. For the river has a personality that's a mixture of an old scholar, a companion and a protector. Thus the affectionate nickname *velho chico* or *chicão* (chico is short for Francisco).

The geographical situation of the São Francisco gave it a prominence in the colonial history of Brazil that surpassed the Amazon. Born from the Serra da Canastre, 1500 metres high in Minas Gerais, the Rio São Francisco descends from south to north, crossing the greater part of the Northeast sertão, and completing its 3160 km journey in the Atlantic Ocean after slicing through the states of Minas Gerais and Bahia, and delineating the borders of the states of Bahia, Pernambuco, Sergipe and Alagoas.

For three centuries the São Francisco, also called the river of national unity, represented the only connection between the small towns at the extremes of the sertão and the coast. Discovered in the 17th century, the river was the best way, and one of the few, to penetrate the semi-arid Northeastern interior. Thus the frontier grew along the margins of the river. The economic basis of these settlements was cattle, first to provide the desperately needed food for the gold miners in Minas Gerais in the 18th century, and later the cacao plantations in southern Bahia.

With cattle came permanent settlements and the civilisation of cattle. Cattle produced a common culture among the region's people, despite the enormous distances between them. This can be seen today in folklore, music and art.

The history of this area is legendary in Brazil: from the tough vaqueiros who drove the cattle, to the commerce in salt (to fatten the cows), the cultivation of rice, the rise in banditry, the battles between the big land owners and the religious fanaticism of Canudos.

The slow waters of the São Francisco ve been so vital to Brazil because in a on with devastating periodic and long ghts, the river provides one of the only guaranteed sources of water. The people who live there know this and thus, over the centuries, they have created hundreds of stories, fairy tale and myths about the river.

One example is the *bicho da água* (beast of the water), part animal and part man who walks along the bottom of the river and snores. The riverboat men must throw tobacco to the bicho da água for protection.

The river's width, varies from two hand-spans at its origins in the Serra Canastre, an empty, uninhabitable region where nothing grows, to 40 km at the Lagoa do Sobradinho, the biggest artificial lake in the world. As a result the Nordestinos believe that the São Francisco is a desert oasis given by God to the people of the sertão for all their suffering in the drought-plagued land.

River Travel

People have always travelled by the São Francisco. In the beginning there were sailboats and rowboats, then came the motorboats which became famous because of the personalities of the *barqueiros* who drove the boats and put *carrancas* on the front of the boats. Carrancas are wooden sculptures that represent an animal-like face between a dog and wolf, with big teeth and open mouth. They are now a popular folk art sold in Salvador and at fairs along the river.

Today, with the river cities linked by roads, river traffic has decreased drastically but it's still possible to travel from Pirapora, Minas Gerais to Juazeiro, Bahia and along the lower São Francisco from Penedo to Pão de Açúcar (see Penedo in Alagoas or Propriá in Sergipe).

The trip from Pirapora to Juazeiro leaves monthly and takes eight to 10 days. The boats are called *barranqueiras*. You need a hammock and rope, but food (rice and beans) is available on board. For schedules call Companhia de Navegação do São Francisco at (037) 741-1744 in Pirapora or (075) 811-2340 in Juazeiro.

It's a rough trip through a harsh land. Distances between towns are quite considerable. Most of the towns are very poor, some quite unusual. Bom Jesus da Lapa is the site of one of the most important religious festivals and processions in the sertão on 6 August.

Sergipe & Alagoas

Sergipe

Sergipe is Brazil's smallest state. It has all three zones typical of the Northeast: littoral, *zona da mata* and sertão. The coastal zone is wide and sectioned with valleys, where many of the towns lounge along sleepy rivers.

What is there to see? There are a couple of interesting historical towns – Laranjeiras and São Cristóvão – and the towns along the Rio São Francisco have a unique, captivating culture – principally Propriá and Neópolis. But the beaches are not up to snuff and the capital, Aracaju, is as memorable as last Monday's newspaper.

ESTÂNCIA
Population: 28,000
Estância, 68 km south of Aracaju, is one of the oldest towns in the state. The city has a certain amount of character and a few historic buildings in the centre, but there's little reason to stop in Estância unless you want to head to the nearby beaches (see the Mangue Seco section in Bahia) or want to avoid spending the night in Aracaju – always a good idea.

Information
Estância has most basic services, including a Banco do Brasil. The June festivals of São João are the big event.

Places to Stay
The town has a couple of simple hotels facing the central plaza. The *Hotel Bosco* ^s rooms for US$2 per person or for ^$1.50 per person without bath. The *smo Hotel Estancio* (tel 522-1404) is renovated and has doubles for US$9 ^h and US$5 without.

^re & Away
^actually a bit off highway 101,

but most buses stop in Estância. There are buses directly from Salvador and São Cristóvão, Aracaju, Propriá and Maceió to the north.

SÃO CRISTÓVÃO
Population: 12,000
Founded in 1590, São Cristóvão is reputedly Brazil's fourth oldest town and was the capital of Sergipe until 1855. With the decline of the sugar industry, the town has long been in the economic doldrums and is trying to become a tourist attraction to bring in some cash.

Things to See
The old part of town, up a steep hill, has a surprising amount of 17th and 18th century colonial buildings along its narrow stone roads. Of particular distinction are the Igreja e Convento de São Francisco with a good sacred art museum (at Praça São Francisco), the Igreja de Senhor dos Poços (Praça Senhor dos Poços, and the Assembléia e do Palácio provincial.

Festivals
Every year the town comes alive for a weekend with the Festival de Arte de São Cristóvão. The festival has both fine and popular arts, with lots of music and dance. The date of the festival changes from year to year.

Places to Stay & Eat
There is no real accommodation in town, but the old part of town has a better than expected Japanese restaurant.

Getting There & Away
São Cristóvão is 25 km south of Aracaju on a good paved road, and seven km off the BR-101. The rodoviária is down the hill below the historic district on Praça Dr Lauro de Freitas.

There are frequent buses to Aracaju and

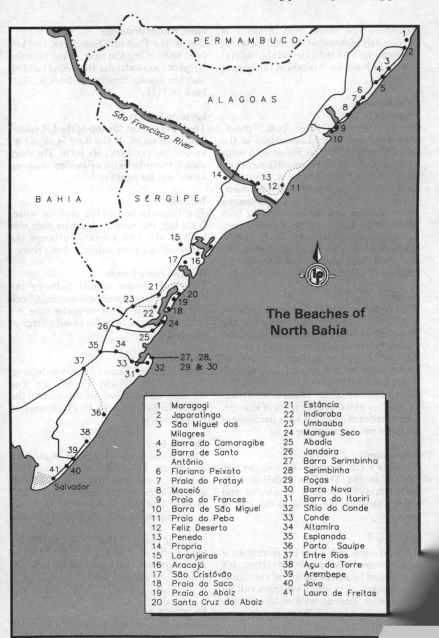

The Beaches of North Bahia

1	Maragogi	21	Estância
2	Japaratinga	22	Indiaroba
3	São Miguel dos Milagres	23	Umbauba
4	Barra do Camaragibe	24	Mangue Seco
5	Barra de Santo Antônio	25	Abadia
6	Floriano Peixoto	26	Jandaira
7	Praia do Pratayi	27	Barra Serimbinha
8	Maceió	28	Serimbinha
9	Praia do Frances	29	Poças
10	Barra de São Miguel	30	Barra Nova
11	Praia do Peba	31	Barra do Itariri
12	Feliz Deserto	32	Sítio do Conde
13	Penedo	33	Conde
14	Propria	34	Altamira
15	Laranjeiras	35	Esplanada
16	Aracajú	36	Porto Sauipe
17	São Cristóvão	37	Entre Rios
18	Praia do Saco	38	Açu da Torre
19	Praia do Abaiz	39	Arembepe
20	Santa Cruz do Abaiz	40	Java
		41	Lauro de Freitas

Estância. The drive from Aracaju is particularly pleasant as the road traverses a plateau with a pretty view of the valleys. Catch the bus from Aracaju at the central rodoviária.

LARANJEIRAS

Population: 5000

Nestled between three lush, green, church-topped hills, Laranjeiras is the colonial gem of Sergipe. Filled with ruins of old sugar mills, old terracotta roofs and stone roads, the town is relatively unblemished by modern development. There are several churches and museums worth visiting and the surrounding hills offer picturesque walks with good views. It's a charming little town, easy to get to and well worth a few hours sightseeing or a day or two exploring the town, the nearby sugar mill and the countryside.

History

First settled in 1605, Laranjeiras became, during the 18th and 19th centuries, the commercial centre for the rich sugar and cotton region along the zona mata west of Aracaju. At one point there were over 60 sugar mills in and around Laranjeiras. The processed sugar was sent down the Rio Cotinguiba about 20 km downstream to Aracaju and on to the ports of Europe. The number of churches are a reminder of the past prosperity of the town.

Information

There is a city tourism office in the city centre, in the Trapiche building, with knowledgeable workers, brochures and guides for hire, but little in the way of services.

Engenho

This old sugar mill a few km from town is semi-restored and in a lovely setting. It's now owned by Paulistas so you must go to the tourism office and have them call for permission. You can walk or hire a guide car to take you there.

Igreja de Camandaroba

Out at the Engenho Boa Sorte, two km from town along the river, is the baroque Igreja de Camandaroba, the second building that the Jesuits constructed back in 1731. back in 1731.

Igreja do Bonfim

This church is at the top of the hill called Alto do Bonfim. If the door is closed go around back and ask to be let in. The short walk is rewarded with a fine view but keep an eye out for snakes.

Trapiche

The Trapiche houses the tourism office. It's a big, impressive structure that was built in the 19th century to house the cargo waiting to be shipped down river.

Gruta da Pedra Furada

This is a one-km tunnel built by the Jesuits to escape their persecutors. Check at the tourism office to make sure it's open. The gruta is in the small village of Machado.

Museums

There is a small Museu Afro-Brasileiro on Rua José do Prado Franco s/n (no number) and a sacred art museum in the Igreja NS da Conceição, Rua Dr Francisco Bragança s/n.

Place to Stay

There is just one hotel in town, *Hotel Edla* on Praça Dr Diniz Gonçalves. It's friendly, safe and quite simple with mostly dorm-style rooms for six to eight people. The bath is down the hall, but accommodation only costs US$1.50 per person.

Out of town, at Km 75 on the BR-101 the *Flecha de Aracaju* (tel 281-1163) is more expensive with doubles for US$5.50 or US$7.50 with air-con.

Places to Eat

Aside from bars, the *Restaurant Gilberto*

is all there is for eats. The shrimp, at least, is not very good.

1	Centro de Criatividade
2	Emsetur
3	Trópicos Hotel
4	Hotel Brasília
5	Galeria Rosa Faria
6	Hotel Serigy/Aperipé
7	Hotel Jangadeiro
8	Prefeitura Municipal
9	Catedral Metropolitana
10	Centro de Turismo
11	Assembléia
12	Palácio do Governo
13	Cacique Chá
14	Posto Telefónico (Telephone Centre)
15	Grande Hotel
16	Hotel Palace
17	Mercado Municipal
18	Ponte do Imperador
19	Terminal Hydroviário

Getting There & Away

Laranjeiras is 15 km from Aracaju and four km off the BR-101. Buses leave from and return to the rodoviária in Aracaju every hour. It's a 20-minute ride with the first bus leaving for Laranjeiras at 5 am and the last returning at 9 pm. Any bus travelling the BR-101 can let you off at the road to Laranjeiras, then you can walk, hitch or flag down a bus for the four km to town.

ARACAJU

Population: 290,000

Aracaju just may be the Cleveland of the Northeast. The city has little to offer the visitor – there is no colonial inheritance – and is visually quite unattractive. Even the beaches are below the prevailing high-standard in the Brazilian Northeast.

History

Some of this lack of appeal stems from the

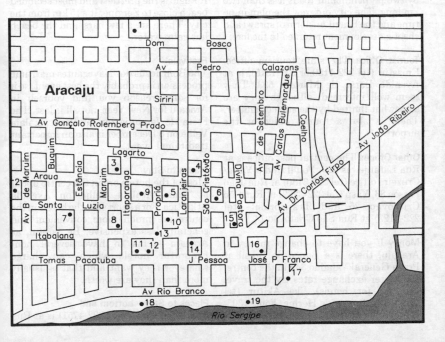

fact that Aracaju was not the most important city in the state during the colonial era. In fact, when it was chosen as the new capital in 1855, Santo Antônio de Aracaju was a small settlement with nothing but a good deep harbour – badly needed at the time to handle the ships transporting the sugar to Europe.

With residents of the old capital of São Cristóvão on the verge of armed revolt, the new capital was placed on a hill five km from the mouth of the Rio Sergipe. Within a year an epidemic broke out that decimated the city. All the residents of São Cristóvão naturally saw this as an omen that Aracaju was destined to be a poor capital. I guess they were right.

Information & Orientation

Aracaju is 367 km north of Salvador and 307 km south of Maceió and was Brazil's first planned city. The plan was a modest one. It called for a grid-pattern intersected by two perpendicular roads less than two km long. The city outgrew the plan in no time and the Brazilian norm of sprawl and chaotic development returned to the fore.

Tourist Office The state tourism office, Emsetur (tel 222-1150 or 222-1315), is at Avenida Barão de Maruim 593. They seem well informed, although they are somewhat limited by the subject matter. There is also a tourist office at the airport.

Other Offices The central post office is at Rua Laranjeiras 229. You'll find a Varig/Cruzeiro office (tel 222-3130) at Rua João Pessoa 86, Vasp (tel 222-3232) at Rua São Cristóvão 26 and Transbrasil (tel 222-2123) at Rua São Cristóvão 14.

Money If you have to change money in Aracaju, there is a Banco do Brasil at Praça General Valadão 341 in the centre. For better exchange rates try the travel agencies (or hotels) like Akitur (tel 222-6537) at Avenida Hermes Fontes 305, Banorte Turismo (tel 222-1142) at

Travessa Deusdeth Fontes 17, Robson Turismo (tel 222-0107), Serigy Turismo (tel 224-3344) or Sergitur Turismo (tel 222-9250), the latter three are at Rua João Pessoa 71.

Beaches

Out on a sand-bar island off the Rio Sergipe, Praia Atalaia Nova (atalaia is Portuguese for watch-tower) is a popular weekend beach. Boats leave frequently from the Terminal Hidroviário on Avenida Rio Branco (near where Divina Pastora hits the river). It's a 20-minute ride across the river.

Praia das Artistas and Atalaia Velha are the closest beaches to the city. They are crowded, with traffic jams on weekends, and built-up with hotels, motels, restaurants, bars and barracas. They are good places for sidewalk seafood.

Further south on the road to Mosqueiro, Refúgio is the prettiest and most secluded beach close to Sergipe. It's 15 km from the city. There are a few bars, and the beach has calm water.

Festivals

The Bom Jesus dos Navegantes maritime procession is probably the best event, so if for some reason you find yourself in Aracaju for New Year, not all is lost. The Festa de Iemanjá out at Praia Atalaia Velha on 8 December is also an important traditional event.

Places to Stay

Most of the hotels are in the centre or out at Praia Atalaia Velha on Avenida Atlântica. For a short stay the hotels in the centre are much more convenient and generally less expensive. Be careful, as Aracaju seems to have several non-Embratur hotels which can charge whatever they want and that is usually more than they are worth.

Places to Stay – bottom end

The *Hotel Capri* (tel 222-4751) is at Rua

Apulcro Mota 573 and the *Ideal Hotel* (tel 224-1374) is on the same street at 677-A. Singles are US$5.50/6.50 and doubles US$6.50/10 without/with air-con. Other possibilities include the *Hotel Siqueira Campos* at Rua Tomar de Gerú s/n (no number) and the *Hotel Central* at Rua Professor Florentino Menezes 24.

Places to Stay – middle
My favourite mid-range hotel is the *Jangadeiro* (tel 222-5115) at Rua Santa Luzia 269. It's in the centre, a convenient bus ride from the rodoviária. New and clean, the hotel serves a good breakfast, has all amenities and charges US$12 for doubles. Nearby at Rua Santo Amaro 269 the *Serigy* (tel 222-1210) is almost as good with singles/doubles for US$13/15. For a bit more, the three-star *Grande Hotel* (tel 222-2112) is close by at Rua Itabaianinha 371. Singles/doubles are US$18/20.

Places to Stay – top end
If you want a five-star hotel in Aracaju, the *Parque dos Coqueiros* (tel 223-1511) out at Rua Francisco Rabelo Leite Neto 1075, Praia Atalaia Velha is the place. Singles/doubles are $60/67.

Places to Eat
Artnatus serves plain vegetarian food downtown at Rua Santo Amaro 282 but it is only open for lunch. For seafood, try the *Taberna do Tropeiro* at Avenida Oceânica 6, Atalaia Velha.

Getting There & Away
Air The major airlines fly to Rio, São Paulo, Salvador, Recife, Maceió, Brasília, Goiânia and Curitiba.

Bus Several buses a day make the five-hour trip from Salvador and the 4½ hour trip from Maceió. Recife is eight hours away and costs US$3. There are frequent buses from all the bigger towns in Alagoas including Penedo.

Getting Around
Airport Transport The airport (tel 223-1929) is 11 km south of town on Santa Maria.

Local Transport The rodoviária (tel 221-1376) is on the west side of town on Avenida 31 de Março. To get there catch a bus heading west, away from the river, on Avenida Barão de Maruim and ask where to get off.

PROPRIÁ
Population: 20,000
Propriá is 81 km north of Aracaju where BR-101 crosses the mighty Rio São Francisco – the river of national unity. While the town is less interesting than the downriver cities of Penedo and Neópolis, it has the same combination of colonial charm and a strong river culture. And it's the easiest place to hop off the bus and catch a boat up or down the river. Market days in Propriá, with goods from up and down the São Francisco, are Thursdays and Fridays.

Festivals
Bom Jesus dos Navegantes on the last Sunday in January is a colourful affair with a maritime procession and *reisado* – a dramatic dance that celebrates the epiphany. It is highly recommended.

Places to Stay
The town's two hotels are near each other facing the church. The *Hotel Imperial* charges by the room not the number of people, with rooms costing from US$5 to US$15. A nice double, for example, with bath and fan costs US$10. It's a very clean place and one of the few hotels in Brazil with a pool table.

The *Status Hotel* (tel 322-1537) has singles with bath for US$5.50 but it's not nearly as nice, although the staff are very friendly.

Boat Trips
Boats go as far as Pão de Açúcar upriver, about a nine hour ride by motorboat, with

stops at all the towns along the way. The *Iolanda* leaves at 6.30 am Saturdays and Tuesdays and for US$1 this may be the cheapest boat in Bahia. The *Iolanda* leaves Pão de Açúcar for the return on Mondays and Wednesdays at 10 am.

There are plenty of other boats which leave irregularly, you can bargain a ride on any of them, including the beautiful *avelas* with their long, curved masts and striking yellow or red sails.

The trip to Propriá, down the river, takes about four or five hours by avela or rowboat and should cost 25c to 50c.

Getting There & Away

Propriá is right off BR-101. There are plenty of buses heading there from the major cities north and south and if the bus doesn't go into town they should stop at the highway from where it's a short walk into town. Off the main highway, there are frequent buses to Neópolis. Despite the 42 km of unpaved road, the bus is quicker than the boat.

To Penedo the paved road is around 98 km. The alternative, if you don't want to sail the river, is to drive, if you have a car, or hitch along a dirt road that is not shown on the maps, but which follows the north side of the river. Find the first dirt turn-off from the highway, just after the bridge, and you're away.

Alagoas

The small state of Alagoas is one of the pleasant surprises of the Northeast. The capital Maceió is a relaxed, modern city, its beaches are enchanting, with calm, emerald waters. Penedo is the colonial masterpiece of the state with a fascinating river culture on the Rio São Francisco.

There is a fabulous stretch of the zona mata. It's a stunning, winding drive through lush valleys of sugar cane, interesting villages like Porto Calvo and an occasional sugar refinery that helps

you remember which century this is. There is a rough dirt road along most of the coast – but there are buses – and because of the slow going there are many undisturbed fishing villages with fabulous beaches shaded by rows of coconut trees.

History

The mighty republic of runaway slaves – Palmares – was in present-day Alagoas. During the invasion by the Dutch in 1630, many slaves escaped to the forest in the mountains between Garanhuns and Palmares. Today, where the towns of Viçosa, Capela, Atalaia, Porto Calvo and União dos Palmares stand, there were once virgin forests with thick growth and plenty of animals. Alagoas today has the highest population density in the Northeast.

MACEIÓ

Population: 400,000

Maceió, the capital of Alagoas, is 292 km north of Aracaju and 259 km south of Recife. A manageable place for the visitor, the city has a modern but relaxed feeling with endless sun and sea.

Women washing clothes outside Maceió

Information

Tourist Office Ematur (tel 223-6931 or 223-6868) the state tourist agency, is at Praça do Centenário 1135 in Farol. They have information booths at the airport, the Calçadão do Comércio on Rua Dr Pontes de Miranda (centro) and at the rodoviária. At the rodoviária booth they have a list of all hotels with prices and will ring around and make a reservation for you.

Post & Telephone There is a post office at Rua João Pessoa 5, Centro and at Avenida Moreira e Silva 391, Farol. Telasa, the phone company, has offices in the centre at Rua Cons Lourenço de Albuquerque 369 and Rua Joaquim Távora 320, as well as Rua Zeferino Rodrigues 207 in Pajuçara.

Money For money exchange check the hotels and travel agents. Aeroturismo (tel 221-4478) at Rua Barão de Penedo 61, Centro is worth a try as are Pajuçara Turismo and Mundialtur, down the same street.

Airlines The major airline offices are in the centre. Varig/Cruzeiro (tel 223-7324) is at Rua Dr Luiz Pontes de Miranda 42, Vasp (tel 223-7188) is at Rua do Comércio 56 and Transbrasil (tel 223-4830) is at Rua Barão de Penedo 213.

Beaches

Maceió's beaches are simply superb. In the city, Praia do Sobral and Avenida are nice (but supposedly polluted) with good bodysurfing. Your best bet is to head north for the best beaches in the Northeast. Protected by a coral reef, the ocean is calm and a deep emerald colour. On shore there are loads of barracas, often jangadas and always sunworshippers.

The beaches to the north are Pajuçara (three km from the centre), Sete Coqueiros (four km), Ponta Verde (five km), Jatiúca (six km), Jacarecica (nine km), Guaxuma (12 km), Garça Torta (14 km), Riacho Doce (16 km) and Pratagi (17 km). You won't go wrong with any of these tropical paradises, but they do get busy on weekends and during the summer when there are many local buses cruising the beaches. The Fátima bus will get you to most of these although sometimes a taxi is worth a few dollars to get to one of the less crowded beaches. The Santuário or Ponta Verde bus goes from the centre to Pajuçara.

Festivals

Maceió is supposed to have a pretty lively Carnival which is still considerably calmer and safer than Rio's. They have active samba clubs and, of course, the beaches. There is a Festa do Mar in December.

Places to Stay – bottom end

The city tourism office (tel 221-8987) can help with inexpensive lodging. Most of the hotels listed below are near Praia da Pajuçara, a couple of blocks from the beach. There are also some very cheap hotels in the centre near the Hotel Flórida.

The best deal in town is the *Rex Pousada* (tel 231-7124) at Rua Dr Antônio Pedro de Mendonça 311. You can call ahead for reservations (not a bad idea during the summer). It's clean and friendly and only 50 metres from Praia da Pajuçara. Rooms are US$5 a double without bath. They don't have single rooms but you can share a room with one other person for only US$2.50.

Pousada Costa Verde (tel 231-4745) is cheap and friendly. They have colectivas, a bed in a shared room, for only US$2 and the pousada is only a block from the beach at Rua Jangadeiros Alagoanos 429, Pajuçara. A great deal if you don't mind a shared room.

The *Ney Hotel* (tel 221-6500) is closer to the centre at Avenida Duque de Caxias 910, Praia Atlântica. They have air-con rooms with baths. Singles are US$6.50 and doubles US$9. It's a very clean and safe hotel.

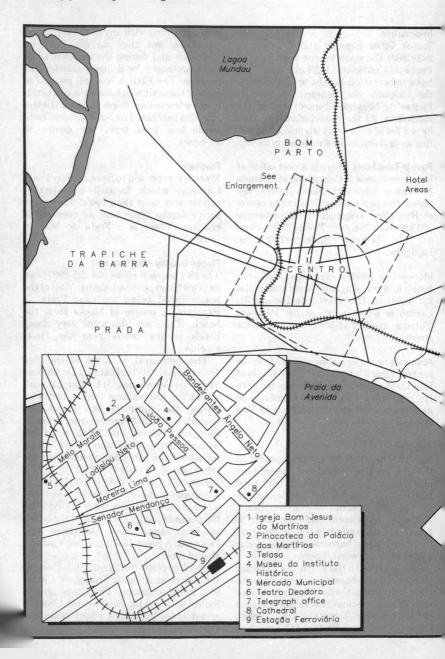

1 Igreja Bom Jesus do Martírios
2 Pinacoteca do Palácio dos Martírios
3 Telasa
4 Museu do Instituto Histórico
5 Mercado Municipal
6 Teatro Deodoro
7 Telegraph office
8 Cathedral
9 Estação Ferroviária

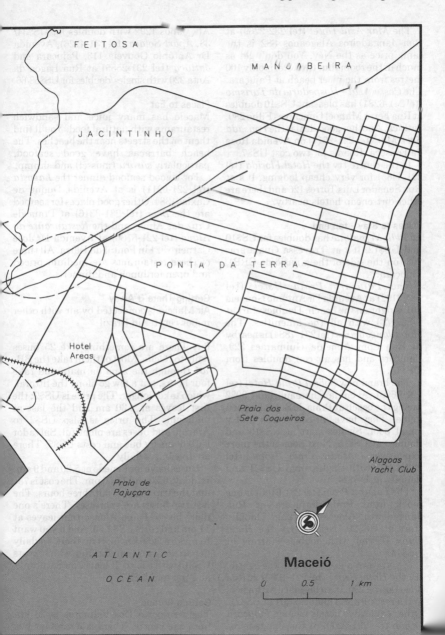

FEITOSA

MANGABEIRA

JACINTINHO

PONTA DA TERRA

Hotel
Areas

Praia dos
Sete Coqueiros

Alagoas
Yacht Club

Praia de
Pajuçara

ATLANTIC

OCEAN

Maceió

0   0.5   1 km

The *Mar Azul Hotel* (tel 232-2269) at Rua Jangadeiros Alagoanos 882 is the same price as the Ney. You don't get as much in the rooms but the hotel is only 100 metres from the nicer beach at Pajuçara. The *Costa Azul – Hospedaria de Turismo* (tel 231-6281) has pleasant US$10 doubles at Rua Ferro Manoel Gonçalves Filho 280, Jatiúca. Another good deal is the *Pousada Sol e Mar* (tel 221-2611) on Avenida Rosa da Fonseca. Rooms for two cost US$7.

In the centre try the *Hotel Florida* (tel 221-4485) for very cheap lodging. It's at Rua Senador Luis Torres 126 and there are other dirt-cheap hotels nearby.

Places to Stay – top end

La Belle Veronique has doubles for US$10 and US$12. It's at Travessa Guajararas 103 (on the side of the ginásio do CRB), Pajuçara.

The *Pajuçara Praia Hotel* (tel 231-3192) at Avenida Dr Antônio Gouveia 261 is right on the beach. Doubles start at US$21/23 with all the amenities. The *Hotel Jangadeiros* (tel 231-7884) is nearby at Rua Com Almeida Guimarães 329, Pajuçara and has air-con doubles from US$16.

The brand new *Sobral Praia Hotel* (tel 221-6665), Avenida Chateaubriand 3022 facing the beach at Praia do Sobral is good value. They have air-con rooms and a small pool. Singles start at US$13 and doubles at US$15. Next door is the more expensive *Jangada Praia Hotel* (tel 223-4102) with singles from US$21 and doubles at US$24.

The *Laguna Praia* (tel 231-6180) is one block from Praia Pajuçara at Rua Jangadeiros Alagoanos 1231. Doubles start at US$20. Nearby, try the *Hotel Buon Giorno* with doubles starting at US$14.

If you want a good hotel in the centre, try the *Hotel Beiriz* (tel 221-1080) at Rua João Pessoa 290. It's a big place with a pool and a restaurant. Doubles start at US$21. Other expensive hotels include *Pajuçara Othon* (tel 231-2200) at Rua Jangadeiros

Alagoanos 1292 with doubles for US$34/38, *Apart Solara* (tel 231-4726), Avenida Dr Antônio Gouveia 113, Pajuçara and *Jatiúca* (tel 231-2555) at Rua Lagoa da Anta 220 with singles/doubles for US$58/66.

Places to Eat

Maceió has many juice and sandwich restaurants with natural food. You'll find them on the streets near the beaches. The beach barracas have good seafood, particularly *sururu* (mussel) and shrimp.

For a good seafood dinner the *Lagosta* (tel 221-6211) is at Avenida Duque de Caxias 1384. Other good places for seafood are the *Bem* (tel 231-3316) at Praia de Cruz das Almas and the *Restaurante do Alípio* (tel 221-5186) at Avenida Dr José Carneiro 321 in Pontal da Barra. All three of these restaurants are medium priced and open for lunch and dinner.

Getting There & Away

Air Maceió is connected by air with other major centres in Brazil.

Bus There are something like 25 buses daily to Recife. Most of them take the BR-101 through the zona da mata and take four hours, but a few go along the littoral, which takes longer. The price is US$2; the first leaves at 4.30 am and the last at midnight. The price is also US$2 to Aracaju and buses are plentiful. Salvador is 10 hours by bus and costs US$5. There are five buses daily.

Buses leave for Penedo at 5.20 and 9 am, midday, 6.20 and 11.50 pm. The cost is 75c and the trip takes about three hours. The last two buses are expresses. There's one daily bus to Paulo Afonso that leaves at 11 pm and costs US$2.50. And if you want to make a 2256 km bus trip there's a daily departure at 7 pm for Rio which costs US$15 with a leito. It leaves on Saturdays at 8 pm for US$35.

Getting Around

The Aeroporto Dos Palmares is 20 km from the centre. There is a circular bus

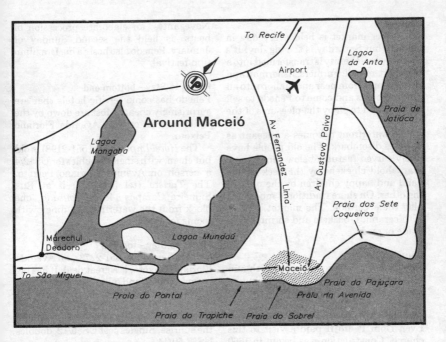

Around Maceió

that stops at the rodoviária, the airport and downtown near the Hotel Beiriz at Rua João Pessoa 290 (get information in the hotel). The new rodoviária (tel 223-4105) is only five km from the centre.

PENEDO

Population: 30,000

Penedo, sitting on a rise above the Rio São Francisco, means great rock. The city has also been called the *cidade dos sobrados* (city of two-storey homes) by the famous Brazilian sociologist Gilberto Freyre. But Penedo's is best known as *capital do baixo São Francisco*, (capital of the lower São Francisco).

Penedo bustles with people from the smaller villages up and down the river who come to sell and buy. These people of the São Francisco have a unique and rich history and culture and Penedo is the best

place to experience the São Francisco, and is also a point of departure for more river travel. It's a fascinating city, 42 km off the BR-101, which is almost untouched by tourism. It is an historic city too, with many baroque churches and colonial buildings.

History

Penedo was founded in either 1535 or 1560 (opinions differ) by Duarte Coelho Pereira, who was descending the Rio São Francisco. He was in pursuit of Caete Indians who had killed the bishop Pedro Fernandes Sardinhaeven. Penedo was the river's first colonial settlement.

Information

There's a tourist information desk and small city museum in the Casa da Aposentadoria, just up from the fort at Praça Barão de Penedo.

Market

The street market is held every day in Penedo, but Saturday is the big day. It's the day when the city is transformed into a busy port-of-call. Farmers, fisherman and crafts people from near and far hop into all kinds of boats and come to Penedo to sell and buy and to enjoy the pleasures of the city.

The waterfront becomes a pageant as families disembark. The old people have finely carved features below funny hats, many hold chickens by the neck in one hand and happy children by the neck in the other. On shore traditional musicians play the accordion. The market is filled with ceramics, baskets and shrimp traps made of reeds.

Churches

Penedo has a rich collection of 17th and 18th century colonial buildings, including many churches. The Convento de São Francisco and Igreja NS dos Anjos is considered the finest church in the state. Even Dom Pedro II paid a visit to this church. Construction was begun in 1660 and completed in 1759. The rococo altar is made of gold. The church is open from Tuesday to Sunday from 8 to 11.30 am and 2.30 to 5 pm. It's at Praça Rui Barbosa.

The Igreja da Senhora das Correntes was completed in 1764. It has some fine work done with azulejos (glazed blue tiles) and a rococo altar. The Church is open daily from 8 am to midday and 2 to 6 pm. You'll find it at Praça 12 de Abril.

The Igreja NS do Rosário was built by slaves and is called the Catedral do Penedo. It's at Praça Marechal Deodoro and is open daily. The Igreja de São Gonçalo Garcia was built at the end of the 18th century and has some of the city's finest sacred art pieces. Currently under restoration, it's on Avenida Floriano Peixoto.

Festivals

The Festa do Senhor Bom Jesus dos Navegantes, an elaborate procession of boats, is held the second Sunday of January. Penedo also hosts a big Brazilian film festival.

Places to Stay – bottom end

Penedo has some terrific hotels that are surprisingly cheap. Most are down by the waterfront on or near Avenida Floriano Peixoto.

The *Hotel Imperial* (tel 551-2198) is old but clean, with singles/doubles for US$2/4 a person on Avenida Floriano Peixoto. The *Turista* (tel 551-2237) is at Rua Siqueira Campos 148. *A Pousada*, one block from the waterfront, is dingy with rooms for US$1.

Places to Stay – top end

São Francisco (tel 551-2273), on Avenida Floriano Peixoto, is a great deal. It has big rooms, is clean and quiet, and has the best showers we had in three months in the Northeast. Make sure you get a room with a view of the river and wake-up early for the sunrise. Singles cost US$6/12, doubles US$7.50/14.

The *Pousada Colonial* (tel 551-2677) at Praça 12 de Abril is more romantic than the São Francisco. It's a beautiful, converted colonial home on the waterfront with rooms for US$7/10 a double.

Places to Eat

There are plenty of bars and lanchonetes where the locals eat. For dining the *Forte da Rocheira* is open for lunch and dinner (until 11 pm) with abundant portions of fish, seafood and meat for US$2 to US$5. The restaurant is in an old fort overlooking the river. Just follow the signs to get there.

Getting There & Away

Buses stop at the waterfront. The town is 42 km off BR-101, 185 km from Maceió and 199 km from Aracaju. There is regular bus service to all coastal points north and south, but much more frequent service to Maceió than to the south.

If you are driving to Penedo, there is a 41 km paved road from BR-101 in Sergipe to Neópolis on the Sergipe side of the river and then a short drive from Neópolis to Passagem where a ferry boat makes the 10-minute river crossing to Penedo every 30 minutes for 50c a car. The ferry stops at night.

There is also a dirt road that goes from BR-101 to Penedo along the north bank of the river. This road is not on any of the maps. The turn-off is the first dirt road north of the bridge. The only difficulty is staying on the right dirt road, but if you choose the fork that's closest to the river and stop and ask every once in a while you should be OK. There are good views of the river and some extremely poor hamlets along the way.

Boat Trips Saturday is the easiest day to find a boat up or down the São Francisco, but it's usually not much of a problem finding a boat any day to any place on the river. If you're going up river you can get a boat as far as Propriá and from there another boat as far as Pão de Açúcar in Alagoas. The beautiful avela sailboats go to Propriá for 25c to 50c, taking four to five hours depending on the wind.

The Penedo to Passagem ferry crosses the river every 30 minutes, but is only of interest if you're driving. In Passagem there's a road to Neópolis and back to the BR-101. A better excursion is one of the motorboat crossings to Neópolis, a few km downriver. Boats start at 5.30 am and continue until 11.30 pm. The 15-minute trip costs 10c and boats leave every 30 minutes or less. Neópolis is an old colonial town on a hill overlooking the river. There are some interesting buildings and some good crafts for sale.

Carrapicho is another close-by excursion. Only four km up river, there are many boats and the town is known for its ceramics. You can also hire a boat and just cruise the river a bit, possibly stopping at a sandbar for a swim. It won't be expensive.

SOUTH OF MACEIÓ

The road is paved from Penedo down to the coast at Pontal do Peba. There is a cheap hotel at the town of Piaçabuçu and a couple of restaurants. Praia do Peba, a couple of km from town, is a disappointing beach, well below the quality of those to the north.

Going south along the coast is a dirt road, so the going is slow. The beaches are deserted until near Coruripe, a small fishing village with a hotel and a restaurant. Another 15 km of dirt road and you reach the coconut-tree lined beach at Poxim which is even more beautiful than Coruripe and the town is even smaller. There is no regular bus service along this stretch of coast.

Marechal Deodoro

Population: 10,000

Marechal Deodoro, Alagoas' state capital from 1823 to 1839, is 21 km south-west of Maceió on the Lagoa Manguaba. Small and quiet, the town sports several good churches, the most famous of which are the Igreja e Convento São Francisco, which was begun in the 17th century and the Igreja de NS da Conceição. For Brazilian history buffs, the old governor's palace and the house where Marechal Deodoro was born are also in town.

Getting There & Away From Maceió you can get a boat on the lagoon at Trapiche or take a bus (they leave every 30 minutes) to Marechal Deodoro.

Barra de São Miguel

Barra is 35 km south of Maceió at the mouth of the Rio São Miguel. The fine beach is protected by a huge reef and there are kayaks for rent. Barra is not too crowded mid-week, but it is being built up with summer homes for Maceió's wealthy.

A big sailboat will take you up the river for three hours for US$6. There are drinks and fruit on board. Boats leave from the dock on the river over at Bar do Tio.

Places to Stay & Eat There are a couple of very expensive hotels in town. The *Pousada Mar e Sol* (tel 272-1159) near the river has doubles for US$11.50. It's overpriced but it is a nice spot.

Bar do Tio has good shrimp and fish dishes for US$3 to US$5. Try the super mussels.

Getting There & Away Barra is reached by paved road with infrequent but regular bus service from Maceió. The last bus leaves Barra for the return trip at 5.30 pm.

Praia do Francês

Only 22 km from Maceió, this is a very pretty, popular weekend beach. The beach is lined with barracas and the ocean lined with reefs. People don't really swim at Praia do Francês as much as wade, the water is that calm. It's a very social beach on weekends, with plenty of drinking, shrimp eating, football and music.

Places to Stay There are several expensive pousadas and restaurants at the beach. The *Hotel do Mar* (tel 231-6820) is cheaper than most. It costs US$10 for a double with bath.

Getting There & Away Buses run from downtown Maceió to Praia do Francês every 15 minutes on weekends.

NORTH OF MACEIÓ

If I had to choose one stretch of the Brazilian coast to spend several days exploring, this would be it. The Alagoas coast north of Maceió, is ideal for independent travellers. The beaches are undisturbed and tropically perfect and the sea is calm and warm. There are several fishing villages with no tourism apart from a simple hotel or two. The coastal road, which is slow dirt along the most secluded stretch, runs within a few hundred metres of the ocean, a rare occurrence along the Brazilian littoral.

From Maceió AL-101 heads north and then divides outside Barra de Santo

Antônio. The main road and most through traffic head inland here on AL-465. It's a stunning drive through sugar cane country (try to stop at Porto Calvo). But if you want to follow the coastal dirt road head down to Barra de Santo Antônio. This road is often in disarray and you have to cross some small rivers on local ferries so check road conditions before departing.

AL-465 passes a large sugar cane plant that processes the sugar cane alcohol that fuels Brazil's cars. The Empresa de Santo Antônio employs about 800 workers in the factory and 4000 in the fields. Tours are possible and worthwhile, but hard to arrange.

A few buses from Maceió go all the way along the coast, but they are less frequent than those that follow the AL-465. Ask for a bus that goes to Porto de Pedras or São Miguel dos Milagres.

Barra de Santo Antônio & Ilha da Croa

Barra is along the mouth of the Rio Jirituba, below a small bluff. Only 40 km from Maceió the fishing village is beginning to see a bit of tourism and beach-home construction. There is a boat that runs back and forth across the river. Little kids will show you some of the sights for a few cruzados.

The best beaches are out on the Ilha do Croa, 15 minutes by motorboat (US$1).

Places to Stay & Eat The *Busque Fazenda Hotel* (tel 293-1131) is a fancy place, with a pool and horses, on the outskirts of town. They have chalets for US$15 plus a pool and horses. For US$14 less you can rent a room at Terezinha's house or just ask around.

Peixada da Rita along the river serves sensational seafood.

Getting There & Away Direct buses to Maceió operate from 4.30 am to 10.30 pm. You can also walk 20 minutes or hire a local cab to the main road and flag down one of the many buses there.

Barra de Camarajibe

This idyllic fishing village, 12 km up the coast, offers fish, beer and beach. Ask around for a place to stay and for a ride in a fishing boat.

São Miguel dos Milagres

A bit bigger than it's neighbours, São Miguel's soft beaches are protected by offshore-reefs and the sea is warm and shallow. There's a petrol station in town.

Porto de Pedras

You've got to catch the local ferry to cross the river here. Porto de Pedras is a lively little fishing village with a road that connects to AL-465 at Porto Calvo. There are bars, restaurants and a good, cheap hotel in town.

Japaratinga

Japaratinga's shallow waters are protected

by coral reef and backed by coconut trees and fishing huts. Under the moonlight you can walk a couple of km into the sea. The town has a petrol station and a telephone.

Places to Stay & Eat The *Hotel Sol Mar* is on the south side of town and has simple doubles for US$4 and singles for US$2 (camping too). Another hotel is being built. A big churrascaria sits by the road and there are several fish places in town.

Getting There & Away There are regular buses to Maceió and Recife (137 km).

Maragoji

Slightly more developed, Maragoji has some weekend homes for Pernambucanos and a couple of cheap hotels. The sea is protected by reefs and it's ideal for swimming.

Pernambuco

RECIFE

Population: 1,200,000

Recife is the country's fourth biggest city and the capital of Pernambuco. The Venice of Brazil, Recife is a city of water and bridges with a stone reef offshore. Its sister city Olinda, was once the capital of Brazil and today is a beautiful enclave of colonial buildings filled with artists, students and Bohemians.

Recife is big, modern and more difficult to negotiate than most cities in the Northeast. The city centre is a confusing mixture of high-rise offices, colonial churches and popular markets. During the day traffic and tourists get lost in the maze of winding, one-way streets. Amidst all the recent development Recife retains a rich traditional side, with some of Brazil's best folk art, including painting and sculpture, dance, music and festivals. It takes time to discover this side of the city, but it's well-worth the effort.

Recife is the port of entry for many flights from Europe and has recently been trying to broaden its tourist appeal. The main beneficiary of these developments has been Boa Viagem, the Copacabana of Pernambuco. Site of the well-to-do nightclubs, restaurants and most of the mid to expensive hotels, Boa Viagem has good beaches which are essential for escaping Recife's muggy heat, but unless you want be right on the beach, Olinda is a cheaper and more interesting place to stay.

History

Recife grew up in the 17th century as the port for the rich sugar plantations around Olinda, the seat of the captaincy. With several rivers and offshore reefs, Recife proved to be an excellent port and began to outgrow Olinda. By the 17th century Recife and Olinda combined were the most prosperous cities in Brazil, with the possible exception of Bahia. The neigh-

bouring Indians had been subdued after brutal warfare, the land was rich with sugar cane and many sugar engenhos (mills), owned by a colonial aristocracy that lived in Olinda. Naturally all the work was done by slaves.

No European country had managed to grab a part of Brazil from the Portuguese, but in 1621 the Dutch, who were active in the sugar trade and knew the lands of Brazil well, set up the Dutch West India Company to grab a piece of the Brazilian cake. A large fleet sailed in 1624 and captured Bahia but a huge Spanish-Portuguese militia of 12,000 men recaptured the city a year later. Five years later the Dutch decided to try again, this time in Pernambuco. Recife was abandoned, the Dutch took the city and by 1640 they had control of a great chunk of the Northeast, from Maranhão to the Rio São Francisco.

The Dutch had hoped the sugar planters wouldn't resist their rule but, to their dismay, many Brazilian planters took up arms against the non-Catholics. After a series of battles around Recife the Dutch finally surrendered in 1654. This was the last European challenge to Portuguese Brazil.

Recife prospered after the Dutch were expelled but in spite of the city's growing economic power, which had eclipsed that of Olinda, political power remained with the sugar planters in Olinda and they refused to share it. In 1710 fighting began between the *filhos da terra* (the sugar planters of Olinda) and the *mascates* (the Portuguese merchants of Recife), the more recent immigrants. The War of the Mascates, as it came to be known, was a bloody regional feud between different sections of the ruling classes and native Brazilians and immigrants. In the end, with the help of the Portuguese crown and their superior economic resources, the mascates of Recife gained considerable political clout at the expense of Olinda, which began its long, slow decline.

More dependent on the sugar economy than Rio or São Paulo, Recife was eclipsed by these two centres as the sugar economy floundered throughout the 19th century.

Information & Orientation

The heart of Recife, containing the old section of town, is along the waterfront in Boa Vista, across the Rio Capibaribe in Santo Antônio and then across to the island of Recife. All are connected by bridges. Olinda is six km to the north, over swamps and rivers, while Boa Viagem is six km to the south.

Tourist Office Empetur, the state tourism bureau has several offices. The convenient airport and rodoviária desks are as good as, or better than any. In the city try the Empetur office at Pátio de São Pedro, Loja 17 and at the Casa da Cultura de Pernambuco. They publish excellent carnival schedules.

The daily paper *Diário de Pernambuco* has hours – often strange ones – for museums, art galleries and churches. You can dial 139 direct for tourist information in English.

Telephone There are 24-hour phone stations with international service at the rodoviária, the airport and in the centre at Rua Diário de Pernambuco 38.

Consulates Both the UK and the US have consulates in Recife:

UK
    Avenida Marques de Olinda 200, Recife (tel 224-0650)
USA
    Rua Gonçalves Maia 163, Boa Vista (tel 221-1412)

Visa Renewal If you need to renew a visa go to the Policia Federal building on Cais do Apolo out on Recife. It's best to call first; try 231-2041 or ask at a tourist office for information.

Airlines The following airlines have offices in Recife:

LAP-Air Paraguay
    Rua Estreita do Rosário 210, Santo Antônio (tel 224-4299)
Nordeste
    Aeroporto Guararapes (tel 341-4091)
Pan Am
    Rua da Concordia 167, São José (tel 224-0061)
TAP
    Avenida Guararapes 111, Santo Antônio (tel 341-0654)
    Aeroporto Guararapes (tel 224-2548)
Transbrasil
    Avenida Dantas Barreto 191, Santo Antônio (tel 224-6166 and 224-7711)
    Hotel Miramar, Rua dos Navegantes 363, Boa Viagem (tel 326-7422 ramal (ext) 130)
    Aeroporto Guararapes (tel 326-2081)
Varig-Cruzeiro
    Avenida Guararapes 120, Santo Antônio (tel 224-8273)
    Othon Palace Hotel, Avenida Boa Viagem 3722 (tel 326-7225 ramal (ext) 645)
    Aeroporto Guararapes (tel 341-4400)
Vasp
    Avenida Guararapes 111, Santo Antônio (tel 222-3611)
    Avenida Manoel Borba 488 (tel 231-3048)
    Aeroporto Guararapes (tel 326-1699)

Bookstores There are several bookstalls along Rua do Infante Dom Henrique. The airport bookshop is a good bet if you are looking for English language books.

Hospital For medical care the Hospital Santa Joana Rua Joaquim Nabuco and the Hospital Restauração are two of the city's best known. We make no promises regarding your chances of surviving a visit to either of these establishments (or any other hospitals in Brazil for that matter).

Museums

With such a long and important history it's not surprising that Recife is loaded with churches and museums, but few are must-sees. The best museums are east of the city centre along Avenida 17 de Agosto (catch the Dois Irmãos bus from Centro).

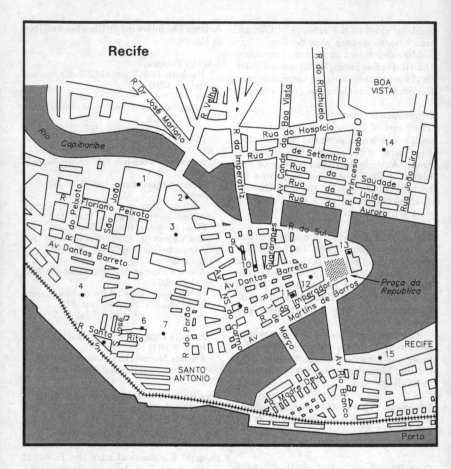

Recife

BOA
VISTA

SANTO
ANTONIO

Praça da
Republica

RECIFE

Porto

The Museu do Homem do Nordeste has an anthropology section about the peoples of the Northeast, a popular art section with some superb typical ceramic figurines, a pharmacy exhibit about the region's rich herbal/indigenous medicine. The Horto Zoobotânico, with a zoo and botanical garden, is in the same neighbourhood.

Old City

To see the old city start over at Praça da República where you'll see the Teatro Santa Isabel (1850) and the Palácio do

Governo (1841). Take a look at the Igreja de Santo Antônio (1753) in Praça da Independência and then the Catedral de São Pedro dos Clérigos on the Pátio de São Pedro, an artists' hangout. There are many intimate restaurants, shops and bars here, all with interesting local characters. On weekends there's often good music.

Walk down Rua Vidal de Negreiros to the Forte das Cinco Pontas opposite the rodoviária. Built by the Dutch in 1630, then rebuilt in 1677, it's open on weekdays

1	Museu do Trem
2	Casa da Cultura
3	Basilica de NS Carmo
4	Forte das Cinco Pontas
5	Terminal Rodoviària de Santa Rita
6	Prâa Dom Vital / Basilica NS da Penha / Mercado Sao Josè
7	Catedral de Sao Pedro dos Clerigos / Patio de Sao Pedro
8	Igreja do Rosario dos Pretos
9	Igreja de NS da Concelaó
10	Matriz de Santo Antonio
11	Phone Company
	12 Capela Dourada/ Convento de Santo Antonio
13	Teatro Santa Isabel
14	Parque 13 de Maio
15	Policia Federal – visas

from 9 to 11 am and 1 to 5 pm. There's a small exhibit of maps and photos of the city.

Nearby, at Praça Dom Vital, is the daily Mercado do São José and the Basilica de NS da Penha. The market has food and crafts from throughout Pernambuco.

Casa da Cultura

The Casa da Cultura de Pernambuco along Cais da Detenção was a huge colonial-style prison that was renovated and redecorated in 1975. It's home to many arts, crafts and trinket shops, but it's certainly not everyone's cup of tea because of its very touristy atmosphere. They do have some good traditional music and dance shows outside. It's open from Monday to Saturday from 9 am to 8 pm, and on Sundays from 3 to 8 pm and the complex contains tourist and phone offices.

Festivals

The Recife-Olinda combination may be the best carnival in Brazil but even if you decide to carnival in Rio or Salvador, Recife starts celebrating so early that you can enjoy festivities there and then go

somewhere else for carnival proper. Two months before the start of carnival there are *bailes* (dances) in the clubs and carnival blocos practising on the streets with frevo dancing everywhere. Galo da Madrugada, Recife's largest bloco, has been known to bring 20,000 people onto the beaches at Boa Viagem in costume and dance.

There are supposedly 500 different carnival blocos in the Recife area and they come in all 'shakes' and colours. There are the traditional and well-organised, the modern and anarchical. There are samba schools, there are afoxés, Indian tribes and maracatus but the main dance of carnival in Pernambuco is the frenetic frevo. The Fundação do Cultura do Recife, which runs carnival, has on occasion organised public frevo lessons for the uninitiated at the Pátio de São Pedro.

Along the Boa Viagem beach the carnival groups practice weekends and as carnival approaches they add *trio elétricos* to the tomfoolery. The week before carnival Sunday, unofficial carnival really starts. Several groups march through the city centre each day and at least one baile kicks off each evening – time to practice that frevo.

Big-time carnival takes place from Saturday to Tuesday, non-stop. The big carnival groups parade in wonderful costumes, singing and dancing. For the parade route and schedule check the local papers or the tourism office. Along Avenida Guararapes there's a popular frevo dance that starts on Friday night and goes on and on.

Places to Stay - bottom end

Most budget travellers prefer staying in Olinda; it's cheap and beautiful, there's lots happening and you can walk everywhere. If you want to stay in central Recife there are a couple of good bets near the Parque 13 de Maio. The *Suiça* (tel 222-3534), Rua do Hospicio 687 has doubles without baths for US$4 and with for US$5.50. It's clean and has a restaurant. Next door the *Hotel 13 de Maio* (222-6338) is similar value. They have doubles without baths for US$5.50 and with for US$7.

Down the road is the busy and friendly *Hotel do Parque* (326-4666) at Rua do Hospício 51. Singles without bath are US$4, doubles without bath are US$6 and with bath they are US$7. A block away the *Hotel América* (tel 221-1300), Praça Amciel Pinheiro 48 has singles/doubles starting from US$6.50/7.50. The rooms have refrigerators and balconies. Also try the *Nassau* (tel 224-3977) at Rua Largo do Rosário 253, which has singles/doubles with bath for US$7/11, or the *Central* (tel 222-1824) at Avenida Manoel Borba 209 with singles/doubles for US$9/10.

For even cheaper lodging try the *Hospedaria Rigor*, Praça 17, the *Hospedaria Senhor do Bonfim* (tel 224-3371), Rua dos Pescadores 8 (near the rodoviária) which has singles/doubles for US$1.50/3. The *Hotel 7 de Setembro*, Rua Matias de Albuquerque 318 (near the Rio Capibaribe) has singles/doubles for US$2/3 without bath.

Places to Stay - middle

If you want the beach, head to Boa Viagem. There are no real cheapies here although you can find moderately priced hotels – they are often full during the summer season. Behind the Rodeo Churrasco, Avenida Boa Viagem 4780, you'll find two super deals. The *Sea View* (tel 326-7238) has good rooms and is reasonably priced for a hotel close to the beach. The *Veraneio* (tel 326-7116) is also close to the beach, with singles for US$12/17 and doubles for US$13/19. Be careful in the back streets around here at night.

Dantas Pousada (tel 326-6201), Avenida Boa Viagem 168, is a good bet. The *Hotel Marazul* (tel 326-1900) is on Rua Prof José Brandão 135 with doubles starting at US$6. For something less expensive try the *Pousada Aconchego* (tel 326-2989), Rua Felix de Brito 382, and the *Albergue Arrecife* (tel 326-7549), Rua Padre

Carapuceiro 132. *Hotel Urupema* (tel 326-0721), with singles/doubles for US$14/16, and *Hotel dos Navegantes* (tel 326-9609), Rua dos Navegantes 1997, with singles for US$12/15 and doubles for US$14/16, are also recommended.

Places to Stay - top end

Almost all the better hotels are in Boa Viagem; there's no reason to stay in the centre of town. Remember it gets very humid in Recife. On Avenida Boa Viagem along the beach the *Jangadeiro* (tel 326-6777) has doubles for US$45 and the *Boa Viagem* (tel 341-4144) for US$50. On the same street the *Recife Palace* (tel 325-4044) and *Othon Palace* (tel 326-7225) –singles/doubles US$39/43 – are the places to stay if you want the best, or at least the most expensive.

Places to Eat

The city centre is loaded with lunch places and at night it's easy to find something to your liking around the Pátio de São Pedro. Always lively, there's a surprising variety of prices and styles. Boa Viagem has the bulk of Recife's good restaurants. Avenida Boa Viagem, along the beach, is a regular restaurant row. Walk here and you're bound to find something you like.

I had my best Chinese dinner in Brazil – which ain't saying a heck of a lot – at the *Grande Restaurante Chinatown* (tel 326-8865), Avenida Boa Viagem 1206. It's open from midday to 3 pm and 7 to 11 pm.

The *Lobster* (tel 326-7593), Avenida Boa Viagem 2612 is a good lobster splurge. They have live music at dinner and stay open till midnight. *Maxime* (tel 326-5314), Avenida Boa Viagem 21 serves traditional seafood dishes at moderate prices; try the lobster (US$6) or one of the local fish like the *cavala* (mackarel) and *cioba*.

Getting There & Away

Air There are flights to most major

Brazilian cities, and also to Lisbon, London, Paris and Miami.

Bus The Rodoviária de Santa Rita is just south of the centre at the corner of Cais de Santa Rita and Avenida Sul (tel 224- 5499). They are opening a three-star hotel in the station. Buses go everywhere. There are many buses to Maceió which takes four hours (US$2); Real Alagoas bus lines has five a day which take the coastal route. Salvador is 12 hours away and costs US$7. Rio is 39 hours and US$23.

Heading north it's five hours to Natal (US$4), 12 hours to Fortaleza (US$7), 23 hours to São Luis (US$21) and 34 hours to Belém (US$26). The frequent buses to Caruaru take two hours and cost US$3.

Getting Around
Airport Transport The Aeroporto Guararapes (tel 341-1888) is 10 km south of the city centre. Taxis cost about US$4 to the centre; catch a regular not a special airport taxi – they are about twice as expensive.

From the airport there are common buses and *micro* buses (more expensive) to NS do Carmo (Olinda) and Dantas Barreto (central Recife). Both routes stop at Boa Viagem. To get to the airport take a bus from NS do Carmo or Dantas Barreto.

Local Transport Recife buses have their destinations written outside the bus. For example, buses to the centre of town say Dantas Barreto. From the city centre to Olinda catch the bus in front of the main post office (Avenida Guararapes 250, just across the Ponte Duarte Coelho) then along Rua do Hospício and up past the Parque 13 de Maio.

Taxis from the centre to Olinda cost about US$2 and take 20 minutes. For a telephone taxi dial 231-7533.

BEACHES SOUTH OF RECIFE
This is excellent beach country. Protected by coral reefs, the sea is calm and the waters are crystal clear, and the beaches are lined with coconut palms and white sand dunes. The coastal PE-060 road doesn't hug the ocean, like the road in northern alagoas, so you have to drive a dozen or so km on an access road to see what each beach is like. There is a frequent direct bus service to all these cities from Recife. From Alagoas just take a coastal bus to Recife and then catch another bus, hitch or walk the dirt access road to the beach. Many of these towns have one or two simple hotels and away from Recife all have excellent camping.

São José da Cora Grande
The first beach crossing into Pernambuco from Alagoas is São José da Cora Grande, one of Pernambuco's finest. It's 120 km from Recife on the PE-060 coastal road. The fishing village is beginning to get some weekend homes but it's not bad yet. There are a couple of restaurants, several bars and two hotels; one is moderately priced, the other a simple pension (*pensão*).

Tamandaré
The next access road goes 10 km to the beach. There's a small fishing village here

with only a couple of bars, no hotel. The beach is idyllic and you can see the old 17th century Santo Iñacio Fort.

More Beaches

The dirt road going north along the coast will take you past the beaches of Ponta dos Manguinhos, Guadalupe, Camela and then to Barra de Sirinhaém where there is a 10-km-long access road back to the main road.

The only lodging in these towns is with the local fishermen. During the week the beaches are practically deserted. Off the coast is the Ilha de Santo Aleixo.

Porto de Galinhas

Seventy km south of Recife is Porto de Galinhas. Among Pernambucos most famous beaches it lies on a pretty curved bay lined with coconut palms, mangroves and cashew trees. Most of the beach, three km from town, is sheltered by a reef, but there are some waves for surfers. The water is warm and clear – you can see the colourful fish playing by your feet. There are plenty of jangada's for rent but they're not cheap (US$4 an hour).

Should you tire of Praia de Porto de Galinhas, head to Maracaipe beach three km away. From here you can sail a jangada to Ilha de Santo Aleixo. The fishermen charge US$10 per hour and take up to four passengers on their boats. The name Porto de Galinhas (port of chickens) came as a result of slave trade which secretly continued after abolition. Upon hearing that the chickens from Angola had arrived the masters of Recife knew to expect another load of slaves.

Places to Stay

Hotel Solar de Porto (tel (081) 326-4154), the lone hotel in town, is a two-star affair (US$18 a double) with a good restaurant. If you want to stay a few days, several houses are available to rent. Most people here either own homes (the celebrities and politicos of Pernambuco), rent for the season or camp out.

Places to Eat

Famed for its seafood, Porto de Galinhas has several eateries but the town's most renowned is *Restaurante do Braz*. Don't miss their lobster, cooked in coconut or tomato sauce or just plain grilled. Other fine restaurants in town – *Peixada do Laercio*, *Restaurante Porto de Galinhas*, *Restaurante de Bras* and *Brisa Maritima* – serve lobster, squid, shrimp and the local fish with coconut milk, pepper and cumin sauces. The locally made genipap liqueur is worth tasting, too.

Gaibu & Cabo de Santo Agostinho

Further up the coast Gaibu is the larger town, but Cabo de Santo Agostinho to the south has one of the state's finest beaches. There are facilities for snorkelling and spear-fishing. Take a walk to the ruins of the Santo Agostinho Fort, it's next to the church.

On a hill between Gaibu and Calhetas (you have to ask around) there's a small, freshwater stream that's used for nude bathing.

Suape & Ilha do Paiva

In Suape a big industrial port is being built. Heading north again, the Ilha do Paiva is popular for its nude beaches. It's nicknamed the island of lovers, take a boat from Barra dos Jangandas. It's worth it.

The mainland beaches here – Candeias, Venda Grande, Piedade – are semi-urban beaches with many barracas, hotels and crowds on weekends. But they are still good beaches, with clean water and sometimes strong surf.

OLINDA

Population: 360,000

Beautiful Olinda. It's up on a hill that overlooks Recife and the Atlantic. After Ouro Preto, it has Brazil's biggest and best-preserved collection of colonial buildings. A living city, a Bohemian quarter and a cultural centre, Olinda has art galleries and museums, music in the streets and the bars, and always some kind of celebration in the works.

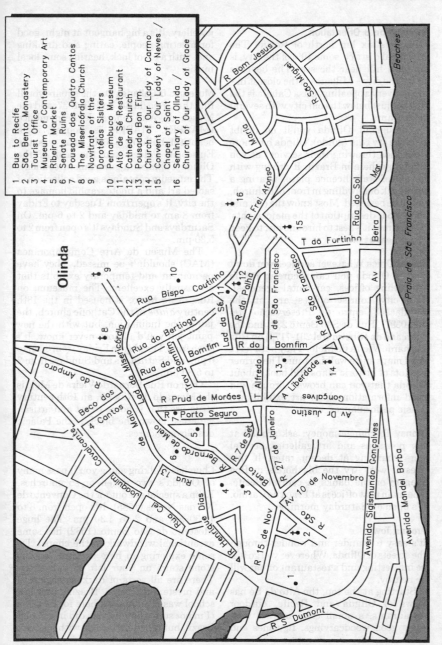

Olinda

1 Bus to Recife
2 São Bento Monastery
3 Tourist Office
4 Museum of Contemporary Art
5 Ribeira Market
6 Senate Ruins
7 Pousada dos Quatro Cantos
8 The Misericórdia Church
9 Novitrate of the Dorotéias Sisiters
10 Pernambuco Museum
11 Alto de Sé Restaurant
12 Cathedral Church
13 Pousada Bon Fim
14 Church of Our Lady of Carmo
15 Convent of Our Lady of Neves / Chapel of Saint
16 Seminary of Olinda / Church of Our Lady of Grace

Information & Orientation

Olinda is six km north of Recife. The historical district, some 10% of the city, is up on a hill near the sea. The beaches along the city – Milagres is the closest in – are not very appealing. Casa Caiada is the district just below the old city with several restaurants.

Throughout Olinda you'll no doubt here the cry *guia* (guide). Olinda has more little kids throwing their services at you than anywhere in Brazil. If driving with an out-of-state licence plate, wearing a backpack or dawdling in front of a church, you'll be besieged. Most know the city and have a pat description of the major sights. Sometimes it's best to hire one just to keep the others at bay.

Tourist Office Whatever services you don't find in Olinda you can secure in Recife (eg airline offices, car-rental agencies). The city tourist offices are at the Fundação Centro de Preservação (tel 429-0397), Rua de São Bento 233, and the Mercado da Ribeira (tel 231-7172) on Rua Bernardo Vieira de Melo. They both have good maps and a walking tour. The former has lots of historic maps and books about Olinda that you can browse through and good information about art exhibitions, music performances, etc.

Money To change money, ask around at the pousadas and art galleries, several were changing at decent rates. If this doesn't work try the big hotels in Boa Viagem or the banks in central Recife. The main post office is at Praça do Carmo. It's open on Saturday mornings.

Around Town

It's easy to wander and wonder through the streets of Olinda. Wherever you go it'll be interesting and a restaurant or bar will be nearby.

Starting at the top, the Alto da Sé has views of Olinda and Recife, outdoor restaurants, a small craft market with some good woodcarvings, figurines and jewellery. It's a big hangout at night, good for meeting people, eating and drinking and, with a bit of luck, hearing some local music.

Museums & Galleries On the square you'll find the Igreja da Sé, built in 1537, and the Museu de Arte Sacra de Pernambuco (MASPE). MASPE is housed in a beautiful building (1696) that was the Episcopal Palace and the seat of the Olinda *Camara* (a government council). The museum contains a good collection of sacred art and a photographic homage to the city. It's open from Tuesday to Friday from 8 am to midday and 2 to 6 pm. On Saturdays and Sundays it's open from 2 to 5.30 pm.

The Museu de Arte Contemporânea (MAC) shouldn't be missed. They have permanent and temporary exhibits that are usually excellent. The museum, on Rua 13 de Maio, is housed in the 18th century *ajube* of the Catholic church, the jail of the Inquisition, but with the new paint job you'd almost never know. It's open from Tuesday to Friday from 8 am to 6 pm, and Saturdays and Sundays from 2 to 5.30 pm.

Over on Rua Bernardo Vieira de Melo is the Mercado da Ribeira, an 18th century structure that is home to art and artisan galleries. Down the block is the Palácio dos Governadores.

Churches Walking along you'll pass many of Olinda's two dozen or so churches. Keep a special eye out for the Convento de NS das Neves (1585). It's open from 8 to 11.30 am and 2 to 4.30 pm. The huge Mosteiro de São Bento (1582) has some exceptional woodwork in the chapel. Do some exploring in here by going up the stone stairs on your left as you enter. There are all sorts of dark passageways and mysterious rooms. Brazil's first law school was even housed here for 24 years (I'm not sure what lawyers did in colonial Brazil, but it had little to do with justice).

The monastery is on Rua de São Bento and is open from 8 to 11 am and 1 to 5 pm.

Also visit the Igreja da Misericórdia (1540) at Largo da Misericórdia with wood and gold work inside. It's open from 7 am to 5 pm. The Convento de São Francisco (1585) is open from 8 to 11.30 am and 2 to 4.30 pm daily.

Beaches
You've got to get out of town a bit for a fine, clean beach. Head north to Janga beach (eight km) or at least Rio Doce (six km), and beyond to Praia do Pau Amarelo, Praia do O, Praia do Conceição and Praia da Maria Farinha (23 km). The road goes along close to the beach but don't be deterred by the ugly development at roadside; the beaches are generally undisturbed except for barracas and crowds on weekends. Enjoy the local small crab siri and big crab caranguejo at the barracas. There are local buses from Praça do Carmo.

Festivals
Olinda's Carnival has been very popular with Brazilians and travellers for several years (see also the Carnival section in Recife). The old historic setting combined with the fact that so many residents know each other provides an intimacy and security that you don't get in big city Carnivals. It's a participatory Carnival; costumed blocos parade through the city dancing to frevo music and everyone else follows. It's easy to meet people and is a very safe Carnival.

There have been complaints of creeping Carnival commercialisation the last couple of years. At the same time, Recife's Carnival has been getting better reviews lately so it's possible to escape to the big city if they mess the Carnival up in Olinda. The tourist office publishes a schedule of events that's worth getting.

Carnival in Olinda lasts a full 11 days. There are Carnival balls (of course), there is a night of samba, a night of afoxé, but everything else happens in the free streets. The official opening ceremonies – with the pomp and ceremony of the Olympic games – commence with a bloco of more than 400 'virgins' (men in drag) and awards for most beautiful, most risque and for the biggest prude.

Everyone dresses for the Carnival so you'll want some sort of costume. The Carnival groups of thousands dance the frevo through the narrow streets. It's very playful and very lewd. Five separate areas have orchestras playing non-stop from 8 pm to 6 am nightly.

Places to Stay
The main choice in accommodation is whether you prefer to stay in the old city, which has fewer hotels, or north of town near the beaches at Bairro Novo or Farol. On the low end there are several fine pousadas and a couple of albergues (hostels). In the old city ask around a bit for cheap lodging. There are several quasi-official pousadas which seem to come and go which are good deals. Albergues have dorm-style sleeping, but sometimes have a few quartos.

Places to Stay – bottom end
If you don't mind dorm-style sleeping, the *Pousada do Bom Fim* (tel 429-1692) has it all. It's in the historic district at Rua do Bon Fim 115. There are eight beds to a room, the place is neat and clean and they let you hang out your washing. A bed costs US$3; they may change money too.

The *Hotel Albergue de Olinda* (tel 429-1592) at Rua do Sol 233 has collective rooms that sleep two to six people for US$3 a head. Showers are down the hall.

Less expensive and more fun, the *Albergue Passageiro de Olinda* (tel 429-3560) is at Praça Dantas Barreto 36. It sleeps six to a room. Ask Marquinhos what's happening in town; he'll know.

The *Hotel Albergue Olinda Beira-Mar* (tel 429-1409), Avenida Beira-Mar 153, is not as good as other pousadas but you do get a private room although they only have double beds (US$5). The other advantage is it's close to the old city. Further out is the *Pensão Albergue Beira-Mar* (tel 341-7402) (can't they think of different names?) at Avenida Beira-Mar 1103.

Places to Stay – middle

The *Hotel 14 Bis* (tel 429-0409), Avenida Beira-Mar 1414 has big, quiet rooms on the waterfront. There's a small pool and all the conveniences and they have rooms at several prices; singles are US$7/12 and doubles US$9/12.

Pousada Barlavento (tel 431-2172), Avenida José Augusto Moreira 1745, is 100 metres from the beach. It's not the cheapest place in town, but it's good value. Doubles with bath go for US$4 (US$5 with air-con). The rooms are comfortable. Similar, but not as good, is the *Hospedaria do Turista* (tel 429-1847), Avenida Beira-Mar 989. Rooms come with a fan and a bath. Singles/doubles cost US$5.50/6.50.

In the medium price range I'd recommend staying in the old city's *Pousada dos Quatro Cantos* (tel 429-0220), Rua Prudente de Moraes 441. It's an historic place in the heart of old Olinda. Apartments for two cost US$14 or US$22 with bath. They have one 'ecological suite' if you're into that kind of thing.

The *Chalé da Praia Hotel* (tel 429-0863), Avenida Beira-Mar 1835 is cheaper and simpler. It's a good deal with singles/doubles with bath for US$5.50/6.50. More expensive is the *Marolinda Hotel* (tel 429-1699), Avenida Beira-Mar 1615. It's clean and attractive; singles start at US$15 and doubles US$17, with TV.

Places to Stay – top end

For luxury sleeping the *Hotel Quatro Rodas* (tel 431-2955) is Olinda's five-star affair. It's north of town, on a so-so beach. They have facilities for everything, there's even baby-sitting and a free bus to Recife. Singles start at US$37, doubles at US$43 and go up to US$100.

Places to Eat

For light eating try a snack at *Alto da Sé* or one of the natural food lanchonetes like *Saúde Lanches Naturais*, Rua de Moraes 211. There are several good restaurants in Casa Caiada, along the beach and an easy walk from the old city. For pizza try *Pizzaria Status*, Avenida José Augusto Moreira 379 or *Ravena Pizzaria* Rua Carlos Leite 140. The *Sol na Brasa*, Avenida José Augusto Moreira, 656 serves regional cuisine daily except Mondays. Try the *linguiça do sertão* for something new and different.

Out in Barra Novo, the *Restaurant Taipei* (tel 429-2504), Avenida Beira Mar 1161 has passable Chinese food. *Restaurante o Rei da Lagosta* (tel 429-1565), Avenida Beira Mar 1255 gets mixed reviews but no one questions the fine view of the sea. Another seafood place nearby is the *Itapoã*.

For fine dining the expensive *Restaurante L'Atelier* (tel 429-3099) at Rua Bernardo Vieira de Melo 91 in Ribeira is supposed to be the best. It has French cuisine and is only open from 7 pm to 2 am.

Entertainment

Alto de Sé has several bars/restaurants open late with a good mix of locals and travellers. The *Canto Luz* is a good choice. In the old city there are several relaxed, hip bars that often have music. Try *Rebicário* in the Praça do Carmo, *Quintal 2* at Praça do Jacaré and *Bar Brasil* at Avenida Bernardo Vieira de Melo 134. Another spot on Praça do Carmo is the *Cheiro do Poro* for serious forró dancing.

Friday and Saturday nights the beach restaurant/bars north of town come to life. The *Ciranda de Dona Duda* on Janga beach is famous for its participatory ciranda. The market at Milagres beach has a folk music show Tuesday nights.

Getting Around

Buses to Recife leave from Avenida Santos Dumont near the corner of Rua 15 de Novembro not far from the Mosteiro de São Bento. Taxis cost about US$3.

BEACHES NORTH OF OLINDA
North of Olinda the beaches of Praias Maria Farinha, Janga and Pao Amarelo are attractive and have good seafood barracas. They attract city crowds on weekends, when there's a bus service from Olinda, but they are rarely crowded. They're the first set of beaches north of the city clean enough to swim in, but the water is thick with seaweed.

IGARAÇU
One of the oldest cities in Brazil, Igaraçu is 35 km north of Recife and 20 km shy of Itamaracá island. Igaraçu is small, untouristed, and full of old colonial buildings.

History
27 September 1535, the day of Saints Cosme and Damião, was a busy day for town hero Duarte Coelho and his men. They managed to fight off both the Potigar Indians at the mouth of the Rio Igaraçu and the French pirates offshore. Later in the afternoon, after a big meal, Duarte Coelho founded the village, naming it São Cosme e Damião in honor of the saints. It later came to be known as Igaraçu.

Information
Igaraçu's tourist office has brochures and beautiful free posters.

Around Town
Historic Section Walking up the hill to the historic section you'll find the Igreja Dos Santos Cosme e Damião dates back to the foundation of Igaraçu and is the oldest standing church in Pernambuco state. Next door on Largo São Cosme e São Damião, the City Museum has sacred art pieces and furniture from the noble families.

The Convento de Santo Antonio (1588) on Avenida Hermes contains the Pinoteca Museum which has paintings depicting folk tales and popular legends. For typical food try the nearby *Restaurante Senzala*.

Engenho Mojope The surrounding area also has a few treasures. The Engenho Mojope, an old (1750) sugar estate with ruins of a mill, *casa grande*, chapel and slave quarters, is now a campground belonging to the Camping Clube do Brasil. It's worth a stop if you're going by car; take BR-101 3½ km south from the Igaraçu turn-off and turn right at the Camping Club sign, the ex-plantation is one km down.

Other Attractions The church of São Gonçalvo do Amarante (1795) 10 km away on Rua Manoel Lourenço in Itapissuma is also worth a peek if you have wheels.

Festivals
Every 27 September the city celebrates its birth and patron saints São Cosme and Damião with *bumba-meu-boi* and the ciranda dance (which actually originated in Itamaracá). The Festival do Coco is held during the last week of November.

Getting There & Away
Buses leave every 15 minutes for Recife's Avenida Martins de Barros.

Ilha de Itamaracá
Only 50 km from Recife, Itamaracá Island is a pleasant and popular weekend beach scene. During the week it's empty. There is a regular bus service to the island but getting to its many beaches takes some time if you don't have a car. There are a handful of hotels, few of which are cheap.

Beaches Itamaracá has a long history and a lot of beach. The better beaches are north and south of Pilar, Itamaracá's town beach. Two km north of town is Janguaribe, an emptier beach with barracas. For still more isolated beaches hike five km further north along the coast to Praia Lance dos Cacões and Fortinho.

Immediately south of town is Praia Baixa Verde and every three km south are more beaches: Praia Rio Ambo, Praia Forno de Cal, Praia de São Paulo and finally Praia de Vila Velha which also is a historic old port near Fort Orange.

Fort Orange Fort Orange was built in 1630 by the Dutch and served as a base in a series of important battles against the Portuguese colonies in Recife and Olinda. It's an impressive bastion, right on the water, but souvenir shops are rearing their ugly little heads.

Other Attractions The Engenho Amparo 18th century sugar plantation is past the island's penitentiary. Further from town is Vila Velha (1526), the first port in the Northeast and its church NS de Conceição (1526). Take a VW Kombi-van to get to these and other distant points from the town of Itamaracá.

Places to Stay The *Hotel Pousada Itamaracá* (tel 544-1152) on Rua Fernando Lopez near the centre of town is a modern hotel with super-clean and comfortable doubles from US$12 to US$18 for more luxurious rooms. The hotel has a pool. For reservations in Recife ring 224-6959. Also on Rua Fernando Lopez, the *Itamaracá Parque Hotel* (tel 544-1027) is nice, but over-priced. Doubles go for US$18 and US$20.

The *Hotel Caravela* (tel 544-1130) on Praça João Felipe de Barros is a two-star Embratur resort hotel with a pool and has US$5.50 singles and US$6.50 doubles. Ocean view rooms with balconies are only US$1 more.

Woodcut prints in honour of São João, from Olinda

Top: Woman selling corn on the street, Recife, Pernambuco (JM)
Left: Colonial village of Olinda overlooking Recife, Pernambuco (JM)
Right: Family transportation, Brazil (JM)

Top: Two men near Natal, Rio Grande do Norte (JM)
Bottom: Genipabu, near Natal, Rio Grande do Norte (JM)

Things to Buy Artisans in Engenho São João, about 10 km in the direction of Igaraçu, make lithographs and carrancas for sale.

Getting There & Away There are 12 buses a day to Recife's Cais de Santa Rita terminal from 4.30 am to 6.40 pm.

Pontas de Pedras

Pontas de Pedras, the last beach in Pernambuco, does its state proud. The water is extremely calm and shallow, (thanks to a reef two km offshore) and is good for bathing and snorkelling. There are restaurants and bars, but no regular lodging in Goiana, 22 km in from the coast at the junction of BR-101 and PE-49.

CARUARU

Population: 165,000

If you like folk art and you wake up in Recife on a Wednesday or Saturday feeling like a day trip, you're in luck. Caruaru, South America's capital for ceramic figurine art, is only a couple of hours away. The fair is a hot and noisy crush of Nordestinos: vendors, poets, singers, rural and town folk, tourists, musicians and artisans. The *zambumba* bands blow *pifanos* and bang on drums, veterans of the Paraguayan war fire rifles up in the hills of Bom Jesus and *sulanqueiros*, Brazilian rag merchants, hawk their scraps of clothing.

Alongside pots, leather bags and straw baskets are representations of strange beasts and mythical monsters crafted by artists as famous as Caruaru's master, Vitalino. It's fascinating to meet the artists and watch them work up in Caruaru's Alto do Moura.

In addition to ceramic artwork you can hear singers and poets perform the *literatura de cordel*: poetry by and for the people sold in little brochures which hang from the fair stands by string (hence the name). The poems tell of political events (the death of Tancredo Neves is likened to a mother giving birth to a nation and then expiring before she can suckle her infant), national figures (Getulio Vargas, Jose Sarney), miracles, and festivals as well as traditional comedies and tragedies (eg The woman who lost her honour to Satan). Although their role in diffusing popular culture is threatened by TV, the literatura de cordel is still written, sold and performed in public by Caruaru's street poets.

Near the fairgrounds, the Casa de Cultura José Conde (the Museum of Popular Art) displays locally crafted pieces made of clay, wood and straw, some dating from last century.

Places to Stay

There are cheap hotels in town like the *Hotel Centenario* (tel 721-1932) at Rua 7 de Setembro 24 and the *Grande Hotel São Vicente* (tel 721-5011) at Avenida Rio Branco 365 which have doubles for US$5 and US$8 respectively.

Places to Eat

Fortunately there's plenty of cachaça and sugar cane broth to quench your thirst and local foods like *dobradinhas* (tripe stew), *chambaril* and *sarapatel* (a bloody goulash of pork guts) appease your appetite.

Getting There & Away

Caruaru is linked by shuttle buses to Recife's bus terminal every half hour

(130 km and two hours east) so there's no reason to stay overnight.

Tracunhaém

If you've missed the fair at Caruaru, the next best thing, some say better, is to be in Tracunhaém for their Sunday fair. The village of Tracunhaém, 40 km from Recife in the direction of Carpina, is Pernambuco's number two craft centre. Look for the ceramic work of master artisans Zezinho de Tracunhaem, Severina Batista and Antônio Leão.

Paraíba, Rio Grande do Norte &
Fernando de Noronha

Paraíba

PITIMBU

Praia Pitimbu has a long broad beach, a coconut grove, some thatched roof houses and a couple of bars frequented by sugar cane farmers, fishermen and jangada sail makers. There are no hotels, but if you look friendly and bring a hammock someone will put you up. The turn-off to Praia Pitimbu is just inside the state border (with Pernambuco), some 50 km before João Pessoa on BR-101. The beach itself is 35 km further east from the turn-off.

JACUMÃ & PRAIA DO SOL

Forty km south of João Pessoa, Praia Jacumã is a long thin strip of sand featuring coloured sand bars, natural pools, potable mineral water springs, a shady grove of palms and barracas (open for business on weekends). Halfway between Jacumã and João Pessoa, Praia do Sol, like Jacumã is also a good place to relax – swaying in a hammock, and sipping coconut milk in the shade. Welcome to the tropics.

The Buraquinho Forest Reserve, operated by the IBDF service, is 10 km before João Pessoa on BR-23.

JOÃO PESSOA

Population: 294,000
João Pessoa is a green, surprisingly cool city full of palms (jangueiros, acacias, mangueiras) and girded by forest preserves. Founded in 1585, the coastal city which is capital of Paraíba lies 120 km north of Recife, 688 km south of Fortaleza and 185 km south of Natal.

Information

There are tourist information stands at the rodoviária, airport and Mercado de Artesanato de Tambaú on Avenida Rui Carneiro in addition to the municipal tourist information centre, SETUR, at Parque Solon de Lucena 671 and PBTUR-Paraíba Turismo S/A at Avenida Getúlio Vargas 301. None of them are particularly helpful.

Igreja São Francisco

The principal tourist attraction is the Igreja São Francisco, considered to be one of Brazil's finest churches. Construction was interrupted by successive battles with the Dutch and French, resulting in a beautiful but architecturally confused complex built over three centuries. The facade, church towers and monastery (of Santo Antônio) display a hodgepodge of styles. Portuguese tiled walls lead up to the church's carved jacaranda-wood doors.

City Museum

The Walfredo Rodrigues city museum in the old powder house (casa da pólvora) on Ladeira de São Francisco has some interesting pictures of the old city.

Beaches

Aside from the rusty remains of battles against the French and Dutch, the beaches are clean. Praia Tambaú, seven km directly west of the centre, is rather built-up, but nice. There are bars, restaurants, coconut palms and fig trees along Avenida João Maurício (north) and Avenida Almirante Tamandaré (south). South of Tambaú is Praia Cabo Branco. From here it's a glorious 15 km walk along Praia da Penha – a beautiful stretch of sand, surf, palm groves and creeks – to Ponta de Seixas, the easternmost tip of South America. The combination of extremely clear water and coral make it a good spot for diving.

Immediately north of Tambaú, there are good urban beaches: Marnaíra, Praia do Bessa I and II, Praia do Macaco (the

surfer's beach) and Praia do Poço. Twenty km north of Tambaú are Forte Santa Catarina, Costinha and Camboinha beaches.

July to November is whale hunting season in Costinha so unless you particularly want to see whales being dismembered those months are a good time to avoid the place. Praia Cabedelo has restaurants and bars and boats to Ilha de Areia Vermelha, an island of red sand which emerges from the Atlantic at low tide. Camping is possible on many of these beaches.

Places to Stay - bottom end

João Pessoa's main attraction is Tambaú beach and that's where many of the hotels are although there are modest hotels in the centre as well. The best deal in João Pessoa – if you can get a room – is the *Hotel Gameleira* (tel 226-1576) at Avenida João Maurício 157 with singles/doubles right off Tambaú beach for US$4.50/6.

In the centre the *Hotel Recife* (tel 221-9966) at Rua Alice Azevedo 208 charges US$5/7.50 for singles/doubles or there's the *Aurora* (tel 221-2238) at Praça João Pessoa 51.

Places to Stay – top end

The *Hotel dos Navegantes* (tel 226-4018) at Avenida NS dos Navegantes 122, Tambaú has doubles for US$16.50. It's close to the beach.

The five-star *Hotel Tambaú* (tel 226-3660) at Avenida Almirante Tamandaré 229 on Praia Tambaú is the city's entry into the world of modern architecture. It's immense. From a distance it bears a passing resemblance to a rocket launching pad. The hotel has basic singles/doubles for US$28/32 and more luxurious rooms for US$40/45.

Places to Eat

The dish to try is crab stew (ensopado de caranguejo) at *Peixada do João*, Rua Coração de Jesus in Tambaú.

Things to Buy

Avenida Rui Carneiro on Praia Tambaú has ceramic, wicker, straw and leather goods for sale. On weekends a food fair is held in front of Hotel Tambaú. The Casa do Artesão Paraibano at Rua Maciel Pinheiro 670, Centro also has craft work for sale.

Getting There & Away

The rodoviária (tel 221-9611) on Avenida Francisco Londres in the lower city and Aeroporto Presidente Castro Pinto Bayeux (tel 229-1009) link João Pessoa to Brazil's state capitals.

BAÍA DA TRAIÇÃO

Despite the peaceful, reef-sheltered waters, coconut palms and gentle breezes, Baía da Traição has a bloody past. Here in 1501, the first Portuguese exploratory expedition was slaughtered by the Tabajara Indians. In 1625 the Portuguese had it out with the Dutch, claimed victory and left some rusty cannons and the ruins of a fortress in their wake.

The fishing village has no regular lodging. The beach is 85 km from João Pessoa. It is better than Barra do Cunhaú.

Getting There & Away

The partially paved turn-off to the beach is 27 km north on BR-101 at Maranguape. Rio Tinto lines runs buses twice daily at 5.30 am and 3 pm from João Pessoa's rodoviária (75c, two hours).

Rio Grande do Norte

BAÍA FORMOSA

The fishing village of Baía Formosa has super beaches, a cheap pousada and practically no tourism. The barrel-chested fishermen sail out on loosely rigged boats, to pursue exotic game fish here.

Backed by dunes, Formosa Bay curves from the village end (on the southern part of the bay) to an isolated point to the north. Parts of the beach have dark volcanic rocks eroded into curious forms by the surf. The beaches further south of town are big, empty and spectacular. Surfing is possible.

Places to Stay & Eat

Hotel Miramar (tel 236-2079) at the end of the road by the waterfront has US$2 dorm beds and US$13/15/16.50 double rooms – the more expensive rooms have bath and air-con. It's clean enough for a cheap-o small town hotel. There are two restaurants to choose from.

Getting There & Away

Seventeen km off BR-101 and 10 km from the Rio Grande de Norte and Paraíba border, Baía Formosa is serviced by one daily bus. The bus leaves town at 6.30 am and returns from the junction with BR-101 at 1.30 pm. Direct buses from Natal's rodoviária leave on weekdays at 7.30 am and 3.30 pm, Saturdays at 11.30 am and 3.30 pm, and Sundays at 7.15 am and 5.30 pm.

BARRA DO CUNHAÚ

Barra do Cunhaú, 10 km from Canguaretama on a dirt track, is a hybrid fishing village/resort town. You can camp in the coconut grove.

Getting There & Away

There are three buses a week on Monday, Thursday and Friday at 3.30 pm from Natal.

TIBAU DO SUL

The small and rocky beaches of Tibau do Sul – Madeira, Caçimbinha and Pipa – are said to be among the finest in Rio Grande de Norte. From Goianinha 75 km south of Natal on BR-101, it's 20 km of dirt to the coast.

BÚZIOS TO SENADOR GEORGINO ALVINO

Along with Ponta Negra, this stretch of coast has some of the best beaches Rio Grande do Norte, a state famous for its beaches, has to offer. Búzios is a lovely beach town 35 km south of Natal. Until the hotel is built, it will continue to be frequented solely by weekenders.

Resist the temptation to get off the bus at Búzios. After Búzios the road is reduced to rugged dirt track, then degenerates into two grooves. It crosses a stream and loses a groove leaving the bus bumping along a goat trail. Aside from the red coastal road, a stone road a few hundred metres inland, and the occasional surfer, there's nothing here but small waves crashing against the coast, white dunes, coconut palms, uncut jungle and pretty little farms. The place is idyllic. Get here before the road is finished and the developers move in.

Getting There & Away From Natal there are two buses a day at 8.15 am and 4.30 pm that go directly to Senador Georgino Alvino, but it's more fun to take a bus along the barely negotiable coastal 'road'. From Natal take one of 10 Auto Viação Campos buses to Búzios (45 minutes).

PIRANGI DO SUL & PIRANGI DO NORTE

Fourteen km north of Búzios, the twin beach towns of Pirangi do Sul and Pirangi do Norte are split by a river which courses through palm-crested dunes on its way to the ocean. It's a quiet area where wealthy folk from Natal have put up their beach bungalows. There are a few hotels and restaurants too. Nearby is the world's largest cashew tree – half a km in circumference and still growing!

BARREIRA DO INFERNO

Twenty km from Natal is Barreira do Inferno (hell's gate), the Brazilian Air Force (FAB) rocket base. The base is open for visits on the last Wednesday of each month from 1 to 3 pm. The tour of the base includes a 30 minute talk with slides and films. Visitors must call 222-1638 extension 206 at least one day in advance.

PONTA NEGRA

Ponta Negra jumps on weekends. The beach is nearly three km in length and full of barracas and sailboats. The water is very calm and safe for weak swimmers. At the far end of the beach is a monstrous sand dune. Its face is inclined at 50° and drops straight into the sea. Bordered by jungle green, the slope is perfect for sand skiing. A good exercise for snow skiers is running down the hill. A good exercise for masochists is running up the hill.

Evening activities consist of beer drinking at the barracas, dancing at the Apple Club and gazing for shooting stars and straying rockets. Ponta Negra is 15 km south of Natal on the Via Costeira, a cobbled coastal route.

Places to Stay

The *Pousada a Beira Mar* at Avenida da Praia 41 (information at barraca number 25) is a clean and bare place frequented by a young crowd. Dorm beds with cold water showers down the hall are US$2.50 per person.

The *Pousada da Praia* (tel 236-2924), a few doors down at number 34, has very clean private rooms with fans and ocean-view balconies. Singles are US$5.50. The showers are communal.

NATAL

Population: 376,000

Aside from endless beaches, there's nothing to go out of your way for in Natal. With aspects similar to many of the major cities of the Northeast, Natal is not a memorable place.

History

In 1535, a Portuguese armada left Recife for the falls of the Rio Ceará-Mirim (12 km north of present-day Natal) where they met strong opposition from the French and their Indian allies. For the next 60 years the territories were no man's land and abandoned until the French (recently expelled from Paraíba) began to use it as a base for attacks on the south. The Portuguese organised a huge flotilla from Paraíba and Pernambuco which met at the mouth of the Rio Potenji on Christmas Day 1597 to battle the French.

On 6 January, the day of *Os Reis Magos* (the three wise kings), the Portuguese began to work on the fortress which they used as their base in the war against the French. The Brazilian coastline was hotly contested and in 1633 the fortress was taken by the Dutch who rebuilt the fortress in stone, but retained the five-point star shape. First under Dutch and thereafter Portuguese occupation, Natal grew from the Reis Magos fortress.

With the construction of the railway and the port (1892) Natal grew into a city which remained relatively small and unimportant until WW II. Recognising Natal's strategic location on the eastern bulge of Brazil, Getúlio Vargas and Franklin D Roosevelt decided to turn the sleepy city into the allied military base for operations in North Africa.

Information & Orientation

Natal is a peninsula flanked to the north by the Rio Potenji and the south by Atlantic reefs and beaches. The peninsula tapers, ending at the Fortress of the Reis Magos, the oldest part of the city. The city centre, Cidade Alta, grew near the river port which was built in 1892.

Bookshops Livraria Walter Pereira (tel 222-0957) Avenida Rio Branco, 590 sells English paperbacks.

Things to See

The pentagonal Forte dos Reis Magos at the tip of the city and the Museu da Câmara Cascudo (tel 222-0923) at Avenida Hermes da Fonseca 1398 are the principal non-beach attractions of Natal. The museum of folklore and anthropology features a collection of Amazon Indian artefacts. The museum hours – Tuesday to Friday 8 am to 4 pm – are interrupted for a marathon three-hour lunch break from 11 am to 2 pm.

Beaches

Natal's city beaches – Praia do Meio, Praia dos Artistas, Praia da Areia Preta, Praia do Pinto and Praia Mãe Luzia – stretch well over nine km from the fort to the lighthouse. These are mostly city beaches, with bars, nightlife and big surf. The ones closest to the fort are rocky and closed in by an offshore reef.

Places to Stay

Natal's hotel areas are in the Cidade Alta and along the city beaches.

Pousada Meu Canto (tel 222-8351) at Rua Manoel Dantas 424, Petrópolis charges US$2.50 per person, but we recommend either staying south on the coast or in town at *Hotel e Restaurante Casa Grande* (tel 222-1513), Rua Princesa Isabel 529. It's directly across from the Macrobiótica. They charge US$3/4.50 for singles without/with air-con and US$4.50/6.50 for doubles without/with air-con.

Pousada Esperança (tel 231-5226), 100 metres from the bus station at Avenida Capitão Mar Gouveia 418 has US$6.50 rooms with hot water showers. The *Hotel Bom Jesus* (tel 222-2237) on Avenida Rio Branco and the *Hotel Santo Antônio* (tel

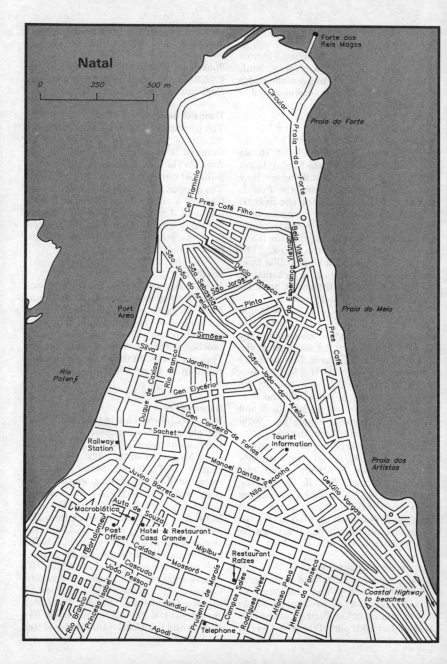

Natal

0   250   500 m

Forte dos
Reis Magos

Praia do Forte

Praia do Melo

Praia dos
Artistas

Rio
Potenji

Port
Area

Railway
Station

Tourist
Information

Macrobiótica
Post
Office

Hotel & Restaurant
Casa Grande

Restaurant
Rafzes

Telephone

Coastal Highway
to beaches

Cel Flamínio
Pres Café Filho
Circular
Praia do Forte
Bela Vista
Décio Fonseca
via Esperança Vianna
São Sebastião
São João do Areial
São Jorge
Pinto
Simões
Silva
Rio Branco
Jardim
Gen Elycério
Duque de Coxias
São João do Areial
Pres Café
Gen Cordeiro de Farias
Sachet
Manoel Dantas
Deconha
Nilo
Getúlio Vargas
Juvino Barreto
Auta de Souza
Bartolomeu
Caldas
Cascudo
João Pessoa
Miplbu
Mossoró
Prudente de Morais
Campos Sales
Rodrigues Alves
Afonso Pena
Hermes da Fonseca
Rio Branco
Princesa Isabel
Jundlai
Apodi

222-2176) on Rua Santo Antônio are two other cheapies in the Cidade Alta.

Natal's fanciest hotels are the *Hotel Luxor* (tel 221-2721) at Avenida Rio Branco 634, with singles/doubles for US$27/30, and *Vila do Mar* (tel 222-3755) on the Via Costeira five km south of town, with singles/doubles for US$39/43.

Places to Eat
The *Macrobiótica* on Rua Princesa Isabel is certainly different. If you're a vegetarian it may be worth it for the rice and beans, but don't expect much from the food or the waitresses.

Restaurante Raízes at Avenida Campos Sales 609 at the corner with Rua Mossoró serves up a rodízio with a choice of 35 regional dishes. *Restaurant Carne Assada do Lira*, Rua Miramar 165 is famous for its carne-do-sol molhada na manteiga de garrafa, a dried meat with a special butter sauce.

Rio Grande do Norte boasts a few good brands of cachaça. Try a shot of Ohlo D'Água, Murim or Carangueijo with a bite of cashew fruit.

Getting There & Away
Air There are flight connections to all Brazilian capitals. Airline offices are located in the Cidade Alta. Vasp (tel 222-7500) is at Avenida João Pessoa 220, Varig/Cruzeiro (tel 222-1535) at Avenida João Pessoa 308 and Transbrasil (tel 221-1805) at Avenida Deodoro 363.

Bus Unlike Recife's beautiful new terminal, the rodoviária is dirty and crowded. There are two daily buses to Salvador (US$8.25, 21 hours), eight daily buses to Recife (US$2, five hours), three regular buses to Fortaleza (US$8, nine hours) and one leito to Fortaleza (US$9, eight hours). There are two buses to Rio. Both take 41 hours, the common bus is US$19, the leito is US$44.

Getting Around
Airport Transport Natal's Augusto Severo airport is 15 km south of town on BR-101.

Local Transport There are municipal buses across from the rodoviária which will take you into the centre to the old bus depot and train station at Praça Augusto Severo. The taxi fare to the centre is US$1.50, to the city beaches it's US$2 and to Praia Ponta Negra it's US$3.50.

NORTH OF NATAL
The beaches immediately north of Natal, where sand dunes plunge into the surf, are beautiful, but not quite as spectacular as the southern beaches.

Praia Redinha
Twenty-five km north of Rio Potenji and Natal, Praia Redinha features 40-metre-high dunes, a good view of Natal, lots of bars and *capongas* (fresh water lagoons).

Genipabu
Five km further north is Genipabu, where golden sand dunes, palm trees and dune buggies converge on a wild little seaside bar. Dune buggy tours will take you along eight km of coastal dunes and palm trees to the lagoon at Pitangui (US$20 per car, up to four passengers).

Places to Stay At Genipabu the brand new *Pousada Genipabu* (tel 221-5672) has spare rooms, good beds and a communal hot shower, singles/doubles are US$18/26.

Getting There & Away Buses to Genipabu and Redinha leave Natal regularly, not from the rodoviária, but from Praça Augusto Severo next to the train station.

Praia Muríu & Praia Maxaranguape
A coastal road is being built which will head north from Genipabu towards Praias Muríu and Maxaranguape, little palm graced bay beaches separated from one another by rivers and hills. The beaches

are readily accessible, but off the beaten track. Muriu is especially nice.

Getting There & Away
Viação Rio Grandense buses from Natal's rodoviária service the area via the town of Ceará-Mirim.

Touros
Sixty km north of Ceará-Mirim is Touros, a fishing village with several beaches, bars and a couple of cheap pousadas.

AREIA BRANCA
The town of Areia Branca, 50 km from Mossoró and BR-304, is a small fishing port. It's possible to visit the super-modern salt docks 25 km away, but only with advance notice.

Places to Stay
The hotel *Areia Branca Praia* is right on Upanema, the town beach.

TIBAÚ
Tibau, 25 km from BR-304, is a bustling resort beach. Truck caravans roll by the surf into Ceará, saving a few km and giving the place a frontier-town flavour. The coast from Tibau, Rio Grande do Norte to Ibicuitaba, Ceará is VW-able at low tide.

Four km west on the coast you come to a river and a friendly outdoor bar. The river's current is swift, nevertheless it's a popular bathing spot. Two men pull you and your vehicle across on a low-tech car ferry – a wooden platform and a piece of rope pegged to both banks – for US$1. Between ferry duty, the float serves as a diving platform for the bathers. Follow the caravan of trucks. From Ibicuitaba the road is paved again.

Fernando de Noronha

Population: 1350
The archipelago of Fernando de Noronha

with its crystal-clear water and rich marine life is a heavenly retreat for underwater sportsmen. The island is sparsely populated and tourism is limited to the one hotel, which is available only through organised tours. A struggle over the future of the island has heated up in recent years. Some want to develop it into a Club Med type resort for the wealthy. Environmentalists want the islands declared a national park and preserved. For now the island's beauty is off-limits unless you have a fair amount of money.

History
Several hundred km off the coast from Natal the archipelago of what is today known as Fernando de Noronha was discovered by the Spanish adventurer and cartographer Juan de la Costa. The islands first appeared on the maps by the name of Quaresma (meaning Lent). A Portuguese expedition under the command of Fernando de Noronha sighted the islands once again in 1504. He was awarded the islands by his friend the King Dom Manoel. It was the first inherited captaincy of the Brazilian colonies.

The islands with their strategic position between Europe and the New World were coveted by the English, French and the Dutch who came to occupy the archipelago. But by 1557 the Portuguese managed to reclaim Fernando de Noronha and build a fortress. All that remains today of the European battles are the ruins of the fortress of NS dos Remédios and a few sunken shipwrecks.

Over the years the islands were used as a military base by the USA during WW II, a prison, weather station, air base and most recently as a tourist resort. There has already been some misguided tampering with the island ecology.

The teju, a black and white lizard, was introduced to eat the island rats which had come ashore with the Europeans in colonial days. Unfortunately, the teju prefers small birds and crab to rat.

The environmentalists want to avoid

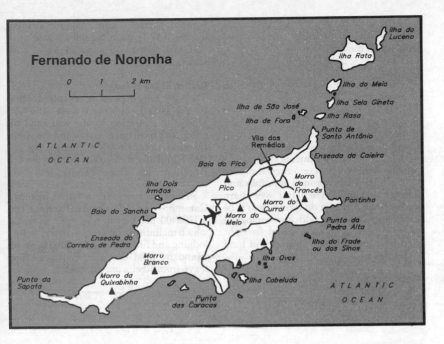

further mistakes and hope to turn Fernando de Noronha into a marine park something like Abrolhos off the Bahian coast. They want to protect the island's natural treasures which include 24 different species of marine birds, two marine tortoises (one, *eretmocheiva imbricata* in danger of extinction), sharks, stingrays, dolphins, whales and a vast number of different fish.

Information & Orientation

The archipelago of Fernando de Noronha lies 145 km from Atol das Rocas, 525 km from Recife and 350 km from Natal. The archipelago is comprised of 21 islands, which together are only 26 square km.

On the largest and only inhabited island, the population is concentrated in Vila dos Remédios. Although Pico hill, the highest point on the island, is only 321 metres above sea level it is well over 4300 metres above the ocean floor, as the island is an extinct volcanic mountain cone. The island-mountain is part of the Dorsal Atlantic ridge, an underwater mountain chain which is over 15,000 km long.

The rainy season is from February to July and the islands are one time zone hour ahead of eastern Brazil. Bring everything you'll need for your stay (eg suntan lotion, insect repellent, magazines, snorkelling gear); there isn't much to buy on the islands.

Diving

You can watch hundreds of dolphins play around incoming boats every morning at Carreiro do Pedra bay or Baía dos Golfinhos or you can take a boat out to the smaller islands or go scuba diving. The Aguas Claras company organise scuba diving excursions with instructors and will rent you equipment. You can dive in the Bay of Santo Antônio where the *Paquistão* and the *Ana Maria* wrecks lie seven metres underwater or at Sapata Point where a Spanish corvette lies beneath 60 metres of water.

Beaches

The island beaches are deserted, clean and beautiful. The beaches of Caiera, Atalaia and Ponta das Caracas have rougher waters than Biboca, Conceição, Praia do Sancho and Baía dos Golfinhos. Cacimba do Padre beach is the only one with fresh water. You can get to Praia do Sancho either by boat or a rugged nature trail which leads through bramble and bush, past almond trees and over sharp rocks. Once at Praia do Santos you'll be lucky to witness an odd meteorological phenomenon: without a cloud in sight rain falls mysteriously on a spot of land 10 metres wide.

Places to Stay

The only hotel is *Vila dos Remédios*. The

hotel/ex-barracks were built for airmen during WW II when Noronha was a way station between US bases in Natal and Dakar.

Getting There & Away

There are only expensive, organised tours to the island, but even these are not always in operation so you will need to check with local travel agents. Independent travel is not permitted. Flights are on VASP and any rumours of free hitches on Brazilian air force (FAB) jets are unconfirmed.

Arrange a tour with a travel agency. Caminhos de Sol Turismo in Recife offers a US$400 per person one week package which includes airfare to and from Recife, lodging and full board and guided tours of island by land and sea. Package tours leave from Recife once a week.

Ceará, Piauí & Maranhão

Ceará

Ceará's pride and glory is its coastline – nearly 600 km of glorious beaches. Any time spent in Fortaleza or inland is time spent away from Ceará's singular attraction, the beach. Don't let anyone tell you otherwise. The beach in this part of the Northeast is more than the happy meeting of sand and water, it is a special way of life. In nearly all of the beach towns, the people of Ceará live out their folklore every day of the year. They make old-fashioned lace work and handicrafts, cook up homemade candies and sweets, sleep in hammocks and live in thatched-roof homes. The fisherman sail handmade sailboats – called jangadas – which have droopy masts and full sails.

Should you stray inland into the sertão, you will see a rugged drought plagued land, a bleak landscape of dust and caatinga, peopled by the poor and proud vaqueiros. These cowboys use their cattle for everything – they eat the dried meat, fashion tools from bone and make clothing from the hides – nothing is wasted. This is the land of big landowners and sertão bandits.

For all its size and wealth of culture, Ceará is a poor and undeveloped state. Poverty and disease are rampant and dengue and yellow fever are endemic. Cars and buses are sprayed for mosquitoes at highway police stations, particularly at state borders.

Festivals & Folklore

A beach to beach regatta of jangadas is held in the second half of July in Fortaleza and the town's folklore week takes place in the Centro do Turismo from 22 to 29 August. There's no need to wait for these events or go to museums to witness Ceará's crafts. The *romaria* (pilgrimage) to Juazeiro do Norte in honour of Padre Cícero takes place on 1 and 2 November. Padre Cícero is a controversial figure of the sertão. Not only was he a curate with several miracles to his credit, but he also exercised a strong political influence.

FORTALEZA
Population: 650,000
According to revisionist Cearense historians, the Spanish navigator Vicente Yanez was supposed to have landed on Mucuripe beach on 2 February 1500, two months before Pedro Álvares Cabral sighted Monte Pascoal in Bahia. Despite the early claim to fame the Portuguese captaincy was first colonised in 1612 by Portuguese sailing from the Azores. Martim Soares Moreno and company settled on the banks of the Ceará river.

The vast majority of the people in this crowded and littered city are miserably poor, the public transport system is a mess, the beaches in town are foul and there are no other sites or attractions to speak of. The weather is good, but not much different from the climate a thousand km north or south along the coast. In all fairness, there isn't much going for Fortaleza other than a few good restaurants and some super beaches 20 km beyond the city limits in either direction.

History
The settlement at present day Fortaleza was hotly contested: it was taken over by the Dutch in 1635, then lost in turn to the Tabajara Indians. In 1639 the Dutch under the command of Matias Beck landed once again, fought off the Indians and put up a fortress. In 1654 the Portuguese captured the fortress and reclaimed the site. A town grew around the fortress which was given the name of Fortaleza de NS da Assunção (Fortress of Our Lady of Assumption). It's not

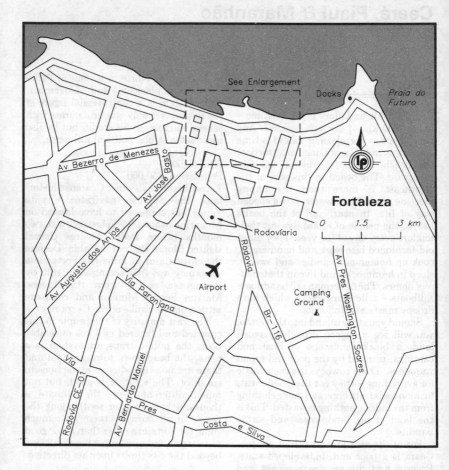

See Enlargement

Docks

Praia do Futuro

Av Bezerra de Menezes

Av José Basto

Fortaleza

0   1.5   3 km

Rodoviária

Av Augusto dos Anjos

Via Paranjana

Airport

Rodovia

Br-116

Camping Ground

Av Pres Washington Soares

Via

Via

Rodovia CE-01

Av Bernardo Manuel

Pres

Costa

e Silva

mentioned in too many history books, but the Indian battles were ongoing and fierce, delaying colonisation for many years.

Information & Orientation

The main hotel strip is on Avenida Presidente Kennedy along Praia de Iracema, Praia do Ideal, Praia dos Diários, Praia do Meireles Praia do Mucuripe, Praia do Náutico, Volta da Jurema and Praia do Titan in one continuous strip of sand to the old light-house of Mucuripe. Praia do Futuro begins at the lighthouse and extends five km along Avenida Zezé Motta to the Hunting & Fishing Club (Clube Caça e Pesca). Cheap hotels can be found on Rua Senador Pompeu. The Central Market is in the city centre.

Tourist Office Emcetur, the state subsidiary of the Embratur tourist organisation has a brochure stand in the Centro do Turismo, right beneath the folk museum and keeping the same hours. There are other

Emcetur branches at the airport and Rodoviária.

Telephone The Teleceará phone station in the airport is open 24 hours; the rodoviária's Teleceará is open from 6 am to 10 pm.

Money When the government cracks down on the parallel exchange, and you're not lodging at a fancy hotel, currency exchange can be very difficult. If this should happen while you're in Fortaleza, ask around.

Museums

The Centro do Turismo at Rua Senador Pompeu 350 is a reformed jail full of artisan shops, a folk museum and Emcetur tourist information stand. The Museu de Arte e Cultura Populares (folk museum) is a minor attraction. There are examples of local crafts as well as full scale displays of a traditional loom, ox and jangadas. The museum is open Monday to Friday 8 am to midday and 2 to 6 pm and Saturday mornings.

Ceará's museum of regional history and anthropology (Museu Histórico e Antropológico) at Avenida Barão de Studart 410, Aldeota is open Tuesday to Friday from 8 am to 5.30 pm, Saturdays and Sundays from 8 am to midday and 2 to 6.30 pm.

Other Attractions

The José Alencar Theatre (1910) is a pastel-coloured hybrid of classical and art nouveau architecture. The building stands before the rodoviária and square of the same name. The Castelo Branco Mausoleum for the military president from Bahia is a yawner on Avenida Barão de Studart. Across the street some of the more sentimental militaries kept pieces of his plane wreck.

Beaches

Fortaleza's city beaches are generally dirty and, with the exception of Praia do Futuro, they are unfit for bathing. There are pleasant beaches within 45 minutes of town (1½ hours or so by public transport), but Ceará's extraordinary beaches all lie further from Fortaleza.

Near Ponte Metálica, the old port, Praia de Iracema was a source of inspiration to Luis Assunção and Milton Dias, Ceará's Bohemian poets of the '50s. Unfortunately this beach is best forgotten. The Praia do Meireles faces the hotel and restaurant strip on Avenida Presidente Kennedy and is a good evening hang out. The same is true of Volta da Jurema.

Fortaleza's colonists first settled at Praia da Barra do Ceará at the mouth of the Rio Ceará. A clean length of sand stretching five km from Avenida Zezé Diogo to the Clube Caça e Pesca and the mouth of the Rio Coco, the Praia do Futuro, is the sole good city beach. Like Rio de Janeiro's Barra de Tijuca it is being built up at an alarming rate. There are barracas which serve fried fish and shrimp. To get there take the buses marked Serviluz or Pr do Futuro.

The beaches immediately north of Fortaleza, Cumbuco and Iparana, are both pleasantly tranquil. Harried travellers can relax from the tensions of tropical living, string up a hammock in the shade of some palm trees, sip coconut milk and rock themselves to sleep. Public transport – a bus from Praça Lagoinha to Cuiaca and then bus from Cuiaca – is a drag. Take a cab.

Places to Stay – bottom end

The Fortaleza tourism office operates a 24 hour alternative (cheap) lodging hotline on (085) 231-1814. They'll try to find you a place for as little as US$2.

The *Hotel Lord* (tel 231-6188) at Rua 24 de Maio 642, right off Praça José Alencar, is far and away the favourite hotel. There are cheaper places, but not this clean. Doubles with hot bath are US$5 or 5.50 with air-con. Nearby is the *Central Hotel* at Rua 24 de Maio 949. The *Pousada da Praia* (tel 224-5935) at Avenida Mons

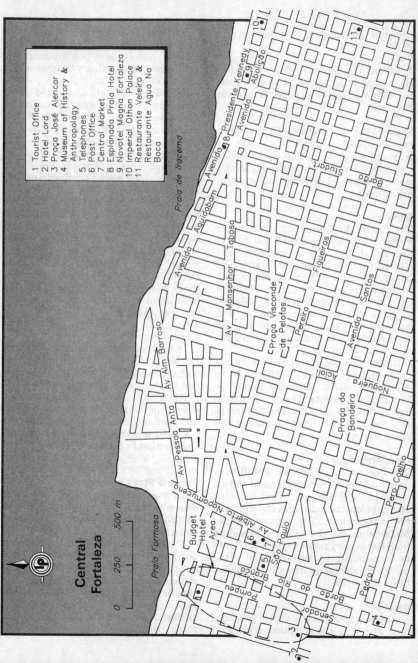

Central Fortaleza

1 Tourist Office
2 Hotel Lord
3 Praça José Alencar
4 Museum of History &
  Anthropology
5 Telephones
6 Post Office
7 Central Market
8 Esplanada Praia Hotel
9 Novotel Magna Fortaleza
10 Imperial Othon Palace
11 Restaurante Veleiro &
   Restaurante Agua Na
   Boca

Tabosa 1315 has doubles for US$6.50 or US$9 with air-con. It's a poor location, but they will change your dollars.

There are many dives on Rua Senador Pompeu like *Tio Patinhas* (tel 221-3081) at 725 with US$4 doubles or *Universo Hotel* (tel 226-9248) at 1152. Singles vary in price from US$1.50 to US$3, doubles US$3 to US$5. Shop around for cleanliness, not price.

Places to Stay – middle
The *Hotel Amuarama* (tel 272-2111) is a surprisingly good two-star Embratur hotel next to the rodoviária. Singles go for US$10 to US$14, doubles US$12 to US$17. The rooms come with air-con, TV and hot showers. The hotel has a café and a pool.

Also nearby is the *Hotel NS de Fátima*, the standard cheap-o rodoviária digs for US$2 per person. The *Jangadeiro Praia Hotel* (tel 224-5653) at Avenida da Abolição 2480, Praia Meireles has US$10 doubles with hot showers and is very clean but noisy. It's located across from the Imperial Othon Palace – take the Serviluz bus. The hotel next door is comparable in quality and a little more expensive.

Places to Stay – top end
There are two five-star hotels facing Meireles beach on Avenida Presidente Kennedy. The *Esplanada Praia Hotel* (tel 224-8555) at 2000 has doubles from US$45 so it's affordable luxury. The *Imperial Othon Palace* (tel 244-9177) at 2500 has singles for US$50.

Novotel Magna Fortaleza (tel 244-1122) at Avenida Presidente Kennedy 2380 is a very slick four-star Embratur hotel with a swimming pool and the usual amenities (TV, air-con, phone, fridge). Doubles start at US$36.

Places to Eat
You can eat well in Fortaleza. There's delicious crab, lobster, shrimp and fish and a fantastic variety of tropical fruits including cashews, coconut, mango,

guava, sapoti, graviola, passionfruit, murici, cajá and others.

There are several local dishes worth tasting. Peixe a delícia is a highly recommended favourite. Try paçoca, a typical Cearense dish made of sun-dried meat, ground with a mortar and pestle, mixed with manioc and then roasted. The tortured meat is usually accompanied by baião de dois made of rice, cheese, beans and butter.

Avenida Presidente Kennedy has several expensive seafood places such as *Trapiche* at number 3956 in Mucuripe. *Restaurante Sandra's* (take a cab from Praia do Futuro) is an OK but overpriced place for a lobster blow-out for US$6.

To have really good food in Fortaleza you must go to Mucuripe or the Aldeota neighbourhood. The Aldeota area near Rua José do Amaral and Rua Coronel Jura is home to the *Restaurante Veleiro* which serves a fantastic peixe a delícia (fish with banana, coconut and cheese sauce, US$3.50). At the aptly named *Restaurante Água Na Boca* (literally water in the mouth) Rua República do Líbano 1084 we recommend the moqueca mixta.

Also in Mucuripe the *Bar do Povo* and *Restaurante Osmar* (Rua São João 147) have been recommended. The barracas at Cumbuco, Prainha and Paracuru beaches out of town serve simple but very good seafood dishes.

Vegetarians can eat at *Caminho a Saúde* at Rua Barão do Rio Branco 1468, Centro or *Restaurante Alvita* a few doors down at number 1486.

Entertainment
Much of the action during holiday season is out on the hotel strip on Avenida Presidente Kennedy. There are outdoor bars and merchants and artists hawking their stuff. *Oba Oba* at Avenida Washington Soares 3199, Água Fria; *Saudosa Maloca* at Avenida Washington Soares 2101 and *Clube de Vaqueiro* (for forró) are three

nightspots with shows, dancing or live music.

Call ahead or pop into the *Imperial Othon* for up to date nightlife information. Basically it's the Praia do Futuro by day, Volta da Jurema by night (best hotels and restaurants) and the fair on Sundays.

Twenty km out of town, *Cel Weyne Centro Espírito Amor ao Próximo* (phone 229-0775 for directions and schedules) doesn't really fit within the rubric of 'nightlife' (or sights for that matter); it's a spiritist-African religious community that holds wild evening ceremonies.

Things to Buy

Fortaleza is one of the Northeast's most important craft centres. Artisans work with carnaúba palm fronds, bamboo, vines leather and lace. Much of the production is geared to the tourist, but there's a fair amount of goods for more typical and poorer urban and sertanejo markets. Among the junk and clothing you can find saddles, bridles, harnesses and images of saints for pilgrims.

Fairs are held about town from Tuesdays to Sundays:

Tuesday
    Praça João Gentil in Gentiláindia
Wednesday
    Praça Luiz Tavora in Aldeota
Thursday
    Praça da Professora
Friday
    Praça Portugal in Aldeota
    Rua dos Tabajaras at Praia Iracema
    Praças Farias Brito, da Igreja Redonda and
    José Bonifácio
Saturday
    Praça Pio IX, Praça Presidente Roosevelt,
    Gustavo Barroso, Cristo Rei and da
    Aerolândia
Sunday
    Praça da Imprensa in Aldeota

You can purchase sand paintings on Avenida Presidente Kennedy, watch the artists work and have them customise your design. Lace work, embroidery, raw leather goods, ceramics and articles made of straw are also available at the Mercado Central, at the Tourist Centre on Avenida Monsenhor Tabosa, the Luiz Tavora Handicrafts Centre, the Centro do Turismo at Rua Senador Pompeu 350, the Central de Artesanato at Avenida Santos Dumont 1500 in Aldeota, the Cooperativa Artesanal de Fortaleza at Avenida Santos Dumont 1589 and the Mercado Central on Rua General Bezerril.

Getting There & Away

Air There are flight connections with all capital cities in Brazil.

Bus Fortaleza is 688 km north of João Pessoa, 537 km north of Natal, 634 km from Teresina and 2805 km from Rio de Janeiro.

The rodoviária is in the direction of the Vila União neighbourhood, about six km from downtown. It's at Avenida Borges de Melo 1630 and Rua Deputado Oswaldo at the Barrio de Fátima.

There's one daily Itapemirim semi-leito bus to Salvador (20 hours, US$10) and Rio de Janeiro (48 hours, US$20). Of the six daily buses to Natal there are leitos and common buses with and without air-con. There are three buses to São Luis (17 hours, US$8).

Empresa Redenção runs 10 buses a day to Quixada (3½ hours) and Quixeramibim (four hours) and 13 buses a day to Baturité (two hours). Ipu Brasileira goes to Ubajara seven times a day (six hours) and four times a day to Juazeiro do Norte (nine hours). The daily bus to Gijoca (for Jericoacoara) leaves at 8 am (US$2.50, eight hours). There are four buses a day to Aracati (for Canoa Quebrada, 2½ hours). For more information call 227-4614 or 227-1566.

Getting Around

Airport Transport Pinto Martins airport is a couple of km further from the rodoviária, in the direction of the Vila União neighbourhood from the centre. From the airport municipal buses go to Praça José Alencar in downtown.

Local Transport Public transport, particularly to beaches north of town, is a mess. If you value your tanning hours, take a taxi. The three main rodoviárias in town are within a few blocks of each other: Praça José de Alencar, Praça Castro Carneiro and Praça Coração de Jesus.

From the rodoviária take the Aguanambe Rodoviária municipal bus to the centre or the Tres de Maio bus to the Avenida Presidente Kennedy hotel and beach strip. Taxis from the rodoviária to the city are US$1.25, to Avenida Presidente Kennedy about US$2.

Tours Protec Turismo Ltda (tel 231-5599) on Rua Major Facundo 814 organises bus tours to beaches south of Fortaleza. One tour spends a day at the beaches of Canoa Quebrada, the second visits several beaches including Morro Branco, Iguape and Prainha. The tours cost about US$5 each, but they're hassle-free and can be a good idea if you're stuck in Fortaleza and don't have time to stay overnight at the beach towns. The buses will pick you up and drop you off at your hotel door. Avoid city tours of Fortaleza.

Car Rental If you intend to rent a car during the summer, reserve in advance.

SOUTH OF FORTALEZA

The coastal road from Fortaleza south to Aracati, CE-004, runs about 10 km inland. It's a flat, dry landscape of shrubs, stunted trees and some lakes. The soil is a sandy white and the towns are poor and small but the beaches have large white dunes and there are many jangadas.

Prainha

Thirty-three km south of Fortaleza via BR-116 and seven km from Aquiraz, is the beach town of Prainha (means little beach). Prainha is very, very nice and the local fisherman will give you rides on their jangadas.

Places to Stay There are two modest hotels in Prainha – the *Aquiraz Praia Hotel* (tel (085) 226-9706), doubles with bath for US$6.50/9.50, and the *Prainha Solar Hotel* (tel (085) 224-4463) are both a bit away from the beach.

Iguape

Iguape, five km south of Prainha, is also a charming little beach with jangadas, a few lonely palm trees and sand dunes breaking the clean line of the horizon. Kids in town ski down the dunes on planks of wood.

In Iguapo, women and children make wonderful lace work. Four or more wooden bobs are held in each hand and clicked rapidly and rhythmically. The bobs lay string around metal pins which are stuck in burlap cushions. Using this process beautiful, intricate lace flowers are crafted.

Save your purchases for Centro das Rendeiras, six km inland, where the lace work is just as fine and cheaper. They also make sweet cakes here from raw sugar cane broth. The broth is boiled into a thick mass, pressed and reboiled in vats.

Places to Stay & Eat There are two pensions in town, but you can easily rent out rooms or houses. The *Restaurante de Iguape*, on the beach near the dunes, serves an excellent breaded fish US$2 and a fair lobster for US$4.

Getting There & Away São Benedito buses to Prainha and Iguarape leave every hour until 8 pm from Praça da Escola Normal in Fortaleza.

Morro Branco

This lovely beach is limited on the coast by the rivers Choro and Piranji and inland by red cliffs. Spurn the annoying child-guides who swarm around beach gringos and instead enjoy the following options:

take a jangada ride to the caves, hike to the cliffs of coloured sands, drink from the natural springs of the Praia das Fontes, or simply savour the sun and surf.

Places to Stay There are two hotels on the beach. *Hotel Recanto Praiano* (tel 224-7118) and *Pousada do Morro Branco* (tel 223-3433) have singles/doubles for US$5.50. *Pousada do Morro Branco* is older than its competitor, but better value. Both hotels serve meals.

Getting There & Away Morro Branco and Beberibe are 87 km south from Fortaleza on BR-116 and CE-004. There are four daily São Benedito buses to Morro Branco from Fortaleza's rodoviária, the first leaving at 6 am, the last at 5 pm (two hours). There are also two daily buses to Aracati.

Aracati

Aracati is a good-size town by the Rio Jaguaribe. If you're stuck there the *Pousada Sandra* (tel 421-0024) near the sacred art museum on Rua Alexandrino Lima 591, is cheap.

The towns south of Aracati, poor little villages often without electricity or running water, are set on stunningly beautiful, wide beaches. There's very little in the way of regular accommodation, but it's easy to camp out on barren beaches.

Canoa Quebrada

Once a tiny fishing village cut off from the world by its huge pink sand dunes, Canoa Quebrada is still tiny and pretty but no longer the shangri-la of the past. There are lots of hip international types running about, but basically the village has

Jangada

peaked. Other than the beach the main attractions are watching the sun set from the dunes, riding horses bareback and dancing forró by the light of gas lanterns.

Hire a horse (four hours US$6 after bargaining) and ride early in the morning; ride north until the telegraph lines, then head inland near a golden ridge of dunes towards villages, ponds, palm fringed lakes and long flat meadows.

Places to Stay The *Lua Morena* is the closest thing to a regular hotel, but US$8 is way overpriced for dark and dirty rooms. The villagers can put you up in a hammock or cot for US$1 or less. Despite the poor lodging, Canoa Quebrada is very crowded in the summer.

There is no electricity in town so flashlights or candles are handy. Take care, bichos de pé are underfoot. Wear shoes all around town and wherever pigs, sheep, and dogs roam freely.

Getting There & Away There are no direct buses to Canoa Quebrada. From Fortaleza's rodoviária take one of four daily buses to Aracati at 7 am, 11.50 am, 2 pm and 5 pm. It's a 2½ hour trip.

Majorlândia

Majorlândia, 14 km south of Aracati, has a wide, clean beach with many barracas and jangadas.

Places to Stay & Eat *Apartamento Beira Mar* (tel (085) 421-1748 Ramal 134) on the beach has US$3/5.50 doubles. It's a good cheap hotel with electricity and is one alternative to the bad accommodation and craziness of Canoa Quebrada. Try *Restaurant Dengo da Bia* for seafood.

Quixaba

Five km further south of Majorlândia on a sandy track are the distinctive, chalky white sandstone bluffs of Quixaba. From the bluffs, cut by gullies between cacti and palms, you can see the pink hills of Canoa

Quebrada. You can rent a jangada and visit the neighbouring beaches.

Places to Stay *Fillo* has clean and quiet rooms to let with electricity.

SOUTH TO RIO GRANDE DO NORTE

For the next 50 km until the border with Rio Grande do Norte, the coast is just a series of primitive little beaches and towns mostly off the maps and definitely out of the guidebooks: Lagoa de Mato, Fontainha, Retirinho and Retiro Grande Mutamba, Ponta Grossa, Redonha and Retiro (waterfall), Peroba, Picos, Barreiras and Barrinha, then Itapuí.

Three buses a day go from Fortaleza to the village of Itapuí; it's a 3½ hour ride. A road continues to Ibicuitaba and Barra do Ceará beach. It's possible to drive from there to Tabau, Rio Grande do Norte at low tide.

NORTH OF FORTALEZA
Paracuru & Other Beaches

About 100 km from Fortaleza on BR-222 and CE-135, Paracuru is a Cearense version of Rio de Janeiro's Búzios. Coconut palms, natural freshwater springs and jangadas complete a tranquil beach picture. Houses can be rented cheaply.

Praia da Lagoinha, a bit after Paracuru, has lots of coconut palms, good camping and a small but deep lagoon near the sand dunes. Have a beer and fish stew at *Bar Restaurante Seu Milton*.

The beaches of Mundau, Guajira and Freicheiras, 125 km from Fortaleza via BR-222, are still traditional fishing areas with unspoiled wide sweeps of sand.

Near the city of Itapipoca, the beaches of Baleia, Pracianos, Inferno and Marinheiros have been recommended as beaches to be explored. They are well off the beaten track, 330 km west of Fortaleza,

Jericoacoara

This latest remote-and-primitive 'in' beach has become popular among backpackers and hipper Brazilians, thus replacing Canoa Quebrada in stature. Jericoacoara is a rough little fishing village where dozens of palms drowning in sand dunes face jangadas stuck on a broad grey beach. It's very hard to get there, so you might as well stay a while. Pigs, goats, sheep, horses, burros and dogs roam the sandy streets at will.

You can boogie at the forró held every evening – just follow the music. You can also climb the sand dunes, hitch a ride on a jangada, or walk to Pedra Furada, a rock three km east along the beach. At low tide the beach route is safer than the hill route. You can also hire horses and gallop 18 km west along the beach from Jericoacoara to the still smaller town of Mangue Seco. Trucks go to Mangue Seco on Monday and Thursday.

Places to Stay & Eat Accommodation is cheap but dirty and there is no electricity or running water – just gas lanterns and running pigs. You can rent a local's house for about US$2.50 or hang your hammock for US$1. There are two restaurants in town, both with cheap, passable food. Frederico the German – the guy with the green jeep – plans to open a pousada and a third restaurant.

Words to the wise: bring a large cotton hammock or bed roll with sheet sleeping sack, as well as bottled water which is sometimes scarce. It's best to avoid bichos de pé and other parasites by not walking the streets barefoot.

Stay clear of the mud-and-straw-walled homes which may harbour Reduvid bugs, transmitters of Chagas' disease. If you do stay in a mud house, sleep with your body and head covered. There is no cure for Chagas' disease, which causes progressive constriction and hardening of the blood vessels – placing increasing strain on the heart.

Getting There & Away There is a gruelling daily eight hour bus ride leaving from Fortaleza's rodoviária at 8 am and arriving 24 km shy of Jericoacoara in Gijoca, roughly by 4 pm. The road(s) to Gijoca are miserable and confusing. The route is best negotiated by a 4WD equipped with over-sized wheels, figa hanging from the rear-view mirror and plastic Jesus on the dashboard.

There is an informal and irregular jeep, pickup truck and sometimes burro service to Jericoacoara. When the bus from Fortaleza arrives, the vehicles fill up and leave en masse. Collective bargaining among the passengers should bring the fare to US$2.50 or less per person.

If you have come by car or even a VW Fusca, take your vehicle no further. Leave it parked in Gijoca where some of the pousada owners can keep an eye on it. The ride over and around sweeping dunes, lagoons, bogs and flat scrub terrain is beautiful, but very hard on people and machines. Transport back to Gijoca usually leaves Jeri after 5 pm.

To get to Jericoacoara from Sobral take a Vale do Acaraú bus to Bela Cruz on an abysmally paved road and intercept the Fortaleza to Gijoca bus there.

Gijoca
Gijoca has a few pousadas (50c per person in hammocks), a sorveteria, a lanchonete, and a fuel station (alcohol on reserve not pumped).

Sobral
Sobral has two minor sights, faded glories from the past before BR-222: the Dom José Museum of Sacred Art on Rua Dom Jose, open Tuesday to Saturday from 1 to 5 pm and Sunday mornings from 8 am to midday; and the São João neoclassical theatre (built in 1880) on Praça Antônio Ibiapina.

Places to Stay Sobral's *Hotel Municipal* on Praça do Figueira has cheap US$6 doubles with cold showers, air-con and frigo-bar.

Getting There & Away There are seven buses a day to Camocim from Sobral. The earliest bus to make the 3½ hour trip leaves at 5.30 am, the last at 7.30 pm.

Camocim

Camocim is a fishing village and beach town set off the river Coreau in north-western Ceará near the Piauí border. The town economy revolves around the salt works and lobster fishing. On Praia das Barreiras and do Faro, two and four km from town respectively, you can sip coconut water while tanning.

Places to Stay & Eat The three pousadas in town, face the ocean. Riverbank restaurants *ODS* and *Fortim* serve the local seafood and typical Cearense dishes. Access to Jericoacoara by sea or beach in a 4WD is difficult but worthwhile. During high season there are boats sailing from Camocim to Jericoacoara – the trip takes eight hours. Half the adventure is getting there.

CANINDÉ

Population: 20,000

Canindé, only 110 km inland from Fortaleza on the BR-020, is the site of one of the Northeast's great religious pilgrimages, O Santuário de São Francisco das Chagas. Since 1775 pilgrims have been coming to Canindé to offer promises and favours to São Francisco de Assis. Nowadays around 250,000 fervent believers arrive each year, most from the sertão, almost all dirt poor. For westerners the festival is both colourful and bizarre, and laced with superstition. You'll see many ex-voto offerings and miracle cures. It's a scene right out of a Glauber Rocha film – Brazil's famous director.

The festival begins 24 September at 4 am, pilgrims continue arriving and things get going in earnest on 30 September with the celebration for the *lavradores* (farm workers), then the celebration for the vaqueiros (cowboys) on

1 October and the *violeiros* (guitarists and guitar makers) on 2 October.

The festivities culminate on 4 October, starting at 3 am when the first of nine masses begins and is followed by a 70,000 strong procession.

UBAJARA

The main attractions of Ubajara National Park are the cable car ride down to the caves and the caves themselves. Nine chambers with strange limestone formations extend over half a km into the side of a mountain. The park and its beautiful vistas, forest, waterfalls and three km trail to the caves are alone worth the visit to the park.

Unfortunately, in 1987 the lower station of the cable car was wiped out by boulders which fell after the winter rains. The station was jerked 18 metres off its foundation and pieces of the teleferique were flung 500 metres into the sertão. The upper station was built on a weak sandstone ledge which is also being undermined by the rains. It's doubtful that it will be repaired soon. Ever since the state stopped paying for electricity in 1982 the lights in the cavern have been turned off and the caves are now locked shut.

Information

The IBDF office, five km from Ubajara proper, has a few brochures and maps.

Places to Stay & Eat

Half a km from the park entrance the *Pousada de Neblina* (tel 634-1270) on the Estrada do Teleférico has US$8.50/14 doubles, a swimming pool and restaurant. It's a good deal and they offer a 30% discount to guests who decline breakfast.

The *Hotel Ubajara* (tel 634-1261) at Rua Juvêncio Luis Pereira 370 is a cheaper hotel in town, with singles/doubles for US$1.30/3.

Getting There & Away

Empresa Ipu-Brasília has seven daily buses from Fortaleza to Ubajara (US$2.50, six hours, 331 km via BR-222 and CE-075). The first bus leaves at 4 am, the last one at 9 pm. There are also bus connections to Teresina, Piauí.

BICO DO IPU

Seventy-five km south-south-east of Ubajara and two km up into the Serra da Ibiapaba mountains from Ipu (waterfall in the Tabajara Indian language), the powerful jet of the Bico do Ipu waterfall drops 100 metres and fans out into sheets of mist and spray.

The Serra da Ibiapaba, a range running along the undefined border with the state of Piauí, forms a rugged terrain of buttes, bluffs and cliffs, overlooking distant plains. There is a sleazy restaurant under the falls, but no hotels in town. It's not worth going out of your way for.

MARANGUAPE

Thirty-eight km from Fortaleza on the way to the Serra de Baturité is the town of Maranguape, famous for its Ypioca brand cachaça. The Ypioca aguardente factory is six km from town, the turn-off is near the Shell station. There is no regular transportation to the cachaça plant, but it's not a bad hike and most of the traffic is headed in your direction.

At the gate, ask for a tour of the 138-year-old plant. Before stepping within the grounds, a pungent sour mash smell assaults the senses. Whirring, clanking, steam-spitting Industrial Revolution era machinery crushes the cane to pulp and mush. The raw sugar cane mash undergoes alcoholic fermentation, is distilled, then aged one to three years in huge wooden casks.

PACATUBA

Pacatuba is a cute little town in the shadow of the Serra de Baturité. The Balneário Bico das Andreas spring is smelly, dirty and not what it's cracked up to be.

Places to Stay The *Pousada das Andreas* (tel 345-1252) charges US$14 for a four-room bungalow that sleeps eight and comes with kitchenette and refrigerator.

SERRA DE BATURITÉ

Ceará's interior is not only harsh and dry sertão. There are mountain ranges which break up the monotony of the sun-scorched land. The Serra de Baturité is the closest mountain range to Fortaleza. A natural watershed, it is an oasis of lush green where coffee and bananas grow clinging to the cliffs and jagged spines of the mountain. The mountain green is cleanly separated from the brown shrubbery of the foothills by a sharp line. The climate is tempered by rain, the evenings are cool and morning fog obscures Pico Alto (1115 metres), the highest point of Ceará. There are a few resorts with mineral pools (thermas) clustered around the town of Baturité 95 km from Fortaleza.

Getting There & Away

Although there's a tourist train heading into the mountains from Fortaleza (leaves Sundays at 7.30 am, make reservations in advance from the station), it's probably not worth touring the area without a car.

Guaramiranga

One of the prettiest villages in the heights of the Baturité mountains is Guaramiranga.

Places to Stay & Eat The CNEC teachers training centre (tel (085) 227-6342 ext 120) right in town has spotless rooms with hot showers, a swimming pool, ping-pong tables and bar. Singles/doubles are US$2/4. It's unmarked and tricky to find (no sign), but it's a great deal. The *Remanso Hotel e Restaurante da Serra* (tel 227-7395, ext 195) is five km from Guaramiranga on the beautiful road to Pacoti. The hotel has nondescript US$7 doubles with hot water showers, a swimming pool and decent food.

Juazeiro de Norte

There's no point in visiting Juazeiro de Norte, 528 km from Fortaleza, except for the pilgrimage and festivals in honour of Padre Cícero on 24 March. On this day Padre Cícero is celebrated in legend and song. The city of Padre Cícero is rich in wood and ceramic sculpture. Look for the work of Expedito Batista, Nino, Cizinho, José Celestino, Luis Quirino, Maria de Lourdes, Maria Cândida, Francisca, Daniel, José Ferreira and Maria das Dores.

Piauí

Piauí is one of the poorest states in Brazil in terms of income and tourist attractions. The odd shape of the state – broad in the south tapered at the coast – is due to a unique pattern of settlement which started from the sertão in the south and gradually moved towards the coast. Piauí is mostly a green state – a transition zone between the Amazon jungles and the bare sertão.

TERESINA

Population: 339,000

Teresina, the capital of Piauí and the hottest city in Brazil, has nothing in terms of tourist attractions.

Places to Stay & Eat

The *Teresina Palace Hotel* (tel 222-2770) at Rua Paiçandu 1219 (no sign), right off the central Praça Pedro II has US$12 doubles with private bath as well as more expensive rooms for US$15. The hotel has a swimming pool, bar and restaurant and serves a good breakfast.

Restaurant *O Pesqueirinho* at Avenida Jorge Velho 6889 on the riverside serves crab and shrimp stew.

Getting There & Away

Teresina has regular bus connections with Sobral (US$2), Fortaleza (US$3, 635 km),

São Luis (US$3, seven hours, 450 km) and Belém (US$6.50, 14 hours, four times a day). Expresso Ipu Brasília also has a leito bus to Belém only on Sundays at 5.30 am (coming from Sobral) which takes 10 hours to Belém and costs US$20.

There are buses to Parnaíba six times a day (US$3, four hours on the executivo bus and six hours on the commercial bus). If you're driving to São Luis the *Pousada Buriti Corrente* (tel 521-1668) between Codo and Caxias (42 km away) on BR-316 at km 513 is a beautiful hotel with US$9 doubles and a small zoo. It's 14 km from an alcohol factory. For tours ask for Sérgio or Marcos.

SETE CIDADES NATIONAL PARK

Only 141 km from Ubajara on a fine paved road, Sete Cidades is a small park with interesting rock formations. The park is open until 8 pm.

The loop around the park's geological monuments starts one km further down from Abrigas. They have no maps or brochures to give away to visitors (you may have better luck with the IBDF in Teresina) but the *Abrigo Hotel* (US$1.25 per bed, OK food) has a map posted. Or speak to the IBDF park director who lives there. The loop is a leisurely couple of hours stroll but bring water because it gets hot and watch out for the *cascavelas* – poisonous black and yellow rattlesnakes.

Sexta Cidade and Pedra do Elefante, the first sites on the loop, are lumps of rock with strange scales. Turn back to the main road and continue to the fork marked by the 'os monumentos' sign post. Quinta Cidade's Pedra do Inscrição (rock of inscription) has red markings which some say are cryptic Indian runes.

Quarta Cidade's highlight is a map of Brazil, a negative image in a rock wall. Seen from above, the formations do appear like cities. The biblioteca (library), arco de triunfo (arch of triumph) and cabeça do cachorro (dog's head) are promontories with good views.

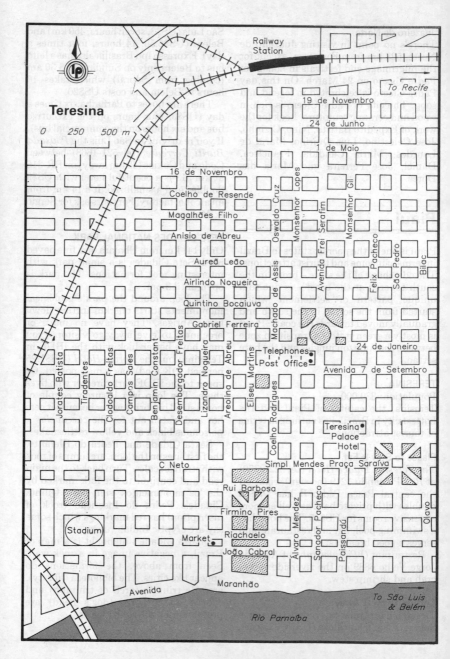

Places to Stay & Eat

The *Hotel Fazenda Sete Cidades*, a two-star Embratur resort hotel has attractive doubles with fans for US$9 and two-room suites with TV, air-con, refrigerators and telephone for US$13. It's a cool and shady spot and the restaurant serves a delicious grilled chicken for US$2.50 . Even if you don't stay overnight it's good for lunch and a quick dip in the pool.

Getting There & Away

IBDF courtesy bus transport to the park leaves from Piripiri at 8 am (26 km) and returns from the Abrigo Hotel at 5 pm. Piripiri is 180 km from Teresina with 16 daily Empresa Barroso buses from 3.30 am to 7 pm. It's a three hour, US$1.25 ride.

THE SERTÃO

The Sertão is a vast and parched land on which a suffering people eke out a meagre existence raising cattle and scraping the earth. There is precious little water, but no shortage of heat and dust.

Periodically tremendous droughts like the great drought of 1877 to 1879 sweep the land. Thousands of sertanejos pile their belongings on their backs and migrate south or anywhere they can find jobs. But with the first hint of water in the sertão, they return. The sertanejos have a strong bond with this land.

Graciliano Ramos' novel *Dry Lives* (Vidas Secas) depicts a family's exodus from the drought-stricken land. Likewise, Glauber Rocha has brought the sertão to the screen. His films are flavoured with violence, religious fanaticism, official corruption and hunger, and the land retains this history. But perhaps the greatest work about the sertão and the quintessential Brazilian novel is Euclides da Cunha's *Os Sertões*.

A Sertão Bus Ride

The bus jolts northwards from the Rio São Francisco into Pernambuco and a caatinga dessert. Here, the roads alternate between pavement and dirt. For hundreds of km the roads will have 50, 100 or 500 metres of dirt then a similar length of pavement.

It's hard to breathe as the fine dust the bus stirs up is everywhere. Many of the people wedged into the bus are standing because there aren't enough seats. After a few hours a man faints with fever, and the bus stops. An infection has spread from untreated wounds in his leg; so I clean the wounds with iodine and bandage them. We splash water on his lips but he is burning up and no one can do anything to help him.

In this outback the living is hard, the people are poor and the animals lean. The rivers have no water. There is no relief from the heat. Through the bus window there are scenes straight from a Hollywood western, with tall, thin vaqueiros on scrawny horses that stumble through the caatinga.

Maranhão

Maranhão, with 324,616 square km, is the second largest state in the Northeast, after Bahia. The area is populated by only three million. Most of the interior is planted with babaçu palm trees, the oil and nuts of which are harvested. This is also the home-state of Brazilian president-by-accident Sarney.

SÃO LUÍS

Population: 185,000

São Luís, the capital of Maranhão, is easy to like. Overlooking the Baia de São Marcos, São Luís is actually on an island, of the same name. The city has colonial charm and a rich folkloric tradition – highlighted by the Bumba-meu-boi festival. Maranhão state must also have one of the most extensive mixes of white, black and Indian in Brazil. There are good beaches out of the city, only 20 minutes away and the São Luísenses are very friendly and quite beautiful.

History

St Louis was the only city in Brazil founded and settled by the French. In 1612 three French ships sailed for

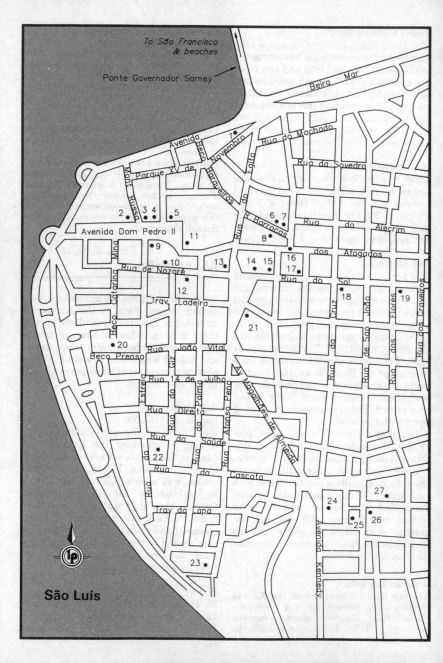

São Luís

1	Ruínas Restaurant
2	Palácio dos Leões
3	Panorama Restaurant
4	Posto de Informação da Pedro II
5	Vila Rica Hotel
6	Solar do Ribeirão Restaurant
7	Posto de Informação do Ribeirão
8	La Bohème Restaurant
9	Varig/Cruzeiro
10	Central Hotel
11	Igreja da Sé Monument
12	Hotel Lord
13	Edifício São Luís Monument
14	Agetur – Agência Marques
15	VASP
16	Largo do Ribeirão Monument
17	Maratur – Maranhão Turismo
18	Museu Histórico e Artístico
19	Casa do Artesão
20	Beco Catarina Mina Monument
21	Igreja do Carmo Monument
22	Cafua das Mercês Monument
23	Igreja do Desterro
24	Mercado Central
25	Centro de Artes de São Luís
26	Athenas Palace
27	Fonte das Pedras Monument

Maranhão to try to cut off a chunk of Brazil. They were embraced by the local Indians, the Tupinambá, who hated the Portuguese. Once settled in São Luís, the French began to expand their precarious colony. With Tupinambá assistance they began attacking tribes around the mouth of the Amazon.

But French support for the new colony was weak and in 1614 the Portuguese set sail for Maranhão. A year later the French fled. The Tupinambá, left to fend for themselves, were 'pacified' by the Portuguese.

Except for a brief Dutch occupation, São Luís developed slowly as a sugar exporting port, and then as a cotton exporter. As elsewhere, the plantation system was established with slaves and Indian labour, despite the relatively poor lands. With the decline of these crops in

the 19th century, São Luís went into a long and slow decline.

In the past decade São Luís' economy has been stimulated by several mega-projects. A modern port complex has been built to export the mineral riches of the Carajás mountains in the Amazon, the world's largest iron mountain. In 1984, Alcoa Aluminum built an enormous factory for aluminium processing – you'll see it along the highway south of the city. The US$1.5 billion investment was the largest private investment in Brazil's history. A missile station is being built near Alcântara, and oil has been found in the bay.

Information & Orientation

The old part of São Luís is on a hill overlooking the bay. This is where the bulk of the hotels, restaurants and sights are. It's easy to get around – despite hills and confusing street layout – because everything is so close. In fact, as long as you're in the old part of town a bus is rarely needed. The most confusing thing about getting around São Luís is the street names, many of them have one too many. There are the new official names that are on street signs and the names that the people use. No two city maps seem to be the same, however, most sites of interest in São Luís are easily reached on foot, so it's no big deal.

Several of the hotels face the Praça Benedito Leite, where local crafts are sold. From the praça, head down the wide and elegant Avenida Dom Pedro II to the waterfront. You'll pass the Palácio dos Leões on the way.

If you do need a bus from the centre of town find the Largo do Carmo. Going north from the old town you cross the Governor José Sarney bridge to São Francisco, the new and affluent area with many restaurants and nightspots.

Tourist Office Maratur is one of the better state tourist offices in the Northeast. They have maps and brochures which list events. Offices are at Avenida Dom Pedro II 206 (near the Palácio dos Leões) and Rua Isaac Marins 141 both in the Centro, at the airport and in Alcântara. Go to the main office (tel 221-1231) at Rua 14 de Julho 88, Centro if you have specific requests or want to use their small library.

Other Offices The Varig/Cruzeiro office (tel 222-5011) is at the Hotel Central building at Avenida Dom Pedro II 268 in Centro. VASP (tel 222-4655) is at Rua do Sol 43 in Centro. Next to the Hotel Central there is also a phone company office.

Livraria ABC at Rua Joaquim Távora 353, Centro has some English-language books. If you have a radio, São Luís has two radio stations that play great Brazilian pop/jazz late at night.

Money There's enough tourism so that you can usually change money at parallel rates, although Fortaleza may be better. Agetur at Rua do Sol 33, Centro is a good travel agency to try, as is the Hotel Centro. For official rates Banco do Brasil is at Avenida Gomes de Castro 46.

Casa de Cultura Popular
They have a pretty good collection of Bumba-meu-boi costumes and masks and artisan crafts from the state of Maranhão. The most interesting museum in town, it's open Monday to Friday from 9 pm to 6 am at Rua 28 de Julho 221.

Palácio dos Leões
Originally a French fortress built in 1612 by Daniel de la Touche, during the reign of Louis the 13th, this is now the state governor's residence and office. You can still arrange visits with the tourist office for Monday, Wednesday, Thursday and Friday afternoons from 2 to 5 pm. The inside has a somewhat seedy, decadent feel and many heavy oil paintings. Next door is the Prefeitura, followed by the *Pizzeria Restaurante Panorama* (with

good view and bad pizza) and a Maratur office.

Commercial District
The old commercial district along Rua Portugal (also known as Rua Trapiche) near the Mercado Grande has fine old Portuguese tile work on old colonial mansions. Don't miss it.

Mercado Grande
The old round market, down toward the bay, is a very interesting side trip. They have dried salted shrimp (eaten with shell and all), cachaça, dry goods, basket work and a few lunch counters for cheap local cooking.

Museu do Negro/Cafua das Mercês
This museum has a limited exhibition documenting the history of slavery in Maranhão that's worth a quick view. The museum, at Rua Jacinto Maia 43, is open Monday to Saturday 1.30 to 5 pm.

The African slaves brought to Maranhão were Bantus. They were used for some general farming of rice and cotton, but particularly sugar farming. They brought their own type and flavour of Candomblé, which is called Tambor de Mina in this part of Brazil. Museum director Jorge Babalaou works at Cafua das Merces and is an expert in Candomblé and Bantu/Maranhense folklore. He may be able to indicate where you can visit a ceremony, but this may be difficult since the major houses, the Casa das Minas, Casa de Nagu and Casa Fanti-Ashanti-Nagô, don't like visitors.

Igreja do Desterro
Notable for its facade, this is the only Byzantine church in South America. It was built by black Jose do Le between 1618 and 1641. There's a small adjoining museum with a display of ecclesiastical garb.

Fonte das Pedras
This marks the spot where, on 31 October

1615, Jeronimo de Albequerque and his troops camped before expelling the French. There are gardens with fountains and fish pools.

Museu Histórico e Artístico de Maranhão
This museum has an attractive display of odd artefacts of wealthy Maranhão families. There are furnishings, family photographs, religious articles, sacred art and President Jose Sarney's bassinet.

Beaches
The beaches are out past São Francisco and they are all busy on sunny weekends. Ponta d'Areia is the closest beach to the city, only 3.5 km away. There are barracas and restaurants here, but the beaches get better if you continue. The water here is choppy and the sand strip is narrow, but for a quick escape from the city it's just right. If you want to stay the night, the *Pousada Tia Maria* (tel 227-1534) back at the point has nice doubles with air-con for US$12.

The next beach, Calhau, is big, broad and beautiful and it's only 7.5 km from the city. The locals like to drive their cars onto Calhau (as well as the next beach, Olho d'Agua) park and lay out their towels alongside their machines. On weekends this means congestion. It's really too bad because these are very good city beaches. Olho d'Agua, 11.5 km from São Luís, has more beach barracas and football games. It's active and fun on weekends. There's one medium-priced hotel, the *Chalet da Lagoa*.

Praia do Araçaji, four km further, is the quietest and most peaceful of these beaches. There are only simple bars and a few weekend beach houses.

Panaquatira is a popular weekend beach on the eastern end of the island. Beach access is solely by car (the bus leaves you six km away), beach camping is permitted and there is a hotel in nearby São Jose de Ribamar. The seven metre tide is very fast, so don't camp close to the water.

Festivals
São Luís has one of Brazil's richest folkloric traditions, which manifests itself during its many festivals. Carnival is supposedly a groove. There are active samba clubs and distinctive local dances and music. Most Carnival activity is out on the streets and the tourist influence is minimal.

São Luís is really famous for its Festejos Juninas and Bumba-meu-boi. I've had the latter explained to me 100 times but still can't figure it out, at least its origins and theme. But who cares. If you go you'll learn, and if it's at all possible you should.

What I do know is the bumba-meu-boi is a fascinating, wild, folkloric festival with a Carnivalesque atmosphere. The festivities revolve about a dance/drama with a prize bull (*boi*), a slave, his lover and master. The origins are eclectic but very Brazilian. Paraders dance, sing and tell the story of the death and resurrection of the bull – with plenty of room for improvisation. Parade groups spend the year in preparation, costumes are lavish and new songs and poetry are invented.

The festivals start on 23 June and go into September. The culmination of the bumba-meu-boi is usually sometime in the second half of June. Give the tourism office a quick call to get the exact date.

The Tambor de Mina on 19 and 20 January for São Sebastião is an important event for the Afro-Brazilian religions in São Luís, as is the Festa do Divino. Joyful events, they feature a kind of dance called the *de tambor*.

Places to Stay – bottom end
There are several very cheap places along Rua da Palma. It's a convenient location, right in the heart of town, but not too safe at night. The *Hotel Lusitano* on Rua da Palma has rooms for US$2 per person, no bath. For the same price, but in a better part of town, is the *Colonial Hotel* at Rua dos Afogados 84. There's no bath and

rooms are partitioned, so it can be noisy, but breakfast is included.

Still cheap, but safer and quieter, the best deal in São Luís is the *Hotel Lord* (tel 222-5544), Rua Joaquim Távora 258, Centro right below Praça Benedito Leite. It's a big, old hotel with clean, comfortable rooms that start at US$8.50/11 a single/ double (air-con extra). The nearby *Central* offers similar accommodation but is way overpriced at US$11/14 a single/double.

At Rua de Saude 178 the new *Hotel São Marcos* (tel 221-4761) has squeaky clean rooms, a parking lot and even a mini-swimming pool, which is nothing to smirk at in muggy São Luís, for only US$6/7 a single/double. The only catch is the sleazy location right off Rua da Palma. Down the hill is the *Athenas Palace* (tel 221-4163) behind the Mercado Central at Rua Antônio Rayol 431. The area is not too safe at night (if you have a car make sure they let you use the locked parking lot behind the hotel) but the hotel is great value with singles/doubles with fan for US$3/5 (air-con is an extra US$1).

Places to Stay – top end

There are a couple of three-star hotels on the other side of the river in São Francisco, not recommended unless you have a car and want something better than the Lord or prefer to stay outside the city centre. The *Gran Hotel São Francisco* (tel 227-1155) is on Rua das Figueiras, with singles/doubles for US$18/22, and the *Panorama Palace* (tel 227-0067) is at Rua dos Pinheiros 15, with singles/ doubles for US$16/20.

There are two five-star hotels, both have all the amenities and rooms start as low as US$30/40 for a single/double. The *Quatro Rodas* (tel 227-0244) is on a bluff above a nice beach out at Praia do Calhau, a 15 minute drive from town. It has singles/ doubles for US$70/76. The *Vila Rica* (tel 222-4455) is very central at Avenida Dom Pedro II 299, with a view overlooking the bay. Singles/doubles are US$40/68.

Places to Eat

The best Maranhense food comes from the sea. They make many of the familiar fish and shrimp dishes of the Northeast and regional specialties include torta de sururu (mussel torte), casquinho de caranguejo (stuffed crab), caldeirada de camarão (shrimp stew) and arroz de cuxá (rice with vinegar, gergelim and shrimp) arroz de jaçanã, arroz de piqui, arroz de toucinho, arroz de couve and arroz doce.

There are plenty of lanchonetes downtown serving typical, cheap food. Across from the Largo do Ribeirão, you'll find a couple of good snack bars with sucos. The main drag through São Francisco has many new restaurants, particularly pizzerias, and bars.

The most important restaurant in São Luís is often the *Panorama* behind the Maratur office on Avenida Dom Pedro II. The dishes are typical, the quality is average or below, and the service is lousy. But on those sticky evenings when the São Luís air is stagnant, the restaurant – on the edge of a hill overlooking the Rio Anil – gets a breeze. This can be cause for a drink and celebration.

For fish, the best place is *Base do Edilson* (tel 222-7210), Rua Paulo Kruger de Oliveira 32. It's only a 10-minute drive from the city centre but worth taking a taxi as it's difficult to find. The restaurant starts serving lunch at 11.30 am and dinner at 7 pm. The portions are not big for what you pay, but very tasty. I'd suggest ensopado de camarão com molho pirão and peixada com pirão, for US$4, but everything's good and it's well worth the trip. Other good restaurants that specialise in similar regional seafood are *Solar do Ribeirão* (tel 222-3068) at Rua Isaac Martins 141, Centro and *Base do Germano* (tel 222-3276) at Avenida Wenceslau Bra's, Camboa. Both are open for lunch and dinner.

In São Francisco *Chapéu de Palha* has some excellent regional dishes for US$3 and up. It's on Rua dos Manaca's Quadra 8, and is open late for lunch and dinner.

Top: Lacemaker, south of Fortaleza, Ceará (MS)
Bottom: Sand dunes, Ceará (JM)

Top: 'Jangadas' on the beach in Ceará (MS)
Left: The day's catch, Ceará (JM)
Right: Fishermen, Ceará (JM)

Out at Ponta d'Areia *Tia Maria* has good seafood and it's a fine place to watch the sunset and drink. Praia da Ponta d'Areia is the closest beach to the city with barracas for food. The *Oriental* is just on the other side of the bridge to São Francisco, with a nice view and typical, greasy Brazilian Chinese food. But if you crave some different cooking they've got it.

Entertainment
Good live music is said to be found at *Ruinas*, near the bridge to São Francisco on Rua 15 de Novembro (only Friday and Saturday). Or try the *Tropical Shopping Center* near Calhau, across the bridge to São Francisco and *Botequim* in São Francisco, *Sobrado* on Rua das Mortas and *D'Gust* on Curva do 90.

Things to Buy
There are lots of crafts around town. The Praça Benedito Leite, has a real hippie craft market. Try the Casa Regional for inexpensive crafts. They have straw weaving (from baskets to bracelets) by the Urubus-Caapor Indians and the Guajajara

Indians, both from the interior of Maranhão state. The Indian tribes of Maranhão live in the south. The Urubus Indians do feather work which is for sale in the FUNAI store on Rua do Sol near the Museu Historico. You can also try the Casa do Artesão at Rua Pereira Rego 122 and Centro de Artes de São Luís on Rua 13 de Maio.

Getting There & Away
Air Air service from most major cities is provided by Varig/Cruzeiro, VASP and Votec.

Bus Buses take 18 hours to Fortaleza or 12 to Belém through Amazon forest.

Getting Around
Airport Transport The Aeroporto do Tirirical (tel 225-0044) is 15 km from the city. The bus marked 'São Cristovâo' costs just 5c for the 30 minute trip.

Local Transport The rodoviária is on Avenida dos Franceses, only four km from

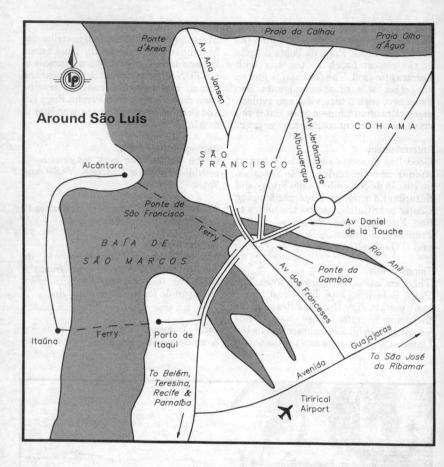

Around São Luís

Ponte d'Areia

Av Ana Jansen

Praia do Calhau

Praia Olho d'Água

Av Jerônimo de Albuquerque

COHAMA

SÃO FRANCISCO

Alcântara

Ponte de São Francisco

Ferry

BAÍA DE SÃO MARCOS

Av Daniel de la Touche

Rio Anil

Ponte da Gamboa

Av dos Franceses

Itaúna

Ferry

Porto de Itaqui

Guajajaras

To São José do Ribamar

Avenida

To Belém, Teresina, Recife & Parnaíba

Tirirical Airport

the city. Catch local buses at Praça Joâo Lisboa.

SÃO LUÍS ISLAND

Exploring the island of São Luís is pure pleasure. There are beautiful beaches and fascinating fishing villages. I seemed to always bump into friendly people who were curious about me as I was about them.

...tara

...the Baía de São Marcos is the old town of Alcântara. Founded in

the early 1600s with extensive slave labour, the town was at the hub of the region's sugar and cotton economy. The beneficiaries of this wealth, Maranhão's rich landowners, preferred living in Alcântara to São Luís.

While the town has been in decline since the latter half of the 19th century, the legacy of this past prosperity is, some say, 'the most homogeneous group of colonial buildings and ruins from the 17th and 18th centuries in Brazil.' The town is very poor and decaying but don't miss the beautiful row of two-storey houses on Rua Grande, the Igreja de NS do Carmo (1665), and the best preserved whipping post in Brazil. You can pick up a list of sites in town.

Places to Stay & Eat Alcântara has the simple *Pousada do Sol*, a couple of restaurants and some unspectacular beaches and islands nearby, but most people find that a morning walking around the city is enough and return the same day.

Getting There & Away The boat from São Luís to Alcântara departs at the Rampa Campos Melo. To get there walk down Avenida Dom Pedro II to the waterfront and turn left. It's a few hundred metres. The boat leaves at 8 am but it's often crowded so get there between 7 and 7.30 am for the 1½ hour journey in an old, one-masted sailboat. Pandemonium reigns as the last passengers and cargo get stuffed below at sailing time. If you want to avoid the crush and sit outside, there's no sitting on the top deck, head to the very front of the boat. The boat leaves for the return trip at 2 pm, but has been known to go a bit earlier.

Praia da Raposa

Out at the tip of the Ilha de São Luís, 30 km from the city, is the interesting fishing centre of Raposa, also known for its basket weaving. It's a poor town built on stilts above the mangrove swamps which gives it an unusual appearance. There are no tourist facilities but the ocean here is pretty and very shallow. There are lots of small fishing boats and it's not too hard to negotiate a ride.

Getting There & Away The frequent buses to and from São Luís take 35 minutes. The last stretch of road is dirt.

São José do Ribamar

Looking out on the Baia de São José, the town is on the east coast of the island, 30 km from the city. There's a busy little waterfront with boats leaving for small towns along the coast. It's a good way to explore some of the untouristed villages on the island. On Sundays buses go from São José to the nearby beach of Ponta de Panaquatira which is reportedly the nicest on the whole island. If you camp at the beach be careful because the tide fluctuates dramatically.

Places to Stay & Eat The only hotel is the *Mar e Sol* with simple doubles without bath for US$5. The hotel has a restaurant with a fine view of the bay.

Getting There & Away Frequent buses from São Luís take 40 minutes and the last one returns at 10.30 pm.

AROUND SÃO LUÍS
Alumar

One of the world's largest aluminium processing plants is on the outskirts of São Luís. Alumar is a cooperative venture between the Brazilian government and a Shell Oil/Alcoa consortium. Bauxite ore is extracted from mines in Para and brought to the Alumar plant for processing. Tours are conducted Saturdays but call 216-1155 a few days in advance. A company bus leaves from Praça Teodoro in São Luís. This might be a good place to change dollars with American employees.

Parque Nacional Lençois Maranhense

It's a real expedition to get to this park and few people seem to find their way there. The park, more accurately a reserve, has absolutely no infrastructure.

In addition to the park's natural attractions, 1550 square km of beaches, mangroves, dunes and local fauna, there is an isolated fishing village within the park. Towns in and about the park include Tutóia, Barreirinhas and Araioses. Since 1981 this parcel of land has been ecological reserve staving off the ruin effects of land speculation. Alth

IBDF authorisation is not required for entry to the park, you should call the São Luís office (tel 221-2126) for more information.

Getting There & Away You can take buses from São Luís to Tutoia on a poor dirt road. You must arrange you own transportation at this point.

THE NORTH
REGIÃO NORTE

The Amazon

History

In 1542 the Gonzalvo Pizarro expedition ran short of food supplies while searching for the elusive El Dorado, lost city of gold. Francisco de Orellana and troops broke off from Gonzalvo Pizarro's expedition in search of food and floated down the Rio Napo all the way to the Amazon.

Geography

The Amazon basin, six million square km of river and jungle, is the world's largest in terms of volume and drainage area. Its flow is 12 times that of the Mississippi, with 12 billion litres of freshwater flowing down the river every minute – enough to supply New York City for 60 years! There are 80,000 km of navigable rivers in the Amazon system. Ocean-going vessels can sail nearly across South America from the mouth of the Amazon, 300 km east of Belém to the Solimões and Marañon rivers, all the way to Iquitos, Peru.

Many of the Amazon's tributaries are enormous: the Rio Juruá is a 3280 km long tributary of the Solimões, the Rio Madeira-Mamoré is 3240 km, the Rio Purus/Pauini is 3210 km (1667 km navigable). The Rio Tocantins is 2640 km and the Rio Negro is 1550 km (only the lower half is navigable and fully explored). For the people who live in the Amazon interior, the rivers are their only roads.

The Amazon region includes the states and territories of Amazonas, Acre, Rondônia, Roraíma and Amapá as well as part of Pará and Maranhão.

Flora & Fauna

The jungle still keeps many of its secrets: to this day major tributaries of the mazon are unexplored. Of the estimated 000 animal species of the Amazon sands of birds and fish and hundreds mmals have not been classified. The have over 1800 species of butterflies, five major groups of primates, four types of big cats and over 200 species of mosquitoes. Biologists are unable to catalogue or identify 30% of the fish they come across in the markets of Belém and botanists still manage to bring back dozens of unclassified plants after each foray into the jungle.

Unfortunately, deforestation is taking place on such a vast scale that countless unknown species of animals and plants will be destroyed. We will lose a genetic library that has already given us so much: rubber, manioc, cocoa, anti-malarial drugs, cancer drugs and thousands more medicinal plants.

The rainforest ecosystem is stratified into five layers of plant and animal life. Most of the activity takes place in the canopy layer, 20 to 40 metres above ground, where plants compete for sunshine and the majority of the birds and monkeys live. The dense foliage of the canopy layer blots out the sunlight to lower levels, while a few tall trees poke above the canopy and dominate the forest skyline. A poorly defined middle layer or understorey merges with the canopy from below and epiphytes hang at this level.

Bushes and saplings up to five metres in height constitute the shrub layer, while the ground layer is composed of ferns, seedlings and herbs – plants adapted to very little light. Ants and termites, the so-called social insects, live here. The leaf cutter ants are farmers and use leaves to build underground nests for raising fungus gardens, while army ants swarm through the jungle in huge masses, eating everything in their path. Fungi and bacteria, the decomposers, keep the forest floor clear. It's tidy in comparison to temperate forests.

The jungle is not homogeneous; plant species vary with the land and its exposure to water. Plants of the *igapo* and

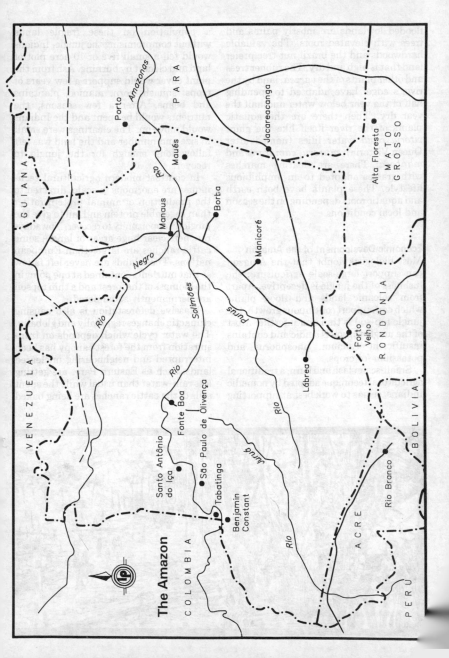

The Amazon

flooded lowlands are mostly palms and trees with elevated roots. The valuable hardwoods and the brazil nut tree prefer land that is high and dry. The rubber trees and other plants of the *varzea*, land by the river's edge, have adapted to spending half of the year below water and half the year dry. Then there are the aquatic plants of the river itself like the giant *vitória regia* water lilies (named after Queen Victoria), *mureru*, *camarans* and *manbeca*. There are floating marshes with grasses adapted to an amphibious lifestyle. These plants have both earth and aquatic roots depending on the season and local conditions.

Economic Development of the Amazon

Most biologists doubt that the Amazon can support large-scale agriculture; the lushness of the jungle is deceptive. Apart from volcanic lands and flood plains which can support continuous growth, the jungle top-soil is thin and infertile. Most of the jungle topsoil is acidic and contains insufficient calcium, phosphorus and potassium for crops.

Small-scale slash and burn, a traditional agricultural technique adopted by nomadic Indians, seems to work best at supporting a population on these fragile lands without compromising the jungle. Indians would fell a small five or 10 acre plot of land and clear it by burning. Ash from the plant cover would support a few years of crops: squash, corn, manioc, plantains and beans. After a few seasons, the nutrients would be spent and the Indians would move on. The clearings were small in size and number and the land was left fallow long enough for the jungle to recover.

In contrast modern agricultural techniques are enormous in scale, directed to the production of animal protein rather than vegetable protein and fail to give the jungle an opportunity to recover. Nowadays ranchers clear huge areas of land – some cattle ranches are larger than European nations. These lands are never left fallow so that nutrients contained at one point in the biomass of the forest and a thin topsoil are permanently squandered.

Massive deforestation is also causing climactic changes regionally and globally. The water cycle which depends on transpiration from the forest canopy has been interrupted and neighbouring uncleared lands, such as Eastern Para, are getting less rain-water than usual while the spent soils of the cattle ranches are being baked

hard and dry. The desertification of the Amazon has begun, and the effects will be global.

Extractive Economics Farming and ranching is almost incidental to the deforestation process. The vast tracts of Amazon land are bought so that the buyers can speculate for the treasures buried beneath the earth, not those growing on it. Since Brazilian law requires that one third of the land be put to use, the owners set fire to the land (killing wildlife indiscriminately), plant some grasses and raise cattle. The government then approves the land rights and the important mineral rights are secured.

The Brazilian government acts as if the forest were an impediment to progress, an asset to be used to pay back the debt incurred during the 20 years of military dictatorship. Encouraged by the IMF and the World Bank the Brazilian government has provided large incentives to coax multinational timber and mining firms to exploit the Amazon. These gigantic projects are designed to yield short-term profits and pay off the foreign debt regardless of environmental and social consequences. The economic plan, in

short, is extractive, and once the forests and precious metals are gone, Brazil will have nothing.

In the '70s, the military government attempted to tame the Amazon with an ambitious highway network. Long roads like the 3000 km Trans-Amazônica were cleared from the jungle and settlers from the Northeast soon followed in the wake of the bulldozers. The roads were said to be safety valves to ease the social tensions and over-population of the drought stricken Northeast. Thousands left the Northeast to build homesteads in the jungle; the majority of which failed. They either perished or left the jungles for the favelas of Manaus and Belém.

The Serra Pelada gold mines west of Maraba, Pará and close by to the Carajás project represent the world's largest mines. The mines are dug by hand and the enterprise rivals the pyramids in scale and epic sweep. Not whips, but the promise of gold drives prospectors to work like slaves. The mine, a huge pit with criss-crossing claims, is a human anthill where 150,000 miners and hangers-on scrape away at the earth. This may change very soon since the Companhia Vale do Rio Doce CVRD which operates the nearby Projeto Grande Carajás claims the mineral rights to the

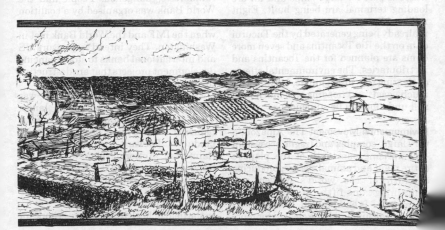

area and is attempting to wrest control of the mines from the prospectors.

If any project defies superlatives to describe its scale, it is the Projeto Grande Carajás Serra dos Carajás, Pará, designed to whittle away Brazil's US$110 billion debt. The multifocal project centres around the world's largest deposit of iron ore, but only US$4.5 billion out of US$60 billion budgeted for the project will be directed towards the extraction of iron ore. The rest of the money will be invested in the extraction of the other metals of the area: manganese, copper, bauxite, nickel and gold, all near the Serra Pelada, and the development of an industrial zone 400,000 square km in area, thus rivalling California in size.

In the tradition of previous Amazonian scaled enterprises, Henry Ford's Fordlândia and Daniel K Ludwig's Jari pulpwood project (which spans an area the size of Connecticut), the Carajás project began with American support. The venture began as a partnership between US Steel and the Companhia Vale do Rio Doce. Since iron has been depressed on the world market, US Steel bowed out of the collaboration. Some of the projects in the works include a 900 km railroad to the Atlantic coast at São Luis, Maranhão, where a port for large ships and an ore loading terminal are being built. Eight million kilowatts of power for the project is already being generated by the Tucurui dam on the Rio Tocantins and seven more dams are planned for the Tocantins and its tributaries. The environmental effects of clearing this much jungle, burning this much wood, and flooding this much land will undoubtably be stupendous.

Environmental Movement The Amazon, a very large, complex and fragile ecosystem – comprising one tenth of the planet's entire plant and animal species, producing one-fifth of the world's oxygen and containing one-fifth of the world's freshwater – is endangered. Unless things change, the jungle will be cleared for more ranches and industries, the land will be stripped for mines and the rivers will be dammed for electricity. Already jaguars, caymans, dolphins and monkeys are threatened with extinction. As in the past, the Indians will die with their forests and the invaluable, irreplaceable Amazon may be lost forever.

Brazil's environmental movement is about 20 years behind those in Europe, Japan and the United States. Rallying behind the slogan 'Vamos a preservar a Natureza' (let's preserve nature), the nascent conservation movement is beginning to make inroads. The environmentalists have demonstrated the benefits to industry of not polluting, and industry is beginning to respond. Nowadays environmental impact studies accompany all major industrial projects.

If the jungle is to be saved it will be through the efforts of groups like these within Brazil and abroad – groups that can educate the public and enlist its support to reduce consumption of tropical forest products, to pressure US and international banks to stop financing destructive development projects and to persuade the Brazilian government to adopt more rational uses for the Amazon.

The Citizens Conference on Tropical Rainforests, Indigenous People and the World Bank was organised by a coalition of US environmental groups last year when the IMF and the World Bank met in Washington. They intend to pressure US and international banks to stop financing development projects that are destructive to the rainforest.

The Rainforest Action Network was organised to protect the jungle lands. Their conservation efforts are directed at reducing consumption of tropical forest products. Forward correspondence to Rainforest Action Network Director, Randall L Hayes, 300 Broadway, San Francisco, California, USA.

Health Care in the Amazon
In the field of health care, there is hope for

the poor of the Amazon. Although to most denizens of the Amazon little or no health care is available, the situation is changing thanks to the efforts of Fundação Esperança (Hope Foundation), founded by the late Father Luke Tupper. The primary health care project is so successful, that the United Nations is using it as a model for health projects in Africa.

The problems of providing health care in the Amazon are manifold. Homesteaders are scattered far apart on minor tributaries and other than river travel there is no transportation network to reach them. The economic resources of these people are scanty.

During its first 10 years, Fundação Esperança's health care programme was centred upon a riverboat fitted with fancy medical equipment and staffed by interns and surgeons. The mobile hospital did not prove very effective. True, 150,000 people were vaccinated, but there was no continuity in health care. After a while the boat would only show up in communities during election years.

In 1978 the World Health Organisation defined the task of cost-effective use of medicinal resources emphasising preventative medicine needs of women and children (formerly overlooked), stressing community participation and education. In the following year the Fundação Esperança (Hope Foundation) began to mobilise rural communities in three areas – improving diet, sanitary practices and medical care. Physicians and nurses were sent into the rural villages but despite the best intentions would not stay very long, as they are overqualified for the task and nearly universally preferred to live in bigger cities.

The third and current approach to health care involves the transfer of information, control and prestige from health care professionals to chosen villagers. These villagers are briefly trained as paramedics in Santarém. They lead their communities in digging wells and developing sanitation, they teach fellow villagers a little hygiene and preventative medicine, treat some things and refer what they can't handle to urban medical centres.

Financial support for Fundação Esperança health project comes from the Interamerican Bank of Development, the Companhia do Vale Doce hydroelectric plant and the Lion's Club. You can also help. Fundação Esperança may not need physicians or health care workers at the moment, but they can always use money. Send cheques addressed to Fundação Esperança, Caixa Postal 222, CEP 68100 Santarém, Pará, Brazil.

Pará

BELÉM
Population: 758,000
Belém is a city with a unique and fascinating culture derived from the peoples and ways of the forest, and animated by the exuberance of the port. The city is easy to get to know: the central area is pleasant, the sites of interest are close by and the people are friendly.

Belém is the economic centre of the north and the capital of the mineral rich state of Pará.

History
The Portuguese, sailing from Maranhão, landed at Belém in 1616 and promptly built the Forte de Castelo at an entrance to the 'river-sea' to prevent French, English, Spanish and Dutch boats from sailing up the Amazon and claiming territory. By 1626 the area encompassed by the present day states of Pará and Maranhão was set-up as a separate colony from the rest of Brazil. It had its own governor, who reported directly to the Portuguese king, and its own capital, São Luis do Maranhão. This remained officially separate from the rest of Brazil until 1775.

The king's decision to create a s

administration for the stretch from Belém to São Luis, the 'east-west coast' as it was called, made sense. Due to prevailing winds and ocean currents along the coast of Brazil, it was extremely difficult for ships to leave Belém and reach Salvador, and the inland route was long and perilous. It was closer to Portugal – the trip from Belém to Lisbon was only six weeks.

Belém itself lived off the *drogas do sertão* (the spices of the backlands). For this the white settlers, most of whom had been poor farmers from the Azores in Portugal, were entirely dependent on the labour of the *filhos do mato*, sons of the forest, the native Indians who knew the ways of the Amazon and could find the cacao, vanilla, cassia and cinnamon for export to Europe. Belém became a relatively prosperous settlement due to these riches and the enslavement and destruction of the Indians. For hundreds of years the settlement survived by striking further and further into the Amazon, destroying tribes of Indians in one slaving expedition after another.

As elsewhere in Brazil, the Jesuits came to the Amazon to save the Indians and install them in *aldeias* (missions) throughout the region. Terrible epidemics killed many Indians and Catholicism killed their culture. The only Indians who escaped fled further into the Amazon along its smaller tributaries.

By the end of the 18th century, as their Indian labour force became depleted, the economy of Belém began to decline. In the 1820s a split between the white ruling classes led to civil war. It quickly spread to the dominated Indians, mestizos, Blacks and mulattos and after years of fighting developed into a popular revolutionary movement that swept through all of Pará 'ke a prairie fire. The Cabanagem 'bellion was a guerrilla war of the tched of the Amazon.

1835 the guerrilla fighters marched lém and after nine days of bloody took the city. They installed a popular government which expropriated the wealth of the merchants, distributed food to all the people and declared its independence. But the revolutionary experiment was immediately strangled by a British naval blockade, Britain being the principal beneficiary of the Brazil trade in the 1800s.

A year later, a large Brazilian force took back Belém. The vast majority of people fled to the interior to resist again. Over the next four years the military hunted down, fought and slaughtered an unbelievable two-thirds of the men in the state of Pará – they killed anyone they found who was black or brown – 40,000 out of a total population of some 100,000. The Cabanagem was one of the bloodiest and most savage of many Brazilian military campaigns against its own people.

Decades later the regional economy was revitalised by the rubber boom. A vast number of poor peasants (*seringueiros*) fled the drought-plagued Northeast, particularly Ceará, to tap the Amazon's rubber trees. Most of the seringueiros arrived and then died in debt.

By 1910 rubber exports were 39% of the national total. Belém grew from a city of 40,000 in 1875 to over 100,000 people in 1900. It had electricity, telephones, streetcars and a distinctly European feel, in the middle of the tropical heat. The rubber boom provided the money to erect the few and beautiful monuments for the city, like the Teatro da Paz.

Climate

Belém is one of the most rained on cities in the world. There is no dry season – October has the least rain – but it rains more often and with greater abundance from December to June. This is not as bad as it sounds, the rain is often a brief welcome relief from the heat.

Information & Orientation

As it approaches the Atlantic, the Amazon splinters into many branches

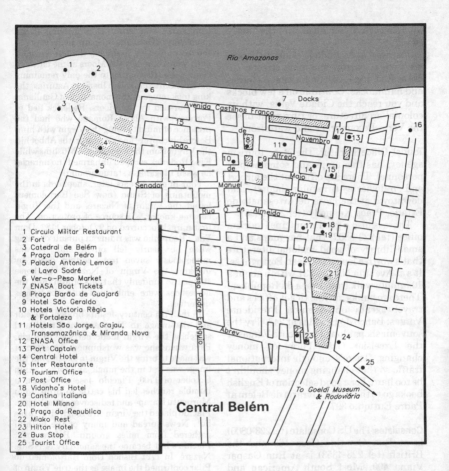

1 Circulo Militar Restaurant
2 Fort
3 Catedral de Belém
4 Praça Dom Pedro II
5 Palacio Antonio Lemos
  e Lavro Sodré
6 Ver-o-Peso Market
7 ENASA Boat Tickets
8 Praça Barão de Guajará
9 Hotel São Geraldo
10 Hotels Victoria Régia
   & Fortaleza
11 Hotels São Jorge, Grajau,
   Transamazônica & Miranda Nova
12 ENASA Office
13 Port Captain
14 Central Hotel
15 Inter Restaurante
16 Tourism Office
17 Post Office
18 Vidonho's Hotel
19 Cantina Italiana
20 Hotel Milano
21 Praça da Republica
22 Miako Rest
23 Hilton Hotel
24 Bus Stop
25 Tourist Office

Central Belém

and forms countless channels, fluvial
islands, and finally, two great estuaries.
These estuaries cut the Ilha de Marajó,
the 'island-continent', from the mainland.
The southern estuary is joined by the
mighty Rio Tocantins and is known as the
Baía de Marajó before entering the
Atlantic.

Belém is 120 km from the Atlantic at
the point where the Rio Guamá turns
north and becomes the Baía do Guajará,
which soon feeds into the massive Baía de
Marajó. It's the biggest port on the

Amazon. From Belém you can set sail for
any place that's navigable on the Amazon
and its tributaries. Distances are great,
river travel is slow and often dull, and you
may have to change ships along the way,
but it is possible and very cheap.

The heart of town is along Avenida
Presidente Vargas from the bay to the
Teatro da Paz in the Praça da República.
Here, you'll find most of the best hotels
and restaurants – expensive and not. The
Praça da República is bigger than m
central Brazilian parks and a good p'

to relax and socialise in the early evening.

Just west of Avenida Presidente Vargas are several narrow shopping streets. Go down Rua Joaõ Alfredo for cheap clothes and hammocks. Continue on a few blocks and you reach the Cidade Velha, with its colonial architecture, or turn right to see the Ver-o-Peso market and waterfront.

Tourist Office Parátur, the state tourism agency, has free maps and some helpful personnel. There are offices at the airport and rodoviária (irregular hours) and downtown at the Feira de Artesanato do Estado, Praça Kennedy (tel 224-9633).

There is also a good municipal tourism office (tel 223-5802) that has maps and a small library of good regional literature that's worth a look if you read Portuguese. It's at Avenida Nazaré 231 within about a 10 minute walk from Praça da República. There are banks, airline ticket offices and travel agents on Avenida Presidente Vargas; Banco do Brasil is at 248. Try the souvenir shops along Presidente Vargas or the Excelsior Grão Pará for money changing. There's enough international traffic so that changing money shouldn't be too hard. For a good selection of English books go to the Nossa Livraria de Belém at Padre Eutiquio 397.

Consulates The US Consulate (tel 223-0800) is at Rua Oswaldo Cruz 165 and the British (tel 223-4353) is at Rua Gaspar Viana 490. Most South American and European countries have consulates in Belém.

Our Lady of Nazaré

The origins of the image of Our Lady of Nazaré, the devotion to the Virgin and the story of how she came to Belém are shrouded in myth and misunderstanding, but many people accept the following as true:

ccording to the Portuguese, the holy image s sculpted in Nazareth in the Galilee. The ge of the Virgin made its way through many

European monasteries before arriving at the monastery of Gauliana in Spain. In the year 714 the forces of King Roderick, the last Visigoth king, were routed by the Moors at the battle of Gaudelette. Retreating to the only remaining patch of Christian soil in Iberia at Asturias, the king took refuge at the monastery of Gauliana. Still pursued by the Moors, Roderick fled to Portugal with Abbot Romano who had the presence of mind to bring the Virgin with him. Before his capture and slaughter, the Abbot hid the Virgin from the iconoclastic Muslims while King Roderick escaped unharmed (no miracle, he wasn't lugging a statue around).

Four hundred years later, shepherds in the mountains of Siano (now São Bartolomeu) found the Virgin of Nazaré, and the Virgin became known as a source of protection. The first miracle occurred on 9 October 1182. Dom Fua's Roupinho was riding in pursuit of a stag when he nearly fell off a cliff he was miraculously saved from certain death by invoking the Virgin of Nazaré. His horse stopped so suddenly that bits of iron from the horseshoes were embedded into the stones underfoot.

In the 17th century Jesuits brought the cult and the image to Northeastern Brazil and somehow the Virgin made her way to Vigia, Pará where she was worshipped. An attempt was made to bring the Virgin to Belém, but the image was lost in the jungle and forgotten. In October of 1700, Placido José de Souza, a humble rancher led his cattle to drink from Murucutu Igarapé and rediscovered the Virgin. Placido placed the Virgin on a rough altar in his hut. News spread and many of the faithful gathered from miles around. Before long, Placido's hut became the sanctuary of NS de Nazaré. In 1721 Bishop Dom Bartolomeu do Pilar confirmed the image as the true Virgin of Nazaré. In 1793 Belém had its first Cirio, and the city has been celebrating ever since.

Ver-o-Peso

Spanning several blocks along the waterfront, this is one big market that goes all day, every day. There's not much for tourists to buy but the display of fruits, vegetables, plants, animals and fish, not to mention the people, is fascinating. It's best to get there early when the boats are unloading their catches at the far end of the market. Watch for the *mura*, a human-size fish.

The most intriguing section is filled with medicinal herbs and roots, dead snakes, jacaré teeth, and amulets with mysterious powers and potions for every possible occasion. There are many restaurants for good, cheap fish and chicken.

Museu Emilio Goeldi

The museum has three parts: the park and zoo, the aquarium and the ethnology museum. The zoo has *manatees*, jungle cats and many strange Amazonian birds like the Urubu Rei. It's great for kids, but a bit depressing unless you're a die-hard zoo fan. The aquarium has a small sample of small fish placed in very small tanks. The select few were chosen from the over 1500 in the local waters.

The highlight here is the museum, founded in 1866. It's billed as the greatest anthropology collection of the Amazon region. This may be, but it is a rather small museum with some silly exhibits (the funniest is a modern Brazilian kitchen that is filled with indigenous Amazonian devices that have made their way into our modern lifestyle). Still, there are good displays of Marajó Indian ceramics, many stuffed birds and old photos. This is also a research facility with a library that's worth exploring if you have a particular interest in the region.

The complex is open Tuesday to Friday 8 am to midday and 2 pm to 6 pm, Saturday and Sunday from 8 am to 6 pm. It's at Avenida Magalhães Barata 376. From the centre, you can catch the Autoclub bus or take a good 30-minute walk. From the Teatro da Paz walk down Avenida Nazaré which becomes Avenida Barata and make a stop at the Basílica de NS de Nazaré.

Basílica de NS de Nazaré

The Basílica is the destination of over one million worshippers a year during the Círio de Nazaré. Built in 1909, the church has a Roman architectural style inspired by the Basílica of St Paul in Rome. Inside there is fine marble and gold, downstairs is a sacred art museum. The church is on Avenida Nazaré and Travessa 14 de Marco; it closes during lunch.

Cidade Velho

The old part of Belém is run-down but authentic. There are many colonial buildings notable for their fine, blue Portuguese tiles. It's a good area in which to walk, drink and explore. The big Antônio Lemos and Lauro Sodré palaces are also in the neighbourhood.

Festivals

Every year on the morning of the second Sunday of October the city of Belém explodes with the sound of hymns, bells and fireworks. The Círio de Nazaré – Belém's festival of candles and Brazil's biggest religious festival – begun in 1793, is a tribute to the Virgin of Nazaré. People from all over Pará and Brazil flock to Belém, and even camp in the streets to participate in the grand event. In 1985 over 700,000 people filled the streets to march from the Catedral Metropolitana (also known as the Igreja da Sé) to the Basílica of Nossa Senhora do Nazaré.

The image of the Virgin, centre-piece of the procession, is placed on a flower-bedecked carriage. While the faithful pray, sing hymns, thank or ask favours of the Virgin, the pious (often barefoot) bear heavy crosses and miniature wax houses, and thousands squirm and grope in their emotional frenzy to get a hold of the 300 metre cord for an opportunity to pull the carriage of the Virgin. Five hours and only 2½ km later the Virgin has come to the Basilica where she remains for the duration of the festivities.

After the parade, there is the traditiona' feast of duck cooked in manioc juice (a Cír de Nazaré without *pato no tucupi* is a' to Thanksgiving without turkey). F there the multitudes head to fairgrounds for mayhem of the secular kind: food, drink, music and dancing. The party continues unabated for a fortnight. On Monday, 15 days after the first procession, the crowd re-congregates for the Recírio parade in which the Virgin is returned to her proper niche and the festivities concluded.

River Excursions

Ciatur travel agency produces 'canned' tours of the Rio Guamá for US$7.50. They do a lively business through the big hotels. In three hours you cruise the river, go down a channel, get out on an island and walk down a path where many have travelled before to see the local flora (rubber, mahagone, asai palms, sumauma, mangoes, cacao trees) and have the rare opportunity to pass a souvenir stand every 100 metres. This voyage into the known is recommended only if you have no time to really see the jungle and rivers.

Places to Stay

With an abundance of two-star hotels at one-star prices, Belém has some of the best hotel deals in Brazil. Most of these hotels are central – along or close to Avenida Presidente Vargas (an ideal location). There are also cheap dives and opulent, old hotels. If you're just passing through there are hotels in front of the rodoviária. All of the hotels that follow are in the central district and have air-con, unless otherwise indicated.

Places to Stay – bottom end

There are very cheap places scattered along the waterfront on Avenida Castello Franca. Try the hotels *Grajau, São Jorge*, and *Miranda Nova*. *Transamazônica* (tel 222-5232) has singles/doubles with bath for $US3/10.50.

For very little more you can get a clean, comfortable room at places like the *Victoria Rêgia* (tel 224-2833) or the *Hotel Central* (tel 222-3011), which are both great deals with singles for US$4 without private bath and air-con, a bit more expensive with. They usually fill-up early.

The *Victoria Rêgia* is at Frutuoso Guimarães 260. The Central (tel 222-3011), a big hotel popular with foreign travellers, is at Avenida Presidente Vargas 290. The *Transamazônica* (tel 222-5232) at Travessa Indústria 17, by the docks, has singles/doubles for US$3/5.50 without bath.

The *Hotel Milano* (tel 224-7211) faces the Praça da República at Avenida Presidente Vargas 640. The staff are very friendly and they have a good safe deposit. Single rooms range from US$9.50 to US$16 for more luxury and a view. If you like the waterfront, the *Ver-o-Peso* (tel 224-2267) – across from the market at Avenida Castilhos França 208 – costs US$6.50 for a single/double. If these are full, try *Sete Sete* (tel 222-7742) at Rua 1 de Março for a small, new room at US$4.50 for one or two.

Places to Stay – middle

If you're travel weary and want to pamper yourself with a better hotel than usual, this is the place to do it. *Vidonho's Hotel* (tel 225-1444), off Avenida Presidente Vargas at Rua O de Almeida 476, is a modern, spic-and-span place with all the amenities of an expensive hotel (colour TV, refrigerator-bar). They have singles/doubles at US$10 which are a good deal for one and great for two.

The *Cambará Hotel* (tel 224-2422), in the Cidade Velho at Avenida 16 de Novembre 300, is in the same league as Vidonho's and has singles/doubles for US$11/12. Also in the Cidade Velho, the *Plaza* (tel 224-2800) at Praça da Bandeira 130 is recommended.

Places to Stay – top end

There is a new and central Hilton (tel 223-6500), which reminded me of the fancy, sterile hotels where the CIA always stays in movies about the Third World. Singles/doubles are US$69/82.

Belém's best hotel is probably the *Equatorial Palace* (tel 224-8855) at Avenida Braz de Aguiar 612, Nazaré. For a bit less money, the *Excelsior Grão Pará* (tel 222-3255) at Avenida Presidente Vargas 718 is good value with singles/doubles for US$20/23. The *Regente* (tel 224-0755) at Avenida Gov José Malcher 485 has singles/doubles for US$14/16.

Places to Eat

The food in Belém is tasty and varied, with a bewildering variety of fish and fruit and, unlike much of Brazil, a distinct regional cuisine that features several delicious dishes. Pato no tucupi is a lean duck cooked in fermented manioc extract, unhas de caranguejo and casquinho de caranguejo are crab claws and stuffed crab, and manicoba is a stew with dried meat.

Three of the best local fish are filhota, pescada amarela and dourada – great fish. And you are no doubt familiar with açai, uxi, murici, bacuri and sapoti, just a few of the luscious Amazonian fruits available.

For cheap vittles, there are loads of snack bars throughout the city with sandwiches and regional juices. The *Ver-o-Peso* market has a thousand and one food stands serving big lunches for small prices. It's a good place to try the local fish.

Vegetarians can try the *Restaurant Vegetariana*, upstairs at Avenida Presidente Vargas 790. You can eat as much as you want for US$1.25 and at street level there's an excellent juice (suco), ice cream (*sorvete*) and sandwich shop. There is decent, cheap pasta at *Cantina Italiana* on Rua Aristedes Lobo off Avenida Presidente Vargas. And for typical Brazilian fare the *Inter Restaurant* has meat, fish, rice, etc for about US$2. It's at Rua 28 de September 304.

Belém has several excellent restaurants where you can do some fine dining for US$2 to US$4. *Lá Em Casa*, *O Outro* (tel 223-1212) are two restaurants at Avenida Governador José Malcher 982, Nazaré which have all the best regional dishes. The *O Círculo Militar* at the old Forte do Castelo has a great bay view and good regional cooking.

The *Izumo* and *Hakata* are good Japanese restaurants and the *Miako*, behind the Hilton Hotel, is one of the best in Brazil, north of São Paulo. And if you don't like Japanese food they have good typical Brazilian plates. *Casa Portuguesa*, Rua Senador Manoel 897 and *Avenida*, Avenida Nazaré 1086 are also recommended.

Entertainment

There's lots of music in town. The best samba clubs at which to shake, rattle and roll on weekends are *Rancho Não Posso me Amofiná* (tel 225-0918), Travessa Honório José dos Santos 764, Jurunas and *Arco-Íris* (tel 226-1926), Travessa Castelo Branco and Silva Castro, Guama. The new kid on the block is *Imperio de Samba 'Quem São Eles'* (who are they) (tel 225 1133), Avenida Almirante Wandenkolk 680, Umarizal which is the closest to the city centre. The price is usually US$1 and they go all year.

Several boats are popular night spots with music, shows and dance. *Mistura Fina* has a younger crowd, *Gemini* and *Lapinha* are reportedly good. The new *Safari Bar* (tel 223-7553) at Avenida 16 de November 528 has a good reputation.

The region has some great traditional music and dance which unfortunately is hard to find in Belém. One place to try is *Samumbia*. There are also performances occasionally arranged for tour groups, which may not be your cup of tea but it's worth doing anything to see and hear the old music and dance. Call the tourism office and tell them you want to see *carimbó* (the origin of which goes back to the Bantu slaves from northern Africa), *lundú* or *siriá*. If you have a cassette player, pick up a tape by the great local musician Pinduca.

If you want to escape the Amazon for a couple of hours, the *Cultural Center Tancredo Neves* often has English movies.

Getting There & Away

Air Belém has airline service from all the

cities of the Northeast and the major cities to the south. There are daily flights to Macapá, Amapá (US$22) and Santarém (US$38), Rio and Manaus. From Belém you can also fly to Caiena, French Guiana and Paramaribo, Surinam.

There is also an extensive network of small prop planes that cover the Amazon region. These air taxis are rather expensive but they will fly you just about anyplace in the Amazon. In Belém the air taxis fly from the separate Aeroporto Julio César. There are several carriers such as Aerotur (tel 233-3786), Kovacs, Bandeirante (tel 233-0986) and Dourado (tel 233-0605).

Bus Belém is a 12-hour, US$6 bus ride from São Luis that passes interesting terrain along the edge of the Amazon forest. It's a 24-hour bus trip from Fortaleza (US$11), 36 hours from Recife (US$15) and 56 hours from Rio (US$23). There are also direct buses from Belo Horizonte, São Paulo and Brasília.

There is one bus a week from Santarém for US$17.50 that is a gruelling, often delayed, two-day trip, only recommended if you are deathly afraid of boats. Frequent buses run to the beaches at Mosqueiro.

Riverboats There are two ways to go boating up the Amazon: with the government-operated ENASA which operates regularly scheduled large passenger boats along four river routes; or with various and sundry small cargo boats that also have a few cabins and hammock space on deck for a couple of dozen passengers (for more boat info see the Amazon section).

ENASA has stopped services to Macapá and cut-back to once a month on their tourist service to Manaus and back. This service seems to be embroiled in controversy – it's not making money – and could be eliminated. It's expensive and what you're paying for are the 'love boat' frills such as a swimming pool, because it's not a good way to actually see the

Amazon (the boat is too far out in the middle of the wide river).

The ENASA office (tel 223-3011 or 223-2995) is at Avenida Presidente Vargas 41. For tickets go to the dock where the boats depart from (right before the Ver-o-Peso on Avenida Castillo França). Both places have the most up-to-date schedule; if you're having any difficulties there are English speakers at the ENASA office who are quite friendly.

Other services from Belém are:

Belém-Santarém-Manaus
Boats leave Belém every Wednesday at 10 pm, and arrive at Santarém on Saturday and Manaus on Tuesday morning. The fare to Manaus is US$30 *clase regional* with food included; sleeping is best in hammocks. The boat holds 600 passengers and is usually crowded. The ship stops at several towns along the way. The return departs Manaus on Thursday night at 8 pm, reaches Santarém on Saturday and Belém a couple of days after.
Belém-Souré
A regular ferry to Souré on the Ilha Marajó departs Wednesday at 8 pm, Friday at 8 pm and Saturday at 2 pm. The boat leaves from Souré for Belém, Thursday at 5 pm and Sunday at 5 pm and midnight. It's a five-hour trip for US$2/4 economy/1st class (the only difference is a separate cabin with more comfortable chairs).
Belém-Tucuruí via Abaetetuba, Cameta, Mocajuba, Baiao
This is a 2½ day trip up the Rio Tocantins to the massive hydroelectric station at Tucuruí. The boat leaves Belém on Friday at 6 pm and returns late Sunday night. The cost for a cabin is US$11, for a hammock US$5. Food is sold on board.
Belém-Breves via Ponta de Pedras, São Sebastiao, Curralinho
This shuttle departs Belém Monday at 6pm and arrives in Breves Tuesday

afternoon. It returns later Tuesday afternoon.

Belém-Amapá

The SUSNAVA line covers the journey in 30 hours for US$6 and goes once a week. Check the schedule at their offices in Belém (tel 223-5355) at Caltilhos França 234.

You can reach Belém from all these destinations and others by the smaller cargo boats that link the ports of the Amazon. They usually have a few very cramped cabins with four, six or eight bunk beds. The better option is to hang a hammock on deck. These boats stay closer to shore so there's more to see. Food is usually included; lots of rice, beans and some meat. Prices are standard and don't vary too much between boats. It's very cheap, US$18 with a hammock or US$22 with a bed from Santarém to Belém. Down river is considerably faster than up, but upriver traffic goes closer to the shore and consequently is more scenic.

To find a boat go down to the docks and climb aboard for information. Most boats take a day or two to load up before they head out. The best place to look is Porto 9 and 10 CDP. They always seem to have a couple of boats getting ready to head up river. The entrance is at the guard station where Travessa Quintino Bocaiúva meets Avenida Marechal Hermes. Boats also depart from the Porto do Sal in Cidade Velho and at the Porto das Lanchas Avenida Castilhos França, between the Ver-o-Peso and the Forte do Castelo.

Getting Around

Airport Transport Val de Cans, the main airport (tel 233-4122), is about 30 minutes from the city centre. It's on Avenida Julio César. Take the Perpétuo Socorro bus, it's quick and, of course, cheap. A taxi costs about US$5. Remember, the air taxis leave from a different airport, the Julio César (tel 233-3868) at Avenida Senador Lemos 4700.

Local Transport The rodoviária is about a 15-minute bus ride from the city. It's at the corner of Avenida Almirante Barroso and Avenida Ceará. From downtown, the Aeroclube bus is one of several that will get you there. For bus information call 228-0500.

ILHA DO MOSQUEIRO

Population: 14,700

Mosqueiro is the weekend beach for Belémites trying to beat the heat. They flock to the island's 19 freshwater beaches on the east side of the Baía de Marajó. It's close enough for plenty of weekend beach houses and some well-to-do Belémites even commute to the city. The island is particularly crowded during summer vacation, which is July, January and February (July is the worst). The beaches are not nearly as nice as over on Marajó or on the Atlantic coast, but if you want to get out of Belém for just a day they're not bad.

Beaches

The best beaches are Praia Farol, Praia Chapéu Virado and the more remote Bahia do Sol.

Festivals

Mosqueiro has a traditional folklore festival in June with the dance and music of carimbó and bois-bumbas, which should be very interesting. In July, there is the Festival de Verão when the island shows off some of its art and music.

On the second Sunday of December is the Círio de NS Do Ó, the principal religious event on the island. Like Belém's Círio, it's a very beautiful and joyous event, and well-worth a special trip if you're in Belém at the time.

Places to Stay & Eat

There are campsites on the island and a handful of hotels. The *Ilha Bela* (tel 771-1448) at Avenida 16 de Novembre 409 has air-con and a restaurant. A room for one or more persons is US$6.50 without bath. The *Hotel Farol* (tel 771-1219 or

Belém 222-5118) is on the beach and is the same price without bath.

The *Sol e Mar Restaurant* at Praia Chapéu Virado is recommended. On the Praia do Murubira is the more expensive *Hotel Murubira* (tel 771-1256 or Belém 223-1448) with singles/doubles for US$14.

Getting There & Away

Ilha do Mosqueiro is a two-hour bus ride and 84 km from Belém. The island is linked by good, paved roads and a bridge. Buses leave from the rodoviária every hour on weekdays and every half-hour on weekends, all day and night and cost 50c.

PRAIA ALGODOAL

Algodoal attracts younger Belémites and a handful of foreign travellers. It's a beautiful spot with dune-swept beaches and at times a turbulent sea. It's very remote, with a small fishing village and a couple of very basic hotels. But all this will change, hopefully not too radically, as it is in the process of being discovered.

Getting There & Away

Algodoal is on the point of a cape northeast of Belém on the Atlantic. Getting there requires a three-hour bus ride from Belém to the town of Marudá, and a boat across the bay. When you get off the boat you have to negotiate with a taxi driver to take you to the other side of the cape.

The road from Belém is not in good condition and buses can be delayed by bad weather. Buses leave Belém daily at 7 and 10 am, 1.30, 3.30, 5.30 and on Fridays 8 pm. The last bus leaves Marudá to return to Belém at 4 pm. There are sometimes additional buses on weekends so call the rodoviária.

Marudá is a poor fishing village with a couple of cheap hotels and a respectable beach, so it's no problem if you're stuck there overnight. Cars cannot make the journey to Algodoal and will have to be left in Marudá.

SALINÓPOLIS

Salinópolis is Pará's major Atlantic coast resort. There are good beaches, like Praia da Atalaia, and some mineral spas. Belém is only three hours away by bus on a paved road. There are plenty of summer homes here and during the July holiday month Salinópolis is very crowded. If you want beautiful deserted Brazilian beach, this is not really the best place to go.

Places to Stay

The *Hotel Salinópolis* (tel 823-1239) is recommended. Camping is easy.

Getting There & Away

There is regular bus service from Belém.

ILHA DO MARAJÓ

The Ilha do Marajó had an ancient Indian civilisation which was famous for its ceramics. The best objects are in Belém at the archaeology museum. The island's 90,000 people live in 12 municipalities and the many fazendas spread across the island.

Geography

Ilha do Marajó has close to 50,000 square km of land, divided into two almost equal-sized regions. The eastern half of the island is called the *region do campos*; it's characterised by low-lying fields with savannah-type flora, sectioned by strips of remaining forest. Various palm trees and dense mangrove forests line the coast. The island's western half, the *region da mata*, is primarily forest.

Climate

Marajó has two seasons: the very rainy, from January to June; and the less rainy, from July to December. During the rainy season much of the island turns into swamp and the region do campos becomes completely submerged under a metre or more of water. The island's few roads are elevated by three metres, but they are often impassable during the rainy season nonetheless.

Fauna

Marajó's sustenance, the herds of buffalo who wander the campos, are well-adapted to the swamp conditions. There are many snakes, most notably large boas. The island is filled with birds, especially during the dry season, including the *guará*, a graceful flamingo with a long, curved beak. The sight of a flock of deep-pink guarás flying against Marajó's green backdrop is spectacular.

Souré

Population: 16,000

Souré, the island's principal town, is on the Rio Paracauari, a few km from the Baía de Marajó – the tide along the city's shore oscillates a remarkable three metres. With regular ENASA boat service and easy access to several of the best beaches and fazendas, it's probably the best place to go on the island. Like all the island's coastal towns, Souré is primarily a fishing village, but it's also the commercial centre for the island's buffalo business.

It's a small town where buffalo are king. They have right of way everywhere in town. The people work around the buffalo, or sometimes with or on them, but never in the way of them.

Legend has it that a French ship was sailing to French Guiana with a load of buffalo picked up in India, but never made it. The boat sunk off the shore of Ilha de Marajó and the buffalo swam to shore. The rest is history.

Today, Marajó is the only place in Brazil where the buffalo roam in great numbers, and there are many of them. These are not the furry American bison that Buffalo Bill and other rough-riders slaughtered on the American plains, but a tough-skinned hairless buffalo that looks like a macho Indian Brahma bull.

There are four different types of buffalo on Marajó. The meat, the dairy, the beast of burden and the hybrid buffalo. The buffalo are better suited than cattle to Marajó's environment because of three qualities: during the wet season, when much of the land is swamp or lagoon, the buffalo can walk on the soft ground with their wide hooves and can swim when the water gets deep; they have a tough three-layered hide that withstands the bites of the island's many snakes and parasite; they can eat almost anything and can get to food under water.

Warning There are *bichu do pé* (feet parasites) in and around the towns and many other nasty parasites. Keep your head on your shoulders and shoes on your feet.

Beaches The bay beaches near Souré are excellent and look more like ocean beaches. The most beautiful beach is also the closest, Praia Araruna is a 10-minute taxi drive from town. Arrange to have the driver pick you up at a set hour and pay then. You can also walk the seven km; get directions in town. At the end of the road, follow two walking bridges across the lagoons to the beach. The bay here, 30 km from the ocean, has both fresh and salt water. At low tide you can walk about five km in either direction along the beach – it's quite beautiful. The beach is deserted during the week and not much more crowded on weekends. There's often a strong wind; in fact one Belémite I met was planning a two-month windsurfing trip around the island.

Like Praia Grande de Salvaterra, Praia do Pesqueiro is close to Souré: 13 km and a 25-minute drive. Ask about buses at Pousada Marajóara. There are a couple of barracas with great caranguejo (crab) and casquinho de caranguejo (stuffed crab) but lousy shrimp. Facing the sea, the best beach is out to the right. Do not swim in the shallow lagoon between the barracas and the sea, there are prickly plants.

Other Attractions Heading upriver, about a 10-minute walk from town, there is an old, simple tannery. They sell sandals, belts, etc, made from buffalo and boa. They were also tanning a jacaré skin when I visited which is illegal but quite common. The stuff for sale isn't very good but it's illuminating to see the way it's made.

Festivals On the second Sunday of November Souré has its own Círio de Nazaré. There's a beautiful procession and the town bursts with communal spirit. Everyone in the region comes to town so accommodation can be difficult to find. The festival of São Pedro with a maritime procession on 29 June is a very colourful celebration. If you're into buffalo culture there's an Agro-Pecuária fair during the third week in September.

Places to Stay There seems to be a tourism industry conspiracy of silence. In Belém, the only information that people are willing to share is 'go talk to MERTUR'. MERTUR is the travel agency that apparently has the Marajó franchise. It's not a bad outfit, but independent travel on the island is really no more difficult than anywhere else in Amazonas. So it's easy to set out on your own.

Souré itself has three places to stay. The *Pousada Marajóara* does most of its business through MERTUR in Belém which arranges package excursions (tel 223-3100). A one-day trip by plane costs US$75. A three-day trip by boat is US$125 for a single and US$190 for a double, food and lodging included. The pousada buses you around to a fazenda with buffalo and the local beaches. If you're in a hurry or want someone else to take care of everything for you it's a good deal, but otherwise there is no reason to take this route. The pousada accommodation is fine, if a bit touristy, and they have the best food in town. The local fish is the best dish but there's also buffalo meat and for dessert don't miss the fantastic flan made from buffalo milk.

The *Pousada Marajóara* (tel 741-1887) is not busy on weekdays and rents doubles for US$14. For about the same price on the other edge of town is the *Hotel Marajó* (tel 741-1472 which is also less crowded on weekends. For cheaper lodging the *Souré Hotel* (tel 741 1202) in the centre of town has apartments for US$6.50/4.50 with/without bath. It's simple but a bit dowdy.

Fazendas The fazendas where the buffalo roam are enormous estates which occupy most of the island's eastern half. They are also beautiful rustic refuges filled with birds and monkeys. Most of the fazendas have dormitories with an extra bunk or a place to hitch a hammock, but not all welcome outsiders. The fazendas listed here have primitive dorms for tourists and will show you around by jeep or on foot.

Fazenda Boa Jardim is reportedly the most beautiful. It's a three-hour boat ride from Souré and a bit less by taxi. Air taxis take 30 minutes from Belém. There's information in Belém at Avenida Presidente Vargas 676 (tel 224-3233). The fazendeiro, Eduardo Ribiera, comes to Souré often so you can also try to track him down in town if you want to stay out at Boa Jardim and maybe get a ride there with him.

Fazenda Providencia is two hours by boat from Souré. They reportedly have beds for a couple of people. MERTUR arranges day trips there on weekends and claims the fazenda is loaded with monkeys. The *Fazenda Jilva* has accommodation for about 20 people. It's a 45-minute flight from Belém.

Information in Belém is at Avenida Presidente Vargas 676 (tel 224-3233). For information about other fazendas in Belém try Paratur, but you will probably have to be insistent because their standard operating procedure is to channel tourists to MERTUR. Another strategy would be to talk to the air-taxi companies like Aerotur at the Aeroclube Julio César in Belém (tel 233-3786). Some of the old pilots know the island very well.

Getting There & Away Aerotur air taxi flies regularly from Belém to Souré. It's a beautiful 25-minute flight, the price varies depending on how many people fly, but standard is US$50. Any of the air taxi companies will fly you to several cities on the island. The price is by the plane load so it's not too steep if you get a group together. A five-seater from Belém to

Souré, for example, costs US$175 so split five ways that's only US$35 a person.

In addition to the ENASA ferry, you can also catch a smaller boat leaving from the docks to and from Belém (no regular schedule). Most of these boats are heading to either Souré or Breves. From Macapá in the territory of Amapá there are boats to Afuá on Marajó. Local fishing boats sail the high seas and it's possible to use them to get all the way around the island and to some of the fazendas.

AROUND ILHA DO MARAJÓ

Salvaterra is a short boat trip across the river from Souré. Shuttle boats go every 15 minutes during the day and cost 10c. Salvaterra has restaurants but no hotel. A 10-minute walk from town, Praia Grande de Salvaterra is a long, pretty beach on the Baía de Marajó. The beach is popular on weekends when the barracas open, but often windy. It's a good place to see the beautiful fence corrals which dot Marajó's coastline (the best view is from a small plane). The corrals are simple fences with netting that use the falling tide to capture fish. The beauty is in the simplicity of the design which – like a Christo sculpture – appears completely harmonious with that environment.

From Salvaterra there is a dirt road that goes to Câmara (24 km) and then Cachoeira do Arari (51 km). Cachoeira do Arari is a very pretty, rustic spot and reportedly has a pousada. To the north, with access only by plane, is the town of Santa Cruz do Arari on the large Lago Arari. The town is completely under water during the rainy season and is famous for it's fishing.

The eastern half of the island is less populated and less interesting for travellers. ENASA boats go to Breves, which has a pousada. Afuá on the northern shore is built on water and also has a pousada. Both cities are linked to Belém by air taxi.

SANTARÉM
Population: 200,000

Santarém is a pleasant city with a mild climate (22 to 36°C), Atlantic breezes, calm waters and forests. The region of Santarém was inhabited by the Tapuiçu Indians. Over three decades after Captain Pedro Teixeira's expedition first contacted the Tapuiçu a Jesuit mission was established at the meeting of the Tapajós and Amazon rivers in 1661. In 1758 the village which grew around the mission was named Santarém after the Portuguese city. Santarém history merges with legends of *garimpos* and Indians, but it is certain that the city was peopled by gold prospectors, Indians, rubber gatherers and Confederate veterans of the US Civil War.

The economy is based on rubber, hard woods, brazil nuts, black pepper, mangoes and fish. More recently soybeans and jute were added to the list and in the past 10 years there has been rapid development with the discovery of gold and bauxite and the construction of the Curuá-Una hydroelectric dam. However, prosperity has passed by the majority of the people.

Information & Orientation

Santarém is in the state of Pará, 2½° south of the equator at the junction of the Tapajós and the Amazon rivers, about halfway between Manaus and Belém (and only 30 metres above sea level). It's the third largest city of the Amazon, but a sleepy backwater in comparison to Manaus and Belém.

The city layout is simple: the Cuiabá to Santarém highway runs directly to the Docas do Pará, dividing the city into old (eastern) and new (western) halves. East from the Docas do Pará where the large boats dock is Avenida Tapajós and the waterfront, which continues to the market place and commercial district near the cheap hotels. The Tropical Hotel is in the new residential portion of town.

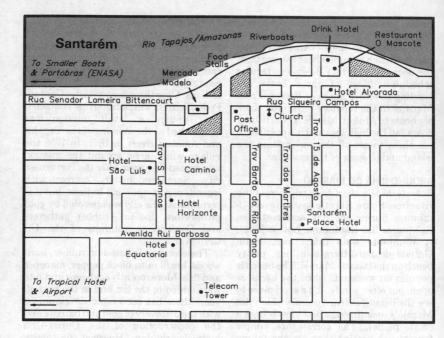

Tourist Office There is no tourist office, but there are two valuable sources of information in Santarém. One is Bill Dieter, an American bush pilot, who flies gold prospectors in and out of the Amazon and the other is Mr Alexander, an expatriate American English teacher who is the author of *Alexander's Guide to Santarém*.

Money Only the Banco do Brasil accepts travellers' cheques.

Airlines TABA (tel 522-1939) is at Rua Floriano Peixoto 607, Varig/Cruzeiro (tel 522-2084) at Rua Siquiera Campos 277 and Vasp (tel 522-1680) at Avenida Rui Barbosa 786.

Waterfront
Walk along the waterfront of Avenida Tapajós from the Docas do Pará to Rua Adriano Pimentel. This is where drifters, loners and fishermen congregate. Include a stop at the Mercado de Peixes (fish market) and the floating market.

Casa da Cultura
The Casa da Cultura at the corner of Avenida Borges Leal and Avenida Barão do Rio Branco features a small collection of pre-Columbian pottery.

Festivals
The Indian Festa do Sairé and the Christian ceremony of NS da Saudé have been celebrated at Alter do Chão since 1880 on 23 June. The Sairé is a vine standard which leads the flower bedecked procession, perhaps in a similar manner in which the Tapuiços greeted the Portuguese or perhaps the manner in which the Jesuits introduced Christianity to the Indians.

The patron saint of fishermen, São Pedro, is honoured with a river procession. On 29 June boats decorated with flags and flowers sail before the city. Fishermen should note that the Tucunare fishing championship takes place during the second half of September and that October and November are the best months for pirarucu at Rio Itaqui and Lago Grande de Curuaí.

Legends of Santarém

Beware of walking the streets after the bells of Cathedral NS da Conceicáo ring, for you may encounter a fire-breathing pig. While you may avoid the pig, at midnight a woman in white kneels at the crossroads to pray; if you set eyes on her you will die.

Places to Stay – bottom end

Hotel São Luis (tel 522-5940), Rua Senador Lemos 118 is cheap but dumpy. Singles are US$4, doubles are US$7 to US$9 and meals and laundry service are available.

Restaurante e Hotel Ponte Certo on the corner of Avenida Cuiaba and Mendoza Fortado is a cleanish place but unfortunately a bit out of the way. Unlike the Hotel São Luis it has baths in its US$7.50 doubles.

Hotel Camino (tel 522-1399), Praça Rodrigues dos Santos 877 near the market, and the *Hotel Central Plaza*, also by the market, asks US$10/15 for doubles with fan/with air-con.

Places to Stay – top end

The *Hotel Tropical* (tel 522-1583) at Avenida Mendoça Furtado 4120 is the only luxury hotel in Santarém. Considering the amenities of a four-star hotel; air-con, swimming pool, restaurant and bar, US$26 isn't unreasonable for doubles.

The two middle range hotels are far inferior in quality but they're adequate. The *Santarém Palace Hotel* (tel 522-1285), at Avenida Rui Barbosa 726, and the *Hotel Nova Olinda* (tel 522-1531), at Avenida Adriano Pimentel 140, charge about US$20 for doubles.

Places to Eat

The local fishes are curimatá, jaraqui, surubins, tucunare and pirarucu. Local dishes use cassava: maniçoba is made from pork and cassava while pato no tucupi is a duck and cassava root concoction.

Restaurante O Mascote on 10 Praça do Pescador off Rua Lameira Bittencourt is Santarém's best restaurant and music hangout. Fried crab is US$2.50 and fish dinners are US$6 and up. Try the peixe calderada and muquequa, and listen for singer/guitarist Vianey Sirotheau. *Restaurant Tapaiu* in the lobby of the Hotel Tropical also has a pleasing menu.

Sorveteria Go-Go at Rua Siquiera Campos 431 offers old favourites and new flavours such as graviola and milho verde (corn) to ice cream fans.

Things to Buy

Fabrica de Redes Aparecida (tel 522-1187) at Avenida Borges Leal 2561 manufactures high quality hammocks, a cheap and handy souvenir of the Amazon. They give factory tours of the 19th century textile works too. Artesanato Dica Frazão, a clothing/ craft store is at Rua Floriano Peixoto 281. The proprietor, Sra Dica, creates women's clothing from natural fibres.

Getting There & Away

Air Santarém's FAB will not give free plane rides to foreigners. Nevertheless it doesn't hurt to try, particularly if you have a letter of introduction from a consulate. TABA flies to the small towns of the Amazon interior while Varig/ Cruzeiro and Vasp connect to Brazilian capitals via Manaus and Belém.

Bus The Transamazônica and BR-163 (Cuiabá to Santarém) cross 190 km south of town at Rurópolis connecting Santarém to the rest of Brazil. Bus travel can be miserable/impossible during the rainy season because about 1800 km of BR-163 between Itaituba and Sinop is unpaved. Most traffic still relies on river transport.

The rodoviária (tel 522-1342) is five km from the Docas do Pará on Avenida Cuiabá. During the dry season there are buses to Cuiabá, Belém (1369 km) via Imperatriz, Itaituba (370 km) and Maraba (1087 km), for the Serra Pelada gold mines.

Riverboats There are daily boats to and from Manaus, but only three to four boats to Belém each week. Boat schedules are firm only *si Deus quiser* (if God wills it), but anticipate 2½ days downstream from Manaus, three days to Belém and 12 hours to Itaituba. The ENASA office (tel 522-2137) is at Rua Senador Lameira Bittencourt 459.

The boat trip is pleasant, and the food is plentiful. It's a breezy ride and the endless view of long, thin, green strips of forest and wider bands of river and sky is OK for the first day, but after a while you'll start talking to your hammock and sucking on the life belts. The river between Santarém and Belém is more interesting, particularly downstream of Monte Alegre at the Narrows, where the boat rides closer to jungle.

Getting Around

The airport is 15 km from the centre and there is no airport bus. You can take a Liberdade bus (well in advance since it's slow) from the centre or one of the private buses that leave from the Tropical. The taxi fare is US$9.

AROUND SANTARÉM
Meeting of the Waters

The meeting of the waters (*aguas barrentas*), where the clear Tapajós and the light brown Amazon merge, is worth a boat excursion or at least a glimpse from land at Praça Mirante near Restaurante O Mascote.

This trip can be combined with a visit up the Tapajos to the village of Alter do Chão, a weekend resort for the people of Santarém. Alter do Chão has good fishing and a beautiful turquoise lagoon which was once a sacred spot for the Tapajos Indians. The village is three hours by boat or 50 km by bus on a dirt road through jungle.

The Tropical Hotel organises a US$25 day tour of the meeting of the waters and Alter do Chão or you can do it yourself by taking a scheduled boat from the town docks or a bus from the rodoviária. The bus leaves at 4 am and returns at 6 pm.

Fordlândia & Belterra

Fordlândia and Belterra, Henry Ford's huge rubber plantations, date from the 1920s. Ford managed to successfully transplant an American town, but his Yankee ingenuity failed to efficiently cultivate rubber in the Amazon. Abandoned by Ford, the rubber groves are now operated by the Ministry of Agriculture as a research station.

For permission to stay overnight at the rubber groves of Belterra phone 522-4076. During the dry season, there is one bus a day from Santarém to Belterra, 60 km south. It departs at 11.30 am returning at 2.30 pm. Travel agents at the Tropical Hotel can arrange trips to Belterra and Fordlândia (50 km further south) even when the roads are closed to buses.

Curuá-Una Hydroelectric Dam

The Curuá-Una Hydroelectric Dam 72 km away on the Palhão Falls is meeting the growing energy needs of a rapidly developing region. It's open to visitors.

River Beaches

Santarém's natural river beaches are magnificent. Like elsewhere in the Amazon, the seasonal rise and fall of the waters uncovers lovely white river beaches and sweeps them clean of debris at the end of the beach season.

Maués

In November the Festa do Guaraná is

celebrated in the town of Maués in Amazonas, the largest producer of guaraná.

The first people to cultivate guaraná were the Saterê-Maûé Indians of the Amazon. Originally the Saterê-Maué lands encompassed the vast stretch of jungle between the Madeira and Tapajos rivers, today the Maûé live in a small tribal reservation. They believe that their place of origin, Noçoquem, is on the left bank of the Tapajós, where the rocks talk. They have a creation myth which ties together the origin of their people and guarana.

Long ago at Noçoquem, in the beginning of all things, lived two brothers and a sister, Ohiamuaçabe. Ohiamuaçabe, also known as Uniai, was so beautiful and wise that all the animals desired her. Of all the animals, the snake was the first to express his desire and act upon it. With a magic perfume the snake enchanted Uniai and made her pregnant. Her brothers were none too pleased and kicked her out of Noçoquem. The child was born far from Noçoquem, but Uniai often told her son about

Aika hunter on the Rio Catrimani

Noçoquem and the brazil nut tree which grew there. Although the brothers had a parakeet and a macaw on guard before the brazil nut tree, the child insisted on tasting the delicious nuts, for as he grew stronger and more beautiful his desire to taste the fruit also grew. Finally he convinced his mother to accompany him to the tree.

The birds spotted the ashes of a fire in which mother and child roasted the delicious brazil nuts. After the birds reported the incident the brothers replaced the inept guard-birds with a reliable monkey guard. Now that the boy knew the path to Noçoquem, he returned to the tree alone the following day. The monkey spied the boy, drew his bow and shot the child full of arrows.

Uniai found her dead child beneath the tree. She buried him and vowed, 'You will be great. The most powerful tree will grow from you. You will cure sickness, provide strength in war and in love.' From the boy's left eye grew the false guaraná *uaraná-hop*, then from his right eye grew the true guaraná *uaraná-cécé* This is why the berries of the guaraná look like eyes.

Days later a child was born from the guaraná tree and emerged from the earth. The child was Uniai's and he was the first Maúé Indian.

To this day the Maúé call themselves sons of guarana, and because of this plant their favourite decorative colours are red and green. The ritual drink of the Sateré-Maúé Indians is *çapo* of guaraná which is prepared from the eye-like berries. The berries, collected before the fruit opens, are dried, washed in running water and cooked in earth ovens. Water is added and the guaraná is moulded into black sticks which are then dried in a smokehouse. The Maúé shave guaraná flakes from the black sticks, using either the raspy tongue of the pirarucu or a rough stone. The flakes are then mixed into water to make the çapo.

The Maúé drink çapo of guaraná on important occasions to affirm the life force, to cure all illness; to gird their strength in times of war and to gird their loins in times of peace. Most Brazilians take their guaraná in the form of a tasty sweetened and carbonated soft drink. Coca-Cola bottles one of the most popular brands of guaraná soda, Taí Guarana. Like Coke, Guarana is a mild stimulant, although unlike coke guaraná is said to have aphrodisiac powers. Brazilians take guaraná to keep themselves up for Carnival. Pharmacies and herbal medicine shops also sell guaraná in the form of syrups, capsules and powders.

Amapá

There's not much to the territory of Amapá other than Macapá, where three-quarters of the territory's inhabitants live. Two chunks of land in the territory have been set aside as biological reserves. Lago Piratuba Biological Reserve is in the eastern corner of Amapá while Oiapoque Biological Reserve is on the border with French Guiana. Cape Orange National Park is on the coastal side of the northern tip of Amapá. The territory's economy is based on lumber and the mining of gold, manganese and tin ore.

MACAPÁ
Population: 150,000
Capital of the territory of Amapá, the city of Macapá lies right where the equator and the Amazon River cross. It is on dirt road BR-156, 570 km from Oiapoque and French Guiana to the north. The territory is divided from Pará by the Rio Javi to the west and the Amazon to the south.

Information
The DETUR provisional tourist information office (tel 222-0733) is on Avenida FAB, Centro Cívico Administrativo. Travellers planning to continue north into French Guiana will require a visa. There are French consulates in Belém, Manaus, Rio de Janeiro, São Paulo and Brasília, but not in Amapá.

Fort São José de Macapá
The fort was built in 1782 by the Portuguese to defend against French invasions from the Guyanas.

Curian
This African village, eight km from Macapá, was founded by escaped slaves.

Festivals
O Marabaixo is an Afro-Brazilian holiday celebrated 40 days after Semana Santa (Holy Week).

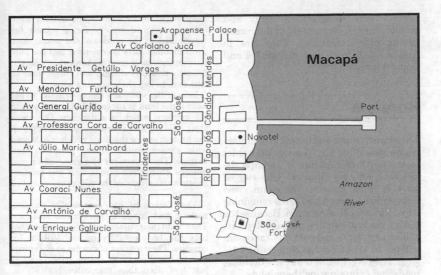

Places to Stay

Cheaper places include the *Mara Hotel* (tel 222-0859) with singles/doubles for US$7/9 on Rua São Jose. The *Arapaense Palace* (tel 222-3366) on Rua Tiradentes is only rated two-stars by Embratur but it does have air-con. Singles/doubles range from US$7.50/10 to US$10.50/12.50 for more luxurious rooms. The *Hotel Tropical* (tel 231-3739) on the same street has singles/doubles for US$1/2.50 with bath and US$1.50/3.50 with air-con as well.

Also known as the Amazonas, the *Novotel* (tel 222-1144) at Avenida Engenheiro Neto 17 is a 4-star hotel on the waterfront. Singles/doubles are US$36/42.

Places to Eat

Eat your meals either at the *Peixaria* (tel 222-0913) at Avenida Mãe Luzia 84 or *Restaurante Boscão* (tel 231-4097) at Rua Hamilton Silva, 997.

Getting There & Away

Air It's possible to fly Air France from Paris to Cayenne, French Guiana. You must then go overland to Amapá. Air France no longer flies to Belém via Cayenne. The Varig/Cruzeiro office (tel 222-1196) is at Rua Candido Mendes 1039. VASP (tel 222-2411) is at Avenida Julio Maria Lombard 115.

Riverboats There is one boat a month to Oiapoque. Boats go to Belém on Tuesday and Fridays, returning from Belém on Thursdays and Saturdays. Senava (tel 222-3648 in Macapá, tel 223-5355 in Belém) keeps Amapá boat schedule and fare information.

AROUND MACAPÁ

Bonito and the Igarapé do Lago, 72 km and 85 km from Macapá, are good places for swimming, fishing and jungle walks. Serra do Navio, four hours and 200 km from Macapá (through beautiful jungle), is the territory's huge manganese plant. Phone 632-6666 for permission to visit.

The Cachoeira de Santo Antonio is a pretty waterfall in the municipality of Mazagão, an 18th century Portuguese village. Lago Piratuba IBDF Biological Reserve and the Maracá Ecological

Station were designed to study and protect turtles, manatees and toucans among other creatures. They are in Amapá's lake region of mangroves and tropical forests.

Roraima

The rugged, remote and beautiful mountain region straddling the Venezualan border to the north of Roraima is perhaps the ultimate Amazon frontier. This rugged land is home to the Yanomani, who represent about one-third of the remaining tribal Indians of the Amazon. Because the Indian lands are sitting on huge deposits of iron, casseterite and gold, the Yanomani will not be kept from the 20th century for long. The government is already building roads and expropriating these lands.

The Yanomani

The Yanomani are one of the newly discovered Indian peoples of the Amazon. Until some Yanomani were given metal tools by visitors, all their implements were made of stone, ceramic, animal hides and plants. They are literally a stone age people rapidly confronting the 20th century.

In 1973 the Yanomani had their first contact with westerners: Brazilian Air Force pilots and religious missionaries. In 1974 and 1975 as BR-210 (Perimetral Norte) and BR-174 cut through the Catramani and Ajarani tributaries of the Rio Negro, people from several Yanomani villages mixed with the construction workers and contracted and died from measles, influenza and VD.

The Yanomani are slight people with Oriental features. Their estimated 18,000 semi-nomadic tribesmen are scattered over 320 villages on either side of the Brazilian-Venezuelan border. They speak one of four related languages: Yanomam, Yanam, Yanomano and Sanumá.

The Yanomani have some curious practices. When a tribal person dies, the body is hung from a tree until dry, then burned to ashes. The ashes are mixed with bananas then eaten by friends and family of the deceased so as to incorporate and preserve the spirit. The mourning ritual is elaborate, one member of the tribe is assigned to cry for a month (as determined by the phases of the moon, since the Yanomani have no calendar and the only number they have greater than two is 'many'). Friendly or allied villages will travel three to four days to join the mourning tribe.

Inter-tribal visits are an opportunity to eat well: if the hunt is successful everyone gets to eat monkey, which is a delicacy. Otherwise tapir, wild pig and a variety of insects make up the protein end of the meal which is balanced with garden fruits, yams, plantains and manioc. The Yanomani also grow cotton and tobacco. Once their garden soils and hunting grounds are exhausted the village moves on to a new site.

The Yanomani are continually warring, making and breaking inter-tribal alliances. They build their villages on high ground so that they can be constantly on the lookout for enemies. Their concept of disease as evil spirits sent by the shamans of enemy tribes, reflects just how deep this inter-tribal hostility is. Disease is cured with various herbs, shaman dances and healing hands. Sometimes the village shaman will enlist the good spirits to fight the evil spirits by using *yakoana*, a hallucinogenic herbal powder.

These days even such remote tribes are close to encroaching civilisation. By FAB plane or air-taxi it's a short hop from Boa Vista to the FUNAI post in the Serra do Surucucu.

BOA VISTA

Population 200,000

Information & Orientation

Boa Vista, the capital of Roraima, is a planned city on the banks of the Rio Branco. Although the city is growing at a bounding pace there is much poverty. Think of the city as an archway so that the base of the archway stands on the Rio Branco and the arch itself is formed by Avenida Major Williams and Avenida Ajuricaba. Avenues radiate from the top dividing the outskirts into wedges.

The government buildings are located dead centre at the intersection of Avenida Ville Roy and Avenida Ene Garcez, while the commercial district runs from the centre of town along Avenida Jaime Brasil

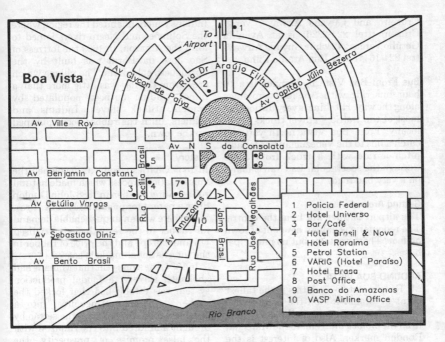

Boa Vista

1	Policia Federal
2	Hotel Universo
3	Bar/Café
4	Hotel Brasil & Nova Hotel Roraima
5	Petrol Station
6	VARIG (Hotel Paraíso)
7	Hotel Brasa
8	Post Office
9	Banco do Amazonas
10	VASP Airline Office

to Avenida Floriano Peixoto on the waterfront.

Tourist Office A Secretaria de Planejamento (tel 224-5810), a provisional tourist office, is at Rua Coronel Pinto 241.

Places to Stay
Cheaper hotels include the *Nova Hotel Roraima* (tel 224-9843) near the Venezuelan consulate and the *Hotel Lua Nova* (tel 224-1242) at Avenida Benjamin Constant 591. The *Hotel Brasa*, also on Avenida Benjamin Constant, is cheaper still.

There are two 2-star hotels in Boa Vista, both with swimming pools, restaurants, bars, air-con and telephones. The *Hotel Tropical* (tel 224-4800) at Praça do Centro Cívico Joaquim Nabuco 53 has singles/doubles for US$16/17. *Hotel Eusebio's* (tel 224-1846) is at Rua Cecília Brasil 1107.

Places to Eat
Peixada do Bigode on Avenida Floriano Peixoto, *Peixada da Tia Quelé* at Rua Edmur Oliva 258 and *Peixada Chopp de Ouro* at Avenida Benjamin Constant 849 are all recommended for fish. If you don't care for that, there are always the two hotel restaurants, *Restaurante Senzala* at Avenida Presidente Castelo Branco 1015 and two steak houses, *Churrascaria Espeto de Ouro* at Avenida Ville Roy 231 and *Churrascaria Paraná* at Rua Sorocaima 702.

Things to Buy
The Centro de Artesanato at Avenida Marechal Floriano 158 and the shop at the airport both sell Indian crafts.

Getting There & Away
Air There are flights to and from Manaus and Georgetown, Guyana by Varig/

Cruzeiro and Guyana Airways. Varig/Cruzeiro (tel 224-2226) is at Avenida Getúlio Vargas 242 while Guyana Airways (tel 224-1644) is at Rua Araújo Filho.

Bus From Boa Vista to Manaus is a 16 hour bus ride with two ferry crossings along the way. Hitching is very difficult as most of the traffic – gravel trucks – run locally. From Boa Vista north you can catch a bus to the Venezuelan border and hitch a ride with a truck from there through the spectacular La Gran Sabana on a very bad road.

Getting Around
The airport is three km from the centre. The rodoviária is half an hour out of town on foot. There are taxis but no municipal buses.

AROUND BOA VISTA
Mt Roraima at 2875 metres is the tallest point in Brazil. It's on the border with Venezuela and Guyana, a three day hike from the *moloca indigena* to the Marechal Rondon marker. Also of interest is the Pedra de Macunaima hanging rock, a source of legends among the Macuxi tribe.

Other points of interest in the area include the Serra de Tepequém, a diamond *garimpo* in an extinct volcanic crater; the Serra do Sol, inhabited by the Igarićs Indians; Estação Ecologíca do Maracá (120 km from Boa Vista); the hieroglyphic fingers of Pedra Pintada; and Lake Caracaranâ on the right bank of Rio Maú.

The upper Rio Branco and Uraricoera are reputed to have great fishing from July to March.

Amazonas

MANAUS
Population: 620,000
Manaus was named after a tribe of Indians which inhabited the region where the Solimões and Negro rivers joined to form the Amazon. In 1669 the fortress of São José da Barra was built by the Portuguese colonisers. The village which grew from the fort was little more than a minor trading outpost populated by traders, Black slaves, Indians and soldiers, until the rubber boom pumped up the town.

History
In 1839 Charles Goodyear developed the vulcanisation process which made natural rubber durable, then in 1888 John Dunlop drew a patent for pneumatic rubber tires. Soon there was an unquenchable demand for rubber in the recently industrialised US and Europe and the price of rubber in the international markets soared.

In 1884, the same year that Manaus had abolished slavery, a feudal production system was established that locked the rubber gatherers, seringueiros, into a cruel serfdom. Driven from the sertão by drought and lured into the Amazon with the false promise of prosperity, the *Nordestinos* signed away their freedom to the owners of rubber plantations, the *seringalistas*.

The seringalista sold the seringueiro goods on credit – fishing line, knives, manioc flour, hammocks – and purchased the seringueiro's balls of latex. The illiteracy of the seringueiros, the seringalista's gun-toting henchmen (*pistoleros*), crooked scales, monopoly of sales and purchases all contributed to the perpetuation of the seringueiro's debt. The seringueiros also had to contend with loneliness, jungle fevers, hostile Indian attacks and all manner of deprivation. Those seringueiros who attempted to escape their serfdom were hunted down and tortured by the pistoleros.

The plantation owners, the rubber traders and the bankers prospered and built palaces with their wealth. Gentlemen had their shirts sent to London to be laundered, ladies sported the latest

Top: Sunset on the Rio Negro, Amazon (KB)
Left: View of the Amazon (VS)
Right: Destruction of the forest, Amazon (JM)

Top: Old man, Santarém, Pará (MS)
Left: On the Rio Negro, Amazon (KB)
Right: On the Rio Negro, Amazon (KB)

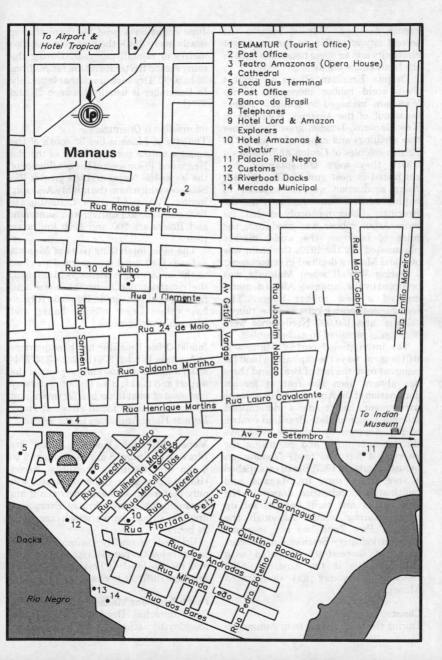

Manaus

To Airport &
Hotel Tropical

1 EMAMTUR (Tourist Office)
2 Post Office
3 Teatro Amazonas (Opera House)
4 Cathedral
5 Local Bus Terminal
6 Post Office
7 Banco do Brasil
8 Telephones
9 Hotel Lord & Amazon
  Explorers
10 Hotel Amazonas &
  Selvatur
11 Palacio Rio Negro
12 Customs
13 Riverboat Docks
14 Mercado Municipal

Rua Ramos Ferreira

Rua 10 de Julho

Rua J Clemente

Rua 24 de Maio

Rua Saldanha Marinho

Rua Henrique Martins

Rua J Sarmento

Av Getúlio Vargas

Rua Joaquim Nabuco

Rua Lauro Cavalcante

Rua Major Gabriel

Rua Emílio Moreira

To Indian
Museum

Av 7 de Setembro

Rua Marechal Deodoro

Rua Guilherme Moreira

Rua Marcílio Dias

Rua Dr Moreira

Rua Marcílio Peixoto

Rua J Paranaguá

Rua Floriano

Rua Quintino Bocaiúva

Rua dos Andradas

Rua Pedro Botelho

Rua Miranda Ledo

Rua dos Bares

Docks

Rio Negro

French fashions. Manaus became the second city after Rio de Janeiro to get electricity and an opera house was built in the heart of the jungle.

Despite Brazilian efforts to protect their world rubber monopoly, Henry Wickham managed to smuggle rubber seeds out of the Amazon. Botanists in Kew Gardens, London grew the rubber tree seedlings and exported them to the British colonies of Ceylon and Malaysia where they were transplanted and cultivated in neat groves. The efficient Asian production was far superior to haphazard Brazilian techniques and the Brazilian rubber monopoly eroded. As more Asian rubber was produced, the price of latex on the world market plummeted. By the 1920s the boom was over and Manaus declined in importance.

During WW II when Malaysia was occupied by the Japanese, Allied demand created a new rubber boom. The seringueiros became known as the 'rubber soldiers' and 150,000 Nordestinos were once again recruited to gather rubber.

The international port of Manaus is still in many ways the capital of a land far removed from the rest of Brazil and there has always been the fear of foreign domination of the Amazon. As a result the government has made a determined attempt to consolidate Brazilian control of the Amazon by creating roadways through the jungle and colonising the interior. It has also made Manaus an industrial city. In 1967, Brazil established a free trade zone in Manaus and multinational industries drawn to the area by tax and tariff benefits set up manufacturing plants. Although the Manaus Free Zone has not spawned Brazilian industry – Brazilian entrepeneurs have not successfully competed with multinationals in the Amazon – the infusion of money has invigorated Manaus.

Climate
During the rainy season from January to June count on a brief but hard shower nearly every day – the area gets over two metres of rainfall per year. During the rainy season the temperature ranges from 23 to 30°C. Dry season weather from July to December is usually between 26 and 37°C.

Information & Orientation
The city of Manaus lies 3° south of the equator on the northern bank of the Rio Negro and 10 km west of the confluence of the lesser Rio Negro and the greater Rio Solimões which form the mighty Amazon. Iquitos, Peru and Leitícia, Columbia are 1900 and 1500 km upriver and Santarém and Belém are 700 and 1500 km down river.

The most interesting parts of Manaus as far as the tourist is concerned are close to the waters edge: Mercado Municipal, the riverboat port, customs house and floating docks. Avenida Eduardo Ribeiro has airline ticket offices, banks and Manaus' fancier stores.

Tourist Office Emantur has headquarters at Avenida Tarumã 379 (tel 232-6324, 234-5503) and tourist information posts at the airport and docks. It's a bit out of the way and most of what it has to offer (maps and brochures) can be found either at Hotel Lord or Hotel Amazonas in the centre.

Money Although business hours are Monday to Friday 8 am to midday, 2 to 6 pm and Saturday mornings, banks (Banco Económico, Banco do Brasil) will only do foreign exchange between 9 am and midday Monday to Friday. Exceptions are the airport banks which are open 24 hours.

US cash is readily exchanged a few points below the parallel rate in São Paulo and Rio de Janeiro. Traveller's cheques are more difficult to change.

Post & Telephone Manaus' post office is on Rua Marechal Deodoro and is open Monday to Saturday 8 am to 6 pm and

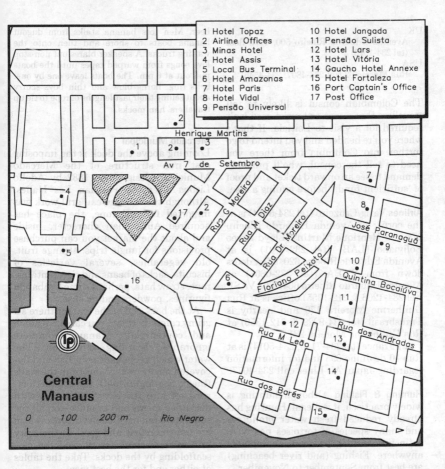

1	Hotel Topaz	10	Hotel Jangada
2	Airline Offices	11	Pensão Sulista
3	Minas Hotel	12	Hotel Lars
4	Hotel Assis	13	Hotel Vitória
5	Local Bus Terminal	14	Gaucho Hotel Annexe
6	Hotel Amazonas	15	Hotel Fortaleza
7	Hotel Paris	16	Port Captain's Office
8	Hotel Vidal	17	Post Office
9	Pensão Universal		

Henrique Martins

Av 7 de Setembro

Rua G Moreira

Rua M Diaz

Rua Dr Moreira

José Paranaguá

Floriano Peixoto

Quintina Bocaiúva

Rua dos Andradas

Rua M Leão

Rua dos Barés

Central Manaus

0   100   200 m   Rio Negro

Sunday 8 am to 2 pm. The Amazon postal system has a poor reputation, and foreign residents in Manaus don't entrust their correspondence to Brazilian correios, but wait for US or Europe bound couriers and friends to take them. For this reason US stamps (as well as vanilla spice) are valuable commodities among expatriates residing in the Amazon.

Embratel, at Rua Barrosso 220, is far more reliable for international communications, and is open daily 8 am to 11 pm.

Consulates It's best to arrange visas to neighbouring countries well in advance through consulates in Manaus.

Bolivia
    Rua Fortaleza 80 (tel 232-0077)
Columbia
    Avenida Eduardo Ribeiro 434, room 31
    (tel 234-6777)
Ecuador
    Rua 6 Casa 6 (Jardim Belo Horizonte)
    (tel 236-3698)
Peru
    Rua Tapajos 536 (tel 234-7900)

UK
    Avenida Eduardo Ribeiro 500, 12th floor
    (tel 234-1018)
USA
    Rua Maceió 62 (tel 234-4807, 234-4546)

The Colombian consul is likely to tell travellers that a visa or tourist card isn't required for a visit to Leitícia. If that's where you're headed and you intend to go further into Columbia from there you need to tell the consul, who'll probably demand to see an onward ticket and proof of 'sufficient funds' before issuing a visa.

Airlines Varig/Cruzeiro (tel 234-5014) is at the corner of Avenida Eduardo Ribeiro 278 and Henrique Martins. Lloyd Aereo Boliviano (LAB) (tel 232-7701) is at Avenida Eduardo Ribeiro 620, a few doors down from TABA (tel 232-0806) at Avenida Eduardo Ribeiro 664. The VASP (tel 234-1266 & 212-1355) office is at Rua Guilherme Moreira 179 and nearby is Transbrasil (tel 234-9229 & 212-1356) at Rua Guilherme Moreira 281.

Air France (tel 234-7115, 234-5014) is at Rua 10 de Julho 695 and for information regarding Japan Air Lines call 234-4077.

Hunting & Fishing Although hunting is widely practised, it is illegal. Hunting has already reduced fresh water *manatees* and many species of tortoises nearly to extinction. Fishing, however, is acceptable anywhere. Fishing (and river beaching) are best from September to November.

Escadaria dos Remédios Port
The Escadaria dos Remédios port by the Mercado Municipal is quite the scene:

most of the people have Indian features, with straight jet black hair and tawny skin. The thin and stoop-shouldered stevedores lug barrels, casks and boxes between the trucks and riverboats whose curved decks are filled with boxes and people and draped with hundreds of hammocks. Fishermen look on from the sidelines while they smoke cigarettes and drink

beer. Men toss banana stalks from dugout banana boats to shore and then onto the waiting trucks. A speaker blares out non-stop love songs from warped tapes until the boats pull out at 6 pm. The boats leave one by one: bells ring, horns blow and thin boys scurry about selling their last lengths of rope to tie up travellers' hammocks.

Mercado Municipal
Looming above the dock is the imposing cast iron structure of the Mercado Municipal, designed in 1882 by Adolfo Lisboa after the Parisian Les Halles. Although the art nouveau grill work was imported from Europe, the place has acquired Amazonian character. Inside and about the market you can purchase provisions for jungle trips: strange fruit, old vegetables, several varieties of biscuits, sacks of beans and rice, lanterns, rope, straw hats, perhaps some Umbanda figurines, powders and incense.

At the back end of the market there's a grimy cafeteria where you can have lunch and contemplate Manaus' complete ignorance regarding sanitation. The water which keeps enormous fish and fly-covered meats cool, drains from the stalls (meat, fish and urinal), flows underfoot, runs off into the river and mixes with discarded meats and produce and all the sewage of Manaus. Urubu vultures swarm around the refuse and roost in the rusty iron work of the cafeteria and the new scaffolding by the docks. Take the tables at either end for the best view.

Teatro Amazonas
The Teatro Amazonas, the famous opera house of Manaus, was designed by Doménico de Angelis in Italian renaissance style at the height of the rubber boom in 1896. More than any other building associated with the administration of Mayor Eduardo Ribeiro this opera house is symbolic of the opulence that was Manaus. The opera is situated off Avenida Eduardo Ribeiro between Rua José Clemente and Rua 10 de Julho. It

may be seen Monday to Saturday from midday to 5 pm.

According to the historian Daniel Fausto Bulcão, there once was a couple who lived in the interior far from the city. The woman was pregnant, and in the course of her pregnancy she had the misfortune to kill a cobra. When her nine months were up she gave birth to two cobras, male and female, which she raised as her own children.

The cobras began to grow and the mother was unable to control her unruly offspring so she threw them into the river. The female cobra earned a reputation for being evil by tipping over river boats, devouring children and drowning adults – killing simply for the pleasure of it. Her brother was of a milder temperament and the two cobras fought continuously. One day brother snake killed his sister, but not without suffering the loss of one eye. He is still alive and well and has grown considerably over the years. It is believed by Caboclos that he now lives beneath Manaus and his enormous head supports the Teatro Amazonas while his body supports the many river beaches of the Amazon.

Palácio Rio Negro

The Palácio Rio Negro, built as a home for eccentric German rubber-baron Waldemar Scholz, now serves as the seat of the state government and is on Avenida Sete de Setembro by the first bridge of the Igarape do Manaus.

British Customs House (Alfândega)

The British Customs House dates back to 1906. The sandy building with its neat brown trim seems out of place in this dilapidated city. The building was imported from the UK in prefabricated blocks and now serves as the Inspetoria da Receita Federal do Porto do Manaus.

Floating Docks

The floating docks also date back to 1906 and were considered a technical marvel when they were first installed, and rise and fall as the water level of the Amazon changes with the seasons.

Amazon Research Institute

The central project of INPA, the National Amazon Research Institute, is a joint study with the World Wildlife Federation to determine the 'minimal critical size of ecosystems', the smallest chunk of land that can support a self-sustaining jungle forest and all its attendant creatures.

The ambitious 20-year project is under the direction of Dr Thomas Lovejoy. Various sized parcels of jungle are studied first in their virgin state and later after the surrounding land has been cleared, creating islands of jungle. Changes in plant and animal populations are carefully scrutinised. It turns out that the complex interdependence of plants and animals and the heterogeneity of species poses a barrier to maintaining an isolated patch of jungle. INPA scientists are also studying aquatic mammals: fresh water manatee, river otter and porpoises. Tanks of these animals as well as the requisite cayman alligator tanks are on display for visitors.

The grounds are open Monday to Friday 8 am to midday and 2 to 6pm, and are located at Bola do Coroado at Estrada de Aleixo 1756, Km 4. A taxi is easier than taking the São José bus. Call ahead (tel 236-9400) to find the topic (and language) of Tuesday's seminar series.

Museu do Homem do Norte (Museum of the Man of the North)

The Museu do Homem do Norte (tel 234-6600, 232-5373) at Avenida 7 de Setembro 1385 is an ethnology/anthropology museum dedicated to the way of life of the river dwelling Caboclos. It's open Tuesday to Friday 9 am to midday and 2 to 6 pm, Saturday 1 to 6 pm.

Museum of the Indian

The Museum of the Indian, at the intersection of Avenida Duque de Caxias and Avenida Sete de Setembro, has exhibits which feature tribes of the upper Rio Negro. It's open Monday to Saturday 8 to 11 am and 2 to 5 pm.

Zoo

The CIGS military zoo boasts more jaguars born in captivity than anywhere else in the world. The animals – tapir, monkeys, armadillos, snakes and birds – were collected by Brazilian soldiers on jungle manoeuvres and survival training programmes. To get to the zoo on Estrada da Ponta Negra at Km 12, near the beach and Hotel Tropical, take a cab or a municipal bus marked Compensa or São Jorge. Zoo hours are Tuesday to Sunday 8 to 11.30 am and 1 to 5 pm.

Praia Ponta Negra

The zoo is near Praia Ponta Negra, the chic river beach of the Amazon, with all the amenities, restaurants and bars. The best time to go is from September to November (sometimes as early as July) when the waters recede, but it's still a popular hangout even when the high waters flood the sand and cleanse the beach for the following season.

If you've missed the beach season, December to February is the best time to visit the waterfalls near Manaus: Cachoeira do Tarumã (15 km by Soltur bus), Cachoeira do Paricatuba and Cascatinha do Amor.

São (Rabbi) Moyal

In Cemitério São João Batista, the general cemetery of Manaus (Praça Chile, Adrianópolis), is the tomb of Rabbi Moyal of Jerusalém. The rabbi came to the Amazon to minister to a small community of Jewish settlers, mostly merchants who had established a cocoa, lumber and rubber trading network. The rabbi died in 1910 and over the years his tomb has become a shrine for an odd Roman Catholic cult. This cult, complete with rosary beads, candles, coins and devoted followers, probably arose with the Jewish custom of placing pebbles on tombs when visiting grave sites. The people of Manaus, unfamiliar with Jews and their ways – of Brazil's 120,000 Jews less than 1000 inhabit Manaus – attribute the mysterious pebbles to the miraculous powers of the dead rabbi. Followers believe that the rabbi is a saint and insist that he does miracles for people who come to him with faith.

Festivals

A folklore festival during the second half of June coincides with a number of saints' days and culminates in the São Pedro river procession. In honour of São Pedro, the patron saint of fishermen, hundreds of regional boats parade down the waters.

Places to Stay – bottom end

There's plenty of cheap lodging ranging from grungy to decent off Avenida Joaquim Nabuco, with some establishments charging as little as US$5 for doubles. The *Pensão Sulista* (tel 234-5814) at Joaquim Nabuco 347, near the junction with Rua Quintino Bocaiúva, has clean doubles for US$3 without bath. Make sure your room has a fan and try to get a room without a tin roof as it gets hot. Breakfast is served after 7 am and there are clothes lines and washing tubs for your laundry.

Other recommended hotels include the *Hotel Vadim* on Joaquim Nabuco and *Hotel Lars* on Rua dos Andradas. *Pensão Universal*, a travellers' hangout with a good cafeteria, is a dumpier hotel than most.

Places to Stay – middle

There is a significant fall off in quality between the top and middle ranges in hotels. Check your rooms for working air-con and showers before paying; these hotels are not bargains. The downtown middle range hotels are clustered near the Hotel Lord.

Hotel Dora (tel 232-4102) at Avenida Joaquim Nabuco 687 has doubles for US$7.50/12 with air-con. Some windowless rooms are available for less. The *Hotel Nacional* (tel 233-7533, 232-3514) at Rua Dr Moreira 59, Centro has barely decent triples with bath and air-con for US$13.50.

Places to Stay – top end

The *Tropical Hotel* (tel 238-5757), eight km beyond the airport and 16 km out of Manaus on Estrada Ponta Negra, is Manaus' premier luxury hotel and is on the Rio Negro's Ponta Negra beach. Doubles at this five-star hotel start at $US62.

The *Hotel Amazonas*, (tel 232-2957/234-7979), a four-star hotel on Praça Adalberto Valle has doubles starting at US$60. The bar of the *Hotel Lord* (tel 234-9741), a few blocks in from the Hotel Amazonas at the corner of Rua Quintano Morais and Rua Marcílio Dias 217/25, is where the wealthier adventurer types used to congregate and exchange old campaign stories. The three-star hotel has recently been refurbished and it looks smart. Doubles start at US$50.

Places to Eat

Before taking a long riverboat ride or foraying into the jungle, splurge on a few good meals in Manaus. The local specialties are tucunare, tambaqui and pirarucu fish served grilled (a la brasa), pickled (escabeche) or stewed (caldeirada). *Chapeu de Palha* (tel 234-2133) at Rua Fortaleza 619 enjoys the best reputation, but excellent fish can also be found at *Restaurante Panorama* (tel 232-3177) at Rua Recife 900. Both seafood restaurants are a bit out of the way in the Adrianópolis neighbourhood.

For surprisingly good pizza and OK ravioli try *Restaurante Fiorentina* (tel 232-1295), Praça Roosevelt 44. Adventurous palates will venture to the street stalls and sample tacacá, a gummy soup made from lethal-if-not-well-boiled manioc root, lip numbing jambu leaves and relatively innocuous dried shrimp.

For desert there's always strange fruit to taste including pupunha, bacaba and buriti. *Pinguizinho*, Avenida Eduardo Ribeiro 523, is a popular ice cream parlour.

Entertainment

Praça do Congresso at the inland end of Avenida Eduardo Ribeiro is the centre of Manaus' nightlife. Bars and restaurants lie along Avenida Eduardo Ribeiro, Avenida Sete de Setembro and Avenida Getúlio Vargas. Manaus is not noted for its nightlife, but it does have its clubs: *Clube Rio Negro, Clube Ideal* and the *Olímpico* are some of the tonier joints.

Things to Buy

Indian crafts are sold at FUNAI's Artíndia, a curious cylindrical wood store at Praça Adalberto Valle. Articles of the Wai-wai and Tikuna tribes vary in price from US$1 to US$5. The store is open Monday to Friday 8 am to midday and 2 to 6 pm and Saturday 8 am to midday. The Central de Artesanato Branco e Silva, on Rua Recife, is another craft shop open Monday to Saturday 9 am to 7 pm and Sunday 3 to 7 pm.

Manaus is a free trade zone. This means that locally manufactured products with foreign labels – particularly electronic goods – are available for less than elsewhere in Brazil. This doesn't mean all that much in the way of savings to foreigners but as a result everyone entering or leaving the city must theoretically go through customs. People entering by bus from the south pass through customs at the Careiro ferry landing. Customs is no problem with smaller river traffic. Travellers arriving via the Manaus airport should declare foreign goods (eg cameras) to avoid a tariff upon departure.

Foreigners can purchase as much as US$1200 worth of tariff-free goods. This amount exceeds that which may be imported tax free into the US and elsewhere. The zona franca commercial district is bounded by Avenida Eduardo Ribeiro, Avenida Sete de Setembro and Avenida Floriano Peixoto.

Getting There & Away

Air From Manaus it's five hours to Miami on Pan Am or Varig and four hours to Rio de Janeiro. There are international flights to: Caracas, Venezuela; Iquitos, Peru; Bogotá, Columbia; and La Paz, Bolivia. There may be Air France flights to Paris via Cayenne, French Guiana. US-bound flights from Manaus are in flux. For a time VASP was defeating restricted flights to the US by operating charter flights from Manaus to Curaçao and Montego Bay with transfers to Miami and Orlando, and LAB still flies to Miami via Caracas. In general it's cheaper to purchase the ticket abroad and have it sent to Brazil by registered mail.

In addition to Brazil's major domestic carriers – VASP, Transbrasil, Varig/Cruzeiro – which have connection to all major cities, air taxis and TABA fly to smaller Amazonian settlements.

Bus All roads from Manaus involve ferry transport. In the dry season, July to December south of the equator, it's possible to travel overland from Manaus southwards to Porto Velho on BR-319 (two daily Andorinho buses, 22 hours and 990 km). In the rainy season river travel along the Madeira takes up the slack (see Porto Velho).

The road from Manaus north to Boa Vista (BR-174) has more unpaved sections but is usually passable. It lies on either side of the equator which means that travellers must contend with two rainy seasons. In addition 100 km of this unpaved road cuts through the tribal lands of the Waimiris. Despite the FUNAI posts there have been Indian attacks on this route.

The daily Andorinho bus to Boa Vista takes 24 hours to negotiate the 770 km. There are two shorter paved roads which end 85 km west at Manacapuru and 290 km east at Itacoatiara.

The rodoviária (tel 236-2732) is four km out of town on Rua Recife and Avenida Constantino Nery. Call them for information on road conditions.

Riverboat Go to Escadaria dos Remédios, the docks by the Mercado Municipal, and poke around. Ports of call are marked on the boats and fares are pretty much standardised according to distance. Although food and drink are included in the passage, it's a good idea to bring bottled water and snacks to supplement the food.

Unless you have cabin space, you will need a hammock as well as rope to string it up. It can get windy and cool at night so a sleeping bag is also recommended. Casa das Redes, a couple of blocks inland from the Mercado Municipal in front of the Hotel Amazonas, has the best prices for hammocks. Spend a few extra cruzados and hang your hammock in the cooler upper deck preferably towards the bow.

The boats usually pull out at 6 pm regardless of the destination. ENASA ferry-catamarans take two days downstream to Santarém (US$20), four days downstream to Belém (US$39 for food, passage and hammock space). Cabin space is up to US$200 per person. Going down river, the big boats go in the faster central currents kilometres from shore. Upriver they stay more along the slow currents by the riverbanks, but not as close as the smaller boats which hug the shore, although there's not much to be seen on the Amazon anyway. If seeing wildlife is a priority, this is not the way to go. The ENASA ticket office (tel 234-3478) is at Rua Marechal Deodoro 61.

If you can't find a boat headed to a given port along the Amazon and tributaries by asking at the Escadaria dos Remédios, avoid the Capitania do Porto – they're of no use – and enquire about hours, fares, distances and ports of call at SUNAMAM. SUNAMAM, the Superintendência Nacional de Marinha Mercante (Merchant Marine Headquarters), is on the 10th floor of the Edifício Manaus on Avenida Eduardo Ribeiro.

Many people have enjoyed cruising the river from Manaus to Iquitos, Peru. The return or outgoing leg can be one of four Varig/Cruzeiro flights a week between Iquitos and Manaus via Tabatinga (US$75). From Manaus it's a seven-day trip on the *Almirante Monteiro* if all goes well. On the *Avelino Leal* and *Cidade de Terezina* it's a week's journey just to get as far as Tabatinga with stops at Fonte Boa, Foz do Jutaí, Vila Nova, Santo Antônio do Içá, Amaturé, São Paulo de Olivença, and Benjamin Constant. From Tabatinga it's three more days and 280 km to Iquitos via Leitícia, Columbia. *Oro Negro* is a recommended boat for this trip.

Travellers coming down river from Peru and Columbia should remember to get their passports stamped in Manaus at the customs house by the floating docks. Another long river trip of interest is from Manaus up the Madeira to Porto Velho.

Remember the waters drop roughly 10 to 14 metres during the dry season and this restricts river traffic, particularly in the upper Amazon tributaries.

Getting Around

Airport Transport Eduardo Gomes international airport is eight km from the city centre on Avenida Santos Dumont. For airport information call 234-8112, 212-1210. The blue and yellow taxis charge about US$8.50, but there's also a municipal bus for 15c that deposits you at Praça XV near the cathedral and a few blocks from the Hotel Amazonas. Beware of the child pickpockets as you get off the bus.

Local Transport There are four municipal bus stations: Terminal Central da Matriz by the Cathedral, Terminal Constantino Nerz, Terminal Manicoré in the Cachoerinha neighbourhood and the Terminal Interbairros transfer station. Manaus has a poor public transport system. With few exceptions it's better to walk or take a taxi than public buses.

JUNGLE TOURS

The number one priority for any visitor to Manaus is to take a jungle tour, to see the wildlife and experience the jungle close at hand. Here it's possible to arrange anything from the standard, but well worthwhile, day trips and overnights to months of travel in the hinterland.

Jungle Tour Operators

Big Operators There are several reputable but pricey jungle tour outfits. Organised tours run upwards from US$100 to US$200 per person per day and are far more expensive than tours you can arrange yourself. The tours use larger boats than those of the independent operators – too big to negotiate the narrow *igarapés* where the wildlife is – but they may have canoe trips included. There are advantages to the organised tours in that they are hassle free, there is nothing to arrange, and English-speaking guides are often available. The larger firms are reputable. Amazon Explorers (tel 232-3052) at Rua Quintino Bocaiúva, 189 has English speaking guides. Selvatur (tel 234-8639) in the lobby of the Hotel Amazonas on Praça Adalberto Valle accommodates large tour groups on huge catamaran boats.

Smaller Operators If you speak Portuguese and don't mind travelling a bit rough, the choice is simple: arrange your own tour with Sivilino Moeira do Santo, an amiable, honest and knowledgeable guide who works out of the Escadaria and goes by the nickname *Capibara*. I've made two trips with him, an overnight to Lake Januária and six months later a five-day tour up the Rio Negro, and if I ever have the opportunity to go again I'll look him up once more.

Moacir Fortes (tel 232-7492) speaks English and his boat is at the Porto Flutuante. He runs a small and first-class operation charging US$65 to US$80 per person per day depending on the number of passengers on board, anywhere from four to 14. Everyone sleeps in a clean cabin with hot showers. His boat is fitted out with canoes and small outboard and has a well stocked bar, a library full of wildlife guidebooks, binoculars and even a telescope on board.

Cláudio da Silva Barreto owns four boats and works out of Mercado Modelo docks. The boats have old outboards which

Humming bird

tend to burn a lot of oil and break down in tight spots. The boats are small enough to go into the igarapés where you can see the jungle and its wildlife close up.

Cláudio operates many of the boats in the Mercado Modelo docks, which cuts into your bargaining power. When serious haggling is called for have Cláudio itemise expenses. Disproportionately inflated estimates can now work to your favour. If the food budget seems unreasonable, buy provisions in and about the Mercado Modelo. If the fuel budget seems too high, offer to pay at the floating gas stations. Subtract the items from your original quote, It's been said that two people can get a boat and guides for two days and a night with food and hammock lodging for US$75. I paid US$110 and I had to bargain hard.

It takes a while to hammer out a deal, change money and arrange supplies and buy provisions. You must allow a few hours for this.

Amazon by River
To see the wildlife of the Amazon – jacarés,

monkeys, hawks, anacondas, toucan and botos – you must leave the major rivers and head for the furos and igarapés, narrow channels cutting through the jungle where the forest brushes up to your face. With an independent operator part of your agreement should include a canoe tour of the igarapés, since noisy motor boats scare the wildlife away. The meeting of the waters is well worth seeing, but not if it detracts from time spent in the igarapés. It can be seen just as well from the free ferry which shuttles between Careiro and the Porto Velho highway BR-319.

Remind your guide to bring fishing gear, straps and cords (to suspend packs) and of course cachaça, sugar and lemons for caipirinhas. My only regret is that I never brought enough cachaça on my jungle tours. Shop for food with your guide and inflict your tastes on him rather than vice-versa. Don't scrimp on water, be conservative and have at least two litres of bottled water per person per day. It's nice to have two styrofoam coolers on board, one to keep perishables from spoiling, the second to keep valuables dry when the weather becomes wet and woolly. Last, but not least, insist on life jackets.

Amazon by Road

Buses are a good way to cover lots of ground cheaply. On Amazon region buses the best seats are three and four, which are the front row on the door rather than the driver side. Usually, these seats are reserved for the ticket taker and his bags so if the bus company won't sell you these get seven and eight instead, the even numbers being window seats on this side. If you have a pair of binoculars and a bird identification book or two, you may well be able to convince the driver and ticket taker, once on board, that you are scientists and need to sit in those front seats. Your ability to do that will depend more on your smiling faces and happy attitudes than anything else. You can improve your view and further prove your scientist story by washing the front window at a gas stop . . . it will probably need it.

Most of the river crossings throughout the back country are simple, motor-driven ferries that take one truck at a time. As it is a slow process trucks are often lined up, especially at night when the ferry isn't operating. The ferries have been known to break down which may take hours, or in the worst cases days, to repair.

As a result of several dirt and paved roads (bringing deforestation along with them) you can arrive in a number of places where wildlife can still be seen. This often involves camping on private ranches at the forest edge where you may see several species of parrots and macaws. In the early morning and, to a lesser extent, the late afternoon, birds and occasionally other animals can be seen. Remember that in the middle of the undisturbed forest you are not likely to see anything, but where the forest is cut away a number of species that would normally take their

Macaw

sun on top of the canopy will instead choose the open edge.

If you go into a forest without trails, go only with a trusted guide or two compasses (if you know how to use them). This sounds a bit obvious, but it is surprisingly easy to get lost just a few metres into a closed forest. A cigarette lighter can also come in quite useful for making small fires and smoke signals if you get lost.

Caterpillars throughout the Amazon

Armadillo

and tropics in general should be avoided, especially the hairy ones. The hairs cause an acid burn that can be quite painful.

Possible Trips

Suggested excursions are an overnight trip to Lake Januária reserve (15 km from Manaus, this standard trip often includes the meeting of the waters) or a three-day two-night trip to Lake Mamori. The latter is especially good when the waters are high, as in recent years when boats could float past the treetops. A glimpse of life at the level of the jungle canopy is far richer than the view from the jungle floor.

A suggested longer tour is 100 km up the Rio Negro to the archipelago of Anavilhanas near Nova Airão. This trip is best from July to December. Regardless of which tour you choose, make sure to take a canoe ride on the igarapés, it's a Disneyland top-price-ticket experience. On a Lake Januária canoe trip I've seen bats on a rotting branch, twisted Tarzan vines and monkeys scattering and crashing over the treetops.

It seems odd that in the millions of square km that make up the Amazon everyone seems to be congregating upon such a small spot, but during the pre-Carnival season Lake Januária's superabundance of wildlife draws hordes of visitors. One thing that cheapens the jungle experience is the feeling of being pumped through a tourist circuit: everyone bangs on the

flying buttresses of the same sambaiaba tree, cuts the same rubber tree for latex-sap, then pulls over to an authentic jungle house where a monkey, a sloth, a snake and a jacaré (alligator) are tied up to amuse visitors.

After a quick bite at a jungle restaurant take the elevated walk to the Vitória Regia water lilies beyond the make-believe Indian craft stalls (10 stores manned by one Indian who follows alongside the group and pushes feathered novelty shop junk). At this point one disregards the water lilies and the Kodak boxes floating alongside and compares notes with his neighbour about how much their respective tour costs, how big their boat is and whether or not it has a flush toilet.

The water lilies, metre-wide floating rimmed dishes adorned with flowers above and protected by sharp spikes below, are lovely despite it all.

Things to Bring

Protect yourself from the sun with a baseball cap or visor, sunglasses, sunscreen and sunblock. Sunscreen is hard to get in Manaus. Little boats floating on big rivers in tropical rainforests can get very wet so bring along a hooded poncho or windbreaker to keep yourself dry. Use Ziplock plastic storage bags to compartmentalise tickets, travellers' cheques and other valuables (unless you prefer to entrust your valuables to a hotel safe) inside your backpack. Ditto for a hammock (fabric is preferable to net), sheet, blanket and some rope. The backpack should be

Scotchguarded, wrapped in a groundcloth or a large plastic bag and suspended above the floor of the boat to be waterproof.

Long-sleeved cotton shirts and light cotton trousers with elastic drawstrings at the ankles keep some of the bugs from nipping. Cloth or rubber thongs and sneakers are also comfortable boat/jungle gear. Bring a day pack stashed with toilet paper/tissues, toiletries, focusing backpackers flashlight, pocket knife, water bottle, a thick novel and plenty of insect repellent.

Don't forget a camera, binoculars and a good birding guide. *A Guide to the Birds of South America* by Meyer de Schanensee (Academy of Natural Science, Philadelphia) is the definitive volume, but it's a coffee table sized book. *A Guide to the Birds of Venezuela* is nearly complete for Amazon birds, and is a more manageable paperback. A detailed map of the area is difficult to find in Manaus itself, but is useful when determining an itinerary.

Finally, anti-malarials, adequate sunblock and pure drinking water should take care of most medical problems.

Tree frog

MANACAPURU
Population: 17,000

It's possible to get an idea of the poverty of life in the interior without resorting to days of river travel. Manacapuru, 85 km west-south-west of Manaus and the Rio Negro, is a river town on the Rio Solimões. The river port and its traffic, the market, the homes and the people of Manacapuru all make for an interesting day trip.

I went to Manacapuru to visit my friend, a 33-year old man who works in Manaus and on the rivers. Manacapuru's residential area is a collection of corrugated tin roof shacks. His home is a three room, eight by 24 foot building elevated by less than two feet off the ground by stilts 'It's ugly, but it's my house.' The house is tiny and spare, but tidy, the floors are rough wood planks; folded hammocks and tinted black and white prints of the matriarch, father and favourite daughter (now living in Porto Velho) adorn the walls.

My friend's extended family lives here; his wife (married since age 15), his mother, two of his six children, his brother, sister-in-law and their child (all three suffering with measles). The entire family is illiterate. There is no running water. Foot wide canals were simply dug into the earth as an open sewage system – not surprisingly the water supply was contaminated. The poor sanitation is not unrelated to the high morbidity and mortality of infectious diseases; of my friend's 14 brothers and sisters only four have survived to adulthood.

Places to Stay

There's are hotels in town in case you miss the boat or the last bus back to Cacau Pirera. The *Hotel Coqueiro* (tel 261-1505) is at Avenida Eduardo Ribeiro 725.

Getting There & Away

It's possible to take the ferry from São Raimundo to Cacau Pirera then the bus to Manacapuru (2½ hours of boat and ferry each way). Although there are daily boats to Manaus from Manacapuru, six hours down the Rio Solimões, only the Thursday and Sunday boats run at reasonable hours.

Take the São Raimundo bus from the Cathedral to the ferry terminal of São Raimundo. There are nine ferries a day in each direction from 5 am to 11 pm, passage is free. Ferry schedules coincide with buses between Cacau Pirera and Manacapuru.

Acre

RIO BRANCO
Population: 100,000

There's no real reason for visiting Rio Branco, capital of the territory of Acre. The city is 544 km from Porto Velho on BR-364. The region is two hours behind Brazilian standard time. The city is built on the Rio Acre which is navigable via the Rio Purus to the Amazon from October to June when the waters are high and the roads are closed. From July to September

the roads are open and river traffic is less. In terms of wildlife diversity, Acre is one of the richest areas in the Amazon and only just being opened up.

Rondônia

Population: 600,000

In 1943, Getúlio Vargas created the Territory of Guaporé from chunks of Amazonas and Mato Grosso. In 1981, the Territory of Guaporé became the state of Rondônia, named in honour of Marechal Cândido Mariano da Silva Rondon, the soldier who tamed the region. A legendary figure, Rondon was honoured by the Indians he helped subdue. He linked Cuiabá, Porto Velho and Rio Branco by telegraph to the rest of Brazil.

In recent years, roads and a gold rush displaced the Nordestinos from the desert

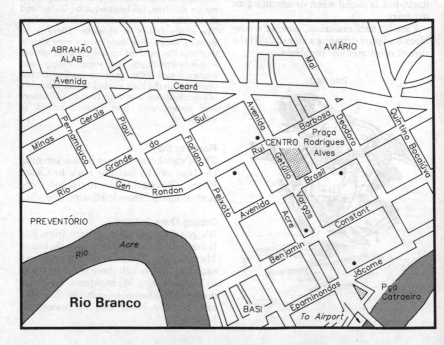

into the jungles and the few remaining Indians from the jungles into the cities. Rondônia's population are mostly poor but hopeful migrants from the Northeast.

Rondônia lies about halfway between the equator and the Tropic of Capricorn and is bounded by Rio Abunã and Amazonas to the north, Rio Juruana and Mato Grosso to the south, Acre to the west and Rio Guaporé/Mamoré and Bolivia to the south-west.

PORTO VELHO

Population: 250,000

Now capital of the young state of Rondônia, Porto Velho is rapidly losing its frontier ways. The streets are getting paved, the Indians are nearly all dead and the jungle is rapidly being felled. Nevertheless, 20th century Porto Velho still has all the elements of the American Wild West - greedy railroad barons, expansive cattle ranchers, fierce Indians, gold prospectors, deadly pistoleros and desperadoes of all stripes.

The newspaper headlines tell the whole story: articles range from the gold strike to taxi cab lynch mobs and examples of rude frontier justice, border cocaine trafficking, Indian attacks against *garimpeiros*, poaching and conflicting land claims settled at gunpoint.

History

Portuguese bandeirantes, hot in pursuit of gold and Indian slaves, crossed the line of Tordesillas and entered what is now known as Rondônia to roam the Guaporé and Madeira river valleys. Since the Spanish were incapable of defending themselves from these incursions, the occupation was officially sanctioned in lofty Latin terms of Uti Possidetis. The Portuguese secured their new possessions by building the fortress of Principe da Beira (1783) at the confluence of the Mamore and Guapore rivers.

The Treaty of Tordesillas was observed more in the breach than the practice; the Portuguese continued to push west and occupy Bolivian lands. The Brazil-Bolivia Treaty of Friendship (1867) and the Treaty of Petrópolis (1901) addressed Bolivian grievances. The Bolivians ceded the region – today the territory of Acre – in return for UK£2,000,000 and the construction of a railway in the upper Madeira to give landlocked Bolivia access to world rubber markets via the Amazon.

The Public Works Construction Company of London had started work on a railroad in 1872, but had abandoned the project after two years due to rampant disease and Indian attacks. These swampy jungle lands earned the unenviable reputation of being the most hostile in the world.

In 1907, the May, Jeckyll & Randolph Company of the US began work on a 364 km railway from the vicinity of Vila do Santo Antônio do Rio Madeira to the Bolivian border and the Rio Mamore. German, Jamaican and Cuban workers and old Panama Canal hands were brought in to do the job. The track was completed in 1912 but thousands of workers had perished – malaria, yellow fever and gunfights had killed one worker for each rail tie on the track. Since the railroad did not go as far as intended (above the rapids of Rio Beni at Riberalta) and the price of rubber had plummeted on the world market, it was effectively useless. However the towns of Guajará-Mirim and Porto Velho grew at either end of the railroad.

During WW II, when the Japanese occupation of Malaysia cut Allied rubber supplies, rubber production in the Amazon picked up briefly once again. In 1958 casseterite (tin ore) was discovered. The mining of casseterite and lumbering now constitute Rondônia's two principal sources of wealth, but other minerals – gold, iron, manganese and precious stones – are also found in the region. In fact, Porto Velho is riding out the tail end of a gold rush; in the space of three blocks of Avenida Sete de Setembro you can find over 30 gold shops, all empty save for the

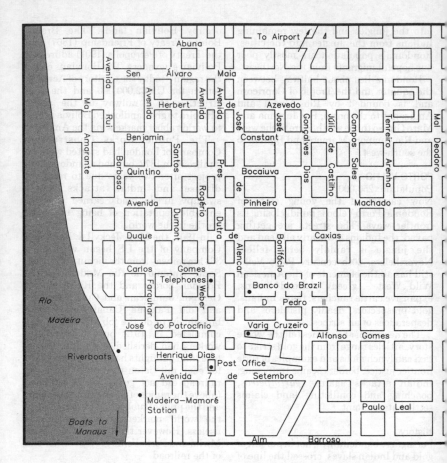

old fashioned powder scales in glass cases. The prospectors haven't seen much gold, but they're still working the old claims and dumping mercury in the river. The economy is completely extractive, and most food is 'imported' from São Paulo, half a continent away.

Information & Orientation

Porto Velho sits on the right bank of the Rio Madeira almost contiguous to the state of Amazonas. The Madeira, a 3240 km long tributary of the Amazon, is formed from the Mamoré and Beni rivers which originate in the Andes. Porto Velho's main street is Avenida Sete de Setembro, which runs from the riverfront docks and Madeira Mamore train station about 19 blocks to Avenida Presidente Kennedy two blocks over from the rodoviária.

Walk along the main drag, Avenida Sete de Setembro, past gun and munitions stores, gold shops, mining supply houses and cheap hotels. The new capital is a little raw: electric wires slump and dangle over muddy dirt roads; scrawny dogs pick

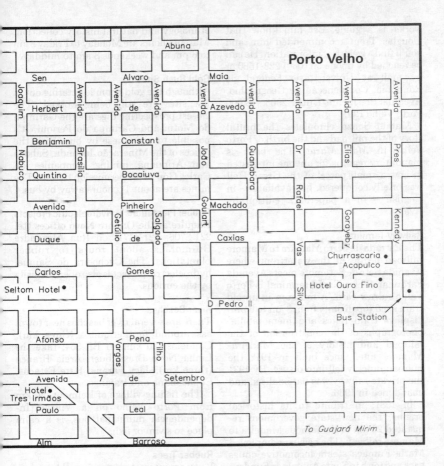

their way through garbage, roaming for scraps; street vendors fry up potatoes and plantains for passers-by. Across the way is the meat, produce and grain market where folk from the interior buy their provisions.

Compra-se ouro signs indicate the gold shops where prospectors bring their gold powder to be weighed and sold. The powder is melted into bullion and smuggled away to avoid government taxes.

Tourist Office There is a DETUR Tourist Office (Departamento de Turismo de Rondônia) at Rua Padre Chiquinho 670, Esplanada das Secretarias. They're very pleasant, but neither Porto Velho or Rondônia have much to offer tourists.

Fluvitur operates two-hour riverboat cruises which leave daily from the train station docks at 4 pm. Baretur (tel 221-6642) runs excursions to the Santo Antonio waterfalls.

Wim Goreneveld, a Dutch ecologist who speaks English fluently, sometimes works as a guide. Let him know that Douglas Trent recommended him and you'll find a wealth of information. He can be reached by phone on (060) 223-1560 or by mail at Universitario Federal de Rondônia, Courdeneçáo de Geographia, Avenida Presidente Dutra 2965, 78,000 Porto Velho RO.

Marcio Souza chronicles the brutal story of the railroad and the birth of Porto Velho in *Mad Maria*. The book is mandatory reading for anyone interested in how a small parcel of the Green Hell was briefly conquered. It is available – in English – in a paperback edition by Avalon.

Railway Terminal

The Estrada de Ferro Madeira to Mamore railroad begins at the waterfront where Avenida Sete de Setembro meets Avenida Farquhar. The railroad terminal is Porto Velho's draw card. A museum in an old train shed (open daily from 8 am to 6 pm) displays train relics and memorabilia, photographs of the construction of the railroad and history of the Madeira-Mamoré line. Once built in 1912 the railroad quickly fell into disuse. By 1931 the private railway was nationalised and abandoned in 1966.

In 1981, in tribute to its historical origins, the new state government re-instated 28 km of the famous Madeira to Mamore railway. The newly re-employed Maria Fumaça steam locomotive chugs back and forth to Santo Antônio on Sundays at 9, 10 and 11 am and 3 and 4 pm. The railroad is closed during the rainy season for maintenance and repairs. Railroad buffs will also get a kick out of the Colonel Church. Built in 1872, this dinosaur was the first locomotive in the Amazon.

Museum Marechal Rondon

Nearby at the intersection of Avenida Sete de Setembro and Euclides da Cunha is the Museum Marechal Rondon which houses a modest archaeology, mineralogy,

ethnology and natural history collection. Museum hours are Monday to Friday 8 am to 6 pm and weekends 8 am to midday.

Gold Rush Sites

Although the gold boom is petering out, a few sites are still being worked. The closest prospecting digs are the Garimpa do Motui and Garimpa do Periqui. It's possible to visit these by bus. Visit the offices of the Mineração Jacunda, Saboca and Aripuanã mining companies on Carlos Gomes for permission to tour. The mines are about 1½ hours away by bus.

Rubber Plantations & Hydroelectric Projects

Enquire at the Oriente Novo offices (tel 221-3706, 221-4471) on Rua Alexandre Guimorães about tours to rubber plantations. The Cachoeira do Samuel hydroelectric project is also open for visits by the curious.

River Beaches

There are several river beaches near town: ask around for Periquitos (three km), Candeias (20 km, off BR-364; take the Linha Novo Brasil bus), Areia Branca (three km), Jacy Paraná, Bate Estacas, Copacabana and Itajangá.

The fishing village of Belmont, 20 km from Porto Velho on a Viação Independencia municipal bus, is a calm place to swim or fish.

Rubber Trees

If you are interested in seeing rubber trees, but aren't inclined to launch an expedition into the wilderness to do so, visit the Parque Circuito on Avenida Lauro Sodre, four km from town on the way to the airport.

Festivals

The Indian legends and traditions were corrupted by Jesuit missionaries to the extent that Indians circulate stories of the Virgin Mary visiting the Amazon. However, theatrical interpretations of authentic Amerindian legends, ritual dances and ceremonies are becoming popular in Porto Velho among students. *A Jara*, *O Mapinguari* and *O Boto* are recent productions of the amateur theatre groups. Call the Teatro Municipal Secretaria do Cultura on 223-3836 extension 136 for information.

Along with the Northeastern settlers folklore was also transplanted from the sertão to the jungle. In June the saints days – São Antônio, São João and São Pedro – are celebrated.

Places to Stay

The *Hotel Ouro Fino* (tel 223-1101) at Avenida Carlos Gomes 2844 has clean, but musty US$4 doubles with fans but no bath. The *Hotel Tres Irmãos*, where Avenida Naçoes Unidas meets Avenida Sete de Setembro, has doubles for US$4/6 with fan/with air-con, but it smells bad.

The *Hotel Vila Rica* (tel 221-2286), Porto Velho's finest, is a five-star hotel at Avenida Carlos Gomes 1616. The *Rondon Palace Hotel* (tel 223-3424) at Avenida Jorge Teixeira 2109 has one less star to its credit.

Places to Eat

Porto Velho is not known for its haute cuisine, but it does have good fish. The best place for fish is *Remanso do*

Tucunaré on Avenida Brasília. *Restaurante Flutuante* (tel 221-6351) on Rio Madeira Estrada de Ferro Madeira-Mamoré on the river bank also specialises in fish. Try the caldeirada of tucunaré and tambaqui.

Churrascaria Acapulco (tel 221-5135) at Avenida Carlos Gomes 2847 serves pizza and rodizio-style barbecues; it's located diagonally across from the bus station. For meats, the locals prefer *O Costelão* on Avenida Lauro Sodré. *Lanches 65*, next door to the munitions shop at Avenida Sete de Setembro 1538, is a clean place for a light lunch. *Roda Viva* (tel 221-6866) at Rua Duque de Caxias 990 serves pizza.

Getting There & Away

Air Both Vasp (tel 221-1035) at Rua Tenreiro Arenha 2326 and Varig/Cruzeiro (tel 221-8139) at Rua José de Alencar 2160 connect Porto Velho to all major Brazilian cities.

Bus By road Porto Velho is connected to: Manaus, Rio Branco, Cuiabá, and the Bolivian border (Guajará-Mirim and Costa Marques).

The only paved roads are BR-364 which connects Porto Velho to Cuiabá 1465 km south-east and Rio Branco 544 km west, and the BR-319 to Manaus 900 km north-east. There are also two dirt roads to the Bolivian border, BR-429 from President Medici to Costa Marques and Principe da Beira and the road to Guajará-Mirim which branches off BR-364 at Abunã.

The Cidade de Borba bus to Manaus costs US$25, takes 22 hours and operates daily during the dry season. Watch your belongings. The bus station (tel 221-2141) is on Avenida Presidente Kennedy. There are daily buses to Cuiabá and also to Manaus, Humaita, Guajará-Mirim and Costa Marques (weather permitting).

Riverboats Given a choice between taking a boat from Manaus to Belém and Porto Velho to Manaus, there's no question that you will see more wildlife on the Rio Madeira. The boat fare of US$25 for the four or five day trip does include three meals a day but you need to take bottled water with you. The boats are small and the ride is long, so check out fellow passengers for unsavoury characters before committing yourself. Some boats go direct to Manaus, others require transfer halfway down the Madeira at Manicoré. The trip takes anywhere from three days to a week depending on the level of the water, the number of breakdowns and how good connections are. From Porto Velho, there is regular boat service to Nazaré, Calama and II de Novembre.

AROUND PORTO VELHO
Santo Antônio

The Madeira terminus of the Madeira to Mamoré railroad was built seven km from the deserted village of Santo Antônio. A small chapel was built there, near the waterfalls of Santo Antônio, after the railroad was completed in 1913. The railroad terminal served as a focus for the city of Porto Velho, which rapidly overtook Santo Antônio in importance.

The fishing village of Teotônio (Km 23 off BR-364, 50 km from Porto Velho), situated by the biggest drop in the upper Madeira, is the site of the annual fishing championship held in August and September.

AROUND RONDÔNIA
Fort Principe da Beira

Fort Principe da Beira was built from 1776 to 1783 on the right bank of the Guapore where the Guapore and Pacás Novos rivers merge to become the Mamoré. The fortress has 10 metre high walls and four towers, each holding 14 cannon which took five years to bring up from Pará. The fortress walls, nearly a km in perimeter and surrounded by a moat, enclose a chapel, armoury, buildings for officers and prison cells where convicts scrawled poetic graffiti. Underground passageways lead from the fortress directly to the river Guapore.

Getting There & Away It's a 10 hour ride to the fort: 278 km on BR-364 to Presidente Medici then 363 km of unpaved BR-429 to Costa Marques and finally another 20 km to Principe da Beira. It's a pretty wild stretch of road and because it has just been cleared, there is a very real risk of disease.

One alternative is a 170 km, three-day boat trip up from Guajará-Mirim. It may still be possible to catch a paddle-boat up the Rio Guapore from Guajará-Mirim to Vila Bela da Santissima Trinidad, Mato Grosso.

Vilhena

Vilhena, at the border between Rondônia and Mato Grosso, is a good access point for the Brazilian frontier. From Vilhena, take another bus east to Juina or further on to Fontanilhas. These are towns straight from the Wild West, complete with Indian wars, gold miners, rustlers and homesteaders. The real treat in the area is north from Juina direct to Aripuana, on a dirt road. There is an alternate route via Juruena, but it is not nearly as spectacular as the direct route, which passes through the mountains.

Just outside of Aripuana are the spectacular Dannelles Falls. A local guide may be able to take you on some longer hikes through the area, which is rapidly being deforested. Note that trees marked with painted bands indicate disputed Indian territory, and you are best off to stay out of these areas. The area around Ji-Parana is particularly rich in animals, but a local guide is essential.

Other Places

Other ideas for excursions closer to Porto Velho include the Lago dos Patos Indian site, the waterfall of Rio Abunã and 3S Indian rock inscriptions, the Salto do Jurau waterfall of the Rio Madeira (Km 132 BR-364) and the birds of Lake

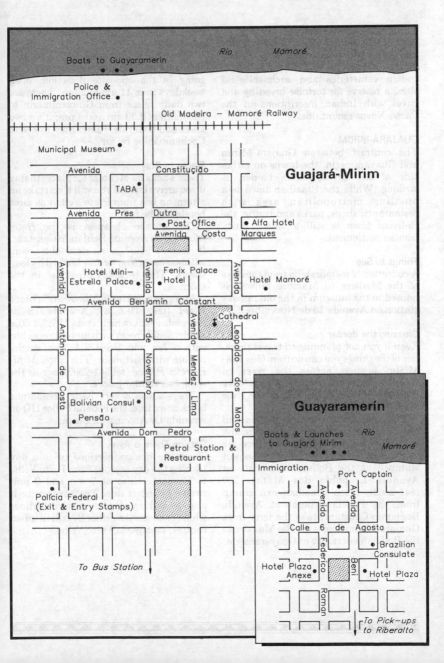

Cuniã Biological Reserve (110 km by water). The tourist office in Porto Velho can help you with details to Pedras Negras, Conçeição and Ilha das Flores Indian cemeteries and archaeological sites, a reserve for tortoise breeding and caves with Indian inscriptions in the Pacão-Novos mountains.

GUAJARÁ-MIRIM

The contrast between Guajará-Mirim and Guayaramerín, the towns on either side of the Brazil/Bolivia border, is striking. While the Brazilian town is a bustling metropolitan area with restaurants, shops, parks and traffic, the Bolivian town is still a small, dusty frontier settlement.

Things to See

A collection of memorabilia from the days of the Madeira to Mamoré railway is housed in the museum in the old railway station on Avenida 15 de Novembre.

Crossing the Border

Even if you not planning to travel there, one of the things you can do from Guajará-Mirim is pop across the river to Guayaramerin, Bolivia. Motorboats leave from the port on either side of the river every few minutes.

If you intend to travel in Bolivia and need a visa have two photographs ready. Regardless of your visa status there are four things you must do: get your passport stamped at the Bolivian consulate at Avenida Leopoldo dos Matos, 239 (541-2862); get a Brazilian exit stamp from the Polícia Federal at Avenida Benjamin Constant; take the ferry from Guajará-Mirim across the Rio Mamoré to the Bolivian sister city of Guayaramerín;

get a Bolivian entrance stamp on your passport.

There is a corresponding Brazilian consulate in Guayaramerín for travellers going in the opposite direction; open weekdays from 11 am to 2 pm. There are two daily buses from Guayaramerín to Riberalta at 9.30 am and 4 pm; it's a two and a half hour ride. Riberalta is linked to Cochambamba by air.

Places to Stay

There's not a lot of choice for places to stay if you arrive late (as you will if you take an afternoon bus from Pôrto Velho) as most hotels will be full.

One of the cheapest is the *Hotel Mamoré* on Avenida Benjamin Constant. It costs US$6/7 a single/double room without bathroom or fan but with clean sheets. This includes breakfast in the morning.

More expensive is the *Fenix Palace Hotel* (tel 541-2326), Avenida 15 de Novembre 459, which costs US$3/4.50 a single/double room without bathroom but with a fan and US$4.50/6.50 a single/double with bathroom. The *Hotel Mini-Estrella Palace* (tel 541-2399), across the road, has similar prices.

There's also a very basic pensão one block down from the Federal Police HQ on Avenida Dr Antonia da Costa.

Getting There & Away

There are bus connections twice a day (during the dry season) from Porto Velho to Guajará-Mirim at 7 am and 9 pm; twelve hour bus ride. The border city is also served by Varig/Cruzeiro airlines which connects it to other Brazilian urban centres, mostly via Pôrto Velho.

THE CENTRAL-WEST

REGIÃO CENTRO-OESTE

Central-West

The Central-West – 1,880,000 square km – is 22% of the national territory but with 10 million inhabitants only 6% of the national population. The region includes the states of Goiás, Mato Grosso, Mato Grosso do Sul and the Federal District of Brasília. This massive terrain, the Mato Grosso, was until the 1940s the last great unexplored area on earth.

Distrito Federal

BRASÍLIA

As an architect, my concern in Brasília was to find a structural solution that would characterise the city's architecture. So I did my best in the structures, trying to make them different, with the columns so very narrow so that the palaces would seem to barely touch the ground.

And I set them apart from the facades creating an empty space through which as I bend over my working table, I could see myself walking, imagining their forms and the different resulting points of view they would provoke.

Brasília architect Oscar Niemeyer

Brasília must have looked good on paper and still looks good in photos, but in the flesh forget it. The world's great planned city of the 20th century is built for automobiles and air conditioners, not people. Distances are enormous and no one walks. The sun blazes, but there are no trees for shelter.

It's a lousy place to visit and no one wanted to live there. Bureaucrats and politicians, who live in the model 'pilot plan' part of the city, were lured to Brasília by 100% salary hikes and big apartments. Still, as soon as the weekend comes they get out of the city as fast as possible to Rio, to São Paulo, to their private clubs in the country – anywhere that's less sterile, less organised, less vapid (Brasília is also one of the most expensive cities in Brazil).

The poor have to get out, they have no choice. Mostly from the Northeast, these *candangos* (pioneers) work in the construction and service industries. They live in favelas, which they call 'anti-Brasílias', as far as 30 km from the centre. This physical gulf between haves and have-nots is reminiscent of South Africa's township system.

Seen from above, which is close enough, Brasília looks like an aeroplane (symbolising the fastest way out of town) or a bow and arrow (signifying the penetration of the interior and the destruction of the indigenous people). The planned city, the *plano piloto* has a population of 400,000 out of a total of 1.2 million and faces the giant artificial Lago do Paranoá. In the plane's fuselage (or the arrow) are all the government buildings and monuments. The plaza of three powers – the President's Palacio do Planalto, the Palácio do Congresso and the Paráciio da Justica – is in the cockpit. Out on the wings are block after block of apartment buildings and little else.

All this is the doing of Brazil's famous urban planner (Lucio Costa), architect (Oscar Niemeyer) and landscape architect (Burle Marx), all three the leading figures in their field. They were commissioned by President Juscelino Kubitschek to plan a new inland capital, a capital that would catalyse the economic development of Brazil's vast interior. With millions of dirt-poor peasants from the Northeast working around the clock Brasília was built in an incredible three years – it wasn't exactly finished but it was ready to be the capital. On 21 April 1960, the capital was moved from Rio to Brasília and thousands of public servants fell into a deep depression.

An inland capital was an old Brazilian

dream that had always been dismissed as expensive folly. What possessed Kubitschek to actually do it? Politics. Kubitschek made the building of Brasília a symbol of the country's determination and ability to become a great economic power. He successfully appealed to all Brazilians to put aside their differences and rally to the cause. In doing so he distracted attention from the country's social and economic problems, gained enormous personal popularity and borrowed heavily from the international banks. His legacy to the country was rampant inflation.

Information

There are tourist desks at the airport and rodoviária. They are not very helpful and frequently closed. If you really need help try a tourist agency, also the best bet for changing money (you're better off changing before coming here). The Hotel Garvey-Park is the travel agency capital of Brasília and most companies have sightseeing tours of the city.

Airlines Phone numbers for the airlines are: Transbrasil 223-4568, Tam 223-5168, Varig-Cruzeiro 242-4111 and Vasp 226-4115.

Things to See

You can rent a car, take a tourist tour or combine a city bus with some long walks to see the bulk of Brasília's edifices. Remember many buildings are closed on weekends and at night. Start at the Memorial JK, open from 8 am to 6 pm. Along with JK's tomb (President Kubitschek) there are several exhibits to see.

Head to the TV tower's 75-metre observation deck. It's open from 9 am to 8 pm and admission is free. The city Cathedral is worth seeing too.

Down by the tip of the arrow you'll find the most interesting government buildings: the Palácio dos Arcos (Itamaraty) is one of the best; the Palácio de Justiça, the supreme court (open Monday to Friday midday to 6 pm); and the Palácio do Congresso (open Monday to Friday from 2 to 5 pm, Saturday and Sunday from 9 am to midday and from 2 to 5.30 pm). The presidential palace is not open to visitors. If you're in town on a weekend the park is fun.

To get a bus tour book at the airport, rodoviária or the Hotel Nacional. Circular buses leave from the city rodoviária.

The Parque Nacional de Brasília is an ecological reserve, everything is in it's natural state, and it's a good place to relax if you're stuck in the city. It's at the end of ASA on the north road. Another good park is the Parque Rogerio Piton Farias where you'll find a swimming pool and small lunch places to grab a snack.

Places to Stay – bottom end

Somehow they forgot to include cheap hotels in the plan although many hotels give discounts on the weekends. Ask at the tourist desk about cheap pensions One central place to ask about is the *Augusta Fraternidade Universalinha Solar*.

For something cheap you have to take the yellow 'Pioneira' buses from the rodoviária out towards Taguatinga. After a 20 to 30-minute ride get off at the Honda car dealership by the name of 'OK Motovéis'. This section is called the SIA and a few hundred metres from the road there are several hotels. The *Hotel Olympus* (tel 234-1211) is cheap for Brasília (US$6 a double) and pretty clean. The *Hotel Aquarius* (tel 233-7122) is more and the *Hotel Rex* is a bit less.

There is a *Youth Hostel* at A W Quadra 704, Bloco M, Casa 35 (tel 259 229), but it's often full.

Places to Stay – middle

Also in SIA the nearby *SIA Park Hotel* (tel 233-3131) is a three-star hotel with doubles starting at US$18. Most of the better hotels are in the city in the 'sector of hotels'. Not only is this much more convenient, but many of these hotels have discounts, particularly on weekends, so you may want to get one of these better hotels for a night.

In the Setor Hoteleiro Sul, Quadra 3

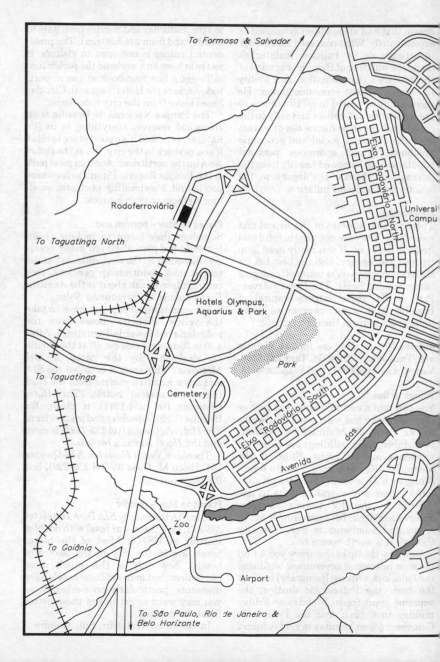

To Formosa & Salvador

Eixo Rodoviário Norte

Universi[...] Campu[...]

Rodoferroviária

To Taguatinga North

Hotels Olympus,
Aquarius & Park

Park

To Taguatinga

Cemetery

Eixo Rodoviário South

Rodoviária das

To Goiânia

Avenida

Zoo

Airport

To São Paulo, Rio de Janeiro &
Belo Horizonte

there are several decent places such as the *Itamarati Palace* (tel 225-6050) with singles/doubles for US$16.50/18, the *Brasília Imperial* (tel 225-7050), the *Riviera* (tel 225-1880) and the *Planalto* (tel 225-6050). All are comfortable and have similar prices. In the same area, the *Continental* (tel 225-7071) is a notch up with doubles starting at US$33.

Places to Stay – top end

The *Hotel Nacional* (tel 226-8180) and *Hotel Carlton* (tel 224-8819) are the city's contribution to five-star lodging. The former has an adjoining shopping mall and the latter is often the home for delegations from the USA. Both have doubles starting at US$65.

Places to Eat

The *Beirute* (tel 243-0397) is worth trying for its Middle Eastern food or go to *Tokyo* (tel 248-3020) for Japanese food. The *Bon de Mais* has plenty of salads, other natural foods and live music, it's at W3 – QA/706.

For nordestino cuisine the *Xique-Xique* (tel 243-0651) has carne de sol and feijoã verde with manteiga da terra. It's at ASA SUL – SLS, 107 Bloco-A/1. *Hoffman com Confalonieri e Também da Silva* (tel 224-9051) is more expensive but quite good. The name combines German, Italian and Portuguese versions of the name 'da Silva' which is the most common name of the Nordeste. The food is Pernambucan, more or less. It's at CLN 102 bloco A/42.

Tiragostas is one of the city's oldest bar/restaurants. A famous meeting point for artists and musicians with outdoor tables under trees. The prices are reasonable and it's at CLS – 109 Bloco-A 2/4.

Getting There & Away

Air With so many domestic flights making a stopover in Brasília it's easy to catch a plane out of the city at almost any time. Almost all Brazilian cities are served and there are Varig flights to Miami. Flying

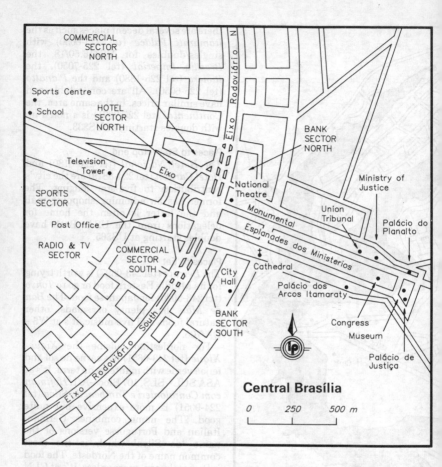

Central Brasília

0   250   500 m

time to Rio and São Paulo is two hours plus.

Bus The giant Rodoferroviária (tel 233-7200) is due west of downtown. There are buses to places you've never heard of. It's four hours to Goiânia, 21 hours to Cuiabá (buses from there to Porto Velho and Manaus), 3 hours to Anapolis, 35 hours to Belém, 12 hours to Belo Horizonte, 19 hours to Rio, 17 hours to São Paulo and 25 hours to Salvador.

Getting Around

Airport Transport The international airport (tel 248-5588) is 12 km south of the centre. There are two buses marked 'Aeroporto' that go from the downtown rodoviária to the airport every 15 minutes. The fare is 35c and it takes 35 minutes.

Local Transport From the downtown rodoviária to the Rodoferroviária (for long distance buses) take the '131' (you can also flag it down along the main drag).

Car Rental There are car rental agencies at the airport and the Hotel Nacional and Hotel Garvey-Park.

AROUND BRASÍLIA
Estancia de Agua de Itiquiara
Itiquiara is the Tupi-Guarani Indian word for water that falls. This 158 metre free-fall waterfall is Brazil's highest. The viewpoint is 450 metres high, from where you can see the valley of the Paranãs to the south. There's forest and several crystal-clear streams with natural pools for a swim, as well as the requisite restaurants and bars.

Itiquiara is 130 km from Brasília; you need a car. Leave through the satellite cities of Sobradinho and Planaltina and the town of Formosa. The road is dirt for the next 35 km. For information in Brasília phone 226-3451.

Cachoeira Saia Velha
This is a pleasant swimming hangout, not too far from the city. Take the road to Belo Horizonte about 20 km. When you reach the Monumento do Candango, a ridiculous statue made by a Frenchman for the people who built Brasília, there's a sign for the waterfall. The road is to the left of the monument.

For US$2 per car they have live music on Saturdays, food and beer and several natural swimming pools, but there is no hotel or camping.

Cachoeira Topázio
This is a pretty fazenda with waterfall, camping facilities, food and drink. To get there, take the road to Belo Horizonte to the Km 93 marker. Turn to the right, taking the other road out to the cachoeira. Entry cost is US$2 a car.

Goiás

GOIÂNIA
Population: 700,000

The capital of the state of Goiás, Goiânia is 200 km south-west of Brasília and 900 km from both Cuiabá and São Paulo. Planned by urbanist Armando de Godói and founded in 1933, it's a fairly pleasant place with lots of open spaces laid out around circular streets in the centre. There are three main zones – housing is in the south, administration in the centre and industry and commerce in the north. The core of Goiânia's economy is based on the commercialisation of the region's cattle.

There's not much for the visitor to see or do in Goiânia although the birds of the Museu Ornitológico are interesting. If you

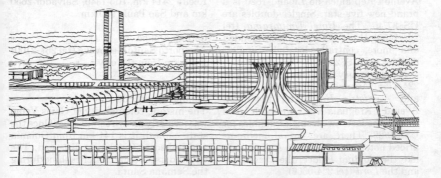

have some time to kill try the Parque Zoologico de Goiânia or the Museu Antropológico at the Federal University. You can also go water skiing at the Jaó Blub on a reservoir.

Excursions from Goiânia include the Caldas Novas hot springs, Lake Pirapitinga, Pousada do Rio Quente and the rock formations of Parauna. All are within a 150 km radius of Goiânia.

Information & Orientation

Turisplan Turismo (tel 224-1941) at Rua 8388 is a central travel agency that sells plane and bus tickets. For major airlines call Transbrasil (tel 223-5844), Varig-Cruzeiro (tel 224-5043) or Vasp (tel 223-4266). If you're interested in an air taxi call Taxi Aereo Goiás (tel 224-1954), Sete Taxi Aereo (tel 224-3559) or União (tel 261-2333).

Places to Stay

There are cheap places across from the rodoviária that have seen too many bad guys in their day but are convenient and usable. For something a bit better near the bus station try the *Itaipu* (tel 223-5655); singles/doubles are US$5/8. In the centre the *Marmo* (tel 225-4575) at Avenida Anhanguera 2680 has doubles for US$3. Also, try the *Principe* (tel 224-0085) nearby at Avenida Anhanguera 2936.

The *Castro Park* (tel 223-7766) at Avenida República do Libano 1520 is a brand new five-star. Singles/doubles are US$37/45. The *Hotel Umuarama* (tel 224-1555), Rua 4 492 is also recommended and more centrally located. Singles/doubles are US$22/28.

For less money the *Cabiuna Palace* (tel 224-4355), Avenida Paranaiba 698, Centro, and *Augustus Hotel* (tel 224-1022), Avenida Araguaia 702, are both good deals – the latter with singles/doubles for US$20/22. There are several medium-priced hotels along Avenida Anhanguera like the *Goiânia Palace*, the *Presidente* and the *Lord* (tel 224-0666).

Places to Eat

Surrounded by cattle, the locals eat lots of meat. The *Churrascaria e Chouparia do Gaúcho* is where the cowboys eat and drink so it's cheap. It's open daily 11 am to midnight and you'll find it at Praça Tamandaré sector oeste.

For good local fish try the *Restaurante Dourado* at Avenida Presidente Vargas 600. Its open from 11 am to 3 pm and 6 pm to midnight. The *Restaurante Baalbeck* at Avenida Presidente Vargas 600 serves Arab food at reasonable prices.

Things to Buy

For superb photographs of Pantanal wildlife contact Décio (tel (062) 224-8000) at Praça Cívico 64 in Goiânia, Goiás.

Getting There & Away

Air In addition to the regular domestic carriers there are several air taxi companies which go any and everywhere in the Mato Grosso and Amazon, but they are expensive.

Bus The rodoviária (tel 224-0350) is at Avenida Anhanguera 4602. The bus to Brasília takes four hours and to Goiás Velho three hours, to Cuiabá 14 hours and Campo Grande 17 hours. Distances from Goiânia to major cities are immense: Belém 2000 km, Belo Horizonte 900 km, Fortaleza 2620 km, Manaus 3289 km, Recife 2414 km, Rio 1340, Salvador 2650 km and São Paulo 920 km.

Getting Around

Aeroporto Santo Genoveva (tel 261-2100) is six km from the city.

GOIÁS VELHO

Population: 20,000

The historic colonial city of Goiás Velho was formerly known as Vila Boa. Once the state capital, it is 144 km from Goiânia and linked to Cuiabá by dirt road. The city and its baroque churches shine during the Semana Santa.

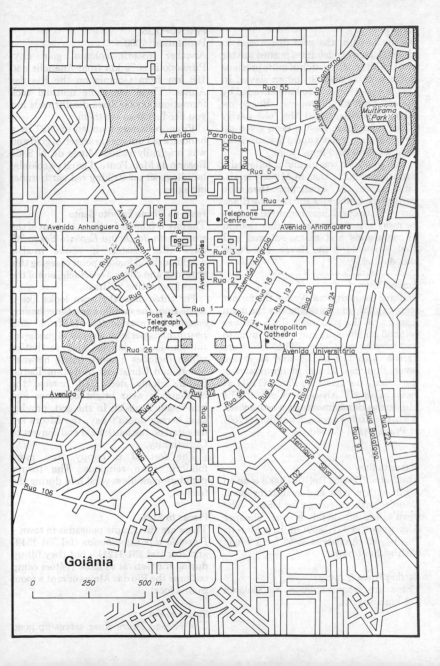

Goiânia

0   250   500 m

History

On the heels of the gold discoveries in Minas Gerais, bandeirantes pushed further into the interior in search of more precious stones and, as always, Indian slaves. In 1722, a bandeira left São Paulo headed by the old Paulista Bartolomeu Bueno da Silva, who was called the 'old devil'. Three years later, having been given up for dead, the old devil and a few survivors returned with gold from Goiás.

The gold rush was on and it followed a pattern similar to that in Minas Gerais. First came the Paulistas, then the Portuguese Emboadas and soon the Black slaves. With everything imported from so far away prices were even higher than in Minas Gerais and many suffered and died, particularly the slaves. The boom ended quickly.

Around Town

Walking through Goiás Velho, the former state capital, you quickly notice the main legacies of the gold rush: 18th century colonial architecture and a large mulatto and mestizo population. The streets are narrow with low houses and there are seven churches. The most impressive is the oldest, the Igreja de Paula (1761) at Praça Zaqueu Alves de Castro. The Museu das Bandeiras is also worth a visit. It's in the old town council building (1766) at Praça Brasil Caiado.

Places to Stay

The *Hotel Vila Boa* (tel 371-1000) is up on a hill with a view and swimming pool. Doubles with air-con go for US$18. The town's second hotel is the cheaper *Alegrama* (tel 371-1360) on Rua Moretti Foggia, which charges $3/$5 for a single with/without bath.

Getting There & Away

There are frequent buses to Goiânia 144 km away.

PIRENÓPOLIS

Population: 7000

Another historic colonial gold city, Pirenópolis is 70 km from Anapolis and 128 km from Goiânia on the Rio das Almas. There are some unusual rock formations in the Serra dos Pirineus but you need a car to see them.

Pirenópolis was founded in 1727 by a bandeira of Paulistas in search of gold and was originally called Minas da N S do Rosário da Meia Ponte. The city's colonial buildings sit on striking red earth under big skies.

Festa do Divino Espírito Santo

The city is famous for the acting out of the story *Festa do Divino Espírito Santo*, 45 days after Easter. If you're in the neighbourhood make a point of seeing this stunning and curious spectacle, one of the most fascinating in Brasil.

For three days the town looks like a scene from the middle ages. *Cavalhadas, congadas, mascardos, tapirios* and *pastorinhos* perform a series of medieval tournaments, dances and festivities which includes a mock battle between Moors and Christians in distant Iberia. Riding richly decorated horses, the combatants wear bright costumes and bull-headed masks. In the end, proving that heresy doesn't pay, the Moors are defeated on the battlefield and convert to Christianity.

The festival is happy, and more folkloric than religious. The town's population swells several fold during the festival.

Places to Stay

There are two simple pousadas in town – *Pousada das Cavalhadas* (tel 331-1313) and *Rex* (tel 331-1121) – but they fill-up during the festival so most visitors camp out near the Rio das Almas or rent a room from a local.

Places to Eat

The *Pensão Padre Rosa* serves-up good

Top: Crocodile (jacaré), Manaus, Amazonas (KB)
Bottom: Crocodile (jacaré), Pantanal (KB)

Top: Jabiru stork, Pantanal (SP)
Left: Cattle, Pantanal (SP)
Right: Stilt house, Pantanal (KB)

regional cuisine. Save room for dessert as they have an assortment of 18 different desserts, each one sweeter than the next.

Getting There & Away

There are bus services from Anápolis and from Goiânia as well as Brasília.

CALDAS NOVAS

Caldas Novas, 190 km from Goiânia and 400 km from Brasília, has more than 30 hot springs with average temperatures of 42° C (107°F). Now a very popular resort, the region has dozens of hotels at all levels of price and luxury. Studies have shown that the healing waters work particularly well with people suffering from high-blood pressure, poor digestion, and weak endocrine glands. For resort information in Rio call 252-6156 or 511-1443.

EMAS NATIONAL PARK

Emas is a relatively small 1300 square km park in the corner of the state of Goiás where it meets the states of Mato Grosso and Mato Grosso do Sul. The park lies along the Brazilian great divide between the Amazon and Paraná river basins, at the head waters of the Araguaia, the Formoso and the Taquari rivers.

The three rivers take divergent paths to the Atlantic. The Araguaia courses north to the equator via the Tocantins and the mighty Amazon. The Rio Taquari travels westward to flood the Pantanal, its water then flows south via the Paraguai. The Rio Formoso changes name midstream to Corrientes and flows into the Parnaiba then the Paraná. The Paraguai and the Paraná flow on either side of Paraguay, meet at Argentina and enter the Atlantic a few hundred km east of Buenos Aires and some 35° of latitude south of the mouth of the Amazon.

Surrounded by rapidly encroaching farmlands, Emas park is on a high plateau covered by grassy plains and open woodlands. There is little foliage to obstruct the sighting of wildlife which includes anteaters, deer, capybara, foxes, tapir, peccaries, armadillos, and blue and yellow macaws. It is the home of endangered wolves, the exclusive sanctuary of the jacamari and other rare species.

The dry season is from July to October but be careful, the area is then dry enough for spontaneous brush fires.

Getting There & Away

Access to the park is tough. Even though it's surrounded by farmland there are no paved roads or regular bus routes. Visitors must arrange with private companies for 4WD or air taxis from as far away as Cuiabá, Goiânia and Campo Grande.

The adventurous types may consider taking BR-364 to Alto do Araguaia/Santa Rita do Araguaia (531 km from Goiânia, 423 km from Cuiabá) then hitching 63 km to Plaça dos Mineiros on a road that's being paved, and then 40 to 60 km further on dirt roads to the park. Be prepared to camp and rough it, although it may be possible to stay at the National Park Headquarters.

Tocantins

On 1 January 1989 a constitutional ammendment creating the new state of Tocantins came in to effect. The new state, which was previously the northern half of the state of Goiás, was supposedly created in order to give the Indians of the region greater autonomy.

At this early stage in the life of the state, very little information is available. There are no official maps printed yet and the site of the state capital has not yet been decided, although there has been ferocious politicking between three or four of the major rival towns. Rumour has it that the previously unheard of town, Miracema do Norte, will be chosen because of its geographical location, rather than its present political status. As of 11 December

·1988, it has held the status of provisional capital.

There is also no governor yet, although a leather armchair has been bought for whomever wins the position. Siqueira Campos, the man who proposed the creation of the state, is strong favourite for the post.

José Freire, one of Campos' toughest rivals, has tried to prove that Campos is in fact a murderer who changed his name in the '60s. He offered a large reward to anyone who could prove this theory by producing the relevant birth certificate and other pertinent papers. Unfortunately he was unable to say what Campos' name had previously been.

RIO ARAGUAIA

The Rio Araguaia begins in the Serra dos Caiapós and flows 2600 km northwards, forming the borders of Mato Grosso, Goiás, and Pará before joining the Rio Tocantins where the states of Goiás, Maranhão and Pará come to a point near Marabá and the fabulous gold mines of Serra Pelada. About 500 km from its source the Araguaia bifurcates into the greater and lesser Araguaia rivers which course west and east respectively then rejoin having formed the largest river island in the world, Ilha Bananal.

The river is not easily accessible so tours are a good idea. The best access from Mato Grosso is via Barra do Garças, about 500 km from Cuiabá. Barra do Garças has the Parque de Águas Quentes (hot springs) and camping facilities are open from May to October. It's a rapidly growing agricultural boom-town of 30,000 people. There are four simple hotels in town.

From the town of Aruaná up to the Ilha do Bananal, the Rio Araguaia is considered one of the best freshwater fishing areas in the world. The region is beginning to attract Brazilian vacationers during the dry season – June to September – when the receding waters uncover white beaches along the riverbank. Many

Brazilians camp on the banks of the river. During the May through October fishing season pintado, pirarucu, pacu, tucunaré, suribim and matrinchã are there for the taking.

If you're serious about fishing and have the money there are tours, arranged in Brasília and Goiânia, where you meet a boat-hotel in Aruanã and sail around the island. If you want to explore the river without a tour catch a boat in Aruanã or Barra do Garças but if you want to get as far north as Ilha do Bananal and don't have a lot of money, it's best to take a bus up to São Felix do Araguaia and hire a boat from there.

ILHA DO BANANAL

The Ilha do Bananal, formed by the splitting of the Rio Araguaia, is the world's largest river island and covers 20,000 square km. Much of the island is covered with forest and a big chunk is an Indian reserve, the Parque Nacional do Araguaia, inhabited by Carajás and Javaés Indians. There is plenty of wildlife but only birds are visible in abundance.

At sunset or sunrise you can reel in all sorts of fish, including dogfish with teeth so large that the Indians use them to shave with. There are also tucunarés with colourful moustaches, ferocious tabarana, pirarucu (a two metre long, 100 kg monster) and several other slimy critters. The river also feeds boto (freshwater dolphin), jacaré, soia (a rare one-eyed fish) and poraquê (an electric fish).

Places to Stay

São Felix do Araguaia São Felix is a town of around 3000 on the Rio das Mortes. It has a few simple hotels. On the river's edge you'll find one called the Hotel Araguaia, which is very simple. You may be tempted to take one of the rooms with air-con, but don't. The electricity turns off at 11 pm, and those closed in rooms turn into ovens. Get a room that has a ceiling open to the hallway.

In town, you can arrange boat rides

from fisherfolk and locals who hang out on the water's edge. A pizzeria and fish restaurant overhanging the water is recommended. In July, the town may well be flooded with tourists from the area looking to 'catch some rays'.

Santa Teresinha Another option to the Ilha is the small town of Santa Teresinha. A small hotel on the water's edge has been attending foreign naturalists who use this as a step-off to the Parque Nacional do Araguaia. Costs in this region, as in all of the Amazon, are higher than what one would expect to pay in Rio or Salvador – so be prepared.

One can visit the park with permission obtained from IBDF (the national parks service) in Brasília, or alternatively from the park director who lives in Goiâna. Of course, if you just show up you may save a lot of time and hassle and get in just the same. The ranger responsible is Sr Bonhilo, who knows the park quite well. There is simple accommodation available on the island but no food other than what you bring. Here, and at any other grossly underfunded national park in Brazil a donation well above the nominal fee should be paid. This should be paid to the ranger on duty. Sr Bonhilo can provide 4WDs and boats.

Getting There & Away

The long and dry road to Ilha do Bananal begins in Barra do Garças, 400 km west of Goiâna. If you don't want to bus Votec flies a small Bandeirante plane (one hour).

Buses leave early in Mato Grosso, not to beat the heat, no one is so presumptuous, but to suffer a bit less. The bus for São Felix do Araguaia leaves daily at 5 am.

It's probably easier to get to the Araguaia from the state of Goiás (Goiânia in particular) than from Mato Grosso. For those without a 4WD at their disposal, the town of Aruanuã, accessible by bus from both Goiânia (310 km) and Goiás, is the gateway to the Araguaia. There is a

campground (open in July). Hire a *voadeiras*, a small aluminium motorboat with guide, to take you to see the river and island.

Mato Grosso

There's a rather well-known story about a naturalist in the Mato Grosso. Disoriented by the sameness of the forest, the naturalist asked his Indian guide – who had killed a bird, put it in a tree and, incredibly, knew where to return for it at the end of the day – how he knew where the tree was. 'It was in the same place,' the Indian replied.

To begin to appreciate the Mato Grosso's inaccessibility and enormity, read the classic *Brazilian Adventure* by Peter Fleming. It also happens to be one of the funniest travel books ever. Fleming tells the story of his quest to find the famous British explorer Colonel Fawcette who disappeared in the Mato Grosso in 1925 while searching for the hidden city of gold. For a more scientific report on the region see *Mato Grosso: Last Virgin Land* by Anthony Smith.

Mato Grosso means bundu, bush, savannah, outback; an undeveloped thick scrub. Part of the highland plane that runs through Brazil's interior, the Mato Grosso is a dusty land of rolling hills and some of the best fishing rivers in the world, such as the Araguaia.

This is also the land where many of Brazil's remaining Indians live. They are being threatened by rapid agricultural development which is bringing in poor peasants from the south and Northeast who are desperate for land, and by a government which is less than fully committed to guaranteeing them their rights. In 1967, an entire government agency, the Indian Protective Service, was dissolved. No less than 134 of its 700 employees were charged with crimes and 200 were fired. In two years the director had committed 42 separate crimes against Indians including collusion in murder, torture and illegal sale of land.

There's a saying in Brazil that 'progress is roads'. Key roads such as the Belém to Brasília and the Cuiabá to Santarém have catalysed the opening of vast stretches of the Mato Grosso to cattle, rice, cotton, soybean, corn and manioc, as well as mining. Goiás, where wealthy ranchers fly from one end of their huge tracts of land to the other in private planes, is one of the fastest growing agricultural belts in the country.

This is Brazil's frontier, the wild west where an often desperate struggle for land between peasants, Indians, miners, rich landowners and their hired guns leads to frequent killings and illegal land expropriation.

CUIABÁ

Population: 200,000

Founded by gold and slave seeking bandeirantes in 1719, Cuiabá has little historic or cultural heritage to interest travellers. The city is a base for excursions into the Pantanal and Chapada dos Guimarães as well as a rest stop to the Amazon and expeditions to Emas National Park and the Rio Araguaia.

The city is actually two sister-cities separated by the Rio Cuiabá: old Cuiabá and Várzea Grande (where the airport is located by the Rio Cuiabá). I found the people here incredibly friendly and gracious.

History

Imagine how hard it was to get here in the 18th century. A Paulista, Pascoal Moreira Cabral, was hunting Indians along the Rio Cuiabá when he found gold in 1719. A gold rush followed but many gold-seekers never reached Cuiabá. Travelling by river over 3000 km from São Paulo took five months; along the way there was little food, many mosquitoes, rapids, portages, disease and incredible heat.

There was usually one flotilla of canoes each year, bringing supplies, slaves and

miners and returning with gold. There were several hundred people in a flotilla, including many soldiers to protect against Indian attacks, but still they often failed. To reach Cuiabá the Portuguese had to cross the lands of several groups of Indians, many of whom were formidable warriors. They included the Caiapó, who even attacked the settlement at Goiás, the Bororo of the Pantanal, the Parecis who were enslaved to mine the gold, the Paiaguá, who defeated several large Portuguese flotillas and caused periodic panic in Cuiabá itself, and the Guaicuru, skilled horsemen and warriors with many years experience in fighting the Europeans.

As a result of being nomadic people in a region without abundant food, the Guaicuru women performed self-abortions, refusing to have children until they were near menopause. On the longer journeys, when the women stayed behind, the Guaicuru men took male transvestites with them as sexual partners. Both women and men could divorce easily and often did, several times a year.

Despite important victories, many Indians had already been killed or enslaved by the time the gold-boom began to fade in the mid-1700s. With the decay of the mines Cuiabá would have disappeared except that the gold never completely finished (garimpeiros still seek their fortunes today) and the soil along the Rio Cuiabá allowed subsistence agriculture while the river itself provided fish.

As in many mining towns, there was tension between Paulistas and recent Portuguese immigrants. In 1834, the small town was torn-apart by the *Rusga* (brawl) when a nativist movement of Paulistas, inspired by wild rumours following Brazilian independence, slaughtered many Portuguese under the pretext that the Portuguese wanted to return Brazil to the rule of Portugal.

Today Cuiabá is a frontier boom town. New roads have opened the lands of the Mato Grosso and southern Amazon,

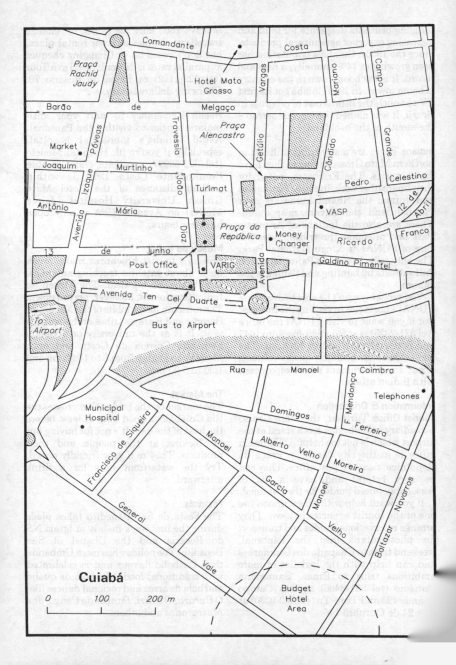

Cuiabá

0   100   200 m

bringing peasants desperate for land and increasing export of agricultural products. Since the 1950s, Cuiabá's population has been growing at 14% annually, a national record. It is *the* boom town in the country of boom towns. In 1969 Cuiabá got its first TV channel, the litmus test of progress in Brazil. It was named the *boca de sertão* – the mouth of the backlands.

Indians There are many tribes still left in northern Mato Grosso, living as they have for centuries. The Erikbatsa, noted for their fine feather work, live near Fontanilles and Juima; the Nhambikuraa are near Padroal; and the Cayabi near Juara. There are also the Indians of Aripuana Park and of course the tribes under the care of FUNAI at Xingu National Park. The only tribe left in the Pantanal which still subsists by hunting and fishing is the Bororo.

You probably won't be able to overcome FUNAI's obstacles to visiting the Indians, but if you want to visit FUNAI the office (tel 321-2325) is at Rua São Joaquim 1047 and is open from 7 am to 1.30 pm. The condition of the building speaks volumes about the government's lack of concern with Indian affairs.

Information & Orientation
Tourist Office Turimat, the Mato Grosso subsidiary of Embratur has a stand at the airport which is not too helpful. The main office is in the city centre in Praça da República, near the post office. They can be very helpful and have a list of reasonably priced guides for the Pantanal.

If you want help with an excursion use one of the tourist agencies in town. They arrange reservations, guides and transport for photo-safaris into the Pantanal, weekend trips to Chapada dos Guimarães and can help with the logistics of more ambitious trips to Emas. Samariana Turismo (tel 321-8466) at Rua Campo rande 423 and Tuiu-Tu (tel 322-9330) at a 24 de Outubro 146.

Money You may be able to change travellers' cheques at a car rental place, but don't count on it. Changing cheques at parallel rates is difficult; try Tavá Tour (tel 322-1122) at Praça do Rosário 70. Changing dollars is easy.

Health Remember to start your anti-malarials prior to visiting the Pantanal. Avoid Cuiabá's municipal hospital, especially if you're ill. Hospital Modelo (tel 322-5599), a private clinic at Rua Comandante Costa 1262, is within walking distance of the Hotel Mato Grosso. University Hospital (Jaime Muller) on Avenida CPA is only open business hours.

Museu do Indio
Cuiabá's tourist brochures make much noise about satellite tracking antennas, but they're no big deal. The Museu do Indio (Rondon) is, however, played down. The museum has exhibits of the Xavantes, Bororos and Karajas tribes and is worth a visit. It is at the university on Avenida Fernando Correia da Costa and open Monday to Friday from 8 to 11.30 am and 1.30 to 5.30 pm.

The Market
The market by the bridge that crosses the Rio Cuiabá is a good one, at least before the heat of the day. It's not for buying but for looking at the people and their products. They're a very friendly crowd. Try the waterfront bars for a drink afterward.

Festivals
The Festa de São Benedito takes place during the first week in July at Igreja NS do Rosaria and the Chapel of São Benedito. The holiday has more Umbanda than Catholic flavour and is celebrated with traditional foods like bola de queijo and bola de arroz and regional dances like *O Cururu, O Siriri, Danças do Congo, dos Mascarados* and others.

Places to Stay – bottom end

Both the *Hotel Plaza* (tel 322-7976) at Rua Antonio Maria 428 and the *Panorama Hotel* (tel 322-0128) at Praça Moreira Cabral have doubles for US$3/8.50 without/with air-con. There are some very cheap hotels across from the rodoviária.

Places to Stay – middle

In the centre, the *Hotel Mato Grosso* (tel 321-9121) at Rua Commandante Costa 2522 has US$7/10.50 doubles with fan/air-con, hot shower and a delicious breakfast. It's the best value in Cuiabá. If that's booked up try *Hotel Almanar* (tel 321-2241), Rua Tenente Colonel Escolastico 150 with US$11 doubles.

Places to Stay – top end

The best of Cuiabá's hotels is the *Aurea Palace Hotel* (tel 322-3377) at Rua General Melo 63. There are two recommended three-star hotels; the *Santa Rosa Palace Hotel* (tel 322-9044) at Avenida Getúlio Vargas 600 and the overpriced *Hotel Exelsior* (tel 322-6322) at number 264.

Places to Eat

A *Integral* at Travessia João Dias 297 near the Turimat office serves vegetarian food. *Terraçus* (tel 322-6816) on Avenida Rubens de Mendoça (CPA) has draft beer and the best pizza in town. *Choparia o Garrafão* on Avenida Rubens de Mendoça is a good place for music, beer and dancing.

O Regionalissimo (tel 321-0603) serves excellent regional food, US$2.50 buffet style – lots of fish and the sweetest of sweets. It's open for lunch and dinner, closed Mondays, and is in the Casa do Artesão, Rua 13 de Junho.

Entertainment

I liked the Cuiabanos and I liked their nightlife. When the sun sets and it cools off a bit, the city comes to life. For some frontier-town fun head down near the bridge over the Rio Cuiabá. The outdoor bars have music and plenty of drinkers until the wee hours, but the centre of activity is on Avenida CPA with plenty of bars with good music and dance.

Things to Buy

There is a craft fair at Praça Santos Dumont and at Casa do Artesão on Rua 13 de Julho. The FUNAI store at Avenida Barao do Melgaço 3944 is open from 7.30 to 11.30 am and 1.30 to 5.30 pm on weekdays and has Indian baskets, bows and arrows, jewellery and headdresses for sale.

Getting There & Away

Air There are flights between Cuiabá and the rest of Brazil with Transbrasil (tel 322-7213), Vasp (tel 321-4122) and Varig/Cruzeiro (tel 321-7433). FAB flies to Porto Velho and Manaus once or twice a month. Pop into the airport for the flight schedule, then bring your visa and passport two days before departure. You may be lucky and grab a free flight on a Vulcan aeroplane.

Make reservations well in advance if you're travelling in July when many Brazilians are on vacation.

Bus Cuiabá's rodoviária (tel 321-4803) is on Avenida Marechal Rondon on the highway towards Chapada dos Guimarães. It's serviced by municipal bus from the city at the Praça da República. There are seven buses a day along the paved road to Campo Grande (11 hours, US$5) and one leito which continues on to São Paulo (24 hours) and Rio de Janeiro (33 hours).

Colibri and Eucatur take the paved road to Porto Velho several times a day (24 hours, time varies). From Porto Velho buses go to Manaus. There are also buses to Santarém in the dry season, but the road is only paved as far north as Sinop and as far south as Rurópolis, Pará. There are three daily buses to Brasília (20 hours, US$8). Goiânia is 14 hours away (US$7).

In the Pantanal there are two daily buses to Barão de Melgaço, 11 to Cáceres

on Empresa São Cristovao and nine daily buses to Poconé (see Poconé).

Getting Around

Airport Transport Marechal Rondon Airport (tel 381-2211) is in Varzea Grande. Municipal buses between the airport and the rodoviária are marked 'CPA2, Rodoviária, Morro da Serra'. Travellers arriving by air in Cuiabá must spend the night there because of flight schedules.

Car Rental The car rental places are in and near the airport. There are often promotional rates so shop around. The best car for the Pantanal is a Volkswagen Golf or Fusca. Note that the Porto Jofre station only has gas and diesel, Poconé and Pousada Pixaim (55 km from Poconé, 85 km from Porto Jofre) have alcohol.

AROUND CUIABÁ

Santo Antonio de Leverger

Santo Antonio de Leverger, Mato Grosso's Cidade Morena, is where Cuiabanos go for river beaching from June to October. It's on the Rio Cuiabá, 28 km south of Cuiabá in the direction of Barão de Melgaço.

Barão de Melgaço

Barão de Melgaço, 35 km south-west of Cuiabá, is, along with Caçeres and Poconé, a northern entrance into the Pantanal. Nearby there are ruined fortresses from the Paraguayan wars and Sia Mariana and Chacororé, two huge bays full of fish. There are three hotels in town.

Another trip by car is 87 km due east

from Cuiabá on BR-070 to sit in the thermal waters of São Vicente or another 100 km further along for the healing warm radioactive waters at Estância Canta Galo de Juscimeira.

Chapada dos Guimarães

After the Pantanal, Chapada dos Guimarães is the region's leading attraction. These rocky highlands are 800 metres up and 64 km north-east of Cuiabá in a beautiful region reminiscent of the American Southwest. Surprisingly different to the typical Mato Grosso terrain, this is a good trip if you have a half-day before setting off for the Pantanal.

Véu de Noiva & the Mirante Lookout

The two exceptional sights in the Chapadas are the Véu de Noiva (bridal veil), 60 metre falls, and the Mirante lookout, the geographic centre of South America. Both are a bit tricky to find. Six km after Salgadeira, which no one can miss, you'll see a turn-off for a swimming hole right after a little bridge. Turn around, go back over the bridge and you'll find a dirt road in a couple of hundred metres on your left. Take that for a km and you'll see the rim of the canyon. The waterfall is to your left.

Alta Mira is eight km from the town of Chapada. Take the last road in Chapada on your right, go eight km and look carefully for a 'capão de Boi' sign on your left. A hundred metres after the sign on your right is a dirt road. Drive a couple of hundred metres to the rim of the canyon. The view is stupendous; off to your right at about 2 o'clock you can see the Cuiabá skyline.

Start walking downhill over the bluff at about 10 o'clock, slightly to your left. There's a small trail that leads to a magical lookout perched on top of rocks with the canyon below. This is Chapada's most dazzling place.

Other Attractions
Driving through Chapada you'll also pass Rio dos Peixes, Rio Mutaca and Rio Claro, and the sculpted rock called Portão do Inferno. Take a waterfall shower at Cachoeirinha and peek into the chapel of NS de Sanfana, a strange mixture of Portuguese and French baroque.

Places to Stay & Eat
Food and lodging in the area ranges from the hotel accommodation and restaurant fare of *Hotel Carinthia & Restaurante Austria* (tel 791-1176) at Avenida Fernando Corea da Costa 1065 and *Hotel São Francisco & Restaurante Costelão* (tel 791-1102) at Praça Wunibaldo 490 .

A spiffy new hotel is being built at the *Salgadeira* tourist complex on the way up from Cuiabá, where there's also camping.

Getting There & Away
Buses leave from Cuiabá's rodoviária every hour to Chapada dos Guimarães, but that's not the way to travel as the interesting spots are a bit out of the way. Ideally you can hitch along with a local – they know the trails, where the hidden rock inscriptions and the waterfalls can be found. Another alternative is for a group to hire a car and explore the area on your own, stopping at different rock formations, waterfalls and bathing pools at leisure.

Around Mato Grosso

CAÇERES
Population: 55,000
The city of Caçeres, founded in 1778 on the left bank of the Rio Paraguai, is an access point for a number of Pantanal lodges. Caçeres is 190 km from Cuiabá on BR-070 and close to the Federal Ecologic Reserve of Ilha Taime.

Places to Stay & Eat
The *Hotel Barranquinho* (tel 322-1122), at the confluence of the Jauru and Paraguai rivers and 18 km from the Pirapitanga waterfalls, is 72 km and 2½ hours from Caçeres by boat. *Frontier Fishing Safari* is 115 km by boat from Caçeres, for information and reservations call (011) 227-0920 in São Paulo.

Safari Fotografico e Pesca (tel 321-6370) is a fishing group that camps on the banks of the Rio Paraquai from May through November, 150 km from Caçeres.

Caçeres itself has a number of modest hotels and restaurants for visitors. *Expeditour* (221-2162), a Pantanal safari outfit with a fleet of three jeeps, has an office in Caçeres at Rua Coronel José Dulce 97.

POCONÉ
Population: 20,000
Poconé is the northern entry point to the Pantanal from Cuiabá and the beginning of the Transpantaneira 'highway'.

In May the pink city of Poconé celebrates the week-long Semana do Fazendeiro e do Cavalo Panteiro with a cattle fair and rodeos. Most of the locals are descendants of Indians and Blacks. Many locals have hunted the *onçea* (jaguar) and have amazing stories to tell.

Places to Stay & Eat
The *Hotel Santa Cruz* (tel 721-1439) is a km from the Texaco station along the Rodoviária Transpantaneira. It charges US$9 for doubles with air-con and hot shower, has a decent restaurant but serves a meagre breakfast. Next door is the *Hotel Panteira*.

The *Hotel Joanna D'Arc* on Avenida Anibol de Toledo, near the rodoviária, ha clean and spare US$5 doubles with far

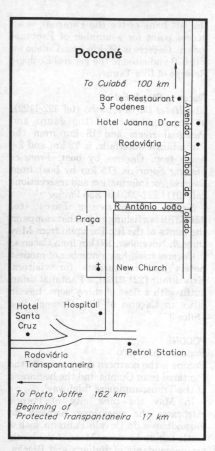

Poconé

To Cuiabá 100 km

Bar e Restaurant •
3 Podenes

Hotel Joanna D'arc •

Rodoviária

Avenida Anibal de Toledo

R Antônio João

Praça

New Church

Hotel
Santa
Cruz

Hospital

Rodoviária
Transpantaneira

• Petrol Station

To Porto Joffre 162 km
Beginning of
Protected Transpantaneira 17 km

Cheapest of the hotels is the *Skala* (tel 721-1407) on Praça Rondon. Singles are US$4/5.50 with fan/air-con and doubles US$5.50/7 with fan/air-con. Some rooms have baths as well for the same prices.

Bar e Restaraunte 3 Poderes, a few blocks from Hotel Joanna D'Arc in the opposite direction from the bus station. It's US$2 for all you can eat of over a dozen hearty dishes.

Getting There & Away

Tut Transportes runs nine buses a day from Cuiabá to Poconé from 6 am to 6 pm and nine in the opposite direction from 6.20 am to 6.20 pm. The 100 km two-hour ride is often packed; get an early seat or you are not likely to be able to appreciate the vegetation typical of the Pantanal's outskirts, *pequís, piúvas, babaçus, ipês* and *buritis*. The bus passes directly by the airport at Varzea Grande.

Pantanal

The Amazon may have all the fame and glory, but the Pantanal is a far better place to see wildlife. In the Amazon, the animals hide in the dense foliage, but in the open spaces of the Pantanal wildlife is visible to the most casual observer. It's not easy to get to and almost impossible to do on the cheap, but if you like to see animals in their natural state, the Pantanal – with the greatest concentration of fauna in the New World – should not be missed.

A vast wetlands in the centre of South America, the Pantanal is about half the size of France, some 230,000 square km spread across Brazil, Bolivia and Paraguay. Something less than 100,000 square km is in Bolivia and Paraguay, the rest is in Brazil, split between the states of Mato Grosso and Mato Grosso do Sul.

The Pantanal – *Terra de Ninguem* – has few people and no towns. Distances are so large and ground transportation so poor that people get around in small aeroplanes or motorboats and 4WD travel is restricted by the seasons. The only road that plunges deep into the Pantanal is the Transpantaneira, a raised dirt road sectioned by 89 small wood bridges, which ends 145 km from Poconé at Porto Jofre. Only one third of the intended route from Poconé to Corumba has been completed because of lack of funds and ecological concerns.

The road and a strip of land on either side of it comprise the Transpantanal National Park. Although the IBDF is

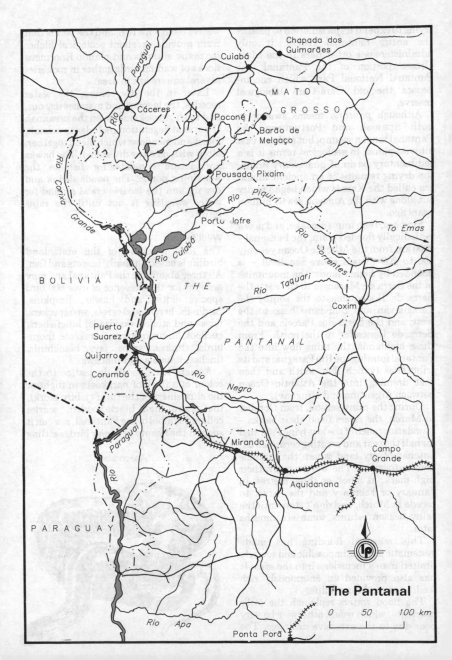

The Pantanal

0   50   100 km

trying to expand its jurisdiction to protect the entire Pantanal region, it only administers one other park in the Mato Grosso portion of the Pantanal, the Pantanal National Park which encompasses the old Cará-Cará biological reserve.

Although *pantano* means swamp in both Spanish and Portuguese, the Pantanal is not a swamp, but rather a vast alluvial plane. In geological terms it is a sedimentary basin of quaternary origin, the drying remains of an ancient inland sea called the Xaraés which began to dry out along with the Amazon sea 65 million years ago.

First sea, then immense lake, and now a periodically flooded plain, the Pantanal – 2000 km from the Atlantic Ocean yet only 100 to 200 metres above sea level – is bounded by higher lands: the mountains of the Serra de Maracaju to the east; the Serra da Bodoquena to the south; the Paraguayan and Bolivian Chaco to the west; and the Serra dos Parecis and the Serra do Roncador to the north. From these highlands, the rains flow into the Pantanal forming the Rio Paraguai and its tributaries (which flow south and then east draining into the Atlantic Ocean between Argentina and Uruguay).

During the rainy season, from October to March, the rivers flood their banks – inundating much of the low-lying Pantanal for half the year and creating *cordilheiras*: patches of dry land where the animals cluster together. The waters reach their high mark, as much as three metres, in January or February and then start to recede in March, and don't stop until the rainy season returns some six months later.

This seasonal flooding has made systematic farming impossible and severely limited man's incursions into the area. It has also provided an enormously rich feeding ground for wildlife.

The flood waters replenish the soil's nutrients, which would otherwise be very poor due to the excessive drainage. The waters teem with fish, and the ponds that form provide excellent ecological niches for many animals and plants. Enormous flocks of wading birds gather in rookeries several square km in area.

Later in the dry season, the water recedes, the lagoons and marshes dry out, and fresh grasses emerge on the savannah (Pantanal vegetation includes savannah, forest and meadows which blend together, often with no clear divisions). The hawks and jacaré compete for fish in the remaining ponds. The ponds shrink and dry up and the jacarés crawl around for water sweating it out until the rains return.

Wildlife

The food economy of the marshland birdlife is based on snails, insects and fish. All three abound in the Pantanal and may account for the presence of over 600 bird species: kites and hawks, limpkins, cardinals, herons and egrets, woodpeckers, ibises and storks, woodrails, kingfishers, cuckoos, hummingbirds, parakeets, thornbirds, shrikes, wrens, jays, blackbirds, finches, toucans and macaws.

A mere list doesn't do justice to the colour of a flock of parakeets in flight or the clumsiness of the *tuiui* (jabiru stork), the metre high black-hooded, scarlet collared symbol of the Pantanal, nor can it suggest the beauty of *ninha* birds settling

Anaconda

Giant Anteater

like snow in the trees or the speed of a sprinting herd of *emus* (latino ostriches). Keep an ear unclogged for the call of the *quero-quero* (I want, I want) bird which is named for its sound to Brazilian ears.

Birds are the most frequently seen animals, but the Pantanal is also a sanctuary for giant river otter, anacondas and iguanas, jaguars, ocelets, cougars, thousands upon thousands of jacaré, Pampas and Marsh deer, giant and lesser anteaters, black howler monkeys, zebu bulls and capybaras, the world's largest rodents.

The capybara is the most visible mammal in the Pantanal. They have guinea pig faces and bear-like coats. They grow up to 63 kg and can be seen waddling in the swampy latter half of the Transpantaneira where they feed on aquatic plants. They are equally at home on land or in water and are often seen in family groups of two adults and four or five young, or in large herds.

The two species of anteater in the Pantanal are endangered and not readily seen. The hairy giant anteater roams the dry savannah ground in search of the hard termite mounds which he'll excavate for 10 to 15 minutes at a time. The lesser anteater, smaller and lighter coloured than the giant, spends most of its time in trees eating ants, termites and larvae. Both are slow footed, with poor vision, but an excellent sense of smell.

The anteater's strong arms and claws,

which keep even the jaguars at bay, offer no protection from the local Pantaneiros who prize their meat. The killing of anteaters has led to an increase in ants and termites in the last decade, and many Pantaneiros now use deadly pesticides to try to destroy the mounds, unaware that the pesticides are absorbed by cattle and wildlife feeding in the area.

With thousands of jacaré sunning themselves on the edge of each and every body of water, it's hard to believe that the jacarés are endangered by poachers who slaughter an estimated one to two million each year.

The jacaré feed mainly on fish; they are the primary check on the growth of the piranha population, which has been growing rapidly due to the jacaré slaughter. The size of an adult jacaré is determined by the abundance of food and varies noticeably: jacaré on the river's edge are often considerably larger than those that feed in small ponds. Although they eat young or injured animals, Jacaré rarely attack people or capybara, and many birds mingle amongst the jacaré in complete peace and harmony.

Visitors to the Pantanal are always fascinated by the passivity of the jacaré. I've seen Pantaneiros swimming in rivers lined with jacaré, but there are times to be on guard. It's not safe to enter the water where there is only one jacaré. It could be a female guarding her eggs or her young. She can attack and, for short distances, run faster than a horse.

Capybara

Howler monkey

During the rainy season you must be careful walking in the water. The jacaré's are not aggressive and will usually swim away before you get close. But if stepped on the jacaré will grab a leg and roll. This has probably never happened to a tourist, and only once in a blue moon does a Pantaneiro suffer this end, but the rare jacaré attack is used nonetheless to justify their slaughter.

The jacaré, not known for their voice, makes one of the strangest sounds in the Pantanal. Every now and then a jacaré will curl its body, with head and tail stretching to the sky, open its mouth and let out a weird, deep rattle-roar. Then, suddenly, thin lines of water shoot up from the jacaré's back, and soon after the jacaré returns to its prior state of inactivity.

The cattle that live side-by-side with all this wildlife graze during the dry season and gather on the little islets that form during the wet season. Amazingly, the cattle live in harmony with the wildlife, as has man until recently.

Jaguars attack only sick or injured cattle, and some eat only their natural prey, capybara and tapir. Nevertheless, many cattle ranchers kill jaguars to protect their cattle. The jaguar are also killed for their skins. They are a highly endangered species and are threatened with extinction, as are the swamp deer and the giant river otter (the 'jaguar of the waters').

The Pantaneiros believe that eating jaguar meat boosts masculine qualities like strength and virility; qualities the traditional hunter of the jaguar, the *zagaeiro*, has in abundance. Using only a *zagara*, a wooden spear with a metal tip, the zagaeiro chases the jaguar up a tree and then taunts the cat until it is ready to leap and attack. At the last moment the zagaeiro plants the spear in the ground and when the jaguar jumps on the man it impales itself, dying instantly.

Driving Along the Transpantaneira The Transpantaneira is the best place we've seen in South America to observe wildlife. The elevated dirt road begins just outside Poconé and extends 145 km to Porto Jofre. Wildlife is drawn to the roadway at all times of the year. During the wet season the roadway is an island, and during the dry season, the ditches on either side of the road serve as artificial ponds drawing birds and game toward the tourist.

Thousands of birds appear to rush out

Jaguar

from all sides, ocelets and capybara seem frozen by the headlights, and roadside pools are filled with hundreds of dark silhouettes and gleaming red jacaré eyes. It's very easy to approach the wildlife; you can walk up to spitting range of the jacarés, and if you are so crazy as to go cheek to cheek with a jacaré you can spot the fleas which live off the lacrimal fluid of their eyeballs.

If you are driving from Cuiabá get going early. Leave at 4 am and you'll reach the Transpantaneira by sunrise, when the animals come to life, and have a full days light to drive to Porto Jofre.

The approach road to the Transpantaneira begins in Poconé (two hours from Cuiabá) by the Texaco station. Follow the road in the direction of *Hotel Santa Cruz* and take the left fork past the gold slurries. The official Transpantaneira Highway Park starts 17 km south of Poconé, there's a sign and guard station at the entrance, but I've seen herds of ema, many birds and jacaré well before the park entrance.

Stopping to see wildlife and slowing for 89 rickety, little, wood bridges, it's easy to pass the whole day driving the Transpantaneira's 127 km – arriving at the *Hotel Santa Rosa* in time for dinner soon after sunset. Weekdays are best if you're driving, there's less traffic kicking up dust.

Hitching on the Transpantaneira is excellent, especially on weekends when the locals drive down the Transpantaneira for a days fishing. I've done the entire route from Porto Jofre to Poconé several times with all sorts of folk: a rancher and his family, Italian tourists, an IBDF park ranger, a photosafari guide, two American birders, an ex-poacher and a photojournalist doing an article on jacaré poaching.

Wildlife is abundant along the length of the Transpantaneira, but reaches a climax in the meadows about 10 to 20 km before Porto Jofre. The flora here is less arid, less scrubby. The birds, jacaré and families of capybara scurry into the ponds along the road. I've seen several toucans, flocks of luminescent green parrots and six blue Hyacinthine Macaws in the big trees that divide the great meadows. There are enormous flocks of birds and individual representatives of seemingly every species.

If you're staying a few days, and I'd recommend at least two or three, prime-time wildlife watching is in the early morning and late afternoon. Plan a daily outing before sunrise and another about an hour before sunset. I drove back to the meadows each day, but there are other places to explore, as well as horses and boats to rent.

To find animals at night a strong flashlight is a great help. Keep an eye out for owls and yellow anacondas. Smaller than their Amazonian relatives, the anacondas still reach 10 metres in length. The anacondas feed on capybara and smaller rodents, birds and even small deer. There are several other snakes in the Pantanal, but poisonous ones are rare.

Poaching According to Dr Maria Padua, a Pantanal biologist and conservationist (though less publicised), poachers are doing more damage to the Pantanal than the Amazon. The Brazilian government has not done much to stem the slaughter of the animals. In 1983, military president João Figueredo dispatched the Brazilian army to defend the natural resources of the Pantanal, but that was only a one-shot deal.

Fifteen IBDF park rangers with only 12 jeeps patrol an area of land one-tenth the size of the Amazon. They are up against a well organised and well funded army of poachers who have aircraft and hidden jungle airstrips, plus corrupt national and state officials on their side. If the poachers do get caught, they suffer nothing more than wrist-slap penalties (US$5 fines or a day in the cell).

Anywhere from 500,000 to two million animals are killed each year in the Pantanal, smuggled over the Bolivian border (where poaching is also illegal, but not even tokenly enforced) and exchanged for cocaine, guns and cash. The slow and fearless jacarés are easily shot at short range. A jacaré skin commands a price of US$200, but only a fraction of it is used. Only the supple, small scaled skin of the jacaré's flanks is used to make fashionable wallets, belts, purses and shoes. The rest of the carcass is useless to poachers and discarded.

A park ranger told me of the hundreds of jacaré carcasses, their skulls in neat piles, crates of handguns and rifles, bags of cocaine and the many jaguar and ocelot pelts found in a recent raid on some poachers who worked two hours by boat from Porto Jofre.

Just as poachers supply the fashion industry with skins, they supply American pet shops with rare tropical fish and birds. A hyacinth macaw will sell for US$5000 in the US; compare that to the minimum monthly wage of the Brazilian and it's easy to see the great temptation for farmers, truckers, government officials, in fact anyone in the area to get involved in poaching. The depletion of the jacarés is causing unchecked growth in the piranha population which in turn will effect the numbers of different fish and bird populations. The environment is delicate and threatened by poachers, mercury in the gold slurries, ever expanding farm and ranch lands, roadways and so on. The hope is that wildlife tourism in the Pantanal will make conservation a profitable enterprise.

When to Go

If possible go during the dry season from April to September/October. The best time to go birding is during the latter part of the dry season from July to September when the birds are at their rookeries in great numbers, the waters have receded and the bright green grasses pop up from the muck. Temperatures are comfortable in the dry season, being hot by day and cool by night, with plenty of rain.

Flooding, incessant rains and deep heat make travel difficult during the rainy season from November to March, though not without some special rewards (this is when the cattle and exotic wildlife of the Pantanal clump together on the small islands). The heat peaks in November and December when temperatures over 40°C are common. Roads turn to breakfast cereal. The mosquitoes are fierce and they're out in force. Many hotels close.

The heaviest rains fall in February and March. Every decade or so the flooding is disastrous, destroying man and beast. In 1988, the southern Pantanal was devastated: fazendas were destroyed, cattle and wild animals drowned and starved, and the city of Corumba was submerged for weeks.

Fishing is best during the first part of the dry season, from April to May, when the flooded rivers settle back into their channels, but Pantanal cowboys have been known to lasso 80 kg fish throughout the dry season and well into December. This is some of the best fishing in the world. There are about 20 species of piranha, many are vegetarians, all are good eating; there is the tasty dourado, a feisty ten to twenty pounder; and there are many other excellent catches: pacu, surubim, bagre, giripoca, piraputanga, piapara, cachara, pintado, pirancajuva and pintado to name a few.

Hunting is not permitted, but fishing – with required permits – is encouraged. Fishing permits are available from the IBDF in Cuiabá and the INAMB in Mato Grosso do Sul. Fishermen can study their quarry at Cuiabá's fish market, at the Centro de Abastecimento.

Guides

If you want to enhance your Pantanal experience, and money isn't a problem, a good guide can identify animal and bird species, explain the diverse Pantanal ecology, and take care of any hassles along the way. But you don't need a guide.

There's only one road to follow and the wildlife is hard to miss.

The tourist office in Cuiabá has a list of local guides. The office is right in the city at Praça da Republica (tel 065-322-5363). The cost of their guides, without a car, is very little (US$10 a day) but you have to pay for their bread and board.

If language or time is a problem and money isn't the guides we recommend are a couple of the best and come with a 4WD. They also know the Central-West (not just the Pantanal) and areas like Emas, Chapada dos Guimarães, Araguaia – and they are fluent English speakers. Vinicius de Albuquerque Maranhao of *Wildlife* works out of Cuiabá, has a couple of 4WDs, an intimate understanding of the Pantanal and a reputation for excellence among professional wildlife photographers. Leave a message at (065) 341-1753 or drop him a line at Caixa Postal 8001 Apt. Mal Rondon Varzea Grande MT 78150.

You can write to Douglas Trent of *Raptimbrasil* (tel (031) 223-3811) Belo Horizonte at Rua Grao Mogol, 502 Belo Horizonte MG. Doug, an American, specialises in nature tours and is active in trying to preserve the Pantanal. For about US$1000 he'll take you to the *Hotel Santa Rosa* for a week and show you the ropes. Christoph Hodina of *Andre Safari & Tours Ltda* (tel (061) 248-3953 or 573-1362) is at Caixa Postal 7020 Brasília 71619 DF.

Places to Stay

Pantanal accommodations are divided into three general categories – fazendas, *pesqueiros* and *botels*. Fazendas are ranch-style hotels which usually have horses for hire and often boats. Pesqueiros are hangouts for fishermen which normally rent boats and fishing gear. A botel, a contraction of boat and hotel, is a floating lodge.

Reservations are needed for all accommodation (unfortunately nearly all are expensive) and usually include transportation by plane, boat or 4WD from Corumba or Cuiabá and good food and modest lodging. More often than not reservations are handled through a travel agent and you must pay in advance. It's also a good idea to call ahead for weather conditions. The rainy and dry seasons are never exact and proper conditions can make or break a trip.

Transpantaneira Accommodation on the Transpantaneira is limited to three points: Poconé, the *Pousada Pixaim* and the *Santa Rosa Pantanal* at Porto Jofre.

The *Pousada Pixaim* (065) 322-0513 has a friendly manager, clean rooms with electric showers, tasty meals (breakfast included in the accommodation price) and the last álcool and gas pump until you return to Poconé – so fill her up!

If you have the money, stay in Porto Jofre where the Transpantaneira meets it's end at the Rio Cuiabá. It's a one-hotel town, in fact it's not even a town. Unless you have a tent to pitch at Sr Nicolino's grounds on the riverfront (he also rents boats), take the turn-off (it's the only one) a couple km to the *Hotel Santa Rosa Pantanal*. For US$25 a person the Santa Rosa will put you up in a clean bungalow that sleeps four and feed you three fish meals a day.

It's nothing fancy, but you get hot showers plus decent food (a choice of fried fish, grilled fish, stewed fish or salted fish). They have a swimming pool and football table: boats (very expensive), horses (expensive) and beer cost extra. reservations are a good idea, the next hotel is probably in Bolivia. *Selva* travel agency handles reservations in Cuiabá (tel (065) 322-0513), or go to Rua Barão de Melgaço, 3594. They also have an office in São Paulo (tel (011) 231-4511). Perhaps you can persuade the manager to let you hang your hammock in the workers' apartments at the edge of the hotel grounds.

Other Pantanal Accommodations There are several fazendas in the northern Pantanal that are off the Transpantaneira. The *Hotel Porto Cercado* is easily reached by car and reasonably priced (tel (065) 322-0178 in Cuiabá and tel (021) 235-6799 in Rio). It's along the Rio Cuiabá about 50 km from Poconé. The expensive *Hotel Cabanas do Pantanal* is 42 km from Poconé (tel (065) 322-1353 in Cuiabá). *Camping Pirigara* and *Pirigara Pantanal Hotel* (tel (065) 322-8961 in Cuiabá) are on the banks of the River São Lourenco and Rio Cuiabá, 45 km from Poconé and about six hours by boat from Porto Cercado.

One of the cheapest places to stay in the Pantanal is the *Pesqueiro Clube do Pantanal* (tel (067) 242-1464 in Miranda). It's 168 km from Corumba in the direction of Campo Grande. They charge about US$10 per person with full board and fishing trips by boats can be arranged. Also in the vicinity of Miranda is the *Miranda Pesca Clube* (tel (067) 242-1323 in Miranda) 5 km from town, and the *Hotel Beira Rio* (tel (067) 242-1262 in Miranda) 8 km from town. The latter has air-con and hot showers and is rigged out like a pesqueiro. It is US$13.50 per person for full board.

There are a few places located downstream of the Rio Miranda and a bit deeper into the Pantanal at Passo do Lontra, 120 km and 2 hours (dry season) from Corumba by the dirt road to Campo Grande. Alternatively you can take the train to Campo Grande and have the lodge pick you up at the Carandazal station. The *Cabana/Pesqueiro do Lontra* (tel (067) 241-2406 in Miranda and (011) 283-5843 in São Paulo) is pricier than many charging US$30 per person including full board. Boat and fishing gear rental is expensive.

Sixteen km from Passo da Lontra is *Fazenda Santa Clara* (tel (067) 231-5797). They charge US$30 per day for full board and cold showers and they have both boats and horses for hire.

Serious fishermen should consider the *Pesqueiro de Severino* (tel 231-1642 and (011) 258-4355 in São Paulo). It's 70 km

south of Corumbá and costs about US$30 per day including meals. Boats and horses are available. Nearby is the *Pesqueiro Taruma* (tel (067) 231-4197 in Corumbá) which is smaller, but well equipped with air-con, hot shower, fridge and boats.

The *Cabana do Pescador* (tel (067) 241-3697 in Aquidauana) is 60 km from Aquidauana in the direction of Bonito – it's situated on higher and drier grounds than most of the other pesqueiros. It's US$12 for full board. *Paraiso dos Dourados* (tel (067) 231-1642 in Corumbá) at Fazenda Morrinhos, 72 km from Corumbá, offers its guests hot water, air-con, fridge, boats and good fishing.

Botels defy any permanent address. *Botel Flory* (tel (067) 231-1968 is a 10-person boat that cruises the Rio Paraguai from Corumba. *Corumbi*, *Trans-Tur* or *Amazonas* (all tel (067) 231-3016) have air-con, hot water and accommodations for eight. *Botel Elvira* (tel (067) 231-4316) docks in Corumbá and for US$40 per day takes 8 people on five-day (minimum) trips to Rio San Lorenzo for fishing and photography. Phone (067) 231-4683 for the eight person *Barco Cabexi*.

The *Cidade Barão de Melgaço* or *CBM* makes long bi-monthly trips through the Pantanal on the Cuiabá, São Lourenco and Paraguai rivers. A US$580 fee includes ground transport to the boat from the airport and the cabins have bath and air-con. For reservations contact Onlytur in Rio at (021) 257-7773 at Rua Siqueira Campos 43, Room 901.

What to Bring

You can't buy anything in the Pantanal so come prepared. The dry season is also the cooler season. Bring attire for hot days, though not brutal, cool nights, rain, and mosquitoes (don't worry they are not terribly vicious). You'll need sunscreen, sunglasses, hat, and cool clothes, sneakers or boots, light raingear, and something for the cool evenings. Mosquito relief means long pants and long-sleeve shirts, vitamin

B-12 and repellent (*Autan* is the Brazilian brand recommended by eight out of 10 Pantaneiros).

Binoculars are your best friend in the Pantanal. Bring an alarm clock to get up before sunrise and a strong flashlight to go hunting for owls and anacondas after sunset. Don't forget plenty of film, a camera, tripod and a long lens – 300mm is about right for the wildlife.

Getting There & Away

From Cuiabá there are three approach routes to the Pantanal; Caceres, Barão de Melgaço and Poconé to Porto Jofre on the Transpantaneira From Campo Grande in the south, the best access is by rail to Corumbá via Aquidauana and Miranda. A third point of entry is via Coxim, a small town on BR-163, east of the Pantanal and accessible by bus or air-taxi from either Campo Grande or Cuiabá.

Since the lodges are the only places to sleep, drink and eat, and public transportation doesn't exist, independent travel is difficult in the Pantanal. There used to be a cement boat from Corumbá to Cáceres that would let you hang a hammock for a couple of dollars but lately they have been refusing guests. You can always try to hitch a ride on a plane with one of the local fazenderos. Driving is less expensive, but not easy. Only a few roads reach into the periphery of the Pantanal; they are frequently closed by rains and reconstructed yearly. Only the Transpantaneira highway goes deep into the region.

It is of course impossible to know everything about travel in the Pantanal, but based on several trips and conversations with literally dozens of Pantanal experts we think the best way to visit the Pantanal, if you're in it for the wildlife and your budget is limited, is driving down the Transpantaneira, preferably all the way to Porto Jofre.

Why the Transpantaneira? First, it's the best place to see wildlife – especially in the meadows near the end of the road at Porto

Jofre. Second, renting a car in Cuiabá and driving down the Transpantaneira to the *Hotel Santa Rosa* at Porto Jofre is less expensive than most Pantanal excursions which require flying, boating or hiring a guide with a 4WD. And third, if you're on a very tight budget, you can take a bus to Poconé and hitch from there (it's pretty easy) and if you have to, return to Poconé for cheap accommodations.

Car Rental In Cuiabá, there are several car rental agencies just outside the airport grounds to your right which are often cheaper than the agencies inside the airport. There is some competition so shop around, and ask about promotional rates. No matter what anyone tells you, you don't need a 4WD to drive the Transpantaneira. The best car is a Volkswagon Golf or Fusca. Flat tires can be a problem, so make sure you have a spare. The Brazilian Gurgel looks like a 4WD but doesn't act like one. Stick with the Golf in the Pantanal.

If you do plan to drive the Transpantaneira, protect yourself by reserving a Golf a few weeks in advance (there's no cost). You can always shop-around for a better deal when you arrive. Don't forget to fill up your tank at Poconé and the *Pousada Pixaim*.

Mato Grosso do Sul

CAMPO GRANDE

Population: 300,000

Founded in 1899 as the village of Santo Antonio de Campo Grande, the city became the capital of Mato Grosso do Sul in 1979 by decree of military president Ernesto Giesel, when the new state splintered off from Mato Grosso. It is known as the 'Cidade Morena' because of its red earth. Manganese, rice, soy and cattle are the sources of its wealth. Campo Grande lies 716 km south of Cuiabá and 420 km south-east of Corumba.

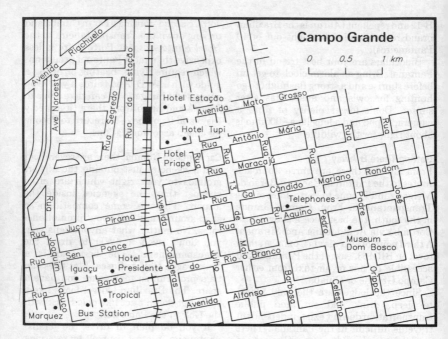

Information

Empresa de Turismo do Mato Grosso do Sul (tel 382-3091) is a tourist office at Avenida Afonso Peña 3149 .

Museu Dom Bosco

The Museu Dom Bosco (tel 383-3994) at Rua Barão do Rio Branco 1843 is open from 7 to 11 am and 1 to 5 pm. It has some interesting exhibits about the Xavante and Bororo Indians.

Places to Stay – bottom end

Hotel Cosmos (tel 383-4271) at Rua Dom Aquino 771 and *Hotel Gaspar* (tel 383-5121) at Avenida Mato Grosso 2 are the budget hotels of note. *Hotel Anache* (tel 383-2841) at Rua Marechal Rondon 1396 has singles/doubles with bath for US$6.50/8.50. The *Village Palace* (tel 624-1954), *Palace* (tel 384-4741) and

Iguaçu (tel 384-4621) hotels on Rua Dom Aquino fall into the mid range.

Places to Stay – top end

The *Hotel Campo Grande* (tel 382-6061), is a four-star inn at Rua 13 de Maio 2825. *Hotel Jandaia* (tel 382-4081) on Rua Barão do Rio Branco 1271 and *Hotel Concord* (tel 382-3081) on Avenida Calógeras 1624 are both three-star hotels in the central area.

Getting There & Away

There are bus and air connections to all major cities. The rodoviária (tel 383-1678) is at Rua Joaquim Nabuco 200 and the Antonio João Airport (tel 383-1942) is seven km from town. There are several air taxis for trips into remote areas of the Pantanal. There are daily trains to Corumbá and São Paulo.

Campo Grande is a departure or arrival

Indian girl in Campo Grande

point for travel to and from Bolivia and Paraguay. See the introductory Getting There chapter for transport details.

CORUMBÁ
Population: 80,000

Corumbá, a port city on the Rio Paraguai and the Bolivian border, is the southern gateway to the Pantanal. Corumbá or Cidade Branca (white city) was founded and named in 1776 by Captain Luis de Albequerque. The city is 588 km north-west of Campo Grande by road or rail. Due to the strategic location near the Paraguayan and Bolivian border (Porto Suarez is only 19 km away), Corumbá has a reputation for drug traffic, gun running and poaching. Go with caution.

Things to See

Corumbá's star attraction is the Pantanal and you can get a preview of the Pantanal from Morro Urucum (1100 metres). Tourists looking for something different might consider a seven-hour boat trip south on the Rio Paraguai to Forte Coimbra, in days gone by a key defence of

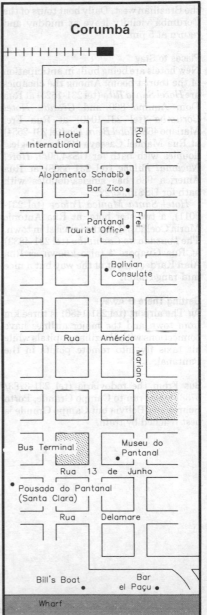

the Brazilian west. Daily boat tours of the Corumbá vicinity leave at midday and return at 5 pm.

Places to Stay

New hotels are being built in anticipation of the tourist boom. Among the cheapies are *Hotel Santa Rita* (tel 231-1525) at Rua Dom Aquino 860 and *Grande Hotel Corumba* (tel 231-1040) at Rua Frei Mariano 468. *Hotel Beira Rio* (tel 231-2554) at Rua Manoel Cassava 109 has singles/doubles with bath for US$4.50/9. *Hotel Nacional Palace* (tel 231-6868) at Rua América 936 has singles/doubles with bath for US$15.50/22.

Hotel Santa Monica Palace (tel 231-3011), a two-star hotel at Rua Antonio Maria Coelho 345, is the fanciest in town. The *Pousada do Cachimbo* (tel 231-4833) at Rua Guapore 4 (also known as Rua Alan Kardec) is out of the way but a nice mid-range hotel.

Getting There & Away

Air The airport (tel 231-1456) is three km from town and the major airlines have connections with Brazilian capitals while air taxis fly into remote points in the Pantanal.

Bus From the rodoviária (tel 231-3783/3738) buses run to Campo Grande, Porto Suarez and Bolivia but Campo Grande is best reached by train.

Riverboats Like Campo Grande, Corumbá is a transit point for travel to and from Bolivia and Paraguay. Boat transport up through the Pantanal is difficult and infrequent. Cement boats are no longer permitted to take foreign passengers, but the *Elsa* still travels every 10 days or so and Barca Tur (tel 231-3016) operates river trips to Cáceres, Cuiabá and Asuncion. Some boats go as far south on the Paraguai as Buenos Aires. Enquire at the Porto Geral. Travel agencies at the Porto Geral will also arrange for transport and lodging in the Pantanal.

COXIM

Population: 25,000
Coxim is a small town about halfway between Cuiabá and Campo Grande on the eastern border of the Pantanal. Coxim's drawing card is the Piracema, when fish migrate up the Taquaria and Coxim rivers, leaping through rapids to spawn. The Piracema usually takes place from November to January, but the fishing (pacú pintado, curimbatá, piracema and dourado) is good from August to December. A fishing licence is required.

Places to Stay

There are a number of cheap hotels in town, one-star and down, plus the *Hotel Grande*.

THE SOUTH

REGIÃO SUL

Paraná

CURITIBA

Population: 1.5 million

Curitiba, the capital of Paraná, is one of Brazil's urban success stories. Like many of Brazil's cities, thousands began to flood into Curitiba in the 1940s. With only 140,000 residents in 1940 the city has grown 10-fold to 1½ million people today. Yet, with the assistance of a vibrant local and state economy, the city has managed to modernise in a sane manner – historic buildings have been preserved, a handful of streets have been closed to cars and there are many parks, gardens and wide boulevards.

Surprisingly, a progressive mayor instituted several incentives, including lower bus prices, to get people out of their cars – and the strategy worked. Traffic congestion was reduced and today there's an ease to getting around in Curitiba. Drivers go slow and stop at red lights, few horns honk, pedestrians cross streets without blood-type identification bracelets and although I haven't researched it, I bet Curitiba's divorce, heart attack, murder and dog abandonment rates are all down.

The local Curitibanos are mostly descended from Italian, German and Polish immigrants. There is also a large university population, which gives the city a young feel. There is also a good music scene.

At 900 metres, Curitiba is atop the great escarpment along the route from Rio Grande do Sul to São Paulo. Due to this location, Curitiba flourished briefly as a pit-stop for gaúchos and their cattle until a better road was built on an alternate route. Curitiba quickly went back to sleep. It wasn't until the tremendous growth of the coffee plantations in northern Paraná at the beginning of the 20th century that the modern city of Curitiba began to take shape.

Like the gaúchos of old, most tourists are just passing through Curitiba. The highway from São Paulo (400 km) to Florianopolis (300 km) and Porto Alegre (710 km) intersects Curitiba, and it's the turn-off for the train ride to Paranaguá and the bus to the Iguaçu Falls.

There's not much here for the out-of-towner, but it's still possible to pass a pleasant day in a park, museum and older neighbourhood waiting for your bus or train to leave. It's an easy city to walk around and if you have errands to do or clothes to buy, this is a good place for it.

Information & Orientation

Tourist Office The tourist information booths at the rodoviária are useless. You can purchase the *Guia Turístico do Curitiba e Paraná* from bookstores, but it's not very helpful.

Money The travel agencies are the best bet for money exchange and information. ABC is at Rua Buenos Aires 178, Brementur is at Rua Candido Lopes 352, Diplomatur is at Rua Presidente Faria 143, Jade and Esatur are at Rua 15 de Novembro 477 and 384 respectively.

Post & Telephone Telepar, the phone company, is at Rua Visconde de Macar 1415. There are good post offices at Rua 15 de Novembro 700 and Rua Marechal Deodoro 298.

Consulates The following countries have consulates in Curitiba:

Bolivia
    Rua Bruno Filgueira 1662 (tel 232-5698)
Chile
    Rua Barão do Rio Branco 63, No 1301 (tel 225-1369)
Paraguay
    Rua Comendador Araujo 143 (tel 222-9226)

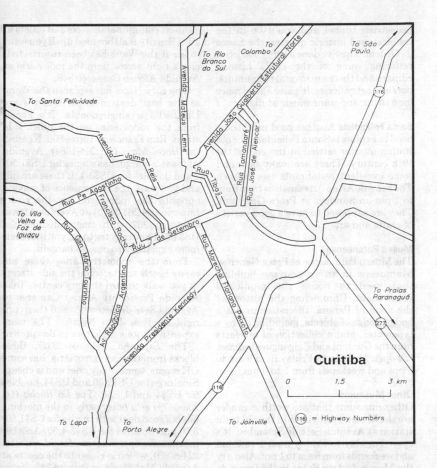

To Rio Branco do Sul

To Colombo

To São Paulo

To Santa Felicidade

Avenida Mateus Leme

Avenida João Gualberto Estrutural Norte

Avenida Jaime Reis

Rua Tamandaré

Rua José de Alencar

Rua Tibají

Rua Pe Agostinho

Rua Francisco Rocha

Rua de Setembro

Rua Marechal Floriano Peixoto

To Vila Velha & Foz de Iguaçu

Rua Gen Mário Tourinho

Av República Argentina

Avenida Presidente Kennedy

Curitiba

To Praias Paranaguá

116

277

0   1.5   3 km

116 = Highway Numbers

To Lapa

To Porto Alegre

To Joinville

Peru

Rua Alameda Dr Muricy 926, 2nd floor (tel 233-4711)

Uruguay

Rua Marechal Deodoro 503, No 303 (tel 233-4161)

Bookshops English books are available at Livraria-Curitiba, Rua Vol da Pátria 205 (Praça Santos Andrade), Rua Marechal Deodoro 275 and Rua 15 de Novembro, and at the Livraria Ghignone, Rua 15 de Novembro 409.

Around Town

Take a stroll in the Passeio Publico where Curitibanos have relaxed since 1886. Because it's right in the centre of town on Avenida Presidente Carlos Cavalcanti the park is always busy. There's a lake and a small zoo. The park closes on Mondays. The Rua 15 de Novembro is the main commercial boulevard and it's good for walking and shopping.

Historic Quarter Over by Praça Tiradentes and the metropolitan Cathedral take the pedestrian tunnel and you'll be in the cobblestoned historic quarter, the Lagoa da Ordem. They've done a very good job of restoring some of the city's historic edifices and there are several restaurants, bars and art galleries. It's also a good place for a drink and some music at night.

Santa Felicidade Another good neighbourhood to explore is Santa Felicidade the old Italian quarter settled at the end of the 19th century. There are many bars and some excellent restaurants (see below). The Feira de Arte e Artesanato is from 8 am to 1 pm on Sundays at Praça Garibaldi. They are supposed to have a good variety of crafts and art.

Museu Paranaense

The Museu Paranaense at Praça Generoso Marques is in an art-nouveau building that used to house the municipal government. Chronicling the history of the state of Paraná, the museum has a hodge-podge of objects, including many a typewriter, and a collection of artefacts from the Guarani and Caigangues Indians. It's open Monday to Friday from 9 am to 6 pm and weekends from 1 to 6 pm.

Other Museums

Other museums that are worth a gander are the Museu Ferroviária in the old train station at Avenida Sete de Setembro. It's open Tuesday to Friday from 1 to 7 pm and weekends from 8 am to 1 pm. Also, try the Museu do Arte Sacra in the Igreja da Ordem (largo da Ordem). It's open Tuesday to Friday from 2 to 8 pm and Sunday from 10 am to 1 pm. There is a Museu de Arte Comtemporanea at Rua Desembargador Westphalen 16, open Monday to Friday from 9.30 am to 6 pm and Sunday from 1 to 5 pm.

Places to Stay – bottom end

The good news is that there are many inexpensive hotels, several right across from the rodoferroviária. The bad news is that the *Wang* – reputed to have the

cleanest communal showers and toilets in all of Brazil – is all boarded up. If you want to see if the Wang has been resurrected, check right across from the rodoviária at Avenida Afonso Camargo 549.

The *City Hotel* has replaced the Wang as the best deal in town. Quartos are US$2.50/3 a single/double. It's across from the rodoviária, on the quiet side street, Rua Francisco Torres 806. Nearby, the *Hotel Maia* (tel 264-1684), Avenida Afonso Camargo, has singles for US$1.50/2 and doubles for US$3/4. If these are full and you want the convenience of staying opposite the rodoviária, try the *Hotel Imperio* (tel 264-3373) at Avenida Afonso Camargo 367 with singles/doubles for US$4/5. They may try to get you into their more expensive rooms, so bargain.

From the rodoferroviária, there are many hotels scattered on the side streets as you walk toward the city centre. Take Avenida Presidente Afonso Camargo to Avenida Sete de Setembro and then turn right on Rua João Negrão. The more expensive hotels are closer to downtown.

The *Espanha* (tel 264-2932), three blocks from the rodoferroviária, has some OK rooms, some dingy ones and is cheap. Singles go for US$2.50 and US$4, doubles for US$4 and US$6. The *La Rocha* (tel 233-6479) gets noisy early in the morning but is a good deal with singles for US$1.50/3.50 and doubles for US$2/4.50. Another inexpensive option is the *Hotel Lotus* (tel 224-8069), which is closer to the centre at Avenida Mal Floriano Peixoto 742. If you plan to stay a while the Hotel Lotus is quiet, clean and friendly and their singles/doubles cost US$3/5.50.

There is a *Casa dos Estudantes* (tel 222-4911) on the Parque Passeio Publico. It costs US$2 a night and you need a student card.

Places to Stay – top end

The *Aeroporto Palace* (tel 223-2444) is at Rua João Negrão 780, on the corner of Avenida Sete de Setembro. It's modern and air conditioned and they have special promotional rates with singles/doubles for only US$9/11. For about the same price, but not as nice, the *Hotel Cacique* (tel 233-8122) is at Rua Tobias de Macedo 26. It's an old classic building on Praça Tiradentes.

Also on Rua João Negrão, at 169, is the *San Martin* (tel 222-5211) with a sauna and singles/doubles for US$21/26. The *Hotel Savoy* (tel 223-7191) at 568, also has a sauna and costs US$18/21 a single/double. The *California* (tel 264-4322) is less expensive, clean and convenient. It's across from the ferrorodoviária at Avenida Presidente Afonso Camargo 279. The *Climax* (tel 224-3411) is also a good deal with singles/doubles for US$17/22, but fills up early. It's in the city centre at Rua Dr Murici 861.

The best hotel in town, the *Iguaçu Campestre* (tel 262-5313), is eight km out of town on the BR-116. Rooms start at US$38 and there are tennis courts and other amenities. The *Araucária Palace* (tel 224-2822) is opposite the performing arts centre, Rua Amintas de Barros 73. Singles/doubles cost US$29/35.

Places to Eat

There is a good assortment of Italian restaurants in Santa Felicidade, many of them inexpensive. The *Bologna* (tel 223-7102) has the city's best Italian food. Moderately priced, it's at Rua Carlos de Carvalho 150 and is open for lunch and dinner daily except Tuesdays. The tortellini has a city-wide reputation. Also in the city centre is the *Arabe Oriente* at Rua Ebano Pereira 26 on the 1st floor. Open daily for lunch and dinner, they have big portions and good food.

There's also a good Japanese restaurant, *Kamikaze* (tel 272-1575) at Avenida Manoel Ribas 6354. They are open daily for lunch and dinner except Mondays, but have the rather rude policy of not serving single customers. The *Yuasu* has inexpensive Japanese meals at Avenida Sete de Setembro 1927. They are open for lunch and dinner daily, except Mondays.

There are several very pleasant, medium-priced restaurants in the Lagoa da Ordem area. It's a good place to walk around, look at menus and see what looks best. The *Super Vegetariano* has self service, fixed price lunches and is open daily except Sundays at Rua Cruz Machado 217.

The *Bar do Stuart* has great small meals and a classy ambience. It's open daily until midnight (except Sundays when they close at 2 pm) at Praça Osório 427. For a good lunch near the rodoviária the *Dragão de Ouro* has big portions at little prices. It's at Avenida Afonso Camargo 451, 1st floor.

Entertainment

The best place in town is the *Camarim Bar*, right next to the Araucária Palace Hotel. It's a small place with great local jazz, informal and cheap and always crowded with a mix of mostly artsy and university types. The music starts late and goes late.

Up in Lagoa da Ordem there are several bars with rock. There's also the *Casa Nilo Samba* at Rua Mateus Leme 65 which has samba and choro. Up the hill, *John Edwards Bar* is at Rua Jaime Reis 212. It's a bit pricey but they have good jazz, blues and bossa nova from Wednesday to Sunday nights. John Edwards, the owner, is an American from San Francisco.

Getting There & Away

Air There are flights to all major cities in Brazil.

Bus The new Rodoferroviária (tel 234-8441) is clean and well organised. The entrance is on Avenida Afonso Camargo. Bus schedules are posted and easy to understand, and some companies even have printed schedules that they hand out.

There are many daily buses to São Paulo (six hours) and Rio (11 hours) and all major cities to the south. There are 12 buses a day to Foz do Iguaçu, the first

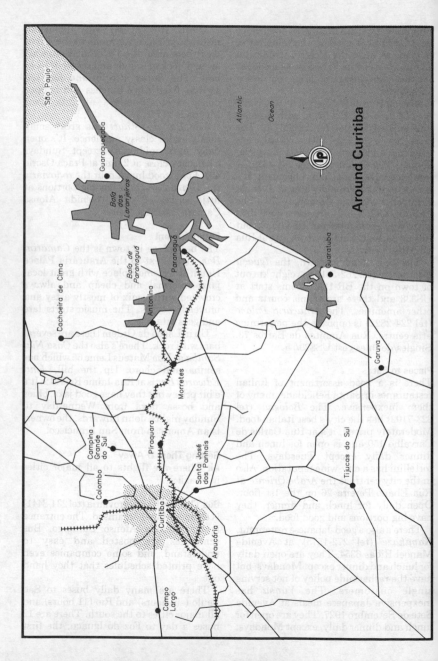

Around Curitiba

leaves at 7 pm and the last two at 9.15 and 10 pm (these are leitos). The price is US$6 for a regular bus and US$12 for a leito.

From Curitiba you can also get direct buses to Asunción (US$12), Buenos Aires (US$36) and Santiago (US$66).

Rail If you miss the train, there are many buses down to Paranaguá on the coast. The train to Paranaguá leaves from the big building behind the rodoviária. The regular train leaves at 7 am and the tourist train at 8.30 am. You can't always get a ticket for the next day's tourist train. For more information about the train ride see the Curitiba to Paranaguá section.

Getting Around

Airport Transport Alfonso Pena Airport is a 20 to 30 minute drive from the city. A taxi costs about US$5 and there are cheap public buses marked 'Aeroporto' that leave every hour or so from opposite the Hotel Presidente on Rua Westphalen. For other information call the airport at 282-1143.

CURITIBA TO PARANAGUÁ

Completed in 1880, the railroad from Curitiba to the port of Paranaguá is the most exciting in Brazil. Leaving from Curitiba at 900 metres, the train descends a steep mountainside to the coastal lowlands. The 110 km track goes through 13 tunnels and crosses 67 bridges. The view below is sublime and, depending on the cloud formations and tone of the sunlight, often surreal: threatening mountain canyons, tropical lowlands, vast blue Atlantic.

When you arrive in Paranaguá three hours later you've just witnessed the world change rapidly and radically: the climate is hot and muggy, often rainy in the winter; the land flat and low until it hits the wall of mountain; the vegetation short, lush and uniform; and the people sturdy, with strong Indian features and faces defined by years at sea.

Getting There & Away

A regular train (comum) and tourist train (automotriz) run daily from Curitiba to Paranaguá and then back to Curitiba. The comum leaves at 7 am and begins the return trip at 4.30 pm. The automotriz leaves at 8.30 am and starts back at 3.30 pm. The air-con automotriz is full of tourists, makes photo stops, and has a recorded description of the sights in Portuguese, English, Spanish and French. Both trains take about three hours each way.

Getting tickets can be tricky. Tickets for the comum train (US$1) go on sale at 6 am and tickets can be bought up to two days in advance for the automotriz (US$3), which often sells out the day before. This means, if you get in to Curitiba late and want to take the train the next day you should go to the station at about 6 am so that if there are no seats left for the automotriz you can get on the comum. Even if tickets for both trains are sold out don't take the bus, yet. Some of the local travel agencies seem to buy a few extra tickets for the automotriz in case they get customers for a tour, and if they don't they come to the train station to sell the extra tickets, so hang around and ask around – you may get lucky.

Tickets are sold at the train station behind the rodoviária. For information you can also call 234-8441 in Curitiba. They sometimes add another train during the busy season so it's often worth a call.

If you can't wait to get on the train, turn around and catch the bus. The trip isn't as stunning as by train but it's still pretty. Try to get a bus that goes along the Estrada da Graciosa. There are many buses daily, the trip only takes 1½ hours and costs less than US$1.

Morretes

Several buses and the train stop at Morretes on the route to Paranaguá. If you like the feel of the place just hop off (the spectacular part of the train ride is over). Founded in 1721 along the banks of the Rio

Nhundiapuara, there's nothing here but a tranquil, little colonial town in the midst of the lush coastal vegetation zone. It's a good place to relax, swim in the river and take some walks, off the beaten track.

Places to Stay & Eat There are three hotels in Morretes. The *Nhundiaquara* (tel 462-1228) is beside the river and has expensive and moderately priced rooms. It also has a good restaurant, which serves the local specialty, barreado, and the local cachaça (called pinga in Paraná). For something cheaper try the *Bom Jesus* (tel 462-1282).

Antonina
Population: 12,000

Antonina is 14 km east of Morretes and 75 km east of Curitiba on the Baía de Paranaguá. There are direct buses linking Antonina, Curitiba and Paranaguá. Similar to Morretes, Antonina is old and peaceful. It's first settlers panned for gold in the river. There's a fine church in the centre, the Igreja de NS do Pilar that was begun in 1715 and rebuilt in 1927. Its festival is held on 15 August.

The beaches along the bay are not very good, but it's sometimes possible to go floating down the Rio Nhundiaquara from Morretes. For information, ask at one of the hotels.

Places to Stay The *Christina Hotel* (tel 432-1163) and the *Monte Castelo* (tel 432-1163) are both reasonably priced. The *Regency Capela Antonina* is expensive.

PARANAGUÁ
Population: 105,000

The train ride isn't the only reason to go to Paranaguá. It's a colourful city, with an old section near the waterfront that has a feeling of tropical decadence. There are several churches, a very good museum and other colonial buildings that are worth a look. Although there has been some renovation, you still feel surrounded by decay. Fortunately, there aren't enough tourists around to destroy this air of authenticity. Paranaguá is also the place to get off for Ilha do Mel and the mediocre beaches of Paraná.

One of Brazil's major ports, Paranaguá is 30 km from the sea in the Baía de Paraná. Goods from a vast inland area encompassing the state of Paraná, and parts of São Paulo, Santa Catarina, Mato Grosso do Sul and Rio Grande do Sul are shipped from here.

The primary exports have been gold, mate, madeira and coffee, and are now corn, soy, cotton and vegetable oils.

Information
There's a tourist information office in front of the train station. They are helpful, friendly and often have maps as well as a list of hotels with prices. A few metres away there is a small telephone office for long distance calls. It's open from 8 am to 10 pm. If you need a travel agency, try Guairacá Turismo at Rua Presciliano Corrêa 129.

Museu de Arquelogia e Artes Popular
Paranaguá's old section is small enough for wandering without a set itinerary. Without much effort you can see most of Paranaguá's colonial buildings and churches, waterfront bars and various markets, but don't miss the Museu de Arquelogia e Artes Popular. Many Brazilian museums are disappointing; this one is not. Housed in a beautifully restored Jesuit school that was built from 1736 to 1755 (the Jesuits didn't get to use the school for long, as they were expelled from Brazil in 1759) the museum has many Indian artefacts, primitive and folk art, and some fascinating old tools and wooden machines, like an enormous basket weaver.

At the front desk the museum has notebooks with descriptions of the exhibits in English. The museum is at Rua 15 de Novembro 567 (near the waterfront), it's open Tuesday to Friday

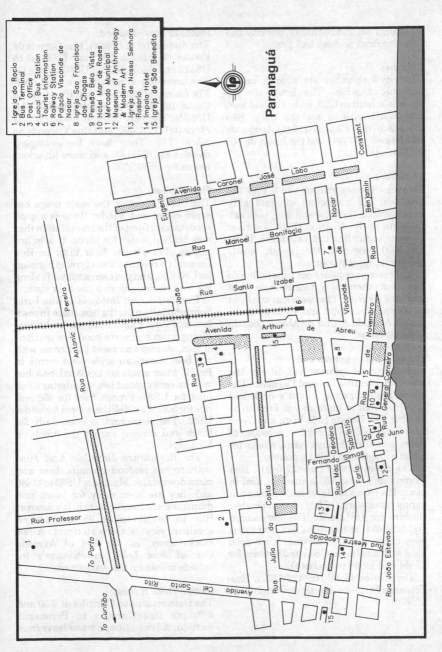

Paranaguá

1 Igreja do Rocio
2 Bus Terminal
3 Post Office
4 Local Bus Station
5 Tourist Information
6 Railway Station
7 Palácio Visconde de Nacar
8 Igreja São Francisco das Chagas
9 Pensão Bela Vista
10 Hotel Mar de Roses
11 Mercado Municipal
12 Museum of Anthropology & Modern Art
13 Igreja de Nossa Senhora Rosario
14 Impala Hotel
15 Igreja de São Benedito

Avenida Coronel José Lobo

Eugenio

Benjamin

Constant

Rua Manoel Bonifácio

Nacar

de

Rua Santa Izabel

João

Antonio Pereira

Avenida Arthur de Abreu

Visconde

Novembro

15

de

General Carneiro

Rua

10 9

Rua

11

29 de Juno

Fernando Mac Simas

Rua Deodoro

Sabrintia

Faria

Rua Costa

13

Rua Professor

2

To Porto

Rua Mestre Leopoldo

Julia

da

14

To Curitiba

Avenida Cel Santa Rita

Rua João Estevão

15

10 am to 5 pm and Saturday, Sunday and Monday from midday to 5 pm.

Churches

The city's churches are simple, unlike baroque churches. The Igreja de NS Rosario's, built in 1578, is the city's oldest. Also worth visiting are the Igreja São Francisco das Chagas (1741) Igreja de São Benedito (1784) and the Igreja de NS do Rocio (1813).

Waterfront

Down by the waterfront you'll find the new and old municipal markets and, depending on the time and day, both can be quite lively. Nearby, there is a river crossing to the Ilha dos Valadares. There are 8000 people on the island; mostly fisherfolk, mostly poor.

There are no regular boat trips to Ilha do Mel, but there is a tourist boat that explores the river. The boats leave daily at 10.30 am, midday, 2 and 4 pm from the end of Avenida Arthur de Abreu, the trip lasts 1½ hours.

Places to Stay – bottom end

The cheapest places are along the waterfront on Rua General Carneiro. The street has character, but it's dark and semi-deserted at night so you need to be careful. The *Pensão Bela Vista* and *Hotel Mar de Roses* (tel 422-6270), a couple of doors away, both have basic rooms for US$2 a single and US$3 a double.

The *Hotel Litoral* (tel 422-0491), Rua Correia de Freitas 66, is the best deal in town. It's rooms are large and open onto a sunny courtyard. They have singles/doubles for US$2/4.50. The *Paranaguá* (tel 422-6414) at Rua Julia de Costa 228 is very clean and disorganised. It's a good deal with singles for US$3 and doubles for US$4 and US$8 (with bath).

The *Karibe Hotel* (tel 422-1177), Rua Fernando Simas 86, has singles/doubles at US$7/9.

Places to Stay – top end

The *Auana* (tel 422-0984), Rua Correia de Freitas 66 has singles from US$4.50 to US$10 and doubles from US$6 to US$14. The lower-priced rooms are a good deal. The *Lider* (tel 422-0588) is at Rua Julia da Costa 169 and has singles/doubles for US$6/9. The best hotel in town, *Dantas Place* (tel 422-1555), is at Rua Visconde de Nácar 740. They have basic singles/ doubles at US$21/30 and more luxurious rooms for US$25/33.

Places to Eat

The *Cafe Itiberê* on the main praça has super coffee and nearby there is a good suco stand in front of the train station that uses bottled water for sucos. It also has pasties. The *Pensão Bela Vista* on Rua General Carheiro serves a typical big meal for US$2.50, and you can eat outside along the waterfront, enjoying the bela vista.

The *Restaurant Bobby* is at Rua Faria Sobrinho 750 and is the best place in town for seafood. They have a traditional dining room and serve good size portions of fish, shrimp and meat that come with the best American style condiments in Brazil. Most meals are US$3 to US$5, but you can easily spend less by ordering a fish fillet for US$1, French fries for 65c and rice for 30c. It's a delicious meal for under US$2. The restaurant is open daily for lunch and dinner, except for lunch on Mondays.

The *Restaurant Danúbio Azul Panorâmico* has seafood upstairs, beer and pizza downstairs. Meals are US$3 to US$6 and they are open daily for lunch and dinner, except Sunday lunch. It's down at Rua 15 de Novembro 95 and has an excellent view of the waterfront. A few blocks away, at the end of Avenida Coronel José Lobo, is *Palhano's* for outside drinks on the waterfront.

Getting There & Away

The train returns to Curitiba at 3.30 and 4.30 pm (see Curitiba to Paranaguá section). All out-of-town buses leave from

Top: Iguaçu Falls, Paraná (SP)
Bottom: Iguaçu Falls, Paraná (WH)

Top: Flower of Iguaçu, Paraná (SP)
Left: Iguaçu Falls, Paraná (WH)
Right: Walkway over Iguaçu Falls, Paraná (WH)

the new rodoviária along the waterfront. The first of many buses to Curitiba leaves at 6 am and the last at 10.30 pm. It costs 80c and takes an hour and 40 minutes. There are many buses to both Antonina and Morretos if you want to stop off on the way to Curitiba (1½ hours to Antonina).

If you're going south, eight buses go to Guaratuba daily, where you can get another bus to Joinville (last one at 5.30 pm). The first bus to Guaratuba leaves at 6.30 am and the last at 11 pm. You can also return to Curitiba for buses south.

To go to the beaches catch the 'Praia' circular at the new rodoviária. There are 15 daily buses that drive 30 km to the coast at Praia de Leste and then go north along the coast past Ipanema, Shangri-lá and finally Pontal do Sul (for Ilha do Mel). The first bus leaves at 5.50 am and the last returns from Pontal do Sul at 8.15 pm. It's 1½ hours to Pontal do Sul.

PARANÁ BEACHES

Descending the Serra do Mar from Curitiba you get a good view of the Paraná coast. The broad beach runs uninterrupted from Pontal do Sul to Caiobá. With the notable exception of Ilha do Mel, these are unspectacular beaches, hot and humid in the summer and too cold in the winter. There's plenty of camping and seafood barracas and each town has a few hotels. Unfortunately condominium blight is on the rise.

Praia de Leste

This is a small, unattractive town with a couple of hotels and the closest beach to Paranaguá, a bit more than 30 minutes away. The beach is open and windy and there's some surfing but the waves are not rough. Fernando and Nilton are a couple of friendly characters at the *Iraja* restaurant (facing the ocean) where it's better to drink than eat.

You can check your luggage in at the rodoviária (25c) if you want to go for a swim. This is where you get buses south to Guaratuba. These get very crowded on summer weekends so get there early.

Pontal do Sul

This is the end of the line and where you get off for Ilha do Mel. The bus stops three km from the canal where boats leave for Ilha do Mel. In between are summer homes and lots of open unused beach. If you get stuck, there is an unattractive pensão where the bus stops. They have rooms for US$2 to US$3. Bargaining may be useful.

ILHA DO MEL

The Ilha do Mel is an oddly shaped island at the mouth of the Baía de Paranaguá that wasn't discovered by the Portuguese until the 18th century. To secure the bay and its safe harbours from French and Spanish incursions old King Dom José I ordered a fort built in 1767. Since then not too much has happened. The few people on the island were ordered out during WW II in the name of national defence and most significantly the island is now part of the *patrimônio nacional*, which has prevented it from being turned into more cheesecake for the rich.

The island is popular in the summer because of its excellent beaches, scenic walks and relative isolation. Its undoing might be that it is becoming too popular, however, Ilha do Mel is administered by the ITCF (Instituto de Terras e Cartografia Florestal) which intends to preserve the island more or less as is. There is no electricity or freshwater on the island, and only a few barracas, campgrounds and fishermen's houses (many rent rooms).

From January to Carnival the island is very popular with a young crowd, but there is still a lot of beach and there always seems to be room for an extra hammock. If you're travelling up or down the coast it's crazy not to visit the island, at least for a day. Many people end up staying much longer.

Information & Orientation

The island has two parts, connected by the beach at Nova Brasília. The bigger part is an ecological station, thick with vegetation and little visited, except for Praia da Fortaleza. The smaller part has the main village on the island, Praia dos Encantados, where the boat drops you off. Nearby on the ocean side are the best beaches – Praia de Fora, Praia do Miguel and Praia Grande. All are reached by a trail that traverses the beaches, coves and steep hills that divide them. The bay side is muddy and covered with vegetation.

The entire island can be walked in eight hours, but the best walking by far is along the ocean side (east) from the southern tip of the island up to Praia da Fortaleza. Bichos de pé are prevalent on the island so keep something on your feet when you're off the beach.

Festivals

Ilha do Mel goes crazy at Carnival. Estimates for last year's attendance were 5000 revellers and before it was over they had run out of food, beer and water.

Beaches & Other Attractions

The best beaches face the ocean toward the east. The furthest, Praia Grande (surfing), is less than a two hour walk from Praia dos Encantadas. The walking is excellent and, except for the interior jungle and the hundreds of sea urchins that cover the beach, is reminiscent of the coast of northern California.

Points of interest include the Grutas das Encantadas, small caves at the southern tip. The Fortaleza de NS dos Prazeres was built in 1769 to guard the bay at Praia de Fortaleza. The Farol das Conchas lighthouse stands at the island's easterly point.

It's possible to catch a boat to another part of the island where, talk has it, there are mermaids. Ask some of the old timers on the island.

Places to Stay

The island's only hotels, the pousadas Dona Quinota and Seu Egidio, are at Praia da Fortaleza. They cost US$10 a person and are often booked on weekends (there's no phone for reservations). There are campgrounds, including a nice one at Praia Grande, with water. People also camp right on the beach, but watch out for the rising tide.

Most people find accommodation with the local fishermen, many of whom have extra rooms in their houses or barracas with hammocks that they rent. A barraca should cost about US$2 but prices fluctuate a lot and you have to bargain. Most of these places are at Praia das Encantadas but Brasília and Fortaleza also have places to rent and bars with food.

Places to Eat

Barracas with food and drink are at Encantadas, Brasília and Fortaleza. On Saturday nights there is music, forró (the great local dance) and when the beer is gone it's time for pinga, the local cachaça. At Encantadas, Lucia is the most popular cook and speaks the best German on the island. Her Bar Delirio doesn't open for coffee until about 10.30 am because she stays open late. Also ask for Dona Maria and Dona Ana, and they'll cook for you with advance notice.

Getting There & Away

Take the praia bus from Paranaguá, or if you are coming from Guaratuba transfer at Praia de Leste for the same bus. The bus stops three km from the canal where the boats leave for Ilha do Mel. There's usually a taxi, which charges monopoly prices, US$2 for the five minute ride, or you can walk or hitch.

If you decide to walk when you get off the bus, return 20 metres to the paved main road and turn right. Follow this road for a little more than a km until it veers right and approaches the sea. Then turn left on a sandy but well-travelled road for

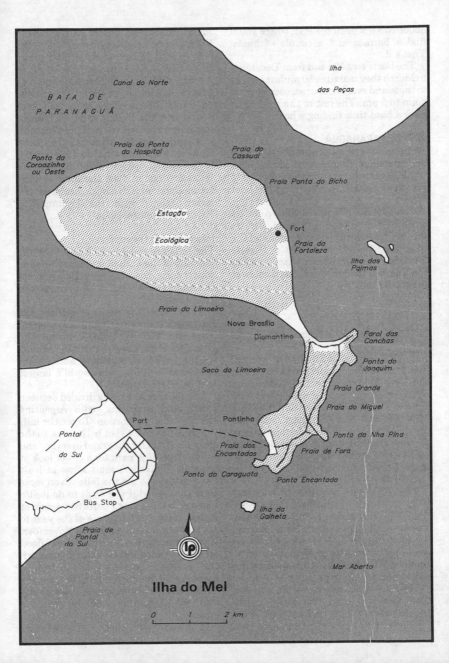

Canal do Norte

Ilha das Peças

BAÍA DE PARANAGUÁ

Praia da Ponta do Hospital

Praia do Cassual

Ponta da Coroazinha ou Oeste

Praia Ponta do Bicho

Estação

Ecológica

Fort

Praia da Fortaleza

Ilha das Palmas

Praia do Limoeiro

Nova Brasília

Diamantino

Farol das Conchas

Ponta do Joaquim

Saco do Limoeira

Praia Grande

Praia do Miguel

Port

Pontinha

Ponta da Nha Pina

Pontal do Sul

Praia dos Encantadas

Praia de Fora

Ponto do Caraguata

Ponta Encantada

Bus Stop

Ilha da Galheta

Praia de Pontal do Sul

Mar Aberto

Ilha do Mel

0   1   2 km

about two km until the end, where you'll find a barraca and a couple of boats. That's it.

The boats cost 50c and from December to March they make the 30 minute voyage to the island every hour or so, usually from 8 am to 5 pm. The rest of the year you'll have a hard time finding a boat.

BAÍA DE PARANAGUÁ

There are several other islands in the Baía de Paranaguá that can be visited, but you'll have to do some scraping around to get there as there is no regular boat service.

The Ilha dos Currais is known for its birdlife, the Ilha da Cotinga for its mysterious inscriptions and ruins and the Ilha dos Valadares for it's Paraná fandango – a hybrid dance that combines the Spanish fandango and the dances of the Carijó Indians.

Foz do Iguaçu

The Rio Iguaçu arises in the coastal mountains of Paraná and Santa Catarina, the Serra do Mar, at the modest elevation of 1300 metres. The river snakes west 600 km, pausing behind the Foz do Areia Cruz Machado and Salto Santiago dams and picking up a few dozen tributaries along the way. The Rio Iguaçu widens majestically and sweeps around a magnificent jungle stage before plunging and crashing in tiered falls.

The 275 falls are over three km wide and 80 metres high, which makes them wider than Victoria, higher than Niagara and more beautiful than either. Neither words nor photographs do it justice; it must be seen and heard. It's what the Romantic poets had in mind when they spoke of the awesome and sublime.

The falls were a holy burial place for the Tupi-Guarani and Paraguas tribes thousands of years before they were 'discovered' by white men. Spaniard Don Alvar Nuñes also known as Cabeza de Vaca (cow's head) happened upon the falls in 1541 in the course of his journey from Santa Catarina on the coast to Asunción. He was the first white man at Iguaçu, and he named the falls the Saltos de Santa Maria. This name fell into disuse and the Indian name of Iguaçu, meaning great waters in Tupi-Guarani, was readopted. No agreement has been made with spelling – in Brazil it's Iguaçu, in Argentina Iguazú and in Paraguay Iguassu – but in 1986 the international commission of UNESCO declared the region (along with the Pantanal) a Patrimonio Internacional.

Information & Orientation

The falls are roughly 20 km east of the junction of the Paraná and Iguaçu rivers, which form the tripartite Paraguayan, Brazilian and Argentine border (marked by obelisks).

The Ponte Internacional bridges the Rio Iguaçu connecting Brazil to Argentina. The Rio Paraná, which forms the Brazilian-Paraguayan border, is spanned by the Ponte da Amizade and 15 km upstream is Itaipu, the world's largest hydroelectric project.

The falls are unequally divided between Brazil and Argentina, with Argentina taking the larger portion. To see the falls properly you must visit both sides, to the Brazilian park for the grand overview and to the Argentine park for a closer look at the falls. Travellers must allow at least two full days to see the falls. Even more time is required if you want to do it at a leisurely pace or visit Puerto Stroessner or Itaipu dam. The best time of the year to see the falls is from August to November. If you come during the May to July flood season you may not be able to approach the swollen waters on the catwalks. Lighting for photography is best on the Brazilian side of the falls in the morning and the Argentine side in the late afternoon.

It's always wet at the falls. The area gets

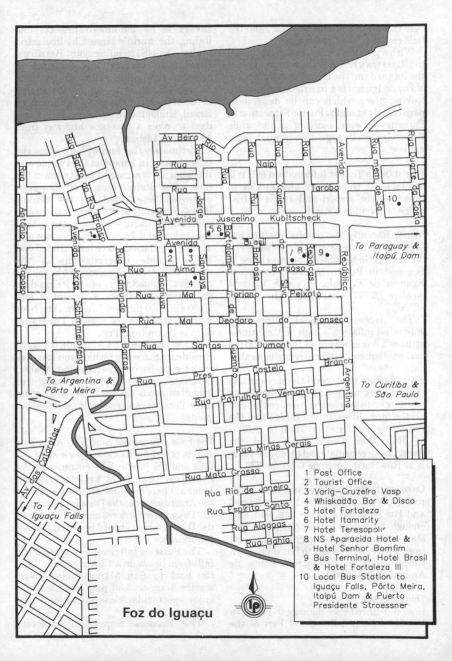

1 Post Office
2 Tourist Office
3 Varig–Cruzeiro Vasp
4 Whiskadão Bar & Disco
5 Hotel Fortaleza
6 Hotel Itamarity
7 Hotel Teresopolis
8 NS Aparacida Hotel &
  Hotel Senhor Bomfim
9 Bus Terminal, Hotel Brasil
  & Hotel Fortaleza III
10 Local Bus Station to
   Iguaçu Falls, Pôrto Meira,
   Itaipú Dam & Puerto
   Presidente Stroessner

Foz do Iguaçu

over two metres of rain per year, and the falls create a lot of moisture.

With a population increase from 35,000 to 150,000 as a result of the construction of the Itaipu dam, the Brazilian border town of Foz do Iguaçu is a frenzied, unfinished-looking place which can be dangerous, particularly at night. Puerto Stroessner in Paraguay is even more of a pit, while Puerto Iguazú in Argentina is much more mellow.

Tourist Office Tourist information in Foz is available at the airport and in Puerto Iguazú at the airport and at the tourist office at Avenida Victoria Aguirro 396

Money Recently the parallel market has been giving more favourable rates in Foz do Iguaçu. Go to Dick's Cambio House in Foz and in Puerto Iguazú to Argecam Agencia de Cambio, Avenida Victoria Aguirre 369/77 across from the tourist office.

The Argentine unit of currency is Australes. Inflation is high in Argentina – although not as severe as that in Brazil – and consequently the currency is weak.

Visas Visitors who spend the day outside of Brazil will not require visas, but those who intend to stay longer must go through all the formalities. In Foz do Iguaçu, the Argentine consulate (tel (0455) 74-2877) is at Rua Dom Pedro II 26 and the Paraguayan consulate (tel (0455) 73-1499) is at Rua Bartolomeu de Gusmão 777.

Crossing the Border Singer and Tigre buses run every hour between Puerto Iguazú and Foz do Iguaçu. Buses will wait long enough for you to get entrance and exit stamps, but not for baggage check. To get from Puerto Stroessner to Foz do Iguaçu, simply walk or bus across Ponte de Amizade (open until 2 am).

Things to See
How did Brazil ever manage to run up a US$110 billion dollar debt? Part of the

answer is by mammoth projects like Itaipu, the world's largest hydroelectric works. The US$25 billion joint Brazilian-Paraguayan venture was designed to generate 12.6 million kilowatts by 1989, enough electricity to supply the energy needs of much of Paraguay and southern Brazil. Enough concrete was used in this dam to pave a two-lane highway from Moscow to Lisbon.

Fortunately the dam will not effect the flow of water in Iguaçu as the Paraná and the Iguaçu rivers meet downstream of the falls. The Itaipu dam has, however, destroyed Sete Quedas – the world's largest waterfall with 30 times the water spilled by Iguaçu, – and created a 1400 square km lake. Local weather, plant and animal populations have been altered and the complete repercussions of the environmental changes will not be felt for decades. Guided tours of the Itaipu dam are given four times a day at 9 am, 10.30 am, 3.30 pm and 5.30 pm. The hour long tours are free of charge. The Itaipu dam is 19 km from Foz.

Across the Ponte da Amizade is Puerto Presidente Stroessner where you can play roulette or baccarat at Casino Acaraz, purchase up to US$150 of duty free imported goods (no great deals) or some nifty Paraguayan lace work and leather goods.

The Falls – Argentine Side The Argentine side is noted for its close-up views of the falls and the jungle. The entrance to the Argentine park is 18 km from Puerto Iguazú. There are three separate walks on the Argentine side: the Passeios Inferiores, the Passeios Superiores and the Garganta del Diablo which should be saved for last for dramatic effect.

The Passeios Inferiores is a view of the falls from below on a 1.5 km circuit. Take the boat to San Martin Island (boat service 8 am to 5.30 pm, US$1.25) and enjoy spectacular close up views of the falls.

The Passeios Superiores' concrete

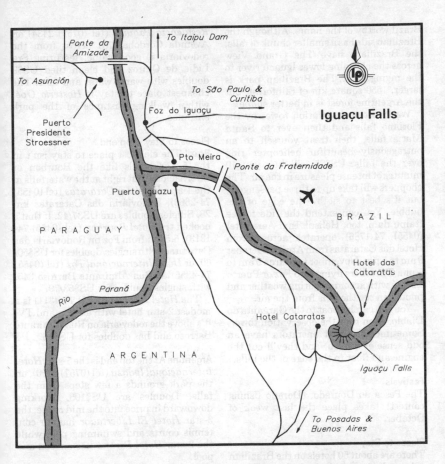

To Itaipu Dam

Ponte da Amizade

To Asunción

To São Paulo & Curitiba

Foz do Iguaçu

Iguaçu Falls

Puerto Presidente Stroessner

Pto Meira

Ponte da Fraternidade

Puerto Iguazu

BRAZIL

PARAGUAY

Rio Paraná

Hotel das Cataratas

Hotel Cataratas

ARGENTINA

Iguaçu Falls

To Posadas & Buenos Aires

catwalks behind the waterfalls used to go as far as Garganta del Diablo until floods a few years back swept them over the edge. The path goes only as far as the Salto Adán y Eva.

There's a dirt road running a few km from the park entrance to Puerto Canoas. From here you can either walk along the catwalks or take a hair-raising boat ride out to Garganta del Diablo (the Devil's Throat) where 13,000 cubic metre of water per second plunge 90 metres in 14 falls, arranged around a tight little pocket.

The view at the precipice is hypnotising. Visitors will be treated to a multi-sensory experience: roaring falls, huge rainbow arcs, drenching mist and in the distance parrots and hawks cruising over deep green jungle. Watch for the *vencejos* (great dusky swifts) which drop like rocks into the misty abyss, catch insects in mid-air, shoot back up and dart behind the falls to perch on the cliffs.

The Falls - Brazilian Side Iguaçu National Park is one of the few national parks in

Brazil worthy of the name. Although the Brazilian side has a smaller chunk of falls, the Brazilians have The Grand View across the churning lower Iguaçu river to the raging falls. The Brazilian park is larger, 1550 square km of rainforest, but the Argentine forest is in better shape.

Walk to the observation tower by the Floriano falls and then over to Santa Maria falls, then treat yourself to an outrageously beautiful helicopter ride over the falls. US$25 will buy you 10 minutes of intense pleasure in the air. The choppers will take up to three passengers, but it's best to sit by the edge of the bubble. You can extend the ride to see Itaipu dam, too. Helisul Taxi Aereo (tel (0455) 74-1786) operates across from Hotel das Cataratas from April to October 9 am to 5 pm, November to March 9 am to 7 pm. Travellers flying into Foz or Puerto Iguazú with accommodating weather and pilots can see the falls from the air.

You can catch a boat to the Garganta do Diablo, from near the observation tower. Sometimes the boat operators have an odd sense of humour and they'll cut the engine and float to the edge of the falls.

Festivals
The Pesca ao Dourado, (Dorado fishing contest) takes place the last week of October.

Places to Stay
There are about 50 hotels on the Brazilian side and 11 more in and about Puerto Iguazú on the Argentine side.

Places to Stay – bottom end
Brazil The rodoviária area has some real cheapies and there are three campgrounds on the Brazilian side. *Camping Club do Brasil* (tel (0455) 74-1013) is the closest to the falls at Rodoviária das Cataratas (eight km from Foz).

Argentina The *Hotel La Cabaña* (tel (0757) 2564) at Avenida Tres Fronteras 434 has US$12 doubles, air-con and pool.

Residencia Paquita (tel (0757) 2434) on Avenida Cordoba, 731 across from the rodoviária is good value, featuring Sra Lidia de Quiroz and clean tiled US$9 doubles with warm water and fans. The cheapest place to stay is *Hostería Opé*, within walking distance of the park entrance.

Places to Stay – top end
Brazil The classiest place to stay isn't in the 5-star hotels like the Bourbon or Internacional but right at the waterfalls in the 4-star *Hotel das Cataratas* (tel (0455) 74-2666), Rodoviária das Cataratas km 28. Singles/doubles are US37/42. If that's booked try *Hotel Bourbon* (tel (0455) 74-1313), 6.5 km from Foz on Rodoviária das Cataratas, with singles/doubles for US$50/60, or *Hotel Internacional Foz* (tel (0455) 74-4855) at Rua Almirante Barroso 345, with singles/doubles for US$63/79.

The *Hotel Luz* (tel (0455) 74-4311) is a modest 2-star hotel with air-con and TV. It's above the rodoviária on Rua Almirante Barroso and has doubles for US$16.

Argentina At the top end is the 5-star *Hotel Internacional Iguazú* (tel (0757) 2790), on the park grounds a few steps from the falls. Doubles are US$105. Working downward in price into the mid range, the 3-star *Hotel El Libertador* has air-con, tennis courts and swimming pool while the 2-star *Hotel Paraná* has air-con and pool.

Places to Eat
Brazil In Foz do Iguaçu, *Restaurante Pei-Kin*, Rua Jorge Samways 765 near the San Rafael Hotel, serves fair Chinese food for about US$3.50.

Argentina In Puerto Iguazú *Restaurant-Parilla La Estancia* at the bus station serves good and cheap *ravioli al tuco* (vegetable ravioli with tomato sauce) for little more than US$1. The restaurant at the *Hotel Libertador* is also good. Dishes are about US$2.

Green leaf tree frog

Jungle Tour

There's more to the 550 square km Argentine park than just waterfalls. If you intend to do a jungle tour, do it on the Argentine side, they do a better job of protecting their park lands than the Brazilians. For an exceptional tour (in Spanish) ask for Juan Manuel Correa of Guembe Tours, Avenida Victoria Aguirre 481, Puerto Iguazú. Arrange the tour (US$6.50 per person) the evening before, pick up a wildlife list and study it. Try to arrive in the park before 7 am (when the entrance fee, about US$1 is waived) or in the late afternoon, the best time to spot birds and wildlife.

Juan – biologist/park-ranger/actor – is very friendly and extremely enthusiastic about his work. Go in a small nature-loving group and bring binoculars and tape recorder (to record the sounds of the jungle). You'll see fantastic butterflies (they congregate about pools of urine and on sweaty handrails to sip salts), parrots, antshrikes, parakeets, woodpeckers, hummingbirds, lizards, three cm long ants, beautifully coloured spiders and all sorts of orchids, lianas and vines.

I saw two species of toucan, but there are four species in the park. Juan explained that their long beaks are deceptive, the beak is so light and spongy that the birds are back heavy and clumsy flyers. The toucans eat fruit, eggs, chicks and leaves of the amba (cecropia adenopus) tree. According to Juan, amba leaves are used to make a medicinal tea which is good for coughs.

There are other creatures in the park including monkeys, deer, sloth, anteaters, racoons, jaguar, tapir, cayman and armadillo, but as is true of other tropical rainforests, large animals are not very abundant and they tend to be nocturnal. You can see them on display at the Natural History Museum at the Argentine park headquarters.

The foliage is lush and lovely. There are 2000 species of plants stacked in six different layers from forest floor grasses, ferns and bushes to low, middle and high tree canopies. The jungle cover in addition to harbouring a wide variety of animals and insects protects the soil from erosion, maintains humidity and moderates temperatures. Tarzan vines, lianas and epiphytes connect and smear the distinction between the forest levels.

Getting There & Away

Air There are frequent flights from Foz do Iguaçu to Asunción, Buenos Aires, Rio and São Paulo. Addresses are Vasp (tel (0455) 74-2999) at Avenida Brasil 845; Transbrasil (tel (0455) 74-3671) at Avenida Brasil 225 and Varig/Cruzeiro (tel (0455) 74-3344) at Avenida Brasil 821.

Aerolineas Argentinas and Austral have daily flights to Buenos Aires for US$80.

Bus From Foz do Iguaçu to Curitiba is 635 km and 12 hours. There are six daily buses on BR-277. There are also buses to São Paulo and Rio.

There are several buses a day from Puerto Stroessner to Asunción (320 km, seven hours).

There are three buses a day from Puerto Iguazú to Buenos Aires (20 hours, US$35). An alternative is to take one of 17 daily buses down Ruta 12 to Posadas (316 km, six hours, US$6), then from Posadas the train to Buenos Aires (1060 km, 20 hours).

Getting Around

The Brazilian airport is 16 km from Foz. The Argentine falls are seven km from the Argentine airport and 18 km from Puerto Iguazú. The taxi fare between airport and city or airport and park is US$10. The bus is 80c.

Santa Catarina & Rio Grande do Sul

Santa Catarina

The Germans and Italians who settled in Santa Catarina in the 19th century, unlike most immigrants throughout the rest of Brazil, owned their own small family-run farms. This European model of land use has produced a far more egalitarian distribution of wealth than in most of Brazil – 83% of the farmland is owned by farmers with less than 1000 hectares.

Many of the state's four million people still own their own rich farmland which, combined with some healthy small scale industry, has created one of Brazil's most prosperous states. This relative affluence, the very visible German presence and the efficient services give the state more the feel of Europe than Brazil, at least in the highlands which are green and pastoral. If Santa Catarina reminds one of Switzerland, it's less because of geography and more because of the sedate middle class consumerism. Most travellers don't come to Santa Catarina to visit a foreign culture – they come for the beaches.

There's no doubt that the beaches are beautiful; they're wide and open with Caribbean-like coves and bays, clear and clean emerald-blue water and views of offshore islands. The water is very warm during the summer months and there are plenty of calm protected beaches for swimming as well as some of Brazil's better surfing spots. The current can be very dangerous in places so be careful.

While there are still fishing villages along the coast, you don't find the kind of fishing villages that predominate in the Northeast. The setting is less exotic and less tropical, the villagers less secluded and less friendly, the escape from western civilisation less complete.

More essential, many of Santa Catarina's beaches have become 'in' vacation spots for well-to-do Paulistas, Curitibanos and Argentines, so during January and February the beaches and hotels are jammed. Several little Copacabanas have sprouted up in beach towns like Camboriú. This growth is changing the face of Santa catarina's coastline at an unbelievable pace. It can be an ugly sight.

Santa Catarina's climate is nice and hot during the Brazilian summer. In the winter the wind along the coast picks up considerably, although it never gets too cold. The best months to go, unless you like the crowds, are March/April and November/December.

Compared to other parts of Brazil this is a polite and proper place, where children are subdued and well mannered. You may be excluded from a restaurant because your jeans are worn, you probably will be excluded from a bar without a shirt and you must wear bermuda short length or long trousers on inter-city buses – no swim suits. What's so unusual about this Brazilian state is not that they have these rules, but that they are respected and enforced.

JOINVILLE
Population 230,000

Imagine a city where blond-haired people stroll through town on clean, well-lit, heavily-policed streets, perusing Bavarian-facaded, neon-named shops full of modern western appliances, with well-manicured lawns, flower festivals and a central park with children playing at night. A city that is polite, efficient and pleasant. Now here's the hard part: imagine this city in Brazil.

Santa Catarina's second largest city, Joinville is described in it's own tourist brochure as 'an industrial city'. The industry, however, is out of the pleasant inner city, which is quite habitable and

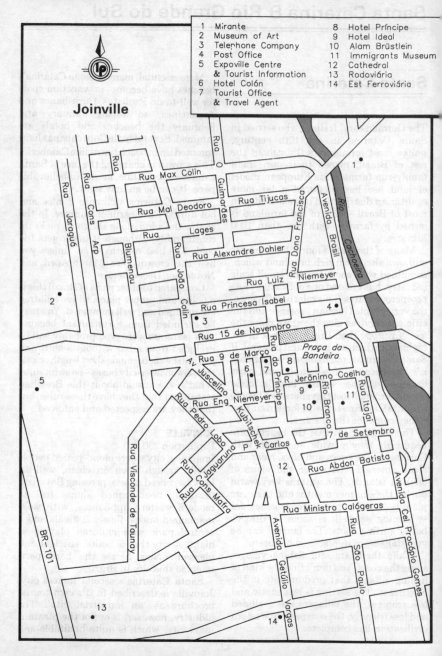

1	Mirante	8	Hotel Príncipe
2	Museum of Art	9	Hotel Ideal
3	Telephone Company	10	Alam Brüstlein
4	Post Office	11	Immigrants Museum
5	Expoville Centre	12	Cathedral
	& Tourist Information	13	Rodoviária
6	Hotel Colón	14	Est Ferroviária
7	Tourist Office		
	& Travel Agent		

Joinville

seems like the kind of place to raise a family. For the traveller, Joinville is relaxed, if unexciting.

Information & Orientation
Joinville (pronounced joyvilee) is on the BR-101, 180 km north of Florianópolis and 123 km south of Curitiba. The road is good and the views are beautiful around Joinville, particularly where the highway traverses the lush coastal mountains. The drive down to the coast at Guaratuba to the north is stunning.

Tourist Office There is a tourist office in front of the Hotel Colón. It's open Monday to Saturday 8 am to 6 pm. They have mediocre maps and silly brochures. There is a travel agency behind the office.

The city is small and most stores and services are concentrated on and around Rua 15 de Novembro and Rua Princesa Isabel. The telephone company and post office are on Princesa Isabel.

Things to See
If you're in town on the second Saturday of the month check out the artisan fair. If you're not, there are a couple of museums. The best is the Museu de Arte de Joinville at Rua 15 de Novembro 1400. It's open Tuesday to Sunday from 9 am to midday and 2 to 6 pm.

Places to Stay - bottom end
The *Hotel Príncipe* (tel 22-8555), Rua Jerônimo Coelho 27, has quartos for US$3.50, singles for US$5 and doubles for US$8. It's clean and the staff are very friendly. It tends to fill up early.

Down the block, the *Hotel Ideal* is very similar. If these are full, try the *Mattes* at Rua 15 de Novembro 811.

Places to Stay - top end
Colón Palace Hotel (tel 22-6188), facing Praça Nereu Ramos, has a pool and great breakfast (try the chocolate milk). Singles/doubles start at US$11/12, more luxurious rooms are US$19/22.

For a little more money, the *Anthurium Palace* (tel 22-6299), Rua São Jose 226 has colonial charm and a sauna, but no pool. Singles/doubles start at US$12/14 with better rooms for US$22/25. The *Tannenhof* (tel 22-8011) at Rua Visconde de Taunay 340 is Joinville's best and most expensive hotel.

Places to Eat
Joinville boasts good German food and is a major chocolate producer. The *Bierkeller* at Rua 15 de Novembro 497 has the city's best value in German food, lots of pork and a feijoada for lunch on Saturdays. Prices are reasonable, about US$3 to US$5 a meal.

The *Pinguim*, is right in the centre off Praça da Bandeira. It's a popular, late-night churrascaria and beer hall and is a good place to meet young people if you don't mind a little noise. Meals cost about US$4.

For quieter dining, the restaurant at the *Hotel Colón* is a good change of pace; it's reasonably priced and has good meat dishes. *Mama Mia*, Rua Rio Branco 193, is recommended. They offer Italian dinners for under US$4. On the same street, *Pinheiro* is more expensive but has the city's best fish.

Getting There & Away
Air There are regular flights from Joinville to Curitiba, Florianópolis, Rio and São Paulo.

Bus It's a 2½ hour bus ride to Curitiba. The first bus, of many that leave daily, departs from Joinville at 5.30 am and the last at 8.25 pm. Several buses leave around 9 pm for São Paulo. The nine hour trip costs US$5. There's a bus at 2.35 and 8.30 pm direct to Rio. The 15-hour journey costs US$11.

Going south the BR-101 runs along the coast and there are many buses serving this route. Most stop at any or all the small beach towns, so it's easy to hop on a bus and get off at whichever beach looks good. If you're going to a set destination, like Florianópolis, the express buses do not stop on the way and are much faster.

Florianópolis is a three-hour bus ride and the express costs US$2.50. The first bus leaves Joinville at 6.30 am and the last at 11.30 pm. Buses to Porto Alegre leave at 1.45 and 7.30 pm, take nine hours and cost US$5. Buses to Blumenau take two hours and are very frequent. There's also a daily 5.05 am bus to Foz do Iguaçu, Puerto Stroessner and Asunción. To Foz, the trip takes 10 hours and costs US$7.

The closest beaches are due east on the Ilha de São Francisco. Many buses make the 1¼ hour, 75c trek, especially on weekends when many Joinvilleians head to these beaches. The first bus leaves at 6.30 am and the last at 8.45 pm. There's also a daily 8 am train that goes down to São Francisco do Sul. It returns at midday.

To get to the coast of Paraná and the city of Paranaguá, you have to catch the bus to Guaratuba. Buses leave at 7.15, 9.30, 10.45 am, 2.30, 3 and 5.30 pm. The trip takes 1½ hours.

Getting Around
The airport is 12 km from the city and the rodoviária is two km out. There's no need to take a cab to the rodoviária, there is a bus stop on the side of the terminal with city buses leaving every 20 minutes or so for central Praça de Bandeira.

JOINVILLE TO FLORIANÓPOLIS
There are many beautiful beaches along the coast but it's being developed rapidly and without controls. In general, the more famous a beach the more developed and ugly. Balneário Camboriú, the area's best-known beach town, is the best example.

São Francisco do Sul
Population: 13,500
This historic city's island setting was discovered way back in 1504 by the Frenchman, Binot Paulmier de Goneville,

but the city itself wasn't settled until the middle of the next century. The city became the port of entry for the German immigrants settling the land around Joinville.

The beaches on the Ilha de São Francisco are good but are some of the most crowded because of their proximity to Joinville and even Curitiba. There is also a lot of surfing. On the up side, there are several cheap hotels in the city and a variety of beaches accessible by local buses.

Both Prainha and Praia Grande to the south have big waves and are popular surfing beaches. Swimming is not safe. Closer to the city, Praia de Ubatuba and Praia de Enseada are pretty and safe for swimming, but developed and often crowded. For another option, ask in town about boats leaving from Capitania dos Portos to the Ilha da Paz.

Places to Stay Praia de Enseada has several hotels and you can catch a bus directly to Joinville. The *Enseada* (tel 42-2122), Avenida Atlântica 1074 is on the beach and reasonably priced. The *Turismar* (tel 42-2060), Avenida Atlântica 1923, is similar with singles/doubles for US$8.50/ 12. In town the *Kontiki* (tel 44-0232), at Rua Camacho 33 across from the waterfront, is reasonable.

Barra Velha
Population: 7000
Driving south from Joinville on BR-101 this is the first point where the road meets the sea. Four km to the south of town, Praia do Grant is popular with the younger set. There are a few hotels and restaurants in town.

Picarras
Population: 3500
Picarras, 14 km to the south of Barra Velha, has a good big beach and several small islands which can be visited. The town is lively in the summer but the campgrounds are often full then.

Places to Stay Apart from the three campgrounds, there are barracas and several hotels, including the cheaper *Real* and the *Itacurumbi*. Ask about houses to rent.

Penha
Population: 7,500
Penha is a big fishing town, so it's not completely overrun by tourism. Only six km from Picarras, the ocean is calm at the city beaches Armação and Prainha. There are simple hotels at these beaches and some very good seafood. The beaches south of these two are less crowded. From Praia da Armação boats leave every half hour or so to the nearby islands of Itacolomi and Feia.

Itajaí
Population: 80,000
At the turn-off to Blumenau, Itajaí is an important port for the Itajaí Valley. There's not much of interest to the tourist and the best beaches are out of town. There are a couple of hotels across from the rodoviária and several more on the main road going out of town to Camboriú. There are plenty of buses coming and going from Itajaí.

Balneário Camboriú
Population: 22,000
This little Copacabana, with sharp hills dropping into the sea, nightclubs with 'professional mulattos' and an ocean boulevard named Avenida Atlântica, is clearly out of control. In summer the population increases 10 fold.

This is Santa Catarina's most expensive town, and here you can meet well-heeled Argentines, Paraguayans and Paulistas who spend their summers in the ugliest beach-hugging high-rise buildings you can imagine. The spoiling of this beachfront is surely a crime against nature.

Outside the city, there is a Museu Arqueológico e Oceanográfico that's worth visiting and a nude beach (a rarity in Brazil), Praia do Pinho, 14 km south of the city.

Porto Belo
Population: 4500
The beaches around Porto Belo are the last good continental beaches before Ilha de Santa Catarina. The Praias Bombas and Bombinhas, three km from town by dirt road, are the prettiest beaches around. For a great walk head out to Ponta do Lobo, 12 km from Bombinhas. From Rua do Comércio in Porto Belo you can catch a boat to the Ilhas de Arvorerdo e João da Cunha. Both islands have fine beaches.

Places to Stay Both Praia Bombas and Praia Bombinhas have barracas and camping and are relatively uncrowded. The *Hotel Bomar* (tel 6-9286), a modest establishment, is at Praia de Bombas along with several other reasonable hotels. There are many campgrounds along the beaches.

BLUMENAU
Population: 150,000
Blumenau is 60 km inland from Itajaí, 139 km from Florianópolis and 130 km from Joinville. Nestled in the Vale do Itajaí on the Rio Itajaí, Blumenau and environs were settled largely by German immigrants in the second half of the 19th century. The area is serene, but the city itself wears its German culture way too loud. Everything is Germanicised with the commercial, but not creative, flare of Walt Disney. The city attracts tourists (mostly from not too far away) but isn't particularly recommended.

Information
The telephone company is on Rua Uruguai near the bridge. The post office is on Rua Pe Jacobs.

Places to Stay & Eat
Hotels in Blumenau are very clean and efficiently run compared to those in the

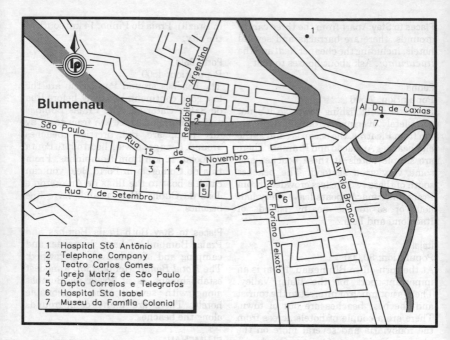

1 Hospital Stô Antônio
2 Telephone Company
3 Teatro Carlos Gomes
4 Igreja Matriz de São Paulo
5 Depto Correios e Telegrafos
6 Hospital Sta Isabel
7 Museu da Família Colonial

rest of Brazil, or in any other country for that matter. The *Herman* (tel 22-4370), Rua Floriano Peixoto 213, has singles starting at US$4. The *Central* (tel 22-0570), Rua 7 de Setembro 1036, has singles/doubles for US$4/6.50.

Moving up the price scale, *Hotel Rex* (tel 22-5877) is conveniently located at Rua 7 de Setembro 640 and has all the amenities and singles/doubles for US$19/28. At number 954 on the same street the *Hotel Gloria* (tel 22-1988) has an excellent restaurant and singles/doubles for US$14/ 18. Nearby, the *Hotel Plaza Hering* (tel 22-1277) is Blumenau's fanciest sleepery with singles/doubles for US$46/52. For reservations from Rio call toll free (011) 800-8618.

Getting Around

The rodoviária is at Rua 2 de Setembro 1222. Take the 'Cidade-Jardim' bus from the city or a taxi for US$3.

FLORIANÓPOLIS

Florianópolis, the state capital, fans out in both directions from the spot where the coast and the large Ilha de Santa Catarina almost connect. The central section is on the island facing the Baía Sul. Over the hill, on the north shore, there is a long row of luxury high-rises, none of which looks more than a couple of years old, and modern restaurants to feed their occupants. The mainland part of the city has the industry. Much of the city's shoreline appears barren due to undeveloped landfill.

The city is modern, with some large structures like the new rodoviária and many works in progress. The island side of the city, where you'll probably spend all your time, has a small city feel. It's easy to get around by foot and there are regular public buses to the island's beautiful beaches.

Information & Orientation

Tourist Office There are tourist desks at the rodoviária and airport which are good for maps, if nothing else. The small white building at the top of Praça 15 de Novembro is a more substantial tourist office, but isn't always open, as is the main state tourist office (tel 44-5822) which is on the mainland side of the city at Rua 14 de Julho, right before the bridge.

Other Offices The phone company is two blocks up the hill from Praça 15. It's open from 8 am to 11 pm Monday to Friday and closes an hour earlier Saturdays, Sundays and holidays. The post office faces Praça 15. The airlines all have offices downtown: Varig/Cruzeiro (tel 22-2811) at Rua Felipe Schmidt 34, Transbrasil (tel 22-0177) at Praça Pereira Oliveira 16 and Vasp (tel 22-1122) at Rua Osmar Cunha 15.

Money Several travel agents exchange money at rates somewhat lower than in Rio. The best place for travellers' cheques is Brusatur at the Ceisa Centre building. Ilha Tur, which also runs bus tours, is a good bet at Rua Felipe Schmidt 27, also try Bretur down the block.

Places to Stay

Hotels in Florianópolis are fairly expensive and fill-up during the summer. Most of the hotels, especially at the bottom end, are in the central district. Out on the island's beaches there are few budget hotels, although it's possible to economise by renting a house or apartment with a group of people. There's lots of camping, which is the cheapest way to go.

Places to Stay – bottom end

All the bottom end hotels are in the centre of town. The *Hotel Sumaré*, Rua Felipe Schmidt 53 is quite good, but often full. They have quartos for US$3/6 a single/double, and a few apartamentos with baths. The place is well-run, the rooms are safe and clean, and there's hot water in the showers.

In the same price range, the *Hotel Colonial* at Rua Mafra 45 is a bit more seedy, but the rooms have a certain flare and the communal showers are hot. Another good bet is the *Felippe* which is often full. It's a couple of blocks past Praça 15 on Rua João Pinto. Other nearby possibilities include: *Hotel Majestic, Hotel Levi* and the *Hotel Cruzeiro*.

For super-cheap lodging the *Dormitório Estrela* on Rua Mafra, near the corner of Rua Bento Gonçalves, is clean. The nearby *Dormitório Tropical* is less attractive.

Places to Stay – middle

The best deal in town is the *Residential Tur Hotel* (tel 23-1388) at Rua dos Ilheus 10, Centro. They have spacious single/double/triple apartments for US$23 with all the usual hotel amenities, as well as a kitchen and laundry room. It's top end quality, without the frills. There is a discount for long stays.

Much less expensive is the *Veleiros Hotel* (tel 23-1329), near the yacht club at Rua Silva Jardim 254. They have a promotional offer of US$8/12 a single/double. A 15 minute walk from the city centre, the hotel has a great view of the bay.

At Avenida Hercilio Luz 66 and 90 respectively, the *Hotel Ivoram* (tel 22-5388) and the *Oscar Palace* (tel 22-0099) are reasonable value. The *Ivoram* has singles/doubles for US$20 or US$27 for more luxurious rooms. Similar accommodation at the *Oscar Palace* costs about US$4 less.

The *Hotel Valerim Center* (tel 22-3280) at Rua Felipe Schmidt 74 has rip-off quartos for US$7 a single, but the apartments are reasonable deals at US$12/19 a single/double.

Places to Stay – top end

The *Florianópolis Palace* (tel 22-9633), Rua Artista Bittencourt 2, Centro, is the five-star hotel in town, and its singles/doubles cost US$72/83. It has everything

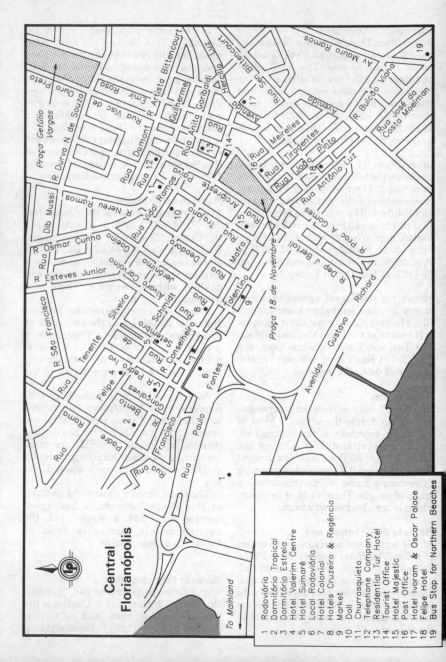

Central Florianópolis

1. Rodoviária
2. Dormitório Tropical
3. Dormitório Estrela
4. Hotel Valerim Centre
5. Hotel Sumaré
6. Local Rodoviária
7. Hotel Colonial
8. Hotels Cruzeiro & Regência
9. Market
10. Doll
11. Churrasquieto
12. Telephone Company
13. Residential Tur Hotel
14. Tourist Office
15. Hotel Majestic
16. Post Office
17. Hotel Ivoram & Oscar Palace
18. Felipe Hotel
19. Bus Stop for Northern Beaches

To Mainland

you'd expect as well as a private beach out at Canasvieiras.

Another central palace is the *Faial Palace* (tel 23-2766), Rua Felipe Schmidt 87. It's a bit less expensive with singles/doubles starting at US$37/43. The *Center Plaza* (tel 22-0188) is also in the central district, at Rua Felipe Schmidt 9. It has singles/doubles starting at US$22/31.

Places to Eat

Macarronada Italiana is a great splurge for some of Brazil's best pasta and formal service. Open daily for lunch and dinner, there's live music Monday to Wednesday at dinner. It's on the Baía Norte at Avenida Rubens de Arruda Ramos 196. Also somewhat pricey, the *Lindacap* (tel 22-0558), Rua Felipe Schmidt 178, Centro and *Martim-Pescador* at Beco do Surfista, about 20 km from the city, are both open for lunch and dinner and are recommended. Martim-Pescador serves seafood, including the island's excellent shrimps. Out at Beira Lagoa, *Ilhabela* has large seafood dishes for about US$4.

There are plenty of cheap lanchonetes in town, many of which are health food oriented – try *Doll-Produtos Natural*. At the corner of Avenida Ramos and Rua Trajano there are three eateries popular with the younger crowd. *DeGrau* has good pizza for US$2 and the crepe place has crepes for only US$1. The third restaurant has local music nightly.

Getting There & Away

Air There are daily direct flights to São Paulo and Porto Alegre, as well as connections to most other cities. Flights to Rio make at least one stop. Watch out for multiple-stop flights, with multiple plane changes.

Bus Costs and times for long-distance buses are: Porto Alegre US$3 and seven hours, Curitiba US$3 and six hours, São Paulo US$6 and 12 hours, Rio US$10 and 18 hours, Foz do Iguaçu US$8 and 16 hours, Buenos Aires US$35 and 27 hours.

There are frequent buses up and down the coast as well as inland to Blumenau, Brusque and Lajes. Travel along BR-101, the coastal highway, is considerably quicker by direct bus. Local indirect buses can be easily flagged down along the highway.

Getting Around

The airport is 12 km south of the city. A cab costs US$7 to US$9. Buses marked 'Aeroporto' shuttle regularly to the airport until 10 pm and leave from centro's first platform. It's a 30 minute ride by bus.

ILHA DE SANTA CATARINA

The east coast beaches are the most beautiful, with the biggest waves and the greatest expanses of empty beach. They are also the most popular for day trips and most do not have hotels. The north coast beaches have calm bay-like water and resorts, with many apartment-hotels and restaurants. The west coast, facing the mainland, has great views and a quiet Mediterranean feel. The beaches here are small and unspectacular.

East Coast

Moving from north to south, Praia dos Ingleses, 34 km from the city, is starting to be developed and could change quickly. The beach is big and beautiful and there are a few hotels and restaurants – nothing cheap. *Sol & Mar* has doubles for US$17.

Praia do Santinho has only a couple of beach houses and barracas and one of the island's most beautiful beaches. The island's longest beach, Praia do Moçambique or Praia Grande is 14 km long and undeveloped. It's hidden by a pine forest from the dirt road that runs a couple of km inland from it. The camping here is good.

Barra da Lagoa, a big curved beach at the end of Praia do Moçambique, is a short bus trip from Florianópolis. It still has many native fishermen. There are more hotels and restaurants here than

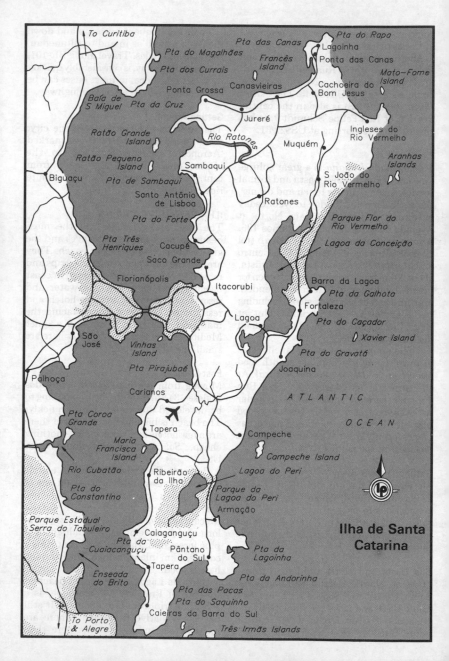

Ilha de Santa Catarina

anyplace else on the east coast, except Praia Ingleses, but there still aren't many of them and they are not modern eyesores. The barracas are excellent, and the beach houses are for rent. This is probably the best beach to head to if you want to stay a few days.

Praia Mole is a surfer beach. Praia da Joaquina hosts the Brazilian surfing championship in January. It has a couple of hotels including *Joaquina Beach* (tel 32-0059) which is simple and on the beach. There are also restaurants, and this is the busiest beach on the island. The crowd is young and hip.

The three main beaches to the south are the most remote and spectacular. Praia do Campeche has a few barracas and the beach is long enough for everyone to find a private patch of sand. Praia da Armação is similar. As at Campeche, the current is often heavy. *Pousada do Sol* (tel 23-4945) has doubles for US$30. Ponta do Sul at the end of the paved road is a small fishing village with one restaurant. The mountains here close in on the sea, which is calm and protected.

North Coast

The north coast is the most developed coast on the island and the beaches are narrow, however, the sea here is warm and calm, incredibly clean and perfect for swimming. Canasvieiras, in particular, has many apartments, families with holiday homes, and nightlife (during the summer). In many ways Canasvieiras is the least attractive beach town on the island and there's plenty more construction on-line.

Canasvieiras has many apartment-hotels. Most are pricey, a few are affordable if you have at least three or four people. There are no real budget hotels, so if you're alone it's expensive. The least expensive place is the *Pousada do Sol* (tel 66-0041) a five-minute walk from the beach on the 'Camping Canasvieiras' road. They have one-bedroom apartments with big kitchens. They'll add another

bed to accommodate up to four people. It's tight, but for US$12 its a good deal. Another possibility is the *Canasvieiras* (tel 66-0106) with doubles for US$14.

A few km west, Jureré is similar to Canasvieiras, but a bit quieter. Out at Praia do Forte there are ruins of the Fortaleza de São José da Ponta Grossa, built in 1750. Jureré has two top-end hotels, the *Jureré Praia Hotel* (tel 66-0108) and the *Canasjuré Club* (tel 66-0175).

West Coast

If you want to explore the west coast, the town of Sambaqui is charming and peaceful. There are a handful of barracas and some beach-goers on weekends. After the town and the barracas, keep walking on the dirt road a few hundred metres for a more private beach or keep going another km for an even more secluded area. Both of these beaches are tiny and cosy, with good views. The road is blockaded soon after this second beach.

The Interior

It's not just the beaches, the entire island is beautiful. Lagoa Conceiça is the most famous region in the interior. The views of lagoon, surrounding peaks and sand dunes make for great walks or boat rides. There are several seafood restaurants at the town of Lagoa – *Ilha Bela* is very good. The town also has some simple hotels which are overpriced, but so is everything outside the city. The *Andrinus* (tel 32-0153) has quartos for two at US$9 and apartments for two at US$16. The *Gaivota* is a less attractive option.

If you're down by Armaçao the Lagoa do Peri is hard to find but fun to explore.

Getting Around

Local buses serve all of the islands' beach towns, but they are infrequent and the schedule changes with the season so it's best to get the times at the tourist office or the centro rodoviária. Also there are additional microbuses during the tourist season that leave from the centre and go directly to the beaches.

The buses for the south of the island leave from the centro rodoviária, platform one (closest to the bay). Buses for the north leave from the corner of Rua José da Costa Moelmann and Avenida Mauro Ramos. To get there, find Rua Antonio Luz at the bottom of Praça 15 and walk away from the centre about seven blocks toward the hillside.

The buses, marked with their destinations, include services for Sambaqui, Lagoa da Conceição, Campeche, Barra da Lagoa, Canasvieiras (Jurerê) Ponta Grossa, Barra do Sul, Ribeirão da Ilha, Pantano do Sul, Ingleses-Aranhas and Ponta das Canas.

The island is one of those places where a one-day car rental is a good idea. With a car, or on one of the bus tours offered by the travel agencies (IlhaTur is a good one), you can see most of the island and pick a beach to settle on.

Another excursion is with Scuna-Sul (tel 22-1806). They have a big sailboat that cruises the north bay for three hours for a reasonable US$10. They leave from near the steel suspension bridge – Brazil's longest.

SOUTH OF FLORIANÓPOLIS

There are a string of beach towns south of Florianópolis.

Garopaba

Garopaba is the first beach town going south. It's 95 km from Florianópolis, including a 15 km drive from the main BR-101 highway. The little town has not been overrun by tourism, the beaches are good and you can still see the fishermen and their way of life. Avoid the next town, Imbituba, it's polluted from a chemical plant.

Places to Stay There are half a dozen hotels. The *Pousada Casa Grande e Senzala* is a good bet with apartments for

US$4.50. Ask about rooms in houses for a cheap sleep.

Laguna

Population: 28,000

Laguna has an active fishing industry and is the centre of tourism for the southern coast. It's an historic city, settled by Paulistas in the 1670s. The city was occupied by the farrapos soldiers and declared a republic in 1839 in the Guerra dos Farrapos, which was fought between republicans and monarchists. If it's a rainy day, take a look at Museu Anita Garibaldi, honouring the Brazilian wife of the leader of Italian unification.

The best beaches in the area are out on the Cabo de Santa Marta, 16 km from the city plus a 10-minute ferry. The ferry operates from 6.30 am to 6.30 pm. There are beautiful dunes here, camping and barracas, but no hotels. For something closer to town, try the Praia do Gi, five km north of town. There are hotels and restaurants along the beach.

From Mar Grosso, the city beach, you can get a boat to Ilha dos Lobos which is an ecological reserve and rather unspoilt. The trip lasts an hour, each way.

Places to Stay Laguna is not cheap. There are several expensive hotels and restaurants. The best place to look for a cheaper hotel is at Mar Grosso. The *Ondão* and *Turismar* are expensive but recommended.

Further South

Continuing south the towns of Tubarão, Criciúma and Araranguá all have a handful of hotels and good beaches, all serviced by regular buses along the coastal route. From Tubarão you can get to several mineral baths including Termas do Gravatal (20 km), Termas da Gurada (12 km) and on the Rio do Pouso (19 km).

The Termas do Gravatal are very popular and have many facilities. The radioactive waters are said to heal rheumatism, ulcers and a variety of other ailments. Unfortunately, none of the four-star hotels on the park grounds are inexpensive. There is camping, however, and you can easily come up for the day from Tubarão.

SÃO JOAQUIM

Travelling east, the mountains are scenic in the winter. São Joaquim is Brazil's highest city, 1355 metres, and one of the few that gets snow. There are a couple of inexpensive hotels on Rua Manoel Joaquim Pinto.

The roads are very precarious but the scenery deserves a slow drive anyway. Bom Jardim da Serra, 45 km from São Joaquim in the middle of the Serra do Rio do Rastro, is a hair-raising but beautiful drive from São Joaquim and there you'll find access to the Parque Nacional de São Joaquim. The park is completely undeveloped, so ask the locals about a guide if you want to explore.

Rio Grande do Sul

PORTO ALEGRE

Population: 1,110,000

Porto Alegre, capital gaúcho and Brazil's sixth biggest city, lies on the eastern bank of Rio Guaiba at the point where it empties into the huge Lagoa dos Patos. It's a modern city, which lives from its freshwater port and commerce. Originally settled by the Portuguese in 1755 to keep the Spanish out, Porto Alegre was never a centre of colonial Brazil and is mainly a product of the 20th century when many German and Italian immigrants arrived.

With little history to discover along its streets and a heavily westernised culture there's little for the foreign traveller in Porto Alegre except the friendly gaúchos and their barbecued meat – the city abounds in churrascarias.

A good place to see gaúchos at play is the big, central Parque Farroupilha. If you're due for some exercise they have bikes to rent. On Sunday mornings the 'Brique da Redencão' – a market/fair – fills a corner of the park with antiques, leather goods and music. After 5 pm, head over to the Rua da Praia, the city's leading meeting place.

Information

Don't forget, Porto Alegre has distinct seasonal weather changes; it gets hot in summer (above 40°C) and you need a good jacket in the winter. City beaches are too polluted for swimming.

Tourist Office Tourist offices are at the rodoviária, the airport, Rua dos Andradas 1234, Praça 15 de Novembro and Travessa do Carmo 84. They seem efficient and publish a monthly guide.

Money There are casas de câmbio in Porto Alegre, so unless there's a government crackdown it's easy to change money and travellers' cheques at parallel rates. Try Exprinter (tel 21-8266), Avenida Salgado Filho 247 or Platine (tel 21-6566), Avenida Borges de Medeiros 445.

Consulates The following countries are represented by consulates in Port Alegre:

Argentina
    Rua Prof Annes Dias 112, 1st floor, Centro (tel 24-6799)
Paraguay
    Praça Dom Feliciano 39, 6th floor (tel 25-0582)
Uruguay
    Rua dos Andradas 1237 (tel 21-2866)

Places to Stay

The *Hotel Praça Matriz*, Largo João Amorim de Albequerque 72 is right in the centre and for US$6 a double you get clean rooms and TV. The *Hotel Henrique*, Rua General Vitorino 182 is less expensive and quite friendly. Doubles cost US$4 and with bath US$5.25. Also in the central district, the *Palacio*, Avenida Vigario Jose Inacio 644 has clean doubles for only US$4.50.

Other recommended hotels which ar

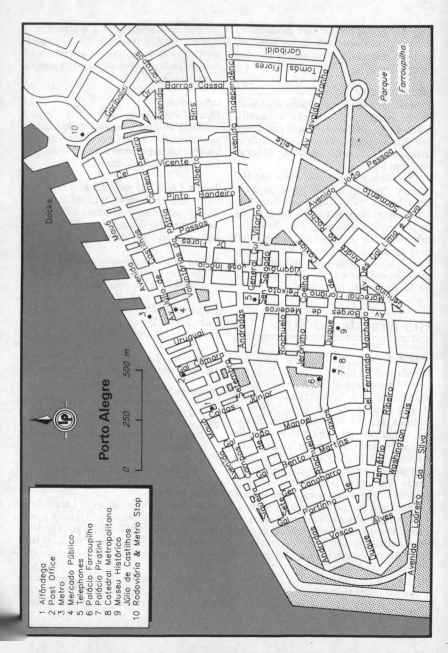

Porto Alegre

0 250 500 m

1 Alfândega
2 Post Office
3 Metro
4 Mercado Público
5 Telephones
6 Palácio Farroupilha
7 Palácio Piratini
8 Catedral Metropolitana
9 Museu Histórico
Júlio de Castilhos
10 Rodoviária & Metro Stop

inexpensive and in the central district include *Rishon* (tel 25-3566), Rua Dr Flores 27, with singles/doubles for US$16/22; *Conceição 2* (tel 24-3987), Rua Garibaldi 165; *Ritz*, André da Rocha 225 and next door *Finks*; and finally *Metrópole* (tel 26-1800) at Rua Andrade Neves 59, with singles/doubles for US$5/6. Near the rodoviária try the *Terminaltur* which has doubles for US$8.50 with air-con and TV.

Two apartment-hotels in the Cidade Baixa have been recommended. *Lar Residence* (tel 24-3442) is at Rua Demetrio Ribeiro 601 while the more expensive *Residence Plaza Catedral* (tel 26-8066) is at Rua Fernando Machado 741 and has singles/doubles for US$18/22.

For something better in the city centre try the *Lido* (tel 26-8233) at Rua Andradas 150, the *Ponte de Pedra* (tel 26-2188) at Rua Fernando Machado 828, with singles/doubles for US$19/21, or the *Plaza* (tel 26-1700) at Rua Senhor dos Passos 154, with singles/doubles for US$33/38. Facing the rodoviária go for the *Hotel Ritter* (tel 21-8155). Three-star singles/doubles are US$25/29 while four-star rooms go for US$30/34.

Places to Eat

Most of the good restaurants are in the suburbs and are a hassle to get to. Meat is the order of the day in the city and wherever you are a juicy steak will be nearby. One place to try for sucos and sandwiches in the city is *Caseiro Natural*, in the subterraneo Malcom. Also try the *Banca 40* at the Mercado Publico. Locals brag about the Portuguese cooking at the *Pulperia*, Trevessa do Carmo 76 at the Cidade Baixa. Meals cost US$3 to US$6 but it's a good splurge.

For German food the *Birklaus* on Rua 24 de Outubro has schnapps or steinegger with good weisswurst (veal sausage). Also try the *Wunderbar* for schnitzel and *Jardim* for morcella sausage.

Getting There & Away

There are international buses to Monte-video (13 hours), Buenos Aires (24 hours) and Asunción (16 hours). Foz do Iguaçu is 18 hours away, Florianópolis 7½ hours, Curitiba 11 hours, São Paulo 18 and Rio de Janeiro 27. Road conditions in the state are generally excellent.

Getting Around

Porto Alegre has a one-line metro that goes from the city centre to the rodoviária and the airport. The central station is by the port and called 'Estação Mercado Modelo'. The rodoviária is the next stop and the airport three further. The metro runs from 5 am to 11 pm.

LITORAL GAÚCHO

The litoral gaúcho makes up a 500 km strip along the state of Rio Grande do Sul - from Torres in the north until Chuí a at the Uruguayan border. Of all Brazil's coast, this is the least distinguished, the least varied. The beaches are really one long beach uninterrupted by geographical variations, wide-open, with little vegetation and occasional dunes. The sea here is choppier than in Santa Catarina, the water less translucent.

In winter, currents from the Antarctic bring cold, hard winds to the coast. Bathing suits disappear, as well as most people. Most hotels shut down in March and the summer beach season doesn't return until November at the earliest, with the arrival of the northern winds.

The big three resort towns on the north coast are Torres, Capão da Canoa and Tramandaí. Torres, the furthest from Porto Alegre, is only three hours away by car. All three have medium-sized airports, luxury hotels and upscale nightlife and they all fill-up in the summer with Porto-Alegrenses, Uruguayans and Argentines. This is not where you go to get away from it all. They also have many campgrounds and cheaper hotels in the towns, but the flavour is much more that of a well-to-do weekend resort than a Bahian fishing village.

Gaúchos in Rio Grande do Sul

Torres

Population: 13,800

Torres is 205 km from Porto Alegre. It is well-known for its fine beaches and the beautiful, basaltic rock formations along the coast. This is good country to walk and explore and if you can get here early or late in the season, when the crowds have thinned-out, it's especially worthwhile. There is also an ecological reserve on the Ilha dos Lobos.

Places to Stay Torres is full of hotels, and has a surprising number of simple places that are reasonably priced. If you're there off-season make sure you get an off-season rate which should be considerably less than the summer price. Campgrounds are plentiful.

Capão da Canoa

This is a smaller resort, 140 km from Porto Alegre, without the glamour and glitz of Torres. The best-known beach is Praia de Atlântida, three km from the town. The beach is big and broad, and there's an active windsurfing scene on the lagoons.

Places to Stay Like Torres, there are several campgrounds here. For less-expensive lodging, ask about the *Acapulco*, the *Johsil*, the *Linhares*, and the *Maquiné*.

Tramandaí

Population: 15,000

Only 120 km from Porto Alegre, Tramandaí's permanent population of some 15,000 swells to half a million in January. On summer weekends the beaches are the busiest in the state and they're good beaches, though not as nice as in Torres. There is a good festival here in late June, the Festa de São Pedro, with a procession of boats on the sea.

Places to Stay There's a lot of camping and several less-expensive hotels in Tramandaí, but reservations are still in order during January and February.

Rio Grande

Once an important cattle centre, Rio Grande lies at the mouth of the Lagoa dos Patos, Brazil's biggest lagoon. To the north, the coast along the Lagoa is lightly inhabited. There's a poor dirt road along this stretch, which is connected with Rio Grande by a small ferry boat.

Cassino

The major beach resort in the south, Cassino is really cold in the winter, but in summer – depending on the currency exchange rates – it's often loaded with Uruguayans and Argentines. At that time of year it's very lively and there's plenty of beach for the asking, you just need to find a way to get there. At the breakwater just north of town you can watch the large ships sail into Rio Grande. To the south, cars zip along the beach so watch out if you're sunbaking. Cassino is 325 km from Porto Alegre and 25 km south of Rio Grande.

Chuí

From Cassino you continue south 200 km on a good paved road to the small border town of Chuí. There are a few simple hotels but several close in the winter. It's much better to pick-up a Uruguayan visa in Porto Alegre or some other major Brazilian city than at the border at Chuí, but it can be done here.

SERRA GAÚCHO

North of Porto Alegre, you quickly begin to climb into the Serra Gaúcho. The ride is beautiful as are the mountain towns of Gramado and Canela, 150 km from Porto Alegre. First settled by Germans in 1824 and later by Italians in the 1870s, the region is as close to the Alps as Brazil gets. Both towns are popular resorts and crowded with Porto Alegrenses in all seasons, but particularly when it's hottest in the big city. There are many hotels and restaurants, particularly in Gramado, many with a German influence. Prices are high for Brazil.

Hikers abound in the mountains here. In the winter there are occasional snowfalls and in the spring the hills are blanketed with flowers. The best spot is the Parque Estadual do Caracol, reached by local buses from Canela eight km away.

Rio Grande do Sul's most magnificent area and one of Brazil's great natural wonders is 70 km north of the town of São Francisco de Paula in the Parque Nacional de Aparados da Serra. The park preserves one of the country's last araucária forests, pine-like trees that stand up to 50 metres tall, but the main attraction is the Itaimbezinho, a fantastic narrow canyon with sheer 120 metre, parallel escarpments. Two waterfalls drop into this deep incision in the earth, which was formed by the Rio Perdiz's rush to the sea.

To get to the Parque Nacional de Aparados da Serra ask for the road to Cambará do Sul. The dirt road is often impassable after heavy rains. Camping is permitted, but check-in at the park office just inside the entrance. The only hotel anywhere near the park is the simple *Paradouro do Itaimbezinho*.

Jesuit Missions

Soon after the discovery of the New World, the Portuguese and Spanish kings authorised Catholic orders to create missions to convert the natives into Catholic subjects of the crown and the state. The most successful of these orders were the Jesuits who created a series of missions in a region which spanned parts of Paraguay, Brazil and Argentina. In effect it was a nation within the colonies, a nation which at its height in the 1720s claimed 30 mission villages inhabited by over 150,000 Guarani Indians. Buenos Aires was merely a village at this time.

Unlike missions established elsewhere these missions succeeded in introducing western culture without destroying the Indian people, their culture and their Tupi-Guarani language.

In 1608 Hernandarias, governor of the Spanish province of Paraguay, ordered the local leader of the Jesuits, Fray Diego de Torres, to send missionaries to convert the infidels and so in 1609 the first mission was founded. Preferring indoctrination by the Jesuits to serfdom on Spanish estates or slavery at the hands of the Portuguese, the Indians were rapidly recruited into a chain of missions. The missions covered a vast region of land encompassing much of the present day Brazilian states of Paraná, Santa Catarina and Rio Grande do Sul plus portions of Paraguay and northern Argentina.

The Jesuit territory was too large to defend and the Portuguese bandeirantes found the missionary settlements easy pickings for slave raids. Thousands of Indians were captured, reducing the 13 missions of Guayra (Brazilian territory) to two. In fear of the bandeirante slavers these two missions were abandoned and the Indians and Jesuits marched westward and founded San Ignacio Miní (1632) having lost many people in the rapids of the Paraná. The missions north of Iguaçu were decimated by attacks from hostile Indian tribes and were forced to relocate south.

Between 1631 and 1638, activity was concentrated in 30 missions which the mission Indians were able to defend. In one of the bloodiest fights, the battle of Mbororé, the Indians beat back the slavers and secured their lands north of San Javier.

The missions, under administration based in Candelaria, grew crops, raised cattle and prospered. They were miniature cities built around a central church and included libraries, baptisteries, cemeteries and dormitories for the Indian converts and the priests. The missions became centres of culture and intellect as well as religion. An odd mix of European Baroque and native Guarani arts, music and painting developed. Indian scholars created a written form of Tupi-Guarani and from 1704 published several works in Tupi-Guarani in one of the earliest printing presses of South America.

As the missions grew, the Jesuit nation became more independent of Rome and relations with the Vatican were strained. The nation within a nation became an embarrassment to the Iberian kings and finally in 1777 the Portuguese minister Marques de Pombal convinced Carlos III to expel the Jesuit priests from Spanish lands. Thus ended, in the opinion of many historians, a grand 160 year experiment in socialism where wealth was equally divided and religion, intellect and the arts flourished – a utopian island of progress in an age of monarchies and institutionalised slavery. Administration of the mission villages passed into the hands of the colonial government and the communities continued until the early 1800s when they were destroyed by revolutionary wars of independence and then abandoned.

Information & Orientation
There are 30 ruined Jesuit missions: seven lie in Brazil in the western part of Rio Grande do Sul, eight are in the southern region of Itapuá, Paraguay and the remaining 15 are in Argentina. Of these 15 Argentine missions 11 lie in the province of Missiones which hooks like a thumb between Paraguay and the Rio Paraná and Brazil and the Uruguai and Iguaçu rivers.

Paraguayan Missions
The missions of Paraguay, long since abandoned, are only now being restored. The most important mission to see is Trinidad, 25 km from Encarnacion. The red stone ruins are fascinating. If you have the time, see the missions of Santa Rosa, Santiago and Jesus.

Argentine Missions
In Argentina, the most important mission to see is San Ignacio Miní, 60 km from Posadas on Ruta Nacional 12. Of lesser stature is mission Santa Maria la Mayor, 111 km away from Posadas on Ruta 110, and mission Candelaria, 25 km from Posadas on Ruta 12 (now a national penitentiary). It's possible to cut across

the province of Missiones to San Javier (Ruta 4) and cross by ferry to Brazil at Puerto Xavier or further south at Santo Tome and ferry across the Rio Uruguay to São Borja Brazil.

The border at Uruguiana, 180 km south of São Borja is more commonly used. Uruguiana is 180 km from São Borja or 635 km from Porto Alegre. Buses operate to Buenos Aires, Santiago do Chile and Montevideo. The Argentine consulate (tel (055) 412-2916) is at Rua Antana 2496 while the Uruguayan consulate (tel (055) 412-1514) is at Rua Domingos de Almeida, 1709

Brazilian Missions

Santo Angelo (200 km from São Borja) has a minor mission museum at Rua Universidade das Missoes 393. São Miguel das Missoes (58 km from Santo Angelo) is the most interesting of the Brazilian missions. Every evening there's a sound and light show. Also nearby are the missions of São João Batista (on the way to São Miguel) and São Lourenco das Missoes (10 km from São João Batista by dirt road).

Places to Stay & Eat

In Paraguay, Encarnacion has a couple of cheap and modest hotels and Chinese restaurants.

Across the Rio Paraná from Encarnacion is the capital of the Argentine province of Posadas. A ferry operates from 8 am to midday, 2 pm until sundown. Everything is more expensive, but the food is better and the lodging (10 hotels to choose from) is fancier.

In Brazil, Santo Angelo (200 km from São Borja) has several modest but proper hotels.

Getting There & Away

Use Encarnacion as a base for the missions of Paraguay. Riza buses leave daily from Puerto Stroessner, 320 km south to Encarnacion and 370 km south-south-east from Asunción on Ruta 1. Either way, it's a pleasant ride through fertile rolling hills, a region where the locals (mostly of German descent) drink a variation of mate called tererê.

Getting Around

This is the sort of travelling that's best done by car but unfortunately car rental fees are expensive and driving a rental car over borders is difficult. It's possible to hire a taxi from any of the three base cities, Posadas, Encarnacion and Santo Angelo. In Paraguay it's as little as US$25 per day.

Glossary

ABCD cities – refers to Brazil's industrial heartland; the cities of São André, São Bernardo, São Caetano and Diadema which flank the city of São Paulo.

abandonados – abandoned children.

abertura – opening; refers to the process of returning to civilian, democratic government which was begun in the early 1980's.

afoxé – music of Bahia with strong African rhythms and close ties to the Candomblé religion.

aguardente – firewater, rot-gut; any strong drink, but usually cachaça.

albergue – a lodging house, a hostel.

álcool – car fuel made from sugar cane; about half the cars in Brazil and all new cars run on álcool.

aldeia – originally a mission village built by Jesuits to 'save' the Indians, now any small village of peasants or fisherfolk.

apartamento – a hotel room with a bathroom.

arara – a macaw.

autódromo – a racing track. *The* race track near Barra in Rio is the site of the Brazilian Grand Prix.

automotriz – tourist train.

avelã – hazelnut.

azulejos – Portuguese ceramic tiles which have a distinctive blue glaze. You will often see them in churches.

bandeirantes – bands of Paulistas (people from São Paulo) who explored the vast Brazilian interior while searching for gold and Indians to enslave. The bandeirantes were typically born of an Indian mother and a Portuguese father.

banzo – a slave's profound longing for the African homeland that often resulted in a 'slow withering away' and death.

barraca – any stall or hut, including those omnipresent food and drink stands at the beach, park, etc.

bateria – any rhythm section, including the enormous ones in the samba parades.

beija-flor – a humming bird; also the name of Rio's most famous samba school.

bicho-de-pé – a parasite that burrows into the bottom of the foot and then grows, until it's cut out. It's found near the beach and in some jungle areas.

bloco – large groups, usually in the hundreds, of singing Carnival revelers in costume. Most blocos are organised around a neighbourhood or theme.

boate or boîte – nightclub; refers to the expensive joint and the strip joint.

bogó – a leather water pouch typical of the sertão.

bonde – a cable-car, a trolley. In Rio there is the 'bonde' which goes from the city centre to Santa Teresa.

bossa nova – music that mixes American jazz with Brazilian influences.

boto – fresh-water dolphin of the Amazon. Indians believe the boto has magical powers, most notably the ability to impregnate unmarried women.

Brazilian Empire – the period from 1822 to 1889 when Brazil was independent of Portugal but governed by monarchy.

bumba-meu-boi – the most important festival in Maranhão; a rich folkloric event that revolves around a carnivalesque dance/procession.

bunda – an African word for buttocks.

caatinga – scrub vegetation of the Northeast sertão.

cabanagem – the popular revolt that swept through Pará state in the 1830s until a large government force defeated the uprising and then massacred 40,000 of the state's 100,000 people.

caboclo – literally copper-coloured, a person of White and Indian mix.

cachaça – Brazil's national drink, a sugar cane rum, also called pinga and aguardente. Hundreds of small distilleries produce cachaça throughout the country.

cachoeira – waterfall.

café – means café da manha (breakfast) or just coffee.

caipirinha – made from cachaça and crushed citrus fruit such as lemon, orange or maracujá.

câmara – a town council during colonial days.

camisa-de-vênus or camisinha – literally cover or shirt of Venus (love), but actually means a condom.

candomblé – Afro-Brazilian religion of Bahia.

canga – a wrap-around fabric worn going to and from the beach and for sitting on at the beach.

cangaceiro – legendary bandits of the sertão.

capanga – a hired gunman, usually of the rich landowners in the Northeast.

capitania hereditária – an hereditary province, estate. To settle Brazil at minimum cost to the crown, the King of Portugal divided Brazil into 12 capitanias hereditárias in 1531.

capivara (capybara) – world's largest rodent, it looks like a large guinea-pig and lives in the waters of Pantanal.

capoeira – a martial art/dance done to the rhythms of an instrument called the berimbau; developed by the slaves of Bahia.

capongas – fresh-water lagoon.

carioca – a native of Rio de Janeiro.

casa grande – the plantation master's mansion.

casa de câmbio – money exchange house.

catamarãs – typical boats of the Amazon.

casal – a married couple; also a double bed.

chapadões – tablelands or plateaus running between river basins.

churrascaria – a restaurant featuring meat, which should be churrasco (barbecued).

Círio de Nazaré – in Belém, this is Brazil's largest religious pilgrimage.

cobra – any snake.

collectivá – a bed in shared room, dorm-style accommodation.

comunidade de base – neighbourhood organisations of the poor led by the progressive Catholic church and inspired by liberation theology. They are involved in many struggles for social justice.

congelamento – freeze, as in a price freeze.

coronel – a rural landowner who typically controlled the local political, judicial and police systems; any powerful person.

cruzado – name of current currency as well as ancient one.

cruzeiro – name of pre-1986 currency.

delegacia – police station.

dendê – cooking oil, the leading ingredient in cuisine of Bahia. It comes from palm tree.

drogas do sertão – plants of the sertão such as cacao and cinnamon.

economic miracle – period of double-digit economic growth while the military was in power during the late '60s and early '70s. Now mentioned sarcastically to point to the failures of the military regime.

embolada – a kind of Brazilian rapping, where singers trade-off performing verbal jests, teasing and joking with the audience. It is most common in Northeastern fairs.

EMBRATUR – federal government tourism agency.

Empire – the Brazilian Empire. Era from 1822 to 1889 when Brazil had declared its independence from Portugal but continued under the rule of a monarchy.

ENASA – government run passenger ships of the Amazon.

engenho – sugar mill or sugar plantation.

escola de samba – these aren't schools, but large samba clubs. In Rio the escolas have thousands of members and compete in the annual Carnival parade. The escolas begin weekend rehearsals around November and continue until Carnival; rehearsals are open to the public.

Estado Novo – the new state. Dictator Getúlio Vargas's quasi-fascist state from 1937 to the end of WWII.

estância hidromineral – spa, hotsprings.

exús – the spirits that serve as messengers between the gods and humans in Afro-Brazilian religions.

facão – a large knife or machete.

fantasia – a Carnivalesque costume.

farinha – a flower made from the root of the manioc plant. Farinha was the staple food of Brazil's Indians before colonisation and remains the staple for many Brazilians today, especially in the Northeast and the Amazon.

favela – slum, shantytown.

fazenda – a ranch or farm, usually a large landholding; also cloth, fabric.

ferroviária – railway station.

ficha – a token. Due to inflation, machines (eg telephones) take tokens not coins.

fidalgos – gentry.

figa – a good luck charm formed by a clenched fist with thumb between index and middle finger. The figa originated with Afro-Brazilian cults but is popular with all Brazilians.

Filhos de Gandhi – Bahia's most famous Carnival bloco.

fio dental – dental floss. This is what Brazilians call their famous skimpy bikinis.

Flamengo – Rio's most popular football team. Also, one of Rio's most populated areas.

Fluminense – a native of Rio state. Also the Rio football team that is Flamengo's main rival.

forro – the music of the Northeast which combines the influences of Mexico and the Brazilian frontier. The characteristic instruments used are the accordion, harmonica and drums.

frevo – fast-paced, popular music that originated in Pernambuco.

FUNAI – government Indian agency.

FUNART – government cultural agency.

fusca – a Volkswagen beetle, long Brazil's most popular car; they stopped making them in 1986.

garimpeiro – a prospector, a miner, originally an illegal diamond prospector.

gaúcho – pronounced gaoooshoo, a cowboy of southern Brazil.

gíria – slang.

gringo – you don't have to be from the USA – any foreigner or person with light hair and complexion, including Brazilians, qualifies. It's not necessarily a derogatory term.

guaraná – an Amazonian shrub whose berry is believed to have magical and medicinal powers, also a popular soft drink.

Iemanjá – the god of the sea in the Afro-Brazilian religions.

igapó – flooded Amazon forest.

igarapés – pools formed by the changing paths of the rivers of the Amazon.

INPA – national agency for research on the Amazon.

jaburú – giant white stork of Pantanal with black head and red band on neck.

jagunço – the tough man of the sertão.

jangada – beautiful sailboat of the Northeast, usually made by the fisherfolk themselves with building techniques passed from generation to generation.

jangadeiros – fisherfolk of the jangadas.

jeito (dar um jeito or jeitinho) – possibly the most Brazilian expression, jeito means to find a way to get something done, no matter how seemingly impossible. It may not be an orthodox, normal or legal way but is nonetheless effective in the Brazilian context. Jeito is both a feeling and a form of action.

jogo de bicho – a popular lottery, technically illegal but played on every street corner by all Brazilians, with each number represented by an animal. The banqueiros de bicho, who control the game, have become almost a kind of mafia and have traditionally helped fund the escolas de samba. Many consider the jogo de bicho the most honest_ and trustworthy institution in the country.

jogo dos búzios – a type of fortune telling performed by a pai or maê de Santo throwing shells.

karaoke – a bar or nightclub where anyone can get up and perform.

Labour Code – labour legislation modelled after Mussolini's system, that's designed to keep government control over labour unions.

ladrão – a thief.

lanchonete – a stand-up snack-bar. They are found all over Brazil.

lavrador – a peasant, small farmer, landless farm worker.

leito – a super-comfortable overnight, express bus.

liberation theology – movement in Catholic church that believes the struggle for social justice is part of Christ's teachings.

literatura de cordel – literally literature of string. Popular literature of the Northeast where pamphlets are typically hung on strings. It is sold at markets where authors read their stories and poems.

maconha – a type of marijuana.

maê-de-santo – female spiritual leader of Afro-Brasilian religions.

maharajás – pejorative term for government employees getting rich from the public coffers, usually army and police officers.

malandro do morro – vagabond; scoundrel from the hills. A popular figure in Rio's mythology.

mameluco – offspring of White father and Indian mother.

manatee or **peixeboi** – literally cow fish, an aquatic mammal of the Amazon rivers that grows to five feet in length, now rare.

Manchete – number two national television station and popular photo magazine.

Maracanã – football stadium in Rio; supposedly world's largest. They say the stadium holds 200,000, but it looks full with 100,000.

mate – popular tea of southern Brazil.

mestiço – a person of mixed Indian and European parentage.

mineiro – a miner, a person from the state of Minas Gerais.

mocambo – a community of runaway slaves; small version of a quilombo.

moço – a waiter or other service type worker.

morro – hill, but used to indicate person or culture of the favelas.

motel – a hotel for sex with rooms to rent by the hour (due to fear of robbery some motels don't rent to male couples).

mulato – a person of mixed Black and European parentage

NS - Nosso Senhor (our father), or Nossa Senhora (our lady).

novela - a soap opera. Novelas are the most popular TV shows in Brazil. They are much funnier with more insights than the American counterparts. From directors to actors to composers, many of Brazil's most talented and famous artists work on novelas.

O Globo - Brazil's number one media empire. O Globo owns the prime national television station and several newspapers and magazines.

Old Republic - period from the end of the Brazilian Empire in 1889 to the coup that put Getúlio Vargas in power in 1930. There were regular elections but only a tiny percentage of population was eligible to vote.

orixás - the gods of the Afro-Brazilian religions.

pagode - todays's most popular samba music.

pai-de-santo - male spiritual leader in Afro-Brasilian religions.

pajé - a shaman, a witchdoctor.

palafitas - houses built on sticks above water, as in Manaus.

paralelo - the parallel, semi-official exchange rate that reflects the currency's market value, not the government's regulated official value.

paruara - Amazon resident who came from Ceará.

pau do brasil - brazil wood tree, which produces a red dye that was the colony's first commodity. The trees are scarce today.

paulista - a native of São Paulo.

PCB - communist party of Brazil.

pelourinho - a stone pillar used as a whipping post for punishing slaves.

Petrobras - the government-owned oil company. Brazil's largest corporation is so powerful that it's called a 'government within a government'.

pinga - another name for cachaça, the sugar cane brandy.

PMDB - the governing party, a loose coalition that encompasses a wide variety of ideologies and interests from far right to centre.

posseiro - a squatter.

pousada - hotel.

prato feito (prato do dia) - literally, made plate (plate of the day). They are typically enormous meals and incredibly cheap.

PTD - the democratic workers party, a social democratic party dominated by the charismatic populist Leonel Brizola.

PT - Worker's Party. Brazil's newest political party and most radical. It came out of massive strike waves of early 1980s and is led by Lula. The PT's support is largely in São Paulo and among industrial workers and the Catholic base communities.

puxar - means pull, not push.

quarto - a hotel room without a bathroom.

quilombo - community of runaway slaves. They posed a serious threat to the slave system as hundreds of quilombos dotted the coastal mountains. The Republic of Palmares was the most famous - it lasted most of the 17th century and had as many as 20,000 people.

rede - a hammock.

Revolution of '64 - the military takeover in 1964.

rodízio - smorgasbord with lots of meat (similar to a churrascaria).

rodoferroviária - bus and train station.

rodoviária - bus station.

sambódromo - the road and bleachers where the samba parade takes place on Rio's north side.

senzala - slave quarters.

Sertão - the drought-stricken region of the Northeast, known as the backlands. It has a dry, temperate climate, and the land is covered by thorny shrubs.

shiita - after the Shiite muslims of Iran, used to describe any zealot or radical, no matter the cause.

suco - a juice bar or juice.

Terra de Vera Cruz - Land of the True Cross. This was the original Portuguese name for Brazil but was soon changed to Brazil. Generations of Portuguese believed Brazil was the work of the devil (who, according to the common wisdom, was very active in the sinful colony).

terreiro - house of worship for Afro-Brasilian religions.

travesti - a tranvestite, a popular figure throughout Brazil and considered by some the national symbol.

Treaty of Tordesillas - the agreement between Spain and Portugal dividing Latin America.

trio eléctrico - literally a three-pronged electric outlet. Also, a musical style that is sort of an electrified frevo played on top of trucks, especially during Carnival in Bahia.

tropicalismo - important cultural movement centred in Bahia in the late '60s.

Tupi – the Indian peoples and language that predominated along the Brazilian coast at the time of the European invasion. Most animals and places in Brazil have Tupi names.

umbanda – Rio's version of the principal Afro-Brazilian religion.

vaqueiro – cowboy of the Northeast.
Velho Chico – old Chico, the fond nickname for the great Rio Saõ Francisco.
violeiros – guitarists and guitar makers.

zona da mata – bushland just inside the littoral in the Northeastern states.

Index

Abbreviations

A	Argentina
B	Brazil
ACRE	Acre
AMAZ	Amazonas
ALA	Alagoas
AMA	Amapá
BAH	Bahia
CEA	Ceará
DF	Distrito Federal

ES	Espirito Santo
FDN	Fernando de Noronha
GOI	Goias
MAR	Maranhão
MINAS	Minas Gerais
MG	Mato Grosso
MGS	Mato Grosso do Sul
P	Paraguay
PAR	Paraná
PARÁ	Pará
PARAI	Paraíba

PER	Pernambuco
PIA	Piauí
RGS	Rio Grande do Sul
RIO	Rio City
RJ	Rio de Janeiro State
RON	Rondônia
ROR	Roraima
SC	Santa Caterina
SER	Sergipe
SP	São Paulo
TOC	Tocantins

Map references are in **bold** type

Ahais (BAH) 236
Abraão (RJ) 131-132
Acre (ACRE) 366
Afuá (PARÁ) 343
Alagoas (ALA) 266-275, **261**
Alcântara (MAR) 322-323
Alcobaça (BAH) 253
Algodoal (PARÁ) 340
Alter do Chão (PARÁ) 346
Alumar (MAR) 323
Amapá (AMA) 348-350
Amazon, The 326-374, **327**
Amazonas (AMAZ) 352-366
Anavilhanas (AMAZ) 364
Anchieta (ES) 158
Angra dos Reis (RJ) 132
Antonina (PAR) 414
Aquidauana (MG) 403
Aracaju (SER) 263-265, **263**
Aracati (CEA) 308
Aracê (ES) 159
Araranguá (SC) 438
Araruama (RJ) 150
Araruna (PARÁ) 341
Areia Branca (RGN) 298
Arembepe (BAH) 232
Argentine Missions (A),
    see Jesuit Missions
Aripuana (RON) 372
Armação (RJ) 153, 154
Arraial d'Ajuda (BAH) 249, 250-251
Arraial do Cabo (RJ) 150-151
Aruanuá (TOC) 387

Bahia (BAH) 202-259, **231**, **261**
Baía de Todos os Santos
    (BAH) 208, 209, 224, **223**
Baía da Traição (PARAI) 293
Baía de Paranaguá (PAR) 420
Baía Formosa (RGN) 293
Balneário Camboriú (SC) 430, 431
Barão de Melgaço (MG) 392, 403
Barra (BAH) 219, 220, 221

Barra de Camarajibe (ALA) 275
Barra de Itabapoana (RJ) 155
Barra de Itariri (BAH) 235
Barra de Santo Antônio (ALA) 274
Barra de São João (RJ) 154
Barra de São Miguel (ALA) 273-274
Barra do Cunháu (RGN) 293
Barra do Garças (TOC) 386, 387
Barra Velha (SC) 430
Barreira do Inferno (RGN) 294
Beaches
    Araçaji (MAR) 319
    Armação (SC) 431
    Armação (Ilha de Santa
        Catarina) (SC) 437
    Arpoador (RIO) 107
    Atalaia Velha (SER) 264
    Atlântica (ALA) 267
    Atlátida (RGS) 442
    Bahia do Sol (PAR) 339
    Baleia (CEA) 309
    Barra (BAH) 215
    Barra da Lagoa (SC) 435
    Barra da Tijuca (RIO) 92, 108
    Barra do Ceará (CEA) 303
    Barra do Farol (BAH) 253
    Barra do Jacuípe (BAH) 232
    Barra Grande (RJ) 138
    Barra Grande (BAH) 224
    Barreiras (CEA) 311
    Bombas (SC) 431
    Bombinhas (SC) 431
    Botafogo (RIO) 107
    Cabedelo (PARAI) 292
    Cabo Branco (PARAI) 291
    Cacha Prego (BAH) 224
    Cacimba do Padre (FDN) 300
    Calhau (MAR) 319
    Campeche (SC) 436
    Candeias (PER) 282
    Chapéu Virado (PAR) 339
    Coroa Vermelha (BAH) 249
    Cumbuco (CEA) 303
    Encantadas (PAR) 418
    Faro (CEA) 311

Beaches *cont*
    Farol (PAR) 339
    Flamengo (RJ) 106
    Fortaleza (PAR) 418
    Forte (RJ) 136
    Francês (ALA) 274
    Freicheiras (CEA) 309
    Futuro (CEA) 303
    Gi (SC) 438
    Grande (PAR) 418
    Grauça (BAH) 253
    Guajira (CEA) 309
    Inferno (CEA) 309
    Ingleses (SC) 435
    Iparana (CEA) 303
    Iracema (CEA) 303
    Jabaquara (RJ) 136
    Janga (PER) 287
    Joaquina (SC) 436
    Leme (RIO) 107
    Mar Grosso (SC) 438
    Marape (ES) 159
    Maria Farinha (PER) 287
    Marinheiros (CEA) 309
    Maxaranguape (PAR) 297
    Meireles (CEA) 303
    Moçambique (SC) 435
    Mole (SC) 436
    Mucugê (BAH) 250, 251
    Mundai (BAH) 249
    Mundau (CEA) 309
    Muríu (PAR) 297
    Pajuçara (ALA) 267, 270
    Palame (BAH) 234
    Pao Amarelo (PER) 287
    Parati Mirim (RJ) 138
    Penha (PARAI) 291
    Pepino (RIO) 108
    Piedade (PER) 282
    Pitinga (BAH) 250, 251
    Placaford (BAH) 215
    Ponta d'Areia (MAR) 319
    Ponta de Panaquatira
        (MAR) 319, 323
    Ponta Grande (BAH) 249

Beaches *cont*
Ponta Negra (AMAZ) 358
Pontal (RJ) 136
Pontas de Pedras (PER) 289
Ponte da Areia (BAH) 224
Porto Suipé (BAH) 234
Pracianos (CEA) 309
Prainha (SC) 431
Redinha (PAR) 297
Salvaterra (PAR) 343
Sancho (FDN) 300
Santinho (SC) 435
Santos (FDN) 300
Seixas (PARAI) 291
Sol (PARAI) 291
Sono (RJ) 138
Tambaú (PARAI) 291
Trindade (RJ) 138
Venda Grande (PER) 282
Vidigal (RIO) 108
Volta da Jurema (CEA) 303
Belém (PARÁ) 331-339, **333**
Belmont (RON) 370
Belo Horizonte (MINAS) 163-164,
162, 165
Belterra (PARÁ) 346
Bico do Ipu (CEA) 312
Blumenau (SC) 431-432, **432**
Boa Viagem (PER) 276, 280
Boa Vista (ROR) 75, 76, 350-352, **351**
Bom Jardim da Serra (SC) 439
Bonito (AMA) 349
Brasília (DF) 376-380, **378-379, 380**
Brazil **10-11, 24**
Brazilian Missions (B),
see Jesuit Missions
Breves (PARÁ) 343
Búzios (PAR) 294
Búzios (RJ) 153-154, **152**

Cabo de Santa Marta (SC) 438
Cabo de Santo Agostinho
(PER) 282
Cabo Frio (RJ) 151-153, **152**
Cachoeira (BAH) 225-229, **226**
Cachoeira de Santo Antonio
(AMA) 349
Cachoeira do Arari (PARÁ) 343
Cachoeira Glass (BAH) 257
Cachoeira Saia Velha (DF) 381
Cachoeira Topázio (DF) 381
Caçeres (MG) 393, 403
Caldas Novas (GOI) 385
Camamu (BAH) 238
Camocim (CEA) 311
Campo Grande (MGS) 403-404, **404**
Campos (RJ) 155
Canasvieiras (SC) 437
Candeias (BAH) 229
Canela (RGS) 443
Canindé (CEA) 311
Canoe Quebrada (CEA) 308-309

Capão da Canoa (RGS) 442
Caraguatatuba (SP) 199
Caraiva (BAH) 249, 251, 253
Caravelas (BAH) 253
Carnival
Maceió (ALA) 267
Salvador (BAH) 215-216
Porto Seguro (BAH) 246-247
Sã Luis (MAR) 319
São João (MINAS) 178
Ilha do Mel (PAR) 418
Recife (PER) 279
Olinda (PER) 285
Rio de Janeiro City (RJ) 108-110
Caruaru (PER) 289-290
Cassino (RGS) 443
Caxambu (MINAS) 182-183
Cáceres (MG) 74, 393-394
Ceará (CEA) 301-313
Centro de Pesquisa do Cacao
(BAH) 242
Chapada Diamantina (BAH) 254,
255, 257
Chapada dos Guimarães
(MG) 388, 390, 392
Chuí (RGS) 443
Conde (BAH) 234, **234**
Congonhas (MINAS) 166-168
Conselheiro Lafaiete (MINAS) 167
Copacabana (RIO) 92, 107, 113,
116, 120, **93**
Corcovado (RIO) 70, 100
Corumbá (MGS) 73-74, 405-406, **405**
Coruripe (ALA) 273
Coxim (MGS) 403, 406
Criciúma (SC) 438
Cuiabá (MG) 388-392, 401, **389**
Cumuruxatiba (BAH) 253
Curian (AMA) 348
Curitiba (PAR) 408-412, 413,
409, 412
Curuá-Una Hydroelectric Dam
(PARÁ) 346

Dannelles Falls (RON) 372
Dedo de Deus (RIO) 70
Diamantina (MINAS) 184-185
Distrito Federal (DF) 376-381
Domingos Martins (ES) 159

Espírito Santo (ES) 156-159
Estancia de Agua de Itiquiara
(DF) 381
Estância (SER) 260

Fazenda Morrinhos (MG) 402
Feira de Santana (BAH) 254
Fernando de Noronha
(FN) 298-300, **299**
Florianópolis (SC) 432-435, **434**
Fordlândia (PARÁ) 346
Fortaleza (CEA) 301-307, **302, 304**
Foz do Iguaçu (PAR) 420-426, **421**

Gaibu (PER) 282
Garopaba (SC) 438
Genipabu (RGN) 297
Gijoca (CEA) 310
Goiás Velho (GOI) 382, 384
Goiás (GOI) 381-385
Goiânia (GOI) 381-382, **383**
Gramado (RGS) 443
Guajará-Mirim (RON) 74, 374, **373**
Guarajuba (BAH) 232
Guaramiranga (CEA) 312
Guarapari (ES) 156-158
Guayaramerín (RON) 374, **373**

Igaraçu (PER) 287-289
Igarapé do Lago (AMA) 349
Iguaçu Falls (PAR) 420, 422-424, **423**
Iguape (CEA) 307
Ilha da Croa (ALA) 274
Ilha de Areia Vermelha (PARAI) 292
Ilha de Itamaracá (PER) 287
Ilha de Paquetá (RIO) 102-103
Ilha de Santa Catarina (SC)
435-438, **436**
Ilha de Santo Aleixo (PER) 282
Ilha do Bananal (TOC) 386-387
Ilha do Marajó (PARÁ) 340-343
Ilha do Mel (PAR) 417-420, **419**
Ilha do Mosqueiro (PARÁ) 339-340
Ilha do Paiva (PER) 282
Ilha dos Lobos (SC) 438
Ilha Feia (SC) 431
Ilha Grande (RJ) 130-132
Ilha Itacolomi (SC) 431
Ilha João da Cunha (SC) 431
Ilhas de Arvoredo (SC) 431
Ilhabela (SP) 200
Ilhéus (BAH) 240-242, **240**
Ipanema (RIO) 92, 107, 114,
117, 120, **93**
Itacaré (BAH) 239
Itaipu Dam (PAR) 420, 422
Itaparica (BAH) 222, 224
Itapoã(BAH) 218
Itatiaia (RJ) 144-149, **145**

Jacumã (PARAI) 290
Janguaribe (PER) 287
Japaratinga (ALA) 275
Jericoacoara (CEA) 309-310
Jesuit Missions 443-445
Candelaria (A) 444
Encarnacion (P) 445
Jesus (P) 444
San Ignacio Miní (A) 444
Santa Maria la Mayor (A) 444
Santa Rosa (P) 444
Santiago (p) 444
Santo Angelo (B) 445

Jesuit Missions *cont*
  São João Batista (B) 445
  São Lourenco das Missoes
    (B) 445
  São Miguel das Missoes (B) 445
  Trinidad (P) 444
Ji Parana (RON) 372
João Pessoa (PARAI) 291-293, **292**
Joinville (SC) 427-430, **428**
Juazeiro (BAH) 258
Juazeiro de Norte (CEA) 313
Jureré (SC) 437

Lago Arari (PARÁ) 343
Lago Piratuba IBDF Biological
  Reserve (AMA) 349
Lagoa Conceiçã (SC) 437
Lagoa dos Patos (RGS) 439, 442
Laguna (SC) 438
Lake Caracaraná (ROR) 352
Lake Cuniã Biological Reserve
  (RON) 374
Lake Januária Reserve (AMAZ) 364
Lake Mamori (AMAZ) 364
Laranjeiras (SER) 262-263
Leblon (RIO) 92, 107, 118, 120, **93**
Lençóis (BAH) 254-257
Litoral Gaúcho (RGS) 441-443
Lumiar (RJ) 143

Macaé (RJ) 155
Macapá (AMA) 348-349, **349**
Maceió (ALA) 266-271, **268-269, 271**
Majorlândia (CEA) 309
Manacapuru (AMAZ) 365-366
Manaus (AMAZ) 352-365, **353, 355**
Mangue Seco (BAH) 235, 310
Manguinhos (RJ) 153
Mar Grande (BAH) 224
Maracá Ecological Station
  (AMA) 349
Maragoji (ALA) 275
Maragojipe (BAH) 230
Maranguape (CEA) 312
Maranhão (MAR) 315-324
Mataízes (ES) 159
Mariana (MINAS) 175-176
Mato Grosso (MG) 387-394
Mato Grosso do Sul (MGS) 403-406
Marechal Deodoro (ALA) 273
Maués (PARÁ) 346-348
Mazagão (AMA) 349
Mico Leão de Una Reserve
  (BAH) 243-244
Minas Gerais (MINAS) 160-185
Miracema do Norte (TOC) 385
Miranda (MG) 403
Mirante Lookout (MG) 392
Morretes (PAR) 413-414
Morro Branco (CEA) 307-308
Morro São Paulo (BAH) 237-238
Mt Roraima (ROR) 352

Natal (RGN) 295-297, **296**
National Parks
  Abrolhos (BAH) 253
  Aparados da Serra (RGS) 443
  Araguaia (TOC) 386, 387
  Chapada Diamantina
    (BAH) 255-256
  Emas (GOI) 385, 388
  Iguaçu (PAR) 423-424, 425
  Itatiaia (RJ) 70, 148-149
  Lençois Maranhense
    (MAR) 323-324
  Monte Pascoal (BAH)
    252-253, **252**
  Pantanal, The (MG) 396
  São Joaquim (SC) 439
  Serra dos Órgãos (RJ) 141-142
  Sete Cidades (PIA) 313
  Tijuca (RIO) 69, 90, 103
  Transpantanal (MG) 394
  Ubajara (CEA) 311
  Xingu (MG) 390
Nazaré (BAH) 231
Nova Airão (AMAZ) 364
Nova Friburgo (RJ) 143-144,
  140, 143

Olinda (PER) 276, 282-287, **283**
Olivença (BAH) 243
Ossos (RJ) 153, 154
Ouro Prêto (MINAS) 168-175, **169**

Pacatuba (CEA) 312
Pantanal, The (MG) 388,
  394-403, **395**
Paracuru (CEA) 309
Paraguayan Missions (P),
  see Jesuit Missions
Paraíba (PARAI) 291-293
Paranaguá (PAR) 413,
  414-417, **412, 415**
Paraná (PAR) 408-426
Parati (RJ) 132-138, **134**
Pará (PARÁ) 331-348
Passo do Lontra (MG) 402
Paõ de Açúcar (RIO) 69, 100
Pedra de Macunaima (ROR) 352
Pedra Pintada (ROR) 352
Penedo (ALA) 271-273
Penedo (RJ) 146-147
Penha (SC) 431
Pernambuco (PER) 276-290
Petrópolis (RJ) 138-139, **139**
Piaçabuçu (ALA) 273
Piauí (PIA) 313-315
Picarras (SC) 430
Pilar (PARÁ) 287
Pirangi do Norte (RGN) 294
Pirangi do Sul (RGN) 294
Pirapora (MINAS) 258
Pirenópolis (GOI) 384-385
Pitimbu (PARAI) 290

Piuma (ES) 158
Poconé (MG) 393-394, 399, 401,
  403, **394**
Poço das Antas Reserve (RJ) 155
Ponta do Lobo (SC) 431
Ponta do Mutá (BAH) 238
Ponta do Sul (SC) 437
Ponta Negra (RGN) 294
Ponta Porã (P) 75
Pontal do Sul (PAR) 417
Porto Alegre (RGS) 439-441, **440**
Porto Belo (SC) 431
Porto de Galinhas (PER) 282
Porto de Pedras (ALA) 275
Porto Jofre (MG) 399, 401, 403
Porto Seguro (BAH) 244-249, **245**
Porto Velho (RON) 367-372, **368-369**
Poxim (ALA) 273
Praça Mirante (PARÁ) 346
Prado (BAH) 253
Prados (MINAS) 181
Praia da Logoinha (CEA) 309
Praia de Leste (PAR) 417
Praia da Forte (BAH) 232-233
Prainha (CEA) 307
Propriá (SER) 265-266
Puerto Canoas (PAR) 423
Puerto Iguazú (A) 422
Puerto Stroessner (P) 422

Quixaba (CEA) 309

Raposa (MAR) 323
Recife (PER) 276-281, **278**
Recôncavo (BAH) 225-231
Resende (RJ) 146
Rio Acre (ACRE) 366
Rio Araguaia (TOC) 386
  Cuiabá (MG) 388
  Emas National Park (GOI) 385
Rio Branco (ACRE) 366, **366**
Rio Corrientes (GOI) 385
Rio Cuiabá (MG) 388, 401
Rio das Ostras (RJ) 155
Rio de Janeiro City (RJ) 86-127,
  87, 88-89
Rio de Janeiro State (RJ) 128-155,
  128, 130-131
Rio do Pouso (SC) 438
Rio Formoso (GOI) 385
Rio Grande (RGS) 442
Rio Grande do Norte (RGN) 293-298
Rio Grande do Sul (RGS) 439-443
Rio Guaiba (RGS) 439
Rio Iguaçu (PAR) 420
Rio Madeira (RON) 368, 372
Rio Mucujezinho (BAH) 257
Rio Nhundiaquara (PAR) 414
Rio Paraguaçu (BAH) 229
Rio Paraguai
  Corumbá (MGS) 405
  Emas National Park (GOI) 385

Rio Paraguai *cont*
  Caçeres (MG) 393
  The Pantanal (MG) 396
Rio Paraná (GOI) 385
Rio Potenji (RGN) 295
Rio São Francisco (BAH) 257-259
  Propriá (SER) 265
  Penedo (ALA) 271
Rio Solimõoes (AMAZ) 365
Rio Tapajos (PARÁ) 346
Rio Taquari (GOI) 385
Rondônia (RON) 366-374
Roraima (ROR) 350-352

Sabará (MINAS) 164-166
Saco (BAH) 236
Salinópolis (PARÁ) 340
Salto do Jurau Falls (RON) 372
Salvador (BAH) 205-222 **206-207**
Sambaqui (SC) 437
Santa Amaro (BAH) 230
Santa Bárbara (BAH) 253
Santa Catarina (SC) 427-438
Santa Cruz Cabrália (BAH) 249
Santa Cruz do Arari (PARÁ) 343
Santa Teresa (ES) 159
Santa Teresinha (TOC) 387
Santarém (PARÁ) 343-346, **344**
Santo Antônio (RON) 372
Saquarema (RJ) 149-150
São Cristóvão (SER) 260-261
São Felix do Araguaia (TOC) 386
São Francisco do Sul (SC) 430

São Joaquim (SC) 439
São João del Rei (MINAS)
  176-180, **177**
São José da Cora Grande (PER) 281
São José do Ribamar (MAR) 323
São Lourenço (MINAS) 183-184
São Luís (MAR) 315-322, **316**, **322**
São Luís Island (MAR) 322-323
São Miguel dos Milagres (ALA) 275
São Paulo City (SP) 186-196,
  188-189, **198**
São Paulo State (SP) 186-200
São Sebastião (SP) 199-200
São Tomé das Letras
  (MINAS) 181-182
Senador Georgino Alvino (RGN) 294
Sergipe (SER) 260-266, **261**
Serra Canastre (BAH) 258
Serra da Carioca (RIO) 90
Serra da Ibiapaba (CEA) 312
Serra da Mantiqueira
  (MINAS) 179
Serra de Baturité (CEA) 312-313
Serra de Tepequém (ROR) 352
Serra de Espinbaço (MINAS) 160
Serra do Navio (AMA) 349
Serra do Rio do Rastro (SC) 439
Serra do Sol (ROR) 352
Serra dos Pirineus (GOI) 384
Serra Gaúcho (RGS) 443
Sertão, The (PIA) 315
Sítio (BAH) 235
Sobral (CEA) 310

Souré (PARÁ) 341-343
Suape (PER) 282
Subaúma (BAH) 233
Sugar Loaf, see Pão de Açúcar

Tamandaré (PER) 281
TAMAR Turtle Reserve (BAH) 233
Tambaú (PARAI) 292
Teresina (PIA) 313, **314**
Teresópolis (RJ) 141-143, **140**
Termas da Gurada (SC) 438
Termas do Gravatal (SC) 438
Tibau do Sul (RGN) 294
Tibaú (RGN) 298
Tiradentes (MINAS) 180-181
Tocantins (TOC) 385-387
Torres (RGS) 442
Touros (RGN) 298
Tracunhaém (PER) 290
Tramandaí (RGS) 442
Trancoso (BAH) 249, 251
Transpantaneira (MG) 401
Tubarão (SC) 438

Ubatuba (SP) 196-199
Uruçuca (BAH) 239

Valença (BAH) 236-237
Vassouras (RJ) 139-141
Véu de Noiva (MG) 392
Vila Velha (PER) 288
Vilhena (RON) 372
Visconde de Mauá (RJ) 147-148
Vitória (ES) 156, **157**, **158**

MAPS

Amazon, The	327	Maceió	268-269
Aracaju	263	Around Maceió	271
Bahia Coast	231	Manaus	353
The Beaches North of		Central Manaus	355
Bahia	261	Natal	296
Baía de Todos os Santos	223	Nova Friburgo	143
Belém, Central	333	Olinda	283
Belo Horizonte, Central	162	Ouro Prêto	169
Around Belo Horizonte	165	Pantanal, The	395
Blumenau	432	Paranaguá	415
Boa Vista	351	Parati Islands & Beaches	134
Brasília	378-379	Parque Nacional de	
Central Brasília	380	Monte Pascoal	252
Brazil	10-11	Parque Nacional do Itatiaia	145
Climate & Rainfall	26	Petrópolis	139
Provinces	24	Porto Alegre	440
Búzios, Cabo Frio &		Porto Seguro	245
Arrail do Cabo	152	Porto Velho	368-369
Cachoeira	226	Recife	278
Campo Grande	404	Rio Branco	366
Conde, The Beaches from	234	Rio State	128
Corumba	405	Beaches of South Rio	130-131
Cuiabá	389	Rio de Janeiro	87
Curitiba	409	Central Rio	88-89
Around Curitiba	412	Copacabana	93
Fernando de Noronha	299	Ipanema	93
Florianópolis, Central	434	Leblon	93
Fortaleza	302	Rio Metro	126
Central Fortaleza	304	Salvador	206-207
Foz do Iguaçu	421	Santarém	344
Iguaç Falls	423	São João del Rei	177
Goiânia	383	São Luis	316
Guajará-Mirim	373	Around São Luis	322
Guayaramerin (B)	373	São Paulo	188-189
Iguaçu Falls	423	Around São Paulo	198
Ilha do Mel	419	São Paulo Metro	197
Ilha Santa Catarina	436	Teresina	314
Ilhéus	240	Teresopólis, Petropólis &	
João Pessoa	292	Nova Friburgo	140
Joinville	428	Vitória	157
Macapá	349	Around Vitória	158

Temperature

To convert °C to °F multiply by 1.8 and add 32

To convert °F to °C subtract 32 and multiply by ·55

Length, Distance & Area

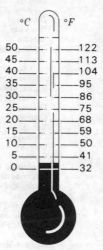

	multiply by
inches to centimetres	2.54
centimetres to inches	0.39
feet to metres	0.30
metres to feet	3.28
yards to metres	0.91
metres to yards	1.09
miles to kilometres	1.61
kilometres to miles	0.62
acres to hectares	0.40
hectares to acres	2.47

Weight

	multiply by
ounces to grams	28.35
grams to ounces	0.035
pounds to kilograms	0.45
kilograms to pounds	2.21
British tons to kilograms	1016
US tons to kilograms	907

A British ton is 2240 lbs, a US ton is 2000 lbs

Volume

	multiply by
Imperial gallons to litres	4.55
litres to imperial gallons	0.22
US gallons to litres	3.79
litres to US gallons	0.26

5 imperial gallons equals 6 US gallons
a litre is slightly more than a US quart, slightly less
than a British one

Guides to Latin America

Chile & Easter Island – a travel survival kit

Chile has one of the most varied geographies in the world, including deserts, tranquil lakes, snow-covered volcanoes and windswept fjords. Easter Island is covered, in detail.

Ecuador & the Galapagos Islands – a travel survival kit

Ecuador is the smallest of the Andean countries, and in many ways it is the easiest and most pleasant to travel in. The Galapagos Islands and their amazing inhabitants continue to cast a spell over every visitor.

Mexico – a travel survival kit

Mexico has a unique blend of Indian and Spanish culture and a fascinating historical legacy. The hospitality of the people makes Mexico a paradise for travellers.

Peru – a travel survival kit

The famed city of Machu Picchu, the Andean altiplano and the Amazon rainforests are just some of Peru's attractions. All the facts you need can be found in this comprehensive guide.

Mail Order

Lonely Planet guidebooks are distributed worldwide and are sold by good bookshops everywhere. They are also available by mail order from Lonely Planet, so if you have difficulty finding a title please write to us. US and Canadian residents should write to Embarcadero West, 112 Linden St, Oakland CA 94607, USA and residents of other countries to PO Box 617, Hawthorn, Victoria 3122, Australia.

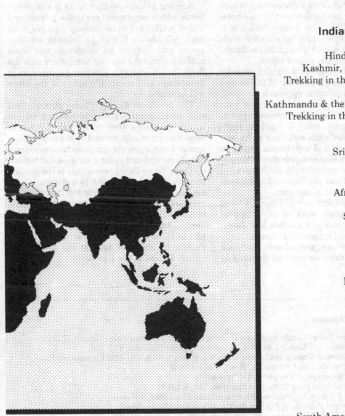

Eastern Europe
Eastern Europe

Indian Subcontinent
India
Hindi/Urdu phrasebook
Kashmir, Ladakh & Zanskar
Trekking in the Indian Himalaya
Pakistan
Kathmandu & the Kingdom of Nepal
Trekking in the Nepal Himalaya
Nepal phrasebook
Sri Lanka
Sri Lanka phrasebook
Bangladesh

Africa
Africa on a shoestring
East Africa
Swahili phrasebook
West Africa
Central Africa

Middle East
Israel
Egypt & the Sudan
Jordan & Syria
Yemen

North America
Canada
Alaska

Mexico
Mexico
Baja California

South America
South America on a shoestring
Ecuador & the Galapagos Islands
Colombia
Chile & Easter Island
Bolivia
Peru
Argentina

Lonely Planet

Lonely Planet published its first book in 1973. Tony and Maureen Wheeler had made a lengthy overland trip from England to Australia and, in response to numerous 'how do you do it?' questions, Tony wrote and they published *Across Asia on the Cheap*. It became an instant local best-seller and inspired thoughts of a second travel guide. A year and a half in South-East Asia resulted in their second book, *South-East Asia on a Shoestring*, which they put together in a backstreet Chinese hotel in Singapore in 1975. The 'yellow book', as it quickly became known, soon became *the* guide to the region and has gone through five editions, always with its familiar yellow cover.

Soon other writers came to them with ideas for similar books – books that went off the beaten track with an adventurous approach to travel, books that 'assumed you knew how to get your luggage off the carousel,' as one reviewer put it. Lonely Planet grew from a kitchen table operation to a spare room and then to its own office. It's international reputation began to grow as the Lonely Planet logo began to appear in more and more countries. In 1982 *India – a travel survival kit* won the Thomas Cook award for the best guidebook of the year.

These days there are over 70 Lonely Planet titles. Over 40 people work at our office in Melbourne, Australia and another half dozen at our US office in Oakland, California.

At first Lonely Planet specialised in the Asia region but these days we are also developing major ranges of guidebooks to the Pacific region, to South America and to Africa. The list of walking guides is growing and Lonely Planet now has a unique series of phrasebooks to 'unusual' languages. The emphasis continues to be on travel for travellers and Tony and Maureen still manage to fit in a number of trips each year and play a very active part in the writing and updating of Lonely Planet's guides.

Keeping guidebooks up to date is a constant battle which requires an ear to the ground and lots of walking, but technology also plays its part. All Lonely Planet guidebooks are now stored and updated on computer, and some authors even take lap-top computers into the field. Lonely Planet is also using computers to draw maps and eventually many of the maps will be stored on disk.

The people at Lonely Planet strongly feel that travellers can make a positive contribution to the countries they visit both by better appreciation of cultures and by the money they spend. In addition the company tries to make a direct contribution to the countries and regions it covers. Since 1986 a percentage of the income from each book has gone to aid groups and associations. This has included donations to famine relief in Africa, to aid projects in India, to agricultural projects in Nicaragua and other Central American countries and to Greenpeace's efforts to halt French nuclear testing in the Pacific. In 1988 over $40,000 was donated by Lonely Planet to these projects.

Lonely Planet Distributors

Australia & Papua New Guinea Lonely Planet Publications, PO Box 617, Hawthorn, Victoria 3122.
Canada Raincoast Books, 112 East 3rd Avenue, Vancouver, British Columbia V5T 1C8.
Denmark, Finland & Norway Scanvik Books aps, Store Kongensgade 59 A, DK-1264 Copenhagen K.
India & Nepal UBS Distributors, 5 Ansari Rd, New Delhi – 110002
Israel Geographical Tours Ltd, 8 Tverya St, Tel Aviv 63144.
Japan Intercontinental Marketing Corp, IPO Box 5056, Tokyo 100-31.
Netherlands Nilsson & Lamm bv, Postbus 195, Pampuslaan 212, 1380 AD Weesp.
New Zealand Transworld Publishers, PO Box 83-094, Edmonton PO, Auckland.
Singapore & Malaysia MPH Distributors, 601 Sims Drive, #03-21, Singapore 1438.
Spain Altair, Balmes 69, 08007 Barcelona.
Sweden Esselte Kartcentrum AB, Vasagatan 16, S-111 20 Stockholm.
Thailand Chalermnit, 108 Sukhumvit 53, Bangkok 10110.
Turkey Yab-Yay Dagitim, Alay Koshu Caddesi 12/A, Kat 4 no. 11-12, Cagaloglu, Istanbul.
UK Roger Lascelles, 47 York Rd, Brentford, Middlesex, TW8 0QP
USA Lonely Planet Publications, PO Box 2001A, Berkeley, CA 94702.
West Germany Buchvertrieb Gerda Schettler, Postfach 64, D3415 Hattorf a H.
All Other Countries refer to Australia address.